EMERGING CIVIL SOCIETY

IN THE ASIA PACIFIC COMMUNITY

Founded in 1970, the **Japan Center for International Exchange** *(JCIE) is an independent, nonprofit, and nonpartisan organization dedicated to strengthening Japan's role in international affairs. JCIE believes that Japan faces a major challenge in augmenting its positive contributions to the international community, in keeping with its position as one of the world's largest industrialized democracies. Operating in a country where policy-making has traditionally been dominated by the government bureaucracy, JCIE has played an important role in broadening debate on Japan's international responsibilities and cross-sectional programs of exchange, research, and discussion. Funding for JCIE comes from private foundation grants, corporate contributions, and contracts.*

The **Institute of Southeast Asian Studies** *(ISEAS) was established as an autonomous organization in 1968. It is a regional research center for scholars and other specialists concerned with modern Southeast Asia, particularly the many-faceted problems of stability and security, economic development, and political and social change.*

The Institute is governed by a twenty-two–member Board of Trustees comprising nominees from the Singapore Government, the National University of Singapore, the various Chambers of Commerce, and professional and civic organizations. A ten-man Executive Committee oversees day-to-day operations; it is chaired by the Director, the Institute's chief academic and administrative officer.

EMERGING CIVIL SOCIETY

IN THE ASIA PACIFIC COMMUNITY

Nongovernmental Underpinnings of the Emerging Asia Pacific Regional Community

A 25th Anniversary Project of JCIE

ISEAS

JCIE 25

Edited by
Tadashi Yamamoto
Japan Center for International Exchange (JCIE)

Co-Published by
The Institute of Southeast Asian Studies (ISEAS)
JCIE

In Cooperation with
The Asia Pacific Philanthropy Consortium (APPC)

Published jointly by

Institute of Southeast Asian Studies *and* Japan Center for International Exchange

Heng Mui Keng Terrace
Pasir Panjang
Singapore 119596

4-9-17 Minami Azabu
Minato-ku, Tokyo
Japan 106

Internet e-mail: publish@merlion.iseas.ac.sg
WWW: http://merlion.iseas.ac.sg/pub.html

First reprint 1996
Revised edition 1996

Cataloging in Publication Data
Emerging civil society in the Asia Pacific Community: nongovernmental underpinnings of the emerging Asia Pacific regional community / edited by Tadashi Yamamoto

1. Civil society—Asia
2. Civil society—Pacific Area
3. Research institutes—Asia
4. Research institutes—Pacific Area
5. Nongovernmental organizations—Asia
6. Nongovernmental organizations—Pacific Area
7. Endowments—Asia
8. Endowments—Pacific Area

I. Yamamoto, Tadashi

HM101 Y21 1995 sls95-53548

ISBN 981-3055-05-7 (pbk)
ISBN 981-3055-06-5

Printed in Singapore by Prime Packaging Industries Pte Ltd

Table of Contents

RESEARCH INSTITUTIONS

PHILANTHROPY

APPENDICES

PREFACE

Background

It has been some time since the concept of a "Pacific Economic Community" or "Pacific Community" started receiving serious attention among some governmental, business, and intellectual leaders within the Asia Pacific region. While this concept became fashionable in the early 1980s, it was also pointed out that the task of some type of community building would be extremely difficult given the fact that the nations bordering the Pacific Ocean show great diversity in size, culture, religion, levels of economic development, modes of political organization, and historical experience. The concept of an Asia Pacific regional community, however, has been attracting renewed and much more serious interest in recent years. One major factor behind this is the remarkable economic development in the Asia Pacific region which has come to be regarded as a center of dynamic economic growth which, in turn, has enhanced an increasingly high degree of economic interdependence among nations in the region, warranting some kind of economic regionalism. For another, the impending formation of regional economic arrangements in other parts of the world, namely, the European Community in Europe and NAFTA in North America, have encouraged the formation of similar regional economic arrangements in this part of the world, either for economic self-protection of the region or for the further strengthening of a free-trade oriented regional economic order.

One of the major characteristics of this emerging "Asia Pacific regional community" is that it has been largely economic-driven, particularly through the dynamic corporate interactions of trade and investment within the region. While this trend is likely to progress given the continued growth of the so-called Asian Newly Industrialized Economies (NIEs) and other emerging economies in East and Southeast Asia, the economic interdependence that has served as an engine of growth among these nations is also a potential source of friction in the region. It is argued in some circles that mere economic interdependence, therefore, is not sufficient as a basis for the regional "community" and that it is hard to bring about such a "community" without some viable shared values or interests or without more stable human and institutional interactions among the nations within this region. It is also pointed out that the European integration could not have been carried out, even to the present stage of development only through governmental negotiations. Instead, the process of integration has been underpinned by multiple layers of nongovernmental interactions including collaborative efforts of research and academic institutions, NGOs, business organizations, and other diverse nongovernmental organizations. It is widely accepted that the human dimension of these nongovernmental interactions is extremely important in generating a "sense of community" and a "community of interest."

Despite the fact that economic interdependence has been an underlining force behind the emerging Asia Pacific regional community, there has been a distinct development of civil society, i.e. non-economic and nongovernmental interactions, in the region in recent years. This trend seems to reflect the growing recognition of the importance of non-economic factors at an advanced stage of economic interdependence, as evidenced, for example, by the increasing importance Japanese corporations attach to stakeholders' interest or by their efforts to become "good corporate citizens" in the East and Southeast countries in which they operate. There is also a noticeable growth of NGOs in Asia Pacific nations in recent years reflecting a significant advancement of the democratization and pluralization process among nations in the region, accompanying a phenomenal economic growth, and a tendency among these NGOs to form collaborative arrangements beyond their own national borders. Such regional cooperation of NGOs has been greatly enhanced by the growing prominence of global issues such as the environment, rural poverty, AIDS, and drug addiction which have become more pronounced since the end of the cold war confrontation which has had regional implications over the past half century. Thirdly, there has been significant growth of a network of policy-oriented scholars and researchers as well as that of research and academic institutions in the region which are becoming more active in jointly addressing themselves to regional economic issues as well as political-security issues.

Objectives

This survey of "Nongovernmental Underpinnings of the Emerging Asia Pacific Regional Community" was proposed in the fall of 1993 in order to assess the state of indigenous development of civil society in each nation in Asia Pacific; to study the present state of development of regional interactions among nongovernmental efforts through the identification of existing networks or collaborative arrangements; to identify major actors for such regional cooperative endeavors; and to explore ways and means of further developing such nongovernmental regional underpinnings in the future. The survey covered three areas, namely, nongovernmental organizations (NGOs), policy-oriented intellectual activities, and organized philanthropy and corporate philanthropy, all of which are involved in international cooperation. There have been some surveys and networking efforts in these three areas of endeavors in the past, and the current survey was designed to build on such past efforts, and, hopefully further enhance them. A central objective of the survey was to provide a basis for accelerating the efforts of enhancing nongovernmental underpinnings of regional community building efforts. It was felt that a more objective assessment and analysis of the degree of the current state of nongovernmental collaborative efforts would make it possible to identify major constraints against and future opportunities for further enhancement of such regional cooperation. It was also expected that the survey would provide a basis for future efforts to build a database on these regional activities.

From the point of view of the Japan Center for International Exchange (JCIE), which was to commemorate its 25th anniversary in 1995, this survey would enable it to bring itself to a new level of efforts in encouraging philanthropic development in Japan. JCIE was fortunate to find close collaborators in the region who had started an initiative to launch the Asia Pacific Philanthropy Consortium. JCIE has been involved in such efforts since 1973 through a series of activities under its International Philanthropy Project. It is felt that, while needs and rationale for philanthropic activities both corporate and organized had been vigorously promoted by a growing number of organizations in Japan through several studies and a multitude of seminars and workshops in recent years, a more action-oriented approach and professionalization of philanthropic activities were desperately needed in order for Japanese foundations and corporations to put into action what they had been learning in the past. This survey project has provided JCIE with an excellent base on which it can launch an ambitious Asia Pacific Agenda Project, also in commemoration of its 25th anniversary, involving multi-pronged research and dialogue activities. This new project is JCIE's modest response to a challenge of strengthening and broadening networks among policy research institutions and intellectual leaders involved in Asia Pacific community building, and it is an effort to enhance the longer term capacity of Japanese and Asian societies to conduct and contribute to quality, objective research and policy dialogue activities relevant to key regional issues.

Methodology

In the first phase of the survey, searches were made on existing materials covering regional networks, collaborative efforts of institutions, and organized efforts being made within each nation within the region. Through the initial phase of the survey attempts were made to identify key players in the region who are involved in nongovernmental regional cooperation. An initial survey involved the scanning of data bases available such as one at the Foundation Center in the United States and interviews with officials of major foundations, NGOs, and research institutions in the United States, Japan, and other Asian nations. As to the countries to be included in the survey, we decided to cover fifteen countries including the United States, Canada, China, Korea, Japan, Taiwan, Hong Kong, ASEAN countries, Vietnam, Australia, and New Zealand.

At the end of the first phase, further exploration of existing or potential regional networking and cooperation was made at a series of workshops JCIE organized on behalf of the Center for Global Partnership (CGP) which was seeking at that time to find its role in enhancing Asia Pacific regional cooperation through support for intellectual exchange and NGO grassroots activities. On 9 and 10 April 1993 a workshop was organized in Singapore to discuss the role of intellectual exchange in enhancing regional cooperation, and another workshop was organized in Jakarta on 11 and 12 April to discuss a similar role for NGOs in the Asia Pacific region.

In the next phase, actual research activities took place. Researchers with expertise in one of the three areas in their respective countries were identified and commissioned with the research. At the same time several JCIE staff members were sent for a series of field trips. Each researcher was provided with the guidelines for the research which was expected to be the basic structure of each country paper, including the history and evolution of NGOs/research institutions/philanthropy in each country, the Asia Pacific orientation of each respective society, major actors, and the status and prospects of Asia Pacific networks. It was truly unfortunate that we were unable to identify a researcher on Malaysia's organized philanthropy in time for this publication. We are aware that drastic changes have been witnessed in Malaysia's philanthropic sector, and we very much wish to include a country paper on this topic when we revise the current volume.

In the final stage, an international symposium was held in Osaka, Japan, on 11–13 December 1994 on the theme of Nongovernmental Underpinnings of the Emerging Asia Pacific Regional Community to discuss and disseminate the results of the survey. Country papers submitted by project researchers were compiled to provide background reading for the conference participants together with the integrative report of the survey project. It was at this conference that the launching of an Asia Pacific Philanthropy Consortium (APPC) was officially announced in order to strengthen indigenous philanthropies in each Asia Pacific nation and enhance philanthropic cooperation in the region, a need repeatedly emphasized in most of the country reports for the further development of the civil society. We are pleased that APPC agreed to extend its cooperation toward the publication of the current volume. Both the integrative report as well as the summary of discussion at the above Osaka Symposium are attached in this volume.

It is our hope that this publication will be a useful addition to the already vigorous discussions and dialogues on the civil society in Asia Pacific. Ultimately, we wish to contribute, through this publication, to the development of civil society in each of the Asia Pacific countries as well as the enhancement of a genuine regional community in the region.

Acknowledgements

First and foremost I wish to thank all the researchers who contributed original and insightful country papers. Without their contributions, the current volume literally would never have materialized. The survey project as well as the publication have been supported by generous funding from various foundations in Japan, the United States, and Taiwan including, in alphabetical order, The Asia Foundation, the East-West Seminar, Ford Foundation, Himalaya Foundation, The Hitachi Foundation, the Japan-U.S. Friendship Commission, John D. and Catherine T. MacArthur Foundation, Rockefeller Brothers Fund, Sasakawa Peace Foundation, Suntory Foundation, Ushiba Memorial Foundation, and Weyerhaeuser Foundation. Special thanks are in order to Professor Chan Heng Chee and her associates at the Institute of Southeast Asian Studies, most notably Dr. Diana Wong and Mrs. Triena Ong, who wholeheartedly endorsed the objectives of this project and agreed to copublish this report on extremely short notice.

Last but by no means the least, I wish to thank my competent and hardworking staff, most notably Makito Noda and Susan Hubbard who deserve to be listed as co-editors of this volume. Hiroshi Peter Kamura, Karin Wilcox, and Noriko Ogawa contributed to the survey project by coordinating among North American and Southeast Asian researchers. Hitomi Komatsu helped me prepare the integrative report by collecting and processing relevant data. Sue Henny and Hazlyn Fortune both read manuscripts and helped us edit the country papers, and Patrick Ishiyama was responsible for formatting the entire manuscript.

Tadashi Yamamoto — Tokyo, July 1995

PREFACE TO THE REVISED EDITION

I am honored to be able to report that this book was awarded the Masayoshi Ohira Award for Outstanding Contribution to Asia Pacific Community Building, by the Masayoshi Ohira Memorial Foundation. It is due to the dedication of the authors of the reports contained within these pages that we received this honor, and I would like to thank all of them for the invaluable contribution they have made.

As I mentioned in the preface to the first edition of this book, we were unable to identify a researcher on Malaysia's organized philanthropy in time for the first publication, but we have since located a very knowledgeable scholar on this subject, Edmund Terence Gomez, of the University of Malaya. Mr. Gomez's paper, "Philanthropy in a Multiethnic Society: The Case of Malaysia," appears in the appendices of this edition. I am pleased to be able to include a report on Malaysian philanthropy, thus making our survey of fifteen Asia Pacific countries complete.

Besides the addition of the report on Malaysian philanthropy, only slight changes were made to the text of this book. I hope that this volume will encourage further development of civil society in each of the Asia Pacific countries and contribute to the formation of a genuine regional community in the Asia Pacific region.

Tadashi Yamamoto — Tokyo, April 1996

Integrative Report

Tadashi Yamamoto
President
Japan Center for International Exchange

I. Introduction

This report provides an integrative summary of papers prepared by a number of researchers, as listed in appendix 1, who have participated in the survey project on "Nongovernmental Underpinnings of the Emerging Asia Pacific Regional Community." The survey was initiated in the spring of 1993, covering fifteen countries in Asia Pacific to assess the development of (*a*) organized and corporate philanthropies, (*b*) nongovernmental organizations (NGOs), and (*c*) independent policy research institutions in these countries, and to identify emerging regional cooperative arrangements and networks among these organizations. It should be noted that the term NGOs, in a broader sense, covers both private philanthropies and independent policy research institutions. In this report, however, the term NGOs refers to those nonprofit and nongovernmental organizations that are active in the field of development issues in third world countries, such as rural development, alleviation of poverty, nutrition and health, reproductive biology, and education; and global issues such as the environment, human rights, refugees, and the population crisis. It should also be noted that "independent policy research institutions" covered in this survey are mostly in the international economic, political, and security fields, and this project focuses primarily on regional networks and collaboration among these research institutions.

This report was initially prepared as background material for discussion at the Osaka Symposium on "Developing Nongovernmental Underpinnings of the Emerging Asia Pacific Regional Community" held 11–13 December 1994. It summarizes the major findings of these country papers as well as key issues that have been raised in connection with efforts for further developing "regional nongovernmental underpinnings." The present form in which this report now appears has been revised and updated since the Sympsoium.

In the first phase of the survey project—January through April 1993—a preliminary search was made on existing printed materials covering private and corporate philanthropies, NGOs, and research institutions in the Asia Pacific nations as well as on regional networks or collaborative efforts among these organizations. On the basis of the preliminary findings, methodology and design of the survey project were explored at two workshops with the participation of experts in the Asia Pacific region who had already been involved in the regional collaborative schemes. On 8–9 April 1993, the first workshop was organized in Singapore to discuss regional cooperation among policy research institutions as well as intellectual exchange activities in general, with twenty experts from eight countries. The other workshop was organized in Jakarta on 12 April 1993, to discuss NGO cooperation in the Asia Pacific region with nineteen experts from six nations. The plans of the survey project were then discussed at the International Symposium on Private Philanthropy in East Asia, held in Seoul, Korea on 19–22 August 1993. In addition to advice and suggestions on the methodology and design of the survey project, participants of the Symposium strongly endorsed the major objectives of the survey, indicating that the survey is consistent with the goals of the Seoul Symposium. The Symposium was a follow-up to an earlier symposium in Bangkok held in August 1989, under the title, "International Symposium on Organized Private Philanthropy in East and Southeast Asia." The key participants of the Bangkok and Seoul Symposia began exploring the possibility of establishing an Asia Pacific Philanthropy Consortium to facilitate philanthropic development and cooperation in Asia Pacific.

Many of the participants of the workshops in Singapore and Jakarta as well as those of the Bangkok and Seoul symposia agreed to participate directly in the survey activities, and others volunteered to facilitate the identification of country researchers, or to assist the researchers with their reports. Therefore, the survey project has truly been undertaken as a regional and multinational collaborative project, though the initiative was taken by the Japan Center for International Exchange (JCIE). In this spirit, it is assumed that the reports received from the researchers on the basis of interviews and data collection along with voluminous reference materials including directories and reports on a number of nonprofit and nongovernmental organizations in the Asia Pacific countries, are considered to be the common property of those interested in future development and cooperation among research institutions, NGOs, and philanthropies in this region. It is hoped, therefore, that these materials will provide a basis for the clearinghouse activities to be carried out by the Asia Pacific Philanthropy Consortium.

The survey project on the "Nongovernmental Underpinnings of the Emerging Asia Pacific Regional Community" was conceived on the basis of several premises. One premise was that the increasing economic interdependence and interaction in Asia Pacific alone will not render itself to "community" building of the region as such. The concept of an Asia Pacific regional community has been gaining greater recognition in recent years, but this emerging Asia Pacific regional community has been largely driven by economic factors, particularly through the intense corporate interactions of trade and investment within the region. While this trend is likely to progress, given the continued economic growth in East and Southeast Asia and recent efforts to institutionalize regional economic cooperation through official forums such as the Asia Pacific Economic Cooperation (APEC) forum, it can be argued that mere economic interaction and linkages are not sufficient as a basis for the regional "community." In fact, it could turn out to be a source of acrimonious economic tensions and conflicts among the nations in the region. It is hard to bring about a "community" without some viable shared visions or interests or without more stable human and institutional interactions among the nations within this region. It should be pointed out that the European integration could not have been carried out through governmental negotiations alone. Instead, the process of European integration has been underpinned by multiple layers of nongovernmental interactions including collaborative efforts of research and academic institutions, NGOs, business associations, and other diverse nongovernmental organizations.

Another premise was that there has been a significant growth of nonprofit and nongovernmental organizations in the countries in Asia Pacific in recent years, and even greater growth is anticipated in the future. Moreover, these organizations have started engaging in closer regional collaborative activities and building networks among themselves, thus providing encouraging opportunities of establishing regional institutional linkages and facilitating individual networks and collaborative relationships, a prerequisite, as discussed above, of community building in Asia Pacific.

A third premise was that, despite a dramatic growth of independent sector organizations in Asia Pacific and extending networks and regional cooperation among them, there is still a considerable number of constraints working against their further development in this region. Indigenous development of the nonprofit sector is a very recent phenomenon in most of the countries in Asia Pacific, including economically more advanced Japan and Korea, and its further growth cannot be guaranteed unless concerted efforts are made. It was also assumed that the regional cooperation of like minded actors in the field will be an effective tool in promoting the indigenous nonprofit sector to overcome many socio-cultural and political impediments.

II. An Asia Pacific "Associational Revolution"?

In a recent article in *Foreign Affairs* under the title of "The Rise of the Nonprofit Sector," Lester M. Salamon maintains that a global "Associational Revolution" is taking place "from the developed countries of North America, Europe and Asia to the developing nations of Africa, Latin America, and the former Soviet bloc."[1] On the basis of extensive research undertaken by the Johns Hopkins Comparative Nonprofit Sector Project covering thirteen countries, Salamon argues that this associational revolution "may prove to be as significant to the latter twentieth century as the rise of the nation-state was to the latter nineteenth." He is referring to "a massive array of self-governing private organizations, not dedicated to distributing profits to shareholders or directors, pursuing public purposes outside the formal apparatus of the state. The proliferation of these groups may be permanently altering the relationship between states and citizens"[2]

The reports submitted by the researchers under the "Nongovernmental Underpinnings of the Emerging Asia Pacific Community" project do underscore a significant growth of the nonprofit sector in Asia Pacific countries in recent years, but a general picture provided by their reports falls short of the rather euphoric tone of Salamon's article. This impression may come, for one, from analyses given in the country reports of this survey project particularly covering newly developing Asian countries where the evolution of the nonprofit sector is a relatively new phenomenon and where there are considerable constraints against the activities of NGOs, independent research institutions, and organized philanthropies. For another, the survey reports in this project portray a relatively less optimistic picture of the nonprofit sector, as they are designed to identify the challenges the nonprofit sector in Asia Pacific is facing, in order to map out future strategies to encourage further development of the independent sector institutions in an indigenous setting as well as greater cooperation among them in a regional context. For example, Salamon's statement that "the relationship between government and the nonprofit sector has been characterized more by cooperation than conflict, as government has turned extensively to the nonprofit sector to assist it in meeting human needs"[3] does not necessarily apply to some of the countries in Asia Pacific where a considerable amount of tension in the relationship between government and the nonprofit sector still persists. By emphasizing increases in public-private cooperation, Salamon's paper, perhaps inadvertently, minimizes the critical issue of the autonomy of nonprofit sector organizations in Asia Pacific, as discussed more extensively later in this report. In fact, some of the country reports reflect concern about a tendency of the government to "turn to" the nonprofit sector, reinforcing a hierarchical relationship where NGOs are reduced to mere subsidiaries of government agencies.

The above cautionary notes notwithstanding, the country reports indicate an impressive growth of the nonprofit sector in Asia Pacific in recent years. In addition to an expansion of the size of the sector, there has clearly been an evolution of the scope and nature of their activities. Many NGOs and philanthropic organizations in these countries have been transforming themselves from traditional organizations that provide charitable contributions and services to the poor, to those that directly involve themselves in the development process or in addressing issues such as the environment and human rights. There also has been a noticeable trend for these nonprofit organizations in many countries to establish networks and associations among themselves. Such trends can be clearly observed through several illustrative cases as shown below.

1. Increasing Size of the Nonprofit Sector

In Indonesia, the growth of the NGO sector since the 1970s has been "phenomenal," as the current estimates of the total number of independent organizations focused on development issues ranges from four to six thousand, even though the report indicates that Indonesian NGOs exist in an environment not as hospitable as many NGO environments in other Asian countries.

In Thailand, the number of associations and foundations registered grew at a reasonably constant rate from 1943, but the number became much larger during the 1980s when the government recognized the role of NGOs in promoting development activities. It is noted that after a very low period for NGOs, from the end of the 1970s to the early 1980s, many NGOs were revived in the latter part of the 1980s, and many new ones were formed, reflecting a more favorable attitude of the government. In 1989, there were 8,408 general nonprofit associations and 2,966 foundations registered with the National Cultural Commission.

In the Philippines, NGOs began flourishing under the emergence of the Aquino government from 1986 to date, and the database of the Department of Interior and

Local Government shows a total of 14,398 NGOs and People's Organizations. With the impending solution of the rightist and leftist insurgencies, the NGOs have gained further impetus, as former hard-liners have sought to rejoin the mainstream of society. In the field of organized philanthropy, a growing number of companies have set up their own corporate foundations, and there are thirty-six of them as of last count.

In China, a *shetuan*, which is a social organization formed voluntarily for common objectives and collectively engaged in economic activities or public affairs, is "more or less comparable to internationally recognized NGOs," according to the Chinese survey collaborator. According to a nationwide investigation conducted in 1991 where all *shetuans* were required to re-register, out of 118,691 applications for registration, 89,969 were granted *shetuan* status, as reported in the *1992 Yearbook of Chinese Law*.

In Korea, the end of the authoritarian regime in June 1987, marks the emergence of increasingly effective sophisticated civic groups led by the younger generation. The main focus of these groups includes issues on public participation in policy formulation, human rights and the environment. In the field of corporate philanthropy, an increasing number of corporate foundations have been established in the last two decades, during which Korean corporations grew along with their national economy.

In Japan, where development of the nonprofit sector has been very slow compared with its phenomenal economic development, there has been a belated but rather encouraging development in recent years. The term NGO*s*, mostly referring to development-oriented NGOs, has almost become a household word in Japan in the past year or two. According to a keyword search on four major Japanese newspapers, the frequency of articles on NGOs has made a quantum jump from 192 in 1990, 291 in 1991, 1,032 in 1992, 972 in 1993, to 1,506 in the first ten months of 1994. Reflecting this general interest in the NGO movement, there has been a marked increase of NGOs or voluntary organizations. Most of the NGOs are not incorporated and, thus, not registered, but it is estimated that the developmental NGOs are about three hundred in number.

In the United States, where there is a tradition of a strong nonprofit sector, there has been a steady growth in the sector in the past decade, despite stagnant economic conditions. In 1984, there were 1,176,000 nonprofit organizations in the United States. By 1990, that number had grown to 1,375,000. Grant-making foundations grew from 25,639 in 1985, 32,401 in 1990, and 35,765 in 1992 (*Foundation Giving, 1994*, The Foundation Center). In organized philanthropies, it is reported that assets of private foundations, not including corporate foundations, grew eight percent in 1992.

2. Evolution of the Scope of the Nonprofit Sector

In the Philippines, the traditional dole-out approach of religious NGOs was eventually criticized as being dependency creating, and NGOs whose activities in the countryside focused on community development began to flourish. Particularly under the Aquino administration, the term *NGO community* became a political reality, and NGOs have gained more influence on every sphere of civil society.

In Thailand, the nonprofit sector has gradually evolved from religious institutions to social welfare NGOs, and more recently to the emergence of development-oriented NGOs. Developmental nonprofit organizations emerged in the latter part of the 1980s, and became more and more active, assuming an important role in the development of Thai society. In more recent years, some NGOs have started working as advocacy groups, concentrating on issues of the environment, people's participation, and democracy.

In Singapore, with the rise of the state came civic groups which dared to have their own vision of a better society. They are issue-oriented, and although their target group is invariably the community, their aims differ from other community service and welfare organizations in that they aim to "be catalytic agents for change through their involvement, education, and mobilization of people to improve their circumstances." This change comes about not through a one-off act of charity but through the implementation of processes that emphasize the autonomy of individuals and/or communities. Research, education, and conscientization are important features of their work.

In Indonesia, in the late 1960s, a new variety of NGOs, oriented toward development as opposed to welfare, emerged as a result of debates around how best to help the disadvantaged in its society. More recently, some NGO activists began to feel that community development programs were not able to obtain maximum impact because of existing inequities, and started establishing advocacy NGOs to respond to these inequities.

In New Zealand, more traditional NGOs have come increasingly to see their roles as supplementing the social welfare provisions of the government, rather than functioning as mainstream providers, though with the economic restructuring of the past eight years or so their potential as mainstream service providers may again come into its own.

Australia has had charitable organizations since the early days of European settlement. However, the emergence of NGOs in the area of sustainable economic development is a relatively recent phenomenon.

In China, with the rapid development of the private economy in various forms, private entrepreneurs have begun to support some of the NGOs that could not have been otherwise established due to the lack of funding.

3. Growing Number of National Networks and Umbrella Organizations

In the Philippines, the mushrooming of NGOs across the nation has resulted in the establishment of networks, coalitions, caucuses, federations, and other associations that seek to rationalize the NGO community's concern and resources. The aggregation process has led to the formation of several national networks, and the organization of the ten main national networks in turn has led to the formation of the Caucus of Development NGO Network (CODE-NGO). Together these networks represent close to three thousand individual organizations.

Philippine Partnership for the Development of Human Resources in Rural Areas (PhilDHRRA) is a national network of sixty-two development NGOs. The Partnership of Philippine Support Service Agencies (PHILSSA) is a national network of fifty NGOs engaged in support service functions such as education and training, research and documentation, legal and technical support, and advocacy.

In Thailand, the NGO-Coordinating Committee for Rural Development (NGO-CORD) has approximately 220 member organizations. Because of its large membership and regional diversity, regional NGO-CORDs have been established for better coordination and flexibility.

The National Council of Social Welfare of Thailand is a coordinating center for the promotion of social welfare organizations in Thailand and has 512 regular members and 125 affiliated members. The Thai Volunteer Service Foundation (TVS) has 400 member organizations that request volunteers to join in activities organized by TVS on a regular basis. The Primary Health NGOs Coordinating Committee (PHC) in Thailand has 20 member organizations.

In Australia, AUSTCARE serves as a special national umbrella NGO for the coordinated provision of emergency and longer term aid, and presently has sixteen members. The Australian Council for Overseas Aid (ACFOA) is a national umbrella organization for Australian-based NGOs that provide funding and human resources for aid and development work outside Australia.

In Malaysia, the Environmental Protection Society of Malaysia (EPSM) has helped build up a coalition of environmental groups through its role as the founding coordinator of the Malaysian Environmental and Conservation Network.

In Indonesia, Wahana Lingkungan Hidup (WALHI) serves as a network of concerned environmental NGOs. Yayasan Anissa Swansthi (YASANTI) provides regional and international linkages to advocate the inclusion of women's issues within the donor agency's programs, and to enhance the exchange of information with other NGOs.

In Japan, the Japanese NGO Center for International Cooperation (JANIC) was organized in 1987 through the initiative of several core NGOs engaged in international cooperation in order to encourage the future development of Japanese NGOs. Since its establishment, JANIC has been active in promoting cooperation among Japanese NGOs and other organizations, human resource and institutional development of NGOs, and public awareness on social issues in developing countries through seminars and publications.

In the United States, the Independent Sector, an association of eight hundred nonprofit organizations, was established in 1980 to create a national forum, encouraging giving, volunteering, and not-for-profit initiatives in order to better serve people, communities, and causes. InterAction was established in 1984, as a voluntary network coordination group for member NGOs, presently 143 in number, with the goals of promoting the status of the NGO sector itself and providing support to enhance their professional capacity and effectiveness.

In Singapore in 1991, SAVE (Society Against Family Violence) was registered as a full-fledged society to serve as an umbrella body for services dealing with various aspects of family violence. SAVE organizes interagency networking and consulting amongst related services for a more comprehensive linkage of services to the victims and perpetrators of domestic violence.

The Association of Foundations in the Philippines is a network of 106 philanthropic organizations in diverse fields. In 1992, the League of Corporate Foundations, also in the Philippines, was formally organized with twelve founding members. A permanent secretariat for the Australian Association of Philanthropy (AAP) was established in 1988 to further promote private and corporate philanthropy which has emerged as a significant sector in the past ten years.

III. Causes of Recent Development of Nonprofit and Nongovernmental Organizations in Asia Pacific

The country papers of this survey project provide analyses of causes of the impressive development of nongovernmental organizations in each respective country in recent years. These analyses are diverse in nature, reflecting a diversity of nations within the region in their level of economic development, in socio-political environments, and in historical as well as cultural background. Yet, a common underlying pattern can be clearly discerned in their discussion of causes and context for the recent development of nonprofit and nongovernmental organizations in Asia Pacific.

1. Rapid Economic Development and the Emergence of a Middle Class

One conspicuous phenomenon common to most of the countries in the Asia Pacific region in the past decade or two has been remarkable economic growth. This in itself explains a growth of philanthropic activities, particularly in the corporate sector in many countries. It is not surprising that Japan's philanthropic activities have been growing since the late 1970s, reflecting the phenomenal economic growth that has made the country one of the global economic powers. Whether Japan's philanthropic development has been commensurate with its economic growth or not, it has shown an impressive advancement. Around three hundred grant-making foundations, or half of the total number, were set up from 1980 to 1992. The number of foundations established from 1980 to 1984 was 94, 138 from 1985 to 1989, and 69 from 1990 to 1992. Corporate contributions have also shown a steady growth since 1984. According to the amount reported to the National Tax Administration Agency, it grew from 267.5 billion yen (approximately US$2.7 billion)[4] in 1984 to 549.1 billion yen (approximately US$5.5 billion) in 1990.

A similar or even faster philanthropic development can be observed in the newly industrialized economies (NIES) in Asia, such as Korea, Taiwan, and Hong Kong. In Taiwan, many foundations were set up during and after the period of its impressive economic growth in the 1980s. The number of foundations in Taiwan almost quadrupled during the period from 1981 to 1990, increasing from 80 in 1981 to 309 in 1990, 45.6 percent of which were established between 1982 and 1988. In countries that have started a growth pattern in more recent years, such as the ASEAN countries, there has also been a clear indication of a significant development of philanthropic activities as discussed in the country papers. In the Philippines, which has had a long tradition of philanthropy, a new pattern of corporate philanthropy has been developing with the strong leadership of the Philippine Business for Social Progress (PBSP). The survey report cites a study of corporate giving in the Philippines which shows 249 companies surveyed giving a total of 295 million pesos (US$11.8 million) in 1992, and 204 companies giving a total amount of 306 million pesos (US$12.24 million) in 1993, a four percent increase from the previous year.

The emergence of the nonprofit sector is often attributed to the growth of the middle class, which has been brought about by economic growth. Lester Salamon argues in his *Foreign Affairs* article that "the global economic growth that occurred during the 1960s and early 1970s...helped create in Latin America, Asia and Africa a sizable urban middle class whose leadership was critical to the emergence of private nonprofit organizations."5 Some of the country reports underscore this point in Asian countries that have witnessed an emergence of the urban middle class. The Thai researcher reports that "most public spirited developmental nonprofit organizations established (in the latter part of the 1980s) were middle class organizations." The Indonesian researcher also points out that "NGOs have been able to reflect on and articulate more general concerns for the environment, human rights and democratization now emerging most obviously, but by no means exclusively, among the middle class."

2. Need for Growth of a "Civil Society" in Responding to Pluralistic Social Needs

Many of the country reports point out, paradoxically, that the rise of the nonprofit sector in Asia is related to negative consequences of rapid economic development in these countries. They point out that "Asian governments have not been able to bring about equitable economic development, thus the NGOs have struggled for alternative development policies and strategies leading towards sustainable development" (Thai report), or "many activists perceive the national development program as favoring the growth of large industries and as programs mortgaging the welfare of future generations for the benefit of a few today" (Indonesia report). Thus, many NGOs consider their role to be that of reflecting concerns about the social and material condition of economically and socially disadvantaged people, and bringing them up to the national political agenda. Such advocacy activities involve "the dissemination of organizational positions on the national level...lobbying in Congress and executive offices with administrative discretion, and efforts to shape public opinion through the media..." (Philippines report). In addition to such an advocacy role, they consider it essential for NGOs to formulate alternative policies and have them incorporated into the national policy-making process. Many NGOs feel that "the ways in which government agencies work in tackling problems may not provide the solution sought...and NGOs may be able to provide an alternative means to tackle development problems" (Thai report). Such alternative policies, in their view, should address the basic systemic problems of economic inequities, environmental degradation, the population crisis, and other issues common to fast developing economies in Asia. Above all, the survey researchers reflect in their reports a growing sentiment that nonprofit organizations, including NGOs and private policy research institutions, should play a vital role in society in Asian countries which have been characterized by a growing pluralism. They report on the increasing awareness among Asians about the need to develop a "civil society" in their countries. As the government's power in these countries has become more decentralized, broader citizen participation in addressing a growing number of domestic and external policy issues has become essential. It is significant that the survey report on China indicates that "the tendency toward decentralization of governance has made it more difficult for relevant government agencies to meet the increasingly diversified social and cultural demands" and, thus, more "popular participation and public funding" is considered necessary. Even in Japan, where government agencies have acted as the sole arbitrator of public interest throughout its modernization process, their failure in recent years to properly address emerging issues such as the influx of foreign workers or growing problems associated with a fast aging society, has prompted the recent emergence of voluntary organizations which are often led by women and young leaders in many local communities. Such a growing role of NGOs and other nonprofit organizations would have been impossible in the cold war period of ideological confrontation where such organizations tended to be seen as advocates of dangerous communist/socialist positions or even subversive elements. Such suspicion on the part of the government or the establishment in these Asian countries may not have completely disappeared, nor has the considerable tension between the public sector and the voluntary sector been dissipated, but the collaborators of the survey reports register a positive trend in their countries toward an advancement of "civil society."

3. Government Recognition of the Roles of Nonprofit and Nongovernmental Organizations

Reflecting a general trend as discussed in the previous section, the government leaders of many countries in Asia Pacific have been giving an explicit or, at least, tacit acknowledgment of the useful functions nonprofit and nongovernmental organizations play in their society. Even in Malaysia where NGOs have shown relatively slow development due to the government's concern that their activities may jeopardize national security, it is reported that "the government is moving towards greater recognition of the role of developmental NGOs and is willing to work with them to promote development." Reflecting a new trend, as discussed above, the report on China indicates that there is an increasingly clear recognition in China that "vertical administration and regulation within government agencies are insufficient and ineffective to satisfy economic, educational, and training needs," and thus, "in many cases the government is now willing to share some of its responsibilities with the newly proliferating NGOs." The following illustrations of governmental actions in Asia Pacific countries underscore the trend toward a greater recognition of NGOs and other independent sector institutions.

In the Philippines, President Ramos' vision of a "Philippines 2000" is seeking the active participation of NGOs. A private sector coalition called the People's 2000 has been organized to support the implementation of the Medium Term Philippines Development Plan. The Local Government Code of 1991 stipulated the participation of NGOs in all levels of decision making with the allocation of specific seats in local development councils.

In Thailand, NGO-CORD has been asked to actively participate in the formulation of the Sixth and Seventh National Development Plans (1986–90 and 1991–95) as well as to serve as a member of several working groups and subcommittees on various development issues.

In Malaysia, the government invited moderate NGOs, such as the Federation of Malaysia Consumers' Association (FOMCA) and the National Council of Women's Organizations (NCWO), to participate in the National Economic Consultation Council to decide on the National Economic Policy after 1990.

In Australia, major NGOs have considerable influence on a national scale in the development of government policy in the areas of health, welfare, and community development. They also actively seek to influence the government in the annual budget allocation of public sources to the nongovernmental and nonprofit sector of health and welfare service providers.

In Japan, as more NGOs have started gaining international recognition in recent years, the government has finally begun to reach out to NGOs. In 1989, a year after announcing an aggregate increase of official development assistance (ODA) over the four-year period of 1988–92 to $50 billion dollars, the Ministry of Foreign Affairs introduced a "Subsidiary System for NGO Projects" and a "Grant Assistance for Grass-roots Projects." Total disbursement through the program has increased fivefold in the past five years from 110 million yen in 1989 to 540 million yen in 1994.

In Singapore, the government is firm in its stand against public welfare programs modeled after those in Europe and North America and has preferred to encourage the private sector in playing a bigger role in contributing to the needs of the community. As Singapore's Community Development Minister Wong Kan Seng said in an articles in *The Straits Times* (23/3/90), willing individuals and community groups should be given the chance to contribute to Singapore's welfare services, while the government's role should be that of a catalyst, providing the basics and necessary funding.

In Vietnam, a policy and drafting committee is now drafting a law on nonprofit groups which seeks to balance encouragement of non-state initiative and state control, and is intended to clarify the confused regulatory environment. The foreign NGO community in Vietnam, The Ford Foundation, and others are providing opportunities for the policy and drafting group to explore diverse perspectives and examples for the functioning of a vibrant NGO sector.

4. Influence of Global and Regional NGO Movements

Development of nonprofit and nongovernmental organizations in countries in Asia Pacific has received a considerable boost from an international NGO movement which has also been accelerated by international organizations such as UNHCR, UNICEF, UNESCO, UNIFEM, WHO, and UNFPA. The Women's Year and Women's Decade announced by the United Nations, for example, have had a considerable impact on women's NGOs throughout the world. The survey report on China indicates that such UN initiatives and related regional and international conferences such as the NGO Forum of Asia Pacific Regional Preparatory Committee in Manila in November 1993, the Women Empowering Communications Conference in Bangkok in February 1994, and the NGO Consultation and Second Preparatory Committee in New York in March 1994 have facilitated the formation of several women's networks cutting across sectors and professions.

Japan's recent surge of interest in the NGO movement has also been closely associated with such international trends to encourage NGO participation in addressing many global issues of development, the environment, refugees, human rights, women's rights, among others. It is said that the United Nations Conference on Environment and Development (UNCED) in Rio de Janeiro in 1992, was a watershed event for Japan's NGO development as it was the first time that a significant number of NGOs participated in an official international meeting.

International crises also have encouraged the development of NGOs and philanthropic organizations. An earlier illustration is the participation of many NGOs from many countries including those in Asia which joined with the UN High Commissioner for Refugees (UNHCR) to provide assistance to refugees at the time of the fall of Saigon and Phnom Penh in 1975. More recent refugee crises in Cambodia and Rwanda have also heightened concerns of Asian countries in assistance through NGOs and philanthropic organizations.

IV. Emergence of Asia Pacific Networks and Cooperative Relations among NGOs

The survey reports from fifteen countries underscore a major premise of the project, s indicated at the outset of this paper, that there has been a growing number of networks and collaborative arrangements among nonprofit and nongovernmental organizations within the Asia Pacific region. Such regional networks and collaborative schemes cover NGOs in diverse areas of activities such as development assistance, environmental issues, and refugees.

For NGOs in Asian countries, particularly among the more recently growing economies, there have been strong motives to develop regional ties with their counterparts. For NGOs of the more advanced economies in North America, Japan, Korea, and Australia, there has also been a trend toward promoting greater cooperative activities in a broader Asia Pacific context. Such a trend among NGOs obviously reflects a growing interdependent relationship among the nations in Asia Pacific. The country reports provide some analyses of this trend of emergence of Asia Pacific NGO cooperation and networks.

1. Impetus of Asian NGOs toward Regional Cooperation and Networks

Many reports covering emerging economies in Asia point out that, at this stage of development, NGOs in these countries believe that joint efforts and closer communication with their counterparts in Asia Pacific will help strengthen their efforts in a significant manner. Modern advanced communication technology and transportation, they believe, greatly facilitate the exchange of information as well as joint endeavors by organizations in the region. They assume that countries within the interdependent Asia Pacific region share common economic, cultural, and political objectives, and they believe this will enhance the effectiveness of collaboration among them.

It is suggested that "with the concept of mobilization and the needs to help strengthen each other, networking among NGOs in Asia has become very strong" (Thai report) and that "the main reason NGOs sought linkages with other NGOs in the region was to forward specific advocacy agendas, and this collective or joint action spurred their interest in developing strong linkages with partners in other Asia Pacific countries" (Indonesian report). Some country reports point out that it is assumed that less economically developed countries within the region can be assisted by more economically advanced countries such as the United States, Canada, Japan, and Korea, among others.

The growing importance of global and regional issues also provides an impetus for greater cooperation among NGOs in Asia Pacific. Global issues such as human rights, the environment, women, migration and refugees, the spread of AIDS, and population growth all pose major challenges to the Asia Pacific region. Widespread concern over these challenges has encouraged the formation of linkages and cooperative arrangements of like-minded NGOs across national boundaries in Asia Pacific. NGOs have become aware of the fact that many Asian countries have similar development problems requiring joint action or support to eradicate the problems that cross national boundaries. Many country reports suggest that during the last decade, networking has become the dominant feature of nongovernment organizations working on specific issues crossing national borders. Moreover, it is recognized that these global issues cannot be effectively addressed by any single country and it is, therefore, essential to form cross-border alliances to seek appropriate solutions.

The establishment of linkages with their counterparts abroad is also regarded as an effective means for NGOs to strengthen themselves in dealing with government controls in their national setting. On this particular point, it is reported that, while Indonesian NGOs have a strong desire and motivation to foster linkages with other NGOs in the Asia Pacific region, many of them expressed dismay that they were more strongly linked with NGOs in the United States than they were linked with NGOs in Asian countries, such as Japan, a country much closer geographically and with greater and larger aid linkages to Indonesia than the United States. This phenomenon can be explained by their perception of reliability when it comes to the needed protection these Indonesian NGOs seek from their foreign counterparts in dealing with their own government's control.

2. Impetus of Japanese NGOs Toward Regional Cooperation and Networks

According to the *Directory of Japanese NGOs Active in International Cooperation 1994*,[6] 141 out of 269 organizations, or seventy-six percent of the total, have programs in Asia, and an additional 26 organizations have programs in Oceania. Such a heavy Asia Pacific orientation of Japanese NGOs has become noticeable in recent years. An increasing number of Japanese NGOs seeks contacts and association with their counterparts in Asian countries in their efforts to participate in activities in these countries. There seem to be several reasons for this trend. One is that Japan's general interest closely follows the growing pattern of economic interactions with Asian countries which generate more exchange of people and information. For another, geographical proximity of these Asian countries as well as cultural familiarity makes these Asian countries more accessible to Japanese NGOs. From the point of view of Japanese NGOs' missions, they feel that they should play a more active role in bringing Japan closer to Asia in a more constructive manner. Many NGOs in Japan are concerned about the unpreparedness of Japanese people to live in the culturally diverse environments that they are increasingly being exposed to as the influx of foreigners in their communities continues to grow. In particular, they feel traditional Japanese prejudices toward Asians have to be overcome, and that the Japanese people should develop greater respect toward the culture and values of their Asian neighbors. They are also conscious of Japan's failure to come to terms with its own history, particularly as it relates to the many Asian countries that suffered from Japanese military aggression during World War II. Therefore, an increasing number of Japanese NGOs, particularly international exchange organizations in local communities, are concerned with public education of the Japanese themselves in these areas. Asian countries also provide opportunities for Japan to play a more active international role, a role which NGOs feel they must fulfill in the region. They are also conscious of the possible negative impact of Japan's enhanced economic presence in these countries, and they feel they should address the problems that may arise from such economic interaction.

3. Growing Interest of North American NGOs in Asia Pacific

According to a recent survey conducted by Katsutoshi Enokida, presently Senior Coordinator at the Center for Global Partnership (CGP), there are presently approximately fifty international NGOs and philanthropic organizations, including about thirty U.S. organizations, that have some form of presence in Japan. They include grant-making or operating foundations, such as the Asia Foundation and the International Youth Foundation; and NGOs active in such fields as development assistance and environmental protection, such as the National Wildlife Federation (NWF), the World Wildlife Fund (WWF), the Nature Conservancy, Conservation International, and Greenpeace. According to the Canadian Council for International Cooperation (CCIC), as cited in the Canadian country paper for this survey, there are approximately thirty Canadian organizations of significant size with development programs in Asia Pacific, out of a hundred and thiry Canadian organizations working in international development. Many of these North American NGOs are active in the Asia Pacific region in close cooperation with indigenous NGOs and regional and national networks among these organizations, as discussed in the previous section. While some U.S. NGOs, such as NWF, hope to "develop relationships with indigenous NGOs in Japan in their effort to lobby the Japanese government to adopt ODA funding policies that are more reflective of sustainable development policies," these NGOs are also interested in making effective use of increasing Japanese ODA funding available to them (U.S. report). Many NGOs from North America have many years of experience and professional expertise that are not sufficiently available for emerging NGOs in Asian countries, and they play an essential catalytic role in advancing the effectiveness of NGO activities in the region. On the other hand, these NGOs from the United States and Canada that are active in Asia have been affected positively by "the network of indigenous or local grassroots organizations which is well advanced in many Asian countries" (U.S. report). Thus, the cooperative relationship between Asian NGOs and NGOs of the advanced economies, particularly of the United States and Canada, in the Asia Pacific region seems to be expanding in a positive way, and the partnership can be characterized as mutually beneficial. These NGOs in the United States and Canada may be contributing to broader Asia Pacific cooperation by stimulating interest among the public in their own countries in the region. The Canadian survey paper makes this point by stating that "Canada spends a large proportion of its overseas dollars in Asia, and Canadians need to be aware of the effects of their involvement. Canadian NGOs can bring the other side of the story of Asian development to the Canadian public, the stories of the grassroots community organizations, which balance the government's emphasis on economic activities." Such public interest is essential as "the lack of interest and the ignorance of this region among the American public in general, except for short-term business interest in certain economies, have negatively affected the public support for American NGO activities in Asia" (U.S. report).

4. Asia Pacific NGO Associations, Networks, and Conferences

There clearly has been an emergence of a number of associations, networks, and other forms of interactions among NGOs in Asia Pacific in recent years, reflecting a general trend in the Asia Pacific countries as has been discussed in this section. This emergence of NGO networks and interactions is reported in most of the country papers of this survey. A common pattern is for networking and association building among NGOs to proceed on a national level, while these national associations and networks reach out to similar organizations in other countries within the region and establish linkages with them. Conversely, in some cases, national chapters of NGOs have been organized in certain fields in response to existing regional associations. Some others have been established through initiatives or encouragement of international organizations such as the United Nations. Some national-level networks and associations promote international linkages with individual NGOs in other countries on their own without going into formal linkages with similar national associations in other countries.

It is anticipated that as regional institutions at the government level are built in the coming years, there will be further growth of regional groupings of nonprofit and nongovernmental organizations. Though many reports cite these regional organizations, networks, and a series of conferences and dialogues, some of the major initiatives are described below to provide a general picture of this development:

CODE-NGO, the largest coalition of major development NGO networks in the

Philippines, has been forging linkages with other development NGOs in Asia. It has also established networks with NGOs in developed countries such as Australia, Canada, the United States, and the European Union in order to influence ODA policies for the Philippines and to set up a mechanism for ODA funds to be channeled to Filipino NGOs.

Yayasan Bina Desa was founded in 1974 to develop linkages and networks among NGOs in Asia, and this has led to the establishment of the South East Asia Development of Human Resources and Rural Areas Forum (SEADHRRA). Yayasan Bina Desa became the Indonesia chapter, INDRHRRA, and along with PHILDHRRA, the Philippines chapter, THAIDHRRA, the Thai chapter, and other DHRRA organizations in Malaysia, Korea, and Japan, has a solid regional network. In turn, PHILDHRRA, a national network of sixty-two development NGOs, has a collaborative arrangement with Canadian NGOs through the Philippines-Canada Human Resource Development Program (PCHRD).

The Asian NGO Coalition for Agrarian Reform and Rural Development (ANGOC) is an Asian regional association of twenty-three development NGOs and NGO networks from eight countries, including Indonesia, Malaysia, the Philippines, and Thailand. It aims to facilitate people-centered development in the region by promoting South-South and North-South dialogue and enhancing human resource development and capacity building of NGOs through research and publications, seminars and workshops, and development education and training.

The Asian Alliance of Appropriate Technology Practitioners, Inc. (APPROTECH ASIA) has established a network committed to the development of appropriate technology and its promotion for grassroots communities. It consists of ten full member organizations and fifteen associate member organizations from the Philippines, India, Bangladesh, Thailand, Indonesia, Sri Lanka, Malaysia, Singapore, and Pakistan. Its major programs include technology dissemination, appropriate technology promotional services, publications and documentation, and information systems development.

The Southeast Asian NGO Consortium for Sustainable Development (SEACON) was founded as a consortium of Southeast Asian NGOs in 1989 and is comprised of three regional networking organizations, namely ANGOC, the Asian Culture Forum on Development (ACFOD), and APPROTECH ASIA, and the representative NGOs of the Philippines, Thailand, Indonesia, and Malaysia. Its aim is to promote regionwide people's participation and social reform in ensuring sustainable development approaches. SEACON has initiated a consultation process in four Southeast Asian countries, through SVITA Foundation in Thailand, the Management

Institute for Social Change (MINSOC) in Malaysia, the Green Forum in the Philippines, and WALHI in Indonesia.

YASANTI in Indonesia, founded to "improve the status of women" has linkages with Tenaganita and Awam in Malaysia, the Asia Pacific Workers Link based in Bangkok (APWLD), PHILDHRRA, and a few Thai NGOs.

ENGENDER in Singapore is the secretariat of a new initiative WEDNET Asia-Pacific, which is a regional research and action network on women, the environment, and development, focusing on women's indigenous knowledge of the environment.

ACFOD is a forum of NGOs in Asia working to promote development based on socio-economic reforms, culture and religion. Its activities range from training NGO staff and volunteers, to research, and raising of public awareness. The member countries involved are Thailand, Bangladesh, India, Japan, Nepal, Malaysia, the Philippines, and Sri Lanka.

Aside from the above illustrations of major regional networks of NGOs, there is an increasing number of regional conferences for NGOs, providing them with the opportunity to share information and establish contacts among themselves. Recent major regional conferences include the following:

The United Nations Economic and Social Commission for Asia and the Pacific (ESCAP), jointly with the Hong Kong Council of Social Services, organized a seminar on Cooperation between Government Agencies and Non-Governmental Organizations in the Planning and Delivery of Social Services in Hong Kong in December 1990. As one of the recent ESCAP endeavors to strengthen the role of NGOs in assisting national efforts to promote social development, the purpose of the seminar was to provide a forum for twenty-three invited experts from government agencies and NGOs from the ESCAP region to consider modalities for cooperation in the planning and delivery of social services.

In 1992, JANIC organized the International Workshop on Human Resource Development for NGOs at the Asian Rural Institute to enhance research and training collaboration among NGOs in Asia Pacific. The Workshop was attended by NGO experts from Bangladesh, Sri Lanka, the Philippines, Indonesia, Malaysia, Thailand, Canada, and the United States.

The Asian and Pacific Regional NGO Symposium was held in Manila in November 1993. Topics included health, labor, agriculture, culture and religion, political empowerment, economic violence, and human rights.

The Asia Pacific NGO Symposium on Social Development was held in Bangkok in July 1994, and was attended by some eighty representatives from NGOs in the

Asia Pacific region. The Australian Council of Social Services (ACOSS), a national umbrella organization, had a leadership role in organizing this symposium.

The Third Asia Pacific NGO Environmental Conference was sponsored by the Siam Environmental Club, the Seoul Eco Club, and the Japan Environmental Council in Kyoto in November 1994 to discuss environmental and development issues in the region. NGO leaders who participated in the Conference decided to establish The Asia-Pacific Environment Council in 1995 in order to promote information exchange and cooperation among environmental NGOs in the region.

V. Emergence of Asia Pacific Networks and Cooperation among Policy Research Institutions

A most dramatic development to underscore the growing networks and collaborative arrangements among policy research institutions and intellectuals in Asia Pacific is the creation of the Council for Security Cooperation in Asia Pacific (CSCAP) in 1994. Its major objective is to create a more structured regional process of nongovernmental dialogue and research on security issues, open to all the countries and regions in Asia Pacific, and it is based on several on-going nongovernmental dialogue channels with the participation of several research institutions in the region. Perhaps the most important dialogue series that contributed to the creation of CSCAP is an ASEAN Institutes for Strategic and International Studies (ASEAN-ISIS) network which was established in 1988, involving five institutes from different ASEAN countries. The founding institutes were the Center for Strategic and International Studies (CSIS) in Jakarta, the Institute of Strategic and International Studies (ISIS) in Malaysia, the Center for Integrative Development Studies (CIDS) of the University of the Philippines (now reorganized as the Institute for Strategic and Development Studies—ISDS), the Institute of Security and International Studies (ISIS) of Chulalongkorn University of Thailand, and the Singapore Institute of International Affairs (SIIA). Significantly, such institutional linkages were established through interpersonal ties that were built between the heads of these institutions through a series of security dialogues since the early 1980s.[7] At the Asia Pacific regional level, CSCAP was preceded by the Asia-Pacific Roundtable (APR) on Security Cooperation, first held in January 1987 as an informal forum on regional strategic and security issues. APR was hosted by ISIS-Kuala Lumpur for the first few years until it was convened by ASEAN-ISIS in 1993, although it is still held in Kuala Lumpur. It was at a meeting of ASEAN-ISIS that the concept of the ASEAN Regional Forum (ARF) was first introduced, which was later formally adopted by the ASEAN governments. As the deputy director-general of ISIS-Kuala Lumpur puts it, CSCAP is an intellectual version and/or underpinning of the ARF, while ASEAN-ISIS plays a similar function vis-à-vis ASEAN itself.

CSCAP, thus, can be regarded as a culmination of "a significant outpouring of academic writing, research and conference activity, especially since 1990," focused on regional security issues. Such nongovernmental activity has been characterized by "a multilateral nature involving simultaneous participation from several Asia Pacific countries."[8] Many of these regional collaborative channels have been of a "blended" or "track two" nature, "involving meetings of academics, journalists, and occasionally politicians" and often including "government officials attending in an "unofficial, private capacity."[9] They have performed important functions in the Asia Pacific region, such as laying the groundwork for formal multilateral government consultations on regional security, once considered to be a sensitive subject to some governments in the region. The informality of dialogues organized by nongovernmental institutions also facilitated a freer flow of ideas and information, uninhibited by governmental constraints. Above all, they have given an impetus for a process of building a community of like-minded intellectual leaders who have been developing a habit of working together and who have been raising the visibility of common security concerns within the region.

Such "track two" efforts are likely to gain greater momentum in the coming years as there is greater recognition by the governments of many Asian countries about the utility of such efforts. Korean Foreign Minister Han Sung-Joo stated in his speech at the Seoul meeting of "Private Philanthropy in East Asia" (held in August 1993) that, "multi-dimensionalism, a major fundamental of Korea's New Diplomacy, involves the diversification of actors as well as of the issue areas. Diplomacy should not be the exclusive domain of the government. It should also be supported by people-to-people diplomacy undertaken by both individuals and private organizations." ASEAN-ISIS was recognized by ASEAN, and its contribution to the organization of ASEAN was specifically cited in the communique of the ASEAN Minister's Meeting in 1993.

Actually, Asia Pacific regional cooperation among nongovernmental research institutions and intellectual leaders was preceded by similar efforts in the economic field in Asia Pacific. The Pacific Forum for Trade and Development (PAFTAD) was established as early as 1968, as a forum for economists and researchers associated with research institutions within the region, and they continue to undertake annual meetings and research projects. The Pacific Economic Cooperation Council

(PECC), with the tripartite participation of business, government, and academic leaders, has sponsored a multinational task force to study diverse issues such as trade, investment, development assistance, science and technology, and energy.

These dialogues and research activities on economic issues have also built networks of intellectuals and professionals in Asia Pacific that will unquestionably play an important role in community building in Asia Pacific, as regional economic interactions will continue to be a dominant force in defining the concept of Asia Pacific. APEC has sought the advice of an Eminent Persons Group headed by C. Fred Bergsten, director of the Institute for International Economics, on the goal of trade liberalization in the region. The Eminent Persons Group has acted as an "agenda setter" for APEC by making proposals that have served as discussion materials for top-level APEC discussions. It thereby underscores the role to be played through joint efforts by nongovernmental actors on issues related to the building of the Asia Pacific regional community.[10]

One major change in the pattern of development of the cooperation among research institutions in Asia Pacific in recent years as compared with the past is a tendency for Asian research institutions to take a strong initiative and to have very active participation in these joint efforts. The development of CSCAP as cited above is a case in point, and it is reported that Asian participants are not quiet partners in international conferences and dialogues anymore. This clearly reflects the evolution of a relationship among nations in Asia Pacific in the post–cold war era where the countries in Southeast and Northeast Asia have been gaining a high degree of self-confidence in managing the growing interdependence on their own, without relying on the leadership of any dominant nation, particularly the United States or Japan. Asia Pacific intellectual interactions have become increasingly multilateral in character with all the participants bringing to the joint fora their respective perspectives on issues of common interest and concern.

Such Asia Pacific regional cooperation among nongovernmental research institutions is most likely to continue growing, as stated in the survey reports: the advanced economies such as the United States, Canada, Japan, and Australia will pay even greater attention to such efforts in the coming years, and many countries in East and Southeast Asia will witness an increase or diversification of research institutions.

In Canada, "a great deal of governmental and academic attention has been directed at raising the content and profile of Canadian connections across the Pacific."

Increased U.S. research interest reflects "the growth of regional economic and political linkages, the institutional manifestations of regionalism, and the implications of regional institutions for economic growth and international security."

The Australian survey report indicates that "the dramatic increase in Asia research centers in the 1990s (fifty-six percent) reflects strong government leadership in driving Australia's engagement with the countries of Asia."

Japan's country report indicates that the number of Asia Pacific related projects carried out by research institutions has increased significantly in the past few years. For instance, in 1992 and 1993, respectively, 128 and 129 projects on Asia Pacific related themes were conducted by Japanese think tanks. The proportion of these projects to all international studies has now risen to almost seventy percent.

Among Southeast Asian countries, where a smaller number of very active research institutions have traditionally played a key role in advancing regional cooperation as discussed before, there are signs of diversification and multiplication of actors in international dialogue and research.

The Malaysian survey report estimates that more than twenty institutions were established in response to the demand for new ideas for Vision 2020 initiated recently by Prime Minister Mahathir. They have reportedly begun to be engaged in international research cooperation and dialogue, particularly in the Asia Pacific region.

The Indonesian report quotes Jusuf Wanandi, chairman of CSIS's Supervisory Board, as saying "the growth and proliferation of nongovernmental organizations is seen as an indication that society does not intend to leave discussion and solution of various developmental problems solely to the government." In this connection, the emergence of the Centre for Information and Development Studies (CIDES) is seen to be "an example of pluralism in the direction of more nongovernmental initiatives" (Indonesian report).

In Hong Kong, "the establishment of the Hong Kong Institute of Asia-Pacific Studies at the Chinese University of Hong Kong in 1990 is the best example of a redirection of research activities."

Similarly, in China in recognition of the importace of the region, the Institute of Asia-Pacific Studies was established in 1988 in the Chinese Academy of Social Sciences, through the merger of the Institute of South Asian Studies and the Asia-Pacific Studies Division of the Institute of World Economy and Politics.

In Thailand, the establishment of the Thailand Institute of Public and International Affairs merits special attention from the viewpoint of the growing civil society. It aims to promote nongovernmental research in public and international affairs by providing existing research institutions with financial and other supports, a totally new development in a society which "has not developed the tradition of privately-funded policy-oriented research."

VI. Challenges for Further Development of Nonprofit and Nongovernmental Organizations in Asia Pacific and Their Cooperation

Despite the impressive growth of nonprofit and nongovernmental organizations in Asia Pacific, they continue to face rather formidable constraints against their activities and against further growth. This is particularly true for rapidly developing economies in Asia, such as the ASEAN countries, but it also applies to economically advanced nations such as Japan. These constraints include the overall attitude of government toward NGOs and policy research institutions; a lack of professional staff in the case of NGOs and a lack of qualified research staff and administrative staff in the case of policy research institutions; and difficulties of raising funds, partly due to a limited number of funding sources and partly due to the absence of tax incentives for individual or corporate contributions.

1. Adjusting the Relationship with the Government

The relationship between the government and the NGOs or policy research institutions in Asia Pacific varies from country to country depending on the country's development process and socio-political dynamics. In the case of some Asian countries that have started their democratization process relatively recently, the development of a civil society may be viewed by the government to undermine social stability or even national security. However, as reported earlier, some Asian governments, such as the Philippines and Thailand, have begun to take a very positive attitude toward NGOs in recent years. In the more advanced Asian countries such as Japan, there seems to be an unshakable assumption on the part of the government bureaucrats that they are most knowledgeable and skillful in resource allocation. Some illustrations of the kind of constraints facing some of the Asian countries are cited from the country reports below:

In Malaysia, NGOs are given relatively limited rein compared to their counterparts in developed countries especially when it is felt that their activities may jeopardize national security, and absolute power is given to the Registrar of Societies to deregister "undesirable societies" at will.

The Chinese leadership, while giving increasing weight to NGOs, continues to emphasize political and social stability with the concern that any loosening of control over NGOs might foster dissenting political forces. It is assumed that the government, faced with the difficulties of drafting new regulations, has preferred to retain its discretion to control the growth of NGOs and restrict the expanding areas of their activities.

In early 1994 the Government of Indonesia drafted a new regulation in the form of a Presidential Decree, which many Indonesian NGOs view as a means to control and regulate nongovernmental organizations and activities. Many Indonesian NGOs fear that the planned Presidential Decree will be used as a weapon, instead of as a tool to strengthen and activate the NGO community in Indonesia.

In Singapore, there is a clause under the Societies Act that specifies that any association that is political in nature must restrict its membership to citizens of Singapore, and must not have such affiliation or connection outside the country as is considered by the Registrar to be contrary to national interest (Societies Act—Chapter 311, 1985). Though not an unusual restriction in view of the fact that Singapore is a nation state, this restriction nevertheless does hamper regional cooperation.

In Japan it is extremely difficult to incorporate NGOs due to stringent government regulations, such as the requirement of basic capital of three hundred million yen (approximately US$3 million) held permanently in the bank. Moreover, the current process for obtaining incorporated status lacks transparency as treatment of the applications depends on the ministry and the personnel with whom an organization must negotiate. Tax incentives for contributions are also extremely limited, making fund raising for NGOs very difficult. Due to these complexities, many policy research institutions sponsored by major corporations often choose not to be incorporated as nonprofit organizations but operate as profit-corporations instead.

2. Need for Institution Building and Development of Human Resources in NGOs andPolicy Research Institutions in Asia Pacific

Partly due to their relatively brief history, most of the Asian NGOs and policy research institutions have a rather meager professional staff running their organizations. With a shortage of competent staff, many NGOs are preoccupied with daily operations and don't have additional personnel who can devote their time and energy to institution building which includes very vital fund-raising efforts. The sudden attention given to the NGO movement in recent years has caused an added demand on a few leading NGO activists to appear in the media, participate in government councils, and carry out a number of other outside chores, not enabling them to concentrate on their own activities. With a growing number of international collaborative schemes and networking efforts, these Asian NGO leaders are facing the even more serious challenge of managing their own time by setting priorities for their activities.

The situation for policy research institutions in most of the Asian countries is quite similar. The fact that a small number of "usual suspects" appears at many international meetings and on research projects underscores a major challenge to these leading intellectuals who have led the Asia Pacific community building efforts through their joint efforts over the years. With growing regional collaborative activities as discussed earlier, the demand on them will continue to rise even more. The encouraging development of a greater interest in North America and elsewhere in Asia Pacific is bound to make it fashionable to stage conferences in the region prominently featuring the "usual suspects." There have been some unsuccessful attempts to train future intellectual leaders and usher them into regional and international fora. Yet, serious exploration should be made to alleviate the current situation.

3. Improving Financial Base of NGOs and Research Institutions

Some of the future challenges discussed above might be readily overcome if there were sufficient funds to operate NGOs or policy research institutions. Indeed, many of the problems facing these nonprofit and nongovernmental organizations are related to the lack of sufficient funding. Professional staff can be increased if there is additional and stable funding. The growing trend for regional cooperation and networking among the nonprofit and nongovernmental organizations in Asia Pacific can be further promoted only if necessary funding is made available. The financial problems will be exacerbated if traditional support from American foundations or international organizations is scaled down as the funds tend to be shifted from economically advancing Southeast and Northeast Asia to other regions in the world, as pointed out by some of the country papers. Yet, indigenous funding sources have not grown sufficiently in Asia Pacific to fill the possible gap that would be created in the funding picture, as reported in the Thai report. On the other hand, there seems to be a new trend for partnership between business corporations and NGOs, as reported in the Indonesian paper, thus offering a new source of funding.

The growing interest of respective governments in nonprofit and nongovernmental organizations, as reported above, may make more public funds available for these organizations. This, however, may create the undesirable situation of the government bureaucrats exerting undue influence on the activities of the NGOs and independent policy research institutions. Even if government funding can be useful, availability of matching funds from other sources including the indigenous private or corporate foundations or individual donations is still important. Thus, philanthropic development in Asia Pacific and regional cooperation on philanthropic development hold the key to the future advancement of Asia Pacific regional cooperation among nonprofit and nongovernmental organizations. Discussion of philanthropic development and cooperation in the region, as stated in the following section, is obviously important. At the same time, as discussed in some of the country reports, iverse modalities of linkages that NGOs may develop with government agencies, corporations, individuals, and private foundations, without losing their comparative advantage as an independent social force will be an important subject for future exploration.

VII. Philanthropic Development and Cooperation in Asia Pacific

The foregoing chapters of this paper focused primarily on two segments of the broader nonprofit and nongovernmental sector in Asia Pacific, namely NGOs and independent policy research institutions, though the third segment of philanthropy was included in the discussion of the overall trend of the sector. As was the case with NGOs and policy research institutions, discussion on private and corporate philanthropy in Asia Pacific is to be based on the survey of philanthropic development in the Asia Pacific nations. However, this discussion will also have to take into account the preceding discussion of new opportunities and demands for philanthropic development arising from the growth of NGOs and policy research institutions in most of the countries surveyed and the expanding network and cooperation among them in the Asia Pacific regional context. Continued development of NGOs and research institutions and their regional cooperation will have to be accompanied by secure financial support for their activities. Hence, philanthropic development and cooperation in Asia Pacific now has an added urgency. Moreover, as pointed out in the previous chapter, the trend of a gradual decline in the longstanding American financial support for Asian NGOs and research institutions will inevitably put a heavier burden on indigenous financial support. Even from the point of view of the new requirement for building closer cooperative relationships and networks among nonprofit and nongovernmental organizations in Asia Pacific, there is the need for combined efforts within the region to secure sufficient funding to further promote such efforts. In short, to build the underpinning of the emerging Asia Pacific regional community, strengthening private and corporate philanthropy in the regional context will be critical.

This survey, as well as discussion on philanthropic development in this paper was preceded by the two symposia mentioned in the introduction to this report, each of which has resulted in a substantive publication of the background papers. One area that attracted considerable attention in the two previous symposia was the subject of corporate philanthropy in this region. The present survey, which emphasizes the Asia Pacific regional context, examines present patterns of development and future prospects for indigenous corporate philanthropic activities in the emerging Asian countries. A related area that was also discussed rather extensively at the Seoul Symposium is the possible development of diverse patterns of philanthropy including new models of publicly funded but privately managed foundations in Asia Pacific. This section will integrate some of the findings of the survey on these areas. Secondly, the prospects for philanthropic activities of Japan and the United States in Asia Pacific will be discussed, as such development will be critical in promoting broader Asia Pacific philanthropic development and cooperation. Thirdly, this chapter will discuss possible mechanisms for facilitating philanthropic cooperation among the Asia Pacific countries.

1. Present Trend and Future Prospect of Corporate Philanthropy in Asian Countries

The discussion at the aforementioned Bangkok symposium pointed to a greater likelihood of future development of corporate foundations in Asia rather than the large private foundation model which is often, and not accurately, considered to be the American model. Given the fact that the phenomenal economic growth in East and Southeast Asia has been corporate-driven, and accumulation of wealth often takes place in large corporate conglomerates, this is a natural evolution. Some of the country reports underscore this assumption.

In Korea, among the 81 corporate foundations listed in the *Directory of Company-Sponsored Foundations of the Federation of Korean Industries*, only nine were established before 1970, whereas sixty-two were set up during the 1970s and 1980s. From 1990 to 1992, ten corporate foundations, or ten percent of the total established in almost half a century, came into existence.

In Taiwan, corporate foundations continued to grow during the period from 1982 to 1990. A total of twenty-six corporate foundations were established between 1982 and 1988, prior to the termination of the Emergency Decree. In contrast, twenty-one corporate foundations were established in the first two years following the lifting of the Emergency Decree, equal to the number of corporate foundations set up between 1972 and 1981. It is anticipated that corporate foundations will continue to gain in importance.

In the Philippines, the League of Corporate Foundations (LCF) was formally organized with twelve founding members. Believing in the important role of corporate foundations to bridge business expertise and social development, LCF was organized with the vision of "promoting and strengthening the commitment of the business sector to social development with its membership improving the quality of life of the communities it serves."

In Thailand, the Chaiyong Limthongkul Foundation, a multi-million dollar foundation, has been funded with profits from the Manager Group. The foundation is "committed to the generation, dissemination, and exchange of knowledge and expertise in public policy, international affairs, arts, and culture."

In Indonesia, Dana Mitra Lingkungan (DML) or Friends of the Environment was established in 1983 by prominent business leaders and environment activists with the support of the then State Minister for Population and Environment. Its objective is to generate environmental awareness among the public, particularly the business sector through the mobilization and management of an endowment fund. Special grant assistance and attention is given to projects submitted by NGOs.

On the other hand, some of the country reports indicate that there is still a great deal of room for future efforts to stimulate corporate giving in their countries. The Thai country report provides analysis of corporate philanthropy on the basis of an extensive questionnaire, and identifies a growing interest held by corporations, though "most firms have neither definite plans nor specific budget allocations for donations as corporate funding is somewhat new in Thailand." In Indonesia, there is an increasing interest among major corporations in making contributions for private causes such as environmental protection, but they continue to be under pressure to make donations for government related projects. These findings reported in the survey suggest that if some appropriate mechanism or policy measure can be taken, corporate philanthropy in Asian countries will have great potential for major development in the future.

In terms of government policies, further growth of corporate or private philanthropy in many Asian countries has been hampered due to the persisting rigid and traditional regulatory regime. Some illustrations of such constraints reported in the survey reports include:

The government in Australia has never provided tax incentives or vehicles to promote the growth of private philanthropy. Current government practice indicates that it would prefer monies by way of taxation so it can determine distribution.

In the Philippines, where corporate philanthropy is more developed than other Asian countries, the legal context for philanthropy has provided fiscal incentives to donors but is still insufficient to allow flexibility, owing to the limited scope and applicability of deductions allowed by the present provisions.

In Taiwan, when foundations are registering with the government, if their statement of mission clashes with the "established policy" or if the government fears they might threaten its "authority," it will deliberately frustrate their efforts by not approving the name of the prospective foundation or by being ambiguous about which government department would be in charge of the foundation-to-be.

In China, the underdevelopment of a legal framework restrains the development of charitable activities. The current tax law implemented in China does not provide tax exemptions for donations from individuals or enterprises. As a result, donations from enterprises account for the smallest portion of foundation revenue.

In Indonesia, NGO-business linkages are considered to be important, but existing tax exemption and deduction regulations do not foster such a relationship. In the absence of effective and commonly recognized incentives for corporate philanthropy, the private sector needs more persuasive reasons why giving money away is in its interest.

A lack of professional expertise is also mentioned in several survey reports as a constraint against further development of corporate philanthropy. These reports point out the prevalence of the ad-hoc approach by foundation executives in grant-making activities. Moreover, some reports indicate that the corporations are found not to be willing to delegate the grant-making authority to the professional staff of the foundation, and the corporate executives tightly control the foundation operations. Improvement of the management of corporate foundations is a topic which interests many corporations and corporate foundations in Asia.

As the Indonesia report points out, there is a need for procedures and mechanisms, other than those that currently exist, to handle resource transfer between business conglomerates and NGOs. The Thai paper reports on the basis of interviews with corporate managers that "business firms indicate their willingness to become more active in philanthropy, but, at the moment, they have not been offered alternatives to give donations to more innovative ideas." These findings suggest that if appropriate mechanisms and approaches are made available, there will be much greater corporate involvement in philanthropic activities in Asia Pacific.

2. Diverse Patterns of Asia Pacific Philanthropic Development

In spite of the encouraging development of corporate philanthropy in Asian countries, its pace of growth, often constrained by domestic socio-political factors, is unlikely to be able to keep abreast with the dynamic growth of NGOs and research institutions in each country and their regional cooperation. Under such circumstances, there has been an evolution of several new patterns of "new forms of publicly endowed grant-making foundations." As reported in Barnett Baron's background paper for the Seoul Symposium in August 1993 "Innovation and Future Directions in East Asian Philanthropy: Strengthening the Public-Private Interface," these new entities have the following characteristics:

First, they are funded from the income earned on endowments intended to provide a secure and steady stream of income to support public interest activities and NGOs. Second, the endowment is typically created from public funds or from a mix of public and private funds. Third, they are governed by autonomous boards of trustees composed largely (or entirely) of private citizens that have the authority and responsibility to oversee the endowment and the distribution of grants.

There have also been some initiatives in the Asia Pacific countries to create mechanisms to facilitate greater private giving. The survey reports provide several illustrations of such innovative approaches including the private use of public funds:

In Australia, the private sector is now seeking new vehicles to promote and encourage philanthropy. One such initiative meeting increasing acceptance has been the growth in Community Foundations, flexible tax-deductible public funds that attract large and small funding in perpetuity to be allocated to community use either through advisory boards (usually prominent local citizens), or through advice from donors. In 1994, three such community foundations were established by ANZ Trustees, a part of the ANZ Banking Group.

In China, the National Science Foundation and the National Social Science Fund were set up by the State Council in the late 1980s for the purpose of encouraging research achievements in the fields of natural sciences and social sciences. The National Science Foundation is managed by the Chinese Science and Technology Commission with a fund of RMB 300 million allocated each year by the Ministry of Finance. It is more of an independent institution with a full-time staff, annual work plan, and an independent review commission. They are also exploring ways to loosen their ties with the government in order to be able to get resources from more diversified channels.

Several Thai philanthropic leaders have committed themselves to establishing the Thai Foundation which, through the Development Support Consortium, will have a unique opportunity to mobilize resources from the government and business sectors as well as the general public for development activities. This consultancy has focused on the most effective way of tapping those resources within the Thai context. Many firms have no intention of establishing their own foundations, and central funds would be a good alternative for firms to support social development activities in financial terms without having to provide personnel and join the time-consuming activities.

Unlike other family foundations, the Tsao Foundation in Singapore designs and runs its own community services. The foundation not only has more autonomy in deciding the ways the funds are to be disbursed, its provision of community service is more flexible than others that depend on external funding.

The Development Cooperation Foundation (DCF) of Thailand was established with initial funding from the Canadian International Development Agency (CIDA). DCF is currently located within the government office of the Department of Technical and Economic Cooperation (DETEC) and governed by a board composed of individuals from government, academia, the private sector, and NGOs.

The Thai Development Fund (TDF) was established with donations from Bread for the World and other European donors. The fund is locally managed by the Thai Volunteer Services (TVS) to make small grants to local community groups such as farmers and villagers.

The aforementioned Barnett Baron paper introduces another model of publicly funded endowment, the Foundation for the Philippine Environment. Initial funding for the Foundation for the Philippine Environment was provided by USAID and the Bank of Tokyo. Through its Natural Resources Management Program, USAID provided US$5 million to the World Wildlife Fund for a debt-for-nature swap while the Bank of Tokyo donated US$200,000 face value debt paper. The proceeds from these transactions have generated approximately US$10 million in Philippine pesos.

As seen in these illustrations, there seem to be many different creative approaches of developing more stable financial resources than are presently available to support nonprofit and nongovernmental organizations which are demonstrating a dynamic growth in Asia Pacific. In particular, there is an assertion that a large nonprofit sector cannot be sustained for long without substantial government support, as quoted in the aforementioned paper by Barnett Baron. In his *Foreign Affairs* article, Salamon asserts that the government–nonprofit relationship has become "one of the most decisive determinants of third sector growth and one of the central challenges of nonprofit management." In this connection, he rejects what he regards to be a "paradigm of conflict" according to which "an inherent conflict exists between 'the State' and the multitude of so-called 'mediating institutions' such as voluntary groups." Although Salamon characterizes this "paradigm of conflict" to be pervasive in American thinking about the nonprofit sector, many NGO actors in Asia seem to feel differently. They are much more conscious than their American counterparts about the inherent conflicts that exist between the government bureaucracy and NGOs in their societies. Nevertheless, they would agree with Salamon's further contention that:

> The task for third sector organizations is to find a *modus vivendi* with government that provides sufficient legal and financial support while preserving a meaningful degree of independence and autonomy. This can be done by mixing government support with other forms of assistance and by clarifying the ground rules under which cooperation with the state takes place.[11]

Thus, the important challenge for the nonprofit and nongovernmental sectors in many Asian countries is to ensure that whatever innovative funding arrangement with the use of public funds is to be made, will be sufficiently counter-balanced by private funding to ensure that their autonomy will be guaranteed. It is imperative, therefore, that concerted efforts be made, in the first instance, to promote private philanthropy in Asia Pacific, particularly if it will enable the development of sufficiently strong nonprofit and nongovernmental underpinnings to the emerging Asia Pacific regional community.

3. Japan's Philanthropic Interest in Asia Pacific

Japanese private foundations and corporate philanthropic activities have been putting an increasing emphasis on Asia-related programs. Motives behind their interest in Asia can be considered to be similar to those of Japanese NGOs. In particular, Japan's growing economic presence in Asian countries has clearly enhanced their interest in activities related to Asia. The most common program among Japanese corporate foundations is scholarship programs to bring Asian students to Japan and supplementary support for financially stranded Asian students already studying in Japan. The foundations that have been active in this field include the Tokyu Foundation for Inbound Students, the Rotary Yoneyama Memorial Foundation, the Hitachi Scholarship Foundation, and the Watanuki International Scholarship Foundation.

The Japan Federation of Economic Organizations (Keidanren) has organized fund-raising schemes for a number of Asia-related projects, including an initiative in 1990 to establish a scholarship fund for junior and senior high school students in poorer rural areas in northeast Thailand, and thirty Japanese corporations have committed two million yen each for eleven years, for a total of approximately five hundred million yen. Recent major grants donated through the Council for Better Corporate Citizenship (CBCC) include: annual contribution of US$72,000 to the Asian Institute of Technology; US$14 million to the UN High Commissioner for Refugees; US$500,000 for the Japan Relief Center for Cambodia; US$4.7 million for Chulalongkorn University; US$1 million for Darma Purusada University; and US$960,000 for ISIS-Malaysia. These figures represent significant growth in corporate support for Asia Pacific related projects and organizations.

Foundation or corporate support for research activities in Asia Pacific has been rather limited in the past. The Toyota Foundation has been carrying out substantial grant-making activities in academic and research areas, and has also been supporting the translation of academic and literary works by Asian scholars and authors into Japanese or other Asian languages, under the project title of "Know Our Neighbors." The Sasakawa Peace Foundation has also been active in supporting joint research in universities and research institutions. Japanese corporations have been providing financial support for several academic and research institutions in Asia. For example, Keidanren has organized an annual contribution by fourteen Japanese corporations to ISIS in Malaysia for four years, for a total amount of 120 million yen since 1991. CGP has started funding multilateral joint activities in intellectual exchange and NGO cooperation in Asia Pacific. In recent years several Japanese foundations and corporations have started supporting NGOs in Asia or their joint projects with their Japanese counterparts.

There has been a discernible trend in recent years for a shift of emphasis in Japanese contributions, which used to favor major universities and prominent research institutions in the United States, over organizations in Asia. There are some emerging patterns of cooperation between Japanese and other private or corporate philanthropies in the United States as well as other countries in Asia Pacific, in providing financial support for nonprofit and nongovernmental activities in Asia. To some of the Japanese philanthropic organizations such collaboration has been helpful to effective grant making in Asian countries where they do not have any particular expertise.

Nevertheless, the growth of corporate philanthropy in Japan has been severely constrained by a very limited availability of tax incentives for contributions. Tax treatment and tight control by the Ministry of Finance over the designation of recipients of preferential tax treatments has limited the number of public interest corporations to 833, less than five percent of all public interest corporations in Japan. If and when these constraints are overcome, Japan's participation in Asia Pacific philanthropic cooperation can become quite substantial.

4. Growing U.S. Philanthropic Interest in Asia Pacific

Philanthropic support from the United States for NGOs and research institutions in Asia has played an indispensable role in sustaining and promoting their efforts in each national setting as well as in developing regional cooperative relationships. Most of the key institutions that have played a central role in promoting Asia Pacific regional cooperation among policy research institutions and NGOs, as described above, are almost invariably the beneficiaries of American foundation support in the form of grants, facilitating activities by their professional staff, and even moral support. Such support has required a long-term institutional commitment rather than a mere personal interest taken by the officers in charge of the region. In this connection, one is struck by the fact that only a few American private foundations have played a sustained role in Asia Pacific over the years, even at present when the Asia Pacific region has become an important national agenda in the United States.

Yet, there are some very positive signs of growing U.S. philanthropic interest in Asia Pacific particularly in the corporate sector. Several illustrations of U.S. corporate philanthropic interest are provided in the U.S. survey report. Perhaps the most eloquent testimony to this encouraging trend is the initiative taken by the Council on Foundations through its Joint Working Group on International Corporate Philanthropy to organize a major conference in Hong Kong from 19 to 22 1995, under the theme of "Corporate Citizenship in East and Southeast Asia" with the participation of a large number of American corporate representatives interested in philanthropic activities in Asia and about an equal number of Asian corporate representatives.

At the same time, a certain trend of a growing number of U.S. corporations working with Asian corporations or nonprofit organizations has been witnessed in recent years. As the U.S. survey report on NGOs indicates, "many American multinational corporations have begun to establish their identity as local corporations and thus changed their giving behavior from giving to American NGOs to either local NGOs or an alliance between local and Asian NGOs." Such a trend in the philanthropic area parallels the increasing number of joint activities of U.S. NGOs and their Asian counterparts.

5. Facilitating Asia Pacific Philanthropic Cooperation

Though philanthropic cooperation in Asia Pacific is considerably underdeveloped, as compared with similar regional cooperation among NGOs and policy research institutions, there have been several new initiatives to promote such cooperation. Some of them provide a facilitating role for foreign corporations and foundations for their grant-making activities in conjunction with their own activities. Others provide similar services through joint efforts of professional staff and information exchange across national boundaries.

In Thailand, the Population and Community Development Association (PDA) has initiated the TBIRD (Thai Business Integration to Rural Development) project to facilitate corporate funding for rural development. Firms are encouraged to provide financial and manpower support for development activities in particular villages. The TBIRD project facilitates foreign corporations' participation in philanthropic activities in Thai villages. Thus far, seven American corporations and one Japanese corporation have participated in this project.

PBSP is a corporate-supported grant-making foundation that receives funding mainly from annual contributions from its member companies which is equivalent to twenty percent of one percent of their net profit before taxes. Through PBSP's grant-making programs, its member companies participate in promoting grassroots efforts to improve the quality of life of the Filipino poor. The member companies can also avail themselves of PBSP's expertise in planning and managing corporate community programs. Presently, PBSP has a total of 174 member companies, including thirteen American and five Japanese corporations and one Canadian corporation.

The Asian Community Trust (ACT) was established by JCIE in 1979 as Japan's first charitable trust based on general fund raising. Patterned after community foundations in the United States, funds raised through eight trust banks are given to NGOs in Asian countries with the joint efforts of ACT's own staff and professional staff of PBSP and of the Foundation for Sustainable Development in Indonesia. As of December 1994, over two hundred and fifty grants worth over 350 million yen (US$3.5 million) have been provided for diverse projects carried out by Asian NGOs.

In addition to these illustrations, there has been an increasing number of concrete cooperative schemes, and network building has been taking place among foundation and corporate executives and professional staff in the Asia Pacific regional context. Some of them take a more organized form, such as the recent visit by members of the Affinity Group of Japanese Philanthropy of the Council on Foundations to Japan at the invitation of Keidanren for a series of meetings with Japanese foundations and NGOs, and some others take place in a more informal manner such as facilitation of a field trip for ACT staff by the regional representatives of the Asia Foundation or the Ford Foundation. These interactions have been mutually beneficial for the foundation and corporate officers and staff in carrying out their respective missions more effectively. Moreover, what is obvious is that these continued contacts and collaborations are gradually generating among the philanthropic actors in Asia Pacific a collegial spirit of working toward common goals with shared aspirations. It would not be too ambitious to expect that the building of a community of those involved in philanthropic activities will underpin broader community building among those involved in nonprofit and nongovernmental activities in Asia Pacific, and, in turn, it will help the eventual growth of the Asia Pacific regional community. It is in this spirit that this survey of the "Nongovernmental Underpinnings of the Emerging Asia Pacific Regional Community" was undertaken as a regional joint project. It is our hope, then, that the product of the regional joint work will provide a basis for continued substantive cooperation among us, and, hopefully, will be carried forward by the joint process of the Asia Pacific Philanthropy Consortium.

Notes

1. Lester M. Salamon, "The Rise of the Nonprofit Sector" in *Foreign Affairs*, July/August 1994, pp. 108–122.
2. Ibid.
3. Ibid, p. 120.
4. International Monetary Fund, *International Financial Statistics*, January 1995 (Washington, D.C.: IMF, 1995). Figures given are based on the end of period exchange rates for November 1994. US$1=98.92 yen.
5. Salamon, op. cit., p. 118.
6. Japanese NGO Center for International Cooperation, *Directory of Japanese NGOs Active in International Cooperation 1994* (Tokyo: JANIC, 1994).
7. Herman Joseph S. Kraft, "Security Studies Institutes in the ASEAN States" in Paul M. Evans (ed.) *Studying Asia Pacific Security* (North York: University of Toronto - York University Joint Centre for Asia Pacific Studies, 1994), p.22.
8. Paul M. Evans, "The Dialogue Process on Asia Pacific Security Issues," in Evans (ed.), op. cit.
9. Ibid., p. 229.
10. Tadashi Yamamoto, "The Role of the Private Sector is Expanding," in *Gaiko Forum*, June 1995 No. 81, p. 13.
11. Salamon, op. cit., p. 122.

CONFERENCE REPORT

Summary Report on the Osaka Symposium on Philanthropic Development and Cooperation in Asia Pacific

Tadashi Yamamoto
President
Japan Center for International Exchange

and

Susan Hubbard
Assistant Program Officer
Japan Center for International Exchange

I. Introduction and Overview

The Osaka Symposium on "Developing Nongovernmental Underpinnings of the Emerging Asia Pacific Community" was held on 11–13 December 1995, bringing together fifty leaders of organized philanthropies, corporations involved in philanthropic activities, nongovernmental organizations (NGOs), and private research institutions from fourteen countries as well as forty participants from nonprofit organizations in Japan. The symposium was organized in order to carry forward two related undertakings that had been set in motion in the nonprofit and nongovernmental sector in Asia Pacific.

For one, the Osaka Symposium was conceived as a follow-up to two previously held symposia on "Organized Philanthropy in East and Southeast Asia," one in Bangkok in August 1989 and another in Seoul in August 1993. The two symposia were designed to study the emerging development of private philanthropy in the fast developing economies in Asia Pacific in order to find ways to further enhance its growth. While developing a common understanding of patterns of development among private philanthropy in the Asia Pacific nations with diverse historical, cultural, economic, and socio-political backgrounds, the participants of the Bangkok and Seoul symposia identified growing opportunities for cooperation among philanthropic foundations and corporations within the region for the further development of private philanthropy in each indigenous setting and also for promoting greater collaborative efforts among them to respond to common challenges in the emerging Asia Pacific regional community.

Secondly, the Osaka Symposium was conceived as the culmination of a comprehensive survey project "Nongovernmental Underpinnings of the Emerging Asia Pacific Regional Community" which was undertaken by the Japan Center for International Exchange in the fall of 1993 to assess the state of development of NGOs, private research institutions, and organized philanthropy within the countries in Asia Pacific and to take a look at regional collaborative activities among those organizations. The JCIE initiative to carry out the survey project was, in a large measure, a response to a consensus view, developed through the deliberations at the aforementioned Seoul Symposium, that there is a need to have a clearer picture of the present state of development of the "demand side" of the nonprofit sector in Asia Pacific in order for the philanthropic activities by the supply side of private foundations and corporations to be effective and relevant. It was assumed that a major surge of NGO activities in the region both in the domestic context and in the regional context is presenting new challenges for philanthropic development and cooperation in Asia Pacific. The Osaka Symposium was designed to review the survey results described in forty-five papers—three each from fifteen Asia Pacific countries covering NGOs, private research institutions, and private philanthropy—and to draw implications for future regional cooperation in the nonprofit sector in Asia Pacific.

The venue of Osaka for the Symposium was decided due, at least in part, to a distinct possibility (which later became a reality) that it will be hosting the Summit Meeting of APEC (Asia Pacific Economic Cooperation) in November 1995. The impetus to promote Asia Pacific regional cooperation of the nonprofit sector parallels the movement on the governmental level to build regional economic arrangements, as exemplified by APEC, which may eventually lead to the emergence of an "Asia Pacific regional community." It was felt, however, that such community building would not be possible merely through intensified economic interdependence but that it should be accompanied by multiple layers of human and institutional interactions and some shared values and interests among the nations within the region. Hence, the interaction of the growing civil society including NGOs, independent research institutions, and private philanthropy in each of the nations in Asia Pacific can underpin such a movement toward a regional community. Foreign

Minister Yohei Kono of Japan sent a message to the Osaka Symposium stating that "promotion of mutual understanding and mutual confidence is essential in managing the interdependent relationship of diverse Asia Pacific nations, and it cannot be achieved by governments alone but requires efforts of the private and nonprofit institutions that you represent."

Discussion sessions at the Osaka Symposium were built around the following themes:

(1) Asia Pacific Community Building and the Role of the Independent Sector
(2) Regional Cooperation Among Research Institutions
(3) Emergence of NGOs and Their Regional Cooperation
(4) Issues of Philanthropic Development in Asia Pacific
(5) Patterns of Japanese Philanthropic Development
(6) Strengthening the Management of Asia Pacific Philanthropy
(7) Future Strategies of Philanthropic Development and Cooperation in Asia Pacific

The Osaka discussion reinforced many of the findings of the Survey on Nongovernmental Underpinnings of the Emerging Asia Pacific Regional Community, as introduced in the preceding Integrative Report. This summary essay on the Osaka Symposium presents several major thrusts of very lively discussion over two days, instead of recording details of each session which may largely duplicate the substance of the Integrative Report.

II. Development of the "Demand Side" of the Nonprofit Sector in Asia Pacific—Dynamic Growth of NGOs and Research Institutions

An underlying theme of discussion at the Osaka Symposium was new trends in the Asia Pacific region and concomitant challenges and opportunities for the nonprofit sector. The Asia Pacific region witnessed major socio-political and economic change in the past decade, reflecting global trends that had been set off by growing economic interdependence and the end of the cold war. The trends have been particularly striking for the region due to very dynamic growth of the East and Southeast Asian economies and the growing economic integration of the region as a whole. The emergence of civil society including NGOs, independent research institutions, and private philanthropy in Asia Pacific was discussed in this context. Recent changes in international and regional environments have had a major impact on domestic societies with implications for local communities, politics, and the environment in all the nations in Asia Pacific, and these changes have provided the civil society institutions with new challenges and opportunities.

As a Thai participant put it, Asians are experiencing two opposing, yet concurrent, trends of globalization and localization. Another participant from Indonesia warned of the danger of ignoring the dialectic between globalization and transnationalization, stressing that making goals global is not necessarily good for everyone in the local community. There are new needs to be addressed through a diversity of enterprise with an interest in local welfare, and NGOs have started playing such a role.

Rapid economic growth in many Asian countries also has brought about serious economic disparity among people within each country. The benefits of new wealth in urban areas attract people from rural areas, but the new benefits are limited and the domestic migrants end up as squatters once jobs and housing are all gone. At the same time, rural areas are losing productive agricultural workers, a situation that exacerbates nationwide hunger and poverty. In addition, rapid economic development can result in the destruction of the natural environment, followed by the destruction of whole communities. These developments have made it clear that the state faces limitations on its ability to solve the problems arising from the recent trends in Asia, leaving a widening space for nonprofit organizations to move in and grapple with new and complex issues.

The recent spurt in growth of NGOs and research institutions in Asia Pacific also reflects the need for better understanding and an effective way to address such a rapidly changing environment and for local communities and citizen groups to take actions to protect themselves or promote desirable change. As NGOs have grown in recent years, they have started assuming more diverse and broader roles than ever before at the national and local levels, thus, further stimulating their growth.

A Filipino participant argued that it has become important for NGOs to start playing an advocacy role in addressing social and economic issues in their communities. As government policies do not bring about reforms that will affect poor people, it has become necessary to train the poor, allowing them access to policy makers and thinkers. A Japanese NGO leader indicated that NGOs in Japan have started voicing their opinions in order to encourage policy change for the good of the people through, for example, mass media, thus, influencing the formation of public opinion. Another possible way of influencing policy would be to send NGO representatives to take part in policy making as was done recently by women leaders of local cooperatives, as cited by another Japanese NGO leader.

Independent policy research institutions in Asia Pacific are expected to play an important role in analyzing the rapid economic and social changes to provide appropriate responses to them, not encumbered by day-to-day involvement in the immediate issues as the government bureaucrats are obliged to do. A Filipino participant emphasized that it is important for NGOs to have their agendas heard by research institutions in order to affect government policy. Another participant stressed the importance of local communities participating in research that pertains to them, as they are the people who best understand local conditions. As a Canadian participant pointed out, however, many research institutions in Asia Pacific are close to the government agenda, and the most successful and active ones have similar opinions and issue identification as the government, making them "regime enhancing" rather than "regime critical." On the other hand, social pluralism is reflected in the emergence of new research institutions in many Asian countries in recent years, and this will provide opportunities for policy research institutions to stimulate more active policy discussion within the society.

The same Canadian participant argued, since governments are generally hesitant to embrace NGOs, it is up to research institutions to bring the two closer together. Though very little of the voice of advocacy groups and NGOs has filtered into research institutions, joint efforts in "softer" issues such as the environment and migration may provide for better and safer linkages of research institutions, NGOs, and government. While it was generally acknowledged that, in an ideal situation, close collaboration between NGOs and research institutions would be desirable, a Thai participant cautioned that the present situation is not an ideal one, and a close relationship could create more problems than solutions. It was also argued by others that NGOs should improve their competence in research activities and information gathering so that they can effectively compete with other sectors of society in the policy-making process.

Some participants indicated that NGOs can make valuable contributions to society in this changing environment not just through social action programs in communities, but also by helping to reshape values. A Japanese participant argued that one means of supporting the underprivileged is by creating new values in society. Another role NGOs have started to play in Asian countries is to urge businesses to pay attention to social issues, and to have them understand that development problems are not going to go away by themselves, and that they will eventually have adverse effects on the business sector.

Participants also discussed the special problems of the development of NGOs in socialist societies. In both China and Vietnam, it was noted, the trend away from highly centralized and rigid state institutions has encouraged the development of institutions that form the beginning of a nonprofit sector. In both cases, however, NGOs are still closely associated with the state and do not have a truly independent voice in policy making.

There was a consensus view at the Osaka Symposium that with the new challenges and opportunities emerging in countries in Asia Pacific, civil society organizations in the region will continue to grow despite some serious constraints they will have to face as will be discussed in the following sections. It was also agreed that the regional cooperation of the civil society in Asia Pacific nations will be essential in sustaining and further developing the vibrant growth of this sector.

III. Managing the Relationship with Governments

One dominant theme that was discussed in almost every session was how the relationship between the third sector and government can best be managed. Many participants from Asian countries pointed out that the biggest obstacle for them has been the lack of governmental appreciation and support for civil society institutions, although this is changing and varies from country to country. In the case of research institutions, governments have encouraged the establishment of institutions supportive of the state. However, this is also a source of problems since real independence by research institutions is not welcomed and may result in funding sanctions.

NGOs have usually been regarded with even more suspicion by governments. There are some NGO movements that have been encouraged by Asia Pacific governments who increasingly recognize that NGOs can be helpful in dealing with many of the newly emerging socio-economic problems that are beyond the ability of the government to handle directly. The end of the cold war has reduced ideological conflicts within Asian countries, and there has been a growing recognition by governments that these organizations can be a positive social force rather than dangerous anti-government elements.

On the other hand, the public sector rarely appreciates the advocacy agendas associated with many NGOs. While experience varies around the region, many governments at the central and local levels regard NGOs as special interest organizations that do not keep the broader public interest at heart, as threats to social unity, or simply as private organizations placing additional burdens on government bureaucrats. One Southeast Asian participant commented that her government now takes a quite positive attitude toward NGOs, but local level government officials frequently still regard them as threats, even seeking to block their funding from foreign sources. On the other hand, an American participant complained that people are generally very cynical about the relationship between NGOs and government, but it is important to recognize that tension between the two is natural and unavoidable. He pointed out that governments usually do not take the initiative in seeking help from the nonprofit sector because they are threatened by the influence that NGOs have over people. NGOs could reduce this perceived threat by helping villages adapt to outside changes and pressures instead of always trying to fight the source of those changes and pressures.

Many participants of the Osaka Symposium stressed that to be effective in Asian countries, the NGO movement must seek to develop cooperative relations with both government and the private sector without compromising its own social agenda. Participants also discussed the dilemmas associated with doing this. Direct confrontation with the government, one warned, is generally not effective. Other participants stressed the importance of both NGOs and research institutions as spokesmen in public debate. Various institutional mechanisms for facilitating cooperation were also noted. In Thailand, for example, a Joint Public/Private Consultative Committee joined NGO leaders with the prime minister and cabinet members and has sponsored a broad dialogue involving politicians, businessmen, community leaders, and academics. In Thailand, according to one participant, "collaboration between NGOs and government is no longer a dream, but a reality." But a participant from another Southeast Asian country stressed the difficulties of dialogue saying that government still retains a monopoly over values. An Indonesian participant pointed out that although the government has given a degree of acceptance to the importance of the nonprofit sector, their policies cannot be relied upon to help the growth of nonprofit organizations. If the government enacts legislation regarding NGOs, the NGOs themselves need to be involved in its formation.

Several participants pointed out that networks of cooperation among the civil society institutions within each nation and across national borders can play a significant role in strengthening their position toward the governments. Japanese NGOs, most of which do not have legal status due to the plethora of government constraints, have formed the National Forum to Create a Legal and Tax System to Support Citizen-based Organizations and have started working with members of the Diet who are interested in taking legislative action. An Australian participant reported on the impact of an international comparative study as a base for recommendations made by the Australian Association of Philanthropy to the government inquiry on philanthropic, legal, and fiscal issues related to the nonprofit sector. The fact that many governments in Asia Pacific have recognized the value of the civil society institutions and have started funding their activities, makes the issue of "source versus governance" even more acute than before, and makes it imperative for the nonprofit organizations to find a *modus vivendi* in their relationship with the governments.

IV. Asia Pacific Regional Cooperation of Civil Societies

There was little disagreement among the participants that collaboration among research institutions as well as among NGOs within the nations in Asia Pacific is one stop toward the building of a regional community. Many participants underscored a trend for both NGOs and research institutions to expand their national and international collaborative activities. A Thai participant argued that in talking about regional networks as a basis of community building, it is important to focus on the community as a "network of networks." Several incentives that account for the emergence of such national and regional cooperation among NGOs and independent research institutions were discussed at the Symposium.

One obvious incentive for broader cooperation is the emergence of what a Japanese participant described as our common agendas, such as sustainable development, national policy making for equitable development and democracy, and local actions for participatory development and good governance. There certainly has been a decline in unique problems, and it has become obvious that solutions to these common problems will be clearer if people work together in their search for answers. Moreover, problems are often transferred across national borders as interdependence among nations grows. A shortage of child care in Singapore, for example, has attracted women from Indonesia, leaving children in Indonesia without their traditional care givers, and thus transferring the child care problem to Indonesia. Indonesia is then faced with solving a problem whose roots are in Singapore, and requires Singapore's cooperation in finding a solution. A participant from Singapore pointed out that what we often consider to be national issues are, in fact, regional issues. One manifestation of this is the Singapore-Jahore-Riau growth triangle which has been formed, among other reasons, for the exploitation of cheap labor.

Because these common agendas can be easily identified, there is a definite need to set up cooperative arrangements among nonprofit organizations within the Asia

Pacific region. This trend has been enhanced by the emergence of electronic information networks. Joint research among research institutions and collaborative work among NGOs have been enhanced in recent years through group conferences and wide access to the fax machine. Electronic mail, a relatively recent development, and more frequent use of the Internet have the potential to allow for cooperative, and more importantly, collaborative work.

A growing sense of regional community is also encouraging collaboration among research institutions and NGOs in Asia Pacific. For example, the emergence of intergovernmental regional organizations spurs similar dialogue and cooperation among the private sector organizations. Encouraged by these factors, the establishment of research consortia in turn engenders more collaboration. A consortium requires multilateral cooperation in all areas, including joint definition of projects and selection of participants. As leadership in the Asia Pacific region is no longer coming from a single power, and other states in the region play an increasingly larger role, it only makes sense that research institutions adopt the consortium structure when pursuing collaboration. A Canadian participant cited a recent consortium on the study of regional security involving planning teams from seven countries as an example of the kind of collaborative work efforts that are emerging.

Several participants also pointed out some practical incentives for more regional collaboration among NGOs and research institutions. Many research institutions and NGOs in the region are facing serious management problems, influenced by a lack of funding, financing, and experts. Cooperation with other institutions in the region is considered to be the most efficient way of looking for a solution to this situation.

On the other hand, several participants acknowledged constraints against regional cooperation among nonprofit institutions. There is an imbalance in the development of research institutions in Asia Pacific and variation in the relationships with their governments. Several countries cannot participate effectively in regional collaborative activities due to a lack of human resources and a paucity of private research institutions. Participants from several countries represented at the Osaka Symposium pointed to problems in creating an environment that is conducive to collaboration among research institutions. Some participants pointed to constraints related to language and cultural factors that inhibit international collaboration. English has become the international language of Asia as well as much of the rest of the world, but many local NGO leaders are not fluent in English. The situation is not as serious in the case of research institutions, but the same problem exists nevertheless due to a lack of human resources. This can be exacerbated as electronic communication advances, since English will be a primary language used on the Internet and other similar systems.

V. Strengthening the "Supply Side" of Civil Society in Asia Pacific

Civil society organizations require a sufficient supply of financial resources in order to meet the challenges arising in this new era. Need is always greater than supply, and that gap will widen as public funding declines in each country, yet NGOs are expected to play bigger roles in addressing new and diverse needs that governments cannot meet alone. Many participants emphasized that while many networks currently deal with the demand side of the nonprofit sector, very few such networks exist on the equally important supply side. In particular, the importance of the development of private philanthropy was often emphasized to advance the efforts of civil society in Asia Pacific. Private philanthropy, although not so important in quantitative terms, makes a critical qualitative difference, allowing NGOs and research institutions to undertake activities of a kind that would not be possible without private philanthropy.

Discussion on funding for the nonprofit sector revolved around three main issues. The first, and most obvious, is quantity. The second deals with the source of funding. It is important for NGOs and research institutions to have diverse sources of funding, so that they do not become too dependent on anyone or anything. Particularly in some of the countries where there is little tradition of civil society organizations operating in the public interest domain, governments invariably try to control the activities they fund. There is only a limited availability of tax incentives for private contributions, as pointed out by participants from many countries including Australia, Korea, and Japan.

Thirdly, the nature of funding is important, as NGOs cannot, for example, survive solely on project funding. According to a participant from the Philippines, very few NGOs receive sufficient operating funds, and they are never sure if they will be able to continue their work for a significant length of time. Several other participants emphasized that donors should be more conscious of sustainability, but they prefer to just make grants for an NGO's projects rather than provide funds that will assure the NGO's longevity.

The participants discussed diverse funding patterns, based on their own experience. There was consensus that individual contributions, both cash and in-kind, will remain an important source. Funds also come from the government and from foreign assistance organizations. Furthermore, it was generally recognized that corporate philanthropy is likely to play a larger role in the Asia Pacific region than private philanthropy in promoting the overall growth of civil society.

Most of the country papers of the Survey on Nongovernmental Underpinnings of the Emerging Asia Pacific Community reported encouraging signs of corporate philanthropy occurring largely as a result of corporate-led economic growth in these countries. Participants at the Osaka Symposium confirmed this general trend, but, at the same time, they recognized that there are continuing obstacles for philanthropic development in most of the Asian countries. The development of corporate philanthropy in Japan was discussed extensively, partly because Japan was the host country of the Symposium, but also because Japan's experience in this field goes back further than that of other countries that have followed a similar pattern of economic growth. There clearly has been a growing awareness of the value of philanthropic activities by Japanese corporations as reflected in the establishment of the One Percent Club and the Council for Better Corporate Citizenship (CBCC), both at the initiative of Keidanren (Federation of Economic Organizations in Japan). Keidanren also has established the Nature Conservancy Fund through financial contributions from its member companies. The development of corporate philanthropy in Japan has been stimulated with the growth of direct investment in foreign countries, particularly in the United States, as these corporations became aware of the need to become good corporate citizens in order to operate effectively in the communities where they have moved their business operations.

As Japanese corporate activities have become more active in Asian countries in recent years, their philanthropic activities in Asia have also increased. Although the number of corporate foundations in Japan has increased over the years, the Japanese participants reported that corporations seem to be emphasizing more direct giving partly to avoid cumbersome bureaucratic procedures in establishing a foundation and to avoid rigid ministry control once established. The difficulties of staffing corporate foundations constitute another reason for the emphasis on direct giving, even though local managers are not necessarily well trained to manage philanthropic giving. Keidanren's Social Contribution Committee and International Exchange Committee have tried to facilitate corporate giving programs, and Japanese Chambers of Commerce in many foreign capitals have also worked together in philanthropic activities. Limited availability of tax incentives for philanthropic giving by corporations, and particularly by individuals, is obviously a major constraint against greater philanthropic development in Japan.

Some of the challenges faced in Japan in developing effective corporate philanthropy were discussed at the symposium, as other Asian countries face similar problems in promoting private philanthropy. In particular, they focused on strengthening the relationship between corporate philanthropy programs and their parent companies and the promotion of professional development. A representative of a corporate foundation established in the United States with Japanese corporate funding discussed a negative tendency of "check book philanthropy" in which donations are made blindly, and no attention is paid to their impact. It is important for people involved in corporate philanthropy to have their case heard by the management of the parent company whenever possible. A Japanese corporate foundation representative discussed difficulties corporate foundations in his country have in forming direct ties with their parent companies, due in part to governmental guidance. This independence makes it difficult to keep the parent corporations interested in the activities of their foundations and, moreover, makes it difficult for the corporate foundations to influence corporations and society.

An American participant stressed that it is critical to consider philanthropy as a professional activity in order to bring about desired results. Too many people believe that those who work in philanthropy do not have to care about what business people do. The need for staff development in further stimulating the growth of private philanthropy in Asia was emphasized by many participants in this context and also in responding to the needs of the "demand side" of civil society in Asia Pacific countries. While participants generally agreed that professional development is essential, they pointed to many behavioral patterns that constrain this development. Too often, people give money without taking ownership of the activity in which they are engaging. An American participant pointed out that too often people refer to philanthropy as a "give-away game." He emphasized the need to regard corporate philanthropy as a "social investment." This way of thinking should help in the professionalization of the nonprofit sector, as "investments" are not looked upon as a job for second class citizens. Being professional means a human resource commitment. Another American participant reported that acceptance of this fundamental point has been growing, and some corporations now invest both human involvement and monetary donations in philanthropy.

A number of specific suggestions were offered on how to strengthen professionalism. A participant from the Philippines suggested that the way in which corporate foundations can build professional skills is to hire full time social development officers, thereby bringing commitment, expertise, and experience to the foundation. This also helps to bridge the difficult gap between NGOs and corporations. A

Southeast Asian participant agreed that in many Asia Pacific societies, as in the United States, foundation work is looked down upon as a non-professional activity, and suggested that the first step toward upgrading professionalism would be to assess what is required to attract qualified managers into this line of work. Other suggestions included investing in short-term training courses and graduate programs, and developing strategies to transfer decision making and other corporate management skills from the corporate parents to the foundations or corporate giving program. Another participant emphasized the need to promote more dialogue between corporations and NGOs to professionalize the staff of both the giving side and the receiving side.

Though the development of private philanthropy, including corporate philanthropy, in Asia Pacific countries has been encouraging, many participants acknowledged that it simply cannot respond to the enormous needs of the demand side in the rapidly growing civil society found in these countries. In this connection, diverse patterns of public-private partnership in providing necessary funding to NGOs and private research institutions were introduced at the symposium as well as in the survey reports. Quite a number of nonprofit organizations in the United States enjoy a healthy partnership with the government. The Asia Foundation is one of these. Two-thirds of the funding for the Asia Foundation comes from the U.S. government, but governance is strictly private.

The Thailand Research Fund receives government funds but is privately managed by a small professional staff, made up mainly of former government officials with an academic as the chairman. The Center for Global Partnership (CGP), established in 1991 with government funding from within the Japan Foundation, has an advisory board made up of leading private citizens from the United States and Japan, and its funding activities have been autonomous, thus far. The Korea Foundation is another example of a foundation that is publicly funded and privately managed. The foundation's income comes mainly from passport application fees that are collected under a new law.

Public-private partnerships present an important challenge in broadening the supply side of the civil society in Asia Pacific. One issue that was raised by an American participant was whether the meaning of "private" refers to the source of the funds or to who sets the philanthropic agenda. This is a critical question as NGOs and private research institutions on the demand side cannot make effective contributions to society in the manner they are expected to do, if they will come under strong government control due to financial dependency. Civil society organizations have to decide for themselves, several participants pointed out, what is the best balance in making use of public and private funds, always taking into account effectiveness in advocacy and innovations on one hand and sustaining of operations on the other.

An American participant asserted that while the United States always makes a clear distinction between public and private, the distinction is not always as clear in Asia. Some Asian participants disagreed with this view pointing out that lack of clarity is created in their countries by the public domain, not the private. Quite often "public-private partnership" means a more hierarchical relationship in Japan with the government controlling the agenda and the private sector merely implementing government instructions. There was a strong consensus among the participants that whatever the degree of influence of the government, it is essential to have sufficiently strong private philanthropy in sustaining creative and necessary contributions of NGOs and private research institutions for further development of Asia Pacific nations and the Asia Pacific region as a whole.

VI. Future Strategies of Philanthropic Development and Cooperation in Asia Pacific

In the concluding session of the Osaka Symposium, the participants discussed how they could best cooperate in order to encourage philanthropic development in Asia Pacific, based on issues and suggestions that were addressed throughout the Symposium. As is the case with NGOs and private research institutions, a network of private foundations and corporations active in philanthropic activities has emerged in several of the countries in Asia Pacific. Such developments are discussed in the country papers of the survey project and summarized in the Integrative Report, as presented in this volume. Examples of such cooperation among philanthropic organizations contributing to overall philanthropic development were discussed at the Symposium.

The League of Corporate Foundations was formed in the Philippines in 1992 with twelve members, and the membership has since doubled to twenty-five. The League provides in-house training seminars, discussion of legal incentives, and sharing of experience in order to help new foundations. The Center for Corporate Citizenship of the Philippines has gathered CEOs from leading companies to decide upon which areas their philanthropic activities should place priority. Keidanren's Council for Better Corporate Citizenship shares information on donees that may be given a higher priority, and they also hold seminars to improve their philanthropic giving. The Foundation Library Center of Japan is attempting to serve as a center of foundation activities and is engaged in information sharing.

The Australian Association of Philanthropy has been able to mobilize its member foundations and corporations in presenting their joint views on legal and fiscal issues in order to obtain better government incentives for philanthropic development. It was pointed out that such cooperation among philanthropic organizations is useful in strengthening their own position in their relationship with the government. At the same time, they can attempt to set a standard for accountability and professionalization of their activities.

In a similar vein there was a general consensus at the symposium that cooperation among leaders of the philanthropic foundations and philanthropic-minded corporations in the region would be a useful contribution to the sector's overall development. The core group of philanthropic leaders that has been working together since 1989 to discuss development of private philanthropy at the aforementioned conferences in Bangkok and Seoul, decided to propose creation of the Asia Pacific Philanthropy Consortium (APPC). The studies presented at the Bangkok Conference were regarded by the organizations as representing "a pioneering international effort aimed at increasing mutual understanding and eventual collaboration among Asian and American philanthropies and those who study them."[1] By the time the Seoul Conference was convened, there was recognition among the aforementioned core group that "a strong network of nonprofit organizations will greatly facilitate the exchange of ideas and joint actions in solving many problems which cross borders. More importantly, the international network will act as a catalyst to stimulate and promote indigenous philanthropic activities in individual countries."[2] It was felt by members of the core group that it would be appropriate to propose the creation of a concrete mechanism for Asia Pacific regional cooperation for philanthropic development.

The Asia Pacific Philanthropy Consortium (APPC) is designed as an informal association of "like-minded institutions, each independent, but jointly pursuing a common objective." It was pointed out at the Symposium that the emphasis of APPC is on strengthening domestic philanthropy through the sharing of experience, rather than on creating a formal regional structure. APPC has four broad objectives: to promote the role of philanthropy in addressing critical issues in Asia Pacific by, among other things, advocating for the nonprofit sector; to increase the flow and effectiveness of philanthropic giving within and to the region; to respond to institutional strengthening needs, through networking, human resource development, and research; and to facilitate efforts by organizations in the region to identify and collaborate in addressing issues of mutual concern.

In terms of its programs, APPC will have four components. The first is a human resource development program through technical support or training in the management of philanthropic organizations and the exploration of innovative funding mechanisms to support Asian NGOs and related public interest causes. The second is research to address critical issues facing the sector and to encourage public discussion of the role of nonprofit organizations in the region. The third component will explore the possibility of creating one or more clearinghouses to share information about the nonprofit sector in the Asia Pacific region, and the fourth will be to facilitate networking and exchanges to put staff and principals of philanthropic organizations in the region in touch with each other to discuss issues of common interest and facilitate international philanthropic cooperation.[3]

In the discussion about regional cooperation in philanthropic development in general and about APPC in particular, several participants argued that APPC should help strengthen the demand side of philanthropy instead of only focusing on the supply side. A participant from Singapore pointed out, for example, that a referral system and information about what foundations focus on would be beneficial for NGOs in identifying possible funding sources. An American participant warned that while focusing on corporate philanthropy is important and may be the main task of APPC, it would be a mistake to overlook the potential of individual donors. Another participant suggested that an additional task for a network of organizations in the region such as APPC might be to set standards through research. A participant from Hong Kong suggested that one task for APPC will be to encourage countries with a more developed philanthropic sector to help less experienced countries hold workshops and conferences. It was also pointed out in the discussion that it will be necessary for more countries of Asia Pacific to establish "national umbrella organizations" in the philanthropic sector before a regional network organization can be established. The core group members responded to these questions by indicating that APPC will and should have a modest beginning and that it does not aspire to be a regional umbrella organization. The organizers of APPC believe that the development of strong national networks is essential before a solid regional network organization can be established. Conversely, however, regional cooperative activities such as those promoted by APPC can stimulate philanthropic networking at the national level.

Close interaction and a strong spirit of sharing among the participants throughout the Osaka Symposium reinforced in the minds of the organizers of the Symposium as well as the core members of the proposed Asia Pacific Philanthropy Consortium that there definitely is emerging a community of people who believe in the critical importance of the nonprofit sector in this new era, and who believe a community of such nonprofit organizations will make a substantial contribution toward the building of a true sense of community in the region beyond dynamic economic interdependence and convergence of political interest. The Osaka Symposium was testimony to this emerging civil society in Asia Pacific and will provide an essential underpinning for the development of the Asia Pacific regional community in the coming years.

Notes

1. Barnett F. Baron (ed.), *Philanthropy and the Dynamics of Change in East and Southeast Asia* (New York: Columbia University, East Asian Institute, 1991), p. 1.
2. Ku-Hyun Jung (ed.), "Preface" in *Evolving Patterns of Asia Pacific Philanthropy* (Seoul: Yonsei University, Institute of East and West Studies, 1994)
3. APPC was formally launched in May 1995, and a secretariat has been established at the Asia Foundation, Manila office with a full-time executive secretary. An executive committee consisting of members from Australia, Korea, Japan, the Philippines, Thailand, and the United States is responsible for the overall management of the consortium, and "lead agencies" within the region will be responsible for specific programs sponsored by APPC.

***NONGOVERNMENTAL ORGANIZATIONS** (NGOs)*

AUSTRALIA

Survey of Major Australian Nongovernmental Organizations (NGOs) Involved in Public Interest and Social Action in the Asia Pacific Region

Jenny McGregor
Director
Asialink Centre

I. History of Australian NGO Involvement in the Asia Pacific Region to Date

1. Outside Australia

Beyond Australia itself, there has been Australian NGO activity in the Asia Pacific region since the 1850s, when the various Christian churches in Australia began to establish missions in non-Christian communities, particularly in the many countries which, like Australia, were then colonies of the British Empire. The Christian missionaries combined humanitarian work for local people with evangelism. For example, the Australian Board of Missions began in 1850 and today is still the official agency of the Anglican Church of Australia for providing mission and related development activities to peoples in the Asia Pacific area, including Australian Aboriginal and Torres Strait Islander people.

NGOs based on the beliefs of the Christian religion still play an active role in aid and development work in the region. Indeed, of the eighty-four members of the NGO umbrella organization Australian Council for Overseas Aid, thirty-three (that is thirty-nine percent) are based in Christianity. The official church agency of the Baptist Union of Australia, Australian Baptist World Aid Inc, through which funds are provided for aid and relief work, is an example. Another is the Society of St Vincent de Paul, a Catholic lay organization (that is, associated with a church but not an official church body) that provides funds for both development and emergency relief.

Before World War II, only a small number of secular Australian NGOs that provided aid and development assistance to the region were in existence. These NGOs had their origins in providing help in emergencies and disasters. The Australian Red Cross Society (1914), Save the Children Fund Australia (1919) and PLAN International Australia (1937) were all established to aid the victims of war in Europe and subsequently expanded their geographic spheres of action.

Since 1945, many secular organizations have been set up by groups of concerned Australians for a wide variety of social and humanitarian purposes. These voluntary NGOs raise funds and provide resources both for development and for aid and relief work.

Three different examples of secular nonprofit NGOs that support development work in the Asia Pacific region today are provided here. The first example is the Australian Foundation for the Peoples of the South Pacific, established in 1968 to support development projects that promote self-reliant communities in the Pacific and Southeast Asia. The second example is Appropriate Technology for Community and Environment Inc, which was set up in 1975 to research, promote and implement technology appropriate for the development of a sustainable global environment and economy. The third example, the Women and Development Network of Australia, was formed in 1981 to help Australian women act together with the women of the Third World on issues of justice, aid and development.

In the area of aid and relief, Austcare was created in 1967 as the special national umbrella NGO for the coordinated provision of emergency and longer term aid and relief to refugees worldwide. In 1994 it had sixteen members, all of which are NGOs in development work in their own right.

In summary, it can be said that Australian NGOs as a group seek to help people who are suffering as a result of war, natural disasters, environmental destruction, poverty, disease, ethnicity, political oppression and other factors that lead to social disadvantage and injustice.

The level of involvement by Australian NGOs in the Asia Pacific region is indicated by the statistics of the Australian Council for Overseas Aid (ACFOA). ACFOA was established in 1965 as the national umbrella organization for Australian-based NGOs that provide funding and human resources for aid and development work outside Australia. The total expenditure of the current eighty-four full and associate members in 1993 is estimated by ACFOA to be A$161.3 million (US$124.2 million).*

* Based on the International Monetary Fund, *Internatinal Financial Statistics*, January, 1995. Figures given are based on end of period exchange rates for November 1994. A$1 = U.S. $0.77

Looking at the activities of ACFOA members in the Asia Pacific region in 1992, it can be seen that a large number of NGOs are funding aid and development projects in all parts of the region (Table 1). For the most part, NGOs fund and support development projects individually rather than in organized cooperation with each other. Where cooperation exists between Australian NGOs, it is generally achieved by the mechanism of a separate umbrella organization. For example, as described above, Austcare is the special umbrella organization for Australian NGOs to provide coordinated help to refugees worldwide.

Table 1: Examples of Involvement and Extent of Australian NGO Activity in the Asia Pacific Region, 1992
(Source: ACFOA estimates of 1992 expenditure)

Region / Country	NGOs	Total A$	US$
East Asia			
Korea	10 NGOs	Total A$ 3.32 million	(US$ 2.6 million)
China	13 NGOs	Total A$ 1.85 million	(US$ 1.4 million)
Taiwan	6 NGOs	Total A$ 0.66 million	(US$ 0.51 million)
Hong Kong	12 NGOs	Total A$ 0.64 million	(US$ 0.49 million)
Indochina			
Cambodia	23 NGOs	Total A$ 17.06 million	(US$ 13.1 million)
Vietnam	20 NGOs	Total A$ 10.76 million	(US$ 8.3 million)
Laos	11 NGOs	Total A$ 3.61 million	(US$ 2.8 million)
Southeast Asia			
Philippines	36 NGOs	Total A$ 20.44 million	(US$ 15.7 million)
Thailand	32 NGOs	Total A$ 15.01 million	(US$ 11.6 million)
Indonesia	27 NGOs	Total A$ 13.92 million	(US$ 10.7 million)
Malaysia	10 NGOs	Total A$ 0.64 million	(US$ 0.49 million)
South Asia			
India	40 NGOs	Total A$ 27.13 million	(US$ 20.9 million)
Bangladesh	30 NGOs	Total A$ 15.91 million	(US$ 12.2 million)
Sri Lanka	21 NGOs	Total A$ 6.64 million	(US$ 5.1 million)
Pakistan	21 NGOs	Total A$ 5.88 million	(US$ 4.5 million)
Pacific			
Papua New Guinea	36 NGOs	Total A$ 29.11 million	(US$ 22.4 million)
Solomon Islands	25 NGOs	Total A$ 7.86 million	(US$ 6.0 million)
Fiji	26 NGOs	Total A$ 4.83 million	(US$ 3.7 million)
Vanuatu	16 NGOs	Total A$ 4.80 million	(US$ 3.7 million)

2. Within Australia

1) Aid and Development Support for Social Groups

There have been charitable organizations in Australia since the early days of European settlement. These organizations have provided services for special groups in Australian society, such as disadvantaged children and families, the physically and intellectually disabled, the homeless, the sick, women's and children's health, war veterans and their families, members of ethnic communities and so on. These nonprofit organizations are run by both religious and secular groups, providing both aid and development support to their target Australian social groups.

Many of these NGOs have considerable influence on a national scale with all three levels of government in Australia. They play an important role in the development of government policy in the areas of health, welfare and community development, as well as actively seeking to influence the government in the annual budget allocation of public resources to the nongovernment, nonprofit sector of health and welfare service providers. Organizations of this kind include the Brotherhood of St Lawrence, the Smith Family and the Salvation Army. They also include national umbrella organizations such as the Australian Council of Social Service (ACOSS), the Australian Federation of AIDS Organizations (AFAO), the Council on the Ageing (Australia) and Family Planning Australia (FPA).

As well as playing a major role in Australian society, many of the umbrella organizations also have both international and regional roles in their respective spheres of activity, as the following three examples show.

First, ACOSS represents Australia on the International Council of Social Welfare (ICSW) and is also a member of the ICSW regional organization for the Asia Pacific region. At present, ACOSS is involved in the ICSW Preparatory Committee for the UN World Summit on Social Development in Copenhagen in 1995. In this role, ACOSS had a leadership role in the organization of the Asia Pacific NGO Symposium on Social Development held in Bangkok in July 1994, which was attended by some eighty representatives from NGOs in the Asia Pacific region.

Second, AFAO is playing an active role in the Asia Pacific region through its support of partnership projects with AIDS organizations in the region. At the time of writing, AFAO is supporting HIV/AIDS education programmes for at risk populations in Fiji, Malaysia, Philippines and Thailand. In addition, AFAO has regional affiliations with the Asia Pacific Council of AIDS Service Organizations, AIDS Concern Hong Kong, Action for AIDS Singapore and the AIDS Research Foundation of India.

Third, FPA has a mission to promote the objectives of family planning associations at both national and international level. FPA is a member of the International Planned Parenthood Federation and is involved in international projects which assist people to achieve reproductive and sexual health and well-being in the context of a sustainable environment. In the Asia Pacific region, FPA is currently supporting projects in Cambodia, Vietnam, Papua New Guinea, Fiji and other South Pacific communities.

2) Aid and Development Support for a Sustainable Environment

The emergence of NGOs in the area of sustainable economic development for Australia is a relatively recent phenomenon. The most influential Australian NGO in this area is the Australian Conservation Foundation (ACF) founded in 1966. ACF's regional work at present is concentrated in Papua New Guinea, in an area where the Australian mining industry has made an impact on the physical environment and on local communities. ACF has affiliations in the region with the Melanesian Environment Foundation and the Wan Ecology Institute.

II. History of Australian Government and NGO Relations to Date

Australian NGOs first began to exert influence as a group over the government in 1965, when ACFOA was formed as the umbrella organization for sixteen Australian NGOs involved in providing aid to foreign communities. ACFOA assumed the role of communicating with government agencies to secure government funding for NGO aid projects and general support for NGOs and their work.

In the 1965–1980 period, ACFOA members were at times in conflict with official government foreign policy in regard to countries such as the then North Vietnam and East Timor. At that time these NGOs were often perceived as public critics of government policy on aid to foreign countries.

Today ACFOA has a close relationship with the government and is one of the key NGO organizations which negotiates with the government for funding and other support for the multiplicity of aid and development projects and programmes of their eighty-four member NGOs. ACFOA estimates that approximately forty percent (some A$60 million or US$46.2 million) of its total 1993 expenditure of A$161.3 million (US$124.2 million) is provided by the Commonwealth Government of

Australia. The agency which has responsibility for the government's relationships with all Australian NGOs is the Australian International Development Assistance Bureau located in the national capital of Canberra.

In the case of the Commonwealth Government of Australia, its relationships with Australian NGOs were fragmented until 1973. Before that time NGOs were obliged to deal with the many Commonwealth departments and authorities which had responsibility for different aspects of NGO aid and development projects. In 1973 the Australian Assistance Development Agency was established under the Ministry for External Affairs as the central Commonwealth statutory body to administer all aspects of Australian aid. In 1975 the Agency changed its name to the Australian Development Assistance Bureau and became an office within the Department of Foreign Affairs. In 1987 its name was changed to the Australian International Development Assistance Bureau, commonly called AIDAB.

In 1994, AIDAB administers seventeen programmes and schemes which provide finance to NGOs to administer and fund their respective aid and development programmes and projects. Table 2 shows the AIDAB programmes. As can be seen, eight of the seventeen programmes provide funds specifically and only for NGO work in the Asia Pacific region.

Table 2 AIDAB Funding Programs for Australian NGOs 1993–94
(Source: AIDAB publication on funding opportunities for 1993–94. Programmes specific to Asia Pacific Region are shown in bold type.)

1. AIDAB/NGO Cooperation Program (ANCP) ....A$12.79 million
2. **Laos NGO Program .... not stated**
3. **Cambodia NGO Special Assistance Program .... A$2.5 million**
4. **NGO: Vietnam-Australia (NOVA) Program .... A$2.5 million**
5. **Philippines-Australian NGO Program (PANGOP) .... A$2.0 million**
6. **HIV/AIDS Initiative-Southeast Asian Region .... A$1.5 million**
7. **NGO Opportunities in South Pacific Region .... Up to A$30,000 per project**
8. **Thai-Australia Northern AIDS Prevention .... A$600,000 and Care Program (NAPAC)**
9. **Thai-Australia Community Assistance Program .... A$1.0 million**
10. Development Education Project Scheme (DEPS) .... under review
11. NGO Environment Initiative (NGOEI) ....A$1.54 million
12. Women in Development Small Grants Scheme ....A$1.54 million
13. Professional Associations Development Scheme .... A$225,000
14. International Seminar Support Scheme .... A$20,000 per seminar grant
15. Emergency and Refugee Programs .... grants as negotiated
16. Southern Africa NGO Participation Scheme ....A$3.7 million
17. Special Assistance Program for South Africans .... under review

Table 3 shows how the AIDAB funds distributed to NGOs under the major programme, the AIDAB/NGO Cooperation Programme (ANCP), were spent by country in the Asia Pacific region. The purpose of ANCP is to support international development assistance activities initiated by Australian NGOs. The ANCP is administered by AIDAB in consultation with the Committee for Development Cooperation (CDC). CDC consists of equal numbers of AIDAB and NGO representatives. Table 3 refers to AIDAB allocations in the 1992–93 year.

Table 3 Distribution of ANCP Funds in the Asia Pacific Region,1992–93
(Source: AIDAB/NGO Cooperation: *Annual Report 1992–93*)

	(A$ '000)	
East Asia		
China	A$ 126.4	(US$97,328)
Hong Kong	A$ 34.1	(US$26,257)
Indochina		
Cambodia	A$ 152.1	(US$117,117)
Vietnam	A$ 330.7	(US$254,639)
Laos	A$ 200.0	(US$154.000)
South East Asia		
Philippines	A$ 794.5	(US$61,215)
Thailand	A$ 804.9	(US$619,773)
Indonesia	A$ 666.9	(US$513,513)
Malaysia	A$ 23.9	(US$18,403)
South Asia		
India	A$ 1,492.3	(US$1,149,071)
Bangladesh	A$ 1,257.9	(US$968,583)
Pakistan	A$ 72.5	(US$55,825)
Bhutan	A$ 27.8	(US$21,406)
Pacific		
Papua New Guinea	A$ 597.6	(US$460,152)
Solomon Islands	A$ 319.1	(US$245,707)
Fiji	A$ 296.7	(US$228,459)
Vanuatu	A$ 66.2	(US$50,974)
Western Samoa	A$ 81.5	(US$62,755)
Tonga	A$ 41.9	(US$32,263)
New Caledonia	A$ 15.0	(US$11,550)
Kirobati	A$ 8.0	(US$6,160)
Tuvalu	A$ 6.0	(US$4,620)
Cook Islands	A$ 4.0	(US$3,080)
Unspecified by Country	A$ 78.0	(US$60,060)
Total Asia Pacific Funds	**A$ 7,726.6**	**(US$5,949,482)**
Total ANCP Funds	**A$ 12,358.9**	**(US$9,516,353)**

III. Future Involvement of Australian NGOs in the Asia Pacific Region

A survey of the relationship of Australian NGOs with the Asia Pacific region and with the Australian government indicates that NGOs will continue to play an important role in assisting local communities in the countries of the Asia Pacific region to develop a sustainable social and economic infrastructure. This conclusion is based on the following findings of the survey.

First, the close cooperation that exists between Australian NGOs and the Australian government in deciding where and how NGOs will direct their efforts suits both parties and, therefore, is expected to continue into the future. On the one hand, the NGO–government partnership enables NGOs to gain as much financial and related support as possible from the government for their work in the Asia Pacific region in a way that does not waste time and money. As has been shown, ACFOA members receive some forty percent of their funds from the government through the central AIDAB agency. At the same time, it enables the Australian government to use a large and experienced body of existing Australian expertise to implement its policy of increasing Australia's social, economic and political relationships with the countries in its geographic region. As has been shown, the government is encouraging NGOs to increase their efforts in the Asia Pacific region by, for example, constructing AIDAB programmes that relate specifically to countries of the region.

Second, many Australian NGOs, particularly umbrella organizations like ACOSS, are members of international NGOs with worldwide policy-making responsibility and strategic influence. These international bodies increasingly identify the Asia Pacific region as a distinct geographic sphere of activity. This means that Australian NGOs like ACOSS are expected to play an increasingly large role in policy making for the whole Asia Pacific region.

Third, in the last twenty years there has been a large increase in immigration to Australia of people from the full spectrum of Asia Pacific countries. Australia's social bonds with the region are a further reason to anticipate that Australian NGOs will continue to support aid and development in the original home countries of its present population.

CANADA

An Overview of Canadian Nongovernmental Organizations and their Work in the Asia Pacific Region

Allan Arlett and Ingrid van Rotterdam
Partners
The Arlett van Rotterdam Partnership

I. Overview of Canadian Charitable Activity

Many countries have reported a significant growth in the number of nongovernmental organizations involved in charitable and philanthropic activity. Canada is among these. The following chart documents the growth in the number of charities officially registered with the Canadian Government and able to issue receipts for income tax purposes. This enables donors to claim tax credits on their income tax return. It is estimated there is at least an equivalent number of entities, involving thousands of individuals, that do not feel the need to establish the legal framework necessary to become officially registered charities with the privilege of issuing official receipts for income tax purposes.

Total Number of Registered Charities in Canada

Year	Total Number
1974	35,113
1980	44,293
1985	53,891
1990	63,186
1992	67,100

The majority of charities, however, have no staff—forty-two percent have staff, and only twenty-three percent have more than five employees. Half of Canada's charities have revenues of less than C$50,000 (US$36,000).[1] Hospitals and teaching institutions account for almost sixty percent of the sector's revenues and fifty-six percent of the employees of registered charities.

While no definitive study has been undertaken regarding the reasons for the growth in the number of charitable organizations, contributing factors include the increase in the demand for services as a result of the economic recession, the changing role of government, the growth of the environmental movement, the recognition of the need to address the previously hidden problems of battered women and child abuse, government policies to de-institutionalize mental health and other services, an increasingly diverse and ageing population, the growth of the self-help movement and consumer advocacy, and the establishment of organizations to address new societal problems such as AIDS.

The consequences of this growth have been extensive. Briefly stated, Canada has a growing number of individuals involved in volunteering their time to charitable activity. A 1991 study for the Canadian Centre for Philanthropy found that 43 percent of Canadians 15 years and older were involved in volunteer activity. This was an increase of 9 percent from studies conducted in 1989 and 1987.

The growth in the number of charitable organizations has had a major impact on the sector itself, causing the Canadian charitable sector to become much more professional and organized. This is particularly true in the area of raising and allocating funds. Where for many years Canadian organizations often had to turn to American-based organizations for their training and information needs, this situation has changed significantly. Under the auspices of the Canadian Centre for Philanthropy, for example, universities and colleges across the country established a national program to train people in management and fund raising for the charitable sector. A growing number of organizations have initiated studies about charitable activity in Canada leading to increased understanding about its role and importance.

The increased number of charities and the subsequent number of requests from charitable organizations have, at least in part, been a key factor in motivating a significant number of foundations and corporations to give serious thought to the way in which they allocate their funds. Donald Rickerd discusses this in his paper.[2]

In 1987, The Canadian Centre for Philanthropy launched a major national program, called Imagine, to encourage individuals and corporations to increase the amount of time and money given to charitable activity. Prior to the launch of the program there were but a handful of Canadian companies giving one percent or more of pre-tax income to charity; now there are some 450 companies which have publicly committed to this figure. As the recession ends, this should result in a significant increase in corporate dollars to charity. The growth in corporate giving is also being fuelled by public opinion polls showing that consumers prefer to make their purchases from companies supporting causes they like. The potential danger for charities is that corporations will seek to gain profile as good corporate citizens through funds tied to marketing and sponsorship opportunities at the price of the less restricted philanthropic dollars.

Earlier we noted the growth in volunteer time. Individual giving, when adjusted for inflation, was on the increase until the recession began in 1990. As the economy improves, signs are promising for individual giving to increase.

As Canadians emerge from the economic recession there are strong reasons to believe that with the right planning, nongovernmental organizations (NGOs) have the opportunity to increase the support they receive from private sources, particularly individuals. NGOs working in the international arena will, however, have a number of very special challenges to address.

II. Our Definition of a Nongovernmental Organization

We are using the following definition from the North South Institute: "NGO" refers to any voluntary, nonprofit agency involved in the field of international development cooperation, or in education and policy advocacy activities related to international development. It is an awkward term and reveals little, but it has the advantage of wide acceptance, not only in the U.N. system where it originated, but also in most industrialized countries and in many regions of the Third World.

III. The Personal Nature of the Information in this Paper

It must be stated that very little of the following information is based on in-depth research. To begin with, there is very little information readily available in written form to easily address the task put to us by the Japan Center for International Exchange. We conducted research in the library of the Canadian International Development Agency (CIDA), the most obvious source of information, but we were unable, by the time of this printing, to arrange an interview with an appropriate CIDA representative. We were, however, able to reach the Canadian Council for International Cooperation (CCIC), and they proved to be very helpful.

Most of the following information is derived from interviews with leaders in the

Canadian NGO community, most of whom were presented with a series of questions prepared by us, and who then provided us with thoughtful, and detailed comments in an interview format. Appendix A is a list of these people who helped us with their opinions and insights.

Furthermore, it must indeed be noted, that much of what follows is opinion and insight gathered from a handful of people—albeit knowledgeable people—and must be read with that in mind.

IV. Canada's Foreign Policy in the Asia Pacific Region as a Context for Canadian NGO Activity

We will set the following information into the broad context of Canada's foreign policy priorities in the region. Within the Asia Pacific region, Canada participates actively in policy development and dialogue on the environment, trade, political matters, human rights, and governance issues. However, Canada's interests in the region have a strong commercial focus. Foreign policy priorities also require that Canada cultivate greater linkages with Asia on political and cultural matters.

V. Number, Type, and Organization of Canadian NGOs Working in the Asia Pacific Region

CCIC tracks approximately one hundred and thirty Canadian organizations working in international development. Of these, there are approximately thirty Canadian organizations *of a significant size* with development programs in Asia Pacific. All told, there are probably in excess of a hundred Canadian organizations working in the region. Appendix B lists the major Canadian NGO players in the Asia Pacific region. These organizations could be categorized in a variety of ways.

By area of activity

- Rural development work—traditional NGO activity; includes primary health care activities
- Social justice—advocacy/human rights organizations doing analysis and critique; help in organizing people to fight poverty
- Single issues organizations—like Operation Eyesight, Help the Aged

By role and structure

- International organizations—such as CARE, OXFAM, World Vision
- Operational organizations—direct implementing role of program by Canadian volunteers and staff
- Partnership organizations—Canadian fund raising but 'local' NGO implementation partners
- Small community based organizations, working in one country or region
- Religion-based institutions

By source of revenues

- Contract agencies that do larger bilateral programs which are funded one hundred percent by CIDA
- NGOs doing smaller 'responsive' programming receiving matching funds through CIDA's NGO program division
- NGOs independent of CIDA funding—as far as we know none on the list in Appendix B and none that we interviewed

1. Canadian coalitions

There has been some organization of NGOs in Canada. Coalitions and councils that work together to address issues in the Asia Pacific region include:

- Asia Pacific Working Group
- Association Quebec des organismes de cooperation internationale
- Canadian Council for International Cooperation
- Canadian Environment Network

2. Church or religion-based groups

The relationship of the church to NGO activity in the region is very important. Canadian churches have a long historic relationship with NGOs in the region and with the development of NGO activity.

- Adventist Development and Relief Agency
- Anglican Church of Canada
- Canada Asia Working Group

- Canadian Catholic Organization for Development in Peace
- Canadian Conference of Catholic Bishops
- Canadian Council of Churches
- Inter-Church Foundation for International Development
- Mennonite Central Committee
- Unitarian Service Committee
- United Church of Canada—Division of World Outreach

VI. Primary Sources of Revenue for Canadian NGOs

Canadian nongovernmental agencies have two primary sources of funding: private donations, usually from individuals; and CIDA. The funding ratio between these two sources can vary widely from agency to agency, depending on their relationship with CIDA.

CIDA disburses funds to NGOs through a number of programs. The vast majority of CIDA funding is government-to-government funding—the so-called bilateral program. Under this program, NGOs are contracted by the government to deliver programs on behalf of the government. The programs are one hundred percent funded by CIDA.

Smaller grants are given to NGOs for their own projects through the partnership branch and NGO divisions of CIDA. This accounts for only 2.5 percent of CIDA funding to the Asia Pacific region. Usually the funds are tied to a matching formula, i.e. for every dollar the NGO raises from other sources, CIDA will match with a certain number of dollars.

Fifty-three percent of total CIDA funding to all of Asia went to the Asia Pacific region—China, Indonesia, Malaysia, Philippines, Thailand, Cambodia, and Vietnam—in 1992. Total funding to the Asia Pacific region in that year amounted to C$208.13 million (US$151.92 million), eighteen percent of which went to China alone. CIDA funding to the Asia Pacific region peaked in 1988/89, then declined for two years, and then increased by five percent in 1992.

Aside from the Canadian public and CIDA, other sources of funding to Canadian NGOs include provincial governments, corporate and foundation grants, the World Bank, and foreign governments. Some of the consortia, councils, and coalitions also charge a membership fee. The International Development Research Council may also fund some NGO research activity.

VII. Funding Challenges for Canadian NGOs

1. Government Funding

The major constraint is perceived to be declining funding, although the recent overall expenditures by CIDA in the region do not support this. This may reflect both a shift in funds to contract agencies and a shift to supporting different types of activities, such as technology transfer, where NGOs traditionally have not been active.

As noted before, the majority of CIDA funding is in the form of contracts through the bilateral program. By becoming a contract agency for CIDA, and carrying on CIDA mandated programs, some NGOs have been able to maintain their size and their levels of activity, in spite of the economic downturn.

Nevertheless, there is general agreement that Canadian NGO programming in the region is not growing. Several organizations had cut back on programming in the Asia Pacific region due to CIDA cutbacks in NGO support. Vietnam, however, is one of the countries that is experiencing growing Canadian NGO involvement.

There is a tension between Canadian NGOs and their main funder, CIDA. NGOs chafe against the mechanics of the funding process. When CIDA goes into policy review, as it has done for the past two years, the dependent organizations can find it difficult to prepare for the future.

Some people argue that the constituency of Canadian NGOs does not have influence in Canada—i.e. people receiving aid from Canadian NGOs do not vote, and so cannot effectively deliver their message to the Canadian government. This highlights the need for Canadian NGOs to develop strong Canadian public support for their work.

2. Private Funding from the Canadian Public

The Canadian NGO community is vulnerable because of its reliance on CIDA funding. There is a need to reduce this dependency—to broaden the base of support. Canadian NGOs need to establish more varied and advanced ways of raising funds.

Unfortunately, the recession and downturn in funds has led development organizations back to disaster relief activities. Many of them started in disaster relief, then moved on to development work in the sixties and seventies. Disaster relief is an effective fund-raising vehicle and has allowed NGOs to maintain their size during the economic downturn. Along with relief work, child sponsorship has grown.

Worldwide, child sponsorship is up from 450,000 to 1.6 million over the last ten years. Although child sponsorship tends to be expensive to administer, this type of NGO activity has also proven to be successful in raising funds.

The raising of funds from the public using disaster relief and child sponsorship messages is controversial in the development community. Our NGO partners around the world also take offence at the impression of unrelieved disaster, or that a child can be separated from their environment. In response, the Canadian NGO community is developing an agreement on ethical fund-raising messages.

These issues may not be as pertinent to the Asia Pacific region. The challenge may be different. There is a perception that the region has moved into a different category of "need" in the donor's mind. The issue here, in terms of raising public funds, is to address the idea that the time has come for the region to take over responsibility for its own development.

It is also felt by some NGOs that the Canadian public regularly requires a new and different sales approach for supporting NGO activity, depending on the current fashion in development. This fashion can be traced somewhat through the U.N. Conferences from Women in Development, to Environment, to Transfer of Technology and to the upcoming theme, Urban Development.

Our personal view is that some Canadian NGOs are frustrated by the need to gain public support for their worthwhile activities, and have avoided designating the necessary resources to educate the public and gain their support. Canadian NGOs do not do enough to inform the Canadian public about their work.

Canadian NGOs should also be linking up with Australian and Japanese NGOs to raise funds from these markets for the region.

XIII. Current Trends in Canadian NGO Activity in the Asia Pacific Region

In recent years CIDA's Asia strategy has shifted away from an isolated project-oriented approach towards broader policy interventions. Strategic themes such as policy dialogue, partnership, institution building, sustainable development, and human rights and good governance have become the cornerstone for CIDA's future planning and programming.

"Canada's aid program seeks to help Asian developing countries create political, economic, social and environment conditions to achieve sustainable development. The aid program is intended to play a catalytic role in transforming the relationship between Canada and Asia to broader based and mutually beneficial cooperation. It builds private sector relationships, establishes new institutions to assist in policy development and creates a base of mutual knowledge and understanding."[3]

Some people believe the focus of Canadian NGOs should be basic needs first of all, and that this type of activity is most welcome in the region. What follows is a description of some of the usual activities of Canadian NGOs in the Asia Pacific region, but bear in mind that meeting basic needs is still the most prevalent activity.

1. Balancing the Needs of Rural and Industrial Economies

In Southeast Asia, rapid integration into the world economy, quick industrialization, and the related environmental effects require an emphasis on private sector collaboration, institution building, economic policy research, and environmental cooperation.

In Asia Pacific, Canadian NGOs appear to be at a point where they must balance their traditional fields of endeavor, for which there is still great need for large segments of the population, with the demands of a rapidly developing and industrialized society facing issues similar in nature to our own society.

However, the shift to urban concerns by Canadian NGOs is hard to detect. There remains a commitment in the Canadian NGO community to rural development and a resistance to becoming involved in urban development.

At this time, the majority of Canadian NGO activity is in rural development. The primary goal is poverty alleviation. NGOs are especially active in food production, human resource development, health, education, water and sanitation, community development, and programs to improve the status of women and increase women's participation in decision making. The emphasis is on capacity building, the transfer of technical skills, and environmental issues.

Environmental concerns are largely addressed through sustainable agriculture activities, which is a growth area. The challenge is to make sure that the effect of sustainable development activities on the lives of people is not negative.

2. Establishing Small Funds so Communities can Help Themselves

NGOs are involved in the creation of an entrepreneurial sector through the establishment of credit lines, and apparently the Canadian banking community has expressed some interest in investing in these loan funds. NGOs, through their growing involvement in loan programs and the establishment of small businesses and cooperatives, are increasingly helping to build an informal economy.

3. Human Resource Development—Skills Transfer vs. Program Implementation

There is a growing emphasis on human resource development, and away from capital development. Indigenous NGOs are very strong in many parts of Asia Pacific. In these environments, Canadian NGOs are moving from direct implementation to transfer of skills. Still, these activities are largely taking place in rural areas.

Canadian NGOs should be building capacity in the region in fund raising, programming skills, accountability mechanisms, report writing, governance skills, and networking. These local NGOs and their regional networks and partnerships will be pushed to find local and regional sources of funding from the so-called booming Asian-Pacific economy. As well, Canadian NGOs can provide resources and facilitate discussions. These may be the more useful roles for Canadian NGOs in the changing relationship with their Asia Pacific colleagues.

Training is needed in less developed countries like Vietnam and Cambodia, to enable them to take advantage of the aid that is available to them. Project management training is needed. Renewed activity in Vietnam is promoting economic, social development, and democratic reform.

In China, efforts are focused at the policy and project levels, particularly in the areas of energy planning and the environment. Transfer of technology is used to assist China to develop its human resources in key areas of development, with agriculture, forestry, energy, and transportation as the major sectors of concentration.

4. Institution Building

There is some activity in institution building, for example in the development of cooperatives and in the development of a financial sector. Canadian NGOs could look at ways to collaborate with the private sector in the region, and to increase assistance to the sector, for example in developing trading and marketing skills. This would be appropriate within the context of putting money into the hands of groups faced with competition constraints, for example, by linking small producer groups with local industries.

5. Development Education

Some NGOs see their primary function as building a constituency in Canada for the cause of development in less developed regions and for educating the Canadian public about development. Relatively speaking, Canada is seen as having a good system for building development education and understanding on the part of Canadians. This may be a useful model for other countries wanting to enlighten their public about the importance of international development work.

6. Cultural Exchange

Cultural exchange is another major area of Canadian NGO activity. For example, Crossroads International sends and receives volunteers to learn about each others' countries.

7. AIDS Prevention

AIDS prevention is a new focus of NGO activity throughout the region. There is a movement to establish a regional AIDS prevention network.

IX. Canadian Development Policy in the Asia Pacific Region—The Emphasis on Business Relationships

Distinguishing between aid and trade, CIDA's aid programs will likely not be oriented to Asia Pacific. However, this is not to say that CIDA will not be heavily involved in the region. The Canadian government will emphasize support toward countries with which it is involved in trade agreements, but the support will take a different form—more toward commercial development than aid in the traditional sense. Therefore, most of CIDA's money in the region goes into technology transfer, for example assisting with building telephone systems.

1. Opportunities for NGOs

Where does this leave Canadian NGOs who do very little within the initiative of technology transfer but who are dependent on CIDA funding? It follows that Canadian NGO activity will become more closely linked with trade. Corporations entering into the region may be supportive of Canadian NGOs, particularly those with branch offices in the region. Not only are these corporations another potential source of development support for NGOs, but they may want to take advantage of Canadian NGO experience in the region.

Canadian NGOs can sell their services and products to Canadian and foreign businesses. For example, B.C. Hydro is using CIDA funding to buy services from World University Services Canada (WUSC). WUSC is recognized as having expertise in identifying and addressing individual and organizational development needs particularly in the transfer of technology through debriefing, evaluation, out-services and other activities. WUSC can be said to bring added value to this work (compared to non-NGO human resource development firms) because of their understanding of intercultural values; they know how to work with people from many different backgrounds and cultures and how to bring these people to work together. From WUSC's perspective, the work they will do for B.C. Hydro fits within their mandate of enhancing understanding and promoting positive change in society.

Looking at corporations as a potential source of funding support, there are opportunities for innovative cross-over programming which can strengthen the business/NGO partnership and provide additional resources for the work of NGOs. An example of this is a 'countervailing' program developed by an energy company in the United States. This company calculated the damaging effects of their activities on the environment. They built into their plans and budget a countervailing program to offset their contribution to the greenhouse effect. They asked NGOs to submit proposals for management of their countervailing program. A major international NGO won the bid and now has access to funds for approximately twenty years from this company for a reforestation program in Africa.

Canadian corporations entering the Asia Pacific region will want to ensure the health of the communities within which they operate and will want to develop the goodwill of the population. They will do this much the same way as they do it now, in their own communities in Canada—through supporting good works. This is the same way that Canadians look to foreign corporate investors, like the Japanese automobile makers, to make a contribution to the Canadian communities in which they operate. All of this would suggest that increasing trade and corporate activity between Canada and the Asia Pacific region opens new opportunities for NGO support.

2. Challenges for NGOs

The economic development and growth in the region will leave many people behind. This, combined with the government abandonment of certain services, will create a need that is not dissimilar from the social needs of developed countries. NGOs can help deflate the negative effects of the investment in the region and can try to ensure that these investments contribute to the development of the majority of the people.

Canada spends a large proportion of its overseas dollars in Asia. Canadians need to be aware of the effects of their involvement. Canadian NGOs can bring the other side of the story of Asian development to the Canadian public—the stories of the grassroots community organizations—to balance the government's emphasis on economic activities.

3. Human Rights

As noted above, the emerging aid framework in the region seems to be shifting to business relationships. Human rights and democratic development are now secondary objectives. However, human rights is seen as a basic premise for development. How human rights is accounted for in development activities is an important ongoing issue.

Political situations in the region can sometimes act as a barrier to effective NGO activities and relations. Some countries, like Indonesia, have heavily controlled environments. In some countries, NGOs may find themselves in conflict situations. Because of the direct link between the development of an effective NGO community and democratic process, restricted human rights can pose a constraint to NGO development and efforts.

4. Need for Political Astuteness

The political environments within which Canadian NGOs function are often complex and, in some Asia Pacific countries, in a state of flux. The strength of NGOs lies in their action-oriented nature, not in their political astuteness. Canadian NGOs need to enter into arrangements with a watchful eye and think carefully through the ramifications of their intervention. NGOs have unwittingly found themselves involved in, and even contributing to, political intrigue.

There are many complex issues to be addressed in the Asia Pacific region. Before intervening, Canadian NGOs should be taking their cues now from organizations in the region.

X. Canadian Development Policy in the Asia Pacific Region—The Emphasis on Regionalization

CIDA's program structure is evolving towards regional approaches respectively in South Asia, Southeast Asia, and China. This shift is following the shape of trading blocks and the movement of economic linkages. The focus will be on regional, intracountry programs.

CIDA has an Asia Regional Institutions Program which supports both intergovernmental and nongovernmental organizations. As these institutions have matured and strengthened, more opportunities have arisen for links between CIDA's ASEAN and Regional Institutions Programs, and regional organizations are increasingly being used to implement all or part of ASEAN projects.

A multiplicity of relationships are developing in the region, accounting for a great deal more movement than ten years ago.

There is growing intraregional activity and cooperation among NGOs. This is another motivation for Canadian NGOs to redefine their roles in the region.

Canadian NGOs need to play a more active role in building regional links in order to build the "people's movement" throughout Asia Pacific and to help people's organizations develop common perspectives and knowledge about trends. For example, they need to understand the objectives of different countries who are investing in the region. And they need to link with NGOs in those "investing" countries to work to ensure that the activities and roles of these investing countries are positive. In this way, Canadian NGOs can also help to build regional and national policies. Canadian NGOs are perceived to bring a consensus building, nonadversarial approach to these discussions.

XI. Canadian Development Work and the United Nations

Generally speaking, very little Canadian development activity in Asia Pacific takes place through U.N. initiatives. When Canadian NGOs work with the U.N., it is usually in the area of disaster relief.

On the other hand, some organizations in the Asia Pacific region are actively developing links with the U.N. For example, the Association of Foundations in the Philippines, with a membership of 106 nonprofit organizations, seeks active involvement in U.N. conferences.

XII. The Different Ways that Canadian NGOs Work with and Through Their Asian Counterparts

Canadian organizations almost always conduct their work through, and in conjunction with, local organizations. Working relationships between Canadian and Asia Pacific NGOs can take many forms and go through many stages of development. The working relationships depend on the stage of development of the NGO community in the "local" region.

For example, most of the ASEAN countries are well organized in terms of local community groups. Canadian NGOs can work through these groups. They assist with organizational development, but the actual implementation of the programs is usually carried out by the local organizations.

In Vietnam, China, and Cambodia, the approaches are different. In Vietnam there is a lack of coordination among the local organizations, and Canadian NGOs work more directly with them in implementation. From its inception, CIDA's China Program has been based on one strategic concept, "the multiplication of contacts at the thinking level." Canada does very little work through and with NGOs in China. Most Canadian third sector contact with China is at the institutional level.

Working relationships are also dependent on the traditional operating methods of the Canadian NGOs. The spectrum would include NGOs like CARE, with their own staffed field offices in the region; and NGOs like the Unitarian Service Committee who work from Canada exclusively using existing "local" groups. A Canadian NGO may also choose to work alone to deliver and implement its own program, or it may work with a variety of partners for its various initiatives. Ways in which Canadian NGOs work with their Asia Pacific counterparts include:

1. Indigenization of NGOs

Sometimes, local NGOs are established to take over the programs developed by the Canadian NGO. For example, in Indonesia, CARE Canada field offices are being prepared for a transition to becoming independent NGOs. This will be done on a phased basis.

An NGO may also assist with the establishment of a local organization. For example, CARE International is helping Indonesia to set up their own Foundation with their own Board to do their own fund raising.

2. Bilateral Organizations

Some organizations have identical programs in both Canada and Asia Pacific countries. Crossroads is an example of this: volunteer committees exist throughout Canada and throughout certain countries in the region. Local volunteers in both countries organize themselves into committees and choose people to send to the other country. Each country, each committee, is responsible for sending and receiving/hosting people. The Canadian Board of Directors raises funds, establishes overall policy, and identifies countries interested in establishing links.

Crossroads is also an example of an NGO whose activities are based almost exclusively on the use of volunteers. There are many of them largely active in the transfer of technical skills.

3. Joint Offices

Some Canadian NGOs may establish a Joint Office with a local partner, which is then staffed by that partner, and through which the Canadian NGO is expected to work. The WUSC China office is an example of this type of arrangement.

4. Bilateral Consortia

Approximately ten years ago CIDA encouraged the establishment of consortia of NGOs in the Asia Pacific region to help make their work easier. Primarily, these groups are intended to help CIDA do work at the grassroots level. Today the main consortia are:

- Philippines Development Assistance Program (PDAP)
- Philippines Human Resources Development Program (PCHRD)
- Indonesia Canada Development Forum
- Cambodia Canada Development Program

These consortia vary widely in their mandates, structures and strengths. For example:

1) ***PDAP:*** CIDA established PDAP, a consortium of Filipino and Canadian NGOs. The Filipino NGOs had first been identified by the Canadian government in the last days of the Marcos regime.

PDAP has a twin committee structure, one in the Philippines and one in Canada. Each committee is equal. A Joint Committee is made up of representatives of both committees. The operating theory is that the Canadian NGOs accept that the Filipino NGOs know what is best for themselves.

PDAP's success can be attributed to a number of things: there was already a history and therefore understanding between Canadian and Filipino NGOs prior to the establishment of consortia; the timing (the fall of the Marcos era); the welcoming and supportive circumstances in both countries; and the compatible cultures and language (many Filipino speak English).

However, it is a challenge maintaining an equal relationship when Canada is the funder. It can also be difficult to determine which country should take responsibility for which area of activity. Because both countries are setting funding priorities, the projects have become scattered. Filipino organizations are looking for more focus, and Canadian NGOs want to spread the resources.

Recently, Filipinos have taken more control of choosing the projects for support. Now the Filipinos will present the projects for the Canadian NGOs to support.

2) ***PCHRD:*** At the same time that PDAP was being established, PCHRD was established by another group of Canadian and Filipino NGOs in response to the perceived limited mandate of PDAP. Some people would point to PCHRD as a better example of a successful cooperative venture. In this coalition, the Filipino community holds more decision-making authority. The two different visions of PDAP and PCHRD provide interesting examples of the options available to cooperative ventures.

PCHRD was designed to put Filipinos in control of the funds. The Philippine office administers and manages the funds. Communities in the Philippines determine their own projects. There is a board in Canada and a Board in the Philippines. The International Executive Committee and Board are weighted with representatives from the Philippines. Filipino groups themselves carry out the training initiatives, which is the primary focus of PCHRD.

3) *Indonesia Canada Development Forum*: In this situation Indonesian NGOs asked CIDA to begin to fund them directly. There was a reluctance to do this on the part of CIDA, due to concerns about human rights issues, the limited ability to influence who would be involved, and the activities and priorities. CIDA preferred to involve Canadian NGOs and initiated a dialogue between Indonesian and Canadian NGOs.

The Canadian and Indonesian NGOs had different goals. The Canadians wanted to work on human rights and democratic development, and the Indonesians wanted money without strings attached. There were also disagreements around whether the money should go to small local NGOs or to the large international NGOs.

Everyone had to compromise their vision. This, in itself, is not necessarily bad, but apparently the process was competitive and adversarial. This may be due to the fact that, unlike the Philippines, there was little historical relationship between Canadian and Indonesian NGOs from which to build and therefore little trust or understanding.

Generally speaking, the development of this consortium has been characterized as difficult.

4) *Canada Cambodia Development Program*: Approximately fifteen Canadian NGOs belong to this consortium. Unlike PDAP and PCHRD this group is primarily involved in direct implementation of its own projects, reflecting the significantly less developed state of Cambodian NGO development. The Canadian NGO experience in Cambodia has also been described as a difficult one.

There was also a consortium for Thailand that has apparently dissolved. This may be due to a shift in priority by CIDA to the Philippines. This highlights to some the importance of building consortia which involve Canadian NGOs. Thus, when CIDA withdraws its funding due to shifting priorities, a link remains between the local and Canadian NGO communities, and the local NGOs are not completely abandoned.

Another challenge facing consortia is responding to changing needs and opportunities. For example, credit development and sustainable agriculture (environmental focus), may be identified as new opportunities to meet changing needs. Yet, the current NGO membership of a consortia may not include the right NGOs to develop these solutions.

5) Local regional cooperative networks: a Canadian NGO can be instrumental in establishing local networks of groups. For example, CUSO has brought local groups together in Indonesia and in Thailand to deliver programs. They also helped establish three regional coalitions that gather and disseminate information to various groups.

An example of a highly successful regional cooperative venture is the NET Foundation (North Eastern Thailand Foundation). This program started with a small number of refugees who were brought together by CUSO for agricultural and literacy training, and a credit scheme was established. The program has branched out to over eighty communities in the region.

Another example of a successful regional cooperative venture is the Congress for People's Agrarian Reform. This is a coalition of peasant farmers in the Philippines. Apparently, they have quite successfully educated and raised awareness about farming issues. This group is supported by PCHRD and has toured Canada.

XIII. Challenges to Effective International Collaborative Arrangements

Based on the experiences of Canadian NGOs that have tried the various collaborative arrangements briefly described above, we can note several challenges:

Reporting requirements: in order to satisfy their own funders and their own evaluation of progress, Canadian NGOs usually require reports from local groups to whom they are providing assistance. This need for reporting, and the inability of a group to report, can affect a collaborative relationship.

Flexibility: there can be weaknesses in an arrangement where a Canadian NGO establishes an "exclusive" working agreement with a partner overseas. This can prevent the Canadian NGO from going directly to the decision makers and from increasing their own understanding of the environment and the options.

Choosing the right partners: a criterion for success in cooperative arrangements is the choice of partners. In choosing partners in developing countries, Canadian NGOs must select target country NGOs that are well-respected and credible in civil society.

Defining roles and responsibilities: when working cooperatively with NGOs in the region, it is also important to do adequate research and preparatory work. Taking the time to define roles and responsibilities is well worthwhile.

Some people feel that success of these cooperative ventures depends on all members of the group having an equal voice, and that no one part of the group dominates the group.

Establishing funding priorities: in terms of the consortia that CIDA has set up for various countries, the tendency to spread funds to many groups is again encouraged. It has also been suggested that there is an inherent tendency to corruption, or at least conflict of interest potential, as the members of the consortia fund each other.

International NGOs: International NGOs, like CARE, assign responsibility for different regions of the world to different country headquarters. This allows for the development of a broad, regional, and comprehensive strategy. This works when each country accepts the structure and follows the instructions of the appropriate lead country. Sometimes adherence to these structures can break down, resulting in wasted resources.

Lack of coordination and rationalization of activity by Canadian NGOs: it is suggested by some people that NGOs in Canada are not well organized. The work that they do is not rationalized. Many NGOs are too small to have a far-reaching effects. Information is not coordinated among Canadian NGOs. Canadian NGOs tend to be generalist organizations. Many of them engage in similar activities. There does not yet appear to be a movement toward coordination, rationalization, or specialization of service in the Canadian NGO community.

XIV. A New Vision for Collaboration

Generally speaking, in many Asia Pacific countries, the local NGOs are so well developed that Canadian NGOs need to find a new role. More equal partnerships are needed now between Canadian and Asian NGOs. Canada is perceived as being open to building partnerships; as having a genuine interest in empowering others.

Canadian NGOs are trying to change the donor/recipient relationship. Where once there was a sense of a need to control programming and funding on the part of Canadian NGOs, there is now a willingness, perhaps a necessity, to develop new relationships.

Canadian NGOs will be doing less training themselves—rather they will facilitate the learning process. There is a move away from on-site implementation and operation of programs. Canadian NGOs will be looked to more for education, help in establishing networks, and provision of funding.

Because of the well-established NGOs in some of the countries, particularly the Philippines, the transfer of skills does not need to be one way—NGOs there can transfer skills to Canadian NGOs. Rapid urbanization, the growing gap between rich and poor, and government relinquishment of certain services to pay the debt, are challenges which Canadians share with people in the Asia Pacific region. This will also contribute to a changing relationship between Canadian NGOs and their Asian counterparts.

It is also to be hoped that, by working together more often, NGOs in Canada and in the Asia Pacific region will have more influence.

In those parts of the Asia Pacific community where there are less sophisticated NGO communities, Canadian NGOs are still needed to assist with the development of the sector.

Finally, it is to be hoped that, by working together more often, NGOs in Canada and in the Asia Pacific region will gain more influence and have a greater impact on their respective communities.

Notes

1. International Monetary Fund, *International Financial Statistics*, January 1995 (Washington, D.C.: IMF, 1995). Figures given are based on the end of period exchange rates for November 1994. US$1=C$1.37.
2. See Donald Rickerd's report "Overview of Foundations and Corporate Philanthropy in Canada" in the philanthropy section of this project.
3. CIDA report, 1993.

Appendix A

List of People We Interviewed to Develop this Document

Tim Brodhead, *J. W. McConnell Foundation*
Tim Draymin, *Canadian Council for International Cooperation*
John Watson, *CARE Canada*
Jacquie Dale, *Canadian Council for International Cooperation*
Denis Leclaire, *St. Mary's University*
Debbie Cote, *Canadian University Services Overseas*
Stephen Kester, *Canadian Hunger Foundation*
Rob McCue, *World University Services Canada*
Marianne Villa Nueva, *Philippine Development Assistance Program*
Etienne Lamy, *Centre canadien d'études et de cooperation internationale*
Jane Gragtmans, *CARE Canada*
Michele Smith, *Philippine Council for Human Resources Development*
Ian Smillie, *independent consultant*
Peter Gillespie, *InterPares*
John Patterson, *Crossroads Canada*

Appendix B

Partial Listing of Major Canadian NGOs Working in the Asia Pacific Region

Association of Canadian Community Colleges
Canadian Cooperative Association
Canadian Crossroads International
Canadian Executive Services Overseas
Canadian Hunger Foundation
Canadian Organization for Development Through Education
Canadian Physicians for Aid and Relief
Canadian Public Health Association
Canadian University Services Overseas
CARE Canada
Centre Canadien d'Étude et Cooperation Internationale
Cody International Institute
Foster Parents Plan
Foundation of International Training
Help the Aged
Inter Pares
HOPE International Development Agency
OSCD/OXFAM Quebec
OXFAM Canada
Planned Parenthood
Save the Children
World University Services Canada
World Vision
YMCA Canada
YWCA Canada

CHINA

Chinese NGOs
A Survey Report

Zhang Ye
Consultant

I. Introduction

This report examines nongovernmental organizations (NGOs) in the People's Republic of China with a view to their interests in and potential for collaborating with their counterparts abroad, particularly in the Asia Pacific region. The first part defines, categorizes, and characterizes NGOs in the Chinese context, tracing their origins and motivations. The second part describes how Chinese NGOs are organized and registered and how they interact with the government. The last part focuses on those Chinese NGOs that are by nature oriented toward the outside world and have already established some external connections. Their achievements and difficulties in promoting activities are discussed.

The observations and information in this report are based primarily on three sources. First, with seven years' working experience as Assistant to the Representative of the Ford Foundation's Beijing Office, I have conducted numerous personal interviews and collected a large amount of notes, minutes of meetings, memorandums, and Foundation reports. One particularly useful report was written by Susan Whiting, with my assistance, for the Ford Foundation in July 1989, entitled *The Nongovernmental Sector in China: A Preliminary Report.* Second, although it is not a common practice for Chinese organizations to provide a written introduction of themselves, some NGOs do have a brochure that describes their purpose and structure. Third, the Chinese Association of Social Organizations (*Zhongguo Shetuan Yanjiuhui*) published two volumes in 1992 and 1993, on "social organizations" (*shetuan*, a concept roughly equivalent to NGO, which will be discussed below). They both contain a good collection of articles on the origins, development, positions, roles, and management of *shetuan.*

Nevertheless, because the research on Chinese NGOs is at a preliminary stage, as they are only beginning to flourish as independent establishments, this report is rather experimental, and expresses my own judgments and opinions without a systematic survey. The assessments and views here are my own and should not be construed as reflecting those of the Ford Foundation or any other organization.

II. Definitions, Origins, and Patterns

In the broadest sense, an NGO can be defined as possessing the following characteristics. First, an NGO enjoys a degree of organizational autonomy that is independent of direct government control. Its leaders are not appointed by the government. Second, an NGO reflects interests that are at least partly separate from those of the state. It may provide an alternative, and in some cases a supplement, to goods and services provided by the government. Third, an NGO is nonprofit by nature. Finally, regardless of its purpose, initiation and participation in an NGO is voluntary

If all these criteria are strictly applied to the Chinese circumstances, few organizations, if any, can be recognized as NGOs. However, Chinese officials have their own definitions. In a recent interview, a senior official in the Chinese Ministry of Civil Affairs divided Chinese NGOs into three groupings: non-state-owned enterprises for profit, government-designated organizations, and social organizations (*shetuan*). In his definition, the second grouping consists of hospitals, academic organizations, and schools that depend on, and at least partially receive, government funding. But their workers are not considered government functionaries, although their offices and facilities are provided, and their leaders are usually designated, by the government. *Shetuan*, the third group, are those loosely incorporated organizations circling around the groups' interests and professional connections. Their members usually work part time for them. They do not depend on government funding.

Furthermore, this official observed that there are currently five types of *shetuan* divided by sectors: culture and arts, medicine and health, social welfare and public services, education and social sciences, and science and technology. According to his statistics, there are now over 1,500 social organizations at the national level, and over 200,000 at the county level and above. In objective terms, only the third group, *shetuan*, is more or less comparable to internationally recognized NGOs. In the Chinese context, *shetuan* are generally defined as "social organizations that are formed voluntarily for common objectives and collectively engaged in economic activities or public affairs." A *shetuan* may or may not be a legal person (body corporate), and is not necessarily nonprofit. Government regulations stipulate that *shetuan* "must not harm the interest of the state," and must be affiliated with a government agency which serves as its parent organization (*guakao danwei*, elaborated below), and supervises the *shetuan*'s activities. Despite all this, in many respects *shetuan* play the role of NGO. Therefore, in the following discussion I will, for expedient reasons, use the term NGO to refer to *shetuan*.

Before the founding of the People's Republic in 1949, four types of NGOs existed in China. The first type was guilds that held together artisans who used customary methods in traditional crafts and were either self-employed or loosely bonded into groups. The guilds offered some wage guarantees, upheld standards of quality, and regulated the entry of workers into a given line of work. The second type was academic associations similar to those in other countries. But they emerged much later than guilds, and those more active ones were mostly formed by Western-educated intellectuals, scientists, and technicians.

Also in pre-1949 China, student associations, trade unions, women's federations, youth leagues, and the like, usually had strong political motivations. They formed the third type of Chinese NGOs. In 1905, Dr. Sun Yet-sen organized the "Revolutionary Alliance" (*Tongmeng Hui*) based on Chinese students studying overseas. The Alliance tried to infiltrate its members back into China to work toward eventual military insurrection against the Qing Dynasty. The Chinese Nationalist Party (KMT) in fact grew out of the Alliance. At a later stage, the Chinese Communist Party followed suit, establishing its own "mass organizations" such as the Workers' Club, which were engaged in overt or covert movements against the KMT.

Religious and philanthropic organizations constituted the fourth type. Among the most influential was Christian organizations supported by foreign churches in China. The leaders of the Christian community were educated in the West or by foreign missionaries in China. For centuries, philanthropy represented a means of lending social status to wealth achieved through dishonorable or questionable means. It was merchants, occupying the bottom of the Confucian social hierarchy, who engaged most actively in philanthropy toward this end.

After 1949, with drastic changes in China's political life, all previous NGOs were either abolished or reorganized. The nature and function of the remaining ones greatly deviated from the past. The professionally oriented NGOs, including guilds and academic associations, were inactive because of the emphasis on political loyalty rather than professional knowledge and skills. During the Cultural Revolution period (1966–76), these NGOs stopped functioning. Similarly, religious and philanthropic NGOs were largely dormant after 1949, and their connections with counterparts abroad were broken.

The organizations that had presumably served the interests of the workers, peasants, women, youth, students, and other social strata or groups, were further centralized and politicized under the Communist leadership, and in reality became peripheral organizations of the Communist Party. For instance, the branch of the Communist Youth League at an enterprise was under the direct leadership of the Party Committee of that enterprise, with the former's funding and personnel being put at the latter's disposal. Thus these kinds of organizations, which are generally referred to as "mass organizations" (*gunzhong zuzhi*) and whose nature has remained the same to this day, may no longer be regarded as NGOs.[1]

During the period of reform and opening since 1978, there has been an unprecedented and increasing interest in reviving NGOs. Several motivations by both the state and the society are evident. First, as the central task of the Communist Party and the government has been proclaimed to be economic development, professional knowledge and skills, especially those of applied science and technology, are being reemphasized. At the same time, in the process of economic restructuring there is an increasingly clear recognition that vertical administration and regulation within government agencies are insufficient and ineffective to satisfy economic, educational, and training needs. The NGOs that first reemerged and revived after 1978 therefore tended to be those professional ones in the industrial, agricultural, and service sectors, in educational institutions, and in science and social science research centers.

Second, with rapid economic growth, the reform process has bred more diverse social and cultural needs, such as welfare, philanthropy, sports, recreation, arts, etc., that require not only popular participation but also public funding. Meanwhile, the tendency toward decentralization of governance has made it increasingly difficult for relevant government agencies to meet these social demands. In many cases, the government is now willing to share some of its responsibilities with the newly proliferating NGOs. For instance, the official media often extols the roles played by the China Foundation for the Handicapped (headed by Deng Pufang, Deng Xiaoping's oldest son), the Children's Welfare Fund, and other NGOs supplementing government provision of goods and services.

The third catalyst promoting NGOs in the reform era is the expansion of non-state-owned enterprises. With the rapid development of the private economy in various forms, private entrepreneurs again have begun to use their wealth to engage in charitable giving or to sponsor popular cultural activities in order to gain public as well as governmental approval and enhance their social status. Their financial support makes possible the burgeoning of some categories of NGOs that could not have been otherwise established due to the lack of funding.

An additional factor giving rise to NGOs is the opening to the outside world. When Chinese government departments and their affiliations interact with foreign institutions, they find in foreign and international NGOs a great reservoir of resources. But under the governmental "cap" it is difficult to communicate with, and gain funding from, these nongovernmental counterparts. This situation has stimulated the creation of ostensible "NGOs" run directly by government agencies. However, with expanding foreign connections and exchanges, these "NGOs" have gradually learned through their experience that it is more efficient and profitable to have their own staff and budget, and to maintain some autonomy. Today some of them have already developed their own domain of interest separate from their "parent" government agency and become more like their counterparts abroad.

It may make sense to divide the existing Chinese NGOs into three categories: NGOs aimed at serving professional interests, including those of science, technology, social science, education, arts, sports, and the like; NGOs aimed at providing social welfare and public services; and religious organizations.

The first two categories of NGOs are both under the supervision of the Chinese Ministry of Civil Affairs or its branches at provincial, city, and county levels. In the Chinese context, religious organizations are never considered a type of *shetuan* or NGO. They are politically more sensitive, and have been bureaucratically under the supervision of the Administrative Bureau of Religious Affairs of the State Council, the Communist Party's United Front Department, and their branches. This paper excludes religious NGOs in the following discussion.

III. Interaction with the Government

A state regulatory framework for NGOs has always existed since 1950. Based on the "Provisional Measures on the Registration of Social Organizations," promulgated in September 1950, the now defunct Ministry of Internal Affairs was responsible for the registration of social organizations. The Ministry was abolished in 1968 during the Cultural Revolution and was not revived until 1977–78, when the Ministry of Civil Affairs took over its responsibilities. In August 1988, the State Council established the Social Organization Department (*Shetuan Si*) of the Ministry of Civil Affairs to take over supervisory responsibility for social organizations. There are indications that the Department now continues to draft new regulations in order to formulate a legal basis for NGOs.

Thus far China has no law governing the formation and activities of NGOs. In the last few years, the Legal Committee on the Standing Committee of the National People's Congress has been working on a number of different drafts of a law, but no such law has been passed. Some observers assume that the government, faced with difficulties in the drafting process, has preferred to retain its discretion to control the growth of NGOs and restrict the expanding areas of their activities.

The rules which now govern the formation and activities of NGOs were enacted in the wake of the Tiananmen incident of 1989. The State Council Order No. 43, promulgated in October 1989, was entitled *The Regulations on the Registration and Management of Social Organizations.* It replaced the aforementioned "Provisional Measures" of 1950. The timing of its formulation indicated the government's concern at that time about the emergence of NGOs outside government control. During the weeks of political storm leading to the Tiananmen incident, quite a few unregistered organizations, e.g., the Beijing Workers' Autonomous Federation and the Beijing Students' Autonomous Federation, had been engaged in agitating activities that challenged the Communist Party's authority.

It is made clear in the Regulations that no NGO may carry out its activities before approval for registration has been granted. The Ministry of Civil Affairs and the Departments of Civil Affairs above the county level are in charge of registration and management of NGOs. A two-step procedure is introduced for registration. First, the "relevant professional leading organs"—in other words the government departments and state-authorized "mass organizations" in charge of particular subject areas—must investigate and decide whether the group should be permitted to register. This essentially gives these organizations veto power. Second, along with this approval, NGOs applying for registration must submit a number of items, including the purpose of the organization, a list of its leading members, the source of funds, the organizational structure, and "other necessary elements."

The document states that "social organizations must abide by the Constitution, the laws and the regulations, and must protect the unity of the state and the solidarity of the nation." Specifically, it forbids the establishment of "identical or similar social organizations…within the same administrative area." This could be cited as a rationale for denying registration to NGOs like labor unions or student unions since government-sponsored associations theoretically already cover these functions on national and local levels.

The Regulations have been implemented effectively. In 1991, a nationwide investigation was conducted, in which all NGOs were required to reregister. A high-ranking official explained that some NGOs had deviated from the correct political line, some had used unlawful means to make profit, and some had avoided government management. These NGOs allegedly "caused elements that damaged social stability and order." According to the 1992 Yearbook of Chinese law, of 118,691 applications for registration in 1991, 89,969 were granted. The process of registration was reportedly completed in the summer of 1992.

Since then, there seem to have been a number of new regulations concerning the registration and management of NGOs, but their contents are not easily accessible, and some stipulations seem to be tentative and changeable. One source says that in November 1992 the State Industry and Commerce Bureau gave permission for the establishment of economic corporations within NGOs (excluding foundations), which had not been allowed in the past. Previously, members of NGOs as such were not considered government officials (cadres), yet a new regulation states that NGOs now can decide upon their own authorized size of cadres according to their economic capabilities, so that government officials can move to NGOs with their previous salary level and political status, and staff members of NGOs can also move to government organs to become officials.

Thus the interaction between the government and NGOs is rather complicated and elusive. It can be better illustrated by describing the formation and functioning of an imaginary academic association, ABC, whose area of interest is Asian-Pacific economic cooperation and whose membership is nationwide. First of all, the initiators of ABC must find a relevant professional leading organ to serve as its "parent unit" (*guakao danwei*). This unit is likely to be a prestigious research institute—an imaginary CBA focusing on Asian-Pacific studies—under the leadership of the central government. Then CBA has to make a report to its superior government department endorsing the founding of ABC, and providing an explanation of its purpose, possible sources of funding, proposed activities, and a list of designated president, vice-presidents, general secretary, and honorary president and advisers.

According to an undocumented rule, at least one actual leading member (the president or the executive vice-president) of ABC has to be a leading official of CBA, and the general secretary of ABC is almost certainly from CBA, so that the former's work is effectively managed by the latter. Because ABC's scope of interest is Asian-Pacific economic cooperation, the honorary positions are likely to be held by distinguished senior officials and retired diplomats with long experiences in this area. The vice-presidents of ABC are likely to be heads of other government-sponsored research institutes and distinguished scholars/analysts/reporters. Having received approval from CBA, ABC submits all the necessary documents to the Ministry (or the local Department) of Civil Affairs for registration. The Ministry usually approves in this case and issues the license.

ABC is a loosely organized professional society with no regular staff and no separate office. The administrative and liaison work is done by the office of CBA. Personnel or structural changes of CBA often cause corresponding changes in ABC. It is likely that CBA—or its superior government department—will allocate a very limited fund (in most cases equivalent to US$400 to 800 annually) for the initiation and maintenance of ABC. Thus ABC has to seek other sources of funding for holding conferences, hosting visitors, and publishing bulletins and occasional papers.

Supposing a group of concerned scholars intends to establish an association of Chinese-Japanese economic cooperation and also wants CBA to be its parent organization, it may not receive official endorsement as a separate entity. Because its scope of interest is only a part of ABC's, it can only be organized as a "professional committee" (*zhuanye weiyuanhui*) subordinate to ABC. The establishment of such a professional committee, also affiliated with CBA, is easier. It is registered in the Department of Civil Affairs as such, but does not need to have a license.

In this sense, most professional NGOs in China are quasi- or semi-official. Even a club for calligraphy has to have a parent organization. As a result, NGOs are politically fragile, and subject to changes of government attention and priority. Nominally, the leaders of NGOs should be elected by their members, but they are in reality appointed by the parent organization or negotiated among the relevant official units. As the main responsibility of NGO leaders is to take care of their respective work units rather than the NGO itself, NGOs often suffer from inertia and insufficient attention. In some cases, the designated leaders of the NGO do not have the necessary professional knowledge, interest, and prestige to make it workable. In addition, many NGOs rely on government funding for their operations. When their parent organizations do not have enough financial resources or willingness to assist them, they may become inanimate.

Despite the close link between NGOs and the government, many Chinese NGOs nonetheless do have their own public space and enjoy a certain degree of autonomy. The fact that NGOs are thriving rather than declining is an indicator of their growing role, popularity, and potential. Chinese NGOs can exert influence on the government in two important ways. First, since most NGOs have their memberships not only in the respective parent organizations but also in other governmental units, they help to establish and expand cross unit, horizontal connections that were very weak before. In the past, Chinese government departments, including government affiliated research institutes, rarely invited people from other units (even if their responsibilities and interests were similar). Although departmentalism was often criticized, there was not enough incentive—and probably not enough experience—to redress the tradition. Now that professional societies have brought together like-minded scholars and workers from different units and promoted scholarship and technological know-how, the leaders of relevant units have started to realize the advantages of these connections. To this extent, it is a good learning experience for government officials, broadening their horizons and providing them with divergent voices that they could not hear within their own realm.

Second, despite the supervision by the parent organizations, many NGOs have their own budget, office space, and even personnel independent of their supervising unit. Therefore, they have the resources to run their own programs, which often generate "spill overs" that benefit the parent unit. In turn, government departments tend to be more supportive of NGOs as long as the mutual benefit is sustained by interaction

However, problems often arise from the close interaction between NGOs and their parent government agencies. Some observers and NGO leaders have warned that "bureaucratization" (*xingzhenghua*) will harm NGOs. In some cases, the NGO's personnel and formation are identical with the parent organization's because the former was created by the latter to seek funding and establish foreign connections in order to take advantage of being registered as an NGO. In some other cases, the leaders of the parent unit are concurrently those of the NGO. Furthermore, there are instances in which the budget of the NGO and that of its supervising body are not clearly divided. Many government officials and NGO leaders have pointed out the deficiencies of the bureaucratization of NGOs, but there will be no easy solutions to these problems as long as all Chinese NGOs have to be attached to a government department.

IV. International-Oriented NGOs and their Activities

In order to illustrate how Chinese NGOs function, especially how they establish and maintain foreign connections, two academic associations are described below. They are selected for case study not because they are representative (associations of this type are not very common in China) but because their activities are somewhat regular and their formation remains stable and is thus easier to describe.

1. The Chinese Association of American Studies (CAAS)

CAAS was founded in December 1988 on the occasion of the tenth anniversary of the establishment of diplomatic relations between China and the United States. It is a national academic organization with multi-disciplinary interests. According to its constitution,

> [T]he main task of CAAS is to contact and unite scholars and specialists in China devoted to American Studies; coordinate domestic bodies and institutions specializing in American Studies; serve as a center for the exchange of information and research by its members; organize symposiums, seminars and workshops on the United States; engage in academic exchanges with corresponding research organizations in the United States and other countries; sponsor commemorative activities of great significance for both China and the United States; and edit and publish *American Studies, CAAS Correspondence* and other results of American Studies.

CAAS adopts a system of institutional membership. This means that only scholarly institutions devoted to American studies are entitled to apply for membership. If individual scholars are working in the membership units, they may participate in CAAS activities. However, as individuals they are not ordinary CAAS members. Yet each member organization nominates one leading scholar or administrator to act as its representative. These representatives constitute the council. CAAS has recruited over fifty institutional members, including such prestigious research institutes as the China Institute of International Studies (attached to the Foreign Ministry), the China Institute of International Strategic Studies (attached to the Chinese military), and the China Institute of Contemporary International Relations. Other member units include university-based research centers, journalist departments, and more specialized academic associations like the Chinese Association for American History.

The council elected a permanent council of no more than thirty members, most of whom are well-established scholars in the field of American studies. In the election the council took into consideration such elements as geographic location, academic sub-field (American politics, economics, foreign relations, society, culture, history, etc.), age, and gender, so that diverse interests would be reflected in the permanent council.

According to its constitution, CAAS shall have an honorary president, a president, a secretary general and several deputy secretary generals. Ever since the founding of CAAS in 1988, Mr. Huang Hua, former vice-premier and foreign minister, has been honorary president, and Mr. Li Shenzhi has been president. At the time when Mr. Li became president, he was vice-president of the Chinese Academy of Social Sciences and former director of the Academy's Institute of American Studies.

Nominally, the permanent council is elected by the council, and has the authority to approve new memberships, decide the activities of CAAS, and nominate the president and secretary general. In reality, however, all these responsibilities fall into the domain of its parent organization, i.e., the Institute of American Studies (IAS) under the Chinese Academy of Social Sciences. The CAAS secretariat is located at IAS, and it has become the norm that a deputy director of IAS is to serve as the secretary general of CAAS, and two to three members of IAS are to serve as deputy secretary generals. The secretariat publishes a newsletter on an irregular basis. The Chinese Academy now gives CAAS an annual subsidy of RMB 4,000 (US$470)[2], which is just enough for printing the newsletter.

CAAS does not run any regular research projects. Like many other similar Chinese NGOs, its activities are organized on an ad hoc basis, depending mainly on initiatives taken by IAS. Up to now, CAAS has cosponsored two large international conferences in collaboration with IAS. The first conference took place in December 1988, when it organized the "Forum on the Occasion of the Tenth Anniversary of the Establishment of Sino-American Diplomatic Relations." An edited book collecting the conference papers was later published in both Chinese and English. The second international forum was held in May 1991 on "The United States and the Asia Pacific Region in the 20th Century." Scholars from many other Asian countries and areas joined their Chinese and American counterparts in Beijing to discuss almost all aspects of American Asian relations. The Ford Foundation, The Asia Foundation, the Rockefeller Foundation, and a few other donors contributed funding to the conference. As a result, the proceedings have been published in an English volume. Incidentally, this conference was one of a series of symposia alternately held in Asian countries, the latest one having been held in Tokyo by the International House of Japan in September 1993.

In addition to the two international conventions, CAAS cosponsored a meeting in collaboration with the Shanghai Institute of International Studies that commemorated the tenth anniversary of the Shanghai Communiqué, a significant document signed by U.S. President Richard Nixon and Chinese Premier Zhou Enlai in 1972. The meeting took place in Shanghai in early 1992 and was attended by over thirty participants from many areas of the Chinese mainland.

Having been supported by the Ford Foundation, a fund is run by CAAS to subsidize the publication of scholarly works in American studies. Up to now, Ford has accumulatively contributed US$50,000 to this fund, which has enabled the publication of over twenty books, and more manuscripts are under review.

In April 1994, a subcommittee within CAAS was founded to focus on the study of Sino-American relations. It is called "subcommittee" simply because government regulation does not allow the establishment of another academic association with similar scholarly interests. In fact, however, although the new organization was registered as a subcommittee of CAAS, it is acting rather independently and calls itself the "Society of Sino-American Relations." Its president is Madame Zi Zhongyun, a senior scholar and former director of IAS. Just like CAAS, this society is also affiliated with IAS and depends on the latter for logistical support. Upon its founding, the society sponsored a symposium that reviewed the development of the study of Sino-American relations in China. The society is also planning to publish a collection of papers on the same subject.

2. The Beijing Society of Comparative International Studies (BSCIS)

BSCIS claims to be a "nongovernmental academic organization." Its objective is to bring together scholars engaged in foreign studies in and around Beijing to promote scholarship and international connections. In the sense that this society only recruits members who are residents of Beijing, it is a "regional" NGO in contrast with a "national" NGO like the aforementioned CAAS. Furthermore, its parent organization is the Institute of Foreign Studies, Beijing Academy of Social Sciences, which is under the leadership of the Beijing Municipal Government. Whereas the Chinese Academy of Social Sciences is considered a "national-level" institution directly administered by the central government (the State Council), the Beijing Academy of Social Sciences is regarded as a "municipal-level" institution (or "provincial-level" because Beijing's status is equivalent to a province). The Chinese Academy certainly enjoys a higher prestige than the Beijing Academy, but the latter is not under the supervision of the former and is administered only by the Beijing Government.

Unlike CAAS, BSCIS accepts only individuals to be members. Since its founding in March 1989, BSCIS has recruited over three hundred members, among whom are scholars, analysts, government officials, and veteran diplomats. In principle, to become a member one should hold an academic title of lecturer or higher, and should be engaged in the research or teaching of international studies. Middle or high level officials in government departments in charge of foreign affairs are also entitled to apply for membership.

One-third of the ordinary members of BSCIS are chosen as council members, and of them forty-six are executive council members. BSCIS has two honorary presidents: Mr. Han Xu, former vice-minister of foreign affairs and ambassador to the United States, and Ms. Gong Pusheng, a retired senior diplomat. Professor Zhang Zhilian, a distinguished historian in French history at Peking University, has been president ever since 1989. There are currently six vice-presidents. Among them three are scholars and the other three are officials working for the Beijing Municipal Government.

Similar to the situation of CAAS, BSCIS depends on its parent organization, the Bleeding Institute of Foreign Studies, for its administrative assistance. The head of the Institute, Mr. Xia Xudong, is in fact in charge of the day-to-day work of BSCIS. Since 1990, it has held four annual meetings, each focusing on a given subject. The society is divided into eight research centers dealing with the United States, Western Europe, Russia and Central Asia, East Asia, the Jews, Ukraine, human rights, and the study of foreign capitals and metropolises. Each center can launch its own research projects.

BSCIS and its research centers have held numerous seminars and received many foreign scholars and diplomats as their guests. A noticeable achievement BSCIS has made is its study of human rights. Despite the tightening of political control following the Tiananmen incident of 1989, BSCIS was able to launch a project on human rights and held a series of seminars to compare different viewpoints on this subject. The result was two collections of articles published by *Foreign Studies Quarterly*, the journal of BSCIS, and an edited book entitled *A Study of International Human Rights*. Although the study is in general quite preliminary, there are some interesting and diverse views expressed by the authors. Indeed, BSCIS was probably the first institution to study the sensitive human rights issue.

Compared with CAAS, BSCIS has been less successful in building up its international connections and soliciting financial support from abroad. Its activities are nonetheless more frequent and cover a wider range of international issues as far as contemporary foreign affairs are concerned.

The cases of CAAS and BSCIS show that a large reservoir of interests and potential exists in promoting Chinese NGOs. Motivations for expanding their activities come from two directions. First, scholars and analysts from different institutions feel the growing need to know each other and institutionalize their horizontal links.

Second, the parent organizations also find it in their interest to serve as the base for an academic association because this position may enhance their prestige and influence. Indeed, the characteristics of Chinese NGOs lie in their indispensable dependence on their parent organizations. On the other hand, Chinese government departments also have felt strong incentives to help establish and maintain NGOs. This phenomenon seems to bode well for Chinese NGOs and their international connections.

Notes

1. Some cases show that changes are taking place in these government-controlled organizations, and thus a more sophisticated understanding of them is needed. For example, the All China Women's Federation (ACWF) is clearly a mass organ of the Communist Party. Yet some representatives of local Women's Federations voice the opinion that their extensive grassroots work and their independent sources of funding have made them NGOs, but that the ACWF is not.
2. International Monetary Fund, *International Monetary Statistics.* January 1995 (Washington, D.C.: IMF, 1995). Figures given are based on the end of period exchange rate for October 1994. US$1 = RMB 8.53.

Philanthropy and NGOs in Hong Kong and Asia Pacific Orientation

Makito Noda
Senior Program Officer
Japan Center for International Exchange

This paper attempts to portray the general features of the philanthropic organizations as well as nongovernmental organizations (NGOs) in Hong Kong.Particular attention will be paid to the Asia Pacific orientation and activities of these organizations, though shortage of systematic information makes the latter task extremely difficult. The author heavily depends on information contained in "Private Philanthropy in Hong Kong" by Alice Ngan Yip.[1]

I. Philanthropy in Hong Kong

In the past two decades, Hong Kong has demonstrated remarkable growth, elevating itself to the status of the ANIEs (Asian Newly Industrialized Economies) or "Four Little Dragons" along with Korea, Singapore, and Taiwan. The chief driving force of Hong Kong's economic development has often been analyzed as the entrepreneurship brought mainly by Chinese immigrants into the textile and garment industries and other labor-intensive, light industries. Acknowledging its crucial importance, Ezra Vogel also underscored the important role played in the course by the Hong Kong government in the form of industrial policy in order to prepare an environment most conducive to free enterprise.[2] Thus, individuals and organizations in Hong Kong have enjoyed, among other things, relative freedom from various regulations as well as low income and corporate tax rates. These elements seem to have some influence on the development of philanthropy in Hong Kong.

Alice Yip writes, "while this low tax rate is instrumental in promoting economic growth, it also means that the Government has a smaller budget to work with. Basic needs have to take priority over offering a comprehensive welfare program."[3] Clearly the priority was placed on economic growth rather than social welfare, the deficiencies of which had to be filled or supplemented by other sources. Thus, the role that philanthropy can potentially play in Hong Kong has been great. This situation, incidentally, has also affected the central nature of Hong Kong philanthropy, i.e., charity and social welfare-oriented activities to "supplement as well as complement the deficiencies of government activities."

In fact, an outside observer will be impressed by the large number of foundations or "charitable funds" as they are often called in Hong Kong. Traditional Chinese ethics encouraging the "haves" to help "have nots," particularly among their immediate relatives and acquaintances, coupled with the above deficiencies in governmental activities, must have paved the way for the entry of numerous philanthropic organizations in Hong Kong.

It would be difficult, however, to grasp an accurate number of philanthropic organizations active in Hong Kong or to systematically trace their activities. This is attributable to Hong Kong's relaxed attitude toward regulations, another industrial policy element that must have contributed to the rapid growth of the Hong Kong economy. According to Alice Yip, "government regulation on the operation and activities of foundations/organisations devoted to philanthropic activities is lax," and "there is no regulation on how, where or when one should spend the money on philanthropy."[4] For these reasons, there is no formal registration or coordinating body for philanthropic activities.Foundations in Hong Kong reportedly prefer a low profile existence to maintain a high level of flexibility in their philanthropic activities. This is because "the majority of foundations in Hong Kong are relatively small and not organized in such a way as to handle a large number of applications." Applications are, therefore, "considered based on an intricate network of personal relationships as well as past beneficiaries for recommendation."While this gives foundations maximum flexibility concerning their activities, it tends to keep liaisons among foundations to the level of insignificance.Coordination among themselves for more effective philanthropy seems to be a major challenge for foundations in Hong Kong when looking to the short-term future.

1. Typology of Philanthropy in Hong Kong

Judging from Alice Yip's report and such publications as the *Directory of Charitable and Trust Funds,* compiled by City and New Territories Administration, and the

Directory of Funding for Social Services, compiled by the Hong Kong Council of Social Service, philanthropy in Hong Kong may be divided into the following five categories:

a. individual donations
b. traditional charity institutions
c. the Community Chest of Hong Kong
d. statutory charitable and trust funds and/or funds administered through various government departments
e. private philanthropy

a. Individual Donations to Public Causes

In a culture that puts emphasis on the virtue of a benevolent rich, successful entrepreneurs, merchants, and businessmen alike are pressured to recycle a part of their wealth to the community.According to Alice Yip, "apart from the foundations, it is not uncommon to see individuals putting up large sums of money for worthwhile causes." These individuals prefer not to establish their own foundations because often times "donations may be made on an one time basis, e.g., setting up scholarships, donation of buildings, etc."[5] This partially explains chains of buildings on Hong Kong university campuses with individual persons' names. It will be another future challenge for Hong Kong philanthropy to more effectively organize these good wills.

b. Traditional Charities

Emergence of traditional charity groups by the name of "I-Tze" and/or "Kuk" date back to the mid- to late-nineteenth century. Originally established as voluntary organizations directly involved in the salvation of the socially disadvantaged, e.g., providing shelter for the poor and the sick, aiding of victims of crimes such as kidnapping, etc., they have developed themselves into sophisticated philanthropic organizations over the years, managing hospitals and providing welfare and educational services.Their main financial sources are, typically, individual donations and fund-raising campaigns as well as government subsidies. One of the most representative organizations of this category is The Tung Wah Group (established in 1851) providing "a wider spectrum of traditional Chinese charities…[including] nonprofit making funeral parlours and…temples and soothsayers' stalls" than any other organization in Hong Kong[6] on top of usual welfare and educational services such as five hospitals, two herbalist clinics, fourteen secondary schools, seventeen homes and hostels for the elderly, and fourteen day nurseries. Another organization very representative of this category, Po Leung Kuk (established in 1878), manages fifteen institutions for residential care for deprived/underprivileged children, mentally retarded people, and unmarried mothers; twenty-five day care nurseries; seven centers for rehabilitation services for the retarded; and fourteen kindergartens; among others.

c. The Community Chest of Hong Kong

The Community Chest of Hong Kong was established in 1968 as the institution that provides an organized approach to fund raising for small voluntary welfare agencies. Money is raised from the public at large to be allocated among member agencies whose activities range from care of the aged to services for families and children.In Hong Kong the great bulk of private welfare work is reportedly provided by those member agencies of the Community Chest. In the first years of operation about HK$5 million (US$4646,000)[7] was allocated to its sixty member agencies. For 1992–93 alone, HK$145 million (US$ 18.7 million) was raised and allocated through 120 member agencies.

d. Statutory Charitable and Trust Funds and Funds Administered through various Government Departments

There are a number of charitable and trust funds in Hong Kong that can be used to provide relief and assistance to members of the general public or of specified groups in the community. Most of these funds are either statutory funds or funds administered through various government departments, and they cover a variety of purposes from charitable to educational, recreational, and agricultural.City and New Territories Administration classifies these funds into the following categories according to purposes:

(1) Agricultural and Fisheries

Agricultural Products Scholarship Fund
Co-operative for American Relief Everywhere Loan Fund
J.F. Joseph Trust Fund
Kadoorie Agricultural Aid Loan Fund
Marine Fish Scholarship Fund
World Refugee Year Loan Fund

(2) Charitable

Brewin Trust Fund
Ellis Kadoorie Hong Kong Ladies Benevolent Association Trust
Emergency Relief Fund
General Chinese Charities Fund
Kwan Fong Trust Fund for the Needy
Li Po Chun Charitable Trust Fund
Lotteries Fund
Samaritan Fund
Sir Robert Ho Tung Charitable Fund
Tang Shiu Kin and Ho Tim Charitable Fund

(3) Cultural and Recreational

Chinese Temples Fund
Hong Kong Jockey Club Music Fund
Sir David Trench Fund for Recreation
Sports Aid for the Disabled Fund
Sports Aid Foundation

(4)Educational

Correctional Services Children's Education Trust
Education Scholarships Fund
Grantham Scholarships Fund
Hong Kong Rotary Club Students Loan Fund
Li Po Chun Charitable Trust Fund
Municipal Services Scholarship Fund
Police Children's Education Trust Fund
Police Education and Welfare Trust Fund
Sing Tao Foundation Student's Loan Fund
Sir Edward Youde Memorial Fund
Sir Jack Cater Scholarship Trust Fund
Sir Robert Black Trust Fund
Social Work Training Fund
The Queen Elizabeth Foundation for the Mentally Handicapped

(5) Other

Correctional Services Department Welfare Fund

As shown above, objects of these funds are essentially social welfare and educational for members of the Hong Kong community.

e. Private Philanthropy

The above-mentioned *Directory of Charitable and Trust Funds* states that funds administered by private bodies are not included in the directory. It continues by admitting that there are a number of such funds in Hong Kong but information on them is scattered. In the absence of a central coordinating body for private philanthropy, as pointed out earlier, this is only to be expected. It refers to the *Directory of Funding for Social Services* compiled by the Hong Kong Council of Social Service, whose first issue was published only in May 1992, as the source of information closest to being comprehensive. The Directory portrays the profiles of the following thirty-one private foundations and funds:

The American Women's Association Ltd.
Brewin Trust Fund*
Caltex Green Fund
The Community Chest of Hong Kong Pilot Project and Agency Development Fund
Duty Free Shoppers Charitable Trust
Ellis Kadoorie Hong Kong Ladies Benevolent Association Trust*
Emergency Relief Fund*
Epson Foundation
Fong Shu Fook Tong Foundation
Fong's Family Foundation
General Chinese Charities Fund*
Hong Kong Jockey Club (Charities) Ltd.
Hong Kong Kidney Patients Trust
Hong Kong University Social Service Group Social Service Fund
Jockey Club Summer Youth Programme Grant
The Keswick Foundation Limited
Kwan Fong Trust Fund for the Needy*
Law's Foundation
Levi Strauss Far East Ltd. Community Involvement Team Grants
Li Po Chun Charitable Trust Fund*
Lotteries Fund*
The Queen Elizabeth Foundation for the Mentally Handicapped*
Samaritan Fund*
The Shell Better Environment Awards Scheme
Sir David Trench Fund for Recreation*
Sir Robert Black Trust Fund Scholarships and Training Grants
Sir Robert Ho Tung Charitable Fund*
Social Work Training Fund*
Subvention Scheme on the Promotion of Civic Education
Tang Shiu Kin and Ho Tim Charitable Fund*
Y's Men's Club of Tsim Sha Tsui Service Together Fund

Those with an asterisk are also included in the *Directory of Charitable and Trust Funds* in which "most of the funds included…are either statutory funds or funds administered through various Government departments." On the other hand, the *Directory of Funding for Social Service* states in its foreword that "there are a number of charitable and trust funds which are used to provide relief and financial assistance to members of the general public or of specified groups in the community in Hong Kong" and explains that "most of them are private funds with scattered information and there is no centralized information about them." Although all of the asterisked ones were established under government ordinance, demarcation between "governmental" and "private" organizations seems to be quite blurred in Hong Kong philanthropy.

Categorizing the above thirty-one "private" organizations according to their objects, one realizes that they are again predominantly social welfare and education-minded groups:

Social Welfare	15
Environment	2
NGO/grassroots support	1
Emergency relief	1
Education	7
Community service	1
Medicare	2
Recreation	1
Other	1

Based on the above, it seems difficult to conclude that those Hong Kong foundations and other philanthropic organizations are very much Asia Pacific oriented. In fact, all of the organizations included in the directory seem to be very domestic in orientation as well as scope of activities. One should note, however, that this directory may not be a comprehensive inventory of private philanthropy in Hong Kong.

In fact, it may have omitted some major foundations, i.e., it does not include any of the foundations that Alice Yip introduced as representatives of various aspects of Hong Kong's private philanthropy. She sees there have emerged two outstanding patterns in recent Hong Kong private philanthropy, i.e., one for education and environmental concerns and the other for tertiary education support. Yip states that "as a result of social pressure to return some of what is taken from the society, all major trading firms…and corporations in Hong Kong have set up foundations or trusts for the benefit of the local community as one of their public relation exercises," and, therefore, "their contributions are mainly local and include environmental protection, scholarships and funds for buildings and auditoriums at tertiary institutions."[8] She goes on to portray, as examples, the Hong Kong Bank Foundation whose principle areas of interest are education and environmental protection in Hong Kong, the Hong Kong Telecom Foundation which supports a host of activities in education and environmental protection, K.P. Tin Foundation, and the Law Foundation (the only institution that is included in the above directory).

In any event, the predominant concern and area of interest of Hong Kong philanthropy, statutory or private, is the immediate community, particularly those issues related to social welfare, the environment, and education.

Another area that Yip discusses as a part of Hong Kong private philanthropic activity is tertiary education. In a territory where government expenditure on research and development is far less than one percent of the total budget (0.06 percent on the average between 1988 and 1992), grants from private sources are very much needed. In response to these needs, "there are a number of foundations that are very active in sponsoring research and related activities at the tertiary institutions."[9] Most representative in this field of activities are the Shaw Foundation, The Croucher Foundation, and the C.C. Hsu Educational Foundation. These foundations make donations for the construction of buildings, auditoriums, libraries, and functional buildings in five of Hong Kong's tertiary institutions; establish endowment funds at these institutions to encourage research in various fields; provide students both inside and outside of Hong Kong with scholarships; make grants for various research projects; and sponsor various academic and intellectual exchange activities based on universities and other institutions of higher education.

2. Asia Pacific Orientation of Hong Kong Foundations

As discussed above, the absolute majority of philanthropic activities of Hong Kong foundations have been confined within the boundary of its territory, particularly in the fields of social welfare, education, and environmental protection. Its cultural heritage and geographic proximity to China have, however, directed some attention of these institutions to East Asian affairs, particularly China. These usually take the form of sponsorship of university-related activities, i.e., research, seminars, symposia, and scholarships.

The Asian Foundation for the Prevention of Blindness may be unique in the sense that it mainly operates in Southeast Asia, conducting and supporting research in ophthalmology, through grants to institutions and individuals, and assists in the training of all kinds of ophthalmic and multidisciplinary staff. The Croucher Foundation shows a strong commitment toward Hong Kong and China. On the belief that liaisons and exchange with academic leaders of China would be "in the best long term interest of Hong Kong in the run up to 1997," the Foundation sponsors joint workshops on topics of mutual interest and provides scholarships for Chinese scholars to spend time in Hong Kong. The C.C.Hsu Educational Foundation, newly established in 1991, sponsored an international conference in 1992 on the "University's Role in the Integration of Knowledge in Technology Transfer" in which more than forty presidents of Chinese, Hong Kong, and North American universities participated.

Li Ka Shing donated more than HK$600 million (US$77.5 million) toward the establishment of a university in Swatow, China. The Pei Hua Educational Foundation was established in 1982 to assist China in the training and development of its professionals by providing professional training. Scholarship programs have been provided by the Shaw Foundation for students from mainland China, Hong Kong, and the ASEAN countries, to further their studies in the United Kingdom and the United States. The Foundation has also made substantial financial contributions to serve the community in Singapore and donated over HK$525 million (US$67.8 million) to more than 240 educational institutions in China.

3. Future Challenges

For Hong Kong private philanthropy to be a more effective social force in the community, better coordination among organizations seems to be crucial for possible collaboration, joint funding, and avoidance of redundancy. For this purpose, some of the "flexibility and freedom" that they have enjoyed may have to be slightly modified.

Although their special attachment to and affinity with China is fully understandable, one may wonder if their rich resources can be made available to other countries in the region.As one of the four little dragons, Hong Kong is encouraged to be more mindful of the Asia Pacific region aside from China.

With 1997 imminently close, Hong Kong philanthropy will be experiencing a unique situation of being predominantly social welfare-oriented private institutions in a market-economy enclave inside a socialist economy. It is difficult to predict how they will be treated under the new rule, especially when, theoretically, there will be no social welfare problem.

II. Voluntary Organizations for Social Services

What is said of the lack of systematic information about philanthropy is more acutely felt about the presence and activities of nongovernmental organizations. One source of information that seems to be more comprehensive than others is the Hong Kong Council for Social Service. The Council, established in 1947, aims to "provide a common meeting ground for voluntary welfare organizations, service clubs, community groups and individuals to work in concert over the development and promotion of voluntary welfare services and in meeting the overall social service needs of Hong Kong."[10] Apparently it is a heavily social welfare-inclined institution, and, therefore, there may be some gap between the concept of NGOs and the organizations that the Council monitors. In the absence of a better alternative, however, the author bases his analysis on the directory compiled by this Council.

The *Directory of Social Services,* compiled by The Hong Kong Council of Social Service, provides information about "public and non-profit-making social services organizations in Hong Kong." It covers 326 institutions that are either member agencies of the Hong Kong Council of Social Service, agencies receiving subventions from the Government of Hong Kong, agencies receiving subventions from the Community Chest of Hong Kong, agencies having been listed in previous editions of the directory, agencies affiliated with the Committees or Divisions of the Hong Kong Council of Social Service, or governmental departments offering social welfare or related service. Therefore, the Directory may contain institutions that normally are not classified as NGOs, while it may omit some of the important components of the NGOs. These 326 institutions provide services that belong to any one of the following categories:

Community Development Services
- Community Center Services
- Community Coordination
- Project-based Services
- Others

Family and Child Care Services
- Day Care Service for Children
- Family Services
- Residential Child Care Services
- Others

Rehabilitation Services
- Coordination and Referrals
- Medical Rehabilitation Services
- Special Education and Training Services
- Vocational Rehabilitation Services
- Social Rehabilitation Services
- Technical Support Services
- Screening and Assessment Services
- Medical Rehabilitation Services
- Special Education and Training Services
- Vocational Rehabilitation Services
- Social Rehabilitation Services
- Technical Support Services
- Sign Language Training/Interpretation Services

Services for the Elderly
- Coordination and Referrals
- Community Support Services
- Employment Services
- Financial Assistance
- Funeral Services
- Housing
- Medical and Health Services
- Residential Services
- Transport Services
- Others

Services for Offenders/Ex-offenders
- Services for Offenders/Ex-offenders
- Services for Probationers

Services for School-aged Children and Young People
- Camps and Hostels
- Children and Youth Centers
- Special Services
- Uniformed Groups
- Others

Services for Other Target Groups
- Services for Alcoholics
- Services for Cancer and TB Patients

Services for Drug Abusers/Ex-addicts
Services for Farmers and Fisherman
Services for Labourers
Services for Patients
Services for Seamen and Servicemen
Services for Refugees
Services for Street Sleepers
Services for Women

Support Services
Coordination and Planning
Funding Sources
Research and Evaluation
Training
Others

The above list implies that there are few, if any, activities or institutions that are oriented toward the wider Asia Pacific region. Bestowed with a number of intricate problems related to the return to China, for example, no doubt there must be some action-oriented, nongovernmental groups that are concerned with such issues as human rights, regional development, cultural and intellectual exchange, etc. Unfortunately, information on these organizations and activities seems to be unavailable.

Notes

1. Alice Ngan Yip, "Private Philanthropy in Hong Kong" in *Evolving Patterns of Asia-Pacific Philanthropy*, edited by Ku-Hyun Jung (Seoul: Seoul Press, 1994).
2. Ezra F. Vogel, *The Four Little Dragons* (Cambridge: Harvard University Press, 1991).
3. Yip, op. cit., p. 114.
4. Ibid., p. 112.
5. Ibid., p. 112.
6. Ibid., p. 115.
7. Based on the exchange rate for July 10, 1995. US$1=HK$7.74.
8. Yip, op. cit., p. 122.
9. Ibid., 125.
10. *The Hong Kong Council of Social Service Annual Report, 1991–1992.*

INDONESIA

Review of the NGO Sector in Indonesia and Evolution of the Asia Pacific Regional Community Concept among Indonesian NGOs

Andra L. Corrothers
Regional Representative for Asia
PACT, Inc. Asia Regional Office
(Private Agencies Collaborating Together, Inc.)
and
Estie W. Suryatna
Representative's Special Assistant

I. Overview of the Indonesian NGO Sector

NGOs in Indonesia are not a new phenomenon; however, the growth of the NGO sector since the 1970s has been phenomenal. While there appears to have been nongovernmental organizations in some form even during the very early Dutch colonial administration, most of these organizations were loose associations or alliances which had only a limited impact on the Dutch colonial masters and on the communities within which they were formed. There were exceptions, however, and some of these organizations formed the foundation of the freedom and independence movement which eventually resulted in Indonesia's independence from the Netherlands.

In the early 1920s, in response to the growing awareness and desire for freedom among Indonesians, nongovernmental organizations (primarily all Indonesian associations) played an important role in developing the intellectual and grassroots movement that fostered the Indonesian independence movement. Such movements as those started by Budi Oetomo, a nationalist educator, were among the earliest such groups which would be familiar today among those studying the NGO phenomenon. These early organizations were followed by the establishment of a series of political organizations attached to the large and diverse system of political parties prevalent in Indonesia in the 1950s and early 1960s; however, many of these organizations were abolished shortly after the coup d'état of 1965. What remained after the abolition of the politically affiliated organizations, were organizations focused on direct welfare, and many of these were focused on specific cultural groups within Indonesia. It was only again in the late 1960s that the foundation of the modern Indonesian NGO sector was established.

II. The Modern Indonesian NGO Sector

In the late 1960s, a new variety of NGO, oriented toward development as opposed to welfare, emerged as a result of debates concerning how best to help the disadvantaged in Indonesian society. These NGOs tried to bridge the gap between the needs of that portion of society and the goals of the national development program. These organizations began their service by attempting to respond to a set of diverse problems articulated at the grassroots level, and then carving out for themselves development roles not assumed by government or business.

During this period, awareness grew regarding the need for more direct people's participation in development. Many NGO activists appeared to agree that the net impact of the government's large-scale and top-down approach was limited in Indonesia, a country known for its cultural diversity and geographic spread (13,677 islands). Some activists of the time felt they could have more direct impact on the poor, as well as remain innovative and flexible, by mounting a grassroots approach.

In the early years of the modern NGO era, more and more charity or relief-oriented NGOs began to adopt a community-based self-reliance approach, although many continued using charitable approaches in their work. Among one of the earliest modern era NGOs in Indonesia was Perkumpulan Keluarga Berencana Indonesia (PKBI).[1] Founded in 1957, it pioneered the concept of family planning during the Sukarno years. It has since moved beyond promoting only birth control and family planning to become very active in other community development activities, including HIV/AIDS prevention and awareness. Despite many ups and downs, PKBI is today one of the largest NGOs in Indonesia.

Formed in the early 1960s, Yayasan Sosial Tani Membangun (YSTM)[2] began its work in savings group (*usaha bersama*, or pre-cooperatives) development. Later, YSTM formed Yayasan Bina Swadaya, which has grown into one of the largest NGOs in Indonesia, providing training for other NGO staff and government officials in community development, pre-cooperative development and management, and other institutional enhancement fields. It also has a widely circulated agricultural magazine, *TRUBUS*, with a wide readership. Through several income-generating units, Bina Swadaya now generates nearly half of its annual budget.

The 1970s witnessed the birth of more development NGOs. These organizations addressed many issues important to both rural and urban Indonesians. Community health, small-scale industrial development, and appropriate technology development were among some of the fields in which these NGOs engaged. Stressing project innovation, this next generation of NGOs was able to impact on national development programs. Yayasan Indonesia Sejahtera, for example, started the concept from which was born the *POSYANDU* (*pos pelayanan terpadu*, or community-based integrated health post), which was later adopted by the government and has become the basis for its internationally known community-based primary health care and family planning programs. Through the years, these NGOs have grown larger. Their credibility has grown a pace, drawing more and more foreign donors to place their confidence in the development approaches of the Indonesian NGO sector.

At about the same time, some NGO activists began to feel that community development programs were not able to obtain maximum impact, as the "playing field" was not level for the poor. Advocacy NGOs began to develop in response to these perceived inequities. NGOs such as the Indonesian Legal Aid Institute and the Indonesian Consumer's Union Institute[3] were founded in this period. Environmental groups such as Kelompok Sepuluh and Wahana Lingkungan Hidup (WALHI) were both products of this generation of NGOs. The action programs of advocacy NGOs are seen by many as complimentary to the approach of the community development NGOs, although their relationship to government has been increasingly strained in recent years.

During subsequent years, many small NGOs sprang up in communities around Indonesia. Many of these disappeared as quickly as they came into being. However, the total number of independent organizations focusing on development issues has grown tremendously since the late 1960s. Current estimates range from between four thousand to six thousand in number. It is very difficult to pinpoint the number, as many do not register with local authorities, and the archipelagic nature of Indonesia makes it difficult to stay abreast of the growth of Indonesia's dynamic NGO sector.

III. The Role of NGOs in Indonesian Society

It is sometimes very difficult for Indonesian NGOs to thrive in the New Order[4] era. Since the coup of 1965, political parties have been forced to fuse and adhere to a prescribed formula. University students, while initially being some of the biggest supporters of the New Order government, were depoliticized through the Campus Normalization regulations of the 1970s. Journalists were forced to submit to self-censorship, midnight phone calls "suggesting" changes in editorial policy, and, occasionally, outright threats to enforce the withholding of certain articles. The *budaya bisu* (culture of silence) became the credo of what some refer to as the tame press. Labor unions, farmers' and fishermen's associations, youth and women's organizations, and all similar popular movements were forced to place themselves under national umbrella coordinating bodies recognized by the government. This last move, known as the principle of *perwadahkan tunggal* (a term originating from Javanese, meaning the only, rightful place), has been one of the tactics most feared by NGO and other activists in Indonesia.

Catalytic to the growth of the NGO sector has been the perceived inability of political parties or other organizations, such as students' organizations, to voice the aspirations and represent the interests of common people. Nor does there appear to be many organizations allowed to act as "pressure valves." "Pressure valve" organizations, of the kind that would allow disaffected persons to vent their disappointment and dissatisfaction with the government and its development programs, or to articulate specific aspirations, have often been funneled into national coordinating bodies, as mentioned above. The Indonesian Lawyers Association is one example. Many activists perceive the national development program as favoring the growth of large industries and as mortgaging the welfare of future generations for the benefit of a few today. Matched with the perceived effectiveness of grassroots organizations, NGOs play a vital role in providing commentary on the social and material condition of economically and socially disadvantaged Indonesians.

In addition, the government bureaucracy of the New Order, which is the employer of choice for many college graduates, has been spurned by some as a lumbering, and often corrupt, development mechanism. For those individuals truly wishing to serve their community in an atmosphere of democratic and participatory conviction, the NGO sector is one of their only choices. For those individuals who look at the development problems affecting poor Indonesians as symptoms of a larger ill, advocacy NGOs provide a mechanism whereby they can test and examine such issues.

Arguably, the major achievement of Indonesian NGOs at the macro level has been the increase in awareness of issues arising from their respective fields of experience to a more prominent place on the national political agenda. The last ten or twelve years has seen a broadening and deepening of this agenda as more NGOs have entered the field and wider segments of the government bureaucracy have been exposed to such ideas. NGOs have also been able to reflect on and articulate more general concerns for the environment, human rights, and democratization, now emerging most obviously, but by no means exclusively, among the middle class.

IV. Interaction between Indonesian NGOs and the Government

Dr. Philip Eldridge, in his working paper No. 55 entitled, "NGOs in Indonesia: Popular Movement or Arm of Government?"[5] describes three NGO models in shaping relations with the Indonesian government. The models, in graphic form, are shown below:

NGO Models			
ORIENTATION	1	2	3
Cooperates with official programs	Yes	Limited	No
Development or Mobilization	Development	Mobilization	Mobilization
Penetration of State Structures	Medium	High	Low
Relations between Small Groups and NGO partners	Semi-dependent	Mutually Supportive	Autonomous
Orientation v. State Structures	Accommodate	Change	Circumvent

Source: Dr. Philip Eldridge, *NGOs in Indonesia: Popular Movement or Ar, of Government,* Working Paper No. 55, The Center of Southeast Asian Studies, Monash University, 1989.

According to Dr. Eldridge, the first model, which he labels "High-level Partnership: Grassroots Development," demonstrates a high degree of participation by the NGOs in official development programs, even though he acknowledges that these

NGOs seek to influence the design and implementation to be more participatory. This approach appears to be strictly development oriented rather than focused on mobilization or advocacy work, and entails linking NGO programs to existing community organizations or creating new organizations for the same purpose. Cultivating cooperation with government officials, this group of NGOs shows little interest in impacting on the "political" process of development, preferring to confine their efforts to influencing policy. Dr. Eldridge believes that most "model one" NGOs originated as small, locally oriented groups, which became involved in large-scale programs as much by accident as by design. He goes on to indicate that these NGOs remain aware of the need to maintain grassroots linkages.

The second model in Dr. Eldridge's paradigm, is described as "High-level Politics: Grassroots Mobilization." Unlike the first model, which appears to have derived its approach from mainstream social work theory, this second model has its foundation in more radical social theory. It is often linked with criticism of the New Order philosophy and favors the promotion of "consciousness-raising" as an approach. These NGOs do not favor cooperation with the government's official development programs, although some have been known to undertake research on behalf of the government. "Model two" NGOs play strong advocacy roles, both in seeking protection and space for local mobilization and on specific policy issues in their respective fields.

The third model, which Dr. Eldridge calls "Empowerment at the Grassroots," can be found among NGOs which have their focus of action at the local rather than the national level. The main difference between this model and the second is that while emphasizing "consciousness-raising" and awareness of rights, this group of NGOs does not focus on campaigns to change policy. This group seeks only minimum contact with government agencies. Dr. Eldridge believes that NGOs described in this model see "social and political changes as ultimately less dependent on 'persuasion' and policy changes by the government as on self-reliant group formation, in the belief that eventually a strong, though informally structured popular movement will emerge."[6] These groups tend to minimize involvement in large-scale networking and to emphasize arrangements requiring personal contact rather than more formal organization.

NGO relations with government have been alternately cooperative and conflicting, with some NGOs being co-opted within government programs, some NGOs in conflict with government programs, and some NGOs experiencing some of both. This fits dynamically within Dr. Eldridge's models, as shown above. However, in Indonesia, there are no rigid mechanisms that harmoniously orchestrate the relationship between the government and NGOs and much distorts the potentially strong linkages that could develop between them. First, there is a perceived conflict and fear on the part of some government officials that effective NGO-based programs might undercut their influence on communities and larger groups of Indonesians. On the other hand, government sometimes seeks to "co-opt" NGOs into national development programs in the hope of increasing popular support and in sharing in the anticipated successes of such programs. Secondly, the Indonesian government has often used a system of "carrots and sticks" to keep the NGO sector under its influence and within the limits of acceptable conduct. This system, which more often than not, limits the capacity of NGOs to maneuver adequately, has resulted in parallel structures which are not conducive to increasing participation in development programs.

From the NGO side, many NGO activists perceive government bureaucracy, and by extension its implementors, as a corrupt and lumbering machine having few meaningful linkages with poor people. Many NGOs dismiss government programs based on this perception. By doing so, NGOs miss valuable linkages and opportunities to bring to scale development programs which they have tested successfully in the field or by actually impacting the policies they aspire to change. The lumping of government programs in such a category is neither realistic nor reflective of the success that the Indonesian government has had in some fields. Furthermore, the high level of informality which NGOs feel obliged to adopt in shaping their organizational structures for purposes of survival tends to inhibit the emergence of accountable democratic structures within their organizations or at the beneficiary level. It also tends to force NGOs to maintain dependence on progressive, influential persons or intermediary institutions (such as international NGO partners or donors). Finally, Indonesian NGOs have had little success in developing networks or federations capable of reducing their dependence on individuals and outside organizations to undertake intermediary roles vis-à-vis government agencies or in developing the foundations of a true movement. Only when Indonesian NGOs can come to grips with the above can they truly have an impact on the system which they criticize and often ignore.

V. Future Prospects to Advance the Asia Pacific Regional Community Concept

The concept of an Asia Pacific regional community has its beginnings in the early

1980s. The concept was founded on the premise that in a new, growing, and interdependent global community, countries contained within or bordering on the Pacific Ocean already possess or strategically should have common economic, cultural, and diplomatic objectives. With communication and awareness development issues making gains in the formerly less economically developed countries within this region, the more economically developed leaders (such as Japan, Korea, China, Taiwan, and the United States) wished to create and take advantage of opportunities provided by increased growth in the region. As noted in the Japan Center for International Exchange (JCIE) proposal for this study, "One of the major characteristics of this emerging 'Asia Pacific Regional Community' is that it has been largely economic-driven, particularly through the dynamic corporate interactions of trade and investment within the region."[7]

In fact, it is precisely because the thrust has almost solely been upon economic linkages that JCIE sponsored this study. "It is argued, in some circles, that mere economic interdependence, therefore, is not sufficient as a basis for the regional 'community' and that it is hard to bring about such a 'community' without some viable shared values or interests, or without more stable human and institutional interactions among the nations within this region."[8] Developing shared values among countries which are as diverse as the countries of the Asia Pacific region will be a challenge that dwarfs the challenge faced in the development of the European Union. It is further recognized that if the Asia Pacific Regional Community is to become successful in creating a sense of shared values or common "community interest," countries within this community will not only have to base linkages and interchange upon the actions of governments and the private sector in the spheres of economics and diplomacy, but also acknowledge the contributions of the nongovernmental sector to this effort in generating a strong sense of community among the countries within the region. Many linkages have already been successfully implemented through various exchange and linkage programs, joint research and academic exchanges, NGO networking and assistance programs, and business organization development. However, much remains to be done before the Asia Pacific Regional Community can take its place among other global blocks of common community interest.

As this part of the study deals specifically with Indonesia, two important questions needing resolution through this study are:

- How can and why should NGOs have a role in the development of the Asia Pacific Regional Community?
- In the context of Indonesia, what more needs to be done to create stronger

linkages among Indonesian NGOs and potential partners in the Asia Pacific region?

1. How Can and Why should NGOs have a Role in the Development of the Asia Pacific Regional Community?

The word *politic*, as defined in *The Random House Dictionary of the English Language* (The Unabridged Edition), means: **1. sagacious in pursuing a policy, 2. shrewd in achieving an end.** This term aptly describes Asian nongovernmental organizations of the current era. Many, though not all, have eschewed the formal political system to achieve their aims. However, their aims are nonetheless political. Kunda Dixit, reporting for *Inter Press Service*, wrote in her article entitled, "NGOs performing bigger role in Asia":

> Asia's drift toward democracy in recent years had raised hopes for a more responsive, welfare-oriented state apparatus, but most governments in the region are so preoccupied with getting re-elected that they seem to have lost sight of the common good. Development experts say democracy has become an excuse for the business and political elite to shuffle the cards every four or five years and cling to power without really devolving decision-making to communities in the countryside. Free elections and multi-party politics have thus legitimized the elite without really addressing the roots of problems like rural poverty, environmental degradation and the population crisis, they add. Even in large countries with a long tradition of democracy like India, there are doubts whether 50 years of elections and heavy government involvement have really made a dent in resolving chronic problems like extreme inequality and landlessness. With such a situation, nongovernmental organizations (NGOs) have found themselves performing their task of stepping in to fill in the gaps left by government neglect or disinterest more frequently.

While Kunda Dixit has hit the nail on the head, so to speak, she did not go so far as to outline roles for NGOs in what David Korten calls "spaceship economies." Mr. Korten, in his book entitled, *Getting to the 21st Century: Voluntary Action and the Global Agenda*, has identified specific roles for NGOs. These four roles are: catalyzing the transformation of institutions, policies, and values; monitoring and protesting abuses of power; facilitating reconciliation; and providing essential community services.[9] The roles are briefly described below:

1) *Catalyzing Systems Change*: The foremost development priority of the 1990s is to

transform the ways in which people perceive their world, use its resources, and relate to one another as individuals and nations. There is a substantial need for leadership and support from government. However, a lead role in catalyzing these changes–through defining issues, creating a new global consciousness, facilitating people-to-people exchange, advocating policy change, building political will, and undertaking experimental initiatives–must come from people taking voluntary action.[10]

2) *Systems Monitoring and Protest*: Many of the changes noted above will require actions to check abuses of power that violate both the law and accepted norms of human behavior, especially by government and business. The key to effective monitoring and protest is a system of citizen surveillance that brings abusive behavior into the open for public scrutiny and action. Abuse feeds on silence, and often the fear of exposure is in itself enough to check the potential abuser. System monitoring and protest are not popular activities among those who are protective of what they may perceive to be their prerogative to abuse the power they hold. It requires courage to monitor and expose this abuse in the face of potential retaliation.[11]

3) *Facilitating Reconciliation with Justice*: Given the current level and prevalence of communal violence and its influence on the lives of millions, attention should be shifted from relief for victims to the protagonists of conflict. Recognizing that violence and a commitment to reconciliation must not be equated with condoning injustice, and that a peace that imposes or sustains injustice works its own violence on the poor and powerless, it must be acknowledged that reconciliation is one of the most fundamental development needs in our contemporary world.[12]

4) *Implementing Large-Scale Service Programs*: A sustainable equity-led growth strategy must be supported by appropriate service delivery systems able to function on a national scale. It has long been assumed that these service delivery programs fall in the province of governments. Family planning services, reforestation (particularly social forestry programs), basic education, and small-scale credit programs readily lend themselves to the more decentralized base of NGO management.[13]

As relationships among the countries of the Asia Pacific region begin to change rapidly in the run-up to the 21st century, so must the way we deal with relationships among institutions and organizations, be they from the governmental sector, the private sector or the nonprofit sector. Even the roles between the various sectors may change; something unforeseen or unanticipated may occur that will help us harmonize the inherent distrust among the sectoral players. Without the underlying values which all cultures acknowledge firmly placed as guideposts along this route of change, and willingness to accept change, entire cultures may be stressed to the point where conflict can arise. As Dr. Korten contends in his book, "the global development crisis rests not with the development industry, but with the great social movements of contemporary society including the peace, environment, women, and human rights movements."[14]

It is precisely for this reason that NGOs must be involved in furthering the aims of the Asia Pacific Regional Community concept. Precisely, because:

- NGOs subscribe to larger concepts (democracy, justice, equality) which form the basis for their actions and programs and which do not depend on geographical or historical boundaries;
- NGOs can, and often do, more readily subvert their organizational interests to the common good of people;
- NGOs are not subservient to short-term nationalist objectives as their goals are generally associated with long-term change and transformation;
- NGOs many times eschew bureaucracy and "old thinking" which hinders acceptance of new situations and the creative resolution of problems; and,
- the NGO value paradigm ensures that people critique and re-examine beliefs, values, objectives and goals in order to ensure that the needs of people are put first.

With NGOs fully participating in the process unfolding in the development of the Asia Pacific Regional Community, the values necessary to create and sustain a sense of broader community interest driving the process can be assured.

2. In the Context of Indonesia, What More Needs to be done to Create Stronger Linkages among Indonesian NGOs and Potential Partners in the Asia Pacific Region?

In the following section of this study, interviews were conducted with some of the largest and most widely exposed NGOs in Indonesia. The focus of these interviews was to provide greater understanding to the readers of this report of the NGOs as organizations and of where they believed they could contribute to the furthering of the Asia Pacific Regional Community. The results of these interviews and a summary of the findings follows.

- The Indonesian NGO community is dynamic and diverse. NGOs range in size and expertise from very small grassroots organizations to large technically skilled organizations. Some are very dependent on donor funds and live a hand-to-mouth existence, while others have either their own source of funds or such a well-established donor base that they are assured of continued existence. Indonesian NGOs exist in an environment which is not as enabling as many NGO environments in other Asian countries. Compared to the freewheeling growth, transition, and contraction of NGO communities in the Philippines or Bangladesh, the number of NGOs in Indonesia has remained relatively stable for a country of its size.

The majority of large well-funded NGOs are based in Jakarta, the nation's capital. As can be seen in the following survey, with only one exception, all the NGOs interviewed were in Jakarta. While there are some larger NGOs based in the larger cities in the outer islands, these are the exceptions, not the rule. The Indonesian NGO community's program interests range from concern for environmental issues, to women laborer's rights, to consumerism, to family planning. The opportunity for sharing expertise and information, exchange and joint action is overwhelming.

- While most of the NGOs interviewed in the survey were clearly in favor of more interaction among fellow NGOs and other institutions in the Asia Pacific Region, it was more difficult to ascertain what motivated them, and why, to seek linkages outside of Indonesia. Several of the NGOs indicated that they sought technical information and resources that would be appropriate or applicable to the Indonesian situation. Others indicated that they sought to broaden their organizational linkages through networking among Asian counterparts to improve program quality. More significantly, the majority of NGOs indicated that the main reason they sought linkages with other NGOs in the region was to promote specific advocacy agendas and that this collective or joint action spurred their interest in developing strong linkages with partners in other Asia Pacific countries.

The stress on an advocacy agenda in linking with other NGOs clearly shows that increased communication among organizations in this region has allowed NGOs to identify development issues requiring joint action to eradicate problems that cross borders and other boundaries. This is most visible in relation to NGOs with organizational advocacy agendas such as WALHI (environment), Yayasan Lembaga Konsumen Indonesia (consumerism) and Yayasan Lembaga Bantuan Hukum Indonesia (human rights and democracy). However, even NGOs with unclear advocacy agendas will seek linkages with other NGOs for mutual protection, thus gaining advantage in strength with numbers. This can be seen most clearly in Indonesian NGOs seeking clear linkages with U.S.-based NGOs, which some Indonesian NGOs hope will afford them some measure of protection should the government decide to lend a greater measure of "guidance" or add restrictions on NGO activities.

- While the desire and motivation for Indonesian NGOs to foster linkages with other NGOs in the Asia Pacific region is strong, Indonesian NGOs are not now consistently nor sufficiently linked to NGO affiliates in other countries. For example, many of the NGOs expressed dismay that they were more strongly linked with NGOs in the United States than they were linked with NGOs in Japan, for example, a country much closer geographically and with greater aid linkages to Indonesia than the United States.

An additional constraint is that many Indonesian NGOs are so strongly focused on Indonesia-specific issues that finding time, energy, and resources to manage relationships with NGOs from outside of Indonesia does not appear to warrant the use of already scarce resources. Many NGO leaders expressed frustration that donors do not also provide support for networking activities among NGOs in the region; therefore, funds to support such activities (phone and fax bills, courier service, travel support, etc.) are rarely included in most donor's project-specific budgets. Some NGO leaders indicated that if funds are not specifically available to support networking activities, then they prefer to devote scarce resources to activities that provide clearer benefits to their organization and their target groups. Donors and other aspiring NGO partners might consider allowing support or developing joint activities within the framework of specific projects or programs to allow for networking and linkage activities. Such assistance might include support for conference attendance, specific-project support funds, joint research projects, etc. It should be noted that in the absence of funds provided by donors or partners specifically for networking activities, many Indonesian NGOs will forego networking in favor of activities that clearly benefit their goals and objectives.

- Some of the NGO leaders expressed the opinion that language and other communication difficulties preclude much of the exchange that would naturally be expected between similar organizations with such close proximity. Language within the Asia Pacific region is diverse. While English might be assumed to be the dominant language of government and business in the region, there are still many NGO activists that have difficulty in expressing and understanding complex ideas in English. Not to be misunderstood for lack of knowledge or stupidity, communication skills, including the capacity to communicate in a common language, form the basis for networking and exchange activities.

Thus, a greater sensitivity to language barriers as a constraint in communication should be demonstrated by potential donors and other aspiring NGO partners when seeking to develop linkages with Indonesian NGOs. Making the effort to translate documents or obtain translation services for regional conferences would go a long way to ease communication barriers and demonstrate genuine interest in the ideas and concepts of potential Indonesian NGO partners. Several of the Indonesian NGO leaders interviewed expressed dismay that their attendance at regional conferences was diminished because they could not express important points sufficiently. One leader indicated that she had begun to reject invitations to conferences because it appeared that the sponsors were more interested in noting some Indonesian participants to justify their agenda rather than providing sufficient services so that the Indonesian participants could participate in the conference fully.

While most NGO leaders interviewed acknowledged that English language skills were extremely important to catalyze communication among potential partners in Asia, they bemoaned the fact that obtaining funds from donors for English language training was even more scarce than support for networking activities. Thus, the lack of English language skills put a damper on efforts made by some Indonesian NGOs to communicate broadly among potential partners in the region and beyond. Additionally, some Indonesian NGO leaders, when contacted first by outside organizations, may fail to respond, or to respond sufficiently, to maintain linkages due to lack of English language skills.

Communication is the crux of any networking or partnership activity. A common language, while not absolutely necessary, will increase the significance of communication. Therefore, encouraging donors to include English language training for NGO activists in their programs is one method to increase the efficacy of networking communication. However, it may be even more efficacious if donors and other potential Asia Pacific regional community partners made additional efforts to communicate, both in written and verbal Bahasa Indonesia.

VI. Significant Trends

The interviews mentioned above were conducted in November and December 1993. Since that time, many developments have occurred which have impacted the NGO community in Indonesia. However, two developments in particular have a bearing on this study.

Japanese Development Assistance and Other Development Linkages

Indonesian NGOs are becoming increasingly critical of official Japanese development assistance. Two questions of paramount importance are often asked by Indonesian NGO staff. These questions are:

- is the amount of official Japanese development assistance sufficient?
- are the mechanisms through which these funds are administered appropriate?

These two questions are significant to the NGO community in Indonesia as Japan has become one of Indonesia's largest development assistance partners. The first question is significant because it is perceived that Japan has developed considerably since the end of World War II, to a large extent, as a result of the assistance it received as part of the reconstruction process. While most NGO staff recognize Japan's unique manufacturing and commercial expertise, many believe that the amount of development assistance rendered to Indonesia is insufficient considering Japan's current status as an economic giant in the region and its trade relations with Indonesia. Some individuals and organizations perceive that the total amount of Japanese development assistance to Indonesia is not in proportion with Japan's current level of economic development, especially considering that Japan was the aggressor in Indonesia during World War II. Additionally, traditional Japanese overseas aid funds are currently administered almost exclusively through the government of Indonesia, where Japanese firms and interests are perceived to benefit just as much as if not more than the host country.

Indonesian NGOs would most likely prefer some portion of official development assistance to be administered through a mechanism in which Indonesian NGOs can either individually or jointly administer a portion of this assistance. Given the nature of official Japanese aid and the low profile advocacy agenda of many Japanese NGOs, in the eyes of some NGOs in Indonesia, these questions may not be resolved satisfactorily in the near future.

Furthermore, Indonesian NGOs have begun to question what benefit they derive from linkages with Japanese NGOs. Many Japanese NGO staff visit or carry out study tours to Indonesia, taking up considerable time and effort on the part of Indonesian NGO staff. However, follow-up by many of the visitors is spotty at best.

While Indonesian NGO staff are naturally gregarious and friendly, clearly after so many visits they are hoping for a deeper or more diverse relationship with the Japanese NGOs that send their staff on study trips to Indonesia. At least one Indonesian NGO staff member mentioned during the survey, "Do they think we are running a tour service here for development tourism?" Afterall, organizational linkages and networking should not be a one-way street, with all the benefits running in one direction.

From the NGO interviews in the following section, it can be concluded that Indonesian NGOs are hoping for four types of linkages with other NGO partners in the Asia Pacific region. These types of linkages are:

- *funding linkages*—Whether a true perception or not, many Indonesian NGOs believe a relatively rich country such as Japan would naturally have NGOs, much like Europe and North America, which can provide funding to Indonesian NGOs. Since such funding relationships have only rarely occurred between Indonesian and Japanese NGOs, many Indonesian NGOs have become disillusioned with this perception.
- *technical assistance linkages*—Many Indonesian NGOs actively seek regional linkages with other NGOs because they are seeking to improve their technical knowledge or to learn new techniques that can be applied or adapted to the Indonesian situation. Unfortunately, it appears that there are few Japanese NGOs that have the capacity to share technical information or skills with Indonesian NGOs.
- *advocacy linkages*—As mentioned above, advocacy linkages are considered to be very important by Indonesian NGOs when they choose to pursue relationships with other Asia Pacific NGO partners. However, Japanese NGOs appear to have very weak or non-existent advocacy agendas in general, making joint regional or issue-based advocacy campaigns nearly impossible.
- *protection linkages*—As has been mentioned earlier in this paper, Indonesian NGOs endure an environment that often challenges their very existence. This less-than-enabling environment has caused many Indonesian NGOs to seek linkages with NGOs in North America or Europe, for instance, to obtain a measure of protection should the situation become extremely deleterious to organizational survival. While it is perceived that North American and European NGOs would be willing to pressure their own governments to take a stand against the Indonesian government on their behalf, most Indonesian NGOs have little faith that Japanese counterparts would do the same.

Thus, while this study, sponsored by a Japanese NGO, seeks to answer the question of what makes Indonesian NGOs seek linkages with other Asia Pacific NGOs, many Indonesian NGOs have asked the question of why they should seek linkages with Japanese NGOs? Other than feelings of solidarity with NGOs in Japan, which surely will not sustain organizational linkages or networking, what can Indonesian NGOs expect to receive in return for increased linkages with Japanese NGOs? The following analysis appears to point to the conclusion that Indonesian NGOs should temper their expectations with regard to linkages with Japanese NGOs. More importantly, Japanese NGOs should review how and in what ways linkages with Indonesian NGOs can be improved in order to instill equity in the relationships they seek.

- Japanese NGOs are perhaps as "poor" or maybe even "poorer" than Indonesian NGOs, in a real sense considering the Japanese economic context. Japanese staff are poorly paid, in the relatively luxurious economy of Japan, and many NGOs survive because their staff are totally voluntary. Additionally, as the government of Japan sees social services as being within its almost exclusive province, few Japanese NGOs have emerged to fill the gaps as has happened in so many developing countries. Thus, the Japanese NGO community is relatively weak in development experience and fund raising. Indonesian NGOs should not look to Japanese NGOs for significant funding linkages in the near future.
- Japanese NGOs appear to have little technical expertise to share with Indonesian NGO staff, and often times have less development expertise than comparable partners from other Asia Pacific countries. The Japanese NGO community is relatively new and many other Asian NGO communities have much longer histories than the Japanese NGO community. Furthermore, few technical experts in Japan have significant overseas development experience, let alone those that have devoted their careers to the NGO community. Indonesian NGOs probably should not look to Japanese NGOs for significant technical assistance linkages in the near future.
- Japanese NGO advocacy agendas are weak or non-existent. NGO relations with the government of Japan, while improving through mutual education, may actually be even less conducive than relations between the government and NGOs in Indonesia, where engagement on issues is still frequent and possible. Until Japanese NGOs can engage their own government in constructive dialogue on domestic issues, their contributions to regional or global advocacy issues is likely to remain weak. Thus, Indonesian NGOs should not look to Japanese NGOs for significant advocacy linkages in the near future.
- Partially due to weak engagement with the Japanese government, Japanese NGOs cannot be looked to by Indonesian counterparts for the protection Indonesian

NGOs seek from linkages with European or North American NGOs. While Indonesian NGOs perceive that NGOs in North America or Europe will exert pressure on their governments to take a stand on democracy issues, including freedom of association, freedom of the press, and human rights, it is unlikely that Japanese NGOs in general would succeed in exerting pressure on a government which they have little success in engaging on domestic or overseas development issues. Thus, Indonesian NGOs should not look to Japanese NGOs for significant protection linkages in the near future.

Therefore, some introspection on the part of the Japanese NGO community is recommended. If Indonesian and other Asia Pacific NGO partners cannot expect Japanese NGOs to support their side of the linkage equation, then perhaps action is due from the Japanese NGO community to strengthen both their own organizational and financial capacity in order to achieve equity with their NGO counterparts in Asia Pacific.

VII. Proposed Indonesian Regulation on NGOs

In early 1994, the Government of Indonesia drafted a new regulation in the form of a Presidential Decree, which many Indonesian NGOs view as a means to exert excessive control and add superfluous restrictions on NGO organizations and activities. An English language translation of this planned regulation is provided as an annex to this report. It should be mentioned here that the regulation has not yet been gazetted by the government at the time of this writing, and the draft may change significantly prior to it's gazetting. The draft regulation has several key sections that many NGOs feel strikes at the integrity of their goals and interests. The regulation covers the following:

- the ways and means of the establishment of NGOs (LSMs called *lembaga swadaya masyarakat*, or NGOs);
- an outline of the fields in which NGOs may operate, and the conditions for obtaining government approval of their legal status through licensing;
- regulations on the principles and aims of NGOs; their functions, rights and obligations; an outline of a mechanism whereby the government provides "guidance" to NGOs;
- an outline of procedures whereby the government can "immobilize" or dissolve NGOs; and,
- an outline of a mechanism which requires NGOs to obtain approval from the

government for specific types of fund assistance from foreign donors.

This planned regulation is strongly opposed by most Indonesian NGOs. In a press conference held on July 22, 1994, the International NGO Forum on Indonesian Development rejected "further discussion of the content of the Presidential Decree."[15] Many Indonesian NGOs fear that the planned Presidential Decree will be used as a weapon, instead of as an enabling tool to strengthen and activate the NGO community in Indonesia. The International NGO Forum on Indonesian Development (INFID) members made the following views public at the above mentioned press conference:

- "On February 11, 1994, the Directorate General of Socio-Political Affairs, of the Department of Home Affairs presented the draft Presidential Decree to a meeting of NGOs in Cisarua, West Java. INFID maintains that the position of the NGO forum at which the draft decree was distributed and discussed is vague, the criteria for participation unclear, and therefore it is unrealistic to expect it to be representative of the views of the wider NGO community. Thus, it is inappropriate to view that meeting as an NGO-government forum for consultation and discussion of issues relating to the regulation of NGO activities."[16]
- "The methods of dissemination of the draft document violated the principles of transparency and the right to obtain information since it was distributed only two hours prior to the conclusion of the two-day meeting mentioned above, ruling out any possibility of "discussion" as suggested by the draft's title. Consequently, the NGOs present at the meeting were not sufficiently prepared to discuss the document or to provide any feedback or comment on its content. Furthermore, it is understood that the Decree (resembling the draft document or in another form) is very soon to be made law."[17]
- "In legal terms, the administration and regulation of NGOs is felt to be adequately dealt with already in Book III of the Civilian Legal Code (granting NGOs the legal status of "Foundation"—*Yayasan*) and in the rulings of various government ministries such as the State Ministry for the Environment and the State Ministry for Social Welfare. If the above were implemented correctly, the issuing of a Presidential Decree would be superfluous."[18]

The utilization of a Presidential Decree to regulate NGOs has also been questioned by many Indonesian NGOs. As the NGOs feel that there are already sufficient laws and regulations governing the NGO sector in Indonesia, the proposed decree appears to have jurisdictional, as well as other flaws, in their view. In a succeeding press conference on 19 August 1994, the INFID members stated, "the draft is overtly aimed at controlling, commanding, and overcoming NGOs' rights to organize, maintain freedom [of] speech, exist, access information and external financial resourcing, disseminate information, and [determine] work partners."[19] The text of both press conference releases and the English language text of the draft decree are included as annexes to this report. While the Presidential Decree has not yet been gazetted for enforcement, the Indonesia NGO community is rife with rumors and anxiety. Needless to say, the NGO community is hopeful that through its advocacy activities, colleagues in other countries will be supportive in this time of potential crisis for the Indonesian NGO community.

Notes

1. See a description of PKBI (Perkumpulan Keluarga Berencana Indonesia) in a later section of this report.
2. See a description of YSTM and Yayasan Bina Swadaya in a later section of this report.
3. Look for descriptions of both these organizations later in this report.
4. New Order: the name ascribed to the post-Sukarno Suharto government which officially began in 1969. The New Order government is noted for the significance of military participation in government, strong emphasis on growth-oriented development policies, stable political and civic life (some would say stagnant growth of), and broad and growing involvement in international affairs.
5. Dr. Philip Eldridge, *NGOs in Indonesia: Popular Movement or Arm of Government*, Working Paper No. 55, The Centre of Southeast Asian Studies, Monash University, 1989.
6. Ibid.
7. Ibid.
8. "The Survey on Nongovernmental Underpinnings of the Emerging Asia Pacific Regional Community," Draft Proposal, Japan Center for International Exchange, February 15, 1993.
9. Ibid.
10. Korten, David C., *Getting to the 21st Century: Voluntary Action and the Global Agenda*, Kumarian Press, 1990, pages 185–207.
11. Ibid.
12. Ibid.
13. Ibid.
14. Ibid.
15. Ibid.
16. International NGO Forum on Indonesian Development, press conference statement, no 134/INFID/1994, 22 July 1994, p. 2.
17. Ibid.
18. Ibid.
19. Ibid.
20. International NGO Forum on Indonesian Development, press conference release, no. 14/INFID/94, 19 August 1994, page 2.

JAPAN

The Evolution of Japanese NGOs in the Asia Pacific Context

Toshihiro Menju
Program Officer
Japan Center for International Exchange
in cooperation with
Takako Aoki
Research Associate
Japan Center for International Exchange

I. Introduction

In the last few years, the term *NGO* has become widely recognized in Japan; almost daily, newspapers carry articles relating to the activities of NGOs. The new atmosphere of NGO acknowledgment is closely associated with the change in sociocultural dynamics with which Japan is faced today.

Toward the end of the twentieth century, Japanese society is undergoing a maturing process. The traditional hierarchical social structure seems to be gradually giving way to a more pluralistic and decentralized system. At least it can be said that an increasing number of people are skeptical about whether or not the long-held dominance of bureaucracy in Japanese society should remain in the coming decades. The outcry for a "civil society" that ensures the direct participation of citizens in the decision-making process, which ultimately determines the societal course of direction, is echoed by more opinion leaders and ordinary citizens who seek an alternative to heavy reliance on bureaucratic leadership. Recent political upheaval and heated discussions focusing on decentralization demonstrate the frustration of the people toward politics and the national government. Under such circumstances, citizen participation in the management of societal affairs has grown, and the number of private and nonprofit organizations is increasing.

In the international arena, although Japan currently faces many challenges, there is an increasing recognition that the national government alone cannot handle increasingly complicated relations effectively, while citizens and the organizations they have formed have the potential to play an innovative and critical role. In the domestic field, economic integration and interdependence have permeated Japanese society. In addition to the economic impact, the number of foreigners who wish to reside in Japan has increased every year, with the majority being Asians and people from developing countries. This new phenomenon has had a gradual but tremendous impact on the fabric of Japanese society. Internationalization now directly influences the everyday lives of the Japanese. In this context, NGO activities as a form of citizens' initiative for strengthening relationships with people in developing countries has gained popular support and enjoyed extensive attention by the mass media.

However, in spite of a seemingly favorable climate for NGO activities, the challenges Japanese NGOs face are formidable. For example, the present legal framework does not allow the majority of NGOs to be legally incorporated, let alone attain the privilege of tax-exempt status. This is one indicator that Japan is still at the beginning stage of a full-fledged "civil society," which inevitably includes an established nonprofit sector. This paper aims at clarifying the evolution of NGOs in Japanese society, and the challenges and opportunities NGOs are confronted with. In addition, the role of NGOs in strengthening partnerships in Asia Pacific is identified, and opportunities to build an Asia Pacific community through NGO collaboration are explored.

Before this research survey of Japanese NGOs was initiated, several meetings were held among staff of the Japan Center for International Exchange (JCIE) to discuss the direction and methodology of the survey. NGOs discussed in this paper basically include organizations initiated by citizens, with a main focus toward international cooperation and the North–South relationship. Besides this general definition of NGOs, we have focused our attention on emerging grassroots international organizations, which are growing rapidly and becoming more involved in issues related to developing countries.

Through consultation with several experts, Ms. Takako Aoki, Research Associate of JCIE, interviewed leaders and staff members of thirty-four organizations throughout Japan from January to June 1994 to collect basic information on NGOs, and wrote a summary of these interviews. The attached list of NGOs is based primarily on her findings. With these data, Mr. Toshihiro Menju, Program Officer of JCIE, completed this paper in November 1994, by incorporating his own findings and interviews with several NGOs.

II. Overview of the NGO Sector

1. Evolution of NGOs in a Changing Japanese Social Environment

In 1960, the first Japanese NGO, the Japan Overseas Christian Medical Cooperative Service was established to provide medical services to communities in Asia, especially Nepal. This organization was created by internationally minded Japanese Christians who shared the Christian desire to help people in need regardless of nationality. Although there are some exceptions, such as the Organization for Industrial, Spiritual and Cultural Advancement International (OISCA), whose underlying faith is rooted in traditional Japanese values, many of the NGOs established during the 1960s and the 1970s were Christian-initiated. For example, the Asian Rural Institute was organized in 1973 by the initiatives of Christians to train agricultural community leaders in Asia and other regions. The Christian Child Welfare Association International Sponsorship Program (CCWA) was established in 1975 to assist needy children and their families through a sponsorship program.

The year 1979 was a watershed for Japanese NGO history. At the time, many Indo-Chinese refugees were fleeing to Japan after a series of wars broke out in Indochina. It was during this period that many Japanese, for the first time, displayed a desire to lend a helping hand and got involved in refugee issues. NGOs such as the Japan International Volunteer Center, Caring for Young Refugees, and the Japan Sotoshu Relief Committee were created by Japanese citizens as a citizen response to the refugee issue. Since then, the number of NGOs has increased, and their activities have encompassed a variety of fields such as rural development, health and hygiene, human rights, and education, to name a few.

The following data illustrates the development of Japanese NGOs. According to the *Directory of Japanese Non-Governmental Organizations Active in International Cooperation 1994* compiled by the Japanese NGO Center for International Cooperation (JANIC),[1] which was established in 1987 to promote cooperation among Japanese NGOs, the number of NGOs established in each five-year period is listed below.

Term	Number	Term	Number
through 1969	10	1985–89	69
1970–74	12	1990–92	28
1975–79	21		
1980–84	46	Total	186

(Source: *Directory of Japanese NGOs Active in International Cooperation 1994*)

This shows that the number of NGOs has increased rapidly from a base of only ten. The Directory contains four categories, namely, Category-I under which the NGO's main activities are technical cooperation, financial assistance, and assistance-in-kind; Category-II which includes organizations that provide support for and cooperate with foreign laborers and refugees in Japan; Category-III which encompasses NGOs whose main purpose is information dissemination, development education, and policy advocacy in Japan; and Category-IV which contains NGOs that facilitate networking between the above NGOs. In sum, the majority of Japanese NGOs are involved in direct assistance of some kind. The number of NGOs in each category (exclusive) is as follows:

Category-I	137
Category-II	10
Category-III	30
Category-IV	9
Total	186

(Source: *Directory of Japanese NGOs Active in International Cooperation 1994*)

In addition to NGOs listed in the *Directory*, it is important to note that many "grassroots international exchange organizations" have been created by citizens in recent years. Many of these organizations were originally formed to promote friendship with foreigners by helping foreign students in Japanese communities, providing home-stays for foreign visitors, and conducting sister city programs, mainly with developed countries. It is sometimes difficult to distinguish these grassroots international exchange organizations from NGOs whose main purpose is international cooperation, due to the fact that grassroots organizations are becoming more involved in activities related to people and countries of the South. However, it can be said that grassroots organizations are deeply rooted in the region in which they exist, and most of the time they promote activities only in their own area. Furthermore, they usually do not have any professional staff, and all the activities tend to be carried out by volunteers.

The rise of NGOs and grassroots organizations became noticeable in the late 1980s when *internationalization* become a household term for describing the international impact and dramatic change Japanese society went through during the same period. Integration of the global economy has escalated, and Japan's international role increasingly became a focus of national discussion. Japanese investment in foreign countries surged, and imports from other Asian countries expanded rapidly. The number of Japanese traveling to foreign countries has been increasing year after year, reaching 11.9 million in 1993. Since the late 1980s, Japan has experienced a new international impact resulting from the sudden influx of foreigners who come to Japan to work, and become residents. The number of legally registered foreign residents in Japan, which was 850,000 in 1985, increased to 1,320,000 at the end of 1993. A change in the immigration law in 1990 induced a rapid increase in South Americans of Japanese origin who are eligible to be employed in blue color positions. In addition to legally permitted foreigners, it is reported that about three hundred thousand foreigners, many of whom come from Asia, stayed in Japan illegally in 1993.

Partly in response to the increase of foreign residents in Japan, grassroots international exchange organizations have expanded rapidly. There is an increasing number of citizens who possess an interest in and experiences related to international affairs, and some of them have organized associations to promote exchange with people in various countries. It is fair to say that internationalization has influenced the growth of NGOs and grassroots organizations. In fact, the term *NGO* has practically become a household word in Japan in the past year or two. According to a keyword search on four major Japanese newspapers, the frequency of articles on NGOs made a jump from 291 during 1991, to 1032 in 1992, 972 in 1993, and 1,506 in the first ten months of 1994.

The increase of NGOs in Japan is also related to international events such as the United Nations Conference on Environment and Development, held in June 1992. It was reported that about three hundred and fifty Japanese from various NGOs visited Brazil for the concurrent NGO meetings. This incident has certainly boosted recognition of the role of NGOs in Japan. More recently, when the United Nations Conference on Population and Development was held in Cairo in September 1994, Japanese NGO members were included, for the first time, in the official government delegation to the conference.

In reference to grassroots organizations active in communities in Japan, a report published by the *Asahi Shimbun* Research Division in 1993, "Current Status of 'Grassroots' International Exchange Organizations," listed 296 such organizations throughout Japan. Organizations covered by this research include grassroots organizations that aim at promoting international friendship, as well as cooperation activities. According to the report, 146 of these organizations were created after 1988, and 46 of these organizations are involved in activities to assist foreign residents in Japan. Through exposure to the conditions of foreign workers in Japan, it is interesting to note that the Japanese are becoming more aware of human rights issues and taking such issues more seriously. Human rights issues have conventionally been regarded as a remote and also sensitive area for many Japanese. However, now that the existence of foreign residents has become so commonplace throughout Japan, the Japanese public is gradually beginning to link these residents to human rights issues. Therefore, in a way, foreign residents have awakened the Japanese to a sense of human rights.

To cope with the surge of internationalization at the local level, many local governments have put internationalization high on their agenda. In addition to the need to internationalize the local economy, there is a growing awareness of the need to create a Japanese society that is more open to foreigners and more compatible with other countries. Interestingly, these local efforts to internationalize regions are taking place in accordance with a movement toward decentralization of government authority in which opinion leaders are discussing the importance of local initiatives for providing services in the rapidly changing social circumstances. Therefore, internationalization and regionalism have been interactively enhanced at the local level. Many local governments established so-called "Divisions of International Relations" within their government structure to deal exclusively with international affairs. At the same time, "International Exchange Associations," semigovernmental organizations, have been created in all the prefectures, by the prefectural governments, and major cities to conduct international activities at the community level. In addition, some local governments set up organizations to promote specific themes with international foci. For example, Osaka Prefecture and Osaka City worked with scholars and local citizens to establish the Asia Pacific Human Rights Information Center in August of 1994 with financial support from both governments. Likewise, the city of Kitakyushu established the Kitakyushu Forum on Asian Women in 1990 to promote exchange with women in other Asian countries. It conducts research on women's issues and has worked with research institutions in China, Thailand, and Malaysia.

In the field of education, educators started a study on development education in the early 1980s, although it has not officially been integrated into school curricula yet. Teachers who are interested in development education have tried to introduce related ideas into classrooms at various levels. Partly due to this development education, the term *global citizenship* has become more commonplace in Japan, and people have come to understand the need for global citizenship in this interdependent world. Japan's younger generation will have more and more opportunities to learn about such things as North-South relations, and they will be expected to play more active and direct roles in international affairs.

There is also a visible increase in coverage of international news, especially NGO-related activities, by the mass media. It is hoped that this will help in educating people about international affairs and in showing them the opportunities for people's participation in global affairs. Thus, the rise of NGO activities, coupled with media coverage, has synergetically led to the enlightenment of people on international affairs. By spotlighting NGO activities, the mass media also points out, intentionally or not, the difficulties and constraints of the national government in handling international affairs, especially in the post–cold war era. It has increasingly become common knowledge that NGO activities supplement the role of the national government in international cooperation.

The development of NGOs and the nonprofit sector in general is an indication of the current emerging "civil society" in Japan. These phenomena benefit the expansion of pluralism in Japanese society and in the devolvement of a more diverse network of individuals to play a role in international affairs. NGOs in Japan have become widely recognized today, and they are currently playing an important role as a platform for citizens to participate actively in international affairs.

2. Government Relations

In spite of the growing recognition concerning NGOs' role in Japan, they are not receiving treatment by the government equal to the degree of current recognition and contributions to society. The government's attitude toward NGOs has been very curt, and this lack of acknowledgment is closely related to the dominant role of the bureaucracy in the governance of Japanese society. There is an underlying assumption among government officials that NGOs are basically unauthorized actors in a society where government is the only authorized organization to promote public interest. Therefore, government bureaucrats could regard NGOs as a potentially disturbing agent, in spite of the favorable appraisal of NGOs in the mass media. This common notion is reflected in burdensome legal and extralegal requirements for nonprofit organizations desiring to receive formal institutional status. Even after they are established, excessive bureaucratic oversights are inevitable, and intense bureaucratic involvement in the organizations' affairs are likely.

Article 34 of Japan's current Civil Code, promulgated in 1896, lodges the right to grant permission for the creation of a registered nonprofit organization with "the competent authorities." The authority referred to is either the national or prefectural government office that handles the area of activity in which the nonprofit organization plans to conduct programs. In order for an organization to be eligible for incorporation, it is generally required to have an endowment of three hundred million yen (US$3 million),[2] an annual budget of approximately thirty million yen (US$300,000), an activity plan, and a board consisting of publicly esteemed individuals. Even with such necessary documents and funds, it normally takes several months to explain the detailed documents accompanying the application to the appropriate ministry before public interest corporation status can be granted.

The ministry exercises discretion over whether or not to grant incorporated status to an applicant, and the exhaustive application requirements discourage unregistered NGOs from seeking it, though remaining unincorporated clearly puts them at a disadvantage in fund raising, tax treatment, and social recognition. According to the *1994 NGO Directory* by JANIC, only 28 NGOs have received legal status out of a listing of 186 organizations.

Once registered as a legal entity, a nonprofit organization is required to submit, before the fiscal period, a budget and outline of proposed activities. After the end of the fiscal period, the organization must again submit a financial report and describe the activities completed. Both are scrutinized closely, and the accounting procedures require that the NGO adhere to rigid guidelines established by the recognizing ministry. It is also possible for ministries to revoke incorporated status if an organization, in their judgment, does not fulfill ministry requirements.

However, along with the growing activism in nonprofit organizations in general, several different groups of citizens' organizations have started making proposals and campaigning to change the legal and administrative framework to one which would allow citizens' organizations to be easily incorporated. The tax exempt status is also a challenge that such groups are striving to attain. The current tax law does not allow for tax-exempted donations to unincorporated organizations, and even in the case of legally incorporated organizations, the type and amount of tax deductible contributions are severely restricted.

Besides the efforts of citizens' groups working for change in the framework of nonprofit incorporation, one hopeful sign for Japanese NGOs is increasing awareness of the need for development of the entire nonprofit sector among certain politicians and the mass media. In spite of this recent awareness and these related efforts, it is difficult to predict at this moment how soon changes leading to a loosening of bureaucratic control over the nonprofit sector will occur, especially considering the stonewalling character of government bureaucracy up until now.

In regards to the field of development assistance, the government is more subject to outside international pressure. Year by year, more NGOs have been recognized internationally for their efforts; national governments and international organizations are prone to seek opportunities to cooperate with them. Under these circumstances, the Japanese government has begun to reach out to NGOs in the last few years. A year after announcing an aggregate increase of official development assistance (ODA) over the four-year period of 1988–92 to 4.9 trillion yen (US$50 billion), the Ministry of Foreign Affairs introduced the "Subsidy System for NGO Projects" and the "Grant Assistance for Grassroots Projects" in 1989. The former is designed to support small programs that Japanese NGOs carry out in developing countries and that are difficult to carry out with ordinary ODA. Total disbursement through the program has increased five fold in the past five years from 110 million yen (US$1.1 million) in 1989 to 540 million yen (US$5.5 million) in 1994.

On the other hand, Grant Assistance for Grassroots Projects is closely tied to the Ministry of Foreign Affairs, and the grants are closely monitored by the ministry-affiliated Japan International Cooperation Agency (JICA) and embassies or consulates abroad. Individual grant values do not exceed five million yen (US$500,000). This grant assistance has also increased rapidly from three hundred million yen (US$3 million) in 1989 to one and a half billion yen (US$15 million) in 1994.

In addition to the more formalized programs of the Ministry of Foreign Affairs, as described above, there are three other forms of support that have been extended to NGOs. In 1992 the outlays were study and aid expenses for Japanese NGOs, twelve million yen (US$120,000); subsidies for groups promoting technical cooperation, more than six hundred million yen (US$6.1 million); and aid through JICA (e.g., support for transportation costs for the Japan Silver Volunteers).

The most unique government initiated program for NGO funding is the Voluntary Deposit for International Aid, administered by the Ministry of Posts and Telecommunications (MPT). This program was first introduced in January 1991. Funds distributed to NGOs are made up of contributions obtained from postal savings accounts. In a specific saving account, depositors voluntarily donate twenty percent of after tax interest earned on their savings deposits. These funds are collected by the MPT and disbursed to projects carried out by Japanese NGOs.

Disbursements have more than doubled during the few years of the fund's existence, outpacing programs of the Ministry of Foreign Affairs. The amount of disbursements has soared: 910 million yen (US$9.2 million) in 1991, 2.3 billion yen (US$23.2 million) in 1992, and 2.4 billion yen (US$24.3 million) in 1993. By the end of July 1994, the number of participating depositors exceeded fifteen million. As of March 1994, this fund has been distributed through 197 NGOs into 261 projects in 56 countries.

The sudden increase of government-related support to NGOs has spurred an increase in their activities; however, some NGO leaders are skeptical and cautious about this government financial support. Apprehensions shared by NGOs toward the government funds concern whether Japanese NGOs can handle it properly without altering their own policy and philosophy. They fear that the funds could misguide NGOs and/or make them dependent on government support. Some NGOs might be led to create programming designed just to please the government. As Japanese NGOs are still financially very vulnerable and Japanese philanthropy as a whole has not developed well in spite of the recent fanfare of mass media on philanthropy, Japanese NGOs may not be prepared to appropriately utilize an increased amount of government funding. Therefore, it is difficult to say that the surge of government financial support will bring forth definite benefits to Japanese NGOs.

Another criticism raised by NGOs concerning government subsidies is the fact that such funds do not cover administrative costs of NGOs and only include direct expenses, excluding personnel expenses. In addition, payment is received from the government only after a project is finished, including the case of the MPT program. Therefore, NGOs have to have enough funds to carry out projects before receiving reimbursements from the government.

III. Evolution of NGO Activity in the Asia Pacific Regional Community

1. Why are Japanese NGOs promoting activities in Asia Pacific?

As discussed above, many NGO activities are targeted toward countries in the Asia Pacific region. According to the JANIC *Directory*, 141 out of 269 organizations (seventy-six percent) have programs in Asia. In Oceania, twenty-six Japanese organizations conduct programs. This notable inclination in Japanese NGO activity in Asia Pacific can be explained by several factors.

First, there is a geographical closeness with other Asian countries that makes NGO activities in the region much more cost effective than in regions such as South America or Africa. Due to the relatively low cost of travel, exchange of information and people is much easier, and consequently, the activities can enjoy comparatively greater interactions of many types.

Second, many Japanese feel that the cultures and traditions in Asia Pacific countries are closer to those of Japan. In looking specifically at East Asia, many Japanese embrace a familiarity with people in the region due to the common cultural threads such as Chinese characters and a diet of rice, in addition to ethnic similarities. This perceived familiarity will help reduce initial psychological barriers toward people in the region that citizens might face when contacting them.

Third, in general, the activities of NGOs will help eliminate biases and stereotypes Japanese hold against people in Asia Pacific. According to our interviews, NGO leaders believe that many Japanese still maintain a superiority complex toward other Asians. The recent influx into Japan of Asians who become laborers, has led to a strengthening of the Japanese prejudice toward all foreign Asians, even though the Japanese are Asians, too. In order to change this tendency, NGO leaders believe activities in Asia Pacific are quite important. Some of them also refer to World War II and the Japanese military invasion in Asia. They believe the atrocities incurred by the Japanese invasion should be appeased by citizens' efforts to the people in other Asian countries.

Fourth, as economic interaction with Asia, especially Japanese investment in the region, has intensified, NGOs believe that exploitation of the local people and the environment by Japanese corporations has been on the increase. In fact, in spite of the sharp decrease of Japan's direct investment in the world, e.g. 6,681 billion yen (US$67,540 million) in 1989 to 3,564 billion yen (US$36,025 million) in 1993, investment in Asia was not affected much, e.g. $8,238 million in 1989 to $6,637 in 1993. Even this figure for 1993 is more than four times larger than that in 1985. Concerning the sudden increase of Japanese investment in Asia, Japanese NGO leaders think that NGOs should address possible problems created by Japanese companies and watch their behavior. They believe that the economic relationship alone will not forge a healthy partnership between Japan and the rest of the Asia Pacific region, and that citizen partnerships should be created as well.

Fifth, in addition to the increase of foreign workers, the number of foreign students who study at Japanese universities and language schools has increased rapidly. In accordance with this increase, grassroots organizations that support foreign students have been flourishing recently. Most of these foreign students come from Asia Pacific, and some of these grassroots organizations have gradually developed into ones to educate a broader range of citizens about Asia Pacific countries. Some such organizations implemented a study mission for citizens to Asia Pacific countries, and the visits have occasionally triggered cooperative spirits, and thus programs with people in the region.

Apart from the focus of NGOs' activities in Asia Pacific, Japanese interest and interaction with the region as a whole have markedly increased. Interest in the Asia Pacific region has been particularly conspicuous in western Japan, especially in the Kyushu region. For example, Hiroshima Prefecture has proclaimed itself the "center for international exchange with Asia," and Fukuoka City has similarly identified itself as the "hub city for Asia." Likewise, there has also been a rapid increase in mutual interest and exchange between Japanese prefectures along the Sea of Japan coast and regions around the Sea of Japan countries. In an effort to strengthen international economic strategies, cities and prefectures are finding ways to enhance relationships within this region. They make a point of their historical and cultural links with the region, and try to reestablish the partnership with communities in the region, which had been disregarded during the cold war era.

2. Current NGO Programs and Networks in Asia Pacific

According to the *JANIC 1994 Directory*, 166 Japanese NGOs have activities targeted at forty-four countries in Asia and Oceania. This outnumbers NGOs involved in Africa (fifty) and those in Latin America (thirty-six). Most organizations that have activities in Africa conduct emergency relief operations. However, in Asia Pacific, NGOs conduct a variety of activities. For example, OISCA, one of the largest and oldest NGOs, assigns volunteers to many projects in the field of rural development, agriculture, education, women's development, environment, etc. in the Philippines, Malaysia, Thailand, Bangladesh, and other countries. On the other hand, Shapla Neer is primarily administering a rural development program restricted to Bangladesh. This organization was originally created by a group of young Japanese volunteers who visited agricultural communities in Bangladesh.

The number of organizations, categorized by country, active in Asia Pacific in the *1994 Directory* is as follows: the Philippines–50, Thailand–46, Nepal–30, Bangladesh–24, India–23, Cambodia–23, Indonesia–18, Malaysia–14, Vietnam–13, Sri Lanka–13, etc. Compared with the figure in the *1992 Directory*, Bangladesh moved to fourth from sixth place, and Malaysia moved to eighth from thirteenth. In addition, Mongolia was listed for the first time in the 1994 edition. Most of the NGOs have projects in developing counties in Asia Pacific and maintain an office(s) in those countries. As many as fifty-six NGOs have ninety-five overseas offices in sixteen countries in Asia Pacific. In addition to overseas activities, these organizations are beginning to make efforts to promote understanding among the Japanese about the current situation in developing countries as well as their own activities.

As has been demonstrated by many NGO projects, agriculture works as a productive bond that connects Japan with other countries in Asia Pacific. Similarities such as farming of rice in Japan and other Asia Pacific countries makes NGOs' activities quite active and attractive to many Japanese. For example, organic farming, which is becoming popular in Japan, is often the theme by which NGOs can offer assistance in educating farmers from Asia Pacific.

Karaimo Koryu Foundation is a unique NGO, located in an agricultural community in Southern Kyushu, that connects agricultural communities in Japan with ones elsewhere in the Asia Pacific region. It invites young agricultural community leaders from Asian countries to Japan for on-site training related to agriculture. The mandate of the organization is twofold: assisting agricultural communities in Asia and reinvigorating the local host communities in Kagoshima. In addition to offering training for Asians, the foundation provides opportunities for exchange between Japanese farmers and Asian trainees so that Japanese farmers can become more internationally minded. In fact, the Asia Pacific Farmer's Network was created on the initiative of the Karaimo staff, and Japanese farmers involved in the network have become enlightened so that they can view the local agriculture from an international perspective. As a result, they have become more active both in international cooperation efforts and their own community development.

Another remarkable trend is the increase in the number of NGOs that assist foreign residents in Japan. The number of foreigners in Japan has been increasing steadily, including those that are illegally overstaying their visa term. Some NGOs deal specifically with illegal foreigners whose human rights are neglected. For example, one NGO offers a shelter for female foreigners. Many of them live in Japan illegally, so they are afraid to report to the police even if they become victims of crime. In the local communities, a number of grassroots organizations offer Japanese-language classes for new foreign residents. Some produce information handouts and booklets in several languages to make daily life easier in the communities.

Since 1992, there has been a noticeable trend to establish networking organizations. For example, the People's Forum on Cambodia, Japan was created by NGOs whose activities were related to Cambodia, and the Nippon NGO Network for Nepal was established as a forum for Nepal-related NGOs. The Japan NGO Network on Indonesia was also formed to facilitate cooperation and dialogue between Japanese NGOs concerned with Indonesia, and their Indonesian counterparts.

In addition to country-by-country networks, Japanese NGOs are expanding their networks in the Asia Pacific region. For example, the Japan Environmental Council, which is concerned with environmental pollution, held the third Asia Pacific

NGO Environmental Conference in Kyoto in November 1994 with other NGOs in the region. During the conference, NGO leaders decided to establish the Asia Environmental Council in 1995. Another example is the first conference of the East Asian Women's Forum held in October 1994, in Kanagawa Prefecture. This forum was established by female participants of the Asia Pacific NGO symposium, held in Manila in 1993, who had common interests in and concerns about the challenges facing women in East Asia, where rapid economic development is affecting the society in various ways. It attracted much attention from the mass media, and more than five hundred people, including NGO staff and local citizens, participated in the Forum. The above cases demonstrate that the environment and women's issues are becoming very important themes in NGOs' recent activities, and that the NGOs are rapidly expanding their networks in Asia Pacific.

3. Why is Regional Cooperation among NGOs Desirable in Asia Pacific?

Japan's interaction with other countries in Asia Pacific is steadily increasing, especially in the economic sphere. Given the irreversible trend of interdependence with that region in particular, grassroots underpinnings in Asia Pacific are essential to developing the viable "Asia Pacific community." At a time when a lot of people from Asia Pacific come to Japan to work as unskilled laborers, and increasing reports of crimes committed by unlawfully residing foreigners are broadcast, it is not difficult to predict that many Japanese will amplify their prejudice toward other Asians if efforts are not taken. If Japan regards the partnership with the Asia Pacific region as a key for its future, it is exceedingly important to furnish a mechanism for establishing an equal partnership between the Japanese and people in the region through which stereotypes and prejudice toward other Asians will be wiped out. In this sense, NGOs have played an invaluable role in redressing the Japanese attitude toward other Asians. With their networks and experience in Asia Pacific, NGOs can increasingly provide truthful information and opportunities for exchange between the Japanese and people in Asia Pacific.

Second, many NGO leaders regard people and culture in Asia Pacific as a useful reference when they review the current situation in Japanese society. They tend to view current Japanese society as unhealthy because it puts too much emphasis on materialism. They believe that the Japanese will be enlightened and will be given an opportunity to review their lifestyle through contact with Asian people and culture. They often praise a simpler lifestyle and spiritual values over economic prosperity. In their view, interactions with certain Asia Pacific countries will provide a chance to review Japan from such a perspective.

NGO leaders also share apprehensions about the current educational system which, they believe, cannot educate children to be global citizens equipped with a balanced view of the world. Therefore, many of them involve students and children in the programs they offer. Terra People Association, located in Kyushu, sends children's groups, headed by their mothers, to experience home-stays in rural communities in Thailand. Through the trip, participants are supposed to gain insights on life and reflect on their own lifestyle through hands-on experience in a different culture and difficult living conditions. They also invite Thai orphans to Japan to cultivate friendships with Japanese children. The PHD Foundation in Kobe also invites trainees from Thailand, Nepal, the Philippines, Indonesia, the Solomon Islands, and other Asia Pacific countries. Trainees are stationed in different regions in Japan to learn various skills as interns in fields such as agriculture and health care. The PHD Foundation also puts emphasis on raising awareness of the need for changing Japanese lifestyles by encouraging local Japanese hosts to be involved in communication with overseas trainees.

IV. Future Prospects

With a rising awareness of "global citizenship" among the Japanese, NGOs can play a significant role in facilitating Japanese partnerships with people in Asia Pacific at the citizen level. NGO endeavors will nourish awareness among Japanese that Japan is a part of the Asia Pacific region. The increasing number of new NGOs in recent years is an encouraging indication that Japanese citizens are trying to interact with other Asians in a positive way. The shift of priority by grassroots international exchange organizations from friendship to international cooperation is also a favorable signal that Japanese people are gradually becoming more enlightened and have more concern for the wellbeing of people in Asia Pacific.

Staff members and volunteers working for NGOs and grassroots organizations are, more often than not, women and young people. They are often concerned with the problems in the current Japanese society. Thus, some NGOs tackle social issues that are common both in Japan and other countries. In order to spread NGO activities, some of those NGO leaders believe that NGOs need more support from citizens rather than the government, because the endorsement and participation of citizens is an integral part of their activities, and without their support, NGOs will lose their raison d'être.

In accordance with the development of NGO activities, it is noteworthy that many local governments are increasingly interested in international cooperation. For many years, more than six hundred and fifty local governments have been involved in sister city (or prefecture) exchange activities with communities in foreign countries; recently they have begun exploring ways to contribute to the development of communities in the South. In a survey conducted in 1994 by the Ministry of Home Affairs, which overseas local government, as many as forty-nine prefectures and major cities out of fifty-nine gave a "very positive" or "positive" response to becoming involved in international cooperation. In fact, the Ministry established a committee in 1993 to study opportunities of international cooperation conducted by local governments, and it is expected to provide guidelines for international cooperation by local governments during the 1995 fiscal year.

This measure will encourage local governments, which have abundant resources for regional development, to participate in international cooperation. However, it will be necessary for local governments, which do not have professional expertise in international assistance, to work with NGOs to carry out successful programs. The unique cooperation between local governments and NGOs offers possibilities for contributions to the strengthening of local governance, including various functions of local governments in the Asia Pacific countries which are often acutely needed in order to provide basic services to grassroots citizens.

At the moment, however, there is still an underlying risk that NGOs and local governments will not be able to cooperate adequately as they have different mandates and views on development. Local governments, just like national governments, are not free from bureaucratic procedures and strict budgetary constraints. Also, many local governments tend to view NGOs and grassroots organizations as minor players in the community. There are, however, some successful examples of cooperation. Kagoshima Prefecture established a training facility, the Kagoshima Asia Pacific Intercultural Countryside Center in 1994 in cooperation with a local NGO, the above-mentioned Karaimo Koryu Foundation, to provide a facility for trainees invited by the Foundation. By the time many Japanese local governments begin to be involved in international cooperation activities, it will be necessary to identify the optimum mechanism of partnership between local governments and NGOs.

In order for NGOs to fulfill their role sufficiently, there are several challenges to overcome. First, NGOs should work as the forerunners in the campaign to change the legal framework of the nonprofit sector. They need to cooperate with other nonprofit organizations and try to involve the mass media and politicians for a successful drive. Second, lack of funds is also a serious challenge for all NGOs. As discussed above, the increase of government subsidies does not necessary guarantee the healthy development of NGOs. Therefore, NGOs need to be well-prepared to make an important judgment on how to utilize government funds without jeopardizing their independence and integrity. At the same time, they should make more efforts to invigorate philanthropic activities in Japan. At present, NGOs often compete with each other by seeking funds from the same donors; they should strategically cooperate to increase recognition of NGOs and their role in society.

Third, NGOs should be more accountable to society by making efforts to develop their human resources. If their activities are regarded as extremist by other citizens, it is difficult to get citizens' support. NGOs have to figure out a sophisticated manner in which to get the message across to ordinary citizens. A guideline for the behavior of Japanese NGOs was compiled by JANIC in November 1994, after a long discussion among NGO leaders. Article five of the guideline prescribes democratic processes of operations as well as disclosure of information on NGO activities. Such efforts will help establish the credibility of NGOs in Japan. In addition to strategic improvement, NGO staff members should be technically trained not only in skills related to development activities, but also in general office duties such as communication, management, bookkeeping, etc. It seems that the staff of NGOs tend to belittle such skills, however, they are important if the NGOs intend to be viewed as organizations accountable to society. It is hoped that individuals with business backgrounds will join more NGO activities.

Fourth, Japanese NGOs should strive to expand their international horizons by expanding networks with NGOs in other countries. Given the future role of Japanese NGOs in international relations, they should possess a broader perspective on the North-South relationship. If they find it difficult at present to undertake a joint program with other NGOs, they should begin by sharing information with them. It is encouraging to note that Japanese NGOs are gradually becoming involved in international forums and conferences more often than before.

The virtue of NGO programs vis-à-vis governmental ODA is the participatory process of development. While ODA is basically one-way assistance from the developed to the developing countries, citizens' international cooperation can bring forth two-way benefits by involving people. Citizen partnerships promoted by NGOs have the potential to implement two-way cooperation, and such efforts will decisively promote the establishment of equal partnerships in the Asia Pacific Community. In sum, NGOs have the opportunity to play a significant role in changing Japan's role in Asia Pacific and in creating a viable Asia Pacific community.

Notes

1. Japanese NGO Center for International Cooperation, Directory of Japanese Non Governmental Organizations Active in International Cooperation (Tokyo: JANIC, 1994).
2. International Monetary Fund, International Financial Statistics, January 1995 (Washington, D.C.: IMF, 1995). Figures given are based on the end of period exchange rate for November 1994. US$1=98.92 yen.

References

Tanaka Haruhiko, *Nanboku Kankei to Kaihatu Kyoiku* [North-South Issues and Development Education] (Tokyo: Akishobo, 1994).

Yamamoto Tadashi, *Government/Nonprofit Organization Relations,* unpublished report for the Johns Hopkins Comparative Nonprofit Sector Project (Tokyo, 1994).

Japan NGO Center for International Cooperation, *Directory of Japanese Non Governmental Organizations Active in International Cooperation* (Tokyo: JANIC, 1994).

KOREA

NGOs in Korea

Hye-Kyung Lee
Professor
Yonsei University

NGOs are not a new phenomenon in Korea. Their legacy stretches as far back as the *Kye* (revolving credit society) and *Hyangyak* (rules and contracts among villagers for mutual support) of the late Chosun Dynasty, across the independence and enlightenment movement during the Colonial years, to the various contemporary activities of citizen groups and organizations. However, the development of these groups has scarcely been documented and they are one of the least understood components of modern Korea. Furthermore, their roles and functions have been grossly downplayed by the government.

In fact, independent NGO activities in Korea have been able to develop only in the limited socio-political space left by the state for legitimate activity. In Confucian tradition, there is no distinction between the state and society. The role of the state is to cultivate the moral values of men through its rites. It is the state that should educate and by so doing transform the behavior of the ruled, not the other way around. People do not determine the role of the state. This Asian version of an organic state contrasts starkly with the notion of a liberal pluralist state, in which the state is believed to be what the civil society makes it. The direction of influence is from society to state, not vice versa. Whereas organic states enjoy more relative autonomy from the civic sector, liberal states tend to concede relative autonomy to the civic sector. It seems fair to say that the pattern of NGO development is in large part contingent upon the state's attitude toward the civic sector in general, and NGO activities in particular. This is the case in Korea.

A further complication arises from the fact that NGOs play different roles in various fields of service. In Korea, the term itself refers to an extraordinarily diverse set of organizations lying between the market and the state. Some NGOs provide services such as health, education, personal services, and arts and culture; others have an essentially representational role, advocating for particular causes or groups. In other words, NGOs do have both service functions and representational functions. Furthermore, the financing, regulatory, and service functions are carried out by the government. It is therefore quite possible for NGOs to create one set of relationships vis-a-vis government with respect to their service functions and another with respect to their representational or advocacy functions. Tensions between these roles are almost inevitable in any society, since government policy is often the principal target of the advocacy activities of NGOs.

The Korean experience of NGOs in the post-Liberation period can be roughly divided into three stages. The first stage is the period before the early 1960s when the primary goal of the state was to maintain security. Most of the NGOs in those days were service-oriented, providing welfare services or implementing development projects for the poor, and they were mostly supported, if not established, by foreign aid.

The second stage began with the de facto authoritarian developmental state which lacked political legitimacy but achieved remarkable success in export-oriented economic growth. It lasted from the early 1960s until 1987 when the authoritarian regime fell with the Great Workers' Struggle (June–September). During this period, the authoritarian developmental state curtailed much of the freedom and civil rights of the dissenters in the name of national security and international competition. In the meantime, there was rapid growth not only in industry, but also in civic social groups which demanded a reduction in the state's relative autonomy. Civic group activities in this period were classified by the government into two categories: advocacy-oriented activities for the promotion of social justice, democracy, and human rights, on behalf of the workers, farmers, and other alienated people in society; and mainly education- and service-oriented groups. While the latter were often actively supported, sometimes initiated, and at other times left relatively less-controlled by the government, the former were labeled as "anti-government" and severely repressed, many eventually being ousted into the underground.

It should be noted at this stage that the formal structure of cooperation between the government and NGOs was established during this period, beginning in the 1980s. All NGOs were expected to register with competent ministries either for establishment as a legally recognized organization or for mere recognition as a public body. As the number of registered NGOs increased and the issues came to require more professional information and management, the ministries began to establish quasi-governmental organizations as an intermediary institute between NGOs and the government. Also during this period, the women's movement expanded, and their organizations became active. For instance, the Ministry of Health and Social Affairs established the Korea Women's Development Institute (KWDI) as a quasi-governmental organization as early as 1983. This was a gesture by the government of support for the women's movement and was not regarded as a challenge against the regime. KWDI activities include not only policy research and support of women's organizations, but also direct services to the community.

In the case of the consumer protection movement, on the other hand, the Korea Institute for Consumer Protection (KICP) was established in 1987 as a special public interest corporation with the Ministry of Economic Planning Board as the competent ministry. KICP conducts activities in policy research, consumer education, dissemination of information, arbitration, and testing, and thereby supports private consumer organizations as well as the government. In the area of environmental protection, the National Institute for Environmental Research (NIER) was established as early as 1978. NIER has confined its functions to research and technology development for the preservation of the environment. Whether these organizations are conducive or detrimental to the development of NGOs is a moot question. In the early years, those NGOs with anti-government inclinations resisted cooperation with these quasi-governmental organizations since they were regarded as an extension of the controlling hand of the government.

The third stage began with the abrupt end of the authoritarian regime in June 1987. New at this stage of evolution of the Korean NGO community was the emergence of increasingly effective and sophisticated civic groups led by the younger generation emphasizing progressive advocacy functions, including efforts to broaden public debate and participation in the formulation of public policy, safeguard or expand the domain of human rights, and safeguard public resources, such as the environment, against the pressures of economic growth. A few very effective NGOs established after 1987 and covered in this survey are as follows: the Citizens' Coalition for Economic Justice, established in 1989 by five hundred founding members, as a citizens' organization to express opinions on general policy issues with a broad focus on economic justice; Korea Women's Association for Democracy and Sisterhood, established in 1987 with a new progressive feminist approach to women's issues; the Korea Action Federation for Environment, established in 1994 by the former opposition movement leaders who view the environmental issue as one related to more fundamental questions of people's right to life and the anti-nuclear and anti-*chaebol* movements. Most of the listed organizations are new additions that are, in fact, leading components of the contemporary NGO community in Korea.

Furthermore, this positive development within the NGO community was accompanied by a remarkable upsurge of public, scholarly, and business attention focused on the role of NGOs, not only as an alternative provider of public services, but also as a vehicle for active citizen participation. Particularly important is that the new democratic government, of which many leaders were themselves active in opposition groups during the Yushin period, is inclined to appreciate the roles of NGOs not as adversaries but as allies. This change may contribute to the development of a more effective mechanism to improve cooperation between the government and NGOs, and perhaps cooperation among NGOs themselves.

As for international cooperation, only a few individual NGOs (with the exception of those Korean branches of international organizations such as the YMCA, YWCA, AAUW, and Amnesty International) are capable of and interested in active horizontal networking. Only a very few appear to be capable of organizing and executing international projects because most of them are seriously understaffed. The quasi-governmental organizations mentioned above have better staff structures, and they are quite active in international cooperation and exchange. They play a major role in disseminating information on international cooperation and organizing and dispatching delegates to international gatherings representing related Korean NGOs. Particularly in the field of environmental protection and women's issues, partly because of the nature of the subjects addressed, and partly because of the history of the movements, international involvement is relatively active. Also, there are a few church-based NGOs mainly focusing on social welfare services by making use of funds from international headquarters and sending gifts and monetary aid to the world's poverty pockets.

MALAYSIA

Nongovernmental Organizations in Malaysia and Regional Networking

Lim Teck Ghee

I. Introduction

This paper is a contribution to the "Survey on Nongovernmental Organizations of the Emerging Asia Pacific Regional Community" being undertaken by the Japan Center for International Exchange. NGOs in Malaysia have played a very important role in the development and progress of the country. However, their contributions have been largely ignored, partly due to the absence of evaluative studies carried out on them. This project hopes to provide a modest input to the study of NGOs in Malaysia and to demonstrate the need for a data base on their activities and achievements, which would not only facilitate future research but would also spur collaborative efforts among these organizations to enable them to deal more effectively with the ever-widening range of socio-economic, political and cultural issues in the country and in the larger Asia Pacific region.

II. Objectives of the Study

The immediate objectives of this study are to evaluate the origins and history of the leading NGOs in Malaysia as well as the objectives and aims of each NGO interviewed for the study. The activities organized by each NGO and the local and regional networks they utilize will also be examined for comparison. Further, they will be evaluated for future promise and potential based on an assessment of past achievements and the breadth of their present network of collaboration with local and regional bodies.

III. Methodology

As the first step towards evaluating various NGOs in Malaysia, a list of leading NGOs was drawn up. These NGOs were divided into five major groups, namely, environmental groups, consumer groups, human rights groups, development groups and women's groups. Simultaneously, a questionnaire was prepared for the purpose of eliciting information on the organizations and their activities. The questionnaire was subsequently administered to a smaller sample consisting of twenty-five organizations with five organizations chosen from each of the major groups. Due to time and resource constraints, the sample was biased toward NGOs located in the Kuala Lumpur area, where follow-up work could be more easily accomplished. Two other methods were used to gather the necessary information. First, personal interviews were conducted with key officials in the organizations, and second, documentary materials such as annual reports and programme reports were solicited from the selected NGOs.

IV. Research Problems

The major problem faced in conducting this research was the lack of positive response from the many NGOs to which the questionnaire was mailed. A total of twenty-five questionnaires was sent out. Unfortunately, only a minority of organizations responded. The other main problem was the return of blank or partially completed questionnaires that required considerable checking with the relevant organizations.

V. Government–NGO Relations

Before summarizing the survey findings proper we must first note the policy of the government towards NGOs in Malaysia and the relationship between these two parties in the recent past.

In dealing with NGOs, the Malaysian government has maintained that it places national security above all other concerns. As such, NGOs are given relatively limited rein compared to their counterparts in developed countries, especially when it is felt that their activities may jeopardize national security, for example when "sensitive" issues such as those pertaining to the government's New Economic Policy or

National Cultural Policy are raised. This explains the absolute power given to the Registrar of Societies to deregister "undesirable" societies at will.

Although it might be argued that the government does not have any formal policy on NGOs, under the Societies Act of 1966, all NGOs are treated as societies and are required to be registered with the Registrar of Societies and to submit audited annual accounts. Amendments to the Societies Act in 1981 divided the NGOs into "friendly" and "political" societies. NGOs labelled as "political societies" were required to obtain the Registrar's approval for foreign affiliation and fund raising. The amendment also prohibited certain categories of people from holding office in these NGOs and provided the Registrar of Societies with the absolute power to register and deregister them in the sense that the Minister's decision could no longer be challenged in court. As a result of public outcry over the amendments, a new bill was passed by Parliament in 1983, providing for a relaxation of the most controversial provisions, including the division of NGOs into "friendly" and "political" societies and the need for societies to obtain the Registrar's approval for foreign affiliation or fund raising.

At present, the government–NGO relationship in Malaysia is characterized by active collaboration at one level and something approaching confrontation at the other. When issues such as welfare policies or youth and child development are taken up, the government is usually appreciative of input from the NGOs and an exchange of information takes place to facilitate the relevant projects. The Federation of Malaysian Family Planning Association, for example, has long worked closely with the government, while the Federation of Malaysian Consumers Association (FOMCA) now sits on a permanent but ad hoc basis on various committees in the Ministries of Trade and Industry, the Ministry of Health, and the Ministry of Finance, to name a few. The government–NGO relationship in such cases borders between overall cooperation and cooperation on what the government perceives to be issues of social welfare that have no underlying political implications or significance.

Tensions arise, however, when some NGOs actively seek to make the political system more accountable to public interests or to make the development process more transparent and people oriented. ALIRAN, the Friends of the Earth Malaysia and the Consumers Association of Penang are examples of these NGOs. The government relationship with these NGOs can be considered difficult at best and confrontational at worst. Besides these organizations, many other NGOs are sceptical about the top-down development approach of the government and fear being subjected to the vested interests politicians may have in their programmes. Further, the inclination of these NGOs to ally themselves with the opposition parties on key national issues has not endeared them to the government.

A major irritant in the existing NGO relationship with the government is the effect caused by the 1986 amendment to the Official Secrets Act, which protects government documents from public scrutiny. This has hampered the free flow of information, even to NGOs that have traditionally cooperated with the government and are dependent on government departments for data and statistics.

There is clearly a need for the government to see NGOs as partners in development rather than as pressure groups out to foment discontent and chaos in the country. The government's recent action to invite moderate groups such as FOMCA, the National Council of Women's Organizations, and even ALIRAN, to participate in the National Economic Consultation Council to decide on the National Economic Policy after 1990, an important national planning occasion, shows that the government is moving towards greater recognition of the role of developmental NGOs and is willing to work with them to promote development. Other occasions which have seen the participation of NGOs include a forum on the Environmental Quality Act, the Taman Negara Advisory Council and the National Unity Board. All these are laudable steps but more important is the dismantling of oppressive laws and legislation that inhibit the participation and growth of the NGO sector.

On the other hand, a number of government leaders have complained that NGOs themselves tend to harbour antagonistic attitudes towards the government and are frequently (and vocally) allied with the opposition political parties on important issues. Rokiah Talib, the chairperson of the National Council for Consumer Protection, believes that there is a need for more patience and understanding among NGOs when dealing with the government. In her opinion, confrontational strategies are counterproductive and further fossilize government antagonisms towards developmental NGOs. Shared decision making in development is a new experience for all in the country, especially a government not known for its liberal policies. In Ms Talib's opinion, the government is open to the NGOs but the latter are in too much of a hurry for change and are oversceptical about the intentions of the government.

Undoubtedly, there are benefits to be derived from greater cooperation between the two groups. For instance, there would definitely be more complementary development efforts and less overlapping of functions, and hence, less waste of scarce resources. The integration of NGOs into the process of national development would be the best guarantee of participatory democracy, as these groups are strategically placed and ideally suited to provide grassroots feedback and facilitate public dialogue because they have their ears close to the ground and their eyes sharp on the government's hands.

VI. Profile of Select NGOs

1. Federation of Malaysian Consumers Association (FOMCA)

Address: 8, Lorong SS1/2A, 47300 Petaling Jaya
Tel: 03-7762009 *Fax:* 03-7762009
Legal Status: Registered with Registrar of Societies

FOMCA was established on 10th June 1973 in Alor Setar, Kedah. FOMCA is a federal body consisting of members of all state consumers associations, except the Consumers Association of Penang. Prior to the birth of FOMCA, there were four consumers associations in the country set up at the state level—the Selangor Consumers Association, the Consumers Association of Penang (established in 1969), the Consumers Association of Sarawak (1971) and the Consumers Association of Negri Sembilan (1971). At that time, these organizations felt that there was a need for a federal association to coordinate the activities of the state bodies. Thus, the initial role of FOMCA was to coordinate the activities of its members. However, as it has progressed and gained more affiliates, the federation has ventured out to include research and representation, and also to initiate related activities.

The objectives of FOMCA include ensuring the continued growth of consumer movements in Malaysia, resolving consumer issues and problems, promoting consumer rights, and acting as an advisory body to the existing consumer organizations in Malaysia and aiding them in their objectives through the provision of information.

FOMCA organizes many seminars, forums and exhibitions on a regular basis to promote consumer awareness. FOMCA believes that the key to consumer protection lies in their education. Knowledge of their rights and responsibilities will enable consumers to protect themselves.

Among the main priorities of FOMCA is research and development, with an emphasis on consumer laws. One of its key functions since its inception has been that of representation. The formation of FOMCA was the manifestation of the express desire of the state consumer associations to extend their influence to the national level and to represent consumer interests within a relationship with the government. Hence, an important distinction in the relationship between FOMCA and the government was the organization's search for the right of representation. One of its early landmark achievements was in 1974, when the Price Control Act of 1946 was amended to include the following subsection:

> The Minister may establish a National Advisory Council for Consumers Protection consisting of such representatives of business, government and other organizations as he may appoint to advise him on various matters.

With this amendment, a National Advisory Council was established, thus setting the stage for a formal relationship with the government. With the government increasingly receptive to NGO opinions on consumer issues, FOMCA representatives regularly meet with government agencies, trade and other nongovernmental organizations, and sit in the following ministries:

- Ministry of Health
- Ministry of Finance (Annual Budget Dialogue)
- Ministry of Post and Telecommunications
- Ministry of Housing and Local Government
- Ministry of Information
- Ministry of Agriculture (Pesticide Advisory Council)

Most important of all, and most indicative of the stature of FOMCA as a representative body, is its membership in the National Economic Consultation Council to decide on the National Economic Policy after 1990, a significant achievement for a development NGO. FOMCA is also a source of valuable feedback and input for the government in making decisions beneficial to the populace. In recognition of FOMCA's contributions and those of its member organizations, the government provides annual financial grants to them, totalling RM 285,000 (US$111,000)* in 1989, to enable them to play their role effectively.

Currently, FOMCA's activities touch on many spheres, including community development, the environment, human rights, women's roles in development, consumerism and health issues. Its main area of concern is, of course, consumerism. However, its leaders believe that all these concerns are interconnected. Human rights, for example, form the basis for consumer protection. A clean environment is promoted as an unassailable right of the consumer. FOMCA also regards women as equal partners in all aspects of life. Under the umbrella of health issues, FOMCA regulates the use and labelling of drugs. One of its major successes in this area has been its development of The Charter for Patients Rights and Responsibilities.

FOMCA's activities at the grassroots and state levels are coordinated by the state consumer associations. At the district level, the state associations will collaborate with the district liaison committees.

As a federal body, FOMCA represents the state consumer associations by highlighting their activities and disseminating that information to the larger public. At the national level, FOMCA cooperates with government agencies and other NGOs. Recently, it has become common for FOMCA to play the role of advisor to various

* Based on the International Monetary Fund, *International Financial Statistics*, January 1995. Figures are based on the end of the period exchange rate for November 1994. US$1 = RM 2.56

government agencies on consumer-related issues.

FOMCA is also involved in active networking with other NGOs. A notable link is that with the Malaysian Environment and Conservation Network, which consists of the Environmental Protection Society of Malaysia (EPSM), the Malayan Nature Society, the World Wildlife Fund for Malaysia (WWFM) and the Centre for Environmental Technology Malaysia.

At the regional and international levels, FOMCA is a member of the International Organization for Consumers Union for Asia and the Pacific (IOCU), with regional offices based on various continents. FOMCA also networks with other regional and international organizations, such as Action for Rational Drugs in Asia and Health Action International.

FOMCA also puts out several publications, namely the quarterly newsletter *Berita Pengguna*, the *Wawasan Alam Sekitar* and *Know Your Medicine*, in its attempt to disseminate information to the public. Various memoranda are regularly submitted to the respective ministries, including one on the "Small Claims Court Procedure" to the judicial authorities and one on "Consumer Credit Regulations" to the Ministry of Finance. Other efforts made to disseminate information include sending representatives to present papers, talks and views at forums, workshops and conventions both locally and regionally. Information is also provided freely to academics and students who come to FOMCA for their research on consumerism and consumer movements in Malaysia.

Based on its existing network at both the grassroots and national levels, FOMCA has the potential to accommodate and develop an even more extensive network in the country. As the NGO with the most extensive relations with the government, and one which has pioneered and fostered the concept of a formal relationship with the government, FOMCA is well placed to lead the way toward greater NGO–government cooperation.

2. Selangor and Federal Territory Consumers Association (SFTCA)

Address: 4B-l, Jalan Pantai Baru, 59100 Kuala Lumpur.
Tel: 03-7822575 *Fax:* 03-2822575
Legal Status: Registered with Registrar of Societies

The Selangor and Federal Territory Consumers Association (SFTCA) was established in 1965. Previously known as the Selangor Consumers Association, it broadened its base to cover the Federal Territory upon the capital city's division from Selangor. SFTCA aims to protect and ensure the rights and the responsibilities of consumers. It also conducts research and makes recommendations to the government and private organizations.

Consumers receive advice, and their complaints are handled. The quality of consumer products is monitored as is their proper pricing. SFTCA also actively advocates better consumer protection laws and simultaneously disseminates information to consumers. SFTCA's other areas of activities include the environment, women's issues, human rights and health concerns.

Since SFTCA is a state body, most of its activities are centred in the State of Selangor and the Federal Territory. Among the activities organized at this level are talks, exhibitions, seminars and forums. Consumer clubs are being nurtured by SFTCA in schools to create consumer awareness at the grassroots level. SFTCA also collaborates with youth and women's rights groups, trade unions and other human interest groups. Frequent publications disseminate information to the public.

At the national level, SFTCA is a member of FOMCA and has links with other state consumers associations. It also has linkages with other NGOs in Malaysia as well as trade unions and academic institutions. At the regional and international levels, SFTCA has established ties with IOCU.

SFTCA has published a wide variety of material, ranging from a quarterly newsletter, the *Berita Pengguna,* to reports on consumer law reform and safety and health standards in agriculture. SFTCA is a well-organized local NGO. Its leaders are mainly academics. As such, a main concern of the organization is research. However, other areas of concern such as the environment, women and human rights are also given importance. The potential of this organization in regional cooperation, especially in the area of research and development, is considerable. There is, of course, a danger that the activities of the many existing consumer bodies in the country may overlap, thus resulting in a waste of resources. As such, there is a need for extensive collaboration between the local consumer bodies, including SFTCA, and agreement on how to establish and operate regional linkages.

3. Sabah Consumers Association (CASH)

Address: Tingkat 3, Lot 1, Bangunan Lijah, Batu 12
Jalan Tuaran, Peti Surat 14859, 88855 Kota Kinabalu, Sabah, Malaysia.
Tel: 088-234616 *Fax:* 088-235158
Legal Status: Registered with Registrar of Societies
The Sabah Consumers Association (CASH) was the last state consumers association to be set up in Malaysia. It was established in 1980. The objectives of the asso-

ciation are to educate the public on the importance of consumerism and the environment and to raise awareness in general.

CASH's areas of activity include efforts towards community development, nurturing of the environment, human rights, the role of women in development and good consumerism. More specific information on its activities was not obtainable.

At the national level, CASH has a great many links by virtue of being an affiliate of FOMCA. CASH is also represented in FOMCA itself, and has elected members on the council. At the regional level, CASH works closely with IOCU.

CASH has no regular publications. However, when an issue of importance to consumers arises, it will normally make a press statement. Its views are also published through FOMCA's quarterly magazine.

CASH, which is located in East Malaysia, has minimal networking contacts with other organizations in Peninsular Malaysia and Sabah. Its ties with international organizations are also weak.

A problem faced by CASH is its small membership. It thus has little influence. The association also runs on a very small budget. However, a cursory glance at the NGO scene in Sabah provides evidence that the consumer movement is slowly gaining momentum. Of some fourteen NGOs surveyed, half had at least two branches outside Kota Kinabalu. These were mostly registered in the 1960s, but more than a few were only registered in the mid-1980s. This shows that the NGO scene in Sabah is not static but evolving. Only one of the fourteen Sabahan NGOs, however, stated that they had been consulted by the government in the past on the formulation of policies and programmes. This demonstrates a definite need to improve links with the government on the part of CASH, for the government may be a source of both resources and influence, thus bolstering CASH's weak areas. The government's more extensive network may also supplement the lesser one of CASH, making for more efficient programme implementation and greater benefits to Sabahan consumers.

At present, the Sabah Council of Welfare Services is perhaps the most noteworthy example of synergetic collaboration between the private and public sector. This council is an umbrella organization for thirteen NGOs, including CASH, which focuses on welfare and community services under the purview of the Ministry of Social Services. Members receive annual grants to subsidize their projects. This points to a division of labour whereby the government has successfully privatized a portion of welfare services, which if undertaken by the government itself, would have entailed far greater cost. Hence, government financial resources have been harnessed and put to good use by NGO expertise and human resources.

4. Environmental Protection Society of Malaysia (EPSM)

Address: P.O. Box 382, 46740 Petaling Jaya.
Tel: 03-7757767 *Fax:* 03-7754039
Legal Status: Registered with Registrar of Societies

EPSM was established at a public meeting at the University of Malaya on 11th January 1974. When registered, it was initially called the Environmental Protection Society, Selangor, until the officials from the organization managed to convince the Registrar of Societies that the membership extended beyond the state of Selangor, resulting in the name being changed to EPSM.

The stated objectives of the organization include preventing the deterioration of the environment as a result of human mismanagement through the control of various activities, initiating measures for the improvement of the environment, and stimulating public concern for the state of the environment.

At the national level, EPSM's efforts have focused on advocacy and campaigning for environmental causes, influencing legislation whenever possible, public education and awareness building, and occasional research on pertinent matters. It has also attempted to build up a local coalition of environmental groups through its role as the founder coordinator of the Malaysian Environmental and Conservation Network.

Its regional activities include participation in the Climate Action Network, Southeast Asia, which is concerned with climate change issues, the exchange of information, and participation in regional campaigns. It is also a member of the Pesticides Action Network, seeking restrictions on the use of chemical pesticides and promoting natural methods of plant disease control.

At the international level, it is part of UNCED, and has taken part in the Climate and Biodiversity Convention and North-South debate as well as South-South cooperation talks. EPSM is also a member of the International Union of Air Pollution Prevention Association.

EPSM's publications include the *Alam Sekitar* (a quarterly magazine in English), *Bahasa Malaysia* (published since 1976) and reports on various studies it has undertaken on environmental and other social issues.

EPSM has been one of the leading environmental NGOs in Malaysia. Among its major handicaps is the lack of active members to promote its ambitious objectives, leading to perhaps a lack of public appreciation for its not inconsiderable achievements; most Malaysians are generally more aware of the more visible WWFM.

5. World Wide Fund Malaysia (WWFM)

Address: Locked Bag No. 911, Jalan Sultan Post Office; 46990 Petaling Jaya, Selangor
Tel: 03-7579192 *Fax:* 03-7565594
Legal Status: Registered under Trustees Ordinance

WWFM is a national charity established under the Trustees (Incorporation) Ordinance in 1972. It is a Malaysian organization and a member of the international WWF family.

The WWF's mission is to achieve the conservation of nature and ecological processes by preserving genetic, species and ecosystem diversity; ensuring that the use of renewable natural resources is sustainable both now and in the longer term for the benefit of all life on earth; and promoting actions to reduce to a minimum pollution and the wasteful exploitation and consumption of resources and energy. WWF's ultimate goal is to stop, and eventually reverse, the accelerating degradation of the planet's natural environment, and to help build a future in which humans live in harmony with nature.

Initially, WWFM focused exclusively on the protection of wildlife in Malaysia, but over two decades its objectives have grown to embrace many aspects and issues related to man and the environment. At the national level, WWFM conducts various field projects on different species and special conservation areas, and engages in policy work and advocacy. Its relations with the authorities are good, WWFM having closely collaborated with the authorities in the identification, formation and administration of various protected areas such as forest reserves, bird and animal sanctuaries and parks. WWFM has also incorporated a human interest angle into its activities whereby it supports advances in the local standard of living while ensuring the adequate protection of the natural resources this requires. While searching for the ideal socio-economic balance, WWFM also educates to promote awareness of the basic fundamentals of environmental protection.

One of its main projects at the regional level is the monitoring of pollution in ASEAN countries. The organization also collaborates with neighbouring countries such as Thailand and Indonesia on environmental education and transnational issues.

WWFM's recent efforts to promote regional cooperation include the establishment of the ASEAN Environmental Office, sponsorship of government staff and private individuals for training courses in the region, sponsorship of a recent Malaysia/Philippines seminar on marine parks, and funding for various Asian Wetland Bureau activities. WWFM's publications include a series of project reports (about two hundred since 1972) and a quarterly newsletter.

The networking prospects of this NGO are considerable. This is due on one hand to its links to WWF International, one of the world's largest and most influential international nature conservation organizations, which has presented WWFM with a ready-made network in the form of other WWF organizations in twenty-two countries; and on the other to the limelight brought to it by its patron, the late Yang Di Pertuan Agong. At the local level, it has a tough job in convincing people that environmental protection need not stunt developmental efforts and that environmental conservation benefits not so much the wildlife or the forests, but man first and foremost.

In terms of cooperation with the government, WWFM has led the way among environmental groups. According to the President of WWFM, Tan Sri Khir Johari, a former minister, WWFM's twenty-one years of cooperating with government bodies has convinced the organization that this cooperation is the key to efficiency and effectiveness.

6. *Management Institute for Social Change (MINSOC)*

Address: B 2114, Jalan Merpati, 25300 Kuantan, Pahang, Malaysia
Tel: 09-5133160 *Fax:* 09-5144982
Legal Status: Registered with Registrar of Companies

The Management Institute for Social Change (MINSOC) was established in 1989. Its objectives are to build the capacity of civil society to achieve development that is socially just, economically viable, environmentally sustainable, politically participatory and culturally vibrant. Its areas of activity include community development, the environment, human rights, the role of women in development, consumerism and an alternative economic paradigm.

At the national level, MINSOC's organized activities include efforts towards capacity and linkage building of people's organizations, networking and support services, training and consultancy services for management and capacity building in general, secretariat support services to the Sustainable Development Network (SUSDEN) and the Malaysian NGO Development Forum, and the running of a Community Resource Information Centre.

At the regional level, MINSOC concentrates on training and consultancy services for management and capacity building and secretariat support services to the Southeast Asian NGO Consortium on Sustainable Development. It is a networking partner of the Asian NGO Coalition and Pesticide Action Network. At the international level, MINSOC engages in training and consultancy services for management and capacity building, is Malaysia's representative to the Canadian Crossroads International Programme, and is also the national focal point for the People Centred Development Forum.

MINSOC's modest list of publications includes a book titled *One Person Size: A Guide to Sustainable Development*, occasional and research papers and a newsletter, *Keeping in Touch.*

MINSOC is a classic example of many developmental NGOs in Malaysia. Its ambitions are wide-ranging but its impact has been minimal. The future of this organization in promoting regional cooperation is comparable to any other organized NGO in Malaysia although with its base in Kuantan, Pahang, where few other organized NGOs are present, it might have a slight edge in highlighting problems peculiar to the less developed eastern part of the peninsula.

7. Sustainable Development Network (SUSDEN), Malaysia

Address: B-2114, Jalan Merpati, Off Jalan Haji Ahmad, 25300 Kuantan, Pahang
Tel: 09-51331A0 *Fax:* 09-5144982
Legal Status: Registered with Registrar of Companies

SUSDEN was established on 16th July 1993. The aim of SUSDEN Malaysia is to create awareness and promote people's participation in achieving sustainable development. SUSDEN's areas of activity include community development, the environment, women in development and consumerism.

Its major activities include organizing awareness-building conferences, seminars and workshops for the general public, the NGO community, the business community and youth groups. It also organizes youth camps for building awareness, assessing environmental impacts, and fostering leadership skills. In addition, SUSDEN is a pioneer in organic farming. According to its officers, it undertakes research, monitors development, advocates policies for change both nationally and regionally, and acts as a community resource and information centre on environmentally sustainable development.

At the international level, SUSDEN is a member of regional NGOs including the South East Asian Consortium on Environmentally Sustainable Development, the Asian NGO Coalition for Agrarian Reform and Rural Development, the Asian Alliance of Appropriate Technology Practices, the Pesticide Action Network, the Wahana Lingkungan Hidup Indonesia and the Asian Cultural Forum on Development. SUSDEN's publications are mainly research papers.

As an off-shoot of MINSOC, the potential of this organization is severely hampered by its dependence on a few officials who are also actively involved in other organizations.

8. Suara Rakyat Malaysia (SUARAM)

Address: 41c, Jalan SS 6/12, Kelana Jaya, 47301 Selangor
Tel: 03-7039266 *Fax:* 03-70327B4
Legal Status: Registered with Registrar of Companies
Suara Rakyat Malaysia (SUARAM), or The Voice of the Malaysian People, is a group committed to the struggle for improved human rights—political, civil, economic, social and cultural—in Malaysia.

SUARAM has its origins in the Support Group for ISA detainees, which was set up in response to the government's mass arrests of social activists in October, 1987. Although all these detainees have since been released, many involved have felt that the campaign to promote and protect human rights in Malaysia needed a more permanent commitment. To this end, SUARAM was formed.

SUARAM's objectives are to protect and promote human rights in the country, campaign for the repeal of all repressive legislation, create public awareness of human rights, organize and set up a resource-based centre to meet the human rights needs of individuals and groups, and to build up a human rights network to further the cause. Its areas of activity include community development, the environment, human rights and the concerns of the indigenous people.

The major activities organized by SUARAM at the national level include human rights consultation (SUARAM regularly organizes workshops on human rights consultation, including a recent one to draft the charter for human rights in Malaysia), *Perjuangan Kenyalang* (a project to create awareness on the plight of indigenous people in Sarawak), and various forums to educate the public on the human rights situation in the country.

At the regional level, SUARAM was the Southeast Asian Coordinator for the Vienna UN Conference on Human Rights, and at the international level, it is actively networking with Amnesty International, the Asian Human Rights Commission, Asia Watch and the International Commission for Jurists.

Its publications include *HAK*, a quarterly newsletter, *A Hidup Agi Ngelaban* (Perjuangan Kenyalang), a book about the concerns of indigenous people, a report titled *Continuing Education of Human Rights Activists* arising from a workshop to develop a curriculum for training human rights activists held in May 1993, which it jointly published with the Asian Forum for Human Rights and Development, and also a series called *The White Papers.*

Since its inception, SUARAM has become one of the leading NGOs in the promotion and protection of human rights in Malaysia. It enjoys the support of the major NGOs in the country. Over the years, SUARAM has become a more organized body. With strong support from other organizations and an enthusiastic staff, it has much potential in promoting regional cooperation.

9. Persatuan Kebangsaan Hak Asasi Manusia (HAKAM)

Address: Tingkat 4, Menara Tun Razak, Jalan Raja Laut, 50350 Kuala Lumpur
Tel: 03-7757767 *Fax:* 03-7754039
Legal Status: Registered with Registrar of Societies
Persatuan Kebangsaan Hak Asasi Manusia (HAKAM) is a relatively young Malaysian NGO. Although its formation was mooted in the late 1980s, it was only officially registered on 14th June 1991 with the Registrar of Societies.

HAKAM aims to promote, preserve, and defend human rights; to campaign for the repeal of repugnant laws and the promulgation of legislation advancing human rights; to redress human rights complaints; and to analyze relevant values and principles within various Malaysian spiritual traditions. To carry out its objectives, it seeks to cooperate with relevant national, regional and international groups.

The main area of concern for HAKAM is the promotion and preservation of human rights in Malaysia and neighbouring countries. To this end, HAKAM has organized human rights discussions in Kuala Lumpur, Petaling Jaya and Kota Kinabalu. Activities organized by HAKAM in 1993 include a forum on the rights of indigenous people, held in Kuala Lumpur; a forum focusing on the Internal Security Act, held in Kota Kinabalu; and "Professor Azmi Khalid: A World Human Rights Day Commemoration Forum", held in Petaling Jaya. HAKAM has not been able to organize any regional or international level activities due to financial constraints.

Cooperating regional and international organizations include the United Nations Centre for Human Rights. HAKAM has no publications to date.

If the regional networking potential of HAKAM were to be evaluated solely on the basis of its performance thus far, the results may not be encouraging, especially since HAKAM, unlike some other organizations, relies entirely on volunteers. However, cooperation with various other local NGOs could enable it to overcome its manpower constraints in setting up regional links.

10. Tenaganita

Address: 28C, Lorong Bunus 6, 50100 Kuala Lumpur
Tel: 03-2913691 *Fax:* 03-2913681
Legal Status: Registered with Registrar of Companies
Tenaganita was established in 1990. However, its active participation and involvement in public issues began only in 1991. Its aims include the empowerment of women, the promotion and protection of women's rights, and the encouragement of women to achieve their full potential in society. Its areas of activity are in community development, human rights, the environment, the role of women in development, consumerism (to some extent) and health-related matters.

Major activities organized by Tenaganita at the national level include various awareness-building forums, seminars and workshops, leadership training, skills training in organizing and mobilizing society, training in legal literacy, services to migrant workers, discussions on violence against women, an anti-pesticide campaign, coordination with local NGOs, and participation in an NGO Council on AIDS.

At the regional and international levels, it is part of the Asia Pacific Forum on Women, Law and Development, the Committee on Asian Women—a regional network for female industrial workers—the Pesticide Asian Network, the Asian Migrant Centre, the Asian Cultural Forum on Development, ARROW, and also the Asia Pacific Bureau on Adult Education.

Tenaganita's publications include *Pesticides—Victims Without Voice* and a Tamil newsletter, *Jothee*, but on the whole its focus is more on action-oriented plans rather than publications.

Tenaganita was one of the few organizations that gave full cooperation to this study. The energy of its members and staff is evident in the number of activities organized by this relatively young organization. Tenaganita is also already playing an important role in promoting regional cooperation, with its members involved with various regional and international organizations.

Whilst the organization's potential for promoting regional networking may be good, a problem it faces is that it is too diverse in the range of issues covered and thus is probably spreading itself too thin.

11. Women's Aid Organization (WAO)

Address: P.O. Box 493, Jalan Sultan, 46760 Petaling Jaya
Tel: 03-7554426, 03-7563488
Legal Status: Not available
The Women's Aid Organization (WAO) opened Malaysia's first refuge for victims of domestic violence in 1982. The aim was to provide a full service for women suffering mental and physical abuse.

Its objectives are to provide, on request, a temporary refuge for women and their children who are suffering from mental and physical harassment, to offer emotional and social support to women who ask for it, and to offer support and after-care to women who have left the centre. It also recognizes and tries to meet the educational and emotional needs of the children involved. To meet its objectives, it encourages research into the causes or ways of preventing the suffering brought on by harassment, and keeps statistics and records that will facilitate further research. Finally, it seeks to educate and inform the public, the media, the police, the courts, the social services and other authorities about the plight of battered women; to enlist the support of professional workers to help such women; and to seek improved legal protection of such women and children. WAO services include running "The Refuge Centre", a shelter for battered women and their children, as well as a centre for all WAO activities relating to families, women and violence. It also runs a Child Care Centre where the children of ex-residents who have decided to live independently are given a home, emotional support and education at local schools; operates a twenty-four hour helpline, to ensure that telephone counselling is available at any time to deal with anything from a crisis situation to basic legal queries; and conducts face-to-face counselling where professional social workers offer counselling sessions to women and their husbands.

VII. Conclusion

The survey shows that NGOs in Malaysia are not generally lacking in cooperation and relationships with organizations from other parts of the world. These efforts are often manifested by the exchange of information, participation in the activities of other organizations, engagement in joint activities, etc. The breadth of issues focused on in these cooperative efforts ranges widely, but they generally mirror similar concerns over problem areas such as the environment, human rights, labour, women and child development, and other related concerns found in many other countries in Asia Pacific.

No attempt was made by the survey to systematically analyze the regional networks that are emerging with the cooperative efforts and activities in which Malaysian NGOs have recently begun to increasingly participate. However, initial examination indicates that the centres of these networks are spread over a number of countries, developing as well as developed, and that the regional networks are mainly based on personal relationships and friendships amongst various leaders of NGOs, in addition to the commonality of interests and concerns over issues found among NGOs in the region.

While not denying the potential of some regional networks to take up issues of a national or regional character more effectively than national organizations can do so by themselves, or the value of the networks in broadening intellectual interaction in the region, it is important that these networks and their activities should not be at the expense of locally based activities. "Regionalizing" or "internationalizing" concerns and activities should only come about after a solid foundation of locally based activities has been established. They must also be justified as a necessity in their own right rather than presumed to be naturally useful. Scarce resources are often unnecessarily devoted to regional or international activities because of their glamour and the immediate benefits they bring to the individuals participating in them. In this sense, NGOs should be no less accountable than the private sector or the governmental interests that they frequently criticize. A transparent database on regional networks, activities and participants, and the work they engage in, would be an important step in monitoring the efficacy of these new initiatives and would help to ensure that the results are commensurate with the resources they consume.

NEW ZEALAND

NGOs and Philanthropy in New Zealand

Peter Harris
Executive Director
Asia 2000 Foundation of New Zealand

Definitions of nongovernmental organizations (NGOs) vary, but tend to focus on nonprofit agencies, especially those in the private sector or those subject to only limited government control, as well as those with a voluntary element to the work they do.

Using this rough and ready definition, it is reasonable to say that the NGO sector in New Zealand is relatively well-developed, and takes a number of forms. Its most traditional consists of the many groups, associations, welfare agencies and charities that owe their rationale to certain South Pacific social mores and practices or, more predominantly, to mores and practices inherited and adapted from Britain and other parts of western Europe. Among these are voluntary welfare agencies like Age Concern that are responsible for caring for the sick, the old, or the otherwise disadvantaged or dispossessed.

During the last few decades these more traditional NGOs have come increasingly to see their roles as supplementing the social welfare provisions of the government, rather that functioning as mainstream providers, though with the economic restructuring of the past eight years or so their potential as mainstream service providers may again come into its own. The parameters of their work and concerns are defined by the 1957 Charitable Trusts Act, which takes a rather narrow view of charity, defining it in terms of the relief of poverty and deprivation, and the advancement of education and religion. Many of them are modelled on similar organizations in the United Kingdom, though some like the AIDS Foundation are recently created and deal with recently-emerging New Zealand concerns.

One particular sub-set of this more traditionally-grounded group of charitable agencies are development agencies like Oxfam that provide development assistance to developing countries or (like the New Zealand Section of Amnesty International) undertake other activities that are primarily targeted abroad, and at less well developed countries. The focus of such agencies' work has sometimes been controversial, since New Zealand's gradual evolution from being one of the OECD's richest countries to being one of its poorest has strengthened the hand of those who want to see more development assistance being directed towards disadvantaged groups at home, rather than abroad.

Alongside this set of agencies and institutions has developed another variety of NGO, the philanthropic trust or foundation. In New Zealand such trusts and foundations draw their inspiration partly from Europe and partly from the United States. They range in purpose from the provision of welfare to the support of health and education. A further growing area of identified need in recent years has been environmental conservation. Such trusts and foundations include those set up by or in memory of private individuals—farmers, business people, lawyers, politicians and others—for example the Norman Kirk Memorial Trust, named after a former prime minister, and the J R McKenzie Trust, set up by the founder of a chain of department stores. Others have been established to promote work in particular fields of study, on particular activities or in particular geographical regions. Examples include the New Zealand Sports Foundation and the Pacific Development and Conservation Trust, the latter a fund set up in 1989 with money paid by the French government after its bombing of the Greenpeace organization's ship *Rainbow Warrior*.

Like other NGOs in New Zealand, such trusts are moderate in size. The largest of them is the Auckland-based ASB Trusts, set up as a result of the restructuring of Trustee Banks in the late 1980s. ASB Trusts disburses some NZ$20 million (that is, US$12.5 million) a year. The majority of the more substantial trusts are, like ASB Trusts, regionally or locally based, scattered among Auckland, Wellington, Christchurch and other small towns and districts.

In recent years the most energetic and imaginative of these trusts have started to operate in a more pro-active and creative manner, somewhat like the more pro-active foundations in the United States, rather than functioning as passive agents of financial disbursement in the more hidebound manner of old-fashioned trusts in Europe. A striking example of this trend is the McKenzie Trust, which seeks to identify emerging social problems and issues and address them with strategically-placed grants.

Many other types of organizations and institutions exist within the NGO sector in New Zealand. These range from informal, often unregistered, voluntary associations of like-minded people at one end of the spectrum, to agencies associated with particular constituencies such as the different Christian churches and the Maori communities, as well as other minority communities such as the South Pacific islanders and the different communities of Asians resident in New Zealand (New Zealand Chinese Association etc.). It is also possible to include in the NGO sector broadly defined a range of larger, more structured institutions and groups, including business-oriented nonprofit organizations and nonprofit bodies closely connected to, or supported by, the government. Business-oriented nonprofit organizations include research and quality testing agencies, trade associations and business councils. Nonprofit bodies closely linked to the government include a number of the so-called Crown Entities, quasi-government organizations partially or wholly dependent on public funds.

The Asia 2000 Foundation of New Zealand is one such Entity. More than eighty percent of its funding currently comes from the government (mainly through the Ministry of Foreign Affairs and Trade), but in many essential respects it is an NGO, and expects to obtain official charitable status very shortly. Like other Crown Entities it is listed on a schedule attached to the New Zealand Public Finance Act, and can only be removed from the schedule and become fully free-standing if and when its funding becomes more diversified.

For a country with a population of only 3.4 million, New Zealand has a remarkably dense and varied civil society, with a wide variety of NGOs the full range and richness of which has only been briefly touched on here. The radical restructuring of government and of the role of government in recent years, which has resulted in among other things in the rolling back of government influence and the curtailment of the comprehensive welfare state, poses challenges for the voluntary sector which it is only just beginning to face. As a recent symposium on the voluntary welfare sector in New Zealand concluded, "Rather than wait for government to recognise how vital the voluntary sector is in achieving their goal of a reshaped state, the voluntary sector must be pro-active in marketing its strengths and needs to government, the private sector and the general public. This requires a solid base of research, information-sharing networks, training, public awareness and advocacy strategies."

Much of this work, some of it local or national in scope but a good deal dependent on advice and assistance from NGOs beyond New Zealand's shores, is still waiting to be done.

PHILIPPINES

Philippine NGOs in the Asia Pacific Context

Segundo E. Romero, Jr,
Vice President
Institute of Strategic and Development Studies

and

Rostum J. Bautista
Research Assistant
Institute of Strategic and Development Studies

I. Overview of the NGO Sector

1. Background

The development of NGOs in the Philippines has been linked to religious missions and lay activities in the far-flung rural areas. The Catholic Church sought to ameliorate poverty at the grassroots level through charity work and social welfare.

These Catholic missions were the oldest type of NGOs. Among the early Catholic organizations that have remained active to this day are Caritas Manila and La Ignaciana Apostolic Center. The tireless work of Christian clergies and volunteers in the Philippine rural areas is indicated by the presence of a village chapel in the remotest *barangays* (the smallest political unit in the Philippines).

The dole-out approach of religious NGOs eventually was criticized as dependency creating. On the other hand, NGOs whose activities in the countryside focused on community development began to flourish. In the 1950s, Dr. James Yen, who founded the International Rural Reconstruction Movement in China, also founded the Philippine Rural Reconstruction Movement (PRRM). PRRM's fourfold program on health, education, livelihood, and self-government remains a powerful model for NGO operations at present.

Other NGOs of this type that mushroomed included farmers' organizations such as the Federation of Free Farmers (FFF) and Sariling Sikap, Inc. The FFF, established in 1953 by a few lay people to organize peasants into a nationwide movement, aimed to protect the interests of and give financial support to small farmers in the rural areas. It is still active today with over two hundred thousand farmer-members and sixty branch offices.

1. Marcos Administration. In the early 1970s, a new breed of NGOs, whose primary activity was "community organizing," sprung up. These NGOs sought to elevate the political awareness of the people to the point where "they themselves determined their future." These NGOs did not stop short of political action, and were consequently viewed by the Marcos administration as front organizations of the Communist Party of the Philippines and the New People's Army.

Many political activists, opposition party members, and mediamen were incarcerated when Martial Law was declared in 1972, but this did not prevent the flourishing of NGOs determined to topple the dictatorship. Many went underground, and most of the issue-oriented and politically active NGOs played a very important role in preparing the groundwork for the eventual fall of the Marcos Administration in February 1986.

2. Aquino Administration. The many cause-oriented NGOs that opposed Marcos were also the primary political actors that supported the ascension to power of President Aquino. The NGO community made up the base of the Aquino political machinery. NGOs were instrumental in institutionalizing "people power," amply recognized in the 1987 Constitution which encouraged the organization and promotion of NGOs and community-based or sectoral-based people's organizations. The 1987–1992 Medium-Term Development Plan likewise recognized NGOs as partners in the national development effort.

NGOs flourished under the Aquino government, gaining in strength and number not only because of their role as agents and catalysts in nation building, but also because they gained the respect of the international community. Donor countries made available funds to support NGOs' developmental work.

The Local Government Code of 1991 has further concretized the participation of NGOs in all levels of decision making. Under the Code, NGOs participate in making the decisions of local development councils. NGOs are allocated specific seats in local bodies. They are also to be given sectoral representation in the local sanggunian (local legislative bodies).

The term *NGO community* is now a political reality. Collectively, NGOs have gained more influence in every sphere of civil society. The mushrooming of NGOs across the nation has eventually led to the establishment of networks, coalitions, caucuses, federations, and other aggrupations that sought to rationalize the community's concerns and resources.

The aggregation process has led to the formation of several national networks, and the organization of the ten main national networks in turn into the Caucus of Development NGO Network (CODE-NGO). Likewise, sectoral networks such as Convergence for a Community-Centered Area Development, Congress for People's Agrarian Reform, and Green Forum-Philippines have been organized. Regional networks include the Association of Social Development Agencies in Region XI, the Multi-Sectoral Alliance for Development and the Associated Council for Coordinated Development in Negros Occidental, the Antique Federation of Non-Government Organizations, Inc., and the Association of Private Voluntary Organizations in Baguio and Benguet, Inc. Further solidarity among NGOs is forged through various compacts, such as the Covenant on Philippine Development by CODE-NGO members and non-members.

The Aquino administration also encouraged NGOs to link with government line agencies and be active partners in the implementation of their projects and programs.

3. Ramos Administration. The Ramos administration continued to support the organizational development of NGOs. NGOs have developed a national reputation for managerial competence to match their cause orientation. President Ramos appointed to his cabinet, leaders or champions of the NGO community, such as Juan Flavier as Secretary of Health, Ernesto Garilao as Secretary of Agrarian Reform, and Angel Alcala as Secretary of Environment and Natural Resources.

The Ramos administration continued the strengthening of NGOs in the Philippines. The main vehicle for this was the implementation of the Local Government Code of 1991. To date, the database of the Department of Interior and Local Government (DILG) shows a total of 14,398 NGOs and People's Organizations being accredited to the local development councils, the bids and awards committees, local school boards, local health boards, and peace and order councils, as well as receiving sectoral representation in local sanggunians.

Several national and regional summits have been held for the purpose of strengthening GO-NGO collaboration. Among the more important ones were the Local Government Unit/Government Organization - People's Organization/Non-Government Organization Conference on Partnership for Local Development, held in Bulacan in October 1993.

The Ramos government has sought to encourage the participation of NGOs in local governance through the Gantimpalang Pampook Project, which aims to recognize exemplary and innovative NGO partnerships with local governments.

President Ramos' vision of a Philippines 2000 also sought the active participation of NGOs. A private sector and people sector (i.e., the NGOs and people's organizations, or POs) coalition called the People's 2000 has been organized to support the implementation of the Medium Term Philippine Development Plan.

Under President Ramos, specific departments have demonstrated the extent to which NGO support could lead to program success. Secretary Juan Flavier of the Department of Health has caught the imagination and awe of Filipinos and foreigners alike in his innovative and highly successful disease prevention programs. Flavier has enlisted the support of NGOs, private businesses, and the media in pushing health programs.

With the impending solution of the rightist and leftist insurgencies, the NGOs have gained further impetus, as former hardliners have sought to rejoin the mainstream of society by organizing livelihood NGOs. The establishment of NGOs has been a standard "re-entry" approach of both rightist and leftist rebels who have returned to the fold of the law.

The continued number of disasters and environmental problems such as the threat of lahar and volcanic eruptions have sustained the importance of NGO work.

Abroad, the plight of Filipina workers, highlighted by unfortunate deaths in India (the Suller case) and Japan (the Sioson case) and those of Filipino seamen who have been involved in an unusual number of fatal accidents in the high seas, have highlighted the role of women's and overseas workers' NGOs.

Environmental and human rights issues have brought the efforts of international NGOs such as Greenpeace and Amnesty International together with those of their local NGO counterparts in stopping the dumping of hazardous wastes in the Philippines and investigating human rights violations. The debt issue in particular has continued to be an enduring focus of coalition building and strengthening among cause-oriented NGOs who belong to the Freedom from Debt Coalition (FDC).

The rise of the NGOs under President Ramos has not been entirely unimpeded. Congress and some local government units appear to have dragged their feet in fully implementing the Local Government Code. Many NGOs fear that their "golden age" may yet be reversible, as traditional politicians who have been adversely affected by decentralization and people empowerment programs attempt to recapture their dominance and influence.

In particular, there have been attempts to manipulate some POs and NGOs to buttress the Ramos administration henchmen's plans to modify the system of governance, from a bicameral to a unicameral legislature, and ultimately, from a presidential to a parliamentary form of government. This move, championed by House of Representatives Speaker Jose de Venecia, eventually was scuttled. The "pork barrel" funds of the congressmen, called the Countrywide Development Funds, were anticipated to be used in manipulating some NGOs to be sympathetic to the administration's designs.

The Congress under the Ramos administration has also failed to enact the necessary enabling law to give due course to the election of electoral representatives to the sanggunians. There was also an aborted move to postpone the May 1994 *barangay* elections.

These political moves have soured the otherwise positive attitude of the Ramos government with regard to the NGOs. However, they do not negate the overall hospitability and fertility of the political, economic, and cultural soil to the further expansion and development of NGOs in the Philippines.

2. Categories of NGOs

1. **Korten's Schema.** The term *NGO* is synonymous with private voluntary organizations in the United States. Korten[1] described the four types of NGOs as voluntary organizations that pursue a social mission driven by a commitment to shared values; public service contractors that function as market-oriented nonprofit businesses serving public purposes; POs that represent their members' interests, have member accountable leadership, and are substantially self-reliant; and government nongovernmental organizations that are creations of the government and serve as instruments of government policy.

2. **CODE-NGO Schema.** NGOs may be classified according to various criteria:[2]

- according to the activities they perform: community organizing for the rural or urban poor, labor organizing, conscientization, skills training, cooperative development, participatory research, appropriate technology, environmental protection. Their activities may be classified generally into organizing, grassroots education, training and research, issue advocacy, and alternative economic endeavors;
- according to the areas they operate in: urban, rural, national, international;
- according to the size or number of staff: big NGO, medium NGO, small NGO;

- according to the sector they service: peasant, labor, fisher folk, urban poor;
- according to their ideological bias: left-leaning, moderate, conservative;
- according to their initiators: business NGOs, political NGOs, church NGOs, academe NGOs, and even government-initiated and organized NGOs.

3. PhilDHRRA's Schema. The Philippine Partnership for the Development of Human Resources in Rural Areas (PhilDHRRA) made the following classification of NGOs: resource NGOs, implementing NGOs—which is further subdivided into four types: welfare organizations, socio-civic and professional organizations, developmental organizations, and issue-oriented organizations—people's/grassroots organizations, and network NGOs.

a. Resource NGOs. These are NGOs that provide funds, material assistance, or technology to beneficiaries. They are sometimes referred to in their literature as tertiary organizations. International funding organizations and big NGOs such as the Philippine Business for Social Progress (PBSP) are classified as resource NGOs.

b. Implementing NGOs. These are NGOs that develop programs and projects and implement a package of services in direct contact with the beneficiaries. The majority of existing NGOs belong to this category, which is further subdivided as follows:

- Welfare organizations—those involved in social work with individuals and groups of children, youth, adults, disabled and aged, etc.
- Socio-civic and Professional Organizations—those involved in diverse civic and professional work in their communities.
- Developmental Organizations—those involved in long-term development work with specific communities. Their concern is to set up viable community structures, raising the level of the communities' competence for problem solving to enable them to participate in the resolution of broad national issues affecting the community's state of affairs.
- Issue-oriented Organizations—those directly involved in advocacy concerns, particularly on social issues. Also referred to as cause-oriented groups, their main concern is citizen mobilization and popular education on the merits of their own particular stand on national issues such as agrarian reform, ancestral rights of tribal groups, labor rights, human rights, etc.

c. People's/Grassroots Organization. This includes indigenous, self-help and people-initiated organizations. Membership may be on a sectoral basis (e.g. women, youth, labor, farmers, landless peasants, urban poor). Concerns are largely community- and issue-specific, and their overriding goal is to build mechanisms for mutual help and assistance towards eventual self-reliance.

d. Networks. These are functionally specialized organizations that link together numerous NGOs, associations, etc. that share a common concern and set of activities. They may include political networks, religious networks, etc. An example of a functional network for agrarian reform and rural development is PhilDHRRA; an example of a network of NGO networks is CODE-NGO.

Philippine NGOs are moving beyond their traditional domain and scope of operation of providing humanitarian assistance in times of emergencies and natural disaster, or delivering basic health and sanitation services to depressed communities. A number have assumed financial intermediary roles between the funding agency and the direct beneficiaries, which include POs like farmers' or fisher folk groups at the grassroots level.

The phenomenal growth in the number and types of NGOs since the EDSA Revolt in 1986 has been difficult to monitor. Government agencies and NGO networks themselves have differing estimates of the number of NGOs in the country.

The proliferation of NGOs has raised concerns about the need to monitor and regulate their activities. Many NGOs have been suspected of being organized for the sole purpose of capturing, for the personal gain of the organizers, part of official development assistance from donor countries as well as funds coming from many foreign foundations and donor-NGOs. "Fly-by-night" and ghost NGOs are as much a concern of legitimate NGOs as of the government and donors.

3. Major Activities

NGOs in the Philippines undertake the following general categories of activities:

1. Action Projects. These activities involve actual implementation of field projects in the countryside. They include the organization of sectoral groups, and community groups, the implementation of reforestation projects, the operation of cooperatives, etc.

2. Policy Advocacy. These activities involve the dissemination of organizational positions on national issues. They include lobbying in Congress and executive offices with administrative discretion, and efforts to shape public opinion through media and mass mobilization events such as demonstrations and rallies.

3. Research. These activities generally apply social science research methods to bear on social problems. They involve community needs surveys, rapid rural appraisal, environmental impact studies, etc. NGOs are generally flexible in their use of research methods in meeting their research needs.

4. Training. Training activities can be directed at POs, other NGOs, and an NGO's own staff. Training activities seek to imbue knowledge (e.g., the provisions of the Local Government Code and the Agrarian Reform Law), skills (e.g., project and financial management), and orientations (e.g., how to deal with urban poor, government workers, foreign donors, etc.)

5. Community Organizing. This generally seeks to make the members of a community realize their situation in the context of the development of the entire society, and eventually to take charge of their own lives, using their collective potential to radically improve their quality of life.

6. Resource Mobilization and Management. Many NGOs are involved as intermediary organizations, obtaining funds from donors, which they distribute to beneficiary NGOs, who in turn distribute the funds to beneficiary POs. Resource mobilization and management involves the husbanding of external and local financial, material, and human resources.

7. Networking. Networking activities seek to establish, extend, and maintain linkages among NGOs in hierarchical and lateral relationships, as well as between NGOs and the government, and with the private (business) sectors. Specific activities involve conferences and workshops, signing of declarations and covenants, public consultation fora, exchange of letters and publications, etc.

4. List Of Cooperating Regional/International Organizations

1. Public Sector. Some of the cooperating regional and international organizations of Philippine NGOs are governmental or quasi-governmental entities. Among these are the following organizations: The U.S. Agency for International Development (USAID), the Japan International Cooperation Agency, The Canada International Development Agency (CIDA), the Danish International Development Agency, and the German foundations—Konrad Adenauer Foundation, the Friedrich Ebert

Stiftung, and the Friedrich Naumann Foundation.

The Philippine Business for Social Progress is the coordinator of the Local Development Assistance Program (LDAP) NGO Support Grants Component funded by USAID that aims to strengthen the local government bureaucracy, debureaucratize local governance and institutionalize people's governance. The LDAP has supported more than thirty projects of individual and network NGOs and POs all over the Philippines.

CODE-NGO has become a partner for the formulation of the CIDA funding mechanism. The process of setting up this mechanism has given the NGOs a chance to discuss many other issues and agree on common positions. It has made the various NGO networks realize the prime importance of coming together. CODE-NGO as a coalition of NGO networks actually emerged from these interactions.

2. Private Sector. Some regional and international cooperators belong to transnational enterprises. These include American, Japanese (Toyota, Bank of Tokyo), Canadian, and European corporations.

The Foundation for the Philippine Environment (FPE) has been established as an endowment fund to provide financial resources to local NGOs concerned with the preservation and protection of the environment. FPE funds came from private institutions such as the Bank of Tokyo and USAID.

PHILGERFUND, in coordination with the Deutsche Welthungerhilfe/German Agro Action, serves as a conduits of German donor funds to address the financial needs of small NGOs in rural areas.

3. People Sector. International NGOs are perhaps the most numerous regional and international cooperators of Philippine NGOs. They include American foundations (Ford, Asia Foundations), Japanese foundations (Asian Community Trust, Japan Center for International Exchange), Canadian foundations (Canada ASEAN Center), and European foundations (Transnational Institute).

The wide range of people sector support for many Philippine NGOs is illustrated by PhilDHRRA. PhilDHRRA has been able to access resources from the Philippines-Canada Human Resource Development (PCHRD) for training and other human resource development projects. It is also part of the Philippine Development Assistance Program (PDAP) mechanism, which enables it to access financial assistance from Canadian NGOs, among them the World Accord, Canadian Lutheran World Relief, Canadian Hunger Foundation, Cardinal Leger and His Endeavors, and Canadian Physicians for Aid and Relief.

PhilDHRRA has also forged ties with the International Labor Organization and the Department of Labor and Employment for assistance in NGO livelihood projects. Ties with the Ecumenical Development Cooperative Society have also been established for livelihood projects and bridge financing.

PhilDHRRA's programs are supported by the Ford Foundation, MISEREOR-Germany, and CEBEMO. Other support agencies are the People's Council for Rural Savings and Finance, the Asia Partnership for Human Development, the United Nations Development Programme, GTZ, CARE, ICCO, Friedrich Ebert Stiftung, Antique Integrated Area Development, and Lutheran World Relief-USA.

PCHRD is a five year-program amounting to C$15 million (US$10.87 million)[3] sponsored by CIDA. The program seeks to develop the institutional capability of the Philippine and Canadian NGO and PO communities to alleviate poverty through human resource development, partnership enhancement, and advocacy. The program started in April 1990.

The fund is managed by the Philippine-Canadian Joint Committee for Human Resource Development, Inc. The body is composed of representatives from nine networks of development NGOs in the Philippines and four representatives from Canada who represent the Canadian Coordinating Committee.

PDAP is the fruit of a partnership among Philippine and Canadian NGOs and an attempt to help the Filipino disadvantaged in addressing poverty, inequity, and structural injustice by providing needed resources. Since its inception in 1986, linkages and partnerships between Canadian and Philippine NGOs have resulted in the support of two hundred and eighty community projects related to agriculture, income generation, and provision of social services.

PDAP supports worthy NGO/PO endeavors through a pooled fund provided mainly by CIDA, and in part by a core group of Philippine NGOs and a consortium of Canadian NGOs. Its first phase, from 1986–89 saw nineteen Canadian NGOs supporting some one hundred Philippine NGOs. Financial assistance support to recipient beneficiaries totaled C$5.8 million (US$4.2 million). The program's second phase runs from December 1989 to November 1995, and it is expected that some PhP 180 million (US$7.54 million)[4] will be committed in the coming years to support community projects before the end of the program.

The Philippine Program Committee, acting as the coordinating and policy-making body of PDAP in the country, regulates project appraisal and monitoring guidelines. The committee is composed of representatives from six Philippine NGO networks, namely the Association of Foundations (AF), ASSISI, the Asian NGO Coalition for Agrarian Reform and Development (ANGOC), NCSD, PBSP, and PhilDHRRA.

PHINCORD has been a recipient of funds from Oxfam-America, the Canadian Catholic Organization for Development and Peace and CEBEMO, amounting to about PhP 6 million (US$251,000).

VICTO, a member of the national confederation, has been a loan and grant recipient of the CIDA, Australia International Development Assistance Bureau (AIDAB), MISEREOR, GTZ of Germany, and CEBEMO.

AF is engaged by the Japan Center for International Exchange (JCIE) as an intermediary for Japanese private foundations. It is one of the Philippine NGOs, in partnership with CIDA and counterpart Canadian NGOs, to manage PDAP aimed at alleviating poverty, inequity, and structural injustice particularly in the depressed communities.

The AF was also chosen as the host NGO for the implementation of the Small Grant Program under the Global Environment Facility.

The World Wildlife Fund, with PBSP, has signed a cooperative agreement to jointly provide technical assistance in the establishment of the FPE.

5. Relationship With Public, Private, and People Sectors

1. Relationship with National Government Agencies. Several national government agencies, notably the Departments of Agrarian Reform, Health, Agriculture, Social Welfare and Development, Trade and Industry, Labor, and Interior and Local Government maintain close cooperative relationships with NGOs, with many of them having accredited NGOs and maintaining NGO desks to deal particularly with NGOs. They have joint projects in which NGOs serve as public service contractors. These national government agencies also have policy consultation relationships with NGOs.

For instance, PhilDHRRA maintains partnerships with the following governmental agencies: the National Economic Development Authority, the Department of Agrarian Reform, the Department of Environment and Natural Resources, and DILG.

2. GO-NGO Workshops and Conferences. As mentioned above, not only have NGOs increased their interactions with their counterparts abroad, they have also increased their cooperation and linkages with the public and private sectors. This is manifested in tripartite conferences and consultative meetings that have been undertaken in the Philippines.

3. Joint GO-NGO Projects. Partnerships between the government and nongovernmental organizations is being encouraged. A lot of GO-NGO joint projects have been spawned in the areas of health, environment, reforestation, agrarian reform, infrastructure development, training, and research.

4. Guidelines for GO-NGO Cooperation and Interaction. There have been several attempts to define the GO-NGO relationship in terms of guidelines and role definition. This has happened even when government and NGOs have been largely suspicious of one another. Today, they have more confidence in each other, and positive, working "critical collaboration" relationships are more the rule than the exception.

5. Exchange of Personnel and Resources. Because of the difference of their perspectives, work styles, sizes, and capabilities of their respective organizations, NGOs and governmental agencies have much to learn from each other. There have been exchanges and enrichment in personnel and resources. Government agencies, especially, learn about the community organizing, social preparation work that is a standard skill among social development NGOs. On the other hand, NGOs learn a lot about financial control and management from government agencies.

6. Consultation Mechanisms. Many consultation mechanisms have become institutionalized, and have been repeated at regular intervals. One such mechanism is the Sta Catalina Forum on decentralization and people empowerment concerns. There are also other fora at different levels, apart from the local special bodies that the Local Government Code mandates.

7. Relationship with Local Governments. NGOs have traditionally served as alternative mechanisms for the delivery of basic services in areas of low government visibility. The complementary role of people's and nongovernmental organizations in local governance is provided for in Sections 34 and 35 of the Local Government Code of 1991:

> Local government units shall promote the establishment and operation of people's and non-government organizations to become active partners in the pursuit of local autonomy (Sec. 34).
>
> Local government units may enter into joint ventures and such other cooperative arrangements with people's and non-governmental organizations to engage in the delivery of certain basic services, capability-building and livelihood projects,

and to develop local enterprises designed to improve productivity and income, diversify agriculture, and spur rural industrialization, promote ecological balance, and enhance the economic and social well-being of the people (Sec. 35).

8. Relationship with Community-Based People's Organizations. Generally, NGOs seek to help others. These are communities, sectors, households, or individuals that may be organized into People's Organizations. Usually NGOs in the rural areas are the ones in direct contact with People's Organizations. City-based NGOs tend to deal more with other NGOs, the private sector, and the government.

9. Relationship with Academe. Many NGOs also have close relationships with academic institutions. Many faculty members and students of the main Philippine universities and colleges (the University of the Philippines, Ateneo, LaSalle) are active in NGOs.

For example, PhilDHRRA's academic and research institution partners include Ateneo de Manila's Human Resource Center, the Institute for Popular Culture, the Asian Institute of Management, the Institute of Agrarian Studies (AST) of the University of the Philippines at Los Baños, and the Mindanao Center for Agrarian Reform and Rural Development.

II. Evolution of the Asia Pacific Regional Community Concept among NGOs

1. Overview

On the whole, Philippine NGOs are local oriented. Only a handful have any international or foreign linkages. This is reflective of the types of domestic concerns they are involved in: community development, local governance, livelihood generation, cultural communities, disaster relief and rehabilitation, and protection and conservation of the environment.

The foreign and international linkages of NGOs are a function of the search for funds, as well as the search for alliances and coalitions in advocating positions on global or international issues such as human rights, the environment, rights of women, labor migration, etc.

There is no particularly strong conception by the NGOs of an Asia Pacific Community, compared to that of the ASEAN, the Southeast Asian, the East Asian, or even the global community. Philippine NGOs have freely shifted from level to level, depending on the problem or issue that is being confronted. Philippine NGOs appear to be equally comfortable in linking with organizations at any of these levels. There is no attempt to limit their conception of region to any one of these.

The Asia Pacific conception of Philippine NGOs may not at all be sophisticated, nor uniform from NGO to NGO. Perhaps what encourages this conception is the increasing interaction with other Asian countries (not part of ASEAN) such as Vietnam and Cambodia, Taiwan, China, Japan, and Korea, and non-Asian countries such as the United States and Canada, which have been important sources of funds, as well as of issues.

The conception of the Asia Pacific region has not been given the attention it deserves among Philippine NGOs. As Jun Wada, Executive Director of the Center for Global Partnership argues:

> One of the most basic issues that requires examination is the definition of the region itself. In an era where the very concepts of regions and regionalism are being reconsidered, is there truly an "Asia Pacific community" that one can point to? While economic integration and interdependence in the region are undeniably strong, is there a community that transcends economic links? If there is a unifying force that bonds these countries, how inclusive and how adaptable is this force?[5]

This issue has largely been ignored so far by Philippine NGOs.

2. Key Factors Influencing NGO Involvement in Promoting the Concept

1. Advances in Transportation and Communication. Advances in transportation and communication may have helped whatever superficial conception of the Asia Pacific region there is among Philippine NGOs. There may have been wider awareness, through satellite television, telephone, and fax facilities, of comparable events in the Asia Pacific region. This is perhaps evident in the newsletters and literature that is available in NGO libraries, such as that of PBSP, the Institute for Strategic and Development Studies (ISDS), PRRM, PhilDHRRA, etc.

It has also been easier to bring together NGO leaders and representatives from Asia Pacific countries for face-to-face meetings, often on short notice. It has allowed NGOs to rotate the hosting of meetings across the Asia Pacific region, giving some tangible survey of and meaning to the region.

2. The Decline of Ideology. The end of the cold war may have encouraged a receptiveness to foreign visitors and influences all around the region. Even China and Vietnam have become favorites, as have the hitherto "remote" Oceania territories. Australia itself has begun to vigorously advocate itself as an Asian nation. These moves have facilitated the networking of NGOs with their counterparts in China, Vietnam, and possibly soon, also Cambodia and Laos.

The international system of the 1990s has truly become hospitable to democratic ferment and civic organizing. Jun Wada notes that

> The NGOs and nonprofit communities are a vital component of the trend towards more pluralistic societies, or what some might call democratization, in Asia. Many countries in the Asia Pacific region have seen an increasing role played by "civil society," as power gradually becomes decentralized and a wider cross-section of citizens participates in addressing domestic and foreign issues. Given the trend, one area that requires particular attention is the encouragement of mechanisms that allow the nongovernmental sector to formulate alternative policy recommendations that can be effectively incorporated into the policy-making process.[6]

3. The Operation of Transnational Enterprises and Organizations. Transnational enterprises have generated interest among NGOs in the Asia Pacific nations. The activities of American, Canadian, Japanese, and European industrial, manufacturing, and service corporations operating in the Philippines presage the activities of their NGO counterparts.

The rise of so-called Growth Triangles in East Asia may serve to develop stronger regional consciousness in the private and people sectors of the nations involved. As economist Dr. George Abonyi observes,

> An important, new related phenomenon is the emergence of subregional economic cooperation among ASEAN countries. This is based not on formal integration among nations, such as NAFTA, but on encouraging limited linkages of complementary economic activities across borders. This need not involve entire countries. Increasingly, adjacent regions within countries that have matching capabilities and resources are lined to form a subregion of economic growth driven by market dynamics. In these groupings, sometimes called "triangles," infrastructure is a critical factor for transforming geographic proximity to economic linkages.[7]

Gonyi also points to the dramatic example of Toyota's integrated ASEAN operations involving Thailand, Malaysia, the Philippines, and Indonesia. This, he says, represents not only a production platform for global exports, but an increasing focus on a Southeast Asian market that is anticipated to double in the next five years. Toyota expects to trade US$100 million among ASEAN affiliates in 1994. Toyota's enterprise in ASEAN is a vivid illustration of the informal, private sector-driven nature of economic integration in Eastern Asia, the central role of investment and transfer of production from East to Southeast Asia and the rapidly growing role of Southeast Asia as a key regional marketplace. Businesses and governments here frame their strategies increasingly in these terms.

Such a ferment may induce greater regional consciousness among NGOs in the region, including those in the Philippines.

In fact, there have been some private sector sponsored international activities in Mindanao to attract attention to the Eastern Growth Triangle, which is the newest proposed subregional economic cooperation zone. The zone links Mindanao (Philippines), Sulawesi (Indonesia), East Malaysia, and Brunei.

The Asian Development Bank also plays a facilitator role in bringing these growth triangles to life, especially the Mekong Subregion, which links Vietnam, Laos, Cambodia, Thailand, and Yunnan province in China. It provides a framework for joint project identification and for mobilizing necessary financial resources.

The orientation of these emerging subregions is outward looking and export-oriented, making increased trade, investment, and development cooperation linkages with countries outside a subregion but within the Asia Pacific region—such as Japan, Canada, the United States, Australia, and South Korea—highly likely.

4. The Prioritization of Global Issues. Global issues such as human rights, the environment, women, migration and refugees, the spread of AIDS, and population growth all pose major challenges to the Asia Pacific region. Widespread concern has induced the formation of linkages of like-minded NGOs across national boundaries in Asia Pacific.

Many experts find it ironical that at a time when the United States and Russia are reducing their arsenals, Asia has become the largest market for arms. The ASEAN Institutes for Strategic and International Studies (ASEAN-ISIS), an NGO accredited with ASEAN, has therefore sponsored confidence-building measures and has focused on security issues in the Asia Pacific region. ISDS is the NGO member for the Philippines. In January 1994, ISDS sponsored a conference on unresolved issues in the ASEAN region. In June 1992, it sponsored an international security conference focusing on the Asia Pacific region.

In the case of women-oriented NGOs, there is a great deal of solidarity across national boundaries. International linkages in Asia Pacific and even beyond are pretty well developed in the women's sector. Such linkages have built up since the generation of international programmatic focus on women's welfare by the International Women's Year (1975), the First Decade of Women (1976–85), and the Second Decade of Women (1986–95). There is a regional action plan that serves as a framework for the programs, projects, and activities of women NGOs in the Asia Pacific region. One of the series of regional conferences in preparation for the Beijing Conference in September 1995 was held in the Philippines.

A great impetus for regional community consciousness among women NGOs has been the fact that women the world over face similar problems. There are experiential links that women suffer as women, efficiently acted on by NGOs because of the few "layers" in their organization unlike the government bureaucracy.

Cultural "faultlines" help reveal commonalities as well as fissures in Asia Pacific orientations. Dr. Sylvia Guerrero of the University of the Philippines' Center for Women Studies, for instance, says that "Western concepts on feminism are tested on Philippine realities."[8]

The same may be said for human rights, where many Asian nations (not so much the Philippines) question the application of universal standards or values.

International conferences focusing on global issues are happening all over the world. Filipino NGOs are represented in many of these conferences. This helps develop global and regional orientations among them. Carolina G. Hernandez, president of ISDS, Horacio Morales, the president of the Philippine Rural Reconstruction Movement and Junie Kalaw of Green Forum, are only three of the many active Filipino participants of such international fora.

5. Governmental Promotion through foreign policy. Governments have sought to create linkages with other Asia Pacific nations, as in the Asia Pacific Economic Council. There have been conscious efforts to build parallel private sector and people sector structures such as PECC, and with respect to the Asian Development Forum, there is the Council for Security Cooperation in the Asia Pacific, involving NGOs.

International agreements and declarations often induce regional NGO action. At the Ministerial Conference on Urbanization in Asia and the Pacific, officials representing thirty-six countries adopted the Bangkok Declaration on Sustainable Urban Development and Management in Asia and the Pacific. The ministers called for the establishment of urban forums to reinforce local authorities and bring in other urban actors such as national governments, local authorities, NGOs and community organizations, the private sector, research institutes, and the media.

6. International Infrastructures for Asia Pacific Regional Cooperation. The operation of international regional organizations like the Economic and Social Commission for Asia and the Pacific (ESCAP) go a long way towards the creation of an Asia Pacific consciousness among governments and NGOs. NGOs and governments seek ways to strengthen cooperation. ESCAP provides the regional coordinating mechanism for intercountry technical cooperation between governments and NGOs. In recent years, ESCAP has closely cooperated with many NGOs in social development concerns in the Asian and Pacific region through regional fora for the exchange of technical views and expertise, research on successful case studies of NGO-government cooperation, and joint convening of national and regional workshops on social development issues.

ESCAP is in a position to integrate the experience of NGOs and government in joint planning, programming, and implementation, in view of its unique role as the only region-wide intergovernmental forum for Asia and the Pacific. Such a consolidated experience will help promote partnerships between NGOs and governments in the region.

Greater ESCAP influence in generating an Asia Pacific consciousness among governments and NGOs seems to be forthcoming. It is being urged to establish a regional network of NGOs and government agencies working in the field of social development, in order to promote the exchange and sharing of national experience, information, and approaches for improved social development policies and programs.

7. Mass Media Interest. Mass media has shown a greater regional interest in its reporting. This has encouraged NGOs to define their work within the larger context of the regional events and conditions. Comparisons of the magnitude of problems and accomplishments are often couched in regional terms.

3. Major Efforts by NGOs and NGO Networks in Enhancing the Concept

1. Networking. NGO coalitions and big NGOs are naturally impelled to seek regional and international linkages. This way, they are able to share resources and insights and gain international reputations. They also get to have a piece of the action, in the implementation of cross-country projects.

As Florencio B. Abad, Executive Director, Union Towards Rural Development and Agrarian Reform said in an ESCAP forum, there is a case for an Asia Pacific NGO community:

> In the last two decades, Asia Pacific NGOs have emerged as major factors in social development efforts. The more successful of them have, in coalition, become legitimate power bases with a substantial grassroots constituency.
>
> In speaking of a development agenda for the year 2000 and beyond, we in the Asia Pacific NGO community must draw on each other's strengths and must continue to be guided by the developmental imperatives that are paramount today in our part of the world. The imperatives of poverty alleviation, of ecological protection, of people empowerment, of peace, and of defense of democratic institutions and human rights.[9]

PhilDHRRA's regional networking is one of the most extensive. PhilDHRRA is a partner of the Center for the Development of Human Resources in Rural Asia (CENDHRRA), along with other DHRRA organizations in Japan, Malaysia, Indonesia, Thailand, and Korea. PhilDHRRA hosted the CENDHRRA Board of Advisers meeting held in June 1992.

Likewise, PhilDHRRA is a network member of ANGOC, which has members in eight countries in Asia and the Pacific. PhilDHRRA participated in the ANGOC-sponsored Asia Development Forum held in Cagayan de Oro City in March 1993.

PhilDHRRA is a member of the Asian-South Pacific Bureau of Adult Education, which promotes people empowerment through education, and likewise of the Innovations et Reseaux pour de Developpement (Development Innovations and Networks).

ISDS maintains a network of linkages with international, regional, national, and local organizations notably ASEAN-ISIS, JCIE, the Seoul Forum for International Affairs, the Asia Australia Institute, Pacific Forum-CSIS, and the Philippine Institute of Strategic Studies.

CODE-NGO continues to forge linkages with development NGOs in developing countries in Asia and sub-Saharan Africa.

In the women sector, Nona Ricafort of the NCWP of the Philippines is the president of the federation of women's groups among ASEAN member states. This Asian Group (of women) meets with its African, American, and European counterparts.

Conferencing is the building block of networking. Joining the conference circuit is a way by which NGOs update themselves on the state of the art in their concerns, as well as get ahead of their competitors. It also allows them greater say in dealing with their respective governments, as well as in acting collectively at the regional level before some regional governmental forum.

2. Conscious Transfer of Technology. NGOs are highly dependent on theoretical and conceptual frameworks and paradigms. They wish to be up-to-date on the latest workable solutions to similar vexing problems like poverty, banking on the pre-entrepreneurial poor, savings mobilization, social marketing, etc.

3. Resource Sharing. NGOs enhance their prestige and marketability by being able to dispense resources generated by other NGOs. Resource sharing as in the establishment and maintenance of databanks and communication networks is the natural way for generating economies of scale, and conserving scarce resources.

4. Policy Advocacy Before International Fora. NGOs are aware that there is strength in unity, and have been careful to adjust their differences and present a common stand before regional and international bodies.

Along this line, FDC in the Philippines assembled NGOs all over the Asia Pacific region to demand the debt-for-nature swap scheme to be adopted by the debt-ridden Third World countries in Asia Pacific.

CODE-NGO and the Green Forum in coordination with the Philippine Development Forum, a network of NGOs advocating Philippine development in the United States, were successful in lobbying for a US$25 million (PhP 597 million) U.S. Congressional allocation for NGO environment initiatives in the Philippines.

CODE-NGO is also cooperating with a group of Swiss NGOs on a "Swiss Debt Relief" program. These Swiss NGOs have successfully lobbied their government for debt relief for the Philippines through a debt-for-development swap scheme.

An example of NGO efforts to forge common orientations and principles on their roles and status as NGOs is the Colombo Statement on People's Empowerment formulated in the Asian Regional Colloquy held in Colombo, Sri Lanka from 7 to 10 July 1992 which sought, among others, to protect and promote Asian cultures and languages, strengthen PO-NGO relationships, promote critical partnership between government and POs/NGOs, promote a new principled partnership with donors, build people's access to information and communication, build and strengthen networking for people empowerment, promote people's institution building and management, promote savings/credit/rural banking and small enterprise development as tools for people's empowerment, promote people's health and education, strengthen advocacy and lobbying.

Philippine NGOs had participated actively in the adoption of a Regional Social

Development Strategy. The strategy is part of the Manila Declaration on a Social Development Strategy for the ESCAP Region Towards the Year 2000 and Beyond. This called attention to "people-centered development" as the crucial factor in dealing with absolute poverty and ensuring distributive justice and popular participation.

5. International Conferencing. NGO leaders are peripatetic. Part of their work is to attend conferences, read papers, report on their work, etc.

The Philippines hosts its share of such conferences. ESCAP organized an NGO/Media Symposium on a Regional Social Development Strategy from 8 to 10 October 1991 in Manila, Philippines. The Government of the Philippines provided the host facilities in cooperation with CODE-NGO. The symposium was attended by 119 representatives from eight media organizations and seventy nongovernmental organizations.

The Manila Declaration on a Social Development Strategy for the ESCAP Region Towards the year 2000 and Beyond was issued in Manila in 1991.

The Asian and Pacific Regional NGO Symposium took place from 16 to 20 November 1993 in Manila, Philippines. Topics discussed included health, labor, agriculture, culture and religion, political empowerment, economic violence, and human rights.

ISDS hosted several international conferences on issues and concerns affecting ASEAN and the Asia Pacific region such as on regional security, human rights, and development of international relations.

ANGOC sponsored the Asia Development Forum (ADF) held in Cagayan de Oro City in March 1993.

The Asian Pacific Regional NGO Conference on Women and Development was held on 16–20 November 1993 in Manila, the Philippines. Topics discussed included health, labor, agriculture, culture and religion, political empowerment, economics, violence, and human rights.

The Philippine Social Science Center hosted the 9th Biennial Conference of the Association of Asian Social Science Research Councils supported by four funding institutions, namely the United Nations Educational, Scientific and Cultural Organization, the Regional Unit for Social and Human Sciences in Asia and the Pacific, the Asian Development Bank, and AIDAB.

PhilDHRRA participated in the ANGOC-sponsored ADF which was held in March 1993, in Cagayan de Oro City, Philippines. ANGOC has members in eight countries in Asia and the Pacific.

Other Asia Pacific focused conferences were:

1988, Bangkok, Thailand: Asia Pacific Call for Action on ESCAP-NGO Cooperation for Economic and Social Development.

14–26 March 1988, Japan: Japanese NGO Center for International Cooperation (JANIC) in cooperation with APPROTECH ASIA sponsored the Second Asian NGO Forum on the theme "The Role of Appropriate Technology in Asian Development." The countries represented were Bangladesh, Indonesia, Sri Lanka, Singapore, Thailand, and the Philippines.

1990, Hong Kong: ESCAP Seminar on Cooperation between Government Agencies and Non-governmental Organizations in the Planning and Delivery of Social Services.

1990, Bangkok, Thailand: NGO/Media Symposium on Communications for Environment.

9–20 July 1991, Japan: A Study Tour on sustainable Agriculture Systems with eight Asian NGO development workers from different countries. Providing the lecture series on Japanese organic farming experts were the Asian Rural Institute and JANIC.

26 Sept.–8 October 1991, Japan: NGO Forum and Field Trip with the theme "People's Participation in Environmentally Sustainable Development." Initiated by APPROTECH ASIA, SEACON and JANIC.

12–13 May 1993, Puncak Pass, West Java, Indonesia: The Canada-ASEAN Centre funded a women in decision-making and leadership meeting, the WE LEAD Meeting.

19–22 August 1993, Jiyunomori-Gakuen, Japan: The First International Federation of Organic Agriculture Movements Asian Conference on organic farming and agriculture. Over forty participants attended the conference.

23–27 August 1993, Singapore: Asia Pacific Regional Conference of the International Council on Social Welfare with the theme family and social development.

1994, Bangkok, Thailand: The Global Forum for Women and the Center for Asia and the Pacific Women conducted Asian and Pacific Leadership Training attended by legislators, local government officials, and NGO leaders. The centerpiece of the training was a simulation game called "Budget-Crisis." Also the promotion of women's effective political leadership.

12–19 February 1994, Sukhothai University, Thailand: Women Empowering Communication. To reassess media-related strategies adopted to protect and increase women's participation in the civil society.

7–14 June 1994, Jakarta, Indonesia: The Second Asian Pacific Conference on Women in Development.

July 1994, The Commonwealth of the Northern Marianas: Sixth Regional Conference of Pacific Women to assess the social, political and economic status of women.

4–15 September 1995, Beijing, China: 4th World Conference on Women: Equality, Development and Peace.

6. Joint Action Projects. The significance, validity, and success of projects is often better appreciated when implemented in similar or different environments. This has induced NGOs to look for cross-national implementation of projects, often with a sponsor or cooperator with region-wide interest or orientation.

7. Cross-Visits and Publications. As part of their documentation, monitoring, and marketing activities, NGOs are very active in research and publications. These publications are usually distributed and exchanged widely across the region. This action may naturally define a region, with its contours dictated by communication and mail costs.

The Philippine Development NGOs for International Concerns publicizes the work of Philippine NGOs abroad. PhilDHRRA is among its members.

4. Public Sector-NGO Promotion of Regional Consciousness

1. GO-NGO Consultations on Regional Issues and Problems. Many regional problems and issues concern both government agencies and nongovernmental organizations. Consultations are initiated with the other side for policy and implementation and problem-solving action in the following issue areas—migrant labor, human rights, the environment, women's rights.

2. Parallel Diplomacy. Nongovernmental organizations often have regional networks that parallel governmental networks. These NGO networks often discuss and arrive at tentative agreements on the same issues and problems dealt with by government. As such, they help define feasible and potential points of agreement or consensus.

3. Joint Regional and International Representation. Often, the governmental and the NGO regional networks consciously seek nongovernmental and governmental representation, respectively, in their activities. Representatives from government and NGOs in effect jointly represent the same country in international and regional fora and activities.

5. Role of NGOs to Further Advance the Regional Community Concept

1. Advocacy and Public Awareness Campaign. The concept of an Asia Pacific region can be strengthened by increasing the international component in the public awareness campaign of NGOs. There must be an effort to put local Philippine problems being dealt with by NGOs in the context of the overall Asia Pacific context, or at least in a comparable foreign country situation.

2. Parallel and Deepening Regional Cooperation Strategies. There must be efforts to start joint projects and deeper involvements beyond conferencing and exchange of reports and points of view. There should be more exchanges that require the pooling of resources and attainment of regionwide objectives.

These efforts may begin at the more proximate regional grouping—ASEAN, which is likewise admittedly low in Philippine NGO focus.

3. Asia Pacific Regional Cooperation Visioning. Apart from solving immediate problems found in their respective societies, there must be some effort and resources that are devoted to long term visioning for the Asia Pacific region. This must be an activity that many or most NGOs must be able to participate in, rather than merely receiving visions second or third hand. Visioning has a regional consciousness-raising value.

4. Benchmarking Overall Regional Cooperation Efforts. A conscious design of monitoring and evaluation indicators for NGO contribution to Asia Pacific regional cooperation is necessary. There must be a conscious attempt to measure progress towards regional consciousness raising. Regional awareness must be accepted as a positive characteristic of all NGOs. Local NGOs need not be parochial.

5. Media. NGOs must be able to project themselves better in the media. They must project themselves and their national and international linkages.

6. Regional Cooperation Impact Statements. One way to induce regional awareness is to encourage NGOs through appropriate incentives to draw up statements of the impact of their key projects on Asia Pacific regional cooperation. This can be in terms of the methodology, or the substantive impact of the project, directly or indirectly, on the region.

7. Regionalizing NGOs. Another way is to identify NGOs on the threshold of international cooperation and assist them in making the transition. Some NGOs are more internationalist than others. There must be a conscious attempt to help NGOs who are developing a more international and regional orientation to make the transition smoothly. There must be, for instance, a new faces program that introduces younger representatives from newer NGOs to participate in conferences and workshops. The well-established NGOs should be able to cut in the new ones in the various conference circuits that are in existence.

6. Major Constraints against NGO Regional Cooperative Efforts

1. Focus on Domestic Concerns. The main constraint is that NGOs are focused on domestic concerns. They have always been this way. It will take tremendous effort to break them from this orientation.

2. Low Regional and International Exposure. Due to a lack of experience in regional and international linkages, many NGOs will consider operation at this level daunting.

3. Lack of Organizational Capacity. To begin with, many NGOs have no resources to spare for regional and international activities. Overseas communications and travel, while already easy and cheap, would still be beyond the capacity of the small NGOs.

4. Lack of Long-Term Organizational Strategies. Many NGOs are barely surviving. They do not have long term strategies. International and regional networking or concerns are definitely out of the question.

5. High Personnel Turn-over. There is high personnel turn-over. Encouraging international and regional linkages are investments that may be difficult to make for staffers, under such adverse personnel conditions.

6. Government Constraints. Some countries are liberal with their NGOs; others are not. It is difficult to deal with human rights NGOs, for instance, in authoritarian countries.

In another sense, excessive passion in NGO advocacy of their positions on issues becomes a "weakness" in forging international linkages, especially when these links are established through governmental channels, because "controversial" NGOs tend to be by-passed by the government.

7. NGO rivalries and parochial orientations. NGOs look at international and regional linkages as opportunities that they would not want to share with rival NGOs.

8. Lack of comprehensive information on the NGO world. Often, it is difficult to link with counterpart NGOs, because information about them and the NGO world in general is not available. In the Philippines, the NGO world is relatively unmapped, and many Philippine NGOs have yet to be networked.

7. Some Measures to Further Enhance the Above Efforts

Some measures that can be considered to further the development of an Asia Pacific consciousness are:

1. Long-Term Programming. Government, NGO networks, and other funding agencies must develop a long term Asia Pacific oriented program. The program should aim for, among other things, greater cross-border exposure for NGO leaders and members, expansion of computer-based cross-border communications networking, and wider tri-media coverage of regional and international Asia Pacific NGO cooperation projects and activities.

2. Specific Fund Facilities. The long-term program must be adequately supported by financial resources. If the development of an Asia Pacific consciousness among Philippine NGOs is important, such must be manifested by the allocation of governmental or donor resources. In other words, we must put our money where our mouth is.

Notes

1. David Korten, *Getting to the 21st Century: Voluntary Action and the Global Agenda* (Kumarian Press, Inc., 1990), p. 2.
2. Fernando T. Aldaba, "CODE-NGO: Unifying the Development NGO Community" in *Development NGO Journal* (Quezon City: Caucus of Development NGO Networks, 1992), p. 1.
3. International Monetary Fund. *International Financial Statistics,* January 1995 (Washington, D.C.: IMF, 1995). Figures given are based on end of the period exchange rates for November 1994. US$1 = C$1.38.
4. Ibid. US$1 = PhP 23.88.
5. Jun Wada, "Director's Message: The Asia Pacific in Transition" in *Center for Global Partnership (CGP) Newsletter,* Volume 3 (New York: CGP, winter 1994), p. 1.
6. Ibid., p. 5.
7. Dr. Georg Abonyi, "Southeast Asia as a Region of Subregions—The Growth Triangles" in *Rapport Quarterly* (Singapore: Canadian—ASEAN Centre, January 1994), p. 7.
8. Dr. Sylvia Guerrero, Pananaw. Quezon City. University Center for Women's Studies, University of the Philippines. September 1990, p. 16.
9. Florencio B. Abad, "Union Towards Rural Development," Keynote Address on NGO/Media Symposium held at the PICC, Manila on 8 October 1991. *Social Development Newsletter.* December 1991. No. 25, p. 11, 12.

SINGAPORE

Nongovernmental Organizations in Singapore

Chan Tse Chueen
Research and Administration Officer
ENGENDER

This report is intended to be a blanket survey of NGOs, *including* independent philanthropic foundations and corporate philanthropic activities, and the points raised apply to them as well. Issues more pertinent to philanthropy are discussed in *Philanthropic Organizations and Corporate Philanthropy in Singapore*, in the philanthropy volume of the *Survey of Nongovernmental Underpinnings of the Emerging Asia Pacific Regional Community*.

I. Narrative Report

1. Overview of NGO Sector

A few notes on the usage of the term *NGO* are necessary. As several writers have pointed out, not only are there discrepancies in many common understandings of the term, even official definitions vary.[1] The World Bank, however, defines NGOs as "all nonprofit organizations with private membership which provide development assistance". This broad definition would effectively include, as Tan & Singh[2] noted, "private foundations, lay and religious aid associations, NGO cooperatives and credit unions", among others. With this as the working definition, the following is a sketch of the NGO sector in Singapore.

1) Evolution of nongovernmental organizations

NGOs have their roots in traditional groupings that preceded the establishment of the state. In Singapore they came in the form of mutual help groups such as clan associations based on surnames, language and provincial origin; numerous others were based on occupation, ethnicity and religious affiliation, and included recreational clubs and school alumni associations. Examples of such earlier groups include the *Raffles Old Girls' Association, Young Women's Christian Association* and the *Singapore Cantonese Women Mutual Help Association.* In modern guises, they appear as registered mutual benefit organizations and cooperative societies, business and professional networks, as well as recreational and hobby clubs.

But recent times have seen the emergence of a type of association that is substantially different from the various permutations of the mutual help group. This process is in large part engendered by formal and mass education. With the rise of the state came civic groups which dared to have their own vision of a better society. They are issue oriented, and although their target group is invariably the community, their aims differ from other community service and welfare organizations in that they aim to "be catalytic agents for change through their involvement, education and mobilisation of people to improve their circumstances".[3] This change comes about not through a one-off act of charity but through the implementation of processes that emphasize the autonomy of individuals and/or communities. Research, education and consciousness-raising are important features of their work. Calling these groups developmental NGOs, Lim[4] describes them thus:

> ...although the organisations might focus on single issues, for example, consumer problems or environmental degradation, unlike the traditional single issue organisations such as trade unions or youth associations, they see their work as explicitly situated in the context of a wider concern for progressive social development and change in the society.

The formation of the Association of Women for Action and Research (AWARE), Nature Society and the Young Women's Muslim Association at different points in Singapore's history is part of this movement that saw a change in orientation of nongovernmental groups.

The relevance of developmental NGOs must be seen in the context of increasing cooperation between the nations in the Asia Pacific region. The formation of APEC, ASEAN, as well as international nongovernmental organizations such as the Pacific Trade and Development Conference, Pacific Basin Economic Council and the Pacific Economic Cooperation Council arise out of, and encourage, such cooperation. Attention is focused on the Asia Pacific region as the next economic powerhouse following the decline of matured economies in Europe and North America. Evidently, the importance of these developmental NGOs in the promotion of a sense of community in the Asia Pacific region lies in the fact that often, in recognition of the transnational consequences of many development projects in the region, these NGOs forge regional links in the pursuit of common solutions.

2) Overall Government–NGO relations—The view of the government

The Singapore state has a highly centralized power structure, with an array of super-efficient bureaucratic arms. Coupled with the government's good management skills and relatively clean slate where corruption is concerned, the stage is set for rather ambiguous relations between the government and the NGOs.

First of all, the legal requirements for the setting up of an NGO in Singapore is worth taking note of. An NGO could be registered under the Societies Act, Mutual Benefits Organizations Act, Cooperative Societies Act, Charities Act or the Companies Act, depending on its legal entity. An NGO which registers itself as a nonprofit company is not accorded any special tax status, unless it is registered as a foundation, that is, a grant-making institution for charitable purposes. The foundation is a public trust where, once it is approved of as a charitable organization, the income of the foundation is tax-free provided eighty per cent of the income is donated in the following year. The implications for regional cooperation within these legalities will be examined in the following sections where appropriate.

The term *NGO* is still very much outside an average Singaporean's vocabulary. Even among those working in organizations that could conceivably be termed as NGOs, a reference to the term sometimes draws blank stares. More often than not, they are described as welfare and social services, charities, societies, voluntary organizations and, more recently, civic groups. This unfamiliarity with the term and with what it means in many other parts of the world is telling for its implications on the political and social climate in Singapore.

The government is adamant in its insistence that any group wishing to have a political voice by way of making commentary on policies should be prepared to join a political party and thereby make its opinions accountable to the general public/electorate. There is precious little political space, outside those official channels sanctioned by the government, available for the general public. The government is impatient with groups that allegedly engage in politically subversive activities in the guise of groups other than political parties. An extreme example occurred in 1987 when sixteen members of a Catholic church group were detained by the Singapore government under the Internal Security Act for propagating Marxist ideas under the guise of welfare activities.

Although there will inevitably be tension in the relations between NGOs and the government, given the structure and perceived role of both sides, it would be foolish to write off that relationship as always confrontational. In the following section on the role of NGOs in society, this relationship will be further explored.

3) Role of NGOs in society—The view of the NGOs

In his paper on NGOs in ASEAN, Lim (1988) was explicit in the many ways that NGOs can and do frequently contribute to the development of a healthy society.[5]

a. Monitoring of the State

NGOs are in a privileged position to engage in the monitoring of the state and its various bureaucratic arms. Indeed, NGOs are often severe critics of government policies as well as the bureaucratic process. The *Nature Society* for example was able to exert some pressure on the government, forcing it to reconsider its development projects. (See section II for more details, under "Nature Society".) With such exercises, NGOs seek to hold the government accountable, and as much as possible check any abuse of power.

b. Channels for alternative visions—Rethinking Development

NGOs can also act as channels through which alternative viewpoints can be heard. In an era of uncertainty spliced with ecological disasters and the time bombs of social disintegration, nobody can hope to be right all of the time. Plurality of views would seem to be the surer path to survival. The general intolerance of the Singapore government of alternative viewpoints has made NGOs wary of getting their knuckles rapped. This unfortunately becomes for the government a means of effective policing, of the NGOs as well as the population at large, through the creation of an imaginary ever-present gaze of the authorities.

On the other hand, these various restrictive controls have also forced NGOs to be more ingenious and creative in their approach to sidestep the trouble spots. Although reluctant to release control, the government nevertheless is not all pervasive in every sphere of life, and there are always loopholes.

c. Information disseminator

Many NGOs, though small and with only limited resources, have managed to harness a great deal of information and knowledge about their chosen areas of expertise. In this role as an educator, solid research and data collection would prove to be helpful. In Singapore, many NGOs organize forums and seminars to reach out to the public, as well as conduct training workshops stressing above all the principles of self-reliance. The NGOs are not only good facilitators of feedback from the grassroots to the policy makers, their research and efforts in trend analysis are often also useful to the government.

2. Evolution of the Asia Pacific Regional Concept among NGOs

1) Key factors influencing NGOs' involvement in promoting the concept

The increasing trend towards economic regionalization in Asia Pacific, for example through trade blocs such as ASEAN and APEC, as well as the many environmental and social problems that are transnational in nature, have led to the necessity of NGOs working at the regional level in order effectively to address these problems.

Some small-scale NGOs find it difficult to manage regional activities simply because it is too expensive. Many grassroots level NGOs are content, therefore, to work within a designated area of influence, so that their resources are not spread too thin. This is partly an erroneous impression because NGOs can be both small-scale *and* regional.

Scarcity of resources is another factor that would prompt NGOs to network and pool together knowledge and expertise. Rather than fighting for the limited pools of funds and human resources, it would make better sense for the NGOs to be working *with* instead of against one another; hence the advantage of forming regional networks.

2) Major efforts by NGOs and NGO networks in enhancing the concept

A survey on the roles, objectives and activities of the ASEAN NGOs by Saravanamuttu & Ahmat[6] revealed that, of the twenty-five affiliated and twenty-five non-affiliated organizations which qualify as ASEAN regional organizations, all but a handful are primarily commercial, industrial and professional organizations. Closer to home, a check through the last four issues of the *Convention/Exhibition Calendar Singapore* shows that almost all the conferences and exhibitions held in Singapore in the past two years, though regional, are of the nature of economic and professional associations.[7] Two typical examples are:

- *Singapore International Conference on Communications Systems*, organized by Institute of Electrical and Electronics Engineers;

- *World Aviation Forum,* organized by the Singapore Aviation Academy of the Civil Aviation Authority of Singapore.

Research and academic exchange is another area where regional cooperation is apparent. Aside from those conferences and seminars organized by official academic institutions in Singapore, independent organizations involved frequently in these activities include the Institute of Southeast Asian Studies and the Information and Resource Centre.

3) Interaction between the public sector and NGOs in the above efforts

In recent years, the government has increasingly recognized the expertise that NGOs possess and have more frequently called upon their professional advice, for example as input into policy making. This is one area of NGO activity that has received some support from the government, and this unquestionably contributes to increased interaction between the NGOs.

3. Future Prospects

1) Role of NGOs in further advancing the concept of the regional community

Both the governments and the private sector in the Asia Pacific region have done much to promote the concept of the regional community, as can be seen by the many governmental and nongovernmental regional organizations. But they are primarily concerned with regional cooperation with regards to issues of economic development and national security, and only secondarily so with development that is sustainable and equitable. The lack of such efforts creates the need for it; NGOs, especially development NGOs, would seem to be eminently qualified to fill that need.

Another area that can increase regional cooperation is the further promotion of voluntary work abroad through the direct transfer of skills and technical know-how to countries where such expertise are needed.

The education of the public about the importance of regional cooperation, above and beyond the economic rationale, is yet another strategy in promoting such co-operation.

2) Major constraints against NGO regional cooperative efforts

There is a clause under the Societies Act that specifies that any association that is political in nature must restrict its membership to the citizens of Singapore, and must not have such affiliation or connection outside Singapore as is considered by the Registrar to be contrary to national interest.[8] Though not unusual a restriction in view of the fact that Singapore is a nation state, this restriction nevertheless does hamper regional cooperation.

For any NGO to even survive, the availability of funds is an important consideration. Therefore, first and foremost, grant-making institutions should be sensitive to the needs of NGOs. Not only should project funding be made available to NGOs, but also programme funding that is essential for the day-to-day running of the organizations. This is especially so for Singapore as overheads are significantly higher than other countries in the region.

3) Some measures to further enhance the above efforts

Increasingly governments are working on closer regional cooperation. Likewise, NGOs should cooperate with the government in order to make an input into the decisions and issues of concern at the regional level.

Funding agencies should make resources available to NGOs in order to enhance their networking, through activities such as the organization of regional workshops based on common issues of concern.

II. Description of Major NGOs

1. Current Structure of the NGO Sector in Singapore

The list of registered societies in Singapore, as on 1st April 1994, totalled 4,562[9] the bulk of which are the 296 registered mutual benefits organizations and 74 registered cooperative societies. Apart from these, there are NGOs registered as companies but which operate with a nonprofit philosophy, and others registered as charitable trust funds.

An overview of the NGO sector in Singapore would require a framework for classification. Here, the categorization used by Tan & Singh[10] is useful in its appropriateness to the Singapore situation. A distinction is made between state NGOs and private NGOs:

1) State NGOs (GONGO)

These are voluntary organizations that are largely managed by people at the grassroots and community level, but which are at the same time conduits of government policy and are located within the state bureaucracy. Their establishment was usually initiated by the government and they generally have easy access to human and financial resources provided by the government. Although the extent of ministerial control varies, these state NGOs are largely coopted by the government and are part and parcel of the state machinery. For this reason, they will not be the focus of this survey.

Some examples in Singapore include:

- the community self-help groups that were set up along official ethnic lines; such as Singapore Indian Development Association, Chinese Development Assistance Council and Council for the Development of Singapore Muslim Community (Yayasan MENDAKI);
- Organizations affiliated to the National Council of Social Services that are welfare organizations such as the Diabetic Society of Singapore, Society for Aid to the Paralyzed, and Home Nursing Foundation; and
- Professional associations like Singapore Professional Centre, Singapore Nurses Association, and Singapore Cancer Society

2) Autonomous NGOs

Autonomous NGOs are the various voluntary associations and societies that were not initiated by the government but by groups of individuals for a specific aim or cause. They may, however, have at some point received financial and technical support from the government. Adopting the classification of Tan & Singh,[11] these organizations may be categorized as follows:

- community-based
- community service
- worker–employer oriented
- women
- youth
- professional

However, this classification by target audience lumps together NGOs with very different aims and methodologies, which are sometimes more important in defining their roles in society.[12] One way would be to differentiate developmental NGOs from other community service and welfare organizations. Consequently, in the description of major NGOs in the following section, my focus is on autonomous developmental NGOs that are issue and research oriented, simply because their potential impact is greater.

2. Description of Major NGOs

In selecting NGOs to include under this heading, the criteria adopted were that they are:

- at least national level NGOs
- development and issue-oriented NGOs
- inclined to regional/international activities

1) Asian Mass Communication Research & Information Centre

Address: 39 Newton Road, Singapore 1130

Tel: 251-5106 *Fax:* 253-4535

Contact person: Vijay Menon, Secretary General

The Asian Mass Communication Research and Information Centre recently coorganized a Seminar on Environmental Television Programmes for Children with the Goethe Institute-Singapore. The Seminar brought together international experts, media practitioners and academics to discuss how environmental messages can be incorporated into children's films and television programmes

2) Association of Muslim Professionals (AMP)

Address: 25 Jalan Tembusu, Singapore 1543

Tel: 346 0911

Contact person: The President

Founded in 1990, AMP aims to play a leading role in the development and long-term transformation of Malay Muslim Singaporeans into a dynamic community, taking pride and place in a larger Singapore society.

Its objectives are the mobilization of Malay Muslim professionals in the formation of a dynamic community; the maintenance of nonpartisanship and independence; as well as in the promotion of education and social action backed by research and training.

3) Association of Women for Action and Research (AWARE)

Address: 64A Race Course Road, Singapore 0821
Tel: 293-5868 *Fax:* 293-6257

Contact person: President, Ms Constance Singam

AWARE is a voluntary women's organization founded in 1985. It is an organization of women working for women. Central to the work of AWARE is the belief that every woman occupies an important place in society and should, therefore, be given the opportunity to maximize her potential. The objective of AWARE is to promote the full participation of women in all areas of social life, through the provision of equal opportunities for both men and women.

AWARE has three broad areas of activity: a women's centre and helpline; research and publications; and public education. Through these activities, AWARE hopes to raise awareness about gender inequalities and works towards eradicating biases arising from such inequalities.

4) Baha'i Office of the Environment

Address: 4 Cooling Close, Singapore 1955

Tel: 441-4592 *Fax:* 441-4592
Contact person: Lynette Thomas
Sub-Committee of the Spiritual Assembly of the Baha'is of Singapore Ltd

Founded in 1991, its objectives are:

- to assist in endeavours to conserve the environment of Singapore;
- to raise the level of environmental awareness among the members of the Baha'i community and the general public in Singapore; and
- to work with both governmental and nongovernmental organizations with a view to sharing information and collaborating on projects to help conserve the environment.

Baha'i view the protection and preservation of the environment in the broadest possible sense linking it to such widely divergent issues as:

- equality of men and women
- world peace and world unity
- abolition of prejudice of all kinds
- universal education
- universal economic sufficiency and the harmony of science and religion

The Baha'i approach to environmental preservation is holistic and integrated. It is based on a new vision for humanity and the natural environment that emphasises spiritual values, unity of effort and the establishment of self-sustaining, ever advancing civilization. The Baha'i commitment to environmental conservation and the maintenance of ecological systems is fundamental.

Since 1990, when the Baha'i Community launched the Arts for Nature exhibition, the Baha'is have been actively involved in efforts to increase public awareness of the need to conserve our environment, and have contributed towards conservation efforts in Singapore. Activities include:

1990: The Arts for Nature: an exhibition of artworks by local artists on the theme of nature. Fourty percent of the proceeds from the sale of the artworks and catalogues was donated to the WWF's Save the Turtles campaign;

1990: Flame of the Forest concert to raise funds for Nature Society;

1990: representation at the ESCAP conference on Environment and Development in Bangkok;

1991: representation at the Women and the Environment conference in Bangkok;

1991: The Banner Project: a display of over eighty banners on the environmental theme by Singapore schools along the Singapore River. A group banner was also painted by children from three different schools as an example of cooperative work;

1991: representation at the Global NGO Conference on Environment and Development in Paris;

1992: collection of about four thousand signatures in support of the Earth Pledge Project; and

1992: accreditation to UNCED; representation at the Earth Summit in Brazil. It was also an active contributor to Rescue Mission Alert, the Children's Education section of the Agenda 21 programme arising from UNCED.

Ongoing Activities: Beach clean-up. The West Coast Park and Beach is the site of regular clean-up activities organized by the Baha'i community. November 1992 marked the official adoption of the beach and park by the Baha'is.

Other activities include:

- consultation with other organizations;
- environmental activity classes for children;
- collaborating with other government and nongovernmental organizations; and
- participation in local, regional and global seminars on environmental issues.

5) *Development of Economy for Women (D.E.W.) Cooperative Credit Union Ltd*

Address: Raffles City P.O. Box 1316, Singapore 9117
Tel: 339 8600 *Fax:* 339 3356
Contact person:
D.E.W. Cooperative Credit Union was established in 1981 with the aim of providing women with the knowledge and opportunities to gain economic independence through money management. With that crucial aim in mind, D.E.W. set about helping women to help themselves as the major first step towards social and economic independence. D.E.W. consists of a group of women who regularly save together and lend to one another from savings at a reasonable rate of interest decided by the members, thus assisting one another through mutual cooperation. The cooperative is owned and controlled by its members. Each member is a shareholder entitled to one vote irrespective of the amount invested or saved. D.E.W. provides its members ordinary and special loans between S$100 to $100,000 (US$68.49 to $68,490),[13] depending on the income of the borrower.

6) *ENGENDER (Centre for Environment, Gender and Development)*

Address: 14C Trengganu Street, Singapore 0105
Tel: 227-1439 *Fax:* 227-7897
Contact person: Dr Vivienne Wee, Programme Director
ENGENDER is an autonomous regional organization engaged in innovative thinking on environment, development and gender issues. Formed in 1992, Engender sees itself positioned at a crucial stage in development history and in a geographical hinterland that is undergoing tremendous social, economic and political change. This climate has produced heightened interest in reviewing alternatives to current development strategies, aimed in a way to prevent mistakes of past development models. Of particular focus are the issues of equity and sustainability in the context of the alarmingly fast rate of resource consumption. Since neither the natural environment nor economic development are static entities enclosed within national boundaries, Engender has, as its broad focus, the environmental, gender and social impact of development processes in the Asian and Pacific region.

ENGENDER's activities include various programmes and projects leading up to the Fourth World Conference on Women. It has been involved in:

- the coordination of workshops on "Women, Environment and Development" at the Asian and Pacific Symposium of Nongovernmental Organizations on

Women in Development (15–20 November 1993, Manila), the first regional NGO preparation for the World Conference on Women;

- collaboration with the Gender and Development Programme of APDC in preparing a "think-piece" on "Gender, Poverty, and Sustainable Development", commissioned by UNDP to be launched at the Conference;
- participation in the GONGO Regional Workshop on "Women, Economics, and Sustainable Development" (26–29 April 1994, Singapore) in preparation for the World Conference.

ENGENDER is also working on the infusion of environmentally and socially sensitive input into the business planning of the private sector, particularly in setting up sustainable living habitats for the working population in new development zones.

ENGENDER's other projects are focused on the development of sustainable livelihoods. These include a poverty alleviation programme "Towards a Women's Skills and Resources Bank", as well as a craft programme intended to organize village craft communities through innovative intervillage cooperation and comprehensive marketing strategies.

ENGENDER was also involved in coordinating a Gender, Health and Sustainable Development Workshop in January 1995.

It is the secretariat of a new initiative, WEDNET Asia Pacific, which is a regional research and action network on Women, Environment and Development, focusing on women's indigenous knowledge of the environment.

7) Environmental Forum for Communicators of Singapore (ECOS)

Address: c/o Singapore National Union of Journalists
Times House, 390 Kim Seng Road, Singapore 0923
Tel: 730-5375 *Fax:* 732 0131
Contact person: Ivan Lim, General Secretary

Founded in September 1993, ECOS' objectives are to raise awareness among communications personnel in Singapore so that through their work, the awareness of the public concerning environmental issues will also be heightened. Nature treks, study tours, a photographic competition and exhibition, publication of a magazine, further seminars, workshops, lectures and film shows, are among its planned future activities. So far, it has organized a neighbourhood nature watch programme for residents of Macpherson Housing Estate. It also recently co-organized a seminar, "Urbanization, Sustainable Development, and the Media", with the National

Council on the Environment and the Asian Mass Communication Research and Information Centre.

8) Information and Resource Centre (IRC)

Address: 6 Nassim Road, Singapore 1025
Tel: 734 9600 *Fax:* 733 6217
Contact person: Executive Director, M Rajaretnam.
Established in 1985 and based in Singapore, the IRC is conceived of as a regional catalyst institution in the definition of its objectives, the materialization of its research and educational programmes, and the networking in human resources. The Centre was set up to undertake work at three broad levels: as an advanced research institution specialized in the study of strategic, topical, and prospective issues related to peace and stability in the region; as a policy-oriented institution promoting relevant rational alternatives for decision-makers for the betterment of national societies and regional cooperative environment; and as a human resource centre capable of mobilizing an important network of experts in the region.

The programme of activities of the IRC includes research focusing on sensitive issues of national and international concerns, which affect the evolution of the nations in the Asia Pacific region, as well as the future of the region as a whole; the organization of discussions and debates between academics, government bodies, and military establishments through its "Asia Pacific Forum" lecture series; initiation of various human resource development programmes; development of a specific programme of publications which focuses on strategic and prospective issues in the Asia Pacific region; and the provision of consultancy services such as feasibility studies on various economic sectors to the business communities within and outside the region.

9) Institute of Policy Studies (IPS)

Address: Honsui Sen Memorial Library Building, NUS, Kent Ridge Drive, Singapore 0511
Tel: 779 2633 *Fax:* 777 0700
Contact person: Professor Tommy Koh
The IPS was set up in December 1987 as the Republic's pioneer think-tank. It brings together concerned minds to promote discussion, research and dialogue on multifaceted issues relating to Singapore's political, economic, social, cultural and his-

torical heritage.

Its many programme activities include:

- an occasional paper series which provides a forum for constructive views of different persuasions to be discussed;
- funding policy-oriented projects; and
- undertaking the publication of research projects directly relevant to Singapore's past, present, and future.

10) Institute of Southeast Asian Studies (ISEAS)

Address: Heng Mui Keng Terrace, Pasir Panjang, Singapore 0511

Tel: 778 0955 *Fax:* 775 6264

Contact person: Professor Chan Heng Chee

ISEAS was established as an autonomous organization in 1968. It is a regional research centre for scholars and other specialists concerned with modern Southeast Asia and its wider geostrategic environment.

The Institute's aim is to nurture a community of scholars interested in the region and to engage in research on the multifaceted problems of stability and security, economic development and political and social change.

ISEAS seeks to stimulate thinking on and the exploration of solutions to some of the major salient issues in the region. In a world increasingly dominated by the forces of globalization and regionalization, networking has become an imperative. The Institute is now strategically placed to assist scholars in this networking process by serving as a centre that provides a congenial and stimulating intellectual environment, encouraging the fullest interaction and exchange of ideas.

To achieve these aims, the Institute conducts a range of research programmes; holds conferences, workshops, lectures and seminars; publishes research journals and books; and generally provides a range of research support facilities, including a large library collection.

11) National Council on the Environment

Address: Environment Building, 11th Floor, 40 Scotts Road, Singapore 0922

Tel: 731-9862 *Fax:* 235-6601

Contact person: Ms Kirtida Mekani, Executive Director

Founded in 1990, the Counil's aims and activities are:

- to educate, inspire and assist individuals, business organizations, and environ-

mental groups to care for and protect the environment;
- to promote greater public awareness and interest in environmental issues and seek public cooperation in protecting and improving the environment; and
- to involve business leaders in a pro-active process of environmental management.
- to organize public lectures by local and international speakers.

This includes forums, seminars and workshops, such as environmental auditing for the business community, and seminars on environmental education for educators in primary and secondary schools. Efforts to work with schools, green organizations and the corporate sector to promote consciousness and action on the environment include the following:
- joint production of an environmental audit handbook for industry, together with the Ministry of Environment, a source book for primary schoolteachers, *Greening Our Young Minds*, with the Ministry of Education; and a quarterly newsletter *elements* ;
- coordination of a programme for the promotion of environmental auditing;
- a nation-wide survey on consumer attitudes to help develop strategies for promoting environmentally-friendly products;
- the planning of a "Great Garbage Seminar" where the reduction of Singapore's garbage volume will be discussed; and
- organization of a biodiversity seminar to educate the public on our natural heritage.

12) Nature Society, Singapore

Address: Sims Drive, #04-04 Pan Island Complex Singapore 1438
Tel: 741-2036 *Fax:* 741-0871
Contact person: Ms Evelyn Eng-Lim, Executive Honorary Secretary

Founded in 1954 as the Malayan Nature Society (Singapore Branch), formal separation from the Malaysian parent organization took place in 1991. It is the only society in Singapore involved in nature and wildlife conservation. Run by volunteers, this nonprofit organization sets out to promote an interest in the natural history of this region and the appreciation of and care for Singapore's natural heritage.

The organization's programmes include monthly talks and walks, field expeditions at home and abroad, research projects and surveys, seminars and forums. The society publishes and co-publishes periodicals, leaflets and books, including its own monthly newsletter *Nature News* and quarterly magazine *Nature Watch.*

The Nature Society's major achievements are:

- the birds sub-group's conservation proposals for wetland bird areas submitted to the government between 1983 and 1990 resulted in the securing of certain areas for conservation, such as Sungei Buloh Bird Sanctuary;
- a masterplan for the Conservation of Nature in Singapore was presented to the government in 1990;
- a conservation proposal for Pulau Ubin island was submitted to the government; and
- a research report entitled, *Proposed Golf Course at Lower Pierce Reservoir—Environmental Impact Assessment in 1992*, opposing the development of a golf course, was also presented to the government.

Current projects include:

- a report on Singapore's endangered plants and animals, commissioned by Asia Pacific Breweries;
- a study of ways to increase the biodiversity of local parks and waterbodies;
- a study of the potential of ecotourism in Singapore and the provision of allied programmes and literature;
- a coral reef rescue project involving relocation of coral reefs; and
- a survey of Pulau Ubin island, and a census of flora and fauna in remaining nature areas.

13) Singapore Action Group of Elders (SAGE)

Address: 19 Toa Payoh West Singapore 1231
Tel: 353-7159 / 292-8663 *Fax:* 353-7148
Contact person: Executive Director

Founded in 1977, the main aims of SAGE are to initiate and organize meaningful programmes, services and activities which provide support, both physical and psychological, to old people. Its programmes include counselling services for the elderly; an employment service; recreational activities for the elderly; local excursions and overseas tours; the organization of local seminars, talks, and international conferences; and the initiation and organization of national campaigns on issues affecting the elderly.

14) Singapore International Chamber of Commerce (SICC)

Address: 50 Raffles Place #03-02 Shell Tower Singapore 0104
Tel: 224-1255 *Fax:* 224-2785
Contact person: Executive Director

Established in 1837, it is the oldest private sector representative organization in the Republic. Its membership is open to companies and individuals of all races and nationalities, as long as they have a place of business in Singapore. Currently forty-five nationalities are represented in the Chamber. These include multinational corproations with operations in Singapore and locally-owned business enterprises. The SICC protects and promotes the business interests of members; maintains constant dialogue with the government; maintains regular contacts with trade organizations around the world; comments on draft legislation, and trading and industrial procedures, when invited by the government; nominates representatives to advisory committees and statutory boards; and assists members in their dealings with official organizations. It also provides a business information service, runs talks and seminars, as well as providing other professional services.

15) Singapore International Foundation (SIF)

Address: 111 Somerset Road, PUB Building #11-07, Singapore 0923
Tel: 738 5955 *Fax:* 738 5234
Contact person: Executive Director, Professor Chan Heng Chee

Founded in August 1991, the SIF has the following goals:

- to further encourage Singaporeans to think internationally, in order to enable Singapore to make a contribution to the international community as a responsible corporate citizen;
- to project Singapore's image abroad by promoting Singapore culture and know-how, by explaining its way of life, its uniqueness, and achievements;
- to help Singaporeans who study, work, and live abroad to maintain links with Singapore;
- to encourage the world's talented to visit and work in Singapore; and
- to develop a worldwide network of friends of Singapore.

As part of its activities, the SIF operates the following programmes:

- publication of a bi-monthly magazine specially designed for the Singaporean living overseas—the magazine keeps readers informed of trends and developments in Singapore;

- the Singapore Volunteers Overseas programme, whose objective is to make a contribution to the developing world by providing humanitarian and technical services as well as to help Singaporeans gain a better understanding of countries in the developing world;
- Singaporeans Overseas/Regionalization programme, whereby SIF maintains contact with more than fifty social and business groups called Overseas Singapore Clubs;
- Singapore International Television, a television service which carries one hour of Singapore-produced programmes daily on the Indonesian satellite;
- links with more than two hundred Singapore student associations overseas are maintained through, for example, providing these organizations with SIF publications;
- an arts and culture programme which promotes Singapore's talent abroad by cosponsoring Singaporean artists in performances and exhibitions overseas; and
- a Friends of Singapore programme, which includes the SIF-ASEAN Visiting Student Fellowship programme, whereby SIF offers a number of fellowships to tertiary level students of ASEAN universities.

16) Singapore Planned Parenthood Association (SPPA)

Address: 116 Lavender Street, #03-04 Pek Chuan Building, Singapore 1233
Tel: 294-2691 *Fax:* 293-8719
Contact person: Executive Director, Mrs Amy Tan

The SPPA is affiliated to the International Planned Parenthood Federation (IPPF), the world's largest nongovernment organization to promote and provide family planning services. The IPPF supports the programmes of its member associations as they work to supplement and complement national programmes in their own countries. The SPPA was formed in 1949, and known then as the Family Planning Association of Singapore. The organization changed its name to SPPA in 1986.

As part of its activities, the SPPA organizes and conducts:

- talks and seminars on topics related to family life education in schools and junior colleges;
- talks, workshops, etc., on love and responsibility, marriage, parenthood, training workshops and teaching programmes on sex education for teachers; and
- training workshops on sexuality counselling for medical, professional and social service groups.

17) Singapore Red Cross Society/International Committee of the Red Cross

Address: 15 Penang Lane, Singapore 0923
Tel: 336 0269 *Fax:* 337 4360

Red Cross work in Singapore began in 1949 and has as its main objectives the furnishing of aid to the sick and wounded in time of war, the improvement of health, the prevention of diseases, and the mitigation of suffering throughout the world. The Red Cross movement supplements official services in the country. Membership is open to all interested in the objectives of the society.

The society's activities and programmes include the medical appliance loan scheme; running the Red Cross Home for the Disabled; cash aid to the destitute and elderly; first-aid service to all schools; attendance at local and national events when requested; running the Red Cross Blood Centre for the collection of blood donations for the National Blood Bank; international refugee relief assistance; international purchase and consignment of regional relief supplies; and the international tracing service.

18) Society Against Family Violence (SAVE)

Address: c/o Singapore Council of Women's Organizations
Blk 24, Outram Park, #03-115, Singapore 0316
Tel: 336-6641 *Fax:* 336-5276
Contact person: President

In 1991 SAVE was registered as a fully fledged society to serve as an umbrella body for services dealing with various aspects of family violence. Its goals are to prevent and reduce the incidence of family violence; to encourage and provide support and therapeutic services to victims of family violence; to encourage and provide support and rehabilitative services to the perpetrators of family violence. SAVE organizes interagency networking and consultation among related services to provide a more comprehensive linkage of services to the victims and perpetrators of domestic violence.

19) Society for the Prevention of Cruelty to Animals (SPCA)

Address: Mount Vernon Road Singapore 1336
Tel: 287-5355 *Fax:* 382-4162
Contact person: Ms Deirdre Moss, Executive Officer

The SPCA has existed since the 1800s, when it was known as the RSPCA. After a period of dormancy, the organization was revived in 1947 and went through a major revamp in 1954 when it relocated to Orchard Road. The organization then became independent and changed its name to the SPCA in 1959. In 1984 it moved its premises to Mount Vernon. The SPCA is highly dependent on public donations, volunteer labour, and media support.

Its aims are to promote respect for animals and a caring attitude towards pets among the public, pet owners and traders, and to reduce the number of unwanted animals, thus eliminating the need to destroy them.

The organization runs a 24-hour emergency service for stray animals, investigates reports of cruelty, collects, rehouses, or if necessary, destroys, unwanted pets and strays, conducts talks for schools and other bodies, and publishes booklets, leaflets and two magazines catering for senior and junior members respectively.

20) Soroptimist International of Singapore

Address: Orchard PO Box 0311, Singapore 9123

Tel: 737-8627 *Fax:* 733-9754

Contact person: Honorary Secretary

The first Soroptimist International was founded in Oakland, California, in the 1920s. On 5th August 1983, the Singapore club was formed. The club supports the Universal Declaration of Human Rights, is officially recognized by the UN, and has been granted consultative or associate status, with right of representation, by a number of UN specialized agencies. Its goals are the maintenance of high ethical standards in business, and in all professional fields, as well as in other aspects of life; to strive for human rights for all people, in particular, to advance the status of women; to develop a spirit of friendship and unity among Soroptimists of all countries; to quicken the spirit of service and human understanding, international understanding, and universal friendship. One of its many programmes includes the assistance to needy students in the form of bursaries.

21) World Vision International

Address: 1 Sophia Road, #04-05, Peace Centre, Singapore 0922

Tel: 334 5835 *Fax:* 334 5848

Contact person: Executive Director, Goh Eng Kee

World Vision is an international Christian organization started in 1950 to help children orphaned by war, widows, the poor, the starving and the sick. Throughout the years, its work has included assisting the Vietnamese boat people in the 1970s, and in the 1980s, assistance to the UN High Commissioner for Refugees in running medical clinics and in looking after the health needs of refugees. In 1984, a branch in Singapore was opened focused on increasing the awareness of people in Singapore and Malaysia on the plight of the poor around the world, their needs, and how they may be assisted; enabling people to offer care and serving as their channel of aid; and seeking to support, encourage and strengthen Christian leadership development.

22) Young Women's Muslim Association

Address: 15 Haigsville Drive, Singapore 1543
Tel: 7440258/7445491 *Fax:* 7481417
Contact person: Executive Officer
The Young Women's Muslim Association was formed in 1952. Its aims are to promote educational pursuits and cultural activities amongst Muslim women and girls, as well as the provision of welfare services to the community; to establish and strengthen the bonds of Islamic sisterhood amongst Muslim women in Singapore; to strive for development and progress of the nation as a whole and women in particular in relation to the socio-cultural, educational and religious fields; and to enhance and promote the welfare of the Muslim family.

III. Conclusion

NGO activities in Singapore, if measured by the provision of social services provided by various voluntary community groups other than the government, would seem to be no worse than any other urban industrial society that eschews the welfare state. But if NGOs were also to include those groups that act as critics and monitors of government policy and those that offer an alternative vision to the way the society is run, then the situation in Singapore is indeed nothing to be ecstatic about. But there is an increase in civic groups in Singapore. A glance at the *Green Directory*, published by the National Council on the Environment,[14] reveals that quite a handful of these are young organizations with young members. There may not be changes overnight, but changes there are.

Notes

1. See, for example, J. Saravanamuttu and Datuk Sharom Ahmat, *ASEAN Non-Governmental Organisations: A Study of their Role, Objectives and Activities* (Kuala Lumpur: Funded by Asia Foundation, 1986).
2. B.K. Tan and Bishan Singh, "Uneasy Relations: The State and NGOs in Malaysia" in *The Role of NGOs in Development.* Monograph 1—Malaysian Case Study (Kuala Lumpur: Asian and Pacific Development Centre, 1994).
3. Ibid.
4. Lim Teck Ghee, "Non-Governmental Organisations and Human Development: The ASEAN Experience" in *Reflections on Development in Southeast Asia.* edited by Lim Teck Ghee (Singapore: Institute of Southeast Asian Studies, 1988).
5. Ibid.
6. Saravanamuttu and Ahmat, op. cit.
7. Singapore Convention Bureau, *Convention/Exhibition Calendar, Singapore*, Vol. 21 No. 2 July 1992; Vol. 22 No. 1 January 1993; Vol. 22 No. 2 July 1993; Vol. 23 No. 1 January 1994 (Singapore: SCB, 1993).
8. Singapore National Printers, *The statutes of the Republic of Singapore—Societies Act (Chapter 311): Revised Edition 1985* (Singapore: SNP Ltd, 1986).
9. SNP, *Supplement to the Republic of Singapore Government Gazette—List of Registered Societies as on 1st April 1994* (Singapore: SNP, 1994).
10. Tan and Singh, op. cit.
11. Ibid.
12. Ibid.
13. International Monetary Fund, *International Financial Statistics* January, 1995. (Washington, D.C.: IMF, 1995). Figures given are based on end of period exchange rates for November 1994. US$1=S$1.46.
14. National Council on the Environment, *Green Groups in Singapore* (Singapore: NCE, 1994).

TAIWAN

The Growing Asia Pacific Concern among Taiwan's NGOs

Hsin-Huang Michael Hsiao
Research Fellow
Institute of Sociology
Academia Sinica

I. Introduction

The purpose of this report is to describe the growing Asia Pacific concern among Taiwan's NGOs by illustrating some selected examples. One of the most significant transformations taking place in Taiwan since the 1980s has been the emergence of a demanding civil society. Being a demanding civil society, Taiwan has witnessed two distinguishable yet related social changes. One is the rise of a social movement sector within the nongovernmental organizations, the other the self-transformation of many already well-established nongovernmental organizations.

By 1994, at least nineteen types of social movements had emerged to make claims on the government for necessary social reforms. Their claims are varied, but four distinct categories can be delineated. The first group consists of movements protesting the government's inaction in the face of new problems such as consumer protection, pollution, rising housing costs, and conservation. A second category of movements has focused on state policies regarding ethnic groups and minority language rights, land control, and cultural identity and preservation. Protests have also risen against inadequate policies in caring for disadvantaged groups, such as the elderly, the handicapped, and veterans, and the treatment of certain religious groups.

A third group of movements has challenged the state's corporatist mode of control over key social groups, such as workers, farmers, students, women, and teachers and intellectuals. Finally, groups have emerged to change the established rules governing politically sensitive issues such as the ban on contacts between people in

Taiwan and Mainland China and human rights violations.

Emerging from the nineteen social movements, there have been more than one hundred specific individual social movement organizations that can be identified in terms of their objectives, social bases, and mobilization strategies. These social movement-oriented organizations have constituted the "new sector" of Taiwan's NGOs. They are, in most cases, grassroots organizations, and very much locally based. Since they are inspired directly by local issues, the orientation of these social movement NGOs has been quite "internal" rather than "external." However, for some social movement organizations, whose major concern is regional or even global in nature, one is likely to find that there is a greater motivation to develop connections with similar NGOs within the Asia Pacific region.

As for those self-transformed "old" NGOs, there is also a growing Asia Pacific concern among some motivated and well-staffed organizations. A few strengthened networking activities are observed.

The following description of such emerging Asia Pacific concern among Taiwan's NGOs is drawn from observation on the recent development in the two types of NGOs—the new social movement NGOs and the old non-social movement NGOs.

II. The New Social Movement NGOs

1. The Consumers' Foundation (CF)

Chairman: Mr. Hsi-Hua Lin
Address: 10F-2, 390, Fu-Hsin South Rd. Sec. 1, Taipei, Taiwan
Phone: 886-2-700-1234, 756-6037 *Fax:* 886-2-706-0247

The Consumers' Foundation (CF) was established in 1980 to support consumer rights. Though it was established in the form of a foundation, CF is actually more like an NGO in that it initiates action and advocates for the consumer movement. The initial endowment was donated by the Taipei International Junior Chamber of Commerce and two private corporations. Since 1981, when CF began publishing the monthly magazine *Consumer Report*, subscriptions have become its most important source of income. CF is still one of Taiwan's most active social movement organizations. The consumer movement led by CF has become a model for other social movements. CF's techniques have been an effective mixture of sounding alarms to the public through media coverage, engaging in policy dialogues with government officials, consumer education through seminars and *Consumer Report*, and legal assistance to consumers injured by negligent manufacturers. The group's consciously depoliticized strategy of avoiding ties with any political force has engendered popular support and trust. The crucial element has been the active participation of a large number of liberal scholars and professionals serving on eleven committees, ranging in subject from food to medical care to consumer education to legal affairs to environmental protection. Many of these liberal scholars have gone on to extend their support and expertise to other emerging social movements. In retrospect, the success achieved by the CF has legitimized the social movements that have followed it.

Since the mid-1980s, CF has endeavored to develop networks with other consumer organizations in East and Southeast Asia. CF has already established sister organization relations with the following Asian consumer groups: Korean Citizen Alliance for Consumer Protection (1984), Consumer Economic Press of Japan (1988), and the Consumer Association of Singapore (1991). With the Hong Kong Consumers Association, Macau Consumers Association, Australian Consumers Association, and the Consumers Association of Penang in Malaysia, CF has also developed close collaborative relationships by exchanging visits and organizing joint seminars. CF has a long history of cooperation and working relations with the International Organization of Consumer Unions (IOCU) and, after more than ten years of dedicated effort, CF finally became a formal member of IOCU in 1993.

2. Homemakers' Union and Foundation (HUF)

Chair: Ms. Hsio-Ling Ong
Address: 4F, 2, Lane 160, Ting-Zhou Rd. Sec. 3 Taipei, Taiwan
Phone: 886-2-368-6211, 6212 *Fax:* 886-2-368-6213

At the end of 1986, a group of activist housewives banded together to campaign for environmental protection and improvement in the general quality of education in Taiwan. With the intention of mobilizing the country's women, they organized the Homemakers' Union and Foundation (HUF). The legal foundation was established in early 1989 with a board of directors and staff composed entirely of women. The endowment came from private donations by the directors and other concerned individuals; no corporate financing was involved. Since then, the Foundation has applied government and corporate grants to specific projects. In many respects, HUF is a de facto social movement NGO.

Though the major concern of this social movement foundation is the environment, it also tackles issues of children's education, safety, and rights; working women's rights; and the worsening problem of juvenile prostitution.

However, the very environmental concern has brought HUF and many other environmental and women's NGOs in Asia Pacific together. For example, HUF has developed a very close affiliation with Japan's Seikatsu Club (Consumer's Cooperative Union) by exchanging visits and conducting joint meetings on community action. It also works with Japan's Tropical Forest Rescue Action Network for a possible joint action on monitoring Japanese and Taiwanese multinational corporations' business practices in Asia Pacific. HUF participated in the East Asian Women's Forum held in Japan in October 1994. Obviously, HUF has already established solid collaboration with Japanese counterparts. In addition to Japan, Mainland China is the next country in which HUF hopes to develop networks. In 1992 and 1993, HUF visited China for a study tour and experience sharing with China's environmental, educational, women's, and children's groups.

HUF is an active social movement NGO in Taiwan and is interested in expanding more fruitful collaborations with many other NGOs in the Asia Pacific region.

III. The Non-Social Movement NGOs

1. World Vision of Taiwan (WVT)

Chair: Rev. Lien-Hua Chou
President: Dr. Jerry Chang
Address: 5F, 30, Chung-Shan N. Rd., Sec. 3, Taipei, Taiwan
Phone: 886-2-585-6300 *Fax:* 886-2-594-9294

World Vision of Taiwan (WVT) was established as a local chapter of the Christians' World Vision International in 1964, originally to serve aborigine villages and orphans in the city. Later, it developed into an islandwide charitable, social work, and community development NGO. Since 1990, WVT has emerged to actively participate in worldwide relief activities, giving international assistance to many other third world countries in Africa, Asia, the Pacific Islands, and Latin America. The 1990s witnessed the transformation of WVT from a benefited to a benefactor organization of world relief efforts. In particular, its campaign of "Hunger 30"—aimed at raising a relief fund for the world's children suffering from hunger, homelessness, and AIDS—has lifted WVF's international visibility and reputation in the international philanthropic world.

2. The Chinese Association for Human Rights (CAHR)

President: Mr. Yu-Jen Kao
Address: 8F, 102, Kuang-Fu South Rd., Taipei, Taiwan
Phone: 886-2-721-0281 *Fax:* 886-2-776-4360
The Chinese Association for Human Rights (CAHR), established in 1979, is similar to many other human rights NGOs around the world. In addition to engaging in human rights advocacy in Taiwan, CAHR has also focused its attention on refugee relief in Northern Thailand and human rights issues in Mainland China. It has also made efforts to initiate an Asia Pacific Human Rights Organization. Since the 1980s, CAHR has developed information networks with more than one hundred human rights NGOs in more than ten Asia Pacific countries. On its immediate agenda is the establishment of the Asia Pacific Human Rights Information Center which will be operated in Taipei.

3. Chinese Society of Comparative Law (CSCL)

President: Prof. Tsung-Loh Huang
Address: 7F-1, 24, Peking E. Rd., Taipei, Taiwan
Phone: 886-2-341-1620 *Fax:* 886-2-341-1620
The Chinese Society of Comparative Law (CSCL) was established by legal professionals and professors in 1970, aiming to strengthen legal research and education and to provide legal services for the public. Though it is a scholarly and professional NGO, CSCL has been playing an effective advocacy role in calling for legal and judiciary reform in Taiwan. The provision of legal aid is another important social service activity. CSCL's international extension has focused on developing affiliations with similar Japanese NGOs by organizing conferences on timely comparative legal issues.

IV. Concluding Remarks

Since 1980, Taiwan's civil society has been mobilized—as reflected in the rise of social movement NGOs and the self-transformed existing non-social movement NGOs—to meet the challenges derived from the new socio-political situations. In retrospect, the majority of social movement NGOs and thousands of non-social movement NGOs are still preoccupied with domestic issues and remain internal oriented in their organizing and programming activities. The major constraints against Taiwanese NGOs' regional cooperative efforts lie in the lack of information about other NGOs in the Asia Pacific region and the shortage of professional manpower to initiate and promote cooperative efforts. Financial difficulties may not be the primary concern. From the experience of the above selected examples, it is clear that strong motivation, keenness about regional and world issues, and effective organizational capability are the key elements for an active NGO regional cooperative effort.

Without doubt, there is a slowly yet steadily growing Asia Pacific concern among many of Taiwan's NGOs. The most effective way to further enhance Taiwanese NGOs' Asia Pacific regional efforts is through active bilateral networking and issue-oriented cooperation between local NGOs and their counterparts in the region.

THAILAND

Nongovernmental Organizations in Thailand

Amara Pongsapich
Consultant

I. Introduction

The traditional form of nongovernmental organizations in Thailand, as in many other countries, has its origins in religion and tends to be seen in the form of philanthropy. From the earliest times, Buddhist monks and their monasteries provided refuge for the needy and the sick, their schools offered education to the public, and their precincts were used for communal activities in all localities. After the Christian missionaries became active during the early Bangkok period, the philanthropic activities they initiated, in the form of hospitals and schools, were also recognized. In addition, missionaries also worked with hill people, slum people, and other socially disadvantaged groups. Karen alphabets, designed by a missionary group, also represent some of the activities of Christian missionaries. The role of Christian missionaries in community development activities has been very important.

Modern forms of philanthropy, on the other hand, were exemplified with the establishment, in 1890, of Sapha U-nalom Daeng, which later became the Red Cross. The Boy Scouts, established during the reign of King Rama VI (1910–25), was also recognized. By the turn of the century, other philanthropic organizations emerged, many of which provided a variety of social services, some more liberal in their political stand than others. During this period, many of the Chinese secret societies were transformed into mutual aid and speech associations, serving the needs of occupational groups and new immigrants.

The 1932 coup d'état changed Thailand from an absolute to a democratic monarchy. This period was also one of worldwide economic recession to be followed by World War II. With the proliferation of diversity within the nonprofit sector, associations were ordered to register with the government under the National Cultural

Act of 1942, in an effort to ensure state control over a growing and potentially threatening sector. The registration did indeed result in control over the activities of these organizations. The activities had to be nonpolitical, and only social and philanthropic activities were allowed.

During this period, organizations based on school alumni and vocations came into existence. Clubs and associations were organized for social and business purposes, but at the same time supported relief activities in times of emergency. The Women's Cultural Club and international clubs such as Rotary, Lyons, and Sontas also came into existence around this time as national networks with branches in the provinces.

During the period after World War II, including the 1950s and 1960s, when the country was under military rule, nonprofit organizations took the form of social clubs and philanthropies. After the student coup d'état on 14 October 1973, nongovernmental organizations emerged to promote social development from a grassroots perspective. Prior to 1973, some of the students found rural summer working camps an outlet for their politico-social propensities. The camps enabled many of the youth from the upper class to familiarize themselves with rural poverty and disparity. The Graduate Volunteer Program at Thammasat University was conceptualized and set up. The Thailand Rural Reconstruction Movement (TRRM) was one of the first "public-interest" nongovernmental organizations to be established. Other new nongovernmental organizations were also initiated at this time. Most of the new organizations, however, did not formally register. They demanded radical reforms to stop the alleged transfer of national resources from the poorer to the wealthier sectors of Thai society.

But the rise of the left wing movement generated a right wing countermovement, which in turn led to the overthrow of the democratically elected government in 1976. Toward the end of the decade, many grassroots nonprofit organizations found themselves branded as communist, and their supporters as communist agents. Since the only nongovernmental organizations tolerated by the government were those representing philanthropic activities of the upper classes, many younger people fled to the jungle to join the Communist Party of Thailand, which offered an alternative vision of economic development.

In 1980, with the fall of the Communist Party of Thailand, the government granted amnesty to those who wanted to return from the jungle "to help bring about development to the Thai nation." Unregistered groups began to revive their activities, and new groups formed. Slowly developmental nonprofit organizations emerged, became more and more active, and assumed an important role in the development of Thai society, despite the many limitations at the earlier stages. Most public-spirited developmental nonprofit organizations established during this period and not registered, are middle class organizations in contrast to the ones developed earlier which are composed of members from the upper class. After the fall of Saigon and Phnom Penh in 1975, came an influx of refugees to Thailand, and refugee camps were established within the Thai borders. Many international nonprofit organizations joined with the United Nations High Commissioner for Refugees to provide assistance and service to refugees. These groups are mostly non-Thai, and they form a distinct group of nonprofit organizations.

The development of Public-Interest NGOs (PINGOs) may be said to be due to two main conditions. First is the degree to which people had been faced with problems arising from or related to "development." The need to understand the poor and to be able to help them help themselves became very apparent. Many individuals and groups of individuals felt the need to join hands and work together. More and more PINGOs were established for this purpose. Second, many committed persons felt that the ways in which government agencies worked and the effort of government agencies in tackling development problems may not provide the solution sought. They believed that NGOs might be able to provide an alternative means to tackle development problems.

Since middle class NGOs had been suspected of being communist in the past, they had to work hard to reinstate themselves. Previously, these NGOs were believed to be competitors and antagonists of government officials. Being antibureaucratic, NGO workers also had negative attitudes toward government officials. The early 1980s was a period of strong tension between NGOs and governmental organizations (GOs). Only recently has there been dialogue, exchanges, and cooperation between the two groups. This is evident in the establishment of the Joint Coordination Committee between GOs and NGOs where representatives of government agencies and of volunteer groups meet regularly. Regional subcommittees have also been designated.

II. Cooperation among NGOs and the Formation of Umbrella Organizations

As mentioned in the paper on philanthropy in Thailand, there are many types of nongovernmental and nonprofit organizations at present. However, only three types are recognized by and legally registered with the Thai government-associations, labor unions and federations, and foundations. In 1989, there were 8,408 general nonprofit associations registered with the National Cultural Commission, 373 commercial associations and a small number of employers' associations registered with the Department of Internal Trade, and 2,773 cremation associations registered with the Department of Public Welfare. The labor groups include labor unions, federations, and councils, and all are registered with the Department of Labor. In 1989, there were 2,966 foundations registered with the National Cultural Commission. Almost half of them focused on funding cultural and educational activities.

In addition, there are also unregistered nonprofit groups organized for specific purposes but without legal status. They may be called projects, working groups, or forums. They tend to be small and dedicated to public welfare, community development, and campaign advocacy issues such as human rights, the environment, and cultural promotion. Grassroots organizations and advocacy groups usually do not register because of the burdensome endowment and membership requirements. Furthermore, many development groups prefer not to register because then they need not report to anyone. They may, on occasion, combine under umbrella councils or coordinating committees.

Umbrella organizations, both registered and unregistered, also form part of the Thai nonprofit sector. However, there are only ninteen registered umbrella organizations, many of which are very specific in nature and do not have much impact on Thai society in general. Seven of the registered umbrella organizations are religious organizations; five are trade or vocational in orientation; three focus on specific target groups, e.g., women, children, and the aged; and the other three are leagues of foundations, associations, and councils of social welfare. It is clear that except for the National Council of Social Welfare and those groups focusing on specific target groups, development-oriented and advocacy groups do not register.

Grassroots organizations and advocacy groups usually do not register because registration requires an endowment fund in the case of foundations and a large membership in the case of associations. As long as they can operate and seek sufficient financial support, they will remain unregistered. When centers and institutions operate as nonprofit organizations, they operate action projects and/or have research or training components in their work plan. The centers and institutions are considered nonprofit as long as there is no profit sharing.

The fact that the government recognized the role of nongovernmental organizations in development activities is evident in the policy on promotion of local organizations in rural development. In the past, although the government recognized that the private sector should play an important role in promoting development activities, action plans to encourage its involvement were not developed until very recently. Private sector involvement was seen in business and investment spheres more than in development spheres.

With economic and social-political development taking place in Thailand, the government is determined to cut their budget and ask the private sector to get involved in development activities at the local and grassroots levels. The 1991 interim government, consisting mostly of technocrats, announced a policy to loosen control of the nonprofit sector. Measures are being taken to revise registration procedures and tax regulations to promote nonprofit sector activities.

There are coordinating groups where existing organizations, foundations, associations, projects, etc., join together as a coordinating body for specific purposes such as working on rural development or pursuing issues of the environment, health, human rights, etc. There are about ten active coordinating bodies which are not yet registered. The most well known of these is the National Coordinating Committee of Nongovernmental Organizations for Rural Development (NGO-CORD) with a total membership of 220 organizations, including regional subcommittees. Others include working groups of children's organizations, primary health organizations, human rights organizations, and slum development organizations. Membership in these other coordinating bodies ranges between ten and thirty organizations.

1. Umbrella NGOs with Specific Target Groups

1) NGOs and women in development

As mentioned in the previous section, the formation of Sapha U-nalom Daeng, or the Red Cross, in 1890 and the establishment of the Thai Boy Scouts more than twenty years later led the way to the formation of other organizations. In general, women's associations appear to be the predominant form of nongovernmental organization. The Women's City Club (Samakhom Satri Thai Haeng Sayam), a liberal group, was formally established in 1932 by the woman editor of *Ying Thai*, a daily women's newspaper. Another founding member and chairperson of the club was a woman with a master's degree from a U.S. university. Although members of the club were middle-class women, they expressed concern for working women, with special concern for the welfare of women of the working class. Headquarters were set up at the office of the Tram Labor Association.[1] In addition to the National Council of Women of Thailand (NCWT), which functions as the umbrella organization for women's organizations (discussed in the paper on philanthropy), there are other groups of women's organizations working on issues of Women in Development and who are not members of NCWT. They are discussed in the paper on philanthropy in Thailand also, but need to be mentioned here as well.

Organizations classified as those working on issues of women in development and deserving mention here include the Thai Girl Guides Association, the Association for the Promotion of the Status of Women, the Women Lawyers' Association of Thailand, the Institute for Gender and Development Studies, the Friends of Women Group, and the Women Foundation. The first three are also members of the NCWT while the other three are not. The Thai Girl Guides Association has long been active, especially in rural areas, in the sphere of nonformal, vocational programs for women. Its latest venture has been the promotion of women as health care providers for the family and community. The Association for the Promotion of the Status of Women has been instrumental in setting up an emergency home for distressed women and children which has offered shelter to many prostitutes escaping from brothels and provided support to battered wives. It operates an occupational training center which may help in the rehabilitation of women who have taken up dubious professions. The Friends of Women Group created greater interest in women's development through its publications and organization of various seminars. They work with women factory workers and provide legal assistance to those in need. The Women Lawyers' Association also provides legal advice to women. The Women Foundation, established and operated jointly with the Women Information Center, also works with battered women and has set up a rescue center for women in distress. The Foundation is also trying to cope with the problem of forced prostitution, especially child prostitution. The group networks with organizations in other countries on the issue of trafficking of women. Collaboration has been established between receiving countries such as Japan and European countries, and supplying countries such as Thailand, the Philippines, and Sri Lanka.

The Gender Research and Development Institute functions to carry out action research and collaboration with both GOs and NGOs, with the objective of more equity and justice in the workplace and the social environment. In addition, many universities have Women's Studies programs on campus. Most of them are informal groups trying to set up curricula on women's studies and carrying out research projects. Most of these university groups are classified as borderline cases of GOs and NGOs. All of them may be said to be working for the betterment of women, attempting to do away with discrimination, and some try to influence government policies on issues related to women. These issues are, for example, the period allowed for maternity leave, leave with and without pay, equal wages, and sexual behavior in relation to AIDS.

When important issues concerning women are recognized, these groups join hands and establish quite a strong network working for causes of concern to all women.

2) NGOs focusing on children and youth

As in the case of philanthropy related to women, organizations working for the welfare of children and youth have been developed since the early stages of philanthropy in Thailand. Part of the reason is the sympathy most people have towards helpless children. Activities related to children and youth range from the provision of food and lodging for orphans and disabled children to scholarships for children in schools, and more recently, to activities helping street children and child prostitutes. The number of organizations working with children and youth remains large, and some kind of organizational body is certainly necessary to facilitate coordination of similar and related activities. Hence, the Council of Children and Youth Development Organizations was formed in 1984.

Similar to the case of women's NGOs, there are also children and youth NGOs that classify their work as nongovernmental, in contrast to philanthropic, in nature. Details of the umbrella organization are included in the paper on philanthropy and will not be repeated here. However, one needs to mention the important advocacy role which children and youth NGOs have played during the last two decades.

The Children Foundation should be recognized as one of the first NGOs working with children that has been able to bring the problem of child malnutrition and poverty to the public through a mass campaign. There are smaller NGOs working on children's issues that have emerged out of the original Children Foundation. They are for example, the Foundation for Children's Development, the Foundation for Slum Child Care, and the Center for the Protection of Children's Rights. Liberal children and youth NGOs carry out advocacy work on issues such as child labor, child prostitution, and children's rights, and demand legal and regulational reform as well as demand that monitoring and control measures be established by the government. An international network is well established, and support can often be sought at the international and local levels because the issues are generally sensitive as well as sensational. Mass media usually cover such activities reasonably well.

2. Issue-Oriented Umbrella NGOs

1) Environmental protection and conservation

The rapidly increasing interest in environmental issues during the past decade has led to the formation of many environmental NGOs. Some are locally based while others are based in Bangkok. Most of the NGOs working on environmental issues are newly established. They include, for example, the Thai Environment and Community Development Association, better known as the Magic Eyes; the Sueb Nakhasathien Foundation, established in memory of a forester who committed suicide for the cause of forestry conservation; the Project on Ecological Recovery, a vocal group that advocates environmental issues very actively; and many other groups who work for the conservation of certain areas. There are also international NGOs such as the World Wildlife Fund, the related Wildlife Fund (Thailand), CARE, and other conservation groups.

There is no single organization functioning as a coordinating body among NGOs working on environmental issues. When coordination is needed, they work with NGO-CORD or other groups. On the other hand, the environmental groups have formed a coalition and several networks. The Environment NGO Coalition initiates movements on certain issues. During the last decade, networking has become the dominant feature of nongovernmental organizations working on specific issues that cross national borders. The groups working on "alternative development" utilize the concept of "mobilization" as a tool to bring people together. Mobilization is the process of making people aware of alternative community development activities different from conventional ones.

The concept of mobilization and the need to help strengthen each other makes networking among NGOs very strong. One of the most powerful networks is the Southeast Asia Forum for Development Alternatives (SEAFDA), established in 1985 out of a United Nations University (UNU) research project. Environmental NGO networks emphasize the role of local and grassroots development activities instead of the predominant concern with economic development which does not give due attention to the socio-cultural basis of such development.

Starting in 1990, the NGO Coalition established a pattern of organizing an annual meeting to discuss environmental issues. A group of environment-oriented NGOs organized a joint public forum called "Environment '33" which took place in 1990 (equivalent to the Buddhist Era 2533). Since then, there has been a meeting every year with the title "Environment '34," "Environment '35," etc. The number of members of the coalition group now exceeds forty, in contrast to thirty-two when it was initiated in 1990.

In 1992, the Thai environment-oriented NGOs, together with SEAFDA, initiated the People's Plan for the 21st Century Campaign in which issues on alternative development were discussed. They also organized the People's Forum. Preparatory meetings were organized prior to the actual People's Forum held during the World Bank and International Monetary Fund (IMF) Meetings in Bangkok in 1992. The People's Forum had an impact on the World Bank/IMF Meeting. It conveyed the message that development activities planned by the World Bank and IMF for the Third World were unacceptable to the NGOs. Along the same lines, the network of environmental groups has also organized movements against dam construction and reforestation plans.

It should be mentioned here that environment-oriented NGOs are not homogeneous. They are very diverse in character, ranging from the pure conservationists (to conserve plants and animals, no matter what), who are not concerned with social impacts, to those interested mostly in the social impacts of development. This diversity may be the reason for the loosely organized form of collaboration without a coordinating body.

2) Health and health-related NGOs

Discussion on the health-related umbrella organization is included in the paper on philanthropy in Thailand as well. However, because of the impact of this organization at the local level, it is necessary to include the discussion in this paper also. Linkages at the international level have not been recognized as yet.

The 1992 data indicate that there are approximately 170 organizations working on health-related issues. Of these, 130 are foundations, 30 are associations, and 10 are not registered. The large number of foundations clearly reflects the dominance of the philanthropic and charity nature of health activities. This group sees no need to organize because charity work can be carried out individually. However, the more liberal groups composed mostly of young and newly graduated doctors and pharmacists were not content with dealing with health issues along the line of charity. They saw the need to advocate certain health issues to inform the public of the harm caused by misuse of drugs and other consumer products.

In an attempt to provide health care to the people in rural areas more adequately, the Ministry of Public Health launched many programs. Two related programs are the provision of rural hospitals at the district level (both thirty-bed and ten-bed) and internship programs where new graduates in the fields of medicine, dentistry, and pharmacology are required to work in rural areas as health professionals for two years. In the late 1970s and early 1980s, after the programs were implemented, these highly motivated young graduates were very ambitious and wanted to help bring about development to the country. Some of them set up a health nongovernmental organization in the district where they worked and recruited volunteers from local clinics and health centers to work on health-related development issues.

The Primary Health NGOs Coordinating Committee (PHC)

In 1981–82, a group of advocacy health-related nongovernmental organizations met and formed a coordinating body under the name Primary Health NGOs Coordinating Committee (PHC). Since the founding members, a few of whom received the Best Rural Doctor of the Year award, were mostly personnel of the Ministry of Public Health fulfilling their internship requirement, there was a strong link between this coordinating committee and the Primary Health Care Office of the Ministry of Public Health. This coordinating body later became a very active health advocacy group. There are about twenty member organizations at present.

The objectives of the Coordinating Committee are:

a. To function as a center to coordinate information to support primary health care development;
b. To coordinate the dissemination of information to the public, and to support public education related to the nature of health problems, and create citizens willing to help solve related problems;
c. To coordinate the dissemination of concepts, activities, and views of primary health NGOs to the public; and
d. To coordinate to promote and improve efficiency in the management of member primary health NGOs with academic and resource support.

Activities of the Coordinating Committee include training programs, seminar and forum sessions, a health development database center, publication of the *PHC Newsletter* (bi-monthly) and *Health Journal* (tri-monthly), and campaign advocacy issues in an attempt to influence certain government policies. The issues advocated include anti-smoking policy, appropriate medical consumption practices, nutritious food, etc.

3. Community Development and Advocacy Organizations

This section includes many umbrella NGOs with multiple objectives which cannot be classified as issue oriented or target group oriented. However, they are all concerned with development issues and the impact of government policies on society, either in relation to specific groups or in general. Some of them are well-established networks, some are loose networks, and some are individual organizations functioning as coordinating bodies for specific networks.

1) The Thai Volunteer Service Foundation (TVS)

The Thai Volunteer Service Foundation (TVS) is a nonprofit organization established to serve the development needs of the country. On 5 April 1980, ninteen development nongovernmental organizations convened and established the Thai Volunteer Service Program with the objective of finding solutions to problems faced by development NGOs. These problems included lack of experienced, capable, and dedicated personnel; lack of funds and other resources for development activities; lack of coordination among NGOs; and insufficient coordination between NGOs and government agencies.

During the initial phases, the project was located at the Chulalongkorn University Social Research Institute as an independent project having its own board of administration and seeking its own funds. In order to secure an official identity, the project was registered as a foundation in 1986, and in 1992 it moved out of the university. There are approximately forty member organizations that request volunteers and join in activities organized by TVS on a regular basis. They are considered to be TVS network members.

The original objectives of the project were to establish an organization to provide support to nongovernmental organizations working on development activities. Support was viewed in terms of training volunteers as well as institution building and financial support if and when necessary. In addition, TVS regularly evaluated situations and identified development activities to be promoted and issues to be advocated. This was to ensure that TVS responded to the needs of the NGOs promptly.

TVS specializes in volunteer training. TVS and the NGOs that request volunteers, recruit volunteers jointly. There are two steps in the recruitment process. First, TVS makes a public announcement and identifies persons appropriate for volunteer work by reviewing application forms and curriculum vitae. The applicants who pass the first round are then interviewed jointly by TVS and the NGOs requesting applicants.

From the beginning, TVS has also tried to help strengthen development-oriented NGOs by organizing technical skill training programs necessary for small NGOs to manage their program activities adequately. In addition, training in organizational management skills has also been organized when the need has arisen.

The formal objectives are as follows:

a. To enable and help improve the capability of dedicated individuals with public interest to have the opportunity to work as volunteers in community development and other social development activities;
b. To help promote efficiency in the management and personnel development of nongovernmental organizations;
c. To help promote coordination among nongovernmental organizations and between nongovernmental and government organizations; and
d. To cooperate with individuals and organizations to identify community development and social development directions for Thailand.

Since 1985, after establishing a reputation for volunteer training and institution building, TVS has shifted its activities more toward the coordination of NGOs through the advocacy of development issues. TVS, together with other NGOs, carries out research activities aimed at collecting baseline data to plan advocacy activities more meaningfully. TVS's research and advocacy activities may be viewed through advocacy issues publicized in the form of seminars and meetings organized jointly with academic institutions or other NGOs. Through these seminars and workshops, TVS and its network try to influence certain government policies such as policies on resource management, infrastructure construction, and government decentralization schemes.

TVS works closely with the NGO Coordinating Committee, to be discussed in the following paragraphs.

2) The Local Development Institute (LDI)/Local Development Foundation (LDF) and Its Networks

The Local Development Institute/Local Development Foundation is an NGO coordination and management model that has evolved from other trial models. In Thailand, bilateral funds have to go through the Department of Technical and Economic Cooperation. Because of this requirement, NGOs usually do not seek funds that are bilateral because this will require extra effort to have the projects approved in terms of activities and amount of financial support for each category of activity. If the donor countries are determined to provide support for NGOs bilaterally, they have to negotiate to set up a special mechanism to manage the funds.

The Canadian International Development Agency (CIDA) attempted many models of channeling funds to NGOs. In the first phase, the Local Development Assistance Project (LDAP) started operating in the late 1980s, out of the CIDA office at the Canadian Embassy. A committee was set up to review and approve projects submitted for funding. Funds were delivered to NGOs directly after approval. A monitoring and evaluation mechanism for each project was also included as part of the program.

In the second phase, LDAP evolved to become the Local Development Institute (LDI) and the Local Development Foundation (LDF). LDI has a clear and definite purpose of functioning as a Thai nongovernmental organization operating under Thai law with flexible and responsive mechanisms so as to be capable of coordinating various forces and networks, as well as synthesizing all the research findings and practical experiences into a relevant body of knowledge and policy, applicable at the national level.

It was in this spirit that LDF was created, with LDI as its operating arm. It was also with the same rationale that LDF and the Department of Technical and Economic Cooperation (DTEC) managed to come to the mutual understanding that GO-NGO working relationships are to be characterized by coordination and cooperation, not by control. LDF/LDI now functions as an NGO with a reasonable degree of autonomy and initiative of its own. As a CIDA-funded government-to-government cooperation project, LDF/LDI is accountable to CIDA as its funding agency, to DTEC as the agency overseeing external assistance, and to the National Education Commission (NEC) in its capacity as LDI's official sponsor. All three government agencies, together with LDF as recipient, form the core of the Project Steering Committee and are responsible for overall project management.

LDI invites proposals for grassroots development activities annually, and has established networks of NGOs working on such activities in the different regions of the country. The proposals are reviewed and improved upon by the regional subcommittees before final approval by the Project Steering Committee composed of members of CIDA, DTEC, NEC, and LDI. Projects are monitored by regional subcommittees with visits from the Project Steering Committee. In addition, LDI also works with regional universities on research projects identified as relevant and essential to the development of the region and the country.

3) NGO-Coordinating Committee on Rural Development (NGO-CORD)

NGO-CORD was formed in 1985 with 106 member organizations joining. Now there are approximately 220 member organizations, not all of which are registered. NGO-CORD itself is not registered. However, the formation was encouraged and supported by the National Economic and Social Development Board. It is now recognized by several government organizations and funding agencies as a major representative of the Thai NGO community. It has been asked to actively participate in the formulation of the national five-year plans as well as to serve as a member of several working groups and subcommittees on various development issues. Because of its large membership and regional diversity, regional NGO-CORDs have been established for better coordination and flexibility.

NGO-CORD has the following objectives:

a. To establish good relationships among NGOs and enhance the roles of voluntary groups working on rural development;
b. To promote understanding and cooperation between NGOs and government bodies working in rural development; and
c. To establish links between NGOs, government organizations, and the general public and to encourage all three to join forces in rural development work.

There are three types of committees in NGO-CORD. The first is the Regional Committee, of which there is one for each of the four regions (North, Northeast, South, and Central). The NGOs in each region select their own representatives to sit on the Regional Committee. The second type is the National Committee, which consists of ten NGOs. There are twenty-two representatives on the National Committee. Last is the Executive Committee, which is made up of five representatives from the National Committee. The National Committee holds meetings every month, the Regional Committee holds its meeting once a year, and the Executive Committee holds meetings twice a month.

NGO-CORD is a small but powerful organization, still seeking an appropriate organizational structure. It runs on small funds from different sources and sets up meetings and seminars among member organizations at regional and national levels. The aim is to promote cooperation in rural development and campaign advocacy, concerning such issues as opposition to dams, environmental protection, and forestry conservation. Attempts are made to consult with local and central government bodies and to form linkages with local people's organizations. NGO-CORD tries to strengthen the work of NGOs and encourages coordination among member organizations, the public, and the government.

Member organizations of NGO-CORD range from community research and development projects, such as the Community Research Project, attached to the

Social Research Institute of Chiang Mai University, and the Kilns for Palm Sugar Project promoted by the Prince of Songkhla University, to large national consortia such as the National Council of Women of Thailand with over one hundred and twenty member organizations.[2] Since NGOs in the Thai context encompass formal and informal groups, both temporary and permanent in nature, it is difficult to provide an accurate number of development-oriented NGOs at any given time. It is common to find newly emerged ones, and the disappearance of old ones. Newsletters are published and distributed as an avenue to disseminate information about member organizations and their activities.

4. Urban Community Development Office (UCDO)

The above examples illustrate efforts at coordination of rural development. Similarly, the need for coordination of urban development was recognized and fulfilled. However, the establishment of the coordinating body of urban nongovernmental organizations has taken a different form from the other umbrella organizations. The Urban Community Development Office (UCDO) was initiated in 1990 when a housing policies subcommittee of the National Economic and Social Development Board appointed a team to research the "Urban Poor Development Fund" and presented the results to the government for approval. After the government approved a 1.25 billion baht (US$50 million)[3] budget, the National Housing Authority issued regulations for the establishment of UCDO to implement the "Urban Poor Development Project." The Urban Poor Development Project is a special unit under the National Housing Authority, but works independently under its own project committee and system of administration. The initial team of seven persons was responsible for the implementation of the project.

The objectives of UCDO are:

a. To strengthen the capacity of the slum dwellers and the urban poor through a process of credit provision; and

b. To help slum dwellers obtain increased and secured income, and appropriate housing, with secured rights and improved environment and living conditions.

The Office divides its functions into three areas: the development function, which aims at developing community organization as well as the managerial capabilities of community or savings groups, career and income generation and enhancement, training programs, and information services; the credit function, which consists of credit provision, credit administration, and credit operation; and the administrative function, which consists of planning and research, evaluation, administration, accounts, and finances. The Office operates under the principle that the people are the main actors in the community development process. Other agencies, both governmental and nongovernmental, should only act as supporters of the people's development process.

Unlike other umbrella organizations, UCDO coordinates activities related to credit and income generation and works with different savings groups and credit unions instead of working with other NGOs. There are twenty-two savings groups and credit unions receiving financial support from the Office.

5. Other Coordinating Bodies on Development

In addition to the five umbrella organizations working on development-oriented activities mentioned in this section, there are a few other agencies forming loose informal networks and operating in an ad-hoc fashion. This phenomenon came about due to efforts made by funding agencies, international nongovernmental organizations, academics, and a number of Thai NGOs themselves to provide support services to the NGO community. Suwana-adth mentions a few. They are the NGO-Resource Development Initiatives; a joint project between the SVITA Foundation, a Thai NGO, and a U.S. consortium called Private Agencies Collaborating Together; the Thai NGO Support Project, supported by Friedrich-Nauman-Stiftung; and the Thai Development Innovative Financing Forum.[4] However, as was mentioned earlier, since these networking bodies are very loose and informal, they may be classified as project-type NGOs, and their project life is short.

III. The Role of Networks of Nongovernmental Organizations in Asia Pacific Today

In the previous sections, it has been shown that the strength of nongovernmental organizations has been both developed and recognized. When people who have agreed upon objectives and goals organize themselves and their objectives, and when those goals are nonpolitical, they are not viewed as threats to the government. But recently in Thailand nongovernmental organizations have also been able to set up political and advocacy goals, but not to the point of joining political parties or becoming involved in parliamentary politics. In some other Asian countries, during the 1960s, they may have joined political parties. In general, nongovernmental organizations may also have an ideology which differs from the government and even becomes anti-government in nature. However, in Asia, many governments viewed people with an ideology different from that of the government as "communist."

Fear of communism provided many governments with the pretext for authoritarian and dictatorial rule. However, despite authoritarian regimes, most governments have not been able to fight communism and at the same time bring about equality and freedom. Examples from Thailand and Indonesia indicate how some governments coped with the problem through regulatory laws. As a result, many people revolted, and alternative government and administrative structures are being sought.

In Asia, in the past, because of the perceived threat of communism, most governments ended up under military rule and became authoritarian in nature. Despite the end of the communist threat, most Asian people are still faced with the problem of authoritative military rule. Furthermore, despite being authoritarian, the governments of most of these countries have not been able to bring about economic development. Nongovernmental organizations in Asia, therefore, have joined hands to work together, to promote both economic development and greater participatory, democratic societies. Networking and international collaboration have proved to have helped strengthen local nongovernmental organizations tremendously. Discussion in this section will focus on the strength of Asian NGOs in two broad fields: the fight against authoritarian military rule and promotion of human rights, and the struggle for alternative development policies and strategies leading toward ecologically sustainable development. However, the two issues go hand-in-hand, and many NGOs work on both simultaneously. Their main objective may be to work on development alternatives, but when political tensions arise, they shift their emphasis to the political issue in pursuit of a more immediate goal.

1. Nongovernmental Organizations Fighting Against Authoritative Military Rule and Demanding Human Rights: The Case of Student and Middle-Class Movements

Communism and military rule have been viewed as the two main antagonistic forces in most Asian societies. However, they are not always antagonistic, and they may also be viewed as mutually supportive, as in the Communist Party of Thailand, which offered an alternative vision of economic development.

In 1980, with the fall of the Communist Party of Thailand, the government granted amnesty to those who wanted to return from the jungle "to help bring about development to the Thai nation." Unregistered groups began to revive their activities, and new groups formed. Slowly, developmental nonprofit organizations emerged, while peasant movements were weak in Asia, student movements were stronger in some countries. Thailand experienced a student-led coup d'état in 1973, which expelled Marshal Thanom and his clan, and the Philippines was able to replace Marcos in 1986.

While students appeared to be a strong pressure group, fighting authoritative governments in Korea, China, Burma, the Philippines, and Thailand, in other countries students have not had such an opportunity, partly because of authoritarian control, but also partly because they have not been empowered. Similarly, labor unions have tried to act as pressure groups in some countries. In Malaysia and Singapore, labor unions were labeled as communist and were subsequently weakened. An observation to be made here is that authoritarian government cannot be dismantled by one riot or revolution or coup d'état. Even after the first successful attempt, the process is not complete. Most authoritarian governments have firm roots in the ground, and there needs to be substantial follow-up strategies in the democratization process.

After the student coup d'état on 14 October 1973, the Thai people became politically active. Many nongovernmental organizations were established by committed people from various professions who viewed social development from the humanitarian point of view. Most of them were not registered, however.

The end of the 1970s and the early 1980s marked a very "low" period for development activities among NGOs. Student and grassroots activities were suppressed. In the latter part of the 1980s, a more favorable condition for nongovernmental organizations came about. Many nonregistered groups revived their activities and many new ones were formed. With a more liberal government attitude, grassroots NGOs have been able to help promote people's participation and self-reliance among local communities. Advocacy NGOs also helped raised awareness on many issues, both political and nonpolitical. They have succeeded in spreading the concept of people's participation and decentralized democracy as well as bringing about political consciousness among the people at all levels.

With the economic boom, many NGO workers turned to the business sector. Many joined large corporate firms, while a few others set up their own enterprises. In other words, many middle class NGO workers who had been suspected of being communist in the past, worked hard to revive themselves in the modern economy.

The 23 February 1991 coup d'état by the military proved to be a serious blow against most Thai people. The Chatichai Government tried to make the public believe that Thailand was one of the newly industrialized countries with a high economic growth rate. If people believed General Chatichai, then there was no reason for a coup d'état.

The Anand Government came in to rescue Thailand for approximately one year. After the April 1992 election, General Suchinda was nominated to become the Prime Minister. General Suchinda, as a leader of the 1991 coup d'état, together with his cabinet, proved to be unacceptable to most Thais. An NGO-organized coalition group led by the Student Union of Thailand and the Democracy Campaign Project worked against the Suchinda government. The core group consisted mostly of members of the Public Interest NGOs. They organized the May rally which was then joined by the opposition political parties. The rally turned out to be one of the most tragic incidents in modern Thai history, with dozens known killed by the military and more than a hundred still missing. It is undeniable that the NGOs who formed the core group that initiated the rally, the opposition political parties who joined the rally later, and the public of mainly young and middle-aged middle-class people, were able to work together and bring down the military leadership in the government.

In the Philippines, the spread of liberation theology of the Catholic Church in general and the critical political and economic problems in the Philippines in particular lead to increased social activism and the establishment of hundreds of Basic Christian Communities during the 1970s. With increasing human rights violations, the Church became progressive and more concerned with human rights abuses by the military. Corruption was another issue leading to the overthrow of the Marcos regime.

Although the Ninoy Aquino assassination triggered the mass movement that followed, Timberman called it "an explosion of nontraditional cause-oriented, sectoral, or mass-based groups."

> The cause-oriented groups were so named because of their concern with particular causes or issues (in contrast to the traditional political parties' avoidance of issue-oriented politics). The sectoral and mass-based groups included unions and labor federations, farmers' organizations, student and teachers' associations, women's groups, human rights lawyers, and other groups with membership ranging from the urban poor to urban professionals.[5]

Reverse economic growth was rapid in the Philippines during 1983–86. Because of the economic crisis in the early 1980s, the Communist Party of the Philippines and the New Peoples Army also expanded. The communist movement benefited from the Marcos government's preoccupation with the political and economic crisis. Anti-Marcos movements reached their peak, and Marcos announced that there would be a presidential election in 1986 "to settle the question of his government's mandate." The election was then followed by a revolution when the public refused to accept the official election results.

Human rights issues now predominate activities of many of the advocacy NGOs. NGOs join hands to help each other advocate basic human rights. The case of Aung San Suu Kyi in Myanmar brought many of the international human rights groups together. Also the case of East Timor and the Indonesian government received full support from many NGOs in different countries. NGO networks now play an important role in bringing about awareness of basic human rights.

2. Role of Nongovernmental Organizations in Seeking Alternative Development Strategies Leading Toward Ecologically Sustainable Development

In the 1970s and 1980s, the search for alternative development strategies was the prevailing slogan criticizing government policies all over the world. Top-down planning, modernization, and diffusion of western technology were development models rejected by progressive nongovernmental organizations. "Self reliance" and "people's participation" were concepts adapted from the Russian and Chinese models. While avoiding Russian and Chinese or Vietnamese communism, multinational capitalism was also rejected. Community development activities were promoted as having income generating activities as the entry point and at the same time educating and mobilizing people with self-reliance and participation concepts.

The Women's Year and Women's Decade announced by the United Nations also helped strengthen women's activities. The concept of promoting more women's participation in the development process and encouraging them to become more economically active was being seen everywhere. The burdens placed on women are being increasingly recognized. Women's involvement in the political sphere is also envisioned. But the most important idea is "empowerment" of women and other minority or disadvantaged groups. Issues of the environment, human rights, land rights, etc., have become the latest buzz-words, and NGOs are now attempting to mobilize people to confront the government on these issues.

In many countries, such as Indonesia and Thailand, the governments also adopted the concept of self-reliance and people's participation in promoting development activities. However, interpretation of the two concepts may be somewhat different between NGOs and GOs. Oakley introduced "forced participation" in contrast to "true participation" in governmental development projects.

Furthermore, Eldridge made a distinction between "development" and "mobilization." If "development" means educating people on specific issues and creating programs to bring about desired changes, mobilization then means making people aware of community development activities different from conventional ones.

"Mobilization" of this kind has become more widespread throughout the Third World as dominant power structures come to be seen as frustrating more conventional community development activity. In Indonesia, the shift coincides with a redirection of strategy by student activists, linked to an Islamic resurgence on both social and political fronts during the 1970s. Compared with India, where distinctions between developmental and mobilization modes of action are more sharply articulated, Indonesian voluntary action groups have shown considerable skill in integrating the two approaches. Since the state represses most overt forms of protest, NGOs have chosen not to operate under the umbrella of official development slogans but to redefine them in terms of paradigms more oriented toward participatory structures and democratic forms of community building.[6]

With the concept of mobilization and the needs for mutual strengthening, networking among NGOs has increased in strength. As mentioned earlier, one of the first networks was the UNU South-East Asian Perspectives Network or SEAFDA. It was established in 1985 in West Java, Indonesia, at a workshop where members of various organizations who were engaged in development programs at the grassroots level, as well as academicians, gathered together. Emphasis was on grassroots development activities which encouraged local initiative. It was felt that there was excessive concern with economic development without due attention given to the sociocultural basis of such development. Adi Sasano criticized mainstream developmental efforts in the Third World as being persistently elitist.

> The situation, despite the impressive rate of economic growth, has strengthened furthermore the economic and political position of the dominant elites, and widened the social and economic disparity between the rich and the poor. Socioeconomic integration between the powerful elites and the powerless majority has hardly been achieved, despite many official statements about the matter as one of the national development goals.[7]

Networking is now the dominant feature of nongovernmental organizations working on specific issues. Many women's networks have been established. Networks of consumers' associations, networks of organizations working on sustainable development, and networks of natural resource conservation groups have been established and maintained through regular exchanges of activities. Movements against dam construction are very strong. NGOs link the Third World with the First World to exchange information on specific dams to be built. Support, both financial and human resource, is pooled to help organize demonstrations or mass rallies. Experiences from the Sardar Sarovar Dam on the Narmada River in India, for example, are transferred to Thailand to help protest against the Pak Mun Dam in Thailand.

According to Claude Alvares, the World Bank–supported Sardar Sarovar dam on the Narmada river will submerge 237 villages and probably claim many human victims. It will cause the displacement of more than one hundred thousand people and destroy more than fourteen thousand hectares of forest. The World Bank also approves of the government's plan to move tribal peoples who refuse to vacate the area. Therefore, the threatened people have decided to drown in the waters rather than being forced to follow the rehabilitation plans. As a result, the Finn Parliament and members of the European and Swedish parliaments have called upon the World Bank by resolution to cease financing the project. Largely as a result of this pressure, the World Bank has recently announced an "independent review" of the environmental and rehabilitation aspects of the dam.[8]

Along similar lines, NGOs in Thailand have been able to stop or postpone construction of the Nam Choan Dam, the Kaeng Krung Dam, and a few other dam construction plans under the responsibility of the Royal Irrigation Department and the Electricity Generating Authority of Thailand.

Environmentalist groups are now fighting for natural resource conservation, arguing that people have the right to keep resources such as forest areas undisturbed. In Thailand, when the Royal Forestry Department proposed developing the Forestry Sector Master Plan with support from FINNIDA through the United Nations Development Programme (UNDP), a protest was made by an NGO coalition. Protest letters were sent to the press and the Ambassador. NGO leaders from the Philippines and India were invited to Bangkok to describe their experiences with Forestry Master Plans in their respective countries. One argument used to fight the project was the claim that the Thai (or Indian or Filipino) Forestry Master Plan would face the same dilemma as the Tropical Forest Action Plan introduced in Brazil where the action plan for tropical forests was based on experiences of evergreen forests in Northern Europe. Biodiversity is much more essential for tropical forests, and monocropping of trees should not be allowed. It is also believed that the promotion of tree plantations will be made to supply soft woods to paper mills and hard woods for furniture factories, both of which are produced to satisfy world, and mainly the industrially advanced world, consumption. The project will benefit the rich countries, while the poor have to sacrifice their natural resources.

Protests against reforestation plans that introduce monocropped tree plantation schemes or other forms of economic forestry are seen in most Third World countries. Local communities are encouraged by NGOs to make their voices heard. Local leaders are identified, and activities are organized to stop forest concessions in these countries. People's movements are now recognized as having sufficient power to have some influence on the decision-making process of some of the governments.

At the moment, discussion on the sustainable development model is increasing. The Green Revolution introduced in India and at IRRI in the Philippines, is said to destroy natural resources of the soil. The use of chemical fertilizers, insecticides, and pesticides should be avoided. Integrated farming where multicrops, fish ponds, animal husbandry, natural fertilizers, and pesticides, etc., exist in a symbiotic relationship, is being introduced to replace the predominant chemical-based, commercial, monocropping pattern. Natural agriculture introduced by Fukuoka in Japan is transported to Southeast Asia as an alternative agricultural practice. The point made by NGOs is that people should have the right to determine their own farming practices without being ordered or directed by agricultural extension officers. Transfer of certain types of technology deemed to be good by the government to all the people must be avoided. Freedom of choice is the message presented here.

IV. Conclusion

It has been difficult to cover all NGOs under the title of this paper. NGO activities are very diverse, and even activities which promote people's participation cover a large variety of topics. In this paper, only the most obvious groups were included with the risk of neglecting some other important ones. Only NGOs involved in issues of development, political movements, and developmental and environmental conservation were selected for inclusion. Those that are social welfare oriented are classified as philanthropic groups and included in the paper on philanthropy. The degree to which NGOs can function for the benefit of the people depends on government policies, whether they control the activities of NGOs or give opportunities for NGOs to promote empowerment of the people.

The role of NGOs in countries in Asia and the Pacific cannot be denied. Networks of NGOs have been established across national borders. NGOs have been sending messages to the governments. However, the degree to which specific governments pay attention to the messages depends entirely on the government. In the future, NGOs will continue to play the role of government advocacy by providing conscious voices to the government, monitoring government activities, and trying their best to work for the benefit of the people. Ideologies may be different, but sincerity and determination are the factors which have helped strengthen NGOs in Asia.

Notes

1. Siriporn Skroebanek, "Movement in Thailand (1855–1932)" in *Satrithat, Vol.* 1, No. 3 (August-October, 1983).
2. Malee Suwana-adth, *The NGO Sector in Thailand and the Potential Role of NGOs in National Development.* A Study Report for the Project on the Role of NGOs in Development-sponsored and supported by the Asian and Pacific Development Center and the Asian NGO Coalition for Agrarian Reform and Development, 1991.
3. International Monetary Fund, *International Financial Statistics,* January 1995 (Washington, D.C.: IMF, 1995). Figures given are based on the end of period exchange rate for November 1994. US$1 = 25.05 Baht.
4. Suwana-adth, op. cit.
5. David G. Timberman, *A Changeless Land: Continuity and Change in Philippine Politics* (Singapore: Institute of Southeast Asian Studies, 1991).
6. Philip Eldridge, "NGOs and the State in Indonesia" in *Prisma The Indonesian Indicator,* Vol. 47 (1990), p. 34–56.
7. Adi Sasano, "NGO Roles and Social Movement in Developing Democracy: The South-East Asian Experiences in *New Asian Visions* Vol. 6, No. 1 (March, 1989).
8. Claude Alvares, "The Narmada Disaster Commences" in *Third World Resurgence.* No. 12 (1991), p. 2–4.

References

Alvares, Claude
"The Narmada Disaster Commences." *Third World Resurgence.* No. 12 (1991), p. 2–4.

Arcillan, S.J.
An Introduction to Philippine History. Third Edition. Manila: Ateres de Manila University Press, 1971.

Asian NGO Coalition for Agrarian Reform and Rural Development (ANGOC)
NGO Strategic Management in Asia: Focus on Bangladesh, Indonesia and the Philippines. Manila: ANGOC, 1988.

Billah, M.M. and Abdul Hakim G.N.
"State Constraints on NGOs in Indonesia: Recent Developments", *Prisma, The Indonesian Indicator,* Vol. 47 (1990), p. 57–66.

Eldridge, Philip
"NGOs and the State in Indonesia" *Prisma, The Indonesian Indicator,* Vol. 47 (1990), p. 34–56.

Gohlert, Ernst

Power and Culture: The Struggle Against Poverty in Thailand. Bangkok: White Lotus, 1991.

National Economic and Social Development Board

Status and Operation of Nongovernment Organizations. Bangkok: NESDB, Rural Development Coordination Division, 1992.

Oakley P. and Marsden D.

Approaches to Participation in Rural Development. Geneva: International Labour Office, 1984.

Pongsapich, Amara

Culture, Religion, and Ethnicity : An Anthropological Analysis of Thai Society. Bangkok: Chulalongkorn University, 1990.

Defining the Nonprofit Sector: Thailand. Baltimore: The Johns Hopkins Comparative Nonprofit Sector Project. Working Paper Number 11 (1993).

Pongsapich, Amara and Nitaya Kathaleeradabhan

Nonprofit Sector and Corporate Funding in Thailand Bangkok: Chulalongkorn University Social Research Institute, 1994.

Skroebanek, Siriporn

"Movement in Thailand (1855–1932)" *Satrithat, Vol.* 1, No. 3 (August-October, 1983).

Suwana-adth, Malee

The NGO Sector in Thailand and the Potential Role of NGOs in National Development. A Study Report for the Project on the Role of NGOs in Development-sponsored and supported by the Asian and Pacific Development Center and the Asian NGO Coalition for Agrarian Reform and Development, 1991.

Sasano, Adi

"NGO Roles and Social Movement in Developing Democracy: The South-East Asian Experiences in *New Asian Vision.* Vol. 6, No. 1 (March, 1989).

Timberman, David G.

A Changeless Land: Continuity and Change in Philippine Politics. Singapore: Institute of Southeast Asian Studies, 1991.

Tongsawate, Maniemai and Walter E.J. Tips

Coordination between Governmental and Nongovernmental Organizations in Thailand's Rural Development. A study of planning and implementation of integrated rural development at the local level. Bangkok: Asian Institute of Technology, Division of Human Settlements Development, 1985. Monograph No. 5.

United Nations

Case Studies on Strengthening Coordination Between Nongovernmental Organizations and Government Agencies in Promoting Social Development. New York: United Nations, 1989.

UNITED STATES of AMERICA

American Nongovernmental Organizations (NGOs) and Their Relationships with the Asia Pacific Regional Community

Yuko Iida Frost
Publisher, International Philanthropy
Consultant, Save the Children

I. Overview of the Nonprofit/NGO Sector in the United States

1. The Definition of NGOs

In the United States, the term *NGO* generally refers to a private nonprofit organization that works in one of the following areas: development of the third world, human rights, the environment, refugees/migration, emergency aid, and population control. Under the broad definition of "development of the third world," some of the specific programs and services that are commonly provided by NGOs are in the areas of health and nutrition, agricultural and natural resource development, early education, literacy improvement, economic opportunity enhancement, development education, and training.

Due to the ambiguity of the definition of NGOs today, it is difficult to measure exactly how many of them exist in the United States. To give a general sense of the nonprofit sector on the whole, in 1993 there were 1,118,131 organizations classified as tax-exempt organizations by the Internal Revenue Service (IRS), of which 575,690 were classified as 501 (c)(3), commonly called "charities." The total number of employees working for NGOs is equally difficult to access. In 1990, about 8.65 million people worked as paid employees in the nonprofit sector while 5.78 million people served as volunteers.[1] However, since the IRS has no regulatory reason to separate NGOs from other private voluntary organizations (PVOs), and there is no known accounting of American NGOs, as a distinct form, it may be worth shifting our attention from a quantitative analysis of NGOs to the basic qualities that define them in practical terms. In fact, it is more *self* identification process by which NGOs distinguish themselves from other PVOs rather than any other external attempt to define this unique sub-group within the independent sector.[2]

One such self identifying process is reflected in the conscious decision to become a member of an NGO support organization such as InterAction, a voluntary network coordination group for member NGOs with the goals of promoting the status of the NGO sector itself and providing support to enhance their professional capacity and effectiveness in carrying out their broadly shared missions. According to its *Member Profile 1993,* InterAction has 143 PVO members, most of whom are involved in "disaster relief, refugee protection, assistance and resettlement, long-term sustainable development, educating the American public about the developing world, and public policy and advocacy."[3] In 1990, the combined financial resources of the member organizations was $2.1 billion.[4] These organizations have together received more than "$1.5 billion each year in private contributions and over $600 million in government funding."[5]

Another sign of self identification is for an organization to register with the United States Agency for International Development (USAID), although some of those registered with the agency include a few grant-making foundations that are not defined as NGOs in the context of this paper. According to USAID, the 390 larger PVOs registered with the government as of October 1993 had received about $2.4 billion in private contributions and $1.5 billion from the U.S. government in the form of grants and contracts. Some of the largest USAID funding in FY1993 went to the Cooperative for American Relief Everywhere (CARE) which received $258.3 million, Catholic Relief Services ($221.2 million), United Israel Appeal ($97.1 million), The Academy for Educational Development ($60.0 million), and Adventist Development and Relief Agency International ($41.3 million).[6]

What primarily differentiates those NGOs registered with USAID from the member organizations of InterAction is their relationship with the U.S. government. While thirty-five percent of InterAction members accept no government support,[7] most USAID registered organizations receive some form of government development assistance grant and actually seek such support.

Donations to those nonprofit 501(c)(3) organizations registered with the IRS are tax deductible. The Tax Act of 1936, allowing corporations and individuals to deduct charitable contributions from their income tax, stimulated the growth of the American nonprofit sector and promoted voluntary assistance activities in the United States and abroad. Among all nonprofits, approximately 88 percent of all the private contributions ($162.2 billion in 1993) come from individuals, 4.7 percent from corporations, and 7.3 percent from foundations.[8] Other sources of funding for NGOs, besides these sources and USAID, include grants from various United Nations agencies and foreign governments.

2. Evolution of NGOs

The history of American development organizations has already been recorded by several scholars such as John G. Sommer, who authored *Beyond Charity: U.S. Voluntary Aid for a Changing Third World*[9] in 1977, and more recently Brian Smith, the author of *More Than Altruism: The Politics of Private Foreign Aid.*[10] They both articulated the evolution and significance of U.S. private overseas assistance activities, which are roughly divided into three periods: the first period until 1900, the second from around the time of World War I through World War II, and the third from 1945 to the present.

The first period, up to the end of the nineteenth century, is characterized by early evangelical/missionary endeavors as well as a plethora of voluntary activities responding to various events overseas. The emergence of NGOs in the nineteenth century is closely related to the evangelical revival, which led to a growing presence of missionaries and their activities overseas. Their goals included more than proselytizing the non-Christian natives; they provided a variety of social and humanitarian services such as education, medical care, and social welfare. One of the earliest examples of American missionaries in Asia includes schools and hospitals built in the Philippines, America's first colony in Asia acquired from Spain at the turn of the century.

Another major philanthropic movement that continues to play an important role in today's development emerged in the mid-nineteenth century—the International Red Cross. The International Committee of the Red Cross was first founded in the 1850s in Switzerland to provide medical aid to victims of wars in Europe and the United States. Created in 1887, the American Red Cross was recognized as a semi-official government agency in 1905, and received an official charter by the U.S. Congress.

The second period came with the two major world wars, from around 1914 to 1945. During this period, increasing numbers of groups, working independently or in coalition with other groups, responded to the disasters abroad by providing emergency relief. Such efforts gathered new strength, commensurate with the growing economic and political power of the United States. One of the early examples is the

American Friends Service Committee (AFSC), founded in 1917 by the American Quakers, which began its activities with relief and medical services first in France and Russia during World War I, then in Germany at the end of the war. AFSC also provided conscientious objectors to war with a non-military and non-violent method of service, such as aid to civilian victims of World War I. American Save the Children, officially called Save the Children Federation (SC/US), was also founded during this period (1932) "to study and interpret the needs of less fortunate children of our own neglected areas and those of other lands, with the aim of furthering their general development and improving conditions that impede their normal development." Unlike other NGOs that began as providers of emergency relief, such as Christian Children's Fund (CCF) which was established in 1937 to help Chinese orphans displaced during the Japanese military invasion in China, or Foster Parents Plan (PLAN) which was created to help children victimized during the Spanish civil war, SC/US applied a long-term approach to improving the well being of children and their families from its inception.

The strength and leadership of American NGOs in the realm of international relations was already apparent in 1945 when the Founding Conference of the United Nations was held in San Francisco to establish a formal consultative status for NGOs. Forty-two selected American NGOs played an official advisory role to the UN conference, and an additional 240 U.S. NGOs participated as observers, outnumbering all the state delegations combined.[11]

The third major phase of U.S. NGO development extended from 1945 to the present day, during which period U.S. NGOs shifted their focus from short-term relief and emergency aid to the contemporary model of designing and implementing long-term self-help development programs.[12] According to Peter Dobkin Hall of the Yale Program on Nonprofit Organizations (PONPO), more than ninety percent of nonprofit organizations existing today were created since World War II.[13] Many of the NGOs created during or immediately after World War II were religiously oriented; those include Catholic Relief Service (CRS), Church World Service (CWS), and Lutheran World Relief (LRW). Unlike the nineteenth century missionary organizations, these new church-supported groups perform completely secular programs even though their creation was aided by their religious denominations and some of their funding sources come from their respective church members. The AFSC and Unitarian Universalist Service Committee (UUSC) also belong to this category. From about the mid 1960s, many organizations that had been providing immediate aid to help refugees, orphanages, and starving populations in many countries during and after World War II, began diverting their resources into more long-term sustainable self-help development programs at the community level. This approach has been continuously reinforced to the present.

CARE, one of the largest and oldest of such NGOs in the United States, for example, began by providing relief assistance for victims of World War II in Europe, and later, in Asia. It now spends nearly $289 million, or sixty-four percent of its total revenue of $451 million, for long-term development programs while only $118 million, or twenty-six percent, is spent for emergency aid.[14] However, emergency relief expenses are difficult to estimate as they can change dramatically by year as regional conflicts and natural disasters create situations that require immediate collection of significant amounts of financial aid.

A growing number of American NGOs are now focusing on "building the capacities of their indigenous partners in the field…offering training, technical assistance, and support to local affiliates and community organizations at the grass roots to strengthen the organizations' ability to carry out their own technically sound, effective development projects."[15] In promoting sustainable development, many American NGOs work with local institutions and groups by getting local governments, local grassroots organizations, and community leaders involved with their work. In other words, they seek to make their own work eventually unnecessary.

As one of the youngest of such NGOs, UUSC began its operations in India in 1981 and the Philippines in 1989 with the goal of promoting the status of women in India and addressing "the imbalances in power between the U.S. and the Philippines as a result of the U.S. bases being situated" in the Philippines. In India, it finds "local groups that work on women's issues—particularly issues related to women's health, reproductive rights and socio-cultural and economic rights improving the status of women… " WSC is planning to phase out of the Philippines, as its primary reason for going into the country—removing the American military presence in the Philippines—no longer exists.[16]

3. The U.S. Government and NGOs

This shift of focus from emergency relief to long-term self help development also marks the beginning of a closer relationship between NGOs and the U.S. government. As the government saw the principles of such development work of NGOs as congruent with and complementary to USAID's fundamental principles of promoting pluralism and democracy overseas, it began to provide support for NGOs for their long-term development work. As a statement by the USAID Advisory Committee on Voluntary Foreign Aid (established in 1948) outlined, "for American PVOs, the emergence of strong and competent colleagues in developing countries presents rich opportunities to multiply growth…The reconfiguring of roles between local and expatriate organizations will and should occur…"[17]

Created in 1961, USAID shifted its focus over the years from countering communism to enhancing the third sector in recipient countries, recognizing the importance of "self-sustaining, civic societies" in its host countries as an indispensable component of their strategy for sustainable development. The most recent paper published by USAID describes this goal:

> It will assist host nations in building indigenous institutions and developing policies that promote openness to trade and investment, support agriculture and rural enterprise, strengthen infrastructure and delivery of services in cities, provide adequate incentives for exports, reinforce the effectiveness and transparency of fiscal and monetary policy and regulations, avoid inefficient import substitution and unwarranted protection, and strengthen the enabling environment for development of the private sector.[18]

As one of the most recent examples of this agenda, USAID has chosen partners from U.S. NGOs to collaborate in building a social environment more conducive to the healthy development of the NGO sector particularly in former Communist countries in Eastern Europe and the Russian Republics. The new initiative will evaluate legal and tax systems and identify areas for change. It will also provide social marketing skills to promote better understanding of the third sector among the public. Finally, it will provide technical assistance in cultivating the professional skills necessary for managing NGOs.[19]

As Table 1 indicates, as of October 1993, 390 PVOs registered with USAID have a total revenue of about $6.2 billion, of which $1.5 billion, or 24.4 percent, comes from the U.S. government. In order to receive U.S. government development assistance funding, NGOs have to be registered with USAID. Some people find irony in this relationship with the government because some of the organizations that had originally started with fundamental distrust in the government's ability and actions in the areas of social welfare, have become increasingly dependent on government financial support.20 In fact, some NGOs have neither sought nor accepted any funding from the U.S. government in order to preserve complete independence. Among those organizations are Human Rights Watch, American Friends Service Committee (AFSC), Oxfam America, and World Neighbors (WN). According to David Elder of AFSC, their organization does not accept U.S. government funds for work overseas since it "often work[s] in countries negatively affected by U.S. foreign and military policy, such as Vietnam and Central America…For independence of action it has been important not to use U.S. government funds."[21] The organizations that were funded by the government were scrutinized and criticized for serving the government's political objectives in Cambodia and Vietnam during the war in Indochina.[22]

Alternative funding sources for those who do not accept government funding include financial support from various private sources including individual contributions, foundations, corporate support, membership dues, programs such as child sponsorship and goods/services sold.

Table 1 Summary of Support and Revenue for
U.S. Private Voluntary Organizations

U.S. Government	US Dollars	Non-U.S. Government	US Dollars
USAID Freight & Food	150,802,893	Other governments and international organizations	387,119,316
PL 480 Food	319,592,738	In-Kind Contributions	820,141,910
USAID Grants & Contracts	727,391,685	Private Contributions	2,392,983,057
Other U.S. Government Grants	313,975,089	Private Revenue	1,072,768,952
Total	1,511,762,405	Total	4,673,013,235

Source: U.S. Agency for International Development, *Voluntary Foreign Aid Programs 1994: Report of American Voluntary Agencies Engaged in Overseas Relief and Development Registered with the U.S. Agency for International Development* (Washington: USAID, 1994), pp. 96–97.

Table 2 shows how much of those revenues are spent for overseas and domestic programs, administration, and fund raising to operate the NGOs registered with USAID. However, it is customary to include salaries and other office expenses related to programs in the program expense line.

Total Expenses	5,952,378,582	
Overseas Program	3,678,107,271	(61.8%)
Domestic Program	1,625,442,777	(27.3%)
Administrative	441,827,809	(7.4%)
Fundraising	207,000,725	(3.5%)

Source: USAID. *Voluntary Foreign Aid Programs 1994*, p. 97.

While the overall relationship between the public sector and the nonprofit sector in the United States has been characterized as more cooperative than confronta tional, and the government has increasingly relied on the nonprofit sector to address social ills, there is a growing perception and concern that less government funding will be available to support U.S. NPOs and that they will have to rely more on either private funding or international resources for their future activities.

4. The Role of NGOs in Societies

One of the most fundamental and historical roles of the U.S. nonprofit sector as a whole is to keep an eye on the public policy formulation process both at the local and federal levels and to make sure that people's voices are heard by the policy makers.[23] Such an action, collectively called *lobbying*, is a basic right guaranteed under the U.S. legal framework. Through lobbying, NGOs attempt to educate policy makers about the conditions of the targeted communities where they work in promoting legislative support for their missions. Bread for the World was created with the primary objective of lobbying the government to assume specific policies that the organization developed based on its research on world hunger. However, some of these missions include areas beyond the provision of third world development. In recent years, NGOs have become more vocal in issues related to human rights and environmental protection, as well.

Human Rights Watch, one of the leading human rights groups with total operating revenues of $7.6 million and five regional divisions (including Asia Watch), not only monitors and publicizes human rights practices of governments around the globe, it also lobbies the U.S. government, other governments, and the United Nations agencies to respond to human rights abuses. In addition, it launches campaigns against governments that violate human rights.

Major environmental organizations spend somewhere around 1.3 percent to 1.5 percent of their total revenues for lobbying, with the exception of 21 percent for Sierra Club in 1992.[24]

In addition to information dissemination and public policy advocacy activities, PVOs have developed many ways of cultivating a more direct relationship with the public. Some NGOs have adopted programs that allow their constituents and supporters directly or indirectly to participate in their organizations' missions whether they be third world development or environmental protection. Some of these programs include a membership system, child sponsorship programs, and volunteer field participation programs. The objectives for providing such opportunities for the public are multifold: (*a*) it allows organizations to establish a direct link with individual supporters; (*b*) it builds awareness among the public about the importance of their missions hence promoting better support; and (*c*) it empowers individuals who tend to perceive themselves as powerless in helping those in needy communities. One of the most appealing aspects to many "foster parents" of a child sponsorship program practiced by organizations such as SC/US and Childreach, for example, is that a sponsor feels he or she is directly helping a needy child and the child's community through the program.

II. Evolution of the Asia Pacific Regional Community Concept among NGOs

1. Key Factors Influencing NGOs' Involvement in the Asia Pacific Region

While the Asia Pacific region has enjoyed the fastest economic growth in the world in recent years, the discrepancy between the wealthy and the needy communities remains disturbingly clear and substantial. Annual per capita income among nations, for example, ranges from $180 in Nepal to $26,930 in Japan.[25] In fact, many in the Asia Pacific regional community suffer directly from the fast industrialization and urbanization, which have caused seriously adverse living conditions. The flow of cheap labor into urban areas, for example, resulted in an insufficient child care and early education system as well as the abuse of women in the work force, the violation of other labor/human rights, degradation of the environment, and lack of attention to the rural economy, keeping most of the areas in this region in severe poverty. Just as such rapid economic growth has generated side effects, the immense cultural diversity of the region is not without negative aspects. The coexistence of many ethnic groups with diverse religious faiths may account for various types of regional conflicts among different ethnic groups and their respective traditions. Similarly, different religious teachings affect population control and women's social and economic status. For example, in an Islamic region, women have less access to social services and economic opportunities.

However, because of the very problems of the Asia Pacific region and the limitation of the public sector in dealing with them, many grassroots organizations have sprung up to address basic needs and inequalities. It is in this economic and social milieu of the Asia Pacific region that American NGOs, working with those local NGOs, have continued to identify problems and implement programs to eradicate them.

Historically, most American NGOs that have worked in the Asia Pacific region began their programs by responding to the urgent needs that arose during some of the major wars that took place in this region. Since the end of World War II, the Asia Pacific region has gone through several prolonged wars that resulted in millions of victims in Korea and Indochina and numerous other regional conflicts that have victimized the lives of many people. American NGOs have responded to some of the disasters in cooperation with the host governments and UN agencies.

In fact, many of the newly created church-oriented NGOs mentioned above left Europe once the war reconstruction was complete, shifting their attention to Asia and other parts of the world. This is mostly due to an increasing amount of government aid available to U.S. NGOs/PVOs during the 1950s and 1960s, resulting from political leaders' perception that the communist influence was spreading fast in Asia and that one of the most effective ways to stop it was to promote pluralism and the local capacity to solve socio-economic problems through the private, rather than the state, network of self-help movements. In fact, during the war in Vietnam, NGOs such as CRS, World Vision, the American Red Cross, International Volunteer Service, and Vietnam Christian Services (a consortium created by CWS, LWR, and the Mennonite Central Committee) provided aid for refugees and other "relief assistance to strategic hamlet programs" with heavy funding from the U. S. government.[26]

Not all American NGOs went along with the U.S. government agendas and objectives in Asia during these periods. The AFSC worked in both South and North Vietnam throughout the U.S. involvement in the Vietnam War, providing medical aid and refugee/rehabilitation programs while designing and implementing peace education as part of its anti-war activities in the United States during the 1960s. Its various forms of humanitarian aid to Vietnam have continued through to the present. AFSC was also in northern India helping Tibetan refugees from 1959 through 1961 when the Chinese invasion caused massive Tibetan migration. This was a significant commitment considering how little attention the international community paid to this regional incident. The AFSC's involvement in Asia dates back to 1923, when it went to Japan to help victims of the Great Tokyo Earthquake, which took more than a hundred thousand lives. It opened offices in China and Pakistan for various emergency relief, refugee/migration, and rural/urban development programs during the 1940s.

In Cambodia, where the twelve-year-old civil war has caused the highest percentage of mine amputees (36,000 out of the total population of 8.5 million), more than fifty NGOs and international organizations have provided health-related services. Handicapped International (HI), the International Committee of the Red

Cross (ICRC), and AFSC opened prosthetic and rehabilitation services in 1991. Organizations such as the Vietnam Veterans of America Foundation, Human Rights Watch, Physicians for Human Rights, the Mines Advisory Group, HI, and Medico International have launched a worldwide campaign to ban the use of mines, of which it is estimated there are eighty-two million scattered in sixty-two countries. Responding to their efforts, the UN General Assembly unanimously approved a "nonbinding resolution calling for a worldwide moratorium on exports of antipersonnel land mines."[27]

As its first program in Asia, SC/US went to Korea in 1953 to help the country ameliorate the conditions of orphans left during the Korean War and the post war adjustment of the society. It now has programs in the Philippines, Bhutan, Nepal, Indonesia, Thailand, Bangladesh, Cambodia, Laos, and mostly recently Vietnam. Many other organizations began their activities in Asia around the same time and grew rapidly.

The growth of the Asian American population and the rise of their social status in American societies have contributed significantly to building a bridge between U.S. NGOs and the Asia Pacific regional community. According to the U.S. Bureau of the Census statistics, Asian Americans are the fastest growing population in the United States, with their total number increasing from 1.5 million in 1970 and 3.7 million in 1980 to 7.2 million in 1990, or nearly three percent of the total population of the United States. As the Asian American population grows rapidly, so does the number of organized activities related to Asia within the United States. The *Asian Americans Information Directory* lists more than 5,200 organizations, agencies, publications, and services concerned with Asian American groups in the United States.[28]

The majority of those groups and activities serve as a link between the Asian American community and their Asian heritage. Some are dedicated to the protection and promotion of the interest of the ethnic groups in the United States, and some are geared more directly toward helping the needy communities in the Asia Pacific region. (Unfortunately, there is no single source of information that distinguishes between the two and quantifies them.)

The Indochina Resource Action Center (IRAC), for example, was created in 1979 to help immigrants and refugees from Indochina in the United States make the transition from "dependent refugees to a responsible Asian American minority . . . [and] serves as a national clearinghouse for information on Indochina refugees, and a technical assistance center for the empowerment of the Indochinese-American community."[29] According to the *InterAction Member Profile 1993,* IRAC attempts to achieve the said mission through its advocacy activities, trying to facilitate an information clearinghouse for the refugees and protecting their human rights both at the first asylum camps and in their home countries.

Organizations that were not created to meet the needs of a particular segment of the American population have developed a special relationship with the Asia Pacific community through the Asian American population. Planned Parenthood of New York City provides services in the fields of population control, family planning, and various public health programs, including HIV testing, counseling, and support services as well as training for health professionals. Motivated largely by the urgent need for family planning programs in the Asia Pacific region and partially by its close relationship with the Asian community in New York City, the organization began its activities in the Philippines ten years ago. Encouraged by the support from a network of local NGOs and the government of the Philippines, Planned Parenthood of New York City plans to expand its programs to countries in the rest of the region, such as Vietnam, Indonesia, Myanmar, Nepal, and India. The major factor that constrains such expansion has been the lack of sufficient funding available for the additional programs in Asia.[30]

2. Major Efforts by NGOs and NGO Networks in Enhancing the Community Concept

Networks of indigenous or local grassroots organizations, well advanced in many Asian countries, have had a positive effect on the activities of many American NGOs.[31] Several sources indicate that there are at least 20,000 to 25,000 NGOs in the seven countries in Southeast Asia.[32] The Unitarian Universalist Service Committee (UUSC), for example, takes advantage of such local strength in the Philippines—where most support comes from "a strong tradition of nongovernmental organizing along with the presence of feminist groups with sophisticated lobbying and advocacy approaches"—that characterizes the local programs. There is also "a culture of networking and working in coalitions that creates a multiplier effect in addressing the issues."[33]

One relief/development organization includes strengthening indigenous programs in its internal ten-year plan. It has increasingly used the local capacities of indigenous organizations in its program implementation. Members of the organization believe that there is less need for a "northern subsidy" to ensure sound program management in the field. It plans to identify existing high-quality indigenous organizations to serve as representatives for some of its programs.

One staff member of Save the Children Federation (SC/US) explained that [in the Philippines] SC/US attempts to coordinate the activities of local NGOs of similar types, which would otherwise work independently and duplicate efforts, for more efficient implementation of programs.

The National Wildlife Federation (NWF) has posted a staff member in Tokyo to develop relationships with indigenous NGOs in Japan in its effort to lobby the Japanese government to adopt Official Development Assistance (ODA) funding policies that are more reflective of sustainable development policies in the Asia Pacific region. It provides Japanese NGOs and their networks with information on ODA policies and assists them in fund raising and advocacy. NWF also funds research projects pertaining to environmental issues of the Asia Pacific region.

The change of donor priority has also contributed to the new phenomenon of American NGOs seeking partnerships with local NGOs. According to Priscilla Li of AT&T Foundation, some American multinational corporations have begun searching for ways in which they can establish their identity as local corporations, and one way of doing so is through changing their giving behavior from one of giving to American NGOs to one of giving to local NGOs or alliances between local and American NGOs.[34] Needless to say, newly created local philanthropic institutions would rather support local NGOs than their U.S. counterparts.

3. Interactions Between the Public Sector and NGOs in the Region

Since the public sector has traditionally had a monopoly in providing social services in most countries in the Asia Pacific region, the recent emergence of NGOs within the cultural context is perceived as a threat or antithesis to the government. American NGOs must be aware of this unique relationship between the public sector and NGOs in the region, which is different from what we have in the United States, where the two sectors are often interdependent and complementary. It is, therefore, imperative that American NGOs first establish clear and positive relationships with the host government before they begin programs. With the exception of emergency relief activities, foreign NGOs are required to obtain government permission and cooperation to implement their programs.

American NGOs have indeed cooperated with other NGOs, UN agencies, and local governments, but no systematic attempt has ever been made by the public sector to promote bilateral collaboration between American NGOs and their counterpart organizations in the Asia Pacific region as envisioned under the Common Agenda.

The Common Agenda, established by President Clinton and Japanese Prime Minister Miyazawa on 10 July 1993 in Tokyo, as part of the Joint Statement on the United States-Japan Framework for a New Economic Partnership, is designed to expand the bilateral relationship beyond the areas that only involve issues related conventionally to national security and trade. As outlined in the Framework, the Common Agenda calls for cooperation on fifteen separate programs aimed at addressing critical global issues in five areas: environmental degradation, technology development, human resource development, population, and the prevention of AIDS. In addition to these areas, Child Health, Alternative Agriculture, Oceans, and Information Exchanges were added under this new program.

Under the Common Agenda, environmental NGOs such as the World Wildlife Fund (WWF), Philippines have already received funding for a joint project with their Japanese counterparts in the Philippines.[35] WWF Philippines and WWF-Japan received $50,000 from the U.S. government and $50,000 from the government of Japan for their joint project to open ten national parks to protect the forest at the site of Subic Bay and training centers for managing the parks.

According to Paul E. White, USAID Minister Counselor for Development Cooperation at the U.S. Embassy in Tokyo, "the U.S. and Japan are encouraging more NGO participation in their jointly supported activities. This goal will be substantially facilitated if NGOs focus on what NGOs do best—working on participatory grassroots programs that are relevant and appropriate to the development needs of the recipients and that are cost effective and sustainable."[36] However, he warns that if American NGOs are only focused on the "dollar value of the cooperation," they would be making a significant mistake as real cooperation should be based on what they can "give" to each other in expertise and knowledge so they can achieve successful development projects in the target community.[37]

III. Future Prospects

1. Role of NGOs to Further Advance the Regional Community Concept

- Building local capacities through cooperation with indigenous NGOs, and local grassroots organizations as well as the local and central governments is considered to be a very effective way of achieving the organizational mission as well as involving local populations in their own development. Many U.S. based NGOs are now involved in such collaboration and partnership.

- Increasing financial support from the Asian philanthropic community to Asia-related programs in educational and other institutions within the United States has helped promote the awareness of the Asia Pacific regional community concept among the non-Asian population. Major universities, for example, have received funding to open or expand their programs on Asia. An environmental organization has started a training program for Asian corporate managers to enhance a sense of compatibility between the economic development and environmental conservation in the Asia Pacific region. A relief organization offers English language programs to the local community of recent immigrants from Southeast Asia.
- The growing number of Asian American community organizations and the scale of their activities has further promoted better understanding of the Asia Pacific region and a sense of local identity, which will in the future be instrumental to adopting more culturally sound policies for American NGOs in planning and implementing programs in that region.
- Forging partnerships with the business sector in the region and involving corporations in the regional activities of NGOs open up new opportunities for both financial security and more effective implementation of programs. For example, The Nature Conservancy (TNC) has successfully involved the "offender," the business community, in approaching the issue of environmental conservation in this region. Rather than taking a confrontational approach, it chose to adopt a cooperative and inclusive policy in tackling regional problems. It received financial support from a powerful funding source while providing opportunities for industries to participate in the process of ameliorating the problems for which they are responsible—opportunities that would have been very difficult to gain access to without such an approach.

Major constraints against NGO regional cooperative efforts

1) The relative lack of interest in and the ignorance of the Asia Pacific region among the American public in general, except for short-term business interest in certain economies, have negatively affected the public support for American NGO activities in Asia. This is manifested in U.S. foreign policies toward Asia. Issues such as human rights in China, trade/industrial policy, the post cold war regional security arrangement, energy policy, and technology transfer, are treated as independent and isolated problems with secondary attention paid next to Europe and the former Soviet Union. Thus, the public's ignorance of and frustration with the re-

gion resulted from the lack of a cohesive and comprehensive "Asia Policy" at the government level, permeating the general public attitudes toward Asia. This has left the vast and important region with less thoughtful attention than is needed.

The clearest manifestation of such sentiment is reflected in American government support for NGOs working in Asia. As mentioned earlier in this report, many American NGOs that have worked in the Asia Pacific region have traditionally received generous support from USAID as well as from private grant-making institutions. Government funding for programs in Asia, however, has continuously declined in the last several years. Of a total of $14 billion, only $316 million,[38] or about 2.3 percent, of the USAID budget in 1994 was spent on this region. The growing tension between the U.S. government and some of the Asian governments in issues such as human rights, regional security, and trade, have contributed largely to this decline. One government official admitted to the *Far Eastern Economic Review* (FEER) that U.S. aid to Asia is very small but that that is the way it should be.[39] Robert Orr, chairman of the American Chamber of Commerce committee on foreign aid residing in Tokyo, also told FEER that he believes there is no reason for Americans to give aid to "rich Asians" and that Japan should take over,[40] as it has done already. Indeed, about sixty-five percent of the total Japanese ODA money was spent in Asia in FY1993.[41] As shown in Table 3, Japan's official aid to Asian countries was about nine times larger than that of the United States in FY1993.

Table 3 Bilateral Comparison of AID to ASIA

(U.S. $ millions)

Receiving Country	Japanese Aid (FY 1993)	U.S. Aid (FY 1994)
Indonesia	1,357	68
China	1,051	1
Philippines	1,031	74
India	425	156
Pakistan	173	3
Bangladesh	163	113
Malaysia	157	1
Thailand	114	6
Nepal	107	30
Sri Lanka	96	36
Mongolia	44	11
Laos	25	2
Cambodia	5	28
TOTAL	4,747	529

Source: Nigel Holloway, "Seed Money: U.S. has a big message but little cash for Asia." *Far Eastern Economic Review* (81/18/94), p. 19.

Compared with their lack of attention given to Asia, USAID began a major initiative in promoting the independent sector in the former communist countries of Eastern Europe and the Russian Republics, as mentioned above.

2) Closely related to the first point, there is a misperception among the American public that the Asia Pacific region has enjoyed monolithic economic growth, and therefore, that the need for the involvement of U.S. NGOs or international organizations is minimal. This has not only left some NGOs with less public financial support, but it has also led some NGOs to begin looking at this region more as a potential funding source rather than a target community for programs. In the absence of fully developed NGOs in many countries in the region, the lack of support from the American NGOs can negatively affect the regional cooperative effort.

3) American NGOs encounter difficulties in entering or remaining in certain socialist and military-led countries in the Asia Pacific region as government restrictions limit the activities of American NGOs. The government of China, for example, has traditionally assumed responsibility for all the social ills leaving little room for private voluntary activities, and it has imposed tight controls over the activities of foreign NGOs.[42] Recently, however, the central government has reduced government subsidies in social services, creating pressure to privatize such services and resulting in the sudden growth of private voluntary groups similar to the PVOs we have in the United States.[43] However, it might take a while before this movement will open the society to foreign NGOs coming into the country. As of this writing, only 24 of InterAction's member organizations (nearly 150 in all) have some type of program in China.[44] Another country that has been difficult to enter is Myanmar; some organizations have been waiting for the optimum time to connect themselves with the community in Myanmar, where military control has made it very difficult to provide social services. The recent release of the opposition leader, Aung San Suu Kyi, is likely to have a profound impact on the improvement of its social standard, and some Western NGOs are already looking at ways of implementing programs in the country.

4) Partnership among northern NGOs and cooperation between American NGOs and local NGOs can be very difficult when the degree of organizational capacity of one NGO is less than that of the other's.[45] The issue of partnering with local organizations is most complex when the partnership is used for fund raising, as some of the newly emerged local philanthropic entities prefer to give directly to local NGOs, rather than to big American or international NGOs that are perceived as having easy access to considerable funding. Some of the local NGOs have indeed earned reputations in competence in carrying out their own programs efficiently, and they are posing unprecedented challenges to U.S. NGOs.

2. Some Measures to Further Enhance the Above Efforts

Following are some recommendations for American NGOs to enhance regional cooperative efforts. These conclusions are drawn from interviews with NGO managers, including Barnett F. Baron of The Asia Foundation; David Claussenius and Alexandria Overy of SC/US; Sherry Dahl of Christian Children's Fund; Giselle Dupuis of The Nature Conservancy; Julie Fisher, a guest scholar at Yale Program on Nonprofit Organization (PONPO); Deborah McGlauflin of Insights in Action; and Sandra Diggs of Food for the Hungry, Inc.

1) "Localize" U.S. NGO activities in the region. In other words, American NGOs should learn to give up direct supervision and administration of their regional programs and either significantly involve local NGOs at the management level or form a partnership in implementing the programs. Some of the field offices of SC/US, for example, are run completely by local managers and staff, with little direct supervision from the head office in the United States. This is an important model for promoting the community concept and a key to building trust in the community by establishing an identity as a local organization of the host country. Re-establishing this identity as a local NGO has to be accompanied by a shift of funding sources from large Western government/foundation funding to locally raised funding, since funding sources often influence the quality and the ownership of the programs. This leads to issues of local capacity building and the responsiveness of programs to the target community, discussed below.

2) Build local capacity by working with local institutions such as central and local governments, private businesses, research institutions and universities, and most importantly indigenous NGOs. A key to sustainable development and the successful implementation of community focused programs is the level of influence NGOs exert on such local institutional strength. A factor that affected TNC's decision to start a program in the Asia Pacific region was the presence of strong local interest in environmental protection issues and local institutional capability. To help increase local capacity, some American NGOs shifted their attention from direct delivery of programs often developed by northern NGOs to the creation of a network of local NGOs through which programs are developed and tested on their own.

3) Use a multisectoral approach, rather than a single sector program. For example, many local environmental NGOs in Asia have teamed up with human rights groups, as they believe that the improvement of Asia's environment cannot be sustained without improving the quality of the lives of those who inhabit the region.46

Likewise, the improvement of children's health and nutrition cannot be sustained without increases in mothers' knowledge of child rearing, education, and health as well as in the level of their income.[47] Thus development programs are becoming increasingly inter- and multi-sectoral reaching out to wider segments of the population through more comprehensive approaches to sustainable development.

4) Become more responsive to local needs by forming alliances with local funding organizations and multilateral or bilateral organizations as alternative funding sources to U.S. government aid. Through cooperative relationships with organizations like The World Bank and the Asian Development Bank, corporate giving programs and private grant-making foundations, and most importantly individuals and the new middle class in the Asia Pacific region, American NGOs can become a more integral part of the process of linking local NGOs and community-focused programs for sustainable development.

IV. Summary

U.S. NGOs will most likely continue to play a preeminent role in the development of the Asia Pacific region. With the scope and quality of their services, as well as their management and organizational skills, many American NGOs have efficiently carried out their missions and promoted the concept of self-help development. Given the long history of the U.S. NGO commitment in the Asia Pacific region, they are expected to stay influential there. However, the recent dynamic growth of indigenous NGOs has generated competition for U.S. NGOs, challenging them to reevaluate their relationship to the region. As international and local donor priority has begun to shift toward more regionally managed programs, many U.S. NGOs have already started repositioning themselves for the new environment.

For an American NGO to provide programs more efficiently and effectively, it must find a competitive niche where it has comparative advantages in quality and technical services. It should work to build a local capacity by getting local/indigenous NGOs, other grassroots organizations, the business sector, and the local and/or central government involved in promoting the sustainability of its programs. Partnerships with the local community and regional NGOs—both operating and grant-making foundations—are thus increasingly vital to sustainable development work as well as securing funding in the regional community.

Notes

1. Independent Sector, *Nonprofit Almanac 1992–1993: Dimensions of the Independent Sector* (San Francisco: Jossey-Bass Publishers, 1992), p. 29.
2. Interview with Deborah McGlauflin, President of Insights in Action.
3. *InterAction Member Profile 1993,* (Washington: InterAction, 1993) p. vii.
4. Ian Smillie and Henry Helmich, (eds.), *Non-Governmental Organizations and Governments: Stakeholders for Development* (Paris: OECD, 1993), p. 305.
5. *InterAction Member Profile 1993,* op. cit.
6. U.S. Agency for International Development, *Voluntary Foreign Aid Programs 1994: Report of American Voluntary Agencies Engaged in Overseas Relief and Development Registered with the U.S. Agency for International Development* (Washington, D.C.: Bureau for Humanitarian Response of USAID, 1994)
7. *InterAction Member Profile 1993,* op. cit.
8. American Association of Fund-raising Council, *Giving USA 1994,* (New York: AAFRC Trust for Philanthropy, 1994), pp. 26–27.
9. John G. Sommer, *Beyond Charity: U.S. Voluntary Aid for a Changing Third World* (Washington D.C.: Overseas Development Council, 1977).
10. Brian H. Smith, *More Than Altruism: The Politics of Private Foreign Aid* (Princeton: Princeton University Press, 1990).
11. Helmut K. Anheier and Kusuma Cunningham, "Internationalization of the Nonprofit Sector," in *The Jossey-Bass Handbook of Nonprofit Leadership and Management,* edited by Robert D. Herman & Associates (San Francisco: Jossey-Bass, 1994), p. 103.
12. U.S. Agency for International Development, *Voluntary Foreign Aid Programs 1994,* p. 5.
13. Peter Dobkin Hall, "Historical Perspectives on Nonprofit Organizations" in *The Jossey-Bass Handbook of Nonprofit Leadership and Management,* op. cit., p. 3
14. *CARE Annual Report 1993: The Challenge,* p. 41.
15. U.S. Agency for International Development, *Voluntary Foreign Aid Programs 1994,* p. 5.
16. Interview with Ms. Shalini Nataraj, International Program of Unitarian Universalist Service Committee.
17. Advisory Committee on Voluntary Foreign Aid, "Responding to Change," USAID, 1990.
18. U. S. Agency for International Development, *Strategies for Sustainable Development March 1994* (Washington, DC: USAID, 1994), p. 6
19. Interview with Jim Kunder, Vice President of Program Development at Save the Children Federation.
20. Sommer, op. cit.
21. Interview conducted in November of 1994 with Mr. David Elder, Coordinator of Asia Programs of American Friends Service Committee .

22. Sommer, op. cit., pp. 94–99.
23. For a brief comparison of the U.S. nonprofit sector with the Japanese counterpart, see Yuko Iida Frost, "A Key to Open Japan?: Japan's Nonprofit Sector on the Move" in *The Brookings Review*, Fall 1993.
24. Linda Kanamine and Paul Overberg, "Leaner Times Test Limits of Movement," in *USA Today*, 19 October, 1994, p. 8A.
25. Isagani R. Serrano, *Civil Society in the Asia Pacific Region* (Washington, D.C.: CIVICUS, 1994), p. 20.
26. Smith, op. cit., p. 64; Sommer, op. cit., p. 97. According to Smith, 94 percent of CRS's total budget of $10.2 million for South Vietnam in 1972 was subsidized by the government.
27. Eric Stover, Allen S. Keller, James Cobey, Sam Sopheap, "The Medical and Social Consequences of Land Mines in Cambodia," in *The Journal of the American Medical Association*, Vol. 272, August 3, 1994.
28. Kare Backus and Julia C. Furtaw, (eds.), *Asian Americans Information Directory*, First Edition (Detroit: Gale Research, 1992).
29. *InterAction Member Profiles 1993*, op. cit., pp. 134–35.
30. Interview with Mr. Peter Purdy, Vice President of International Programs and Director of Margaret Sanger Center International of Planned Parenthood of New York City.
31. Interview with David Claussenius, Director of Asia/Middle East regions of Program Operations at Save the Children.
32. Julie Fisher, *The Road from Rio: Sustainable Development and the Nongovernmental Movement in the Third World* (Westport, CT: Praeger Publishers, 1993), pp. 89–91. Those seven countries are Bangladesh, India, Indonesia, Nepal, the Philippines, Sri Lanka, and Thailand.
33. Interview with Ms. Shalini Nataraj, International Program of Unitarian Universalist Service Committee.
34. Interview with Priscilla Li of AT&T in November 1994.
35. "Conversation with Common Agenda Grantee," an interview with Hon. Ceoso Rokue, head of World Wildlife Fund Philippines, in *International Philanthropy* Vol. I No. 6, pp. 12–13.
36. Paul E. White, "Insider's View," in *International Philanthropy*, July 1994, Vol. I, pp. 1–2, 13.
37. Ibid., p. 13.
38. Spending includes food handouts and Peace Corps volunteers, the total budget was $526 billion.
39. Nigel Holloway, "Seed Money: U.S. Has a Big Message But Little Cash for Asia," in *Far Eastern Economic Review*, 8118/94, p. 19.
40. Ibid.
41. Ministry of Foreign Affairs, *Japan's ODA 1993: Annual Report*, (Tokyo: Assoc. of Promotion of International Cooperation, 1994), p. 44.
42. Isagani R. Serrano, op. cit., p. 14.

43. Barnett F. Baron's speech on "The Emergence and Potential Role of Asian NGOs and Grantmaking Philanthropies" at Yale School of Management on 1 November, 1994.

44. *InterAction Member Profiles 1993,* op. cit., p. 334.

45. Interview with Mr. Peter Purdy, Vice President of International Programs and Director of Margaret Sanger Center International of Planned Parenthood of New York City.

46. Fisher, op. cit., p. 105

47. Save the Children, *Ten-Year Strategic Framework for 1993.*

VIETNAM

The Emergence of a Nonprofit Sector and Philanthropy in the Socialist Republic of Vietnam

Mark Sidel[1]
Program Officer for Vietnam
The Ford Foundation, Bangkok

The post-1986 Vietnamese policy of reform and renovation (*doi moi*), the acceleration of economic reform policies, the retreat of the state from provision of social services and from many aspects of control over daily life, and the greater political and economic space now available for policy research, social action, social and religious service, and other work have resulted in a rapidly growing number of policy- and development-oriented initiatives in Vietnam. Many of these are largely outside the state sector. In total, such groups now number at least in the hundreds, more are forming, and new regulatory efforts are underway at the central level.

A variety of Vietnamese groups are seeking space from the Vietnamese state, and they are among the most exciting, dynamic sectors of a dynamic economy and society. This chapter provides some background to the development of these groupings, provides a typology for such groups, examines some common problems many face, and reviews the rapidly changing regulatory structure in which they function.[2]

I. New Policy- and Development-Oriented Groups

Nongovernmental organizations is not yet the most accurate term to apply to the range of Vietnamese research, social action, religious, community, and other groups discussed here, which are attempting to find, maintain, and work with some space from the Vietnamese state.

A variety of factors have contributed to the development of this range of policy-

and development-oriented initiatives. The economic reform process itself has spurred the formation of many such groups. The Vietnamese Party and state are no longer the sole, and in many cases not even the dominant, providers of education, health, and other social services for Vietnam's rapidly growing population. Economic reform has led to declining state expenditures on important elements of social services (in terms of total proportional outlay within the sector and, generally, within institutions). In some ways this has been as much a matter of conscious choice—a reform "policy option"—as of necessity.[3] A more generally open political atmosphere has also contributed to the growth of new initiatives.

A variety of newer policy- and development-oriented initiatives and groups have emerged in Vietnam since the mid to late 1980s. One category is *newer, more independent policy research and teaching groups.* These range from well-established groups such as the Center for Natural Resources and Environmental Sciences at Hanoi University (led by Professor Vo Quy) to newer initiatives such as the Center for Gender, Family and Environment in Development in Hanoi (led by Professor Le Thi Nham Tuyet).

A second category is *Ho Chi Minh City and other southern social activism and social service networks,* which were influenced by French and particularly American training and assistance in the 1950s and 1960s. These groups include the Social Work Research and Training Center (led by Ms. Nguyen Thi Oanh) and the Center for Pediatrics, Development and Health (led by Dr. Duong Quynh Hoa), both in Ho Chi Minh City. Such organizations range from local, service-oriented charitable organizations, to groups concerned with sustainable development, to organizations somewhat more directly critical of Party and government policies and of corruption.

It may be useful to consider the policy research groups in the north and the social action/sustainable development groups in the South as one broad category, expressing differences between northern and southern politics and a sense of what is possible in the north and the south. In the north, policy research is an important route to more autonomous social and political activity, while in the south, social action and social service (including, at times, charity work) lead to more independent activity.

The policy research option in the north, and the space for social service and social action in the south, reflect earlier politics. In the Democratic Republic of Vietnam between 1954 and 1986 (when *doi moi* began), policy research was virtually the only expression of creative social thought acceptable to the authorities.[4] In the south, social action and social service institutions, along with religious groups, have often had a larger range of political space than have policy research groups. There are also important differences, discussed below, in the northern, more research focused sector between more established groups (such as the Hanoi University Center for Natural Resources and Environmental Studies [CRES]) and newer, much less well established groups (such as the Center for Gender, Family and Environment in Development).

A third, related category is a series of *quasi-public/quasi-private and private universities and other educational institutions*, most of which are in Hanoi, Ho Chi Minh City or other southern cities. The Hanoi and Ho Chi Minh City Open Universities, still within the state system but largely self-financed through higher tuition rates, are gradually opening the tertiary education sector. Private universities, business and vocational schools, and other post-secondary institutions (such as Thang Long Universities in Hanoi and Ho Chi Minh City, the Business Management Institute in Hanoi, and numerous private educational institutions in Ho Chi Minh City) have also been quite successful since about 1990, first in Ho Chi Minh City and later in Hanoi.

A fourth category among these new initiatives or groupings is *senior leader–supported patronage groups supporting training and research projects.* This is a particularly difficult category to analyze. At one level these are social service groups which merely happen to have elite support. But such an open-faced simplistic definition begs further analysis. At another level, these groupings are intended to contribute to elite power retention through patronage and social service, while substituting voluntary for now scarce state funds for specific projects.

Groups in this sector include scholarship-granting, academic research and social service groups headlined (though not necessarily headed on a day-to-day basis) by such patrons as Prime Minister Vo Van Kiet (Fund for Young Talents of Vietnam), General Vo Nguyen Giap (Vietnam Fund for Supporting Technological Creations) and former Foreign Minister Nguyen Co Thach (Programme Volontaire de Vulgarisation des Progres Scientific-Techniques pour les Familles Rurales).

A fifth category is *professional and business associations*, such as the national and local science and technology associations, social science professional associations, consultancy services (such as that operated by former southern government economist Nguyen Xuan Oanh in Ho Chi Minh City), small business development groups (such as the Non-State Economic Development Center), and other organizations.

A sixth grouping is *peasant associations and collectives.* Here we can identify two types: "traditional" state-founded peasant associations, and voluntary community groups formed in the years since 1986, to help peasants cope with aspects of rapid economic reform. Closely related, but present as well in urban areas, are *ethnic and clan groups.* Discouraged or dissolved throughout much of the 1954–86 period, such groups seemed nonetheless never to have died out. Their "new" prominence in the *doi moi* era may result from strengthened activity, but it may also reflect merely a gradual reemergence into the public sphere. Examples of both these subcategories can be found in the ethnic Chinese (*hoa*) community of Ho Chi Minh City, where *hoa* community groups serve that population, and clan groups serve large but specific families. These various groups are only beginning to receive the attention they deserve, and will be the subject of considerable research in the years ahead.[5]

A seventh category is state-recognized and unrecognized *religious groups, temples and churches—Buddhist, Catholic, Protestant, Cao Dai, and others.* A key feature of the "politics of society"[6] in the *doi moi* era has been the measured greater freedom accorded such groups, combined with continuing state attempts to exercise broad control over religion and, in the Buddhist and other contexts, at times more specific or direct control.

An eighth series of groups is the traditional Party-led *mass organizations and trade unions,* such as the Women's Union, the Youth Union, and the Peasants Union. The mass organizations had primarily a mobilizational and control function for much of the 1954–86 period. They are now struggling to find a new and more representational role under *doi moi,* and, in many cases, beginning to take some more direct responsibility for social service and development activities, particularly in the countryside. The trade unions are also now under significant representational pressure from workers dislocated as a result of economic reforms or engaged in disputes with state, private, joint venture, or wholly foreign-owned firms.[7]

A final category includes *political activism groups* challenging the Party and state. These opposition groups are neither permitted nor tolerated and have generally been suppressed or coopted. Two examples are General Tran Van Tra's veterans group, founded in the late 1980s and later coopted by the authorities, and Doan Viet Hoat's Freedom Forum, which put out several issues of a journal seeking more rapid political reform and was closed in the early 1990s. Hoat and several colleagues were sentenced to long prison terms. A typology of this sector would be entirely incomplete without groups, such as these, which are suppressed or coopted, as well as the initiatives which are allowed to exist.

1. The Policy Research Context in the North, and the Social Activism/Social Service Context in the South

Northern policy research and training institutions and southern social activism and social service groups, which have developed some enhanced autonomy from the Party and government in the *doi moi* era, are important examples of the Vietnamese policy- and development-oriented initiatives.

Among the organizations that typify the development of this sector in the north are Hanoi University CRES, (headed by Professor Vo Quy), and the Center for Gender, Family and Environment in Development (CGFED) (headed by Professor Le Thi Nham Tuyet).[8]

Of the various northern institutions that could be cited as examples of more autonomous policy research groups, Hanoi University CRES is among the oldest and most prominent. CRES engages in environmental and resource management policy research and training relating to Vietnamese upland, lowland, and wetland agriculture. Its core activity—now underway for over twenty years, and the source of much of CRES' and Vo Quy's extensive influence—is the annual six-month environmental and resource management training course conducted by CRES. Out of this course and related training activities has grown a network of academics, government officials, local officials, scientists, and others around Vietnam with whom Vo Quy and his colleagues have remained in close touch, in some cases for decades.

From the training base, Quy and CRES have expanded into policy research on upland, lowland, and wetland agriculture, including sometimes controversial work. But it is central to CRES' success and to Vo Quy's influence that the core activity is training, and that Quy remains directly active as a biological scientist working in mammal and bird research.

CRES is structured as a research division of Hanoi University, itself a tertiary education unit governed by the Ministry of Education and Training.[9] That structure provided initial security for sometimes controversial policy research activities and continues to provide a quite secure and highly autonomous base for training, research, foreign collaboration, and other activities.

The Center for Gender, Family and Environment in Development is a considerably newer group, founded by the anthropologist Le Thi Nham Tuyet in the early 1990s. Professor Nham Tuyet is a social scientist of many years seniority in Hanoi, who earlier worked with the Center for Women's Studies in the National Center for Social Sciences and Humanities, and the Hanoi Teachers Training University, where she helped to found a gender studies program. Branching out on her own upon retirement, she has gathered a small core of perhaps four to six full-time researchers and a considerably larger group of part-time research associates into a broad-based young policy research center concerned with gender, the environment, and development.

CGFED is engaged in its own research; collaborative research with Swedish, Thai, American, and other scholars and groups; consulting work for international NGOs and bilateral, and other aid agencies; and other activities. The role Professor Nham Tuyet plays for CGFED is directly analogous to that which Vo Quy plays for CRES—a dominant founder and the source of most initial domestic networks and foreign ties. But over its twenty years of work, Vo Quy has succeeded in developing and encouraging several younger scholars to develop research, training, and funding subcenters of their own,[10] and today CRES is a much more complex, diffuse, and diverse organization than in its early days.

Professor Nham Tuyet's center is much younger, and there has yet been no similar development of strong younger personnel. Nham Tuyet and Professor Nguyen Minh Luan, a sociologist and ethnologist formerly affiliated with the National Center for Social Sciences and Humanities, remain the key research personnel, and the remainder of the staff, generally much younger and with less research experience–in some cases little directly relevant to training—remain somewhat in the background.

While CRES is structured as an academic research unit of Hanoi University, the Center for Gender, Family and Environment in Development is structured as a science and technology research institution and registered with the Hanoi Municipality. CGFED's registration and existence in this channel is a concrete example of the important role played by the legislation authorizing science and technology research institutions in the early 1990s, discussed further below. Such legislation has been one important channel through which new policy research and other groups have been legalized or legitimized.

The southern context has been, not unexpectedly, quite different. In the south, three key social activist and social service groups include the Social Work Research and Training Group, headed by Ms. Nguyen Thi Oanh (recently replaced by the Social Development Research and Consultancy Group[11]); the Catholic Committee for Solidarity; and the Center for Pediatrics, Development and Health, headed by Dr. Duong Quynh Hoa.

In the south, the more flexible route to quasi-autonomous work appears to have been through social service and social activism rather than policy research.

The Social Work Research and Training Group worked with abandoned and abused children and in other forms of community service; the Catholic Committee for Solidarity has served as a bridge between the post-1975 regime and southern Catholics and has carried out social service work; and the Center for Pediatrics, Development and Health has engaged in health and social development work in Ho Chi Minh City and several southern provinces.

2. Issues Facing Policy- and Development-Oriented Initiatives, North and South

The problems facing these groups mirror issues facing the range of Vietnamese initiatives and groups seeking space from the state.

Many of the policy- and development-oriented groups (including CRES, CGFED, and the Center for Pediatrics, Development and Health) are the virtual creation of a single individual, and now face difficult problems of generational transfer of leadership. Many such groups (but generally not CRES) also suffer from perennial core funding difficulties, leading to significant dependence on foreign funding for specific projects, often to the exclusion or delay of core organizational, institution building, training, and research activities. A surprising number are unregistered, or registered in quite tenuous ways.

II. The Context for Organized Domestic and Overseas Vietnamese Philanthropy

While Vietnamese policy, development, charity, and other initiatives and groups largely outside the state sector are developing rapidly, organized philanthropy is developing considerably more slowly in Vietnam. That is to be expected in a nation barely eight years into a reform process from a hardline socialist base, and with per capita income measured at about two hundred dollars per year.

Key sources of funding available for the wide range of activities outlined above include private citizen contributions, state contributions, remittances from Vietnamese living abroad, and foreign bilateral and multilateral and foreign private and NGO/PVO funding.

Private citizen contributions are rising in Vietnam, but only to narrowly defined activities. Such activities include local peasant associations and collectives, ethnic and clan groups, private schools and universities (for tuition), and religious groups and temples. State contributions are in decline across the board.

Remittances from overseas Vietnamese to Vietnam are increasing each year. They now total, it is estimated, perhaps six hundred million dollars per year from the United States alone, with substantial additional funds from overseas Vietnamese residents in France and elsewhere. Most of these funds are channeled directly to individual families, small business development, and small and medium scale joint ventures, not to direct philanthropic activity. Nor does the Vietnamese community abroad, with several notable individual exceptions, have wealth approaching that of the overseas Chinese.

Foreign bilateral and multilateral and foreign private and NGO/PVO funding is increasing each year. Many of the initiatives and groups described in this chapter receive substantial funding from bilateral, multilateral, and private sources. While such aid is in many cases not considered "philanthropy," the dependence of many Vietnamese groups seeking space from the state on foreign funding of various kinds makes this an important sector to include and consider.

III. The Regulatory Context

Comprehensive state regulation of the rapidly growing number of policy, development, and other groups has lagged behind the rapid development of the sector. A number of overlapping statutes and regulations govern the sector. Rather than retarding the development of initiatives and groups (other than dissident or oppositional political groups, which the state will not tolerate), this plethora of overlapping, confusing, often contradictory laws, decisions, circulars, and regulations has created space for at least dozens and perhaps hundreds of groups to claim at least quasi-legal status.

In this sense, regulatory confusion has been an advantage for the development of the sector. The overlap and confusion arises out of three primary sets of laws and regulations. The first is a series of restrictive regulations governing the establishment and operation of associations and similar groups (adopted in 1957 after the liberal *Nhan Van Giai Pham* movement of intellectuals for greater openness in Vietnamese society was ended by the authorities). These are now regarded as out-of-date and inappropriate for Vietnam's era of reform, but they have not yet been formally abrogated and continue to provide at least a political rationale for the formation of associations and similar groups.[12]

Broad policy regulations were promulgated in 1989 and 1990 on mass organizations and associations.[13] The 1989 and 1990 enactments were intended to encourage greater non-state activity than the 1957 enactments. Five years later they are regarded in Vietnam as insufficient both to encourage and to regulate the rapid growth of the sector, but they too served as implicit or explicit legal and political "covers" for many groups formed in the 1988–93 period.

Finally, and perhaps most important in recent years, many groups have registered, claimed quasi-legal status, or claimed enhanced quasi-legal status, under a decision and circular issued in January and November 1992, which allow the formation of organizations to promote scientific research and technological innovation and exchange.[14] Groups such as the Center for Gender, Family and Environment in Development in Hanoi and the Social Development Research and Consultancy Group in Ho Chi Minh City have registered under this general rubric.

There are no tax incentives presently available for such groups, or for private giving and other forms of philanthropy.

A policy and drafting committee is now active in Hanoi, drafting a law on nonprofit groups which seeks to balance encouragement of nonstate initiative and state control, and is intended to clarify the confused regulatory environment. The foreign NGO community in Vietnam, the Ford Foundation, and others are providing opportunities for the policy and drafting group to explore diverse perspectives and examples for the functioning of a vibrant NGO sector.

Notes

1. Program Officer for Vietnam, The Ford Foundation; formerly Program Officer for Chinese Law and Legal Reform, The Ford Foundation (Beijing) (1988–90); Assistant Professor of Law, Lewis and Clark Law School (1990–94). The Ford Foundation, Vietnam Program, Central Chidlom Tower, 22 Soi Somkid, Bangkok, Thailand (*fax:* 662-254-7174).
2. The literature on this sector in Vietnam is sparse indeed. Reports based on direct observation include Zarina Mulla and Peter Boothroyd, *Development-oriented NGOs of Vietnam* (Centre for Human Settlements, University of British Columbia and National Center for Social Sciences and Humanities, 1994); and Carole Beaulieu, *Is it an NGO? Is it a civil society? Is it pluralism wriggling along?* (Report CB-26 to the Institute of Current World Affairs, October 1994). Secondary discussions include many of the papers presented at the 1994 Vietnam Update conference convened by the Research School of Pacific Studies at the Australian National University, including Adam Fforde and Doug Porter, *Public goods, the state, civil society and development assistance in Vietnam: Opportunities and prospects*; Ben Kerkvliet, *Politics of society in Vietnam in the mid 1990s*; Borje Ljunggren, *Beyond reform: On the dynamics between economic and political change in Vietnam*; Lu Phuong, *Civil society: From annulment to restoration*; David Marr, *The Vietnamese Communist Party and civil society*; Nguyen Ngoc Giao, *The media and the emergence of a "civil society"*; Nguyen Ngoc Truong, *Grassroots organizations in rural and urban Vietnam during market reform: An overview of their emergence and relationship to the state*; Phan Dinh Dieu, *Doi moi—Scientific work and the development of information technology in Vietnam*; and Tran Thi Lanh, *The role of Vietnamese NGOs in the current period.*
3. State revenues (largely now derived from taxes) are actually increasing, which makes the declining role of state expenditures on education, health, and other social services even more striking.
4. Academic research without direct policy implications was weak in the war and post-war eras, and academic activism not considered contributory to policy formulation (such as the *Nhan Van Giai Pham* movement of 1956–57) was not tolerated.
5. These developments are worthy of extensive further work. Professor Nguyen Ngoc Giao writes, for example, "[i]n the countryside as well as in the urban areas, there has been an unprecedented proliferation of religious cults and especially the return of the cult of the ancestors, festivals and traditional clothing....the regeneration of family clans (the restoration of the clan house, the altar to the ancestors in each home, the reconstruction of the family archives, the drafting of a *toc uoc* (a clan convention) that reinstitutes clan hierarchy, establishes rights and duties toward each member of the clan, their place of residence....)—and at the same time, the revival of outdated traditional clothing, the restoration of a sense of solidarity that was long forbidden, and of referential values which anchor individuals who find themselves at sea in a society of crisis." Nguyen Ngoc Giao, *The media and the emergence of a "civil society,"* presented to the 1994 Vietnam Update conference, Australian National University. Another initial paper on this sector is Nguyen Ngoc Truong, *Grassroots organizations in rural*

and urban Vietnam during market reform: An overview of their emergence and relationship to the state, presented to the 1994 Vietnam Update conference, Australian National University.

6. That most apt term is Ben Kerkvliet's, from Kerkvliet, *Politics of society in Vietnam in the mid-1990s,* presented to the 1994 Vietnam Update conference, Australian National University.
7. Carole Beaulieu provides one picture of the situation. "No independent union such as Solidarnosc has appeared in Vietnam. Wildcate strikes that broke out in the South in mainly foreign-owned factories have alarmed the official Vietnam General Confederation of Labor Unions (VGCLU). The Union leadership has shown a determination to respond to new needs, supporting an association of bicycle rickshaw drivers, for example, talking about creating an association for restaurant cooks, pushing for higher wages for workers in foreign-owned companies. More recently they have won a battle to enshrine the right to strike in a new Labor Code. 'We must adapt to our new role in a market economy,' [said] Chau Binh Nhat, assistant director of VGCLU's international department. 'Otherwise the workers will desert us.'"Carole Beaulieu, *Is it an NGO? Is it a civil society? Is it pluralism wriggling along?* (Report CB-26 to the Institute of Current World Affairs, October 1994).
8. Other groups include the Centre for Environmental Research, Education and Development (CERED), headed by Dr. Nguyen Huu Ninh; the Institute of Ecological Economy (Eco-Eco), headed by Professor Nguyen Van Truong, and perhaps Toward Ethnic Women, headed by Ms. Tran Thi Lanh. Toward Ethnic Women views itself, it appears, more as an action-oriented sustainable development group than as a center-oriented policy research institution. The two groups mentioned in the text, CRES and CGFED, have received support from the Ford Foundation.
9. The recent merger of Hanoi University, Hanoi Foreign Languages College and Hanoi University for Teachers of Foreign Languages into the Hanoi National University does not seem to have had any significant structural, political or operational effect on CRES.
10. Deputy Director Le Trong Cuc, an internationally known specialist on the uplands, is an example. Professor Cuc directs the CRES uplands work, manages (with Neil Jamieson) the Winrock/CRES uplands collaboration, is a founder of the new uplands working group in Hanoi, is a regular research collaborator with domestic and foreign colleagues, and attracts considerable funding from domestic and foreign sources. Professor Quy has encouraged Professor Cuc and a few similar senior research and training personnel to develop their own academic, policy, and administrative roles and encourages a high degree of autonomy in their work.
11. The Social Development Research and Consultancy Group, recently formed, will serve as an NGO resource center in the south, consult for domestic and foreign groups on development and social policy issues, and conduct research on social development problems. It is led by personnel from the Catholic Committee in Solidarity, the former Social Work Research and Training Group, and other Ho Chi Minh City social service and social activist groups. Pham Dinh Thai, who has worked for many years in the Catholic Committee for Solidarity and was trained in theology and development in Scotland and England, is manager of the new group.

Ms. Nguyen Thi Oanh, a renowned social activist in Ho Chi Minh City and leader of the Social Work Research and Training Group, is chair of the advisory board. Initial funding has been provided by Bread for the World and Radda Barnen (Swedish Save the Children).

12. These included the *Luat quy dinh quyen tu do hoi hop (Luat so 101-SL/L/.003 ngay 20-5-1957)* [Law stipulating rights to meet and gather (Law no. 101/SL/L.003 of May 20, 1957]; *Nghi dinh quy dinh chi tiet thi hanh Luat so 101-SL/L.003 ve quyen tu do hoi hop (Nghi dinh so 257-TTg ngay 14-6-1957)* [Decision stipulating implementing rules for Law no. 101-SL/L.003 on the rights to meet and gather (Decision no. 257-TTg of June 14, 1957]; *Luat quy dinh quyen lap hoi (Luat so 102-SL/L/.004 ngay 20-5-1957)* [Law stipulating rights to form associations (Law no. 102/SL/L.004 of May 20, 1957]; *Nghi dinh quy dinh chi tiet thi hanh Luat so 102-SL/L.004 ve quyen lap hoi (Nghi dinh so 258-TTg ngay 14-6-1957)* [Decision stipulating implementing rules for Law no. 102-SL/L.004 on the rights to form associations (Decision no. 258-TTg of June 14, 1957].

13. These include *Chi thi so 01-CT ngay 5-1-1989 cua Chu tich Hoi dong Bo truong ve viec quan ly to chuc va hoat dong cua cac Hoi quan chung*; [Instructions 01-CT of January 5, 1989, of the Chairman of the Council of Ministers on the management of organization and activities of mass organizations]; *Thong tu so 07-TCCP ngay 6-1-1989 cua Ban To chuc Chinh phu huong dan thi hanh Chi thi so 01-CT ngay 5-1-1989 cua Chu tich Hoi dong Bo truong ve viec quan ly to chuc va hoat dong cua Hoi quan chung*; [Circular 07-TCCP of January 6, 1989 of the Government Commission for Organization and Personnel implementing Instructions 01-CT of January 5, 1989, of the Chairman of the Council of Ministers on the management of organization and activities of mass organizations]; *Chi thi so 202-CT ngay 5-6-1990 cua Chu tich Hoi dong Bo truong ve viec chap hanh cac quy dinh cua Nha nuoc trong viec lap Hoi* [Instructions 202-CT of June 5, 1990, of the Chairman of the Council of Ministers on implementation of state regulations on the formation of associations]. These and the 1957 statutes are available in *Phap luat ve quyen hoi hop, lap hoi va tu do tin nguong cua cong dan* [Law and regulations on citizens' rights to meet and gather, form associations, and freedom of beliefs] (Law Publishing House (Hanoi), 1992).

14. *Nghi dinh so 35-HDBT ngay 28-1-1992 cua Hoi dong Bo truong ve cong tac quan ly khoa hoc va cong nghe* [Decision 35-HDBT of January 28, 1992 of the Council of Ministers on the management of science and technology]; *Thong tu lien bo so 195-LB ngay 13-11-1992 cua Bo Khoa hoc, Cong nghe va moi truong—Ban to chuc-can bo Chinh phu huong dan dang ky hoat dong cua cac to chuc nghien cuu khoa hoc va phat trien cong nghe* [Joint circular 195-LB of the Ministry of Science, Technology and Environment and the Government Commission for Organization and Personnel promulgating implementing regulations for registration and activities of scientific research and technological development organizations]. These regulations are available in *Cac van ban phap luat ve khoa hoc cong nghe* [Legal texts on science and technology] (National Political Publishing House (Hanoi), 1993).

RESEARCH INSTITUTIONS

AUSTRALIA

Australian Research Institutions

Jenny McGregor
Director
Asialink Centre

I. Historical Evolution of Interests in the Asia Pacific Regional Community

It could be said that Australia's interest in the Asia Pacific region was first created, or imposed, by the British in the colony's early days when Australia was made part of the Diocese of Calcutta. The transfer of British colonial officials across the Empire also had an impact as did the writings of "Chinese" Morrison, an Australian doctor and correspondent for the London *Times* who walked across much of China in the 1890s, visited Japan, Burma, Indochina and Siam, reported the Siege of Peking in 1900, and helped to make Asia more of a reality for Australian readers of the *Times*. The return of those Australian soldiers who, as part of the British Expeditionary Forces, helped to raise the Siege of Peking also raised Australians' consciousness.

Other factors, such as the arrival of thousands of Chinese in the 1860s, 1870s and 1880s to work on the gold fields in Victoria and Queensland, and then in some cases to stay on as shopkeepers and market gardeners, the presence of Afghan camel drivers and Indian travelling tinkers, and the alliance of Japan with the Allies in World War I, all had some impact. But it cannot be said that Australia developed any serious, sustained interest in Asia until after World War II. It was the impact of the war, and of those who returned from its Asian arena, that first created a focused curiosity and a desire to learn and teach Asian languages and cultures.

1. World War II

In particular, Japan and Indonesia (then the Dutch East Indies), for very different reasons, were the two countries which first inspired a range of intellectuals to explore, study and advocate the teaching of their languages and cultures to Australians and, by extension, those of other countries in the region. Australians fighting in New Guinea, Malaya and Singapore, those interned in Changi, or who laboured on the Burma Railroad, added to the awareness of Australia's "near north" (a term not current until the 1980s), and as their stories unfolded after the war, created both positive and negative attitudes to various Asian peoples and places.

Despite the fact that popular Australian thinking continued to be flavoured by reminiscences of World War II, powerful countervailing attitudes nevertheless also emerged, and it was largely these which fuelled the development of the field which came to be known as Asian Studies.

Three exceptional individuals whose interest in Asia was generated by the war went on to become champions of closer relationships between Australia and its Asian neighbours. These men inspired a generation of scholars and officials who would later play major roles in forging closer ties:

- Professor William McMahon Ball, whose first experience of Asia was in Japan towards the end of the war, went on to advocate, and be a founder of, Radio Australia, as a necessary link between Australia and the region surrounding it, making an early break from the thinking which assumed that the BBC Overseas Service could adequately represent Australian attitudes and culture. In the same vein, he encouraged and helped to develop the Australian Diplomatic Service after the war. As professor of the Department of Political Science at Melbourne University from 1949 to 1968, McMahon Ball remained throughout his life a spokesman for Australian rapprochement with Asia. Among his books were *Japan—Enemy or Ally* (1949), *Nationalism and Communism in East Asia* (1956) and *Australia and Japan* (1969). Professor Ball educated and inspired a generation of Australian university students who went on to develop and extend his interest in Asia, including many in the Australian diplomatic service, academia and journalism, who are still influential in the Australian community.
- Sir Edward "Weary" Dunlop, was a medical practitioner, surgeon and officer in the Royal Australian Army Medical Corps, who survived the Burma Railway with a humanity and humility which made him a hero to the men who lived and died in the camps, to those who survived the war and then to the entire country. His lifelong postwar advocacy of educational and cultural exchanges, and the development of links with the countries of the region, has made an enormous impact on Australian thinking.
- Kenneth Myer, eldest son of the founder of the Myer retailing empire, served in

the Navy during World War II, and at the end of the war his ship stopped in Hong Kong, Shanghai and Tokyo on the way home to Australia. The impact of this first experience of Asia energized the young man with a vision of the value to Australia of Asian cultures, and Asian markets, and led to the formation of the Myer Foundation, which between 1964 and 1976 funded hundreds of Asia Pacific fellowships providing for about a dozen students a year to study in Asian countries. Among those were a number of influential future Indonesianists as well as the current head of the Asian Law Centre at Melbourne University. Kenneth Myer's enthusiasm for and practical assistance in business, the arts, communications (particularly through his chairmanship of the Australian Broadcasting Corporation) and scholarship are among the most important influences in this period in shaping Australia's postwar involvement with Asia.

2. Postwar

Events as well as individuals added to the developing awareness of Australia's neighbourhood in the early postwar period, contributing not only an emotional impetus, but an intellectual focus for the arguments in favour of a regional outlook. The Indonesian struggle against the Dutch led to a general sense of fellowship with Indonesia's anti-colonialists which not only marked the start of Indonesian Studies in Australia, but infused the nascent concept of Australia as a "newly independent" nation in a region with a similar background.

Numbers of both the Dutch colonizers and their Indonesian subjects had been evacuated to Australia during the Japanese occupation of the Indies, including several hundred Indonesian political prisoners of the Dutch. Australia refused the Dutch request to intern them, and their participation in Australian life for a number of years, especially in the larger cities, strengthened the sympathetic feelings of many ordinary Australians for their cause; feelings strengthened by the empathy of Australian soldiers serving in Indonesia at the end of the war. The public climax of this empathy came in September 1945 when Indonesian seamen in Australia, who had been employees of the Dutch, refused to take three Dutch ships that had been stranded in Australia during the war, out of their Brisbane port, and were supported first by Brisbane's Australian dockworkers and then those of the whole country. The Australian workers' aim was to prevent the Dutch from shipping military equipment, supplies and troops to the Indies to resume control of the country. Indonesian public opinion was expressed by a committee of Indonesian freedom fighters who had spent the war years in Australia, led by spokesman Dr Ali Sastroamidjojo.

After the first Dutch "police action" in Indonesia in July 1947, Dr Sastroamidjojo appealed to Australian Prime Minister Ben Chifley, who agreed to refer the case to the United Nations. Chifley's action was strongly supported by Australian public opinion. Australia participated in the conference on Indonesia held in New Delhi in January 1949, and cosponsored the new nation's admission to the United Nations in 1950.

Among those young Australians, who met and befriended Indonesians and supported their cause towards and after the end of the war, were many for whom links with Indonesia and the study of its language and culture were to become the focus of their lives. Numbers of young Australian women married Indonesians and became involved with the freedom struggle, among them such stalwarts as Molly Bondan, who later became an adviser to the new Indonesian government, Ailsa Zainnu'din, who came back to Australia with her husband to teach Indonesian Studies, and Joan Hardjono, who became an academic in Indonesia, specializing in questions of land reform, and returning to Australia annually for conferences and other academic interaction.

Monash University student, Herb Feith (Politics), became the first (1954–56) of a stream of young Australians to spend time in Indonesia under the volunteer graduate scheme and then encourage others to do the same. Feith, and Jamie Mackie (Research School of Pacific Studies, Australian National University [ANU])), a Colombo Plan student in Indonesia in 1956, and John Legge (professor emeritus, Monash), who went from Cornell University to Indonesia in 1956 (all later founder members of the Asian Studies Association of Australia), were among those students who founded Indonesian Studies in Australia. They have remained intellectual stimuli to the development of one of the most sophisticated such studies in the world. Indonesian Studies in Australia have supported the creation, despite times of trouble, of firm government links, exchanges of military, academic and public service personnel, of artists, and of a pool of Australians fluent in Bahasa Indonesian and expert in fields ranging from the arts through science and technology. The proximity of Indonesia has been, of course, a particular advantage, with parts of the country, such as Bali, being magnets for students wanting cheap holiday travel, thus exposing many for the first time to an Asian culture and language which has led them into further study.

3. A Sense of Self

Wartime experiences, therefore, created the first extensive contact between Australians and Japan, Indonesia, New Guinea and parts of Southeast Asia, and were the catalyst for the interest in an Asian regional community which has developed ever since the end of the war. Allied to this interest was the growing sense among Australians of being a nation in their own right, not merely a British appendage, an attitude which was sparked by the war-engendered shift from England to America as a "great and powerful friend", and fuelled by the postwar development of Australian studies in history and literature, both hitherto ignored as unworthy of serious academic study. Crucially, and dramatically, the development of a sense of community with the geographic region of Asia was, therefore, a twin to the development of a sense of self among the Australian population.

It was partly because Australia had started to understand that its place and its future international role, both politically and economically, were unalterably linked to the countries which surrounded it, and not to the England that some still called "home" after the war (although they had always lived in Australia), or to Europe or to America, that the country slowly began to realize an identity different from the heritage of most of its settlers. An increasingly uncomfortable feeling, that Australia had grown past adolescence and must mature in its own way, forced intellectuals' thoughts to begin to turn realistically outward, not to the other side of the globe, but to the countries it was growing up amongst and would continue to live with. The excitement of growing up became entwined with the excitement of discovering new cultures, new ideas and new friendships.

II. Asian Studies and "The Region"

In 1960 Bruce Grant, Australia's first foreign correspondent based in Asia, opened the Singapore office of *The Age* and the *Sydney Morning Herald*, with a brief to cover the entire region. The appearance of regular news stories and features, written for the first time from an Australian viewpoint, about and from individual Asian countries, and covering cultural and political events and interactions, including the Vietnam War, had a profound effect on Australian newspaper readers, from the man in the street to government officials and the academic hierarchy.

Such journalism helped to popularize the formal Asian Studies initiated by universities in the 1950s, when Indonesian language teaching was introduced at

Melbourne and Sydney universities (1956), with staff funded by the Commonwealth government concerned that Indonesian was taught nowhere in Australia. The choice of Indonesian reflected not only the political events and student involvement described above, but the new awareness that Australia was not in fact part of Europe, that its nearest neighbour was not the cosy, easily understood Great Britain of many Australians' fond imaginings (Australians at that time were still British citizens, with British passports), but a country about which it has been written that "no two neighbours anywhere in the world are as comprehensively unalike as Australia and Indonesia. We differ in language, culture, religion, history, ethnicity, population size and in political, legal and social systems. Usually neighbours share at least some characteristics brought about by proximity over time, but the Indonesian archipelago and the continental land mass of Australia might well have been half a world apart."[1] This realization was also a challenge to understand, which stirred the spirits of the new generation of undergraduates.

Adding to this ferment was the beginning of the public debate about Australia and "the region". Some of this was sparked by an academic argument between traditionalists and innovators in Asian Studies, which has informally been described as a battle between the SOAS and the Cornell models. The School of Oriental and African Studies in London (SOAS), still enormously respected as a source of Asian scholarship and a producer of academic Asianists, tended to be, especially in the immediate postwar period, still "antiquarian and heavily linguistic", to quote one Australian Asianist. Its academics studied the past, and believed that unless one knew two or three Asian languages one was not a scholar. A number of SOAS graduates held key positions in Australian universities in the 1950s and 1960s, people such as the Malay scholar Cyril Skinner (Monash University), the Sinologist Harry Simon (Melbourne University) and the South Asianist A. L. Basham (ANU), and their impact on the new field of Asian Studies was immense.

In contrast was the new generation of Australian students of Asia, exemplified by John Legge, whose years at Cornell helped to influence him towards the "area studies" approach to studying and teaching about Asia, looking, for example, at "Southeast Asia" or "East Asia", and linking politics, language and culture with a study of history. Legge had been one of the young men inspired by war service in Indonesia, and after a period at Melbourne University teaching Indonesian history, became the foundation professor of history at Monash University and later dean of arts, developing the pioneering Centre of Southeast Asian Studies, the oldest such research institute in Australia, where students from many disciplines and countries working on graduate degrees could gather and exchange ideas. The newness of the university and the need to offer intellectual inducements to both staff and students was a factor in the innovatory decision to focus on Asia at an Australian university, and this plus Australia's proximity to Asia began to attract a new generation of scholars from Europe and America, who worked within the "area studies" concept.

Such catalysts as SEATO, created in 1954 under the aegis of the United States and the first grouping linking Australia formally with countries in Asia (Pakistan, Philippines, Thailand, Laos, Cambodia and South Vietnam), the decision in the 1950s to turn towards Japan as a trading partner in the knowledge that Australia's "special trading relationship with Britain was doomed",[2] and the concept of Japan, India and Australia as a triangle balancing China,[3] all added incrementally to the sense of the region's importance for Australia's future, and supported the development of regional academic studies. One political commentator notes "the enthusiasm in official circles in Washington and Canberra [in 1968–69] for an Australian role in regional developments in Southeast Asia", although by 1972 "no sense of a defence community [had] emerged". Indeed, he continued, "regionalism is not a source of inspiration for anyone looking at Australian defence and foreign policies at this moment" although "a sense of region can always be revived either by opportunity or danger".[4]

In academia, however, things were different, as exemplified by the establishment in various universities across Australia of Asian language teaching and accompanying studies, or studies alone. In 1948, Canberra College created a department of Far Eastern History and in 1952 a School of Oriental Languages, which became the Faculty of Oriental Studies in 1962. In 1952 the University of Tasmania offered a year-long course on China, Japan and Indonesia. Indian Studies were introduced at the University of Western Australia at this time (in Perth, on the Indian Ocean), while Japanese, the anomaly, was still being taught at Sydney University, where it had been the first Asian language introduced at an Australian tertiary institution, in 1918. British Sinologist, Michael Lindsay, after living and teaching in China from 1937 to 1945 (the latter years in Yenan), joined the recently established ANU in 1951 and worked there throughout the 1950s. Japanese was introduced at the ANU in 1952. By 1955 Indonesian was also being taught at Canberra University College.

Indeed, an influence on Australian government policy towards Indonesia was Prime Minister John Gorton's wife, Bettina, who studied Indonesian in Canberra, sparking her husband's interest in the country, which led to the signing of a cultural exchange agreement during what was possibly the first visit to Indonesia of an Australian prime minister.

At Melbourne University, the study of Chinese and Japanese started in the early

1960s when Ken Myer offered personally to fund a chair of Oriental Studies. The position was filled by British Sinologist Harry Simon. Courses began in 1962, and further expansion was supported by the Myer Foundation, the first Australian foundation to acknowledge and underwrite the importance of Asian Studies. A Department of Indian Studies was established at Melbourne University the following year, in 1963.

The Ingelson Report records that this period had two noteworthy features: that most developments were the result of direct Commonwealth government funding, and that few students were attracted and the studies were "generally peripheral to the teaching and research activities of the institutions in which they were located".[5]

Nevertheless, the significance of this new field of study, and the enthusiasm and quality of its practitioners, brought Australian universities to the attention of academics and their institutions throughout the world. For example, throughout the 1970s and 1980s Monash University was known abroad primarily because of its Centre of Southeast Asian Studies, with its pioneering teaching, its graduate students from Australia and throughout Southeast Asia (over three hundred students have received their graduate degrees through the Centre since its founding), its publication of hundreds of books, studies and research papers, and its weekly seminars attended by visiting specialists from throughout the world. In addition, it spearheaded many of the debates into which Australian Asianists entered on subjects such as "does 'Asia' exist?"; the importance of teaching Asian languages and studies in Australian schools and universities, and how this might best be done; the problem of overcoming Eurocentricity in the teaching of Asian Studies; the need to encourage the federal and state governments to support such studies; whether "studies" were more important than languages; whether languages should be taught at all without concomitant studies; the notion of "priority languages" (Japanese, Chinese and Indonesian versus the other Asian languages?); the concept of "the region" versus such descriptives as "the Pacific rim"; and, eventually, the question of whether Australia was, or could be, or should be, "part of Asia". Publications and exchanges of staff and students created strong links with such institutions as Cornell University, SOAS, Leiden and, increasingly, Asian universities such as the universities of Malaya and Indonesia.

Social liberty and the increasing ease of travel of the 1960s encouraged young people to explore the countries of the region. Few at this stage ventured as far as East Asia (not only because of the distance, but because Australian university summer holidays coincide with the winter in Japan, China and Korea). In addition to the nearest Southeast Asian countries, a fascination with Indian culture and religion sent thousands of young Australians to the subcontinent, beginning the tradition of backpacking. For the first time the cultural artefacts of an Asian country became commonplace in Australian cities, with Indian clothes, incense, vegetarianism, and such uncommon practices as pierced noses, entering Australian homes through their teenagers and young adults. Many among these went on to university study of Asia, although Indian Studies were still relatively rare in the 1970s. However, they had swept across the continent from Perth to Melbourne University in the early 1960s, and the South Asianists had formed Australia's first national association of Asianists by the early 1970s.

1. Setbacks and Responses

The early 1970s also saw the initial postwar interest in Asia peak, and in the universities the number of students studying Asia and Asian languages began to drop. Economic stringencies and the influx of the children of European migrants into universities turned students' thoughts towards "practical" subjects (the government and universities had not yet publicly linked the study of Asian languages and the knowledge of Asian cultures to the development of the Australian economy) and towards the histories and languages of their heritages; the study of European Renaissance history, French and German increased, and Greek and Italian Studies were initiated. Any general public idea of Australia as being part of an Asian "region" seemed to be weakening, if it had existed at all. Indeed, the Asian Studies Association of Australia reported in 1978 that "enrolments in Asian Studies departments and Asian language courses in universities have never risen above three percent of total enrolments in university humanities and social science departments".

It was just at this time, however, that anxious lobbying by Australian Asianists, combined with the growing governmental interaction with Asia politically and militarily, and an increasing awareness of trade opportunities, combined to produce the first major report on Asian Studies in Australia. The then Minister for Education and Science, Malcolm Fraser (later prime minister), spurred on by his Prime Minister John Gorton's interest, established in 1969 the Commonwealth Advisory Committee on Teaching Asian Languages and Cultures, chaired by Professor J. Auchmuty, (a classicist, not an Asianist) which in mid-1970 produced its report, "The Teaching of Asian Languages and Cultures in Australia" (the Auchmuty Report). Although this document created a certain level of public debate on the question of Asian Studies in Australia, the general indifference supported its argument that there was little public awareness of any potential influence of Asia on Australia, while the report's intellectual framework was a confident assumption that as a leading country in the region, Australia of course made a contribution to Asia and not vice versa (the nature of this contribution was not discussed, and it may be assumed that the assumption rested largely upon perceptions of Australia's "Britishness"). Although the report linked increased teaching about Asia with better relations between Australia and Asia, there was no clear direction as to how such teaching could be increased or improved to a particular end; it was simply assumed that such studies would continue to develop.

The report focused on schools rather than universities, and on the need to develop and improve the study of languages, making no distinction between language and cultural studies. It did, however, note the danger of Eurocentrism in the teaching about Asia as well as the need for "parity of esteem" of Asian and other studies, although it gave no guidelines as to how this might be achieved. Nevertheless, the report cited the importance of national approaches to curriculum development, coordination between universities and state education authorities, and the need to develop teaching materials and educate teachers, including the provision of opportunities for teacher education in-country. In response to the Auchmuty Report, the government established the Asian Studies Coordinating Committee in 1972, with A$1.5 million (US$1.2 million)[6] to be spent on the development of teaching materials and travel grants for teachers. However, once the money was disbursed, the committee was disbanded in 1978, with no ongoing government commitment to Asian Studies replacing its activities.

One of the critics of aspects of the report was then dean of Asian Studies at ANU, Professor Sydney Crawcour, a specialist in Japanese economics. He argued that a distinction had to be made between Asian languages and Asian Studies if the education system were to produce a greater awareness of Asia among schoolchildren. Asian Studies, rather than language studies, should be emphasized in schools, he said, because the learning of language demanded a high degree of concentration and skill. Crawcour continued to argue throughout the next decade that language teaching to any meaningful level could most successfully be done at tertiary level, and that the important task in Australia was to increase the general knowledge of Asia through non-language studies in the schools.

None of this discussion, however, increased the number of students undertaking the study of Asia or Asian languages at tertiary level, nor offered a platform for the national expression of ideas and for debate on the issues which continued to arise, nor gave a coherent voice to the growing number of Asianists at Australian tertiary and secondary institutions. In 1971, at a Canberra meeting of the International Association of Orientalists, the idea of an Australian organization modelled on the American Asian Studies Association was mooted.

2. The Asian Studies Association of Australia

No organizational activity was forthcoming, however, and at a meeting of ANZUS in Canberra in 1974 a number of Asianists set up a committee, chaired by Professor A L Basham, head of the ANU Department of Oriental Civilization, which organized the Asian Studies Association of Australia (ASAA). Its first conference was held at Melbourne University in May 1976, attracting more than four hundred people who approved a constitution. At its second conference in 1978, the ASAA voted to set up a committee to assess the "crisis" of the weaking interest in Asian Studies among university students. The chairman was Stephen FitzGerald, recently returned to the ANU from his post as first Australian ambassador to the People's Republic of China,

The report, "Asia in Australian Education" (the Fitzgerald Report), differed from the Auchmuty Report in its assertiveness, partly the result of the ASAA's existence as a lobbying body. It also differed in expressing a series of ideas for the development of Asian Studies based on an assumption not only of the importance of the Asian region to Australia, and the growing influence of Asian cultures on Australian life, but of the need to integrate the study of Asia and Asian languages into the normal school curriculum. Moreover, it asserted that the study of Asia should not be optional, but should be a "hard" (employment-oriented) subject, like science and mathematics. Rather than being taught as a "core" subject, Asian Studies should be moved into the "mainstream" by including it in the range of normal subject areas. The study of Asia, the Fitzgerald Report stated, was a matter of Australia's national survival and it noted Asia's "economic, strategic and political significance" to the country. The report also underlined the need to change community perceptions about Asia, and assumed that this could be done with a combination of academic and government initiatives.

3. The Asian Studies Council (ASC)

Primary among these, the report recommended that the government establish an

Asian Studies Council to make Australia "an Asia-literate society" by initiating and coordinating reforms in the national approach to the study of Asia and by conducting a campaign to make the public aware of these changes and of their importance—and the importance of Asia—to themselves and their children. To ensure implementation of the Fitzgerald Report, the ASAA set up four lobbying committees, on national curriculum, the media, information resources and the arts. In April 1985, the Minister for Foreign Affairs, Bill Hayden, announced the establishment of an Asian Studies Council working party, which set up the council, chaired by Stephen Fitzgerald. In 1988, the council released its "National Strategy for the Study of Asia in Australia", which called for "a revolution in Australian education".[7]

Although its emphasis was practical, based on the fact that "Asia is central to our trade, our foreign relations and our future", arguing that "the proper study of Asia and its languages is about our national survival in an intensely competitive world", its focus, significantly, linked back to the postwar equation of "the region" and an individuated Australia. The National Strategy argued that teaching about Asia must take place within an Australian context, and that Australian national needs alone should be the criteria which determined the reform of the educational system, not outworn nineteenth century notions. It quite specifically targeted the country's British educational inheritance as being incapable of reflecting the reality of present-day Australia, and decried the fact that this heritage still went largely unquestioned despite its irrelevance to current needs.

In its early stages the ASC concentrated on primary and especially secondary education, and emphasized language studies which, it insisted, should incorporate a study of Asia. This was because students learning an Asian language had a greater incentive to study about Asia and this, they believed, was therefore the most effective way of raising the overall level of learning about Asia in the schools. The council administered a federal fund called "Asian Languages and Studies" as a component of the national policy on languages, which had been set up in 1987, and determined that "priority languages" were Chinese, Japanese and Indonesian, with a second level of Korean, Thai, Vietnamese and Hindi. It set up a national language curriculum project, to develop a uniform curriculum and teaching materials throughout the country for these languages, and divided responsibility for their development among the states: the Japanese language project was assigned to Queensland and Western Australia; Chinese to Victoria; Indonesian to South Australia and the Northern Territory; Korean and Thai (for years eleven and twelve) to the ACT; and Vietnamese (for primary schools) to South Australia.

In relation to the study of Asia, the ASC took up Stephen FitzGerald's emphasis on "mainstreaming", asserting that Asian Studies should be incorporated into existing subjects in order to reach all students. It agreed with FitzGerald that special Asian subjects, or optional units, created the idea of a "soft option", which encouraged students to think of such studies as unimportant. In a similar style to that used for language materials, the ASC assigned the development of politics materials on Asia to the Asia Education Teachers' Association; history to the History Teachers' Association of Victoria; geography to the Geography Teachers' Association; and economics to the Victorian Commercial Teachers' Association.

Numbers of other initiatives were spearheaded by the ASC, including a Chinese-language television programme for secondary students, produced by Griffith University and the Asian Business Centre (ABC); a nationwide workshop and conference on Asian Studies in schools (1990); a history textbook for years evelen and twelve; and the Asia-wise project, a TV series and the publication of monthly newssheets for schools, including stickers saying, "I'm Asia-wise", produced by the Tasmanian Department of Education and the ABC.

In 1991 the ASC was disbanded, despite intense lobbying by the ASAA and other bodies for a continuation of its engendering activities, and its projects were taken over by the Commonwealth Department of Employment, Education and Training (DEET), under the ministership of John Dawkins, a man with his own forceful vision of the directions which Australian tertiary education should take. In 1992, under a new minister, Kim Beasley, the Asia Education Foundation was announced, to "coordinate and promote Asian Studies across the curriculum in schools throughout Australia".

4. The Ingleson and Garnaut Reports

One of the ASC's most important influences on the continuing development of the concept of "the region" was its commission of a report on the tertiary sector, produced in 1989 as "Asian Studies in Higher Education" under the research directorship of John Ingleson (the Ingleson Report).

The following year, Professor Ross Garnaut (Economics, ANU) produced for the government, "Australia and the Northeast Asian Ascendancy" (the Garnaut Report), an examination of the implications for Australia of "the emergence of Northeast Asia as one of the three main centres of world production, trade and savings", which concluded that "the Northeast Asian economies are more closely complementary to Australia in their resource endowments and in the commodity composition of their trade than any other economies on earth", and that because of "proximity, complementarity, migration and investment...Australians are placed in more intimate contact with people from Northeast Asia than is any other community of European origins and traditions".[8]

While the Garnaut Report contended that the challenge of Northeast Asian ascendancy to Australia "includes the need to comprehend Northeast Asian social, economic and political institutions and languages",[9] the Ingleson Report was asserting that although Asian Studies had suffered "some severe setbacks", especially in teacher education, "no other country outside Asia teaches the three major Asian languages of Japanese, Chinese and Indonesian in schools as extensively as Australia. Australian tertiary institutions as a whole teach a far higher percentage of subjects with reference to Asian countries than any other western country." It added, "Most importantly, there is a sense of commitment to teaching about Asia among Asian Studies specialists. Most understand that, for Australians, knowledge of Asia really does matter".[10]

The impact of these two reports, especially on tertiary institutions, of the numerous specific recommendations for improvements to the tertiary teaching of Asian languages and studies outlined in the Ingeleson Report, created the third, and greatest, push towards public acceptance of the concept of "our" region, Australia's links to it, and the permanence of the relationship. Among the offshoots of the Ingelson Report has been the National Asian Languages Scholarship Scheme, and of the Garnaut Report, the Targeted Institutional Linkages Programme, which supplied government funds to establish student and staff exchange programmes with Asian universities.

A dissenting minority report was submitted by a member of the Ingelson inquiry, J V Neustupny, professor of Japanese Studies at Monash University. Among his arguments is a correction to the mainstreaming concept, put strongly by Ingleson as a refusal by those who teach about Asia to either want or accept "being relegated to an Asian Studies ghetto". Tertiary institutions must ensure, says Ingleson, that "the study of Asia and its languages becomes part of mainstream teaching and research activities...[Teachers] must closely relate to their discipline colleagues if the study of Asia is to be accepted as a normal part of the teaching programs of discipline departments".[11]

To this Neustupny replied that although the Ingleson Report correctly emphasizes that "Asia" is not a clearly defined unit, "a number of features that different Asian societies and civilisations share make it not only possible but imperative to deal with Asia within a single academic frame-work."12 Among these are that Asia "is a clear term of reference, whether we agree or not, for the majority of the Australian population" and also "tends to be a term of reference for people from Asia, who recognise their mutual affinities". He describes "Asia" as "a number of vast areas of influence (Islamic, Indian, Chinese, etc.) which partly overlap" and cites the formation of political and economic alliances and trade interconnections, as well as "common socio-economic features" such as late industrial development and the importance of family in social life. Although Australia needs people who understand individual Asian countries, Neusteupny added, "it also needs graduates who possess a wide picture of individual regions of Asia, and an understanding of the shared Asian sensitivities and socio-economic and cultural problems." He goes on to emphasize the importance of "area studies" and describe how they might ideally function.

5. The Region

Although this dissention can be seen as a narrow academic desire to limit Asian Studies to self-contained departments of "comparative Asian Studies" without interference from "the disciplines", and to argue for strongly-held beliefs about "methodology", in particular the correct methodological basis of Japanese language teaching in Australia, "the communicative approach",[13] it can also be positioned within the argument for a "region", and by implication, a region to which Australia may belong. Certainly concepts such as "shared Asian sensitivities", "political and economic alliances" and "trade interconnections" are echoed not only in cultural or economic terms, but in discussions of how "Australia's 'region' in security terms" is to be perceived, with Australia's current Foreign Minister, Gareth Evans, and his co-author Bruce Grant, indicating that "any discussion of security in our region" must look not only at the South Pacific, Southeast Asia and "the eastern reaches of the Indian Ocean", but at Northeast Asia, Indochina and South Asia as well.

Evans and Grant use the term "the Asia Pacific region", but they give a cogent description of the reason why the focus of intellectual debate is on "Asia" as the area which is, or is not, "our" region:

> The great turn-around in contemporary Australian history is that the region from which we sought in the past to protect ourselves—whether by esoteric dictation tests for would-be immigrants, or tariffs, or alliances with the distant great and powerful—is now the region which offers Australia the most. Our future lies, inevitably, in the Asia Pacific region. This is where we live, must survive strategically

> and economically, and find a place and role if we are to develop our full potential as a nation.
>
> The problem for Australia in fully realising this role does not lie in the 'Pacific' so much as in the 'Asia' component. We have thoroughly well-established working relationships with the United States, Canada and the Pacific Island countries, and are as well placed as any to develop such links with any of the Pacific rim Latin American nations who may in the future choose to reach out into the Asia Pacific region…it is with the Asian countries in our region that the risks of misunderstanding and non-acceptance are very much higher.
>
> It is not surprising that this should be so, given that for most of the two hundred years since European settlement, Australia has fought against the reality of its own geography. We thought of ourselves, and were thought of by just about everyone else, as an Anglophonic and Anglophilic outpost—tied by history, language, culture, economics and emotion to Europe and North America. On the other hand, that perception has been under assault for some time. A long series of developments, stretching back now for several decades, has been gradually changing the picture…[14]

After discussing "the distorting lens of old prejudices and fears…which live on in muted form", they note that "It is one thing to recognise that our future lies in this region. It is another to know how to manage that future…" And, citing "the diversity of the Asian region", they add that "Asia" is a European concept and enumerate "six or more important and distinct cultural traditions, dozens of significant cultures of lesser influences, and a multitude of living languages". As part of the process of both jettisoning old baggage and becoming familiar with the new, they conclude that "a major effort is being made to systematically educate current and future generations of young Australians about the region in which they live…"[15]

This division of "Asia" and "Pacific" and the designation of "Asia" as "our region", about which as much education as possible is desirable, is, for the complexity of reasons given, the definition of "the region" most likely to be understood and accepted by the general public and by intellectuals and educators. When discussing the larger area within which the region resides, the term "Pacific Rim", whose parameters are far more remote—in both distance and concept—is conventionally used. In terms of academic disciplines, Asian Studies, not "Asia Pacific regional studies" are those pursued, individually by country or together across disciplines and comparatively. Generally the South Pacific is regarded as a separate area of study, and Australia's "neighbourhood", and other studies such as American or South American are undertaken separately, while Asia is "the region".

Another aspect of the search for "the region" or for "Asia" can be found in the course "Images of Asia" taught in the English Department of the University of Western Australia. The course "looks at the construction of the concept of 'Asia' in texts ranging from colonial texts like Kim to contemporary Asian writers like Kuo Pao Kun and Nayantara Saghal".

6. Tertiary Research Centres

Curiously, the various studies and reports described in the preceding pages, which have so greatly influenced the development of Asian Studies in Australia, have uniformly ignored a group which perhaps more than any has developed and promoted the concept of area, comparative and regional studies, and which is in its various manifestations the home of the intellectuals most vigorously engaging the general public, undergraduates, teachers, business and government in a continuing shaping and sharpening of the portrait of "the region": the nation's tertiary research centres. As indicated above, the earliest of these began more than twenty-five years ago; the most recent have been founded in 1993, and more are being planned.

From a small beginning focusing on Southeast Asia, but primarily Indonesia, they have grown to bodies attached to universities in every state and territory, and covering most conceivable countries, groups of countries and themes. They have argued on all sides of the "regional" debate, and individual scholars and postgraduate researchers have produced a range of theses and studies, journals and other publications, and organized regular seminars and conferences. Each of these research institutions has established, through its university, links with a range of Asian universities, some through the Targeted Institutional Links Programme mentioned earlier, and they host academic, government and business visitors from abroad as well as from within Australia, creating a network of like minds and interests which often also interact with Asian alumni of Australian universities in their home countries.

As of 1993 there were forty-five of these institutes or centres of Asian Studies, with interests ranging from Peace Studies to Eastern Indonesia. Whatever their focus, and although some of their staff may differ about whether Australia is or is not "part of" Asia, or may argue about what "part of" means, none argue against the notion of "region", or of Australia's membership in it, though they may debate the "regional identity". The great change which has taken place in Australian thinking since World War II, is that Australia is acknowledged as belonging to its geographic not its historic region, both in terms of its community membership and its own identity.

Many of the more recent institutes or centres have been established as initiatives of the government. Centres such as the National Korean Studies Centre, the National South Asian Studies Centre, the National Thai Studies Centre, Murdoch University's Asia Research Centre, the Key Centre for Asian Languages and Studies, and the Asia Education Foundation, are examples of the federal government allocating funds and calling for tenders from universities around Australia to establish the centres as new facilities or extensions of existing bodies.

The dramatic increase in Asia research centres in the 1990s reflects strong government leadership in driving Australia's engagement with the countries of Asia. The number of university-based Asia research centres increased by fifty-six percent in the 1990s with government funding an important catalyst.

The government view has, however, been shaped to a large extent by intellectuals from the universities and from the older Asia centres. Academics from the ASC played a critical role in advising the government on the future needs of Asian Studies and languages in Australia; academics also played a major role in advising the government on economic and strategic relationships in the region. Much of the strategic economic research undertaken by the Department of Foreign Affairs and Trade in the region is contracted to university-based Asia centres and Asia academics through the government's East Asian analytical unit.

The Australian university-based Asia centres in the 1990s are extremely diverse. Some focus purely on research and teaching whilst others have a role in education of the broader community. Some are country based, others issue based. Some are entirely funded by their university, others depend on a mix of corporate, government, philanthropic and university funding. One, the Asia-Australia Institute (AAI) at the University of New South Wales has a mission to promote the formation of an "Asian community" and a place in it for Australia as an equal, Asia-educated and contributing partner. The AAI is generously funded by the University of New South Wales and receives support from the corporate sector and from the government for particular projects.

One example of the AAI's strategy of promoting the "Asian community" was the Asia young leaders' forum, sponsored jointly with the Institute of Southeast Asian Business (Asean Institute), held in Kuala Lumpur in October 1993. The theme which its one hundred young executives from the public and private sector discussed was "How can the leaders of tomorrow shape Asia into the next century?". In his opening address, Malaysia's Finance Minister, Dato'Seri Anwar Ibrahim, said, "When I refer to Asia, I include Australia, of course." The forum covered such areas as business and the environment, resolution of regional conflicts, and the shape of Asia tomorrow. Among the other speakers was the Queensland Premier, Wayne Goss. Stephen Fitzgerald, chairman of the AAI, said he hoped the forum would become an annual event, to enable "young leaders from the emerging elites of Asia to discuss the issues that will critically shape the Asian region in the twenty-first century, and to assess the nature of the leadership, institutions and strategies needed to manage those issues." A second young leaders forum took place in October 1994 in the Philippines.

The AAI also held their inaugural leaders forum in Queensland in 1993 which brought together fifty eminent people from twelve countries to discuss the theme "APEC in Asia—Does it matter? Will it count?". The second leaders forum, held in Bali in September 1994, addressed the theme: "The Asianization of Asia".

Another example of work which aims to enhance the emerging Asian community is a series of nine working papers produced by the Academy of the Social Sciences in Australia and published by the AAI with such titles as "Perceiving Citizenship", "Perceiving Business Ethics", "Perceiving Education", "Perceiving Human Rights", "Perceiving Industrial Relations". In its description of the project, the Academy said, "In order to ensure Australia's full participation in the developing 'Asian' community, Australians need to acquire not only knowledge of Asian societies, but also an appreciation of the ideas and values that underpin Australian approaches to the world."

Other recent examples of Australian research institutes' activities relating to the future of the region, including Australia, have been a conference organized by Murdoch University's Asia Research Centre in August 1993 on changing diets and food consumption patterns in Asia and the opportunities these offer for Australian suppliers; and a joint project on the aquaculture of the trochus shell by the Northern Territory University and Universitas Nusa Cendana, Kupang, Timor, funded by the DEET Targeted Institutional Links Programme, which will re-seed hatchery-produced juveniles in Kupang and Ambon with the aim of setting up a method of standardized mass production.

The above is a small sample of the continuous interaction between Asian research institutions in Australia on topics ranging from science to the arts, which exemplify the concept of a regional community. It is activities such as these, and many more, in research centres throughout the country, which indicate the degree of development that has occurred in the evolution of the regional community concept.

Further evidence, which can well serve as the coda to this narrative, is the assessment of Australia's foreign minister, Senator Gareth Evans, in an interview in March

1994, that Australia is joining Asia culturally, politically and economically, much more quickly than the government had expected. Australia "now looked less odd" as an Asian nation than it used to. "The 1980s was a remarkable decade of transition for Australia", he said, and found that "now you go anywhere in the Australian business community and they are just incredibly Asia-conscious and Asia-focused at every level", with the understanding that jobs and growth are based in the region "permeating the Australian consciousness". He added that the region's political cultures were also converging.

Using the term "region", without feeling any need for explanation or definition, as the normal description of Australia's part of the world, he assumed, also without finding it necessary to explain or justify, that Australia's relationship with the region would naturally continue to develop into the future. Unconsciously making the distinction between "region" and "Asia Pacific" described above, he said that Australia's role in establishing the Asia Pacific Economic Forum in 1989 had "established its regional credentials as an independent force", and that it was "not impossible that the forum could be expanded into a Pacific-wide trade area, although no-one foresaw an Asia Pacific version of the European Union." It seems clear that the work of Asianists and other Australian opinion-shapers have, over the postwar period, educated the general public to accept that Australia belongs to a regional community and that the term "the region" is now interchangeable with "our region".

Notes

1. Gareth Evans and Bruce Grant, *Australia's Foreign Relations in the World of the 1990s* (Melbourne: Melbourne University Press, 1991). Page 185.
2. Ibid., p. 26.
3. Ibid., p. 19.
4. Bruce Grant, *The Crisis of Loyalty* (Sydney: Angus and Robertson, 1972), p. xv.
5. John Ingleson, *Asia in Australian Higher Education* Vols 1 & 2, 1989, p. 34.
6. International Monetary Fund, *International Financial Statistics*, January, 1995 (Washington, D.C.: IMF, 1995). Figures given are based on end of the period exchange rates for November 1994. A $1 = US$0.77.
7. Ibid., p. 33.
8. Ross Garnaut, *Australia and the Northeast Asian Ascendancy* (Canberra: Australian Government Printing Service, 1988).
9. Ibid., p. 3.
10. Ingleson, op.cit., p. 35–36.
11. Ibid., p. 37.
12. J V Neustupny, *Strategies for Asia and Japan Literacy* (Melbourne: Japanese Studies Centre, 1989, p. 4.
13. Ibid., p. 12.
14. Evans and Grant, op. cit., p. 326–327.
15. Ibid., p. 326–328.

Bibliography

Australian Education Council. *Relationships Between Australia and Asia Languages and Cultures.* Canberra: Asian Studies Council, 1988.

Ball, W Macmahon. *Australia and Japan.* Melbourne: Thomas Nelson, 1969.

Basham, A L. *The Wonder that was India.* London: Fontana Collins, 1954.

Broinowski, Alison. *The Yellow Lady.* Melbourne: Oxford University Press, 1992.

Evans, Gareth and Bruce Grant. *Australia's Foreign Relations in the World of the 1990s.* Melbourne: Melbourne University Press, 1991.

FitzGerald, Stephen, et al. *A National Strategy for the Study of Asia in Australia*, Asian Studies Council. Canberra: Australian Government Printing Service, 1988.

Garnaut, Ross. *Australia and the Northeast Asian Ascendancy.* Canberra: Australian Government Printing Service, 1989.

Grant, Bruce. *The Australian Dilemma.* Sydney: Macdonald Futura, 1983.

____________. *The Crisis of Loyalty.* Sydney: Angus and Robertson, 1972.

____________. *What Kind of Country?* Melbourne: Penguin Books, 1988.

Greenwood, Gordon and Norman Harper eds. *Australia in World Affairs 1961–1965.* Melbourne: Cheshire, 1968.

Ingleson, John. *Asia in Australian Higher Education..* Vols 1 & 2, 1989.

McKay, Elaine, ed. *Challenges and Opportunities: Our Future in Asia.* Melbourne: Asian Studies Association of Australia, 1988.

______________. *Towards an Asia Literate Society.* Melbourne: Asian Studies Association of Australia, 1988.

Neustupny, J V. *Strategies for Asia and Japan Literacy.* Melbourne: Japanese Studies Centre, 1989.

Stargardt. A W. *Australia's Asian Policies: The History of a Debate 1839–1972.* Hamburg: Institute of Asian Affairs, 1977.

CANADA

Canadian Research Institutions and Asia Pacific

Paul M. Evans[1]
Director
University of Toronto - York University
Joint Centre for Asia Pacific Studies

I. Introduction

In an era in which regional connections and identities are the apparent successors to the cold war international order, Canada faces some fundamental challenges. With a small population, middle power aspirations, and a global foreign policy, what is Canada's region? Once described in the 1960s as "a regional power without a region," Canada in the late 1990s is in fact a global actor spread (thinly) across several regions.

This said, a great deal of governmental and academic attention has been directed at raising the content and profile of Canadian connections across the Pacific. Canada increasingly sees itself as an Asia Pacific country. Commercial links are important and growing. In human terms, more than half of the roughly 220,000 new immigrants to Canada each year now come from Asia. Their presence is of growing importance in the cultural, economic, and social lives of the urban centres in which they live. The level and quality of collaborative and policy-relevant research in Canada focusing on contemporary topics in what we now call Asia Pacific has expanded substantially in the past decade.

Efforts to strengthen research and other connections have faced two recurrent difficulties. The first is the limited resource base in Canada, both human and financial. The second is the problem of achieving sustained high-level attention in business and government. Pulls across the Atlantic through a myriad of historical and institutional connections and southward through an integrated economy (more than seventy-five percent of Canada's trade is with the United States) make Asia Pacific only one of Canada's priorities.

High-level Canadian policy makers have sometimes been described at home and abroad as being "inattentive and intermittent"[2] in focusing on Asia Pacific issues the same can be said of Asian policy makers' interest in Canada, with the risk that Canada will be perceived as a marginal player in the area. The "inattentive and intermittent" concern is of course similar to the one often voiced about Washington's role in Asia. However, because of its large economic and military role in the region, few would describe the current or medium term role of the United States as "marginal." Canada faces the task of creating and sustaining a Pacific policy presence in ways different from its southern neighbour. The policy areas of special Canadian interest are multilateralism, regional institution building, preventive diplomacy (including peacekeeping and cooperative security), and developmental assistance.

In looking at current trends in the research component of Canadian connections across the Pacific, I need to make four initial observations which set some boundaries. First, there does not exist any kind of national inventory of research being conducted in Canada related to Asia Pacific. As I will argue later, such an inventory would be extremely valuable. In preparing this essay I contacted about twenty research organizations and funding agencies in Canada and relied upon my partial knowledge of about ten more. My observations here are thus based on an empirical base that is neither comprehensive nor systematic.[3]

Second, defining *research* is a tricky business. By research I have in mind the process of investigation, writing, and publication of original work designed to advance knowledge and action. It is of course difficult to detach research from related activities including training, network building, and various forms of exchange including conferences, workshops, and the like. For example, graduate education and other training programs often produce research and researchers, involve large amounts of money from diverse sources, and are a growing component of the trans-Pacific world. My focus here, however, will be restricted to research in the sense of a specific kind of end product which normally takes the form of some kind of report, essay, or book. It differs from journalism, the source of the vast bulk of information and analysis, mainly in the time permitted for investigation and in the form of ensuing publication.

Third, even within this restricted definition of *research* I will focus on only a small domain. My primary concern is research that is conducted on a collaborative basis at universities and nonprofit research institutes and which examines contemporary issues and problems. I will pay special attention to the work that focuses on topics that are closely linked to governmental policy concerns. This means that much, if not most, scholarly research conducted in Canada will be outside the boundaries of the study. This is a significant exclusion because of the volume and quality of work that is being done by individual researchers on an array of topics in several disciplines. It is also an important omission because scholarship and research in these areas, whatever its policy relevance, produce trans-Pacific academic networks which have proven durable and which are expanding. One such mechanism is international professional associations. A second is the myriad of individual contacts arranged through research trips, teaching assignments, and other forms of scholarly exchange. Together they are a significant element of the nongovernmental underpinnings of trans-Pacific connections.

My definition entails a disciplinary bias in favour of the more policy- or action-related sciences, especially economics, political science, environmental studies, and business administration; practitioners of which tend to be adept at creating structures for promoting collaborative research on issues of current national concern. Further, I will exclude another world of activities from the study; that is the work of private sector, profit-oriented research organizations that work on Asian topics. These include a large and growing number of consulting companies and research divisions within corporations.

Fourth, the geographic boundaries and constituent principle of "Asia Pacific" are open to multiple interpretations and indeed constitute what some describe as "contested terrain."[4] For about a decade Canadian officials and business leaders have tended to prefer the unhyphenated "Asia Pacific" which they see as explicitly linking North America and Australia to those countries in Asia that are on or closely linked to the Pacific. Through such instruments as the Asia Pacific Foundation of Canada created in 1984, the objective has been to expand Canadian connections across the Pacific and to help create a region of which Canada is an integral part. This means placing emphasis on the trans-Pacific dimension rather than the more narrowly Asian which is now apparent in a variety of contemporary usages of "Asia Pacific" and "Pacific Asia."[5]

"Asia Pacific" and its variants have only begun to surface in university curricula, scholarly discussion, and substantial research in the past four or five years. For most Canadians, in government and outside, the more likely vocabulary for describing the topics of their attention are individual countries or regional groupings such as "Asia," "East Asia," or "Southeast Asia." For example, there is not any professional organization in Canada on "Asia Pacific Studies," but there is a "Canadian Asian Studies Association." This reflects the inevitable inertia of academic practice, especially in the creation of national organizations. But from the perspective of research funding, it also reflects the fact that a principal source of support for research and university activities is Canada's governmental agencies for developmental assistance. "Asia Pacific" has entered the lexicon and world view of Canada's decision-making elite, but in the specific area of developmental assistance the more convenient definition of the region is "Asia," an area that connotes recipients in need rather than countries moving quickly ahead. So far as the public purse is concerned, "Asia" remains as important as "Asia Pacific."

For present purposes, Asia Pacific will primarily refer to Canadian activities focusing on East and Southeast Asia, a region I prefer to call Eastern Asia. I will not be assessing here the array of institutes and projects in Canada that focus on the United States, Latin America, Australia, New Zealand, or Canada itself unless those project explicitly relate to developments in Eastern Asia. I have also excluded in most instances "South Asia" from the study. This too is a significant exclusion considering the substantial communities in Canada of South Asian origin and historical connections through the Commonwealth.

II. Level And Scope of Research Activity

The number of individuals and institutions involved in research on Eastern Asia and Asia Pacific is difficult to estimate. The Canadian Asian Studies Association, composed primarily of faculty and graduate students, has a total membership of 300, of whom 211 identify their primary area of interest as Southeast Asia or East Asia. A more extensive inventory of "specialists/researchers" compiled by the Asia Pacific Foundation of Canada (APF) includes 1189 names. Of these 1127 are based in Canada.

There is no national research institution in Canada focusing on Asia or Asia Pacific. There is not, for example, a Canadian equivalent of the East-West Center in Hawaii, which receives substantial funding directly from Congress, or the Research School of Pacific Studies at the Australian National University. At the national level, the APF occasionally supports research programs but is only at an early stage of developing in-house capacity for promoting research and creating research networks. The Canadian Institute of International Affairs (CIIA), unlike the Japan Institute of International Affairs, (JIIA) does not have a capacity for commissioning or conducting research. Neither the APF nor the CIIA currently organizes the kinds of policy study groups organized by the JIIA or the Asia Society in the United States.

Nor is there a preeminent Canadian institution measured in terms of scale of operation, comprehensiveness, or international reputation. Rather, collaborative research projects are located at a number of institutes across the country. These fall into four main categories.[6]

a. *University-based research centres concentrating on Asia or Asia Pacific.* These include GERAC, the Groupe d'etudes et de recherches sur l'Asie contemporaire [Study and Research Group on Contemporary Asia] (Laval University); Centre d'études sur l'Asie de l'Est [Centre for East Asia Asian Studies] (University of Montreal); Centre conjoint pour le recherche sur le communication Asie Pacifique [Joint Centre for Asia Pacific Communications Research] (University of Quebec at Montreal and Concordia University); Centre for Canada-Asia Business Relations (Queen's University); Asian Pacific Research and Resource Centre (Carleton University); Joint Centre for Asia Pacific Studies (University of Toronto and York University); Brock Centre for Canada and Asia Pacific Studies (Brock University); Institute for Northeast Asian Studies (University of Regina); Institute for Asian Research (University of British Columbia), which includes five centres focusing on China, Japan, Korea, Southeast Asia and South Asia; the Centre for Asian Legal Studies (University of British Columbia); and the Centre for Asia Pacific Initiatives (University of Victoria). Three of the above (the Joint Centre for Asia Pacific Studies, the Institute for Asian Research, and the Centre for Asian Legal Studies) each have research programs, not including administrative salary lines, of more than C$400,000 (US$290,000)[7] per year.

b. *University-based research institutes that are not exclusively Asia-focused but that undertake substantial research programs focusing on Asia.* Among them, the Centre for Foreign Policy Studies (Dalhousie University); the Deutsch Centre (Queen's University); the Norman Paterson School of International Affairs (Carleton University); the Human Rights Research and Education Centre (University of Ottawa); the Centre for International Studies and the Centre for International Business (University of Toronto); the Centre for International and Strategic Studies (York University); the David Lam Centre for International Communication (Simon Fraser University); and the Centre for Human Settlement and the Institute of International Relations (University of British Columbia).

c. *Private, nonprofit organizations that are not university-based and that undertake major programs on Asia.* One example is the Canadian Centre for Global Security, which has done work on Asia Pacific security questions including non-proliferation. A second is the Conference Board of Canada. The major programs operated by the Conference Board focusing on Asia Pacific include the Applied Economic Research Institute Linkage program which connects seven research institutes in Canada to nine counterparts in China. The linkages focus on twelve project areas (for example Sino-North American trade and balance of payment modeling). Another project is connected to APEC's Working Group on Human Resource Development in the areas of business management, industrial technology, and the creation of a network for economic management and an educational forum. A third organization is the North-South Institute, engaged in "research for a fairer world," which is currently managing projects on Asia Pacific Economic Cooperation, specifically related to the human resource development working group network on economic development management; NGO research, including a gender equality linkage program with the Economic Research Institute of the State Planning Commission in China, and a program on global restructuring and women leading into the 1995 World Conference on Women to be held in Beijing. A fourth is the Institute on Governance, also located in Ottawa, which, as part of its mandate, undertakes "action research" including the situation papers linked to its regional governance network.

d. *Government-funded organizations that support research but that also have in-house research capacity.* The largest and most active is the International Development Research Centre (IDRC). Established in 1970 by the Parliament of Canada, IDRC provides funding to researchers in universities, government, business, and nonprofit organizations for applied research intended to improve the quality of life in the areas of human health, economic and social well-being, food and nutrition, the environment and natural resources, and information and communication in the developing world. The total amount of funding for approximately one hundred projects in Asia since 1990 has been in the range of C$36 million (US$26 million), not including in-house research.

In quantitative terms, the total number of current projects related to specific countries in Asia, regional dynamics, or thematic issues, probably exceeds 250. Based on information provided by several funding agencies, there are probably in excess of 150 research projects with annual budgets of more than C$100,000 (US$73,000).

The range of research topics is exceptionally broad even when reduced to those concerned with contemporary issues with direct or implied relevance for government. The International Development Research Centre in Ottawa has a database that includes more than one hundred "macro-thesaurus descriptors" of projects it supports. They include the following:

economics, including trade, investment, economic reconstruction, economic policy, competitiveness, export promotion, planning, policy, industrial cooperatives, and tourism; sustainable development, including food security, nutrition, rice, urbanization, rural development, agriculture (mixed farming, hills, mountains, shifting cultivation, cultivation practices, on-farm research, poultry, animal production, sheep, small ruminants, crop production, plant breeding, vegetables, coconuts, garlic, bamboo, bananas, weeds, weed control) education, water supply, groundwater, hydrogeology, management development, evictions, housing conditions, aflotoxins, community development, hydrams, and energy consumption; regional cooperation; the environment, including environmental protection, ecosystems, maritime resources, water resources, resource management (fisheries, forests, aquaculture, fish genetics, fish parasites), pollution, toxic waste disposal, waste management, drinking water, botanical pesticides, ferrocement rainwater catchment systems, and vortex wind machines; science and technology, including remote sensing, technological change, pharmaceutical industry, bioengineering, data processing, information services, and earthquake dam safety; health, including disease control, maternal and child health, primary health care, lower class, low cost housing, breast feeding, AIDS, hepatitis B, measles, malaria, and lung fluke infection; communication, including diffusion of innovations, library science, women's radio, and urban transport; and good governance, including policy making, statutory laws, customary laws and village practices, regional development, law of the sea, and exclusive economic zones.

To this list could be added the several projects funded from other sources in the areas of political security (including cooperative security), immigration and refugees, economics (especially trade and investment), and law.

III. Funding Sources

Unlike the United States, there are few private foundations in Canada that support Asia Pacific long-term public policy, training, and research programs; and few research institutes with endowments or major *long-term* funding from governmental, or a mix of governmental and private sources. Canadian researchers and institutes occasionally find support from foreign-based organizations such as the Ford and Rockefeller Foundations in the United States as well as organizations in Asia including the Japan Foundation, the Korea Foundation, and the Chiang Ching-kuo Foundation. A handful of Canadian-inspired projects have received support from the Centre for Global Partnership, though successful projects have necessarily included American and Japanese participants.

The main funder of research is the Canadian public sector, federal and provincial. Almost all Canadian universities are publicly funded with these two levels of government playing a major role in providing infrastructure, faculty appointments, graduate student assistance and the like.

The federal government funds private research in several ways. One is through institutions it supports financially but does not manage. A prime example is the Social Sciences and Humanities Research Council (SSHRCC). SSHRCC supports the work of individual Canadian scholars through "research grants" and collaborative "strategic grants" (aimed at creating networks and original work in areas defined to be national priorities), both on a peer-assessed, competitive basis. Total SSHRCC funding for strategic and research grants with a geographic coding for "Asia" (including South Asia) was approximately C$2 million (US$1.5 million) in 1992–93; C$1,700,000 (US$1.2 million) in 1993–94; and C$1,675,000 (US$1.2 million) in 1994–95. Research grants comprised at least eighty percent of the total each year and averaged between C$15,000 and C$20,000 (US$11,000 and US$15,000) per year per project. Strategic grants averaged between C$26,000 and C$44,000 (US$19,000 and US$32,000) per year per project. Of all of the grants awarded by the SSHRCC between 1992 and 1994, only two amounted to more than C$70,000 (US$51,000) per year.

The government also has direct programs administered by line ministries. The funding provided is normally on an annual basis for task-specific research programs. Rarely is it provided in the form of endowments. "The Pacific 2000 Program" was created by the Conservative government in 1989 with the intention of making Canada more competitive in Asian markets. Administered by the Department of Foreign Affairs and International Trade, its annual expenditures varied between C$12 and C$18 million (US$8.8 and 13.1 million). The amount targeted for research through the Japan Science and Technology Fund has been as high as C$3 million (US$2.2 million) per year; and that through the Asia Pacific Research International Education Fund has ranged between C$700,000 and about C$370,000 (US$511,000 and US$270,000) per year, of which about C$150,000 (US$109,000) is directly tied to the APEC Working Groups. The Pacific 2000 Program was terminated in 1995, with a small annual fund of about C$350,000 (US$255,000) preserved to provide support to a smaller number of projects on a competitive basis. Another program administered by the Department of Foreign Affairs and International Trade (DFAIT) between 1992 and the summer of 1994 was the Cooperative

Security Competition Program, with an annual budget of about C$1 million (US$730,000) to support research on policy-related topics on international security of which Asia Pacific constituted one part.[8] DFAIT also has a modest in-house research capacity through the Asia and Pacific Branch and the Policy Planning Branch.

The Canadian International Development Agency (CIDA) also has a limited in-house research capacity and commissions a large number of studies through consultants and contract research. Some of that research is funneled through university-based research institutions and at least five institutions have multi-year funding arrangements with CIDA's Asia Branch. CIDA also funds the Canada-ASEAN Centre in Singapore which for four years has awarded research grants to institutions, professors, and graduate students for work focusing on Southeast Asia.

The Asia Pacific Foundation of Canada occupies an unusual position. Funded principally by the federal and provincial governments, its objective is to increase knowledge of Asia in Canada and knowledge of Canada in Asia. Its head office is located in Vancouver and it operates regional offices across Canada and in five Asian cities. Although active in funding and operating programs in the field of education, it has not played a major role in undertaking or sponsoring research. This is changing to the extent that the Foundation has recently created a new position at the vice-presidential level tasked with playing a catalytic role in creating a research network of institutes and individuals across the country and finding innovative ways of bringing their findings to the attention of a larger audience in government and business. One part of this research network, the APEC Studies Centre, will be based at the Foundation and staffed by research interns. The APF is also taking the lead in establishing two working groups composed of academics, government officials, and representatives of the business community. The first is focusing on the cultural aspects of trade dispute mechanisms and the second on the fit between economic and security issues.

At risk of uttering heresy, my impression is that research on contemporary issues is not under-funded in Canada. This is not to suggest that there are many worthy projects that are unable to locate appropriate support and that research institutions spend a great deal of time drafting proposals for comparatively small grants. It is to say that medium-level, medium-term funding is less serious a problem on Asia Pacific topics than it is, for example, on African or Middle Eastern ones.

The research funding problem in Canada is less of volume than of type. First, with reference to Asia Pacific, funding tends to be focused on contemporary problems and issues, and policy-and problem-oriented rather than basic research. This orientation is understandable in light of the fact that the Canadian public purse is the provider of the vast majority of funding. It also reflects the fact that the very concept of "Asia Pacific" is relatively new and is itself a government and business driven idea. An interesting consequence is the distribution of research by subject area. Developmental assistance funds distributed through large players such as the Canadian International Development Agency and the IDRC constitute a hefty share, probably approaching two thirds, of the money that flows into the research community. Considering the wide definition of the topics that are deemed to be relevant to Canada's ODA, this is less confining than it would first appear. But should these agencies take a narrower approach to their mandate and responsibilities as some are requesting, the consequences for the research community would be substantial.

Second, for all of the money spent on research, conferences, network building, and related activities, very little is spent on sophisticated and detailed studies of Canadian public policy options. There are no Canadian equivalents of the Brookings Institution, the Council on Foreign Relations, the American Enterprise Institute, or any number of other policy-related think tanks based in the United States which, while they might do contract research funded by government, rely principally upon private support. A partial exception is the Conference Board of Canada, which receives substantial private sector funds (about seventy percent of its budget) and has undertaken occasional studies of public policy issues concerning Canadian involvement in Asia Pacific, though these have been exclusively on economic topics. While it is tempting to think the absence of privately funded, comprehensive research institutes reflects the realities of the central role that government and government-funded agencies play in the research process, it is worth noting that the Australian National University in Canberra is government supported and yet at the same time plays a vigorous role in providing policy support and review for government on a full range of policy issues.

Third, a major problem is locating high quality, well-trained personnel for policy-relevant research. The vast majority of research is done by university-based faculty members, whether they do this through private contracts or collaborative research programs. To the best of my knowledge, only one university in Canada has research professorships of the kind that exist at the Australian National University.[9]

IV. Trends

1. Funding

Whatever the consequences of government funding of research, the grim reality is that the level of government support is almost certain to decline. Yet Asia Pacific is a priority area of government and the site of a rising tide of Canadian economic and social connections. This will mean that the Canadian research community will increasingly turn to private sources in Canada and to sources abroad, particularly in the United States, Japan, Korea and other parts of Asia.

Lest our Asian and American friends be inclined to find new locks for their vaults, there is the potential for something positive to follow. One of the challenges to the major funding agencies around the Pacific will be to support genuinely collaborative, cross-national research programs. In the areas I know best, mainly political, economic and security studies, there has been a great deal of parallel research in support of the proliferation of conferences and workshops in the past decade. But there have been very few collaborative projects that include joint design and implementation of research programs. This kind of collaboration is difficult to achieve for reasons of language, theoretical starting points, operating logistics, and the large injection of funds that are required. It has been difficult to arrange these programs even in situations where funding sources are already in place and the number of participating countries is restricted to two.[10] Despite these difficulties, multinationally designed and executed programs are now widely recognized as a valuable and necessary next step.

While government funding has been provided to a variety of institutes across the country, there has been some ambivalence about setting up high-profile, national-level research institutes or think tanks. In 1992 the Conservative government dismantled several of the federally funded institutes with an interest in Asia Pacific, among them the Canadian Institute for International Peace and Security, the Economic Council of Canada, and the Science Council of Canada. There is some indication that the current Liberal government might reinvent one or more of them. Yet in an era of stringent fiscal austerity that the Canadian government has entered, it appears very unlikely that any new institute will receive significant funding. The decentralized character of Canada's research capacity is thus likely to continue into at least the medium-term future.

2. Researchers

Most of the policy- and problem-related research focusing on Eastern Asia is not conducted by Asian specialists with extensive field work in Asia, capacities in Asian languages, and a commitment to long-term connections to a specific part of Asia. Rather, it is increasingly a province of specialists with a thematic, technical, or comparative expertise who are some of the most active players on a variety of topics, especially in the areas of economics, business administration, law, and the natural sciences. For example, the Applied Economic Research Institutions Linkage program, funded by CIDA and administered by the Conference Board of Canada, has virtually no connection to the research community in Canada that focuses on China or the (smaller) Chinese community that focus on Canada or North America.

The new wave of research interest and non-traditional researchers is a sign of the growing significance of the region and reinforces the adage that "Asia is too important to be left to Asian specialists." But it has also caused an unfortunate level of resentment at several universities and research institutes between traditional area specialists (especially in the humanities, language and literature, linguistics, and history) and the thematic specialists. In an era of increasingly scarce resources, it is probably inevitable that some of these tensions will arise. The challenge remains of linking the area specialists and the thematic specialists more effectively. At many of the most active research institutes across the country, the problem is being addressed in some creative and imaginative ways. At the University of Montreal, for example, very useful connections have been developed between the East Asian Studies Centre and the Business School in the areas of curriculum and research design. In another area, security studies, this fusion is beginning to take place on a national basis and is paying some handsome dividends as seen in the activities of the Canadian Consortium for Asia Pacific Security.[11]

3. Topics

The facts of funding mean that a large, perhaps disproportionate, percentage of applied research is linked to the general thrust of Canada's developmental assistance programs. The consequences of this orientation are less damaging than might first appear because of the very broad definition of developmental assistance that is currently employed. Far from being restricted to poverty alleviation, aid programming in Asia is built around the concept of "sustainable development." This involves creating partnerships with developing countries that involve elements of human resource development, market-based economic development, attention to the environment, gender relations, national and regional institutions, and human rights and good governance. The analytic and research support that is necessary to guide and support this range of activities is equally broad, moving from demographics and economic mapping, through to such areas as cooperative security.

It is impossible here to list the cutting-edge work at Canadian institutes on Asia Pacific topics. Let me suggest that the thematic concerns of Canadian researchers tend to reflect changing circumstances at home and across the Pacific. One area where domestic priorities have generated some innovative new work is in gender relations. Another is environment. A third is human rights and good governance. A fourth relates to economic issues, including regulatory environment, investment flows, technology transfer, and cross-cultural management issues. One trend that runs across these areas has been the increasing tendency to treat them in a comparative, regional context, rather than as restricted to a single country or jurisdiction.

The rise of regional multilateral institutions has added a new dimension. Organizations such as the Pacific Economic Cooperation Council (PECC) have been in existence for more than a decade and have generated a large body of multi-national research. The Pacific Forum on Trade and Development (PAFTAD) has proven to be a creative and durable institution for promoting forward-looking economic research. APEC in particular is generating an unprecedented demand for detailed, technical research through its working groups and their quickly expanding activities. The creation of an APEC Studies Centre housed at the Asia Pacific Foundation is an important step in better mobilizing limited resources to focus on a range of issues related to the APEC agenda.

This organizationally driven demand has not yet produced a substantial or systematic corpus of research findings or basic information. The fact that the level of institutionalization of Pacific international organizations is rather restricted means that research is geographically decentralized. For example, there is not an OECD equivalent, and the task of preparing economic forecasts is handled through mechanisms like the Pacific Economic Outlook (PEO) which is assembled from contributions from several countries. The Canadian contribution to the PEO is funded by DFAIT, managed by the Canadian Committee for the PECC which is based at the APEC secretariat in Singapore, and produced by the Conference Board of Canada. It appears likely that the PEO might well be blended into the APEC process in the near future.

What it has produced is an ever proliferating series of working groups, task forces and conferences. The need for quick production or research on increasingly technical questions is intense and growing. From my experience, meeting this demand is more and more difficult, in part because of an inevitable shortage of authors who have technical expertise combined with a sense of policy context, and in part because of the limited capacity of overburdened government officials to absorb, much less direct, research undertakings. The expansion of research programs has had the unintended consequence of making a considered contribution to policy making more difficult.

One of the areas where the growth of multilateral institutions and processes is having a pronounced catalytic effect on research in Canada is in the area of security studies. Asia Pacific security studies in Canada have been given a boost, with comparatively small amounts of additional funding, by the proliferation of channels for regional dialogue since 1990. Canada has attempted to play an active and, intermittently, leading role in shaping the post-cold war security agenda in the region. The research community in Canada has generally been supportive of these initiatives, and there has been a surge of activity related to research, conferences, and other exchange on a range of geographic and thematic security problems.[12] The task of linking this work to governmental policy and priorities remains significant.

4. Organization

The Canadian research community focusing on Eastern Asia is both larger and better organized than it was a decade ago. Part of this has been because of the development of the university-based research centres which have expanded in number and level of activity. Most depend heavily on contract research and service programs funded by outside agencies for their well being, indeed survival through the overhead component of grants and awards. The same can be said for the university-based research institutions which are thematically defined but which do work on specific Asia Pacific topics.

Considering the fact that research expertise in Canada is geographically dispersed, loosely concentrated in three parts of the country—the Vancouver-Victoria area, Southern Ontario, and Montreal-Quebec—one of the more promising trends has been the development of research consortia. The creation of mechanisms for inter-institute cooperation has been a general objective of national funding agencies for the past few years. There have been some very successful examples in the policy areas of environmental studies, but as a general rule there is little contact among institutes in different parts of Canada, a problem that is especially acute in working across the linguistic divides of French and English

With reference to Asia Pacific issues, two recently created networks deserve special mention because of the breadth of their membership and the range of topics they examine. The first is the Pacific Economic Research Consortium established in 1992 to enable Canadian economists specializing in applied and policy research to develop linkages with East and Southeast Asian and other Pacific Rim research institutions. It is designed to enable research scholars from Canadian universities to work with Canadian research organizations outside the universities, including the Conference Board of Canada, the IDRC, and the North-South Institute, in projects involving partners in other Pacific Rim countries. One example of this cooperation is the Applied Economic Research Institute Linkage program with China that is being funded by the CIDA and administered by the Conference Board of Canada. The second is the Canadian Consortium for Asia Pacific Security (CANCAPS) created in December 1993 with about sixty participants from across the country. CANCAPS organizes an annual meeting, small working groups, and publishes a quarterly newsletter and occasional policy papers.

In addition to expanding collaboration among individual researchers and institutes in Canada, both consortia aim at promoting linkages in the area of policy research across the Pacific. CANCAPS, for example, is closely connected in its objectives and organizational structure to the Canadian member committee of the Council for Security Cooperation in Asia Pacific (CSCAP). CSCAP was founded by ten leading research institutes in Asia Pacific with an interest in international relations and security studies. CSCAP now is composed of fourteen member committees and is sponsoring four working groups, one of which on "Enhancing Security Cooperation in the North Pacific/Northeast Asia" is cosponsored by Canada and Japan. The activities of CANCAPS and CSCAP are establishing new connections between Canadian institutes and counterparts in other parts of the Asia Pacific region, especially the ASEAN Institutes of Strategic and International Studies (ASEAN-ISIS).

A challenge within Canada and across the Pacific is to move from parallel research projects to genuinely collaborative ones. Here there have been some promising developments. In one example, the David Lam Centre for International Communications has been working with the Lijiang County Minority Peoples Cooperative Enterprise on a collaborative research and development project sponsored by the IDRC. In another, the Centre for International Studies at the University of Toronto is engaged in a three-year project with the Berkeley Roundtable on

International Economics and Saitama University in Japan to examine foreign direct investment and diffusion of technology in East Asia.

V. Conclusion

The major actors in creating what can alternatively be conceived of as a web of trans-Pacific connections or the base for an emerging trans-Pacific community have, until very recently, been nongovernmental. They have included private firms, universities and nongovernmental organizations. One hypothesis is that these nongovernmental processes will recede in importance as governments come to play more dominant and leading roles in the creation of a multilateral institutional infrastructure across the Pacific. Some feel this is already occurring in the economic area, with PECC or APEC facing a diminished future because of the rapid development.

My own view is that nongovernmental associations have the potential to play a durable and effective role regardless of the development of formal governmental organizations. There is reason to believe that institution building Asia Pacific-style will follow its own trajectory rather than replicate the process that has developed in Europe or North America. There are very real limits on the pace and scope of institution building in a region that is as diverse as Asia Pacific in the realms of religion, culture, ethnicity, political systems, and level of economic development. In the absence of a pressing will for any form of political and social integration to accompany economic and security interactions, institutional development will not necessarily lead in the direction of "community" as the word is normally used. In other words, there are severe constraints on how much governments can do.

The research process plays several roles in the evolution of Asia Pacific. One is to support and occasionally guide formal governmental efforts in a wide array of areas ranging from trade policy to the management of human rights issues. A second is to engage in a kind of critical questioning of government policies and regional dynamics. A third, whatever the influence on government thinking and action, is to serve as a species of trans-Pacific actor that establishes linkages and fosters understanding across great distances and great divides. Rather than coming to an end, nongovernmental networks are only just beginning to hit stride in establishing long-term personal relations, trust, and durable institutional linkages.

This leads to five specific challenges that the Canadian research community must face in advancing Asia Pacific cooperation in the remainder of the decade.

- To move from parallel to collaborative research projects within Canada and across the Pacific;
- To diversify funding sources beyond the Canadian government and to establish more programs that receive funding from sources in two or more countries;
- To ensure that basic research is not ignored in the face of pressing needs for action-oriented, instrumental research;
- To find more creative ways to link area specialists to thematic specialists; and
- To provide more timely and concise information and analysis to government officials and business leaders and to contribute more effectively to the discussion of public policy options.

While the prescription might seem parochial, Canadians first need to know more about what they are already doing. Part of this will depend upon the results of the JCIE project which will present the most comprehensive picture to date of the nongovernmental philanthropic and research activities around the Pacific. These results will provide a useful comparative perspective from which we can evaluate the structure and future direction of Canadian activities.

As a starting point, we also need a detailed and systematic study of the projects, research institutes, and funding sources focusing on Asia Pacific that are already in place.[13] It seems clear that no one inside or outside government has a systematic and comprehensive sense of what is now being done. The purpose of such an inventory would be to suggest complementarities, potential areas for cooperation, and gaps in the current patchwork of programs and activities. It would be of value to the research community in Canada, to funding agencies in Canada and abroad, and to the federal government which, like almost all Canadian organizations, is being forced to do more with less.

Without wishing to undervalue the enthusiasm or energy which characterize the current phase of trans-Pacific research cooperation, I will end on a cautionary note. History suggests that the relationship between governments and private associates are not always positive. In comparing contemporary policy networks in Canada to the earlier era of the Institute of Pacific Relations, Larry Woods perceptively notes that

> a societal policy network can assist the state in the absence of requisite bureaucratic capabilities in a particular issue area, but that this network, having served and perhaps even incorporated the state sector, can be easily abandoned by the state when those capabilities are captured or political circumstances diminish the network's utility.[14]

This is not an argument for abandoning collaborative ventures between government and the research community. This is neither realistic in the light of current funding patterns nor helpful in the face of current needs. It is to suggest that research institutions and networks must be active in serving national needs while at the same time be vigilant in preserving their independence and autonomous character.

Notes

1. The author wishes to thank Shirley Yue for research assistance and Charles A. Barrett, Karen Minden, and William A. Nielson for their thoughtful comments on an earlier draft.
2. The words chosen by two Canadian political scientists, David Dewitt and Brian Job. See their comprehensive overview, "Asia Pacific Security Studies in Canada," in Paul M. Evans, ed., *Studying Asia Pacific Security: The Future of Research, Training and Dialogue Activities* (North York: University of Toronto - York University Joint Centre for Asia Pacific Studies, 1994).
3. I am hesitant to get into the matter of the unconscious factors which have shaped this essay. Let me merely state that I am a male, forty-something social scientist (more specifically political scientist), teaching in English at a university in central Canada, and directing an area-based research centre.
4. I've examined in detailed fashion the origins and implications of some of the formulations of "Asia Pacific" in my essay "The Concept of Eastern Asia," soon to appear in a volume edited by Colin Mackerras, *Eastern Asia: An Introductory History*, 2nd edition (Sydney: Allen Unwin, forthcoming). For a different point of view see Arif Dirlik, "The Asia Pacific Idea: Reality and Representation in the Invention of a Regional Structure," *Journal of World History*, Vol. 3, No. 1 (Spring 1992).
5. Consistency is a challenge. Canadian officials have supported formal institution building through such organizations as the "Asia Pacific Economic Cooperation." And contrary to the penchant and rationale for "Asia Pacific" the Liberal Government shortly after its election in October 1993 a new position of "Secretary of State for Asia Pacific."
6. It is possible that a fifth category, *non-university institutes of higher learning*, will deserve more attention in the future. Most important here are the community colleges across Canada that are increasingly active in international linkages and training programs with an Asia Pacific dimension. One of the most active and successful has been Capilano College in British Columbia. The Associates of Canadian Community Colleges (ACCC) is a participant in the APEC Human Resource Development Networks Projects along with the Conference Board of Canada and The North South Institute. It is also the Canadian lead institution in the network on "Human Resources in Industrial Technology."
7. International Monetary Fund, *International Financial Statistics* January 1995 (Washington, D.C.: IMF, 1995). Figures are based on the end of the period exchange rates for November 1994. US$1=C$1.37.
8. The programs and approach of the Department of National Defense are carefully assessed in Dewitt and Job, "Asia Pacific Security Studies in Canada," op. cit. The total amount of funding devoted to outside research on Asia is minimal, probably less than $100,000 per year.
9. There are four such positions attached to the University of Victoria's Centre for Asia Pacific Initiatives.
10. The example I have in mind is the Centre for Global Partnership which was established to promote Japanese-American exchange.

11. See Evans, *Studying Asia Pacific Security*, op. cit., especially Ch. 18, David Dewitt's "Summary of Discussion."

12. The origins, pattern, and implications of these developments for Canada are carefully examined in Dewitt and Job, "Asia Pacific Security Studies in Canada," in Evans, op.cit. On the effects of the dialogue process see my essay, "The Dialogue Process on Asia Pacific Security Issues: Inventory and Analysis," ibid., pp. 297–318.

13. The only vaguely similar study with which I am familiar was published in 1986 on Canadian academics connecting with China. See Martin Singer, *Canadian Academic Relations with the People's Republic of China Since 1970*, Vols. I and II (Ottawa: International Development Research Centre, 1986).

14. Lawrence T. Woods, "The Asia-Pacific Policy Network in Canada," in *The Pacific Review*, Vol. 7, No. 4 (1994), p. 436.

CHINA

Status of Research Institutions in China

A Trend Report

Shohei Muta
Program Officer
Japan Center for International Exchange

and

Makito Noda
Senior Program Officer
Japan Center for International Exchange

I. Introduction

As a result of recent government policy changes, there have been substantial reorganizations in many Chinese research institutions. The Chinese Academy of Social Sciences (CASS) established an Institute of Asia Pacific Studies in 1988 by merging the Institute of South Asia Studies and the Asia Pacific Studies Division of the Institute of World Economy and Politics. However, the Institute is still strong in South Asian (India and Pakistan) studies. The Shanghai Academy of Social Sciences (SASS) also established an Institute of Asia Pacific Studies in 1991, separating four research departments (Japan and Korea, Southeast Asia, Taiwan, and Hong Kong) from the Institute of World Economy.

Since the beginning of 1993, the central government has been undertaking drastic social reforms that require contributions in the area of policy studies from various governmental think tanks and academies. It seems that the central government and the Party leaders are ready to hear policy advice from specialists beyond the government policy planners.

The most urgent topics discussed are economic-related issues, and many different institutions are participating. The Chinese leadership is well aware that in order to maintain economic development, China must have stable relations with neighboring countries. The immediate concern of Chinese leaders is how to integrate the Chinese economy into the world market economy within the fast-growing Asia Pacific region.

Since the introduction of the Social Science Research Project for the Eighth Five-Year Plan by the State Education Commission in 1991, a majority of research projects conducted by major research institutions in China have followed governmental project guidelines. The Project contains the following priority topics:

> Asia Pacific regional development and China toward the next century; structural adjustment in Asia Pacific economic relations; the Asia Pacific regional community and its future; historical studies of China-Japan relations after World War II; political and economic relations between China and Southeast Asian countries; unification of the Korean peninsula and the security of Northeast Asia; Asia Pacific economic cooperation; economic relations between the Chinese coastal region and Hong Kong and Macao; South Asian regional cooperation; and the China–India border conflict.

The government seems to be convinced of the importance of research projects on Asia Pacific regional development and security issues as a national priority.

II. The Intellectual Infrastructure in China

1. Impact of the Cultural Revolution on Social Sciences in China

Many institutions active in independent research were shaken to their intellectual foundations during the Cultural Revolution. Though they resumed their activities in the early 1980s, many of them still suffer from this set-back. The most profound impact has been the notable absence of a generation of intellectuals due to a ten-year alienation from formal educational training and isolation from the international intellectual community.

There are two groups of intellectuals in China; i.e. one group that belongs to the old school of thought trained under Marxism and Maoist ideology, and the other which belongs to a new generation who are western educated and immune to Communist dogma.

Most of the scholars who regularly communicate with the outside world belong to the latter, younger generation. However, the researchers and academics belonging to the former are more senior and thus hold stronger positions in research offices of the State Council, and these individuals also have close contacts with government leaders, sometimes as a result of personal relationships. In addition, recently, scholars belonging to the old school have started exchanging their views with outside scholars out of necessity. The success of economic reform depends very much on open communications between these influential government researchers and young "sophisticated" western trained researchers.

The economic reform policy pursued by the present Party leaders relies on western trained scholars for ideas. Most of these western trained scholars were educated in the early 1980s, and some are now in their late thirties. They are versed in foreign languages, especially in English, and are accustomed to western-style discourse.

Intellectual discussions and expressions of opinions are said to be mostly unfettered, except for those relating to politically sensitive issues. Where economic reform is concerned, the government encourages intellectuals to discuss and express their opinions freely.

2. Emergence of New Intellectual Leaders and the "New Social Force"

Chinese society traditionally has functioned through personal and informal contacts. This is also true under the present socio-cultural system. The Chinese leaders usually form informal research groups or "private advisory groups" recruited through their affiliations with educational institutions. From these groups they obtain policy ideas. The recommendations of these groups are usually more influential than the ones brought up by formal bodies such as government think tanks.

In order to cope with newer sets of problems associated with industrial development, government leaders have been urged to develop a new intellectual infrastructure for industrial development. The government has to rely solely on the new generation of scholars with educational backgrounds in the West in fields such as industrial policy and financial management. Even in the late 1970s, the government started establishing new research institutions such as those in the framework of CASS. It seems that the end of the cold war and the introduction of a market economy into China have been accelerating the substantial reorganization of many of these research institutions.

3. Infrastructure Support for Intellectual Dialogue and the Role of American Foundations

As early as 1966, the Committee on Scholarly Communication with China (CSCC), formerly the Committee on Scholarly Communication with the People's Republic of China, was established by the American Council of Learned Societies, the Social Science Research Council, and the National Academy of Sciences in order to facilitate Sino-American academic exchanges in the fields of science, engineering, social science, and humanities.

After the normalization of diplomatic relations, American foundations and academic associations stepped up their efforts to assist China's international studies, which were underdeveloped and strongly influenced by Marxist paradigms.

In 1984, a consortium of three American foundations formed the Committee on International Relations Studies with the People's Republic of China (CIRSPRC). The Committee originally consisted of the Ford Foundation, the Rockefeller Foundation, and the Rockefeller Brothers Fund. The Rockefeller Foundation later left the consortium and, in its place, the Henry Luce Foundation and the MacArthur Foundation joined. CIRSPRC has been supporting human resource development through scholarships for Ph.D. and M.A. candidates and visiting scholars to the United States. It also sends American scholars to China for lectures and teaching at Chinese institutions.

Presently, American foundations, as well as U.S. government agencies and some American corporations, have given grants to institutions in the United States to support academic conferences and policy dialogues with Chinese scholars and analysts. American organizations actively involved in intellectual dialogue with China include the Brookings Institution, the Pacific Forum, the Asia Society, the Atlantic Council of the United States, the RAND Corporation, and a number of universities such as Stanford, Berkeley, and Johns Hopkins. Also, Johns Hopkins University runs the Hopkins-Nanjing Center on Chinese and American studies jointly with Nanjing University.

4. Information Access to the Outside World

Because of the increased demand for information related to the Asia Pacific region, many research institutions are building up a collection of books and basic materials such as statistics on various countries in the region. Many institutions are eager to exchange their publications with foreign counterparts as a means of obtaining the latest information.

Among them, information on Japan and the United States is the most needed, obviously because of the actual and potential impact of these two major powers in the region. Research institutions in Beijing and Shanghai are relatively well informed on contemporary U.S. issues due to active assistance, financial and otherwise, by American foundations, universities, and the U.S. government.

For example, the library of the Institute of American Studies, CASS has fifty thousand books, one hunderd foreign language (mainly English) and five hundred Chinese language journals, and three American (*Washington Post*, *New York Times*, and *Herald Tribune*) and fourteen Chinese newspapers. The collection is constantly updated and well equipped. The library also regularly receives U.S. government documents from the Embassy in Beijing.

On the other hand, information on contemporary Japan is very limited. With the exception of the very few financially stable institutions, such as the Center for Japanese Studies at Fudan University in Shanghai, which has received ten million yen (US$100,000)[1] from a Japanese corporation for the purchase of Japanese books, the majority of Japanese studies institutions cannot procure Japanese government publications and documents.

As one of the few exceptions, the library at the Center for Japanese Studies is new but also equipped with basic reference material on Japan—twenty thousand books and basic journals such as the *Monthly Report of the Bank of Japan*. The Center has received several private collections of books by Japanese scholars. However, because of the appreciation of the yen, it is difficult to import Japanese books. The Center has benefited from the Japan Foundation Book Donation Program, but because the program is awarded annually to different institutions and universities, the Center cannot expect to benefit from the program continually, making it difficult to obtain annual publications such as white papers and statistical year books. Additionally, the list provided by the Japan Foundation is more focused on humanities related publications, which are not always relevant to the needs of scholars in the Center.

III. The Role of Various Institutions in Policy Discussion

When the government announces a new economic policy in China, many intellectuals and institutions active in government economic policy making become busy preparing detailed policy studies and policy recommendation "drafts" related to the new policy. The Party leaders also give some weight to the opinions of their personal advisors.

However, the final policy recommendations will be decided by the research offices of the ministries. The officials at those ministerial research offices are not yet exposed to the outside world. Because of their isolated position, they are not always well informed of the present international realities and, it is said, they tend to place importance on opinions and recommendations that support their way of thinking. Their unrealistic attitude toward policy planning sometimes causes confusion in the implementation of new policies. Recently, the Chinese government has begun to listen to recommendations from more independent research institutions, in an attempt to avoid shortsighted policy plans drawn up by ministerial research offices.

What follows is a typology of Chinese research institutions in the order of their impact on procedural policies, or their "importance."

1. Government Institutions (Think Tanks)

Government think tanks such as the International Trade Research Institute of the Ministry of Foreign Trade and Economic Coordination and the China Institute of International Studies (CIIS) of the Ministry of Foreign Affairs are under the direct control of their respective ministries or the State Council itself. The researchers have more chances to participate in direct policy discussions and have access to government information. But as the quid pro quo they have less freedom in expressing independent opinions. Their findings tend to faithfully reflect the government's views or "party lines."

However, some of them are allowed to have more autonomy in deciding research topics, especially concerning economic fields. There are also institutions established by the government but encouraged to seek funding from foreign foundations for their research activities. Such government think tanks are often engaged in the study of current issues. Many of the foreign affairs related institutions belong in this category, including the China Institute of Contemporary International Relations (CICIR), which is the largest government think tank on foreign relations, and the China Center for International Studies (CCIS), formerly the Center for International Studies of the State Council. Other institutes in this category include the Development Research Center of the State Council, the Economic Research Center under the State Planning Commission, and the Chinese People's Institute of Foreign Affairs under the Foreign Ministry.

2. Institutions Affiliated with the Military

The People's Liberation Army has maintained significant interest in, and influence on, China's foreign policy, particularly its defense and strategic studies and security relations. Not much is known about their organization or programs, but the China Institute for International Strategic Studies, the Foundation for International Strategic Studies, and the Institute of Strategic Studies all directly belong to the National Defense University.

3. CASS Institutes

CASS was established in 1977 as the national center for social science research. It is made up of thirty-one research institutes, three research centers, two publishing houses (for books and journals), and a graduate school with about four thousand research staff. Most of the research staff have university teaching experience and regular contact with the universities. The research staff sometimes move between government research institutions and universities and back again. CASS researchers are given freedom to conduct their research under much longer time frames than are researchers at other institutes.

CASS positions its research between pure academic and policy studies and places priority on economics, social and political development, international relations, and legal issues. In the field of Asia Pacific studies, CASS has the Institute of Asia Pacific Studies, the Institute of World Economy and Politics, the Institute of Economics, the Institute of Finance, and the Institute of Industrial Economics. Aside from these functional/disciplinary institutes, CASS also has newer regional institutes such as the Institute of American Studies and the Institute of Japanese Studies.

The main financial source of these CASS institutes has been the government. However, as a result of recent reforms, the government encourages fund raising from other sources such as foreign foundations and emerging "private business sectors." The Ford Foundation, whose China office has an annual budget of RMB 6 billion (US$700 million),[2] supports almost forty percent of CASS exchange activities with the United States, mostly through CSCC.

The institutions affiliated with CASS draw major research funding from the national research budgets that provide funds for government designated key projects. Because of ideological sensitivity, the study of social sciences in China has traditionally been in a weaker position compared with that of natural sciences. The Natural Science Foundation, which allocates funding for natural science research, thus takes a larger share of the budget than the National Social Science Fund, which allocates state government funding among the social science research institutions.

Therefore, competition for funds within CASS is much greater than within research institutions dealing with natural science.

4. University Affiliated Research Institutions

Many of these are still teaching and training institutions for postgraduates. However, recently, some university affiliated research institutions have strengthened their research capability on policy-related issues. In the field of international relations, Peking University has the Institute of International Relations in the Department of International Politics under the dynamic directorship of Dr. Yuan Ming. In the fields of finance and fiscal policy, where specialists are scarce within government think tanks, the government has to rely on policy-related studies from university research institutions such as those attached to the Shanghai University of Finance and Economics (SUFE). Affiliated with the Ministry of Finance, SUFE is a "State Priority University" for academic research on finance and business for the State Council. Research topics and their priority follow the State Council's policy.

5. "Nongovernmental" Research Institutions

Any research organization in China has to obtain the majority of its funding from either the central or local government. However, recently, the central government has begun to encourage even government research institutions to look for supplementary funding sources, allowing them more autonomy in their activities. Although no institution can be called nongovernmental yet, the Institute of Asian Economic Studies was established very recently at SUFE with major funding from a private textile company in Beijing. Additionally, institutions that are categorized as "informal research institutions" have emerged. They are loosely connected with particular government agencies and staffed chiefly by retired diplomats, military officers, and journalists. Their funding sources vary from the government to foreign foundations. The Institute of Global Concern is a typical example of this category.

6. Shanghai and Other Regional Centers for Asia Pacific Studies

Aside from the previously mentioned Beijing-based institutes, there are important institutions in other areas, particularly Shanghai. Shanghai has been playing a unique and important role in Chinese foreign relations. Generally speaking, Shanghai is regarded as more innovative and experimental than Beijing. Accordingly, oftentimes new policies and plans are first tried in this city. In 1988, for example, the Shanghai government was authorized by the State Council, in its economic development plan, to experiment with various new market-oriented reforms.

Research institutions located in Shanghai are also more likely to be in tune with current trends. Thus, as early as 1984, a seminar on "The Prospect of Development in the Pacific Region and China's Modernization," cosponsored by six Shanghai research institutes, was held. The discussions covered the current situation and the political position of the Asia Pacific region, the influence of the emergence of the Asia Pacific region on China's modernization and on Shanghai's development, and Asia Pacific economic cooperation. The six institutes included the Shanghai Institute of International Studies, the Center for American Studies at Fudan University, the Institute of Asia Pacific Studies of the Shanghai Academy of Social Sciences, the Asia Institute, the Chinese Institute for Peace and Development Studies, and the Shanghai Council for Strategy and Policy.

Research institutions in Shanghai receive funds from various sectors and are financially better off than their counterparts in Beijing. In addition, the buildings they are housed in are new and modern compared with institutions in Beijing.

There are many other research institutions affiliated with provincial governments or universities that conduct research on issues related to the Asia Pacific region, including the Institute of Asia Pacific Studies in Fuzhou, Guangzhou, and Dilian. There are institutes of Japanese studies at universities such as Hebei, Jilin, Liaoning, and Northeast Teachers' University. There are also a few university institutions for Korean and Southeast Asian studies—the Institute of Asia Pacific Studies in Fuzhou, Guangzhou, and Dilian.

IV. Problems and Obstacles in Promoting Intellectual Exchange with China

1. Language

Despite the fact that many institutions focus on the Asia Pacific region, as a whole researchers tend to concentrate on a single country and are not well versed in regionwide issues. Many specialists in international studies are trained in the United

States and are fluent in English, but it is very rare to find a Japan specialist, for instance, who can communicate effectively in English, making it difficult for him to participate in an international research project. This may be attributable to the compartmentalized approach traditionally adopted by Chinese institutions.

2. Funding

Research institutions have recently been encouraged by the government to look for alternative sources to augment government funding. Many are looking for foreign foundation grants. Because of the underdeveloped legal framework, it has been difficult for foreign foundations to establish their presence in China. Under these unfavorable conditions, the Ford Foundation and other major American, German, Canadian, and Australian foundations, as well as the Japan Foundation, have been active and have already established themselves as recognized entities among Chinese scholars. However, the shortage of funding sources for international activities has become the bottleneck for more active participation by Chinese institutions. In order to improve the situation, China has to introduce a legal framework in which nonprofit and nongovernmental organizations can operate more effectively.

Looking at the positive side, the recent move by the government to allow and urge research institutions to look for other financial sources may have a positive impact on promoting more independent policy research in China.

V. Major Research Institutions in China

1. Institutions in Beijing

a. CASS Institutes

Chinese Academy of Social Sciences (CASS)

CASS was established as a national research center for social sciences. It has thirty-two research institutions and fifteen research centers with five thousand research staff. When necessary, research units are established temporally for interdisciplinary research topics. CASS places priority on economics, social and political development, international relations, and legal issues. Presently, six institutions are focusing on economics, and eight concentrate on international and world affairs. Regional studies such as American and Japanese Studies have been added recently.

There are about one hundred CASS-affiliated research associations and societies including the National Association of Social Sciences.

CASS manages twenty-four formal exchange programs, mostly with European institutions. In the Asia Pacific region, CASS frequently interacts with such organizations as The Japan Society for Promotion of Science, The Korea Foundation, The Institute of Southeast Asian Studies (Singapore), The Council for Social Sciences and The International Development Research Centre (Canada), and The Australian Association of Social Sciences. It also has working relationships with the Korean Sejong Institute, the Korea Development Institute (KDI), and Japan's National Institute for Research Advancement (NIRA).

CASS's main financial source has been the government. As a result of recent reforms, however, the government now encourages CASS to raise its own funds from other sources such as overseas foundations and newly emerging private business sectors. It receives annual support from the Japan Foundation, particularly in the form of book purchases.

CASS includes the following relevant institutions:

Institute of American Studies (IAS), CASS

The Institute of American Studies was established in 1981, as an independent academic research institution within CASS. The Institute takes its own independent initiative in choosing research topics. Although the Institute has interests in various aspects of U.S.-China relations, it is presently placing more emphasis on economic relations. Recently, the Institute was involved in topics such as U.S. economic relations with mainland China, Hong Kong, and Taiwan, and political implications for the countries involved. Research work on the Asia Pacific region naturally involves a number of Japanese scholars. Recent Asia Pacific related projects include: a study on economic and security issues related to the "Greater China" and issues on nuclear nonproliferation (jointly with the Institute of Global Conflict and Cooperation at the University of California at San Diego); a 1992 conference on U.S.-China in the Asia Pacific and American studies in the Asia Pacific (jointly with the International House of Japan and the Jefferson Institute of the United States) and a study on U.S.-China relations in the 1970s (jointly with the East-West Center).

Additionally, the Institute plans to conduct a project that will deal with trilateral interactions among China, the United States, and Japan in the post–cold war era.

Institute of Industrial Economics (IIE), CASS

The Institute of Industrial Economics (IIE) was established in 1978 within CASS in order to create the academic infrastructure needed to pursue industrialization. IIE primarily works for the State Council and the Chinese Communist Party. The main areas of concern mostly deal with industry-related subjects such as macro-economic analysis, industrial management, energy, and high-tech industry. Although IIE places emphasis on domestic economic development, it maintains very strong interests in Japanese industrial policy and policies of other emerging economies in the Asia Pacific region. Recently, IIE has gone through a major organizational restructuring to meet demands for studies related to the introduction of market mechanisms into the Chinese economic system. IIE has started to pay more attention to industrial strategy after joining the GATT under the on-going Asia Pacific economic integration. IIE has scholar exchange programs with the Institute of Developing Economies, Tokyo, Tufts University's Fletcher School of Law and Diplomacy, and the Pacific Forum-CSIS.

The Institute of Asia Pacific Studies, CASS

As a result of the merger between CASS's Institute of South Asia Studies and the Asia Pacific Studies Division of the Institute of World Economy and Politics, the Institute of Asia Pacific Studies was established in 1988. The Institute is the largest academic research institution devoted to regional studies. While South Asian studies (India and Pakistan) remain a major focus, the Institute has added American studies to deal with issues such as trade in the Pacific. The Institute has eight senior research staff, twenty-five junior research staff, and ten assistants.

The Institute has recently completed four projects—"Four Little Dragons," "Korean Peninsula and Northeast Asian Security," "Yellow Sea Projects," and "Asia Pacific Economic Cooperation"—while it is currently conducting ten major research projects, mostly on economic issues, related to the region. With Sasakawa Peace Foundation support, the Institute plans to launch a research project on socialism and economic transformation. The Institute will also launch a study project on Sino-Japanese relations after World War II with support from the Toyota Foundation. The Institute plans to publish a series of books on such topics as *Japan, from Economic Giant to Political Giant*, *Economic Development in the Coastal Region and Hong Kong*, and *Asia Pacific Economic Cooperation: Vision and Reality* The Institute has maintained various exchange programs with overseas institutions including The International Center for the Study of East Asian Development, Kitakyushu; The Institute of Developing Economies, Tokyo; Sakura Research Institute, Tokyo; Korea Development Institute; the Association of Contemporary Chinese Studies (Korea); the East-West Center, Honolulu; the Institute of Southeast Asian Studies, Singapore; and Thailand's Chulalongkorn University.

b. Other Beijing Institutions

China Center for International Studies (CCIS)

CCIS, known as the Center for International Studies of the State Council until 1988, was established in 1982. It is a governmental think tank focusing on international affairs and security issues. Under the first Director General, the late Huan Xiang, the Center was very close to the political leadership and played an influential role in Chinese politics. As a result of the current political reform, however, CCIS has begun to take a more independent stance. Yet, the government remains the sole beneficiary of most of the CCIS studies, although it has been taking a more autonomous approach gradually.

China Institute of Contemporary International Relations (CICIR)

CICIR is a comprehensive research institution conducting policy-oriented research for the government on strategic, international, and economic issues. CICIR was established in 1960 through the initiatives of Mao Zedong and Zhou Enlai as an institution to provide the government with policy studies. Presently, CICIR has a research staff of four hundred, and it is one of the most active government think tanks. The Institute consists of seven regional divisions and three comprehensive divisions (world politics and economics, international VIP profiles, and the Editorial Board). The Asia Pacific region is covered by related regional divisions such as Northeast Asia (Japan and the Koreas), the United States and Canada, and South and Southeast Asia. Most of the research topics are decided by the Institute itself, but as a government think tank, it conducts research and provides reference materials commissioned by various ministries. Japanese and American studies are the strongest sections in the Institute, although there is a growing interest in the Asia Pacific region. Most of their publications are confidential reports to the government except for a periodical in the Chinese language and an English monthly, *Contemporary International Relations.* The Institute has maintained exchange programs with several overseas institutions, including The Japan Institute for International Affairs (JIIA), The Asia Forum, The Sigur Institution, George Washington University , and ASEAN-ISIS.

China Institute for International Strategic Studies (CIISS)

CIISS was established in 1979 to promote research and dialogue on international strategic questions. CIISS is more of an association, whose membership consists of retired military officers, retired diplomats, and scholars. It publishes quarterly journals in Chinese and English. Financially, the Institute receives funding from the government and the People's Liberation Army. The Institute undertook a China-Japan-U.S.-Russia conference in 1992, a China-Japan conference, a study on Japan-Russian relations, and a joint conference with the Singapore Institute of International Affairs. The Institute has annual meetings with the United Nations Association of the United States, the Russian Academy of Science's Far Eastern Institute, the Institute for International Policy Studies (Japan), and the Research Institute for Peace and Security (Japan). The Institute has established contact with about thirty academic societies and seventy research institutions abroad.

China Institute of International Studies (CIIS)

CIIS was established in 1956 in order to provide the Ministry of Foreign Affairs with analytical and objective views on international issues. Approximately ninety percent of its work is only for internal circulation with the exception of a Chinese language journal on international studies. Among some one hundred staff members are about twenty assigned to the Japan and Korea section. CIIS holds regular meetings with its Japanese counterpart, the Japan Institute of International Affairs. After diplomatic normalization with South Korea, CIIS initiated joint meetings with the Korean Institute for Security Studies. It also holds annual meetings with the Brookings Institution and accepts visiting scholars from various institutions in the world including the International Institute for Strategic Studies.

Chinese People's Institute of Foreign AVairs (CPIFA)

CPIFA was founded in 1949, with encouragement from Zhou Enlai, to promote people-to-people diplomacy. Besides its English quarterly, *Foreign Affairs Journal,* CPIFA's main function is to promote international exchange of academics, opinion leaders, and private citizens. CPIFA has been very active in various exchange programs with other Asia Pacific countries including the United States. CPIFA maintains regular contacts with the Institute for International Policy Studies in Tokyo and has held regular seminars with the National Committee of U.S.-China Relations for the last fifteen years.

2. Institutions in Shanghai

Shanghai has played a unique role in the recent political and economic development of China. Because of geographical distance, scholars in Shanghai seem to be freer to speak about security and strategic issues than their counterparts in Beijing. It has been said, for instance, that scholars in Shanghai have played a very critical role in encouraging Beijing leaders to promote diplomatic relations with Indonesia. Their influence has not been confined in security and international relations areas. They have been equally influential in the economic fields, particularly because it is easier in Shanghai, a provincial capital, to discuss ideas that are still politically sensitive such as the introduction of a share-holding system for state-owned enterprises. Prominent institutions in Shanghai include:

The Center for Japanese Studies, Fudan University

Fudan University's Center for Japanese Studies is directly administered by the President of the University and it has held department status since 1990. The Center is composed of three divisions (politics, economics, and culture) and maintains a research staff of seven. The Center organizes joint studies and an annual joint symposium with Japanese scholars of various Japanese universities. Recent study themes include: "Inflation and Commodity Price in the Post-War Period" (1991), "Japanese Corporations and their Strength" (1992), "Japanese Economic Development and the Role of Government" (1993), and "National Insurance in Japan" (1994).

Institute of Asian Economic Studies, Shanghai University of Finance and Economics

The Institute of Asian Economic Studies was established with financial help from a private textile enterprise in Beijing. For this reason, some in China refer to this institute as the first "nongovernmental" research institution in China. The Institute is engaged in a one-year joint research project with the Hong Kong University on issues concerning China, Southeast Asia, and other Asian countries.

Institute for International Studies, Shanghai International Studies University (SISU)

The Institute for International Studies was established in 1980 as the Institute for Soviet Studies. After the collapse of the Soviet Union, it changed its name to the present one in May 1992. It houses about twenty research staff members drawn from a pool of professors of the University.

The Institute's current works are mainly concentrated on Russian and German studies, but it plans to expand its research scope to the Asia Pacific region.

The Institute of World Economy, Fudan University

Fudan University's Institute of World Economy (known until 1978 as the Institute of Capitalist Countries) was established in 1964. There are eight departments including American, Japanese, and Asia Pacific studies, with a research staff of thirty-five. The Institute has traditionally conducted research on individual countries, but it has recently shifted its focus toward regional economic development, with Asia Pacific as the most important region. The current main focus of research is trade and investment in Asia Pacific, and the Institute has recently completed projects including "Japan's Direct Investment in the 1990s" and "U.S.-Japan Trade Friction."

The Shanghai Academy of Social Sciences (SASS)

SASS was established in 1958. The Academy is the largest regional comprehensive social science research center in China,with a research staff of eight hundred. Among its sixteen attached institutes, the Institute of Asia Pacific Studies, the Institute of World Economy (North American studies), and the Institute for Peace and Development are involved in Asia Pacific regional studies. Additionally, SASS operates the Shanghai Center for International Studies which works closely with the Shanghai government and the China Center for International Studies in Beijing to function as a catalyst for international and interregional cooperation among research institutions.

The Institute of Asia Pacific Studies, separated from the Institute of World Economy in 1992, has four research departments (Japan and Korea, Southeast Asia, Taiwan, and Hong Kong) and a research staff of thirty. The major focus of its research has been Asia Pacific regional cooperation. The Japan and Korea Department focuses on Japan's economic presence in the Asia Pacific region, while the Southeast Asia Division concentrates its research on overseas Chinese in Southeast Asia and the concept of the "Greater China Economic Zone." It has not conducted joint research with its Asia Pacific counterparts.

Shanghai Institute of International Studies (SIIS)

The Shanghai Institute of International Studies (SIIS) was established in 1960 as a "local independent research institution" following suggestions from Zhou Enlai to promote academic study of the West, primarily the United States and her allies. Zhou Enlai wanted to maintain a window of contact with the West in order to be informed of developments there, but thought it would be difficult to have such an institution in Beijing. Over the last twenty years, however, the Institute's focus has expanded from the United States to include the Asia Pacific region. Presently, the

Institute has seven research departments: Japan, America, Western Europe, Former Soviet and Eastern Europe, Asia Pacific (East and Southeast Asia), Asia-Africa (including South Asia and the Middle East), and Comprehensive Research (United Nations, Asia Pacific economic cooperation) and it houses 106 full time staff (80 research staff) members.

Recently, priority has been given to research related to politics and economies of the Asia Pacific region. It has been constructing new centers, next to the current facilities, for exchange activities with Japan, Australia, and Korea. The objective of establishing those centers is to provide means and venues for research institutions in the Shanghai area to become more involved in Asia Pacific studies and to promote exchange activities between those institutions and related institutions in the three countries.

SIIS's main budget comes from the Shanghai Municipal Government. Although SIIS has autonomy in deciding research topics, it takes into consideration the needs of the Shanghai government and the Foreign Ministry in Beijing. SIIS has also received funds from overseas sources such as the Ford Foundation and Japan's National Institute for Research Advancement (NIRA). The Institute has maintained close working relations with the Institute of East Asian Studies at the University of California, Berkeley and other major U.S. think tanks such as the American Enterprise Institute, the Atlantic Council, the Brookings Institution, and the RAND Corporation. Besides the above think tanks, SIIS has conducted academic exchange programs with Princeton University's Center of International Studies, the Pacific Forum, NIRA, the Institute of Development Economies (Tokyo), the Japan Institute of International Affairs, the Institute of Social Sciences of Waseda University (Tokyo), the Institute of Strategic and International Studies in Malaysia, the Centre for Strategic and International Studies in Indonesia, the Association of International Relations in Singapore, Chulalongkorn University in Thailand, and other major institutions in Europe and the former Soviet Union.

SIIS stresses the importance of applied and policy research, and priority is given to foreign policy issues. In December 1993, SIIS cosponsored a joint conference with Daito Bunka University, Seoul University, two universities from Taiwan, and a North Korean research institution on "East Asian Economic Cooperation and its New Framework."

Notes

1. International Monetary Fund, *International Financial Statistics*, January 1995 (Washington, D.C.: IMF, 1995). Yen figures given are based on the end of period exchange rate for November 1994. US$1=98.92 yen.

2. IMF, op. cit. RMB figures given are based on the end of period exchange rate for October 1994. US$1=RMB 8.53.

HONG KONG

Survey of Research Institutions in Hong Kong

Yue-man Yeung
Director
Hong Kong Institute of Asia Pacific Studies
The Chinese University of Hong Kong

I. Evolution of Interests

Research institutions in Hong Kong, whether located at tertiary institutions or outside them, have long-standing interests in the affairs of the Asia Pacific region, particularly in China and Hong Kong. They have organized over the years a large number of conferences, research projects and other related activities, involving academics, policy makers and other professionals in Hong Kong as well as elsewhere. There is, therefore, no question that the research institutions and academics in Hong Kong have been playing a traditional role in shaping public opinion in this territory and outside. A major vehicle in this has been through research publications, scholarly meetings and participation in community affairs.

The manifold ways in which research institutions and their scholars have contributed to the development of this community are manifested in diverse ways. Many of our academics have played active roles in advising the government and its policy-making committees as members or in other capacities. For example, in key development sectors such as housing, transport, the new airport, town planning, health and social services, just to name a few, some members are invariably academics, who make their due contributions. The highest decision-making bodies in Hong Kong—the Executive Council and the Legislative Council—have also benefitted from the participation of academics as members, either through appointment by the governor or through elections. Academics contribute as well to major policy making, acting as think-tank members, part-time or full-time, in the Central Policy

Unit. It is clear, therefore, that from these many roles, academics have been influential in the process of intellectual development as well as in policy making in Hong Kong.

A more enhanced role for researchers and research institutions in Hong Kong has occurred with the government's policy rapidly to expand tertiary education over the last few years. At the same time, much greater emphasis has been placed on research at tertiary institutions, with the view that both the quality and the quantity of research activity should be greatly improved to train Hong Kong's own manpower to meet the challenges of a technological age and an increasingly interdependent global economy in the twenty-first century.

II. Attitudes towards the Asia Pacific Community

Because of Hong Kong's strategic geographical situation, it has played its bridge functions extremely well over the years. This was particularly important in the period when China pursued a policy of self-imposed isolation from the international community between 1949 and 1978. During this period, there were some research institutions set up in Hong Kong whose primary focus was on gaining an understanding of development in China without the opportunity of being there. Examples of research institutes set up for this purpose were the Universities Service Centre (which has recently been transferred to the Chinese University of Hong Kong in modern premises and expanded holdings), with support from a consortium of American universities, and the now defunct Union Research Centre.

With the gradual opening of China since 1978 and a more relaxed political atmosphere between China and Taiwan, increased trade and economic cooperation among the three territories, with Hong Kong playing a service and intermediary role, have increased by leaps and bounds during the last few years. Research institutions and their activities focused on this evolving and rapidly developing southern China region involving Fujian, Guangdong, Taiwan and Hong Kong have consequently increased. Many research institutions recently set up in Hong Kong have their geographical orientation towards this emerging region.

Concomitantly, Hong Kong is fully aware of rapid development and growing opportunities in countries within the Asia Pacific region. Parallel efforts are directed at cultivating contacts and networks within this area. For this reason, Hong Kong has participated actively in the Asian-Pacific Economic Cooperation forum (APEC), the Pacific Economic Cooperation Council (PECC), the Pacific Basin Economic

Council, etc. It is widely recognized that the continued prosperity and development of Hong Kong is dependent on continued and growing links with countries in the region. Consequently, there is a growing awareness and understanding of development in the Asia Pacific region. The establishment of the Hong Kong Institute of Asia Pacific Studies at the Chinese University of Hong Kong in 1990 is the best example of a redirection of research activities. Similar activities are also being carried out in other research institutes in Hong Kong.

At another level, there is a growing demand, especially from foreign universities, to network with local tertiary institutions in the exchange of staff and students. The recent formation of the University Mobility in Asia Pacific, with the participation of most countries in the region, is a mechanism being devised to enhance development in this respect. Hong Kong is a member of this informal network and, through it, there is scope for more activities of scholarly exchange.

III. Major Actors

Along with the growing perception of Hong Kong as a vital part of the Asia Pacific region and the increasing profile of regional activities, there has been no lack of new and existing organizations whose aim is to promote a regional intellectual research dialogue. The emphasis on the southern China region, with Hong Kong, Taiwan, Guangdong and Fujian being the focus is obvious but, increasingly, other parts of East Asia such as Japan and Korea have increased markedly in the frequency of their dialogue with institutions in Hong Kong.

The orientation towards the growing intellectual and scholarly dialogue with institutions in China has been facilitated by tertiary institutions since 1978, when China adopted an open policy and economic reforms. The government and private organizations have been providing funds for this kind of exchange to be promoted and expanded. Also, in the tripartite format of PECC, several leading research institutions, through their membership in the Hong Kong committee for PECC, are in close contact with similar research institutes in the region. It should also be noted that because of the perception of the Asia Pacific region as a growth centre in the world in the foreseeable future, there have been many requests to initiate scholarly exchange and contact from institutions in countries outside the region. Hong Kong institutions would generally welcome this growing network of contacts but they also have to review their own institutional capacity to be able to respond favourably to them.

IV. Future Prospects

With the general forecast that the Western Pacific Rim will grow in stature in economic terms in the remainder of this century and into the next, more and more political and economic activities and organizations have been focused on expanding cooperation among countries within the region and with those that lie outside it. It is often perceived in Hong Kong that as it will be returned to China in 1997 under the "one country, two systems" concept, Hong Kong must maintain, indeed increase, its international character if it is to remain a vibrant financial, service and transportation centre in the region. Consequently, research institutes in Hong Kong have a critical role to play in maintaining this international flavour of the territory and to maintain its existing strengths as a key metropolitan centre in this part of the world.

Because of Hong Kong's return to China in 1997, existing links with Commonwealth institutions and countries may have to be reviewed. Hong Kong institutions would certainly prefer to have the existing links maintained and strengthened but these have to be reviewed by Commonwealth professional and other organizations as the case may be. It can be anticipated that with the further integration of the territories in southern China, the existing merits of Hong Kong in its functional contacts with institutions in Taiwan and South China will be maintained. At the same time, it should be noted that institutional contacts between Hong Kong and Southeast Asia are not as strong as they should be. This is perhaps one direction along which future efforts should be devoted for promoting institutional contacts for the good of the parties concerned.

INDONESIA

Policy-Oriented Research Institutions in Indonesia
From the Viewpoint of Asia Pacific Intellectual Cooperation

Makito Noda
Senior Program Officer
Japan Center for International Exchange

I. Indonesia's Asia Pacific Orientation

On 16 November 1994, President Suharto hosted a meeting for leaders of the eighteen members of the Asia Pacific Economic Cooperation (APEC) forum in Bogor, indicating Indonesia's interest in and concern over the region. Analyzing how Indonesia decided to host this second meeting of the informal APEC summit seems to reveal at least some elements of Indonesia's orientation toward Asia Pacific.

The first twenty years of Indonesia's history as an independent state were full of political instability and economic decline, culminating in an abortive coup d'état in 1965 by a group of army officers followed by the massacre of some 750,000 alleged members of the PKI (Communist Party of Indonesia) which was suspected of being behind the uprising. President Suharto, who steered the republic through this turmoil, has since enforced what is termed New Order (as opposed to Old Order under the Republic's first president, Sukarno) and developed a highly centralized authoritarian government, effectively containing domestic dissidents and promoting economic development. As a result, "Survey of Indonesia" in the 17 April 1993 issue of *The Economist* declares that "Mr. Suharto's 'New Order' regime has been associated with stability and progress, rather than stagnation and collapse. Even many of those who chafe at the restrictions imposed under his rule acknowledge that there is something to be said for stability."[1] At the same time, President Suharto attempted to mitigate the tensions in Southeast Asia, which was a legacy of his predecessor's *konfrontasi* policy, culminating in the establishment of the Association of Southeast Asian Nations (ASEAN). In twenty-five years, President Suharto has also scored high in this endeavor. The Economist Intelligence Unit report, describing the degree of Indonesia's integration in the ASEAN institution, analyzes that "Indonesia has until recently been content not only to focus its foreign policy within the regional context of ASEAN but also to permit most of its wider foreign policy initiatives to be taken under the auspices of this organization."[2]

Thus, when the time came for Indonesia to assert itself more actively in the international arena, for such reasons as the need to review its external relations because of the end of the cold war system and the desire to advocate its own approach to human rights and freedom of press, President Suharto found that Indonesia could afford to pay more attention to external affairs without worrying about causing adverse effects on domestic stability or alarming its neighboring countries.

Secondly, Indonesia has always been a very active leader of the Non-Aligned Movement (NAM). The Movement, essentially a product of the rift between the two cold war blocs, could have lost its relevance and/or meaning in the wake of the cold war. Instead, under Indonesia's stewardship, the Movement was saved from obsolescence and obtained new relevance by shifting its emphasis from focusing on political and ideological issues to acting as a voice for developing countries in the debate on global economic issues. President Suharto's trip to Tokyo during the G-7 Tokyo Summit and his persistence in trying to have Indonesia involved in the summit as a representative of the NAM nations is regarded by some as a valuable effort to place the concerns of third world countries on the international agenda.

On the other hand, when the leaders of the APEC member nations gathered in Seattle for the first time in an informal forum, APEC was praised as the first regional institution that encompasses not only the great gap in political ideology but also that between the rich countries in the North and the developing nations in the South. President Suharto himself characterized APEC as "a model of the North-South cooperation between developed and developing worlds."[3] Thus, as the Chairman of the Non-Aligned Movement and the representative of the South, it was logical for President Suharto to host the second APEC summit in Jakarta.

In addition to the above two elements, another, more political factor should be mentioned in reference to APEC's Jakarta summit meeting. While domestic stability and economic growth have been achieved under the new order through centralized governmental control, this has not been accomplished without restricting political freedoms (e.g., freedom of press and freedom of assembly), delaying political modernization, and increasing the disparity of wealth. Although the Suharto government itself acknowledges the need to advance various deregulations, it believes that the process should be an evolutional, gradual one that can be achieved in the longer run. A major political show such as the APEC summit can project the image of President Suharto as a great statesman dealing on an equal footing with such great powers as the United States, China, and Japan, and, thus, temporarily fend off the consequences of the domestic political frustration. A member of the Indonesian diplomatic corps in Jakarta reportedly claimed that "the success of the Bogor Summit will deprive energy of domestic dissidents for at least one year."[4]

As all of the above elements are expected to persist in the foreseeable future, and particularly because Indonesia has to review fundamental concepts that had been central to its foreign policy in the post–cold war era and to work out how the four major powers in the region—i.e., China, Japan, Russia, and the United States—can be accommodated constructively in the ASEAN subregion; it looks as though Indonesia's positive attitude toward Asia Pacific will also continue in the years to come.

II. Circumstances Surrounding Research Institutions in Indonesia

Because of its highly centralized "developmentalist" governance, the Suharto government has not been open to proposals and suggestions from various sources in terms of its policy formation and planning. M. Hadi Soesastro of the formidable Centre for Strategic and International Studies (CSIS, Jakarta), in his interview with researchers from the Sasakawa Peace Foundation, revealed that the Indonesian government is not willing to hear suggestions from outside and that policy matters have been in the monopoly of the bureaucracy and other government agencies. Furthermore, when a meeting was organized for the Japan Center for International Exchange (JCIE) among heads of major Indonesian research institutions by CSIS in August 1993, the participants agreed that there is no direct channel through which research institutions can exercise direct influence on government policy, particularly its foreign policy, because President Suharto ultimately decides foreign policy no matter what his advisors or bureaucrats advise. The channel through which research institutions can be heard is limited to the personal relationships that institution leadership has cultivated with government officials and other policy makers, which, incidentally, seems to be a general pattern throughout the ASEAN countries.

They added a footnote, however, by explaining that one possible exception to this pattern may be the national security and defense policies in which the army, legally a "source outside the government," does have President Suharto's ears. Particularly since Major General Suharto's crushing of the coup attempt in 1965, the military has been openly endowed with *dwifungsi* or "dual function" which grants the military a major role not only in the country's external defense but also in its socio-political management. Its experience during Indonesia's struggle for independence, its crucial role in maintaining the unity of the nation during the post-independence turmoil (including the 1965 coup), and the historical fact that it does not owe its creation to any act of government or political party, have created "a sense of entitlement within the military to a special role in the political arena."[5]

It is suspected that this special role of the military may have a role to play in the sense of vulnerability that research institutions in Indonesia seem to have vis-a-vis the government. A senior member of a governmental research institution admitted that the position of research institutions in Indonesia is rather vulnerable because they are in a sense at the mercy of the government when and if they are found "unnationalistic." This view is further endorsed by a senior officer of an American foundation stationed in Jakarta who, in comparison with other Asian countries, finds it to be a particularly Indonesian phenomenon for intellectuals, including research institutions, to be so mindful of acceptance by the government. The Indonesian research institutions circle is essentially made of a small number of enclaved, Western trained intellectuals who have witnessed the potential of independent research institutions in the countries of their education and training. They are also well connected with the international intellectual networks to which they are often invited, and where they may speak very freely. Back in Indonesia, however, they find themselves at the mercy of the government, and, consequently, they cease to be an effective voice advising the government. In a country where nongovernment initiatives can easily be interpreted as anti-governmental, research institutions, according to this foundation staff, are very vulnerable to governmental intervention in the form of approval/disapproval of projects and severance of financial support (as in the case of institutions that had been heavily dependent on Dutch contributions before the government decided to severe all financial ties with the former colonizer).

Due in part to this sense of vulnerability, but, also, partly because of the frustration out of a sense of futility in the face of "bureaucrats who will not read a report longer than five pages,"[6] quite a number of sincere researchers in Indonesia are left professionally unconsummated. Those who strongly wish their findings to be read by those engaged in the national policy must employ something similar to Washington's Heritage Foundation's "flash report," a very brief summary and direct policy proposal. Additionally, those working for governmental research institutions are not allowed to circulate their research findings on a commercial basis. Because of these reasons, it it is not rare for fellows and senior members of governmental research institutions in Indonesia to join nongovernmental institutions on the side, mainly for the purpose of publishing their research results. For the same reason, the boundary between universities and research institutions, too, is very narrow and obscure. Some add to this grievance list the fact that monetary compensation for intellectual works is very low, particularly among college professors. According to participants of the CSIS-JCIE meeting, it is, therefore, not at all unusual for a single researcher to wear many hats concurrently.

But Indonesia watchers would agree that the overall trend, despite occasional setbacks and stagnation, is definitely toward more decentralization and greater participation in politics. A senior government institution fellow admits that nongovernmental initiatives are clearly on the rise in Indonesia. In recent years, Indonesia has witnessed the development of nongovernmental organizations as well as political parties and the parliament. Jusef Wanandi, chairman of the Centre for Strategic and International Studies, stated in a recent discussion that the growth and proliferation of nongovernmental organizations is seen as "an indication that society does not intend to leave discussion and solution of various developmental problems solely to the government."

In this connection, a recent phenomenon that has caught all the Indonesia watchers' imagination is the emergence of the Centre for Information and Development Studies (CIDES). Established in early 1993, it aims to address more or less the same national and international issues that have traditionally been "monopolized" by CSIS, which, as an ASEAN-ISIS member, is supposed to more or less represent Indonesian national interests. At first glance, therefore, the emergence of CIDES seems to be an example of the advancement of pluralism in the direction of more nongovernmental initiatives.

While this first impression is very attractive and certainly contains elements of truth in it, closer scrutiny is required to fully appreciate the background and meaning of this phenomenon. It is widely known that CIDES was created by the dynamic Research and Technology Minister B.J. Habibie. Minister Habibie has been the key person in the rivalry in the Suharto government between the traditional "technocrats" (famous "Berkeley Mafias") and the newly emerging "technologue camp" which, under the leadership of Habibie, tends to see Indonesia's future in the light of high technology industry. Thus, the establishment of CIDES may have an element of political rivalry between two camps within the Suharto government.

But more importantly and, to some extent, alarmingly, CIDES is talked of in relation to the fissure between Chinese catholic intellectuals on one hand and Muslim intellectuals on the other. In the multi-ethnic and multi-cultural society of Indonesia, President Suharto has made very deliberate efforts to maintain the balance between the Muslim majority (eighty percent of the total population) of the nation and non-Muslims, particularly the economically powerful Chinese Indonesians. The rise of Islamic fundamentalism has always been an imminent danger to national integrity and stability, and, together with the Chinese population whose degree of cultural assimilation to Indonesian society has been much higher and deeper than other societies with similar backgrounds, it has caused the government to constantly downplay the Islamic elements so much so that there has been latent frustration among the Muslim majority who believe that they deserve more.

Against this background, Minister Habibie created the 40,000-member strong network, Organization of Indonesian Muslim Intellectuals (ICMI), in December 1990, linking Muslim politicians, civil servants, the army, and the universities. In the face of a stark disparity between rich and poor, which is seen by some to parallel ethnic (Chinese Indonesians and *primbumi* Indonesians) and religious (Christian and Muslim) differences, economic growth through development of high tech industries seems to be attracting the interest of the Muslim population. In order to ensure that Muslims achieve greater wealth and success, ICMI is helping to found a set of new institutions. One of them is CIDES which is widely seen as Minister Habibie's answer to CSIS, which is perceived as being dominated by Chinese Indonesians and Christian intellectuals.

Therefore, there are some elements of racial/ethnic tension as well as political rivalry behind the establishment of CIDES, which everyone in the Indonesian circle seems to be talking about. In light of the above, funding organizations, including overseas foundations, have not fully determined if they should endorse CIDES by funding their programs. However, as one foundation representative admits, at the very least, the emergence of competition that can lead to excellence through competition, even for funding, is welcome and should be encouraged, albeit with caution.

III. Profiles of Major Research Institutions in Indonesia

Indonesian research institutions can be divided into four categories: those that are part of the National Institute of Sciences (LIPI), those affiliated with various national universities, military-related institutions, and independent institutions. Since the current survey focuses chiefly on nongovernmental institutions, the first three categories will be analyzed very briefly, followed by a more detailed study of independent institutions.

LIPI was established in 1967 as a government institution directly under the President of the Republic, to whom it must report. LIPI is fully financed by the government, although it was assisted by a grant from the Ford Foundation at its outset. It is expected to be developed into a national academy of sciences in the near future. LIPI is divided into different centers and departments, including a section on social sciences and humanities that comprises the Centre for Social and Cultural Studies, the Centre for Economics and Development Studies, and the Centre for Politics and Area Studies, all of which have programs related to Asia Pacific. The Centre for Economic and Development Studies has traditionally maintained close working relations with such regional institutions as the Institute of Developing Economies, Tokyo; the Kyoto University Center for Southeast Asian Studies; the Asia Pacific Development Centre, Kuala Lumpur; the Foundation for Asian Management Development, Tokyo; and the Institute of Southeast Asian Studies, Singapore. The Centre for Politics and Area Studies includes a Regional and International Affairs Division which is headed by Dr. Dewi Fortuna Anwar, who is one of the principle researchers of the aforementioned CIDES, a typical case of an Indonesian scholar "with many hats."

Various universities in Indonesia have their own research institutions that conduct policy-oriented programs with an Asia Pacific orientation. Bandung Institute of Technology, for instance, has the Centre for Environmental Studies which conducts research on Indonesian and regional environmental issues to formulate policy recommendations as well as the Centre for Planning Studies for development planning, regional planning, and development policy. Bogor Agricultural University maintains the Centre for Development Studies which emphasizes the role of agriculture, women, and human resources in the development process. The Centre of Economic Research of Gadjah Mada University, on the other hand, is more macroeconomic oriented but also conducts research on environmental economics. The largest and most prestigious university, the University of Indonesia, also has a number of research institutions including the Centre for Research of Human Resources and the Environment that functions as the key point of regional intellectual and information networks such as the Association for Collaboration of Environmental Study Centres in Indonesia, the ASEAN Region Conference on Environmental Education, and the University Consortium on the Environment connecting York University, the University of Waterloo, and the University of Toronto in Canada with Gadjah Mada University, the Bandung Institute of Technology, and the University of Indonesia. The University of Indonesia also houses the Institute for Economic and Social Research at the Faculty of Economics, which conducts research and other related activities in the fields of economic and social development, economic policy, national and regional planning, and regional development.

According to a study by Herman Joseph S. Kraft, the Institute of Strategic Studies of Indonesia (ISSI or LPSI in Bahasa Indonesian) is a private research institution established in 1987 by alumni of the National Defense College of Indonesia and maintained by support from private contributors in Indonesia. Its aim is to provide a forum for discussion of strategic issues in terms of "national resilience," which covers economic, military, political, and social issues, with the idea of formulating findings as an alternative source of input for senior government officials and functionaries. The Institute is a living example of the Indonesian military's strong interest and sense of entitlement in national policy matters, particularly in defense and security-related issues.

Turning to the nongovernmental sector, due to the highly centralized, developmentalist nature of the political system, independent research institutions are an underdeveloped and underutilized resource in Indonesia.

CIDES is the newest and arguably the most controversial organization. Established in early 1993, CIDES aims to contribute to the process of national development as well as to address challenges of other developing countries through various activities that are designed to both identify development issues and facilitate policy action to deal with them. It claims to "support the efforts to improve the quality of human resources for participation in the process of a people-based national development...(and) to study and develop different models of local-based development to strengthen the complimentary interrelationship between informal and formal sectors,"[7] emphasizing the need for more majority-based (thus, presumably more Muslim oriented) development methods. More specifically, CIDES has been conducting research and dialogue programs in the areas of: cooperation on development among developing countries; development of human resources (particularly the improvement of the productivity level of Indonesian work forces as the main input in the value-added process of the national economy); regional economic cooperation with an emphasis on the development of the Growth Triangle; policy of development of science and technology within a sustainable economic growth scheme; human rights protection in the perspective of the development of Pancasilabased democracy; and the development of local resources in terms of local autonomy. Although its leadership claims that CIDES is a more development-oriented institution and, therefore, it is not a direct competitor of CSIS, CIDES also conducts a dialogue series on various issues expected in the course of development, including such topics as "political system and political parties," "political institutionalization and leadership," "press ethics in Indonesia," "the Dual Function and its implication," and "the Indonesian foreign policy in the post–cold war era."

The Centre for Policy and Implementation Studies is characterized as "an independent foundation funded by the government,"[8] however some label it as a governmental institution. Established in 1986 on the basis of the former Development Programme Implementation Studies, which was a government agency, it is fully financed by the Department of Finance. It is an interdisciplinary research and policy advising center, designed to have the capacity for combining macro and micro approaches in analyzing development policies and programs. The Centre conducts research in order to analyze the actual workings and outcomes of government policies and other programs undertaken by the government, on which it can advise the government on ways to improve both policy formulation and program implementation. With some sixty researchers, the Centre conducts studies in such areas as rural banking, employment in the urban informal sector, urban waste recycling, higher education, and public health. It is a member of the Asia Forum network of think tanks convened by the Nomura Research Institute and its Tokyo Club Foundation for Global Studies.

By far the most world-renowned among Indonesian research institutions is CSIS, Jakarta, established in 1971 together with the Yayasan Proklamasi (Proclamation Foundation) which sponsors CSIS and its activities, a unique arrangement that enables CSIS to finance all of its study projects in-house. Two Indonesian Army generals who were personal assistants of President Suharto were particularly instrumental in the foundation of these two institutions. CSIS aims to undertake policy-oriented studies on both domestic and international affairs. As one of the founding member institutes of the ASEAN-ISIS network, naturally ASEAN ranks high in CSIS's order of priorities, but it has also maintained a particular interest in the broader Asia Pacific region. With some fifty research staff under four research departments, recent and current research topics include intra-ASEAN economic cooperation, political economy of deregulation and liberalization in Indonesia, the future direction of Pacific economic cooperation and the role of Indonesia and ASEAN, human resources development issues in Indonesia, labor issues especially in light manufacturing "footloose" joint-venture enterprises, implications of the changing global environment for Indonesia's diplomacy and foreign policy, perceptions in other ASEAN countries on Indonesia's role and position in Southeast Asian regional politics, and new strategic thinking in the major Asian powers of Japan, China, and India.

CSIS also frequently organizes national and international (bilateral as well as multilateral) conferences and dialogues. Among eighteen regular bilateral conferences are ones with Japan (since 1973), the United States (since 1974), Korea (since 1979), New Zealand (since 1981), Australia (since 1982), Vietnam (since 1984), Singapore (since 1986), and Malaysia (since 1988). Aside from individual books, CSIS publishes *The Indonesian Quarterly* whose recent titles include "The Asia Pacific Security Dimension" (1994), "ASEAN and The Asia Pacific" (1994), "ASEAN and the South Pacific" (1991), "The Asia Pacific in the 1990s" (1991), "Some Perspectives on Southeast Asia and Asia Pacific" (1990), and "Focus on the Pacific" (1990).

Aside from ASEAN-ISIS and CSCAP, CSIS also serves as Indonesian national committee for the PECC.

The Institute for Economic Studies, Research and Development is a nongovernmental research arm of the Indonesian Chamber of Commerce and Industry. The Institute's chairman, Mr. Mohammad Sadli, himself admits that it has not been very active in terms of research and information dissemination, particularly internationally, since the Institute's publications are in Bahasa Indonesia. Instead, it has assumed the role of an instrument of policy dialogue between businessmen and the government through various meetings and conferences.

IV. Future Prospects

As discussed in the above sections, the long-term trend in Indonesian politics is toward greater deregulation and decentralization from the governmental viewpoint, along with greater political participation by private citizens. When government leaders openly criticize certain aspects of "western democracy" such as freedom of press and freedom of assembly, this process is necessarily a slow, evolutionary one.

Nevertheless, it has been reported that the number of nongovernmental organizations has been rapidly increasing. In the realm of research institutions, recent years have witnessed the establishment of LPSI and CIDES, a trend that is hoped to continue. If the emergence of new institutions is somehow related to the political power game, as CIDES has allegedly exemplified, it will not be surprising to see the emergence of more institutions as the issue of President Suharto's successor becomes imminent.

Against this background, there will be an increasing need for private funding sources to support these institutions as well as their activities. Contributions from American foundations in this field are well known and well respected. It is said, for instance, that support from the Ford Foundation was truly indispensable to the establishment of the National Institute of Sciences, a gigantic governmental institution that aspires to grow into a national academy of sciences. German foundations, particularly Friedrich Neuman Stiftung, have also been supportive of Indonesian independent research institutions. These funding organizations will certainly not be able to meet the increasing demand for funding, which must be filled by other Asia Pacific organizations including foundations of the region's richest country, Japan.

Notes

1. "Survey of Indonesia" in *The Economist* (17 April 1993).
2. The Economist Intelligence Unit, *The ASEAN Countries: Economic Structure and Analysis* (London: The Economist Intelligence Unit, 1989).
3. *Nihon Keizai Shimbun* (17 August 1994).
4. *Mainichi Shimbun* (7 November 1994).
5. An Indonesian participant of the 5th ASEAN-Japan Dialogue Program, 1992–1993.
6. A participant of the CSIS-JCIE meeting of heads of research institutions.
7. From CIDES brochure.
8. Alan J. Day (ed.), *Think Tanks: An International Directory* (Essex: Longman Information & Reference, 1993.

JAPAN

Research Institutions in Japan
From the Perspective of the Asia Pacific Intellectual Network

Makito Noda
Senior Program Officer
Japan Center for International Exchange

I. Typology of Research Institutions in Japan

The current survey aims to reveal the status of contributions to the intellectual underpinnings of the Asia Pacific community, provided by independent research institutions through their research and dialogue activities as well as networks with their overseas counterparts in the region.

The role of independent research institutions in international relations in general and the underpinnings of the global community in particular is well known. One only has to recall the special roles played by such actors as the Royal Institute of International Affairs in London and the Council on Foreign Relations in New York, in creating a sense of community between intellectual and opinion leaders across the Atlantic following the end of World War II. The positive role in international and diplomatic relations played by independent institutions is not confined to the experience of western countries. It is well known among Asia watchers that the ASEAN Regional Forum, the first regionwide intergovernmental forum on security affairs in Southeast Asia, is actually the brainchild of a series of meetings of the ASEAN Institutes of Strategic and International Studies (ASEAN-ISIS), a group of independent research institutions on security and international affairs representing each ASEAN country. This may be the most recent and yet classical case of nongovernmental institutions affecting formal diplomacy.

The current survey attempts to give a critical review of the status of Japanese research institutions against these "potentials" vis-à-vis Asia Pacific cooperation.

Research institutions in Japan can be divided into the following categories:

a. governmental research institutions, including those affiliated with individual ministries (e.g., the Ministry of Finance's Institute of Fiscal and Monetary Policy and the Defense Agency's National Institute for Defense Studies);
b. quasi-governmental institutions such as the Institute of Developing Economies and the National Institute for Research Advancement (NIRA);
c. research institutions affiliated with public and private universities, including Kyoto University's Center for Southeast Asian Studies and Sophia University's Institute of International Relations for Peace and Development in Asia; and
d. independent research institutions or "think tanks" including profit-making corporations (e.g., Nomura Research Institute) and nonprofit organizations.

Although occasional references are made to programs of quasi-governmental institutions and university-affiliated institutions, the major focus of the current survey is placed on independent research institutions, particularly those with policy-oriented intellectual activities in the broad field of social sciences (political science, economics, international relations, socio-anthropology, etc.).

II. Brief History of Independent Research Institutions in Japan

Any literature on Japanese think tanks refers to what is called "the first year of Japanese think tanks" (*shinku tanku gannen*) of 1970, and most, in fact, takes off from this point to explain the history of Japanese research institutions. This does not mean that there had been no research institutions before 1970. To be sure, there were a few research institutions before the introduction of the western (mostly American) concept of "think tanks" in the late 1960s. While think tanks aspire to be interdisciplinary in their approach to deal with broad, policy-related areas, whether they have succeeded or not, the principle aims of these early institutions were to collect and analyze insights and information on narrower and more specific areas.

The rush to establish think tanks in Japan, often referred to as the "First Think Tank Boom," in the late 1960s and early 1970s, was a direct result of admiration on the part of Japanese business and government leaders' for the successful landing on the moon under the Apollo Project. This event was followed by waves of Japanese visitors to the RAND Corporation, the major force behind the Project, in hopes of adopting research and development systems developed by RAND. During this period, an almost religious belief in the omnipotence of systems analysis and systems research was born among the Japanese, resulting in the launching of think tanks, one after another. A quarter of a century later, the term *think tank* is somehow still affiliated with systems analysis, even though most of the newer institutions have applied a much more diverse approach.

But more than this, a certain element at the genesis of think tanks has haunted Japanese research institutions more gravely. Most of the more prominent of the hundred and twenty think tanks established in this first boom—Nomura Research Institute (1969) and Mitsubishi Research Institute (1970), to name several well-known representatives—were set up as profit-making corporations with capital and concepts provided by the business sector. As such, they were expected to fill the research and development needs related to the corporate activities of their parent corporations. As a result, think tanks were handicapped in pursuing independent, objective policy research from the very beginning,[1] a handicap which has never been overcome by research institutions in Japan. The government also launched a number of their own think tanks which were, almost by definition, policy oriented, but they were not large enough to constitute the mainstream of Japan's think tanks.

However, he first boom was short-lived, effectively put to an end because of the oil crisis. Meanwhile, local governments became fascinated by the potential of think tanks, leading to the local dispersion of the first boom. By the mid-1980s, when the local echo of the first boom was about to subside, major corporations located at the center of the boom, particularly those in the financial, information, and communications industries, revived their interest in their own research institutions, leading to the emergence of 12 institutions in 1985, 11 in 1986, 12 in 1987, and 12 in 1988, a period usually referred to as the "Second Think Tank Boom." Tsutomu Numajiri of the *Asahi Shimbun* believes that behind the scenes of this second boom was corporate realization of the urgency to obtain independent capability for mid- to long-term projection, in addition to the conventional short-term forecast, especially in the face of imminent financial and information liberalization and internationalization.[2] As such, these new think tanks tended to have an even stronger business orientation than the first boomers. It is noteworthy that most of the major, large-scale think tanks (forty-four of them) were established sometime during these two booms, again making the collective orientation of Japanese think tanks very much business oriented.

Since the peak year of the second boom, the incidence of new establishments located at the center decreased to six in 1989 and four in 1990. However, as in the case of the first boom, new think tanks are being born one after another in local areas such as Fukuoka, Kochi, Niigata, Miyagi, and Kagoshima prefectures. The number of think tanks established in local areas since 1980 is almost equal to the number established in Tokyo for the same period (74 in local areas compared to 79 in the metropolitan area). Since 1990, more think tanks have been launched in local areas. This phenomenon fits very well with the recent tendency among local areas to push for greater autonomy and self-determination. In particular, internationalization is regarded as one desirable direction for such developments, resulting in an increase in the demand for long-term planning and study of local international interactions, a demand which local think tanks must meet.

III. Status of Japanese Research Institutions

In this section the status of independent research institutions or think tanks in Japan will be examined with a five-year historical perspective where necessary. The only source of systematic information on Japan's research institutions is NIRA, and what follows is constructed mainly on the basis of NIRA's *Think Tank Yearbook* for the years between 1989 and 1993. The *Yearbook*'s trend analysis is based on a questionnaire filled out and returned by individual research institutions, the number of which fluctuates every year. In 1989, 183 institutions were included, 344 institutions in 1990, 191 institutions in 1991, 198 institutions in 1992, and 403 institutions in 1993. The number of projects included in the trend analysis also fluctuates. Thus, a year to year comparison of absolute numbers (e.g., number of institutions, number of projects, number of researchers, etc.) does not make much sense. Instead, trends of proportions to the whole should be compared.

1. Institutional Set-up

In order to compile the 1993 edition of its *Think Tank Yearbook,* NIRA sent questionnaires to 625 institutions in May 1993, leading to the conclusion that there are at least 625 think tanks identified by NIRA as independent research institutions or think tanks in Japan. NIRA defines think tanks as those institutions with independent legal status (which excludes sporadic voluntary organizations, central and local government agencies, and institutions affiliated with universities and corporations); those institutions whose principle activity is general research in the fields of policy science, social sciences, and humanities; and those institutions which have already completed at least one project.

Of these 625 think tanks, NIRA obtained information on 403 institutions. As one can conjecture from the above brief history, the mainstream think tank in Japan has been and still is a corporate, profit-making entity. Of 403 institutions 196, or 48.6 percent, are corporations, while 156 research foundations and 50 membership associations constitute the nonprofit sector which comprises 51.1 percent. When one compares the operational scale of these institutions, however, the predominance of corporate institutions should be obvious. Of 23,568 staff members in 403 think tanks, 19,214 individuals, or 81.5 percent of the total, work for research corporations. Of 10,163 researchers, 8,096 or 79.7 percent work for corporations. The think tank industry in Japan is a ¥500 billion (US$5 billion)[3] industry in terms of revenue, of which research corporations contribute ¥420 billion, (US$4.2 billion) or 83.7 percent. Almost forty percent of those research corporations have their own parent corporations, banks, manufacturers, and insurance and securities houses, with which they are affiliated. In other words, in Japan the mainstream think tank is a profit-making corporation, responsible for meeting the needs of its parent corporation.

Tokyo has retained the highest concentration of think tanks, having more than sixty percent of the total number of institutions in 1993. Even though more think tanks have been established in local areas in recent years, in terms of number of employees, which indicates research capability, in 1993 Greater Tokyo reported having 84.1 percent of the entire work force and 83.6 percent of total research personnel. As new institutions are continuously established outside of Tokyo, this disproportionate concentration may be corrected in the future.

2. Notes on Researchers

In 1993, a total of 23,568 individuals were employed by 403 think tanks, and of these 10,163 were researchers. Therefore, an average of twenty-five researchers would be expected to be engaged in research activities in each of the 403 think tanks. However, it has been revealed that in 1993, 50.4 percent of think tanks had less than ten researchers and when combined with those having ten to twenty researchers (24.2 percent), they comprise the absolute majority of 74.6 percent. In 1989, those with under twenty researchers numbered 70.1 percent, while in 1990 it was 53.2 percent, and in 1991, 54.1 percent of all think tanks operated with less than nine researchers. The majority of Japanese think tanks, therefore, are very small in terms of their in-house research staff.

In terms of recruits, the proportion of fresh graduates from higher education institutions has been on the rise, from 49.6 percent in 1989 to 45.1 percent in 1990, 55.1 percent in 1991, 65.7 percent in 1992, and 65.8 percent in 1993. This phenomenon probably signifies the fact that think tanks have gradually established an image for themselves as a viable career. The average age of employees in Japan's think tanks has been declining, partly reflecting the increasing number of fresh recruits, from 38.6 in 1990 to 38.3 in 1991, 37.6 in 1992, and 34.8 in 1993. In Japanese society, a society with a traditional seniority system, think tanks are still a very new phenomenon.

3. Research Projects

When one's attention turns to the substance of research work, the very domestic and predominantly business orientation of Japanese think tanks becomes obvious. In the past five years, more than half of their research work has been in the three areas of "land development/planning," "domestic economy," and "industry," starting with 53.5 percent in 1989 to 57.6 percent in 1990, 59.3 percent in 1991, 54.2 percent in 1992, and 53.8 percent in 1993. In particular, the predominance of research projects on land development/planning has been outstanding, occupying 28.9 percent, 32.4 percent, 27.9 percent, 25.1 percent, and 25.6 percent respectively between 1989 and 1993. It is reported in the 1993 *Yearbook*, though, that projects on environmental issues have been constantly increasing in recent years, while those related to citizens' livelihood, transportation, and natural resources and energy have also been on the rise.

One can tell a lot about the nature and, particularly, the limitation of research projects by finding out if they are self-initiated studies or contractual projects commissioned by outside clients. In the case of Japanese think tanks, three-quarters of all projects in the past three years have been contractual projects, the largest proportion of which (26.6 percent in 1993) comes from their parent corporations, followed by other corporations, local governments, and the national government.

Finally, it has been revealed that almost all of their research projects are short in terms of project duration. In the past five years, about 95 percent of all projects were completed within a year, i.e., 94.3 percent in 1989, 95.7 percent in 1990, 93.7 percent in 1991, 93.0 percent in 1992, and 93.0 percent in 1993. The highest concentration is found in the projects with a duration of between six and twelve months; 36.7 percent in 1989, 45.7 percent in 1990, 41.2 percent in 1991, 43.9 percent in

1992, and 38.1 percent in 1993. It is hard to imagine a full-fledged study with long-term perspective being completed in a year. More importantly, almost a quarter of all projects (27.9 percent, 23.8 percent, 21.6 percent, 21.3 percent, and 27.7 percent, respectively from 1984 to 1993) lasted less than three months.

4. Think Tanks' International Programs and Their Own "Internationalization"

Based on the above observations, one cannot expect too much from Japanese think tanks in terms of their international orientation. As the entire research work of Japanese think tanks is classified in the fields of land development and planning; citizens' livelihood; welfare, public health, and education; transportation; communication and information; natural resources and energy; environmental issues; politics and administration; domestic economy; industry; international affairs; culture and fine arts; and science and technology, research projects on international affairs have constantly kept a low profile, occupying 5.7 percent in 1989, 5.6 percent in 1990, 4.0 percent in 1991, 5.1 percent in 1992, and 5.3 percent in 1993. Although the absolute number of projects seems to be increasing (from 56 in 1989 to 62, 133, 191, and finally to 213 projects in 1993), it is undeniable that the degree of attention given to international affairs has been far too low for a country like Japan which has grown to be a world power.

In terms of collaboration with overseas institutions, which is by far the most effective means to becoming a part of the international intellectual community, past achievements of Japanese think tanks have not been remarkable, either. The number of joint research projects with foreign counterpart institutions has been more or less stagnant, amounting to 14 cases in 1989, 16 in 1990, 28 in 1991, 22 in 1992, and 29 in 1993.

Equally discouraging observations can be made about foreign researchers employed by Japanese think tanks. On one hand, the number of foreigners working in Japanese think tanks is increasing, from 43 in 1989 to 117 in 1993, the highest number foreign researchers have attained so far. On the other hand, 117 is still merely 1.2 percent of the entire number of researchers working in Japanese think tanks. Judging from the nationality of those foreign researchers, Japanese think tanks have shown a strong Asia Pacific orientation. Until 1991, the United States supplied the largest number of foreign researchers in Japanese think tanks, but in 1992, this was overtaken by the Chinese. In 1993, thirty-two Chinese and thirty Americans were employed in Japanese research institutions. Asian researchers (including Chinese, Korean, Filipino, Malaysian, and Australian) occupy more than fifty percent of the entire number of foreign researchers working in Japan.

Thus, it can be concluded that much is to be desired of Japanese research institutions in terms of their international programs as well as their own internationalization.

IV. Policy Research and Research Institutions

It has been established that policy making is dominated by the government, particularly by the national bureaucracy. Government ministries in Japan often function as think tanks, formulating plans and policies themselves and hearing nongovernmental views only when necessary through policy advisory councils they establish within themselves. Frequently, those ministries crammed into Tokyo's Kasumigaseki area are referred to as "the world's largest think tanks" or, simply, "Kasumigaseki Think Tanks."

Japan owes a lot to this policy elite group, for her present success, economic and otherwise. After all, it is the national bureaucracy that has steered Japan through the dynamic process of post–World War II reconstruction and development. It seems to have worked particularly effectively because throughout this period the Japanese single-mindedly pursued essentially one thing—rapid development in endeavoring to become a leading citizen of the world. Now that this goal seems to have been attained, however, the traditional dominance of policy planning and formulation by the national bureaucracy, no matter how competent and excellent it may be, has become highly questionable.

Against this background, university and independent research institutions seem to be the only alternative source of policy research and deliberation, equipped with intellectual capability, as well as necessary information. Japanese universities, however, cannot be expected to play this role for various reasons: the "ivory tower" syndrome inherent to Japanese universities where anything outside of academic inquiry is not respected; their tendency to become too compartmentalized according to faculties organized to conduct interdisciplinary projects; the lack of professors who are well informed on developments in the nonacademic "real" world; and, last but not least, their lack of a crucial research infrastructure such as research and clerical assistants and secretariat functions.

Thus, it is up to independent research institutions or think tanks to present themselves as the rare alternative for policy planning and proposals. To be sure, pressures from private citizens on such research institutions to grow into viable sources for the development of alternative policies have not been strong so far. Long accustomed to being unilateral recipients of policies decided elsewhere, ordinary Japanese voters have not developed a sense of efficacy in terms of national policy. For Japan to become a more mature democracy, this attitude of the Japanese toward participation in policy making must be improved.

It must be admitted that independent research institutions in Japan have not been very effective in this field, either. To summarize the status of Japanese think tanks developed in the previous section, the following observations can be made:

a. think tanks are typically profit-making corporations with a strong mandate to serve the research and development needs of their parent or affiliated corporations, making their independence almost academic;
b. they rely heavily on research contracts commissioned by local and national governments as well as private corporations, making it extremely difficult for them to be critical of these clients;
c. they survive by conducting numerous short or "quick" projects as short as a few weeks in duration, hardly long enough to enable indepth or comprehensive studies; and
d. as far as foreign affairs are concerned, they are not well enough connected or well enough exposed to international scholarship to develop their own information channels aside from diplomatic channels.

Because of these elements, unfortunately, research institutions in Japan have not fulfilled one of the most important social missions imposed on them so far.

V. Asia Pacific Related Activities of Japanese Research Institutions

1. Notes on Methodology

As discussed above, the *Think Tank Yearbook*, compiled by NIRA, is without a doubt the most comprehensive, if not the only, source of systematic information available on the status and activities of independent research institutions, or think tanks, in Japan. Utilizing the subject index of research project titles by individual institutions, one can construct a list of Asia Pacific related projects for each year, as long as the title includes key words that implicitly or explicitly indicate this regional orientation. The first half of this section is based on an original analysis, using data thus collected.

In contrast to the above, more "macroscopic" approach, one can also single out major research institutions that are known to have a strong orientation toward international relations and/or foreign affairs and try to analyze the Asia Pacific related programs of each of these institutions. What follows are some of the observations found by utilizing these two methods.

2. Asia Pacific Related Projects of Major Think Tanks in Japan

In February 1991, the Japan Center for International Exchange (JCIE) conducted a survey on the status of U.S.-Japan intellectual exchange activities including the activities of major research institutions using a similar method. In the study, an inventory was taken on research projects and other intellectual exchange programs related to U.S.-Japan relations conducted by institutions in the United States and Japan for the last five years. The study found, among other observations, the following trends which provide a reference against which findings of the current study can be compared:

a. there were very few (much less than one percent of total projects conducted in one year) policy-oriented, social-scientific inquiries into various aspects of American society or U.S.-Japan relations;
b. these projects actually included more ad hoc conferences, symposia, and seminars, typically taking advantage of visits by prominent foreign scholars and other intellectual leaders; and
c. the themes of these programs were predominantly economic in nature.

The same study also found hopeful signs of growing joint and collaborative work (such as joint research and cosponsored research conferences) conducted by major Japanese institutions with their American counterparts.

Since the United States is by far the most prominent actor in Asia Pacific and, at the same time, the most important Asia Pacific partner for Japan, one can expect to find a similar trend in Japanese research institutions' activities vis-à-vis Asia Pacific. A wide deviation from the above findings may indicate the changes that must have taken place in the three years since the previous study.

It should be noted at the outset that there is a certain risk associated with heavy reliance on the *NIRA Think Tank Yearbook* because of the method applied in compiling the data. The yearbook is solely dependent on a questionnaire filled out and returned by think tanks identified and selected by NIRA as "independent research institutions/think tanks." NIRA itself openly admits that it is not an exhaustive listing because, for instance, quasi-governmental institutions such as the world renowned Institute of Developing Economies are not included from the beginning. In terms of continuity, too, some institutions may cease to return the annual questionnaire for one reason or another, suddenly eliminating familiar names from the inventory. However, more importantly, in this listing a project can mean a wide range of activities, from a full-fledged, multi-year, serious intellectual inquiry to an almost casual essay on specific topics that is typically circulated in pamphlet form to supporting members. Thus, one is not presented with a comprehensive picture of the scope and scale of individual projects, making the latter kind of "project" look as prominent, if not more so, as the former type. Nevertheless, the fact remains that this yearbook is by far the most reliable source of information on Japanese research institutions.

Counting all the Asia Pacific related projects (defined here as projects whose titles include either name(s) of individual Asia Pacific countries or such terms as "ASEAN," "Southeast Asia," "East Asia," "Far East," "Asia," "Pacific," "Pan Pacific," and "Asia Pacific") listed in annual compilations of NIRA's *Think Tank Yearbook* for the years between 1989 and 1993 (which is the most recent issue at the time of this writing), it is revealed that the number of relevant projects has not only been larger than expected but it has also been expanding rather significantly, as follows:

Year	Total Number of Projects	Number of Asia Pacific Projects (percent of total)
1989	2,733	61 (2.2)
1990	3,070	88 (2.9)
1991	3,298	85 (2.6)
1992	3,761	128 (3.4)
1993	4,036	129 (3.2)

In 1989, when only twenty projects could be classified as programs for U.S.-Japan intellectual exchange, which is supposed to be a crucial element of Japan's Asia Pacific intellectual interactions, the above figures would have been rather impressive. At a glance, they may not strike observers as significant, but they have to be appreciated in the context of Japanese research institutions where, because of their organizational affiliations, activities have been predominantly domestic and micro-level oriented. In fact, in the last three years, 1991–93, the number of projects classified by NIRA as "international affairs" was, respectively, 113 projects (4.0 percent of the total), 191 projects (5.1 percent), and 213 projects (5.3 percent). Since some of the projects identified in this study as Asia Pacific oriented are not classified by NIRA as related to international affairs, the proportion of Asia Pacific related projects may be somewhat overemphasized if we divide the number of Asia Pacific related projects by the above number of international affairs projects. (For instance, a project on strategic municipal financing policy in Asia was classified as "national land development and use" in the *1993 Think Tank Yearbook.*) However, it should be obvious that Asia Pacific related projects have occupied the majority of projects on international affairs conducted by Japanese research institutions in recent years.

As can be deduced from the above findings, projects on the United States and U.S.-Japan relations occupy only a portion, a small portion at that, of Asia Pacific related projects. In fact, one remarkable development in the last five years seems to be the increasing regional and/or multilateral orientation. Contrary to initial expectations, there have been more projects dealing with Asia and/or Asia Pacific as a region than projects on any individual country in the region or Japan's bilateral relations with it. China and the United States have been the most frequently studied during the period, with related annual projects numbering 7, 12, 6, 13, and 12 consecutively and 7, 7, 7, 10, and 10 projects respectively from 1989 to 1993. All the other countries in the region have received much less attention than these two superpowers. On the other hand, the number of projects that deal with ASEAN and Southeast Asia, East Asia and Asia, and Asia Pacific and Pan Pacific have steadily increased. The number of projects on East Asia and Asia, for instance, has increased from 8 projects in 1989 to 13 in 1990, 17 in 1991, 35 in 1992, and 35 in 1993. Equally, the number of projects which deal directly with Asia Pacific have expanded from an insignificant 6 projects in 1989 to an impressive 25 projects in 1993, after numbering 14 in 1990, 13 in 1991, and 20 in 1992. These facts seem to indicate a more regional and multilateral orientation of Japanese research institutions vis-à-vis this area, reflecting, perhaps, an awareness of the significance of the concept of Asia Pacific cooperation.

In terms of the substance of projects, the heavy economic orientation which was identified in the previous study on the U.S.-Japan exchange is also found in Asia Pacific studies. Counting the number of projects that can be characterized as "economic analysis and study" from their titles, 27 were discovered in this study, out of 89 projects on Asia Pacific in 1989 (or 30.3 percent), 68 out of 88 (77.3 percent) in 1990, 53 out of 85 (62.4 percent) in 1991, 85 out of 128 (66.4 percent) in 1992, and

84 out of 129 (65.1 percent) in 1993. More than three-fifths of the entire number of Asia Pacific projects have always been economic in nature, which must be a reflection on the nature of Japan's interest in and relations with the region. It is undeniable that, for a deeper understanding of and better balanced relations with the region, there is a shortage of noneconomic analysis.

On the other hand, one noticeable change in the substance of Asia Pacific research is the decline in the number of projects that can be categorized as developmental studies, i.e., the study of various aspects of development in developing countries. In earlier years, this kind of study must have occupied a major part, if not the majority, of studies on the Asian region, but in the last five years, the number of projects that can be regarded as conventional developmental studies has drastically declined to 17, 13, 11, 3, and 11 projects respectively. On the other hand, the number of projects with a specific focus on such issues as the environment, financial markets, and high technology, has steadily increased. This reflects changes in the status of the region in Japanese minds. Asia Pacific is no longer a developing area that needs the full attention of development studies. It has developed into an region where Japan can pursue other economic interests, i.e., partners in trade, manufacturing, and regional economic management.

A more encouraging phenomenon, from the viewpoint of the current study, is the impressive expansion of policy-oriented projects during the past five years. This observation was made when, in this study, macroscopic Asia Pacific research projects were singled out, with longer-term analysis and projection of individual nations and/or the region as a whole, the kind of research work whose conclusions are directed at relevant policies of national governments (as opposed to corporations). Single-issue, short-term technical studies as well as project-specific feasibility studies, which seem to compose a major part of "developmental studies," have been excluded. As was disclosed at the outset of this chapter, it is rather risky to judge the nature of individual projects only by the title and implementing agency. Even when efforts were made to be very selective, as many as 33 projects that seemed to be heavily policy oriented in 1989 were counted. This is fifty percent of the total of Asia Pacific related projects. In 1990, the figure became 43 projects, 32 in 1991, 48 in 1992, and 43 in 1993. Even though its proportion has been slightly declining, partly due to the sudden jump in the number of relevant projects in the past two years, it is encouraging to find out that more than one-third of Asia Pacific related projects have been more or less policy oriented rather than purely academic/scientific or short-term business oriented, particularly against the background of the relative shortage of policy-oriented activities among Japanese research institutions as discussed in previous sections.

Another development that has become increasingly more visible is a sudden increase of locally based and/or locally oriented projects, defined here as those projects that are either conducted by locally based institutions or dealing with Asia Pacific relations with specific localities within Japan. Such projects have expanded from 6 in 1989 to 7 in 1990, 6 in 1991, 13 in 1992, and suddenly 21 in 1993. Projects conducted in 1993 by locally based institutions include:

- research on software technology transfer and international division of labor using Asia as a model region, by the Kansai Institute of Information Systems in Osaka
- a survey on the means to promote international exchange with the Asia Pacific region by Kansai Inter-Disciplinary Studies, Inc. in Osaka
- research on Asian needs and the role of Kyushu, by the Kyushu Economic Research Center in Fukuoka
- planning of an Asian cultural and regional strategic research center and planning of an Asian frontier research center by the Associates of Regional Planners, Kyushu in Fukuoka
- an international seminar on international exchange around the Sea of Japan by Research Advancement of Regional Planning, Inc. in Shimane Prefecture
- a survey on the means for strengthening the functioning of the Osaka Bay area toward the hub base of Asia by the Daiwa Research Institute, Inc. in Osaka
- research on a program to promote international exchange with Asian countries by Chugoku Regional Research Center in Hiroshima Prefecture
- research on key actor ports for international exchange around the Sea of Japan, by the Chubu Region Development Research Center, Inc. in Nagoya
- research on the Sea of Japan Economic Zone Scheme and the role of Niigata Prefecture, by the Economic Research Center of Niigata
- planning of a joint research center on Asian affairs by The Hirogin Economic Research Institute in Hiroshima Prefecture
- a survey on the status of regional development projects in the Russian Far East and Northeast China and their implications on Hokkaido and a survey of energy resources in the Russian Far East and Eastern Siberia, by the Northern Regions Center in Hokkaido
- research on economic interaction between Asia and the Hokuriku region by the Hokuriku Research Institute of Economics in Toyama Prefecture

It should be obvious that the above indicates that these localities began to have their own direct dealings and interaction with the Asia Pacific region. More than that, they seem to be based on the realization that their localities are a part of the larger Asia Pacific community.

Projects conducted by Tokyo-based institutions but whose substance is related to specific localities within Japan also suggest that Asia has become a part of their daily lives. For instance, a survey was conducted by the Daiwa Institute of Research, Inc. on American, Australian, and New Zealand high schools where Japanese students study, and a survey was conducted on the areas in ASEAN where Japanese businessmen are stationed by the Hitachi Research Institute.

These projects reflect the overall trend in Japan toward more international interactions based on localities or "internationalization" of local areas that has been going on for some time. It seems to be only natural for these local regions to be interested in Asia Pacific first since their primary international contacts and intercultural activities tend to be with students, illegal and legal workers, and other visitors from neighboring Asian countries. To them, Asia Pacific may not be a remote abstract anymore.

In addition to the above "macroscopic analysis," using the NIRA reports, this study applied a more microscopic process, looking into recent programs of selected individual institutions. For this purpose, the following institutions, well-known for their international programs, were selected:

American Studies Foundation, Inc.
Asian Forum Japan
Asia Pacific Association of Japan
Asian-Pacific Center
Association of Promotion of International Cooperation
Foundation for Advanced Information and Research, Japan
Global Industrial and Social Progress Research Institute
Institute of Developing Economies
The International Center for the Study of East Asian Development
International Development Center of Japan
The International House of Japan, Inc.
Institute for International Policy Studies
Japan Center for Economic Research
Japan Center for International Exchange
Japan Economic Foundation
The Japan Forum on International Relations, Inc.
The Japan Institute of International Affairs
Japan Research Institute

Mitsubishi Research Institute
National Institute for Research Advancement
Nomura Research Institute
Research Institute for Peace and Security
Sakura Institute of Research, Inc.
Sasakawa Peace Foundation
Tokyo Club Foundation for Global Studies

Profiles of the above institutions are compiled in a separate directory.

In the past three years, these twenty-five institutions have conducted some 120 projects, in some way related to Asia Pacific, according to information provided in their annual reports and other publications. Of these 120 projects, only 45 were research and study projects, while the remaining 75 were seminars, conferences, and symposia. This finding seems to endorse the observation made previously about U.S.-Japan intellectual exchange as a weak point, but, overall, the proportion of research activities to other types of activities does not seem to be overly distorted, considering a good research project is normally accompanied by an international conference or two.

Of the total of 120 projects (research projects and conferences), those that are economic in nature are limited to a surprisingly low 35 projects, while the majority of the projects focus more generally on international relations in the region. Only 17 projects dealt with U.S.-Japan bilateral relations, but it is important to note that the number of projects that try to analyze regional cooperation (including that of the United States and Japan) in tackling global and common issues, such as the global environment, run up to the level of eight projects in the past three years while those on U.S.-Japan relations in the Asia Pacific region count as many as five projects. Traditionally, Japan's international relations have been centered around the U.S.-Japan relationship, and thus, one would expect Asia Pacific study to be a kind of spin-off from American studies or studies on U.S.-Japan relations. The above result clearly shows that issues concerning Asia Pacific have been picked up as topics of study quite independent of U.S.-Japan relations.

More significantly, there are 22 projects that give direct reference to Asia Pacific, while those that attempt to deal with ASEAN and East Asia as a region total 43 projects. In other words, more than half of the relevant projects seem to be related to Asia Pacific (or East Asia for that matter) as a region.

To again follow up on the findings of the previous U.S.-Japan intellectual exchange survey, of 120 projects (both research projects and symposia), 8 projects were cosponsored and co-organized by overseas institutions in the Asia Pacific region, including the Asia Society, Harvard University, the Center for Strategic and International Studies, the National Bureau of Economic Research, Winrock International, the Overseas Development Council, Aspen Institute, The American Assembly, and the Council on Foreign Relations of the United States; and the Korea Development Institute, the Chinese Academy of Social Sciences, the Centre for Strategic and International Studies, Jakarta, and the Institute of Strategic and International Studies, Kuala Lumpur. Considering the mounting pressure on their Japanese counterparts for joint research and additional collaboration provided by American and other institutions, this figure is by no means satisfactory.

Lastly, further evidence for what was observed in the above macroscopic analysis of locally based and/or locally related projects is given with the introduction of two new research institutions that are specifically designed to deal with Asia Pacific affairs, i.e., The International Center for the Study of East Asian Development and the Asian-Pacific Center, both of which are located in Kyushu. Considering the long historical interactions that these cities in Kyushu (Kita-Kyushu and Fukuoka) have had with the Korean peninsula and others in the Asian region, it is not surprising that East Asia and the Asia Pacific region have been selected as their chief target of analysis and interaction. It is encouraging to see that these Kyushu-based institutions are active in research and intellectual exchange activities in a variety of fields outside of economics.

3. Interactions and Networks with Overseas Institutions in the Region

As observed above, Japanese research institutions' interests and involvements in the study of Asia Pacific seem to be genuine, and Asia Pacific studies occupy the majority of international studies by Japanese think tanks. One can perhaps refer to several reasons behind this upsurge of interests in Asia Pacific affairs including:

a. the increasing, predominantly economic, importance of the Asia Pacific region, particularly East and Southeast Asia, for Japan's economic survival;
b. the growing sense of political responsibility commensurate to its economic power and presence in the region;
c. the growing presence of Asia Pacific in the social life of the Japanese through students and workers; and
d. a review of Japan's Asian identity, part of which may be triggered by the weariness of incurring a backlash from the West, particularly the United States.

Since the above conditions are expected to continue in the years to come, projects on Asia Pacific undertaken by major research institutions in Japan are also expected to continue to increase.

However, in terms of networking with their counterparts in the region, the picture is not altogether optimistic. Intellectual underpinnings to interregional community creation are provided more effectively by joint works between institutions and personal relations among institution leaders. From this point of view, despite the growing number of Asia Pacific related policy research projects, Japanese research institutions' contributions to the intellectual underpinnings have been rather limited. Among Japanese institutions, only the Japan Institute of International Affairs (JIIA) and the Nomura Research Institute are part of formal networks among research institutions in Asia Pacific. JIIA, as the research arm of the Ministry of Foreign Affairs, has represented Japan at various gatherings, including the Pacific Economic Cooperation Conference (PECC) and the Conference on Security Cooperation in the Asia Pacific (CSCAP). Through the former network, JIIA has been linked with various PECC national committees of member countries, most of which are research institutions such as the Centre for Strategic and International Studies, Jakarta (CSIS, Jakarta) and the Institute of Strategic and International Studies, Kuala Lumpur (ISIS, Kuala Lumpur). In the latter network, JIIA has been a member of a group of regional research institutions concerned about security issues, namely CSIS, Jakarta; ISIS, Kuala Lumpur; the Institute of Strategic and Development Studies, the Philippines; the Singapore Institute of International Affairs; the Institute of Strategic and International Studies, Chulalongkorn University; the Seoul Forum for International Affairs; JIIA; and the Pacific Forum/CSIS, U.S. The core of CSCAP is ASEAN-ISIS, and, aside from natural cohesion provided by ASEAN solidarity and a sense of shared destiny, ASEAN-ISIS is, in a nutshell, based on personal relationships and friendship among the individually charismatic, founding leaders of these member institutes. Aside from the question of the "fairness" of this situation, it has proven to be very difficult for directors of JIIA to be members of the hard-core because, as career diplomats, they will leave from the directorship of JIIA in two to three years, leaving their successors the task of constructing their own personal relationships from scratch.

The Nomura Research Institute and its affiliate, the Tokyo Club Foundation for Global Studies, has maintained the Asia Forum of networks, bringing together major think tanks in the region. This network includes the Brookings Institute; the Centre of Asian Studies, Hong Kong; the Center for Policy and Implementation Studies, Jakarta; the Korea Development Institute; ISIS, Kuala Lumpur; the Center for Research and Communication, the Philippines; the Institute of Southeast Asian Studies, Singapore; the Chung-Hua Institution for Economic Research, Taipei; and the Thailand Development Research Institute.

JCIE has maintained good personal relationships with scholars and other experts of international relations in ASEAN countries, Korea, and China, who are, more often than not, concurrently leaders of major research institutions in their respective countries and regions through such fora as the ASEAN-Japan Dialogue Program, Korea-Japan Intellectual Exchange Program, and others.

When a field study trip was made by JCIE to major research institutions in five ASEAN countries, interviewees were requested to enumerate Japanese institutions that they regard as their collaborators or regular contacts. The most frequently mentioned institutions include, aside from the above three, the Institute of Developing Economies, Sasakawa Peace Foundation, the Center for Southeast Asian Studies, Kyoto University, and, from quite a different viewpoint, the Japan Foundation, and the Japan International Cooperation Agency. The absence of genuinely independent research institutions that can be long-term partners of this type of intellectual network is increasingly becoming as apparent to the international community as it is to the intellectual community in Japan.

Notes

1. Hajime Ishida. *Seisaku Keisei to Nippon-gata Shinku Tanku* [Policy Formulation and Japanese Think Tanks] edited by the Urban Institute (Tokyo: Toyo Keizai Shimpo-sha, 1993).
2. Ibid.
3. International Monetary Fund, *International Financial Statistics*, January 1995 (Washington, D.C.: IMF, 1995). Figures given are based on the end of period exchange rate for November 1994. US$1=98.92 yen.

KOREA

Research Institutions in Korea

Ku-Hyun Jung
Director
Institute of East and West Studies

The research institutions dealt with in this survey cover mostly social science areas; natural science and engineering research firms are not included. There are three types of research institutions in Korea—government-supported organizations, corporate research institutes, and university-affiliated organizations. In this short report, each type of research institution will be briefly sketched with an emphasis on activities related to the Asia Pacific region.

Governmental Research Institutions

Government-supported research institutions are currently the most visible and financially secure type in Korea. Almost all government ministries have at least one research institution or think tank to back up their policies and to do some quick work for them. This survey contains data collected from twelve such governmental research institutions. Some of these are more prestigious than others, such as the Korea Development Institute, which was established in 1971 and has been involved in economic decision making throughout Korea's period of high-paced economic growth in the past three decades.

Most of these research institutions collaborate with foreign research institutions. Their international exposure is certainly affected by their primary research task. Institutions like the Korea Institute for Industrial Economics and Trade, the Korea Institute for International Economic Policy (KIEP), and the Sejong Institute are internationally oriented and organize international conferences, especially with other institutions in Asia Pacific. Some other institutions, such as the Consumer Protection Board and the Korea Information Society Development Institute tend to focus more on domestic issues. In general, as economies become more interdependent globally, most institutions have become linked with foreign institutions in one way or another. In January 1995, KIEP was designated by the Korean government as the National Research Center for APEC and is thus expected to perform a more active role in regional research collaboration with other institutions in the region.

Most of these governmental research institutions are staffed by research fellows with American and other foreign Ph.D.s and master-level degrees. Directors tend to be scholars, rather than ex-bureaucrats. While, in terms of personnel, these research institutions are fairly independent of the ministries that established them, in terms of research projects, they have to first cater to the needs of bureaucrats in the ministries, which also oversee the institutions. In this sense, governmental institutions tend to be short-term oriented and less than objective in some of their work because they cannot openly oppose the policies of their related ministries.

In December 1994, the Korean government implemented a major governmental reorganization. The Economic Planning Board, which has been the major economic ministry during the rapid economic growth of the past three decades, merged with the Ministry of Finance. In addition, the Ministries of Construction and Transportation also merged into one ministry. There is speculation that a second-phase reorganization could involve some non-economic ministries in the future. It is possible that some of the research institutions reported on in this survey will merge with each other, and some will be downsized as well.

It is difficult to evaluate the cost and benefit of governmental research institutions because they are not judged by their performance in the market. These research institutions, however, should be given credit for having employed many young Ph.D.s who studied at home and abroad but could not find gainful employment. It is noteworthy that Korea has a relatively abundant supply of foreign Ph.D.s and sometimes has an oversupply of them relative to positions available. A major problem with governmental research institutions is that they are too bureaucratic and thus very inflexible. This factor may present problems in developing cooperative relationships with foreign research institutions. All in all, the role of governmental research institutions in Korean society and the economy is expected to slowly diminish in the future.

Corporate Research Institutions

Corporate research institutions are younger than government-supported institutions, but they have grown rapidly in recent years. For example, Samsung Economic Research Institute was established in 1986 and currently employs about a hundred and twenty researchers, including eleven Ph.D.s. Four major business groups (Samsung, Hyundai, Lucky-Goldstar, and Daewoo) have incorporated research institutions which do some macroeconomic forecasting, industry study, and foreign area studies. As Korean companies have become more aggressive in overseas markets in recent years, their research work on foreign markets has also increased. Since their history is very short, these corporate research institutions have to rely heavily on financial contributions from their sister companies.

Since these institutions are for-profit organizations, they cannot be expected to produce substantial research reports related to public policy or public interest. For the same reason, potential collaboration by these research institutions with other research centers in the Asia Pacific region would also be of limited scope. Some of these research institutions are involved indirectly in regional collaboration since they support corporate participation in the Pacific Basin Economic Cooperation (PBEC), the Pacific Economic Cooperation Council (PECC), and other bilateral and multilateral dialogues in the region. As Korean business involvement in the region is likely to increase rapidly in the form of direct foreign investment and trade, corporate research institutions and corporate philanthropic activities are expected to be more active in the international arena in the future.

University Research Institutions

There are many university-affiliated research institutions in Korea, but they are generally poorly endowed. This survey includes eight such institutes which are internationally oriented. Several of them have full-time researchers and additional graduate assistants, but most university research institutions are staffed by regular faculty members who do work for research institutions on a part-time basis. Professors in Korean universities have a relatively heavy teaching load, and very few universities have professors who specialize in research.

In terms of international exchange, however, university institutions are the most active. For example, the Institute of East and West Studies at Yonsei University organizes more than ten bilateral and multilateral conferences each year, in addition to regular seminars and frequent visits by foreign scholars. In particular, the Institute has organized an international conference on Asia Pacific Economic Cooperation annually since 1993. In addition, it is involved in a multilateral research consortium on Northeast Asian Economic Cooperation with five other research institutions in the subregion. This initiative is supported financially by the Sasakawa Peace Foundation in Japan. The Institute for Sino-Soviet Studies of Hanyang University is also active in research collaboration in the region, mainly with China and Russia. The Institute for Far Eastern Studies of Kyungnam University has been active in research collaboration with Indonesia, and the Center for Asia Pacific Studies of Kyunghee University has been active in China studies in recent years. The Center for Area Studies of Seoul National University has been acting as a coordinating body in managing government research grants for foreign area studies for the last few years.

Since university research institutions are independent from the government or private firms, they have the potential to formulate a research agenda on their own and make some concrete contributions to the society. However, these activities require financial and human resources which the institutions lack. There is room here for private foundations to support these university research institutions to perform more public policy-oriented research as well as more academic research which cannot be done by government or corporate research institutions.

Looking into the future, the potential for research collaboration in the Asia Pacific region is expected to be most promising with university research institutions. There are at least two reasons for this optimism. First, Korean universities are expected to go through a major transformation in the next decade. Student turmoil and campus unrest which have characterized Korean universities in the past are now largely gone, and universities are busy charting a course for their future. As the global village becomes more and more a reality, it is only natural that they place high priority on globalization and international collaboration in the future. As a result, academic exchanges between Korean universities and their foreign counterparts, especially in the Asia Pacific region, are expected to mushroom in the coming years. In addition, research activity, not only by individual faculty members but also by research institutions, is expected to receive higher priority in university fund allocation.

Second, government support of research institutions is expected to increase in the future. Recently, the Korea Research Foundation, a public foundation, started a new program of identifying and supporting key university research institutions. Several research institutions included in this survey have been designated as such. Especially with the decreasing role expected for governmental research bodies, university research institutions are expected to play a more active role as think tanks and centers for international research collaboration in the future.

MALAYSIA

Research Institutions in Malaysia
From the Perspective of the Underpinnings of the Asia Pacific Community

Makito Noda
Senior Program Officer
Japan Center for International Exchange

1. Malaysia's Asia Pacific Orientation

To discuss Malaysia's attitude toward the Asia Pacific community, one must start with what seems to be its preoccupation with East Asia. Prime Minister Datuk Seri Dr. Mahathir Mohamad has advocated the so-called "Look East Policy" since his inauguration in 1981, seeking a model for Malaysian economic development in East Asian forerunners such as Japan and Korea, particularly for the purpose of emulating work ethics and practices. Together with members of the "Singapore School" (see Singapore country report), most notably Lee Kwan Yew, Prime Minister Mahathir has been one of the most visible and outspoken advocates of the "East Asian" way of development. As such, Malaysia has been actively promoting ties with its Far Eastern neighbors. At the same time, however, due to its Islamic orientation, Malaysia has also pursued closer relations with Islamic countries. This "double identity" seems to coexist in Malaysia apparently without causing an identity crisis on the part of the Malaysians.

One element that may be able to connect these two is the fact that Prime Minister Mahathir is openly critical of what he sees as U.S. attempts to dominate Asia, or the Orient for that matter, by imposing its own set of values on Asian countries and, in fact, more generally, of the "Western challenges to its sovereign jurisdiction…reflected in acts of intervention by Western governments and private organizations in issues where they believe intervention to be morally required and politically laudable, including issues over trade and intellectual property rights, human rights, the environment, and even over arms acquisition."[1] To Mahathir, what seems to be a sudden surge of interest in the Asia Pacific Economic Cooperation (APEC), which received nothing short of a cold shoulder when first proposed by Australia, appears to be another case of U.S. ambitions to control Asia or intervene in Asian affairs. It is also well known that the prime minister has been highly critical of the American government's approach to its economic friction with Japan. Reportedly, he believes that what happened to Japan can and will happen to the Asian NIEs and, subsequently, to other ASEAN countries, or "sisters of NIEs" as their economic presence begins to be felt by Americans. The East Asian Economic Caucus (EAEC) proposal, which includes all of APEC's East Asian countries but excludes APEC's "Western" governments such as the United States, Canada, Australia, and New Zealand, can be viewed in this conjunction. This may, at least partially, explain why Malaysia's current interest in the Asia Pacific seems to emphasize the "eastern arch of the Pacific Rim,"[2] which coincides with the proposed members of the EAEC.

However, this should not be interpreted as Malaysia's general antipathy toward a greater Asia Pacific community. In fact, the current "bias" for East Asia seems to reflect Prime Minister Mahathir's personal philosophy more than the general attitudes of Malaysians. The defense minister in the Mahathir administration, Najib, for instance, is well known for his open endorsement of a wider Asia Pacific grouping that includes the United States. Mohamed Jawhar bin Hassen, Deputy Director General of the Institute of Strategic and International Studies (ISIS), which is supposed to be quite close to Mahathir, claims that "ISIS is very much supportive of the Asia Pacific community concept and it can be said about Malaysia in general." He continues to state that the Asia Pacific community and East Asian community are not "mutually contradictory or exclusive," and, in fact, they are "mutually complementary." Furthermore, it is a well-know fact that one of the leaders of the next generation, Defense Minister Najib, is very much in favor of an Asia Pacific grouping that includes the United States.

2. Circumstances Surrounding Research Institutions in Malaysia

1) The Role of Intellectuals in Policy Making

Malaysia has been a predominantly government-led society where practically everything is done by the government or conducted under rather tight government control and regulation such as the recently reinforced Official Secrets Act, the Polic Act (which regulates public meetings), the Printing Presses and Publications Act, the Internal Security Act, and the Societies Act (which governs the formation of political parties and other societies). Policy research is no exception to this general rule. In fact, research projects in Malaysia are supposed to be approved by the Social and Economic Research Unit of the Prime Minister's Office at least six months before launching.[3] In this climate, nongovernmental policy research is not, if anything, encouraged. The absence of change of government has also minimized the potential role of research institutions in national policy formulation. Malaysian politics have been dominated by the United Malay National Organization (UMNO), representing the largest ethnic group, the Malays, and UMNO has headed each coalition government since the country's independence in 1957. Thus, the research circle's channel for policy influence in Malaysia has been limited to informal and personal relationships between intellectuals and government leaders and policy makers.

Yet, the 1980s saw the evolution of quite a number of research institutions in Malaysia. Since this seems to have followed the inauguration of Prime Minister Mahathir, it has been suggested that his reservations about the dominance of policy making by the national bureaucracy may have contributed to this phenomenon. Mahathir's aversion to the bureaucracy, it is argued, has gradually undermined the latter's policy capability. In fact, together with the adoption of Vision 2020, described below, this weakened national bureaucracy, in terms of policy capability, seems to have contributed to the emergence of new research institutions in recent years.

2) Private, Nongovernmental Research Institutions

Among some ten major policy-oriented research institutions in Malaysia (according to the criteria of the current survey), a few of them are characterized by international directories as nongovernmental organizations, including the Institute for Policy Research (IPR), ISIS, and the Malaysian Institute of Economic Research (MIER), while all the others are registered as governmental or semigovernmental. In fact it has been pointed out, even by Malaysian intellectuals, that all research institutions in Malaysia are more or less "government" institutions. As an institution designed to advance the relevance of Islamic beliefs and principles in the development of policies and goals, IPR always boasts heavy participation of national government leaders in their programs. ISIS is world-renowned as "one of the three largest nongovernment think tanks in ASEAN and in Southeast Asia," but its independence is at best described as "technically a private institution"[4] due, among others, to the fact that it was granted an endowment by the Malaysian government when it was set up. Its Director General, Nordin Sopiee, himself admits that "most of the important work we do is somewhat confidential."[5] MIER may be closer to the familiar concept of nongovernmental institutions, though "it was first mooted in the Prime Minister's Panel and later promoted by the Council of Malaysian Invisible Trade."[6]

3) "Islamic" Policy-Oriented Institutions

One of the unique features of the Malaysian research circle seems to be the presence of policy-oriented research institutions that have very strong religious, Islamic, orientations. Against the background of a potential threat to domestic stability from Islamic fundamentalism, these relatively new institutions attempt to emphasize the relevance of Islamic teachings to the elements of modern economic development and social progress. The most representative of them are IPR above (established in 1985) and the Institute of Islamic Understanding Malaysia, which was created by the Malaysian federal government in 1992.

4) Impact of Wawasan 2020 (Vision 2020)

Wawasan (*Vision*) 2020 is a plan recently initiated by Prime Minister Mahathir which, in essence, aims to turn Malaysia into a fully developed nation by the year 2020. Since it is a rather ambitious scheme, calling for minimum annual growth of seven percent for the next thirty years, its implementation requires all kind of intellectual reinforcement and support. Its success, for instance, depends a lot on a stable security environment in Southeast Asia, requiring a greater number of security studies than before. H.J.S. Kraft analyzed that this new situation "led to the establishment of a variety of think tanks all over the country" and, in fact, he claims that "1993 saw the flowering of think tanks in Malaysia. It was estimated that more than twenty institutions were established in response to the demand for new ideas for Vision 2020."[7]

It has also been pointed out that individual political leaders tend to establish their own research institutions in order to reinforce their own policy capability. While, for that matter, ISIS is supposed to be very close to Mahathir, contenders for the leadership of the next generation have begun to have their own equivalent. Defense Minister Najib, for instance, is the founding patron of the newly established Malaysian Strategic Research Centre, while the more Islamic Institute for Policy Research (IKD) is often referred to as "Anwar's institute," underlining the role of Deputy Prime Minister Anwar Ibrahim, Mahathir's heir apparent, who leads IKD's board of trustees. With the succession race becoming harsher, new institutions may continue to be established by other political leaders.

3. Profiles of Major Research Institutions in Malaysia

What follows is a profile of major policy research institutions in Malaysia which have already been or have the potential to be members of the Asia Pacific intellectual network. The inventory includes not only nongovernmental, independent institutions, which is the prime concern of the current study, but also some semigovernmental or quasi-governmental organizations and one intergovernmental institution.

1) Institutions on Security Studies

Partly reflecting the sudden emergence of security-related research institutions after the announcement of Vision 2020, the number of security/strategy-related institutions that have evolved is more than one would expect from a country of Malaysia's size. Most prominent among them, of course, is the *Institute for Strategic and International Studies (ISIS) Malaysia*, which celebrated its first ten-year anniversary as a legal entity last year (even though it was first established as a company limited registered under the Companies Act in 1965). Modeled after the Centre for Strategic and International Studies Jakarta, ISIS was conceived out of Prime Minister Mahathir's desire to have a source for "the second opinion" on foreign policy because of his apprehension to total reliance on the bureaucracy. ISIS was initially financed by an endowment from the government, but for the past three or four years, it has been completely independent of government financing. Having nearly one hundred full-time research and support staff, the need for fund raising has led Director General Nordin Sopiee to describe ISIS as a "foreign policy entrepreneur." ISIS has established itself as a key institution in the development of international relations studies (including security as well as international economic studies) in Malaysia. It has contributed policy inputs on defense and security issues, and foreign affairs, and it is believed to have "played a key role in elaborating the government's plan to lift Malaysia into the rank of the developed nations by 2020,"[8] i.e., Vision 2020. ISIS has, for a long time single-handedly, represented Malaysia's intellectual link to the Asia Pacific, being the founder of the annual Asia Pacific Roundtable on Security Cooperation (the largest annual informal dialogue mechanism on security in the Asia Pacific region with more than two hundred participants). ISIS is also the founding member of the ASEAN Institutes of Strategic and International Studies (ASEAN-ISIS), by far the most active regional network among research institutions. As discussed elsewhere, ASEAN-ISIS has provided a basis for the larger, somewhat more formal, Council on Security Cooperation in the Asia Pacific, including Korean and Japanese counterparts, for which ISIS Malaysia also serves as one of the founding members. Additionally, ISIS is the Malaysian secretariat of the Pacific Economic Cooperation Council and Pacific Basin Economic Council.

Preceding ISIS's emergence, the *Malaysian International Affairs Forum (MIAF)* has been instrumental in organizing seminars and discussions on issues of international affairs since 1978, supported by the academic community around Kuala Lumpur. MIAF, however, does not support a professional staff or a well-developed infrastructure, being a voluntary society of like-minded scholars. Likewise, its policy impact on Malaysia's foreign policy has not been as significant from a comparative point of view.

Within the Universiti Kebangsaan Malaysia (Malaysia National University), the *Strategic and Security Studies Unit* was started by Zakaria Haji Ahmad in 1987. The Unit aims to study and analyze all aspects of national and regional strategic and security developments mainly in the Asia Pacific region. From its inception, it has attempted to promote informed debate of policy options by supplying objective studies.

The newest addition to Malaysia's security studies circle is the *Malaysian Strategic Research Centre (MSRC)*, established in September 1993. Its inaugural mission has been to look at the implications of the Vision 2020 for Malaysian foreign and defense policies. It aims to work in the fields of defense and foreign affairs, economics, resource management, and science. It is an independent, nongovernmental organization but maintains close ties with the government, particularly with the office of Defense Minister Najib Tun Razak. Despite its brief history, it has already conducted a number of international symposia, inviting participants from other countries in the Asia Pacific region, including Japan.

2) Economic Development and International Economics

Most internationally-renowned in this category is the Asian *and Pacific Development Centre (APDC)*, a center for research, training, and information dissemination on women, agricultural development, industrial development, international trade, energy, regional cooperation, economic and social development, environmental management, public administration, poverty, and rural development established by the UN institutions in 1980. However, APDC is an intergovernmental organization supported and managed by the governments of the Asia Pacific countries which signed ADPC's charter. Aside from independent research activities, APDC functions as a hub of the Asia Pacific network among institutions and individual researchers in development fields. It houses the Association of Development Research and Training Institutes of Asia and the Pacific, and its *Directory of Research and Training Institutions and Organizations on Economic and Social Development and Planning in Asia and the Pacific* is probably the most comprehensive information source in this area. Its major concern in recent years, however, has been the imminent withdrawal of funding from the UNDP, creating a gap which will have to be filled by other sources including private philanthropy. Aside from regional and extraregional governmental contributions, APDC has been funded by such philanthropic organizations as the Ford Foundation, Noyes Foundation, and the World Wide Fund for Nature, but lacks strong support from the Japanese philanthropic community.

Reflecting the strong autonomy enjoyed by the State of Sabah, the city of Kota Kinabalu has three major, semigovernmental institutions on development and public policy, i.e., Institute for Development Studies, Institute for Policy Research, and Institute of Policy Studies. What applies to Kuala Lumpur and other parts of the Federation does not seem to apply to this special region, requiring separate research centers. Among them, the *Institute for Development Studies* conducts research on economic policy, economic and social development, social policy, rural development, public expenditure and other government policies. But its intellectual scope tends to be limited to the Sabah area.

The *Malaysian Institute of Economic Research (MIER)* may be one of a very few independent, nongovernmental institutions in Malaysia. Established in 1985, it has an independent board of trustees that includes representatives from the private sector, scholars, as well as government officers. It serves both private business' and the Malaysian government's needs by conducting economic forecasts and macroeconomic analysis and planning, surveying business conditions and consumer orientation, etc., and providing economic policy proposals to the government. In fact, according to Lee Kim Pian, MIER's Institute Secretary, MIER representatives are regularly invited to government conferences on the budget, securing a direct channel for MIER with the government through which it can exercise its influence on the latter's policy.[9] Even though MIER has a strong inclination toward national and, subsequently, subregional (i.e., ASEAN) orientations, one major funding source is the Canadian International Development Agency whose presence is very much felt throughout ASEAN and which is deeply appreciated for its support of, among other things, institution building.

3) Other Public Policy Institutions

One of the unique features of the Malaysian research circle is the attempt to make Islamic teachings, Malaysia's national religion, compatible with social and economic development, and, thus, provide the predominantly Muslim nation with alternatives to the Islamic fundamentalism that has the potential of fatally destabilizing the nation. For this particular purpose, the *Institute of Islamic Understanding Malaysia (IKIM)* was established by Prime Minister Mahathir himself in July 1992. Its priority is stated as the "elaboration of the theoretical and theological basis of an Islamic work ethic in the context of perceived cultural barriers among Muslims to the achievement of Malaysia's rapid development targets"[10] but, more specifically, it addresses "the same national and international issues as ISIS but from an Islamic point of view."[11]

In the private sector, the *Institute for Policy Research* (IPR, but IKD as an acronym in Malay) was established in 1985 to conduct systematic research on economic and social development, and the relevance of religious beliefs and principles to the development of policies and goals. It is essentially "a training and education institution with a strong inclination toward Islamic teaching,"[12] and as such, is very much interested in links with the Arab world as well as fellow third world countries. Nevertheless, it has conducted joint projects with other ASEAN institutions, including the International Symposium on Interaction for Progress: Modernization of Vietnam and ASEAN Cooperation, cosponsored with Singapore's Information and Resource Center, a partner of the ASEAN-ISIS network, and the Study Group on ASEAN-Vietnam Cooperation jointly organized with the Information and Resource Center, Thailand's Institute for Security and International Studies, and the Institute for Long Term and Regional Planning, Vietnam. It also sponsored a Regional Islamic Science Conference for the Asia Pacific in 1987.

4. Future Prospects

In terms of an intellectual network with Asia Pacific countries, until very recently, Malaysia has been represented solely by ISIS Malaysia. Although it remains the most frequent and influential link to international intellectual networks, a number of new research institutions have been established in recent years, particularly in response to the need caused by the launching of Vision 2020. They have gradually begun to engage themselves in international research cooperation and dialogue, particularly in the Asia Pacific region, providing the Asia Pacific intellectual network with alternative Malaysian partners.

As the number of research institutions increases, already severe competition for limited financial resources is expected to increase. Particularly if these research institutions, new and old, wish to retain their relatively independent status, the importance of nongovernmental funding sources will be critical. It is noteworthy that many Malaysian research institutions, even those with a strong domestic orientation are financially supported by European and Canadian foundations and agencies on top of American philanthropic organizations. For the sake of providing a more complete picture of Asia Pacific intellectual networks, greater contribution by the Japanese nongovernmental sector seems to be vital.

Notes

1. Herman Joseph S Kraft, "Security Studies in ASEAN: Trends in the Post–Cold War Era," in *Studying Asia Pacific Security*, edited by Paul M. Evans (North York: University of Toronto - York University Joint Centre for Asia Pacific Studies, 1993), p. 14.
2. Lee Kim Pian, Institute Secretary, Malaysia Institute of Economic Research, in an interview in August 1993.
3. Takahiro Suzuki and Makiko Ueno, *Sekai no Shinku Tanku* [Think Tanks of the World: Linking Knowledge with Public Policy] (Tokyo: SIMUL, 1993), p. 189.
4. H.J.S. Kraft in his unpublished directory of security institutions in ASEAN countries, 1993.
5. "ISIS Malaysia: The First Ten Years," in *ISIS Focus* (July, 1993), p. 5.
6. MIER *Annual Report* 1992.
7. Kraft, "Security Studies...," op. cit., p. 15.
8. *Think Tanks: An International Directory*, 1993.
9. In an interview in August 1993.
10. Alan J. Day (ed.), *Think Tanks: An International Directory* (Essex: Longman Information & Reference, 1993).
11. Kraft, "Security Studies...," op. cit., p. 16.
12. Mahamed Ezam Mohd Nor, Deputy Director, IKD, in an interview in August 1993.

NEW ZEALAND

Research Institutions in New Zealand

Nicky Thomson
Programme Manager, Business
Asia 2000 Foundation of New Zealand

New Zealand is a small country with a population of only 3.4 million people which nonetheless has a well-developed research capability. This capability can be grouped into three general institutional areas—the Crown Research Institutions, the universities and a small group of independent research-based organisations focusing largely on policy and economic matters. This paper briefly describes those three institutional areas, but it should be noted that in New Zealand not all research is generated from a centre of excellence in a particular institution and much significant work is the result of individual scholars researching in a variety of fields.

One group of institutions is the Crown Research Institutes (CRIs), set up in 1992 as government-owned companies with a clear focus on servicing the technology and innovation needs of important sectors of the economy. The organisations are based on the skills of staff from a wide range of backgrounds and take the place of several former government departments. They have the freedom to operate as commercial organisations and offer a rich and flexible resource for providing large, medium and small organisations with technology and innovation services. The CRIs undertake a wide range of research, technology development and consulting for private companies within New Zealand and overseas. They also undertake strategic public good centred science for government.

The company structure allows the CRIs to borrow funds and to form both joint ventures and subsidiary companies in order to fully exploit the commercial potential of new developments for the benefit of New Zealand. The nine CRIs are based around four productive sectors of the economy. The Institute of Environmental Science and Research Limited (ESR) works in the human resource and environmental health sector. Industrial Research Limited supports a range of technology development in the industrial sector. Landcare Research New Zealand Limited., the National Institute of Water and Atmospheric Research Ltd. (NIWA) and the Institute for Geological and Nuclear Science Limited undertake environmental and resource management research. The New Zealand Pastoral Agriculture Research Institute Limited (AgResearch), New Zealand Institute for Crop and Food Research Ltd, The Horticulture and Food Research Institute of New Zealand Ltd (HortResearch) and New Zealand Forest Research Institute Limited (NZ FRI) support the land-based industries.

New Zealand has seven universities each of which has particular areas of expertise in terms of research. Each university also has a commercial company or office to service outside inquiries for research cooperation contracts and consultancies. The oldest, the University of Otago, was established in 1869. Its particular strengths are sciences and health sciences and areas of research excellence include animal gene molecular biology, animal disease management, marine science, natural products chemistry, protein chemistry and spatial information. The University of Canterbury, established 122 years ago, is renowned for its earthquake engineering work, and also for its work on drying processes for industry, and on geochemistry and the formation of granites. Other areas of particular strength include history and anthropology and the University is in the process of setting up a new centre for Asian studies.

New Zealand's largest university, the University of Auckland, is well known for its Geothermal Institute. Other areas of research excellence are gene technology, surface materials science, marine science, geophysics, applied optics and developmental medicine. Auckland University's New Zealand Asia Institute comprises four centres: the Korea Studies Centre, Japan Studies Centre, China Studies Centre and the ASEAN Studies Centre. Each of these centres will have input into the APEC (Asia Pacific Economic Cooperation) Study Centre recently established in New Zealand and based at the University of Auckland as part of a network of APEC Study Centres around the Asia Pacific region. This Centre is intended to be a vital part of efforts to turn the Asia Pacific region into a free trade area. It will focus on economic and trade issues and will liaise with interested scholars in New Zealand and throughout the region as well as with sister APEC Study Centres.

Victoria University of Wellington's School of Architecture does research in building performance and energy efficiency. The University also excels in the research areas of managing the environment, innovation, petroleum science, and seismological studies. The Institute of Policy Studies was established by Victoria University of Wellington from which it receives financial support. Other funding comes from institutions and enterprises in the public and private sectors in the form of direct grants for projects or fellowships, and staff secondments. The Institute promotes the study, research and discussion of current issues of public policy, both foreign and domestic. As a link between academic research and public policy, it provides opportunities for independent, detached study and for neutral and informed discussion of issues that are important to New Zealand. There are also two semi-autonomous research centres within the Institute: the Health Services Research Centre, promoting independent research into health services, and the Centre for Strategic Studies, which belongs to the network of strategic studies institutes in the Asia Pacific region, and shapes a New Zealand input into them.

Massey University has a very strong faculty of Agricultural and Horticultural Science and has developed particular strengths in computer control and modeling, computer systems for schools, DNA vaccine receptor technology, ion exchange resin, metabolism of alcohol and molecular systematics. Massey University also renowned for its excellence in the social sciences.

The University of Waikato's areas of research expertise include managing environmental change, interdisciplinary water science and resource management. The University has a strong education department which focuses on science, technology and mathematics education. Lincoln University, established as an agricultural college in 1878 and the most recent to become an independent university, excels in the research areas of animal transgenics, plant protection/integrated pest management, land, water and farm management, agroforestry and other land use options, plant and animal production, and ecology and conservation.

Research in New Zealand is also supported by independent institutions. Included in this group are the New Zealand Institute of Economic Research (NZIER), a non-profit incorporated society that provides quality economic research material, economic advice and forecasting services for its members. It works on the premise that in today's world business planning and strategy cannot be done without the right information. It supplies research information covering all aspects of commerce, industry and trade with macroeconomic research and forecasting as the central part of its business, but the Institute also carries out individual company research and contract research in a wide range of areas.

The New Zealand Business Roundtable (NZBR) is an organisation of chief executives of major business firms, committed to contributing to the overall development of New Zealand. With a focus on major national issues the NZBR aims to make a pro-active, professional and well-researched contribution to policy formation which it does in part by issuing policy papers. These consistently espouse an economic perspective that stresses the value of the market and the need to limit the role of government in society.

PHILIPPINES

Policy-Oriented Research Institutions in the Philippines

From the Perspective of Asia Pacific Intellectual Cooperation

Makito Noda
Senior Program Officer
Japan Center for International Exchange

I. Asia Pacific Orientation of the Philippines

Compared with its ASEAN neighbors, the Philippine's international initiatives have not been very outstanding in recent years. Indonesia has been an aggressive leader of the refurbished non-aligned movement, while Malaysia has advocated for the East Asian Economic Caucus, Singapore has represented the East Asian way of development and democracy in various international fora, and Thailand has functioned as a bridge between ASEAN and Vietnam and other Indo-Chinese countries. Compared to these epoch-making initiatives by other ASEAN partners, the Philippines has not shown any internationally visible performances, except, perhaps, for the termination of the agreement with the United States regarding the latter's military bases in the Philippines. While the withdrawal of one of the largest overseas military bases from Southeast Asia is undeniably a major event, it was nevertheless the termination of something that already existed rather than the creation of something new.

Several factors seem to lie behind this low profile of the naturally extrovert Filipinos in international interactions. First and foremost, every Philippine watcher would point to negative legacies of the Marcos regime, which, in short, damaged the very unity of the nation, deepened distrust of politicians and the political system among citizens, as well as devastated the economy. President Corazon Aquino, when enthroned by the "People's Power" cum "EDSA Revolution," thus, had to face the reality that "the national government she inherited was comatose and bankrupt; foreign debt payments sapped the government's extremely limited resources; and local government had ceased to function in many parts of the country." On top of all this, the communist insurgents still possessed a formidable capability to challenge the new government politically and militarily.[1] Under these circumstances, the top priority of the government would naturally be to restore a semblance of national unity, which cannot be accomplished in a short period of time. Secondly, restored democracy under President Aquino was also a period infested with a lot of military coup attempts, which sucked up the already depleted energy of the government. As if these obstacles were not tough enough, the Philippines in the late 1980s and early 1990s was hit by waves of natural calamity, including a volcanic eruption and several devastating typhoons. Some include damages caused by typhoon-related floods in the list of Marcos' negative legacies since they were worsened by destroyed forests, a result of thoughtless development planning.

In other words, as David Timberman describes it, "the Philippines has been preoccupied with its internal affairs for most of the last fifteen years. Too few Filipinos have focused their attention on their nation's diminishing position in the world."[2] Simply put, the Philippine leaders could not afford to pay too much attention to events and changes outside of their immediate national threats.

This situation, however, is expected to change as the domestic conditions stabilize and national unity is gradually restored under the less charismatic but, perhaps, less idealistic Ramos government. Since the memory of the Marcos autocracy is still too fresh in the minds of Filipinos, any achievement that President Marcos and his groups accomplished tends to be brushed away, including diplomatic relations. This makes it difficult to speak of the "trend" in attitudes and policies of the Philippine government, again including international relations, due to this presence of a twenty-year vacuum. Nevertheless, the long-term trend seems to be rather obvious.

Foreign policy in the first years of Philippine independence can be summarized as "a way of expressing 'loyalty to America,'" and the international role of the Philippines was "defined primarily in terms of the American relationship,"[3] Toward the end of the 1950s, however, Filipinos became aware of the critical stares that its Asian neighbors cast on its close association with the United States or its "excessive Americanization,"[4] leading to a "new-found awareness of Asia."[5] In the following twenty years, this Asian identity gave birth to a sense of nationalism and, ironically, anti-Americanism among some, particularly intellectuals. As a result, by the late 1970s, Philippine foreign policy had begun to give increasing prominence to ASEAN. At the 1976 ASEAN Summit in Bali, the Philippines was found to be "ASEAN's most enthusiastic supporter."[6] When most of Marcos's past achievement was denied, this importance attached to ASEAN survived the "EDSA Revolution." Thus, Segundo Romero, Vice President of the Institute of Strategic and Development Studies writes, "Clearly, the Philippines wants to continue its peaceful and friendly relations with its neighbors, without which its chosen path of development in democracy would not be possible."[7]

This trend has been further consolidated by the end of the cold war, which simultaneously reduced the importance of this island nation to U.S. strategy and, from a Filipino point of view, deprived it of the established chart of its future course in the international community. The rejection of the continued presence of two U.S. bases on its land in 1992 was a natural outcome of these sequences. Alex Brillantes of the University of the Philippines labels this decision "a real basis for a marked shift in the country's foreign policy" toward a new, 'economic diplomacy' specifically in terms of increasing economic relations with neighboring Asian countries."[8] Brillantes believes this "new economic diplomacy" is a cornerstone of the Ramos government for the same reason that Romero explains the importance of ASEAN to the Philippines. Thus, it is expected that the Philippines will have no other recourse than deepening and widening its orientation toward Asia Pacific.

II. Circumstances Surrounding Independent Research Institutions

Despite the wide-spread image of the Philippines as an Asian copy of American society, independent research institutions have not established themselves as an integral part of policy deliberation, not even in the field of international relations. More than that, in fact, there are few institutions that are active in policy-oriented international studies. A general preoccupation with domestic issues and problems, which has long distracted Filipinos' attention from international relations, certainly must have played some role in this dearth of intellectual activities. Intellectual apathy to the Marcos government whose policies and programs were, despite Marcos's attempts to "neutralize them through incarceration, cooptation or gentle wooing,"[9] intellectually unjustifiable also must have discouraged Filipinos from developing policy-advisory institutions.

However, eight years after the fall of the Marcos government, there are several new factors that seem to promise a greater role to be played by independent research institutions, particularly in international relations in the years to come.

One of the major changes in Philippine politics brought about by Mrs. Aquino was the increased role of the military, caused by the government's heavy reliance on the armed forces for protection from coup attempts by its own radicalized segments on one hand and the need to coopt the military in the system of governance on the other hand. One consequence of this has been "the increased influence of the military in governance and policy-making."[10] This is particularly true in the fields in which national security is involved, including foreign and strategic relations. Thus, the armed forces will continue to "assert their right to have a major say in shaping government policies, particularly on the wide range of issues related to national security."[11] In order to counter this development and to minimize the role of the military in policy making, the civilian government must establish its credibility and civilian authority on national security affairs. Security affairs nowadays, particularly in the post–cold war era, are highly complicated issues that require experts to anatomize and propose prescriptions. Thus, there will be an increasing demand for intellectual capabilities on the part of civilians that can contribute to this end.

Secondly, somehow related to the above first factor, the nature of national security concerns has dramatically changed. According to Herman Joseph S. Kraft, the mainstream of security discourse in the Philippines "did not have any guiding framework (except perhaps anti-communism) and was largely focused on two issues, the communist insurgency and the U.S. facilities in the Philippines."[12] Now that the threat of communist insurgency has become almost academic, and the U.S. bases have finally withdrawn, a total review of the national security policy will be required, calling for more objective research capabilities with fresher perspectives. In fact, the armed forces has quickly established an Office of Strategic and Special Studies, a research arm of the Armed Forces of the Philippines that aims to "conduct studies and conferences on various security issues in the Asia Pacific region as a form of policy input to our political and military decision-makers,"[13] reminding us of the military's desire to have a say on government policies. As if to respond to this development from the civilian side, the Ministry of Foreign Affairs' Foreign Service Institute established the Center for International Relations and Strategic Studies in 1993 in order to deal with various issues and problems with foreign policy implications, global and regional strategies, and management of foreign affairs. Its current thrust is the assessment of the present geo-economic and geo-political environment of international relations, particularly in the Asia Pacific region.

Thirdly, inadequacy of the bureaucracy in its capacity to streamline policy planning and implementation has become widely recognized. According to Romero, "the highly centralized nature of government has put tremendous pressure on the 1.7 million strong government bureaucracy to deliver basic services to the people. Over the past half-century, administration after administration has sought to reorganize government and streamline the bureaucracy, to make it more responsive, honest, and capable. Despite these efforts, the bureaucracy has remained overstaffed but under manned."[14] In the meeting among heads of major research institutions in Metro Manila organized by Professor Carolina Hernandez of the Institute of Strategic and Development Studies (ISDS) in August 1993, it was agreed that "it has been clearly revealed that the government and its agencies and institutions are incompetent in many areas and respects, which must be supported and supplemented by the private sector." In light of this critical deficiency, the Aquino government, breaking with the past tradition, increased the role that non-governmental organizations and the private sector played in public affairs, on both the local and national level. In fact, by 1993, some NGOs "have assumed the tasks of governance, specifically in the delivery of basic services and active local development work, and have gained legitimacy and acceptance at the local level."[15] On the national level, they have been consulted in the drawing up of the Medium-Term Philippine Economic Development Plan and Philippine Assistance Plan. This acceptance and even encouragement of an increased role of NGOs and other private organizations in public affairs was also reflected in the discussion among heads of independent research institutions who all agreed that (compared with the Marcos administration to which they kept silent because of the widespread sense of inefficacy and despair) "post-1986 governments have begun to actively seek advise from every possible source." Foreign policy and external relations is certainly one area where supplementary or alternative sources of policy proposal are very much desired.

Additionally, in light of the fact that there are quite a number of highly competent research institutions attached to universities, particularly the big three of the University of the Philippines, Ateneo de Manila University, and De Lasalle University, prospects of these institutions leaving the university and becoming "independent" are believed to be high. It has been pointed out that this is mainly due to the gap of income that these institutes can earn from contractual projects and the budget allocated by the university, perhaps signifying the high demand for the kind of intellectual service these institutes can offer.

For these and perhaps other reasons, it is expected that the Philippines will witness the emergence of an increasing number of independent, nongovernmental research institutions, including those very active in Asia Pacific related fields.

III. Profile of Major Independent Institutions

There are only two institutions that are relevant to the current survey of policy-oriented institutions with particular emphasis on the social-scientific inquiry of Asia Pacific. There are some institutions that are affiliated with universities or government ministries, but they are excluded from the current study.

1. The *Center for Research and Communication* (CRC) of the Southeast Asian Science Foundation, Inc. was established in 1967 as an independent nonprofit institution devoted to research, communication, and professional training programs in economics, business, education, and other related fields. CRC encourages pluralism among its two hundred full-time staff members. Its major areas of research include economic policy and forecasting, industry monitoring, regional economics, agribusiness, urban planning, and international and strategic studies. Of particular relevance to the current survey is CRC's *Institute for International and Strategic Studies* (CRC-IISS) which was established in 1986 to focus on international relations and security. It provides a forum for discussing issues to help shape public opinion and chart the course of policies of major political actors in the Western Pacific region. CRC-IISS's areas of interest include internal and external security of the Philippines, political and economic cooperation among nations in the region, and the role of major powers in Asia Pacific.

2. The *Institute of Strategic and Development Studies* (ISDS) was founded in 1991 by a group of academics based at the University of the Philippines in order to contribute to international and regional peace and cooperation and human well-being through cooperative research and advocacy, discussion, publication, and training activities. ISDS is unique in its approach to issues from local, national, and international levels, through its Local Resources Development Program, Government Performance and Democratic Governance Program, and Strategic and International Studies Program, respectively. ISDS is the Philippine counterpart of ASEAN-ISIS and the newly established CSCAP. As such it is closely related with four other ASEAN-ISIS members, the Seoul Forum for International Affairs, the Pacific Forum/CSIS, the Japan Institute of International Affairs, as well as the Japan Center for International Exchange. ISDS's current and recent projects include "ASEAN into the 21st Century," "The Politics of Economic Policy-Making: AFTA and the Philippines," "The Philippines and the Law of the Sea," and "The Philippines into the 21st Century."

In addition to the above institutions, there are two powerfully policy-oriented institutions, *Congressional Research and Training Service, Inc.* and the *Philippine Center for Policy Studies*, but their works are not particularly related to Asia Pacific so far.

Notes

1. David Timberman, *A Changeless Land* (1991), p. 375.
2. Ibid., p. 385.
3. David Wurfel, *Filipino Politics: Development and Decay* (1988), p. 178–179.
4. Ibid., p. 179.
5. O.D. Corpuz, "Realities of Philippines Foreign Policy" in *The United States and the Philippines*, edited by Frank Golay (Englewood Cliffs: Prentice Hall, 1966), p. 53.
6. Wurfel, op. cit., p. 182.
7. Segundo Romero, "The Major Challenges Facing the Philippines in the 1990s," unpublished paper presented at the Sixth ASEAN-Japan Dialogue, 1992.
8. Alex Brillantes, "The Philippines in 1992: Ready for Take Off?" in *Asian Survey*, February, 1993, p. 228.
9. Wurfel, op. cit., p. 178.
10. Timberman, op. cit., p. 380.
11. Ibid.
12. Herman Joseph S. Kraft, "Security Studies in ASEAN: Trends in the Post–Cold War Era," in *Studying Asia Pacific Security* (1994), p. 16.
13. Arugay, Captain Artemio R., in his letter to JCIE, 17 August, 1994.
14. Romero, op. cit., p. 8.
15. Brillantes, op. cit., p. 229.

SINGAPORE

Research Institutions in Singapore

From the Perspective of Asia Pacific Intellectual Exchange

Makito Noda
Senior Program Officer
Japan Center for International Exchange

I. Asia Pacific Orientation of Singapore

It has been established that Singapore as a sovereign, independent nation is endowed with several critical constraints. First of all, it is a very young republic with a history of less than thirty years. Surrounded by Malaysia and Indonesia, the world's largest Muslim nation, it is, literally, a Chinese island in the Malay sea. Moreover, it is totally devoid of any resource, except for a pool of highly educated human resources. These constraints have necessarily made this island city-state a very vulnerable entity whose national security is directly and crucially affected by a capricious international environment. As such, Singaporeans have always been very concerned about their external relations. This is evidenced by the large number of individuals attracted to public seminars on international affairs organized by various institutions, to the extent that, according to Chan Heng Chee, organizers occasionally have to "turn down the applicants by hundreds."[1]

As a small, weak state, it also must manage friendly relations with the superpowers, particularly the United States in view of possible domination of the region by China or Japan. It is believed in Singapore that "the emergence of an unfriendly regional power seeking regional hegemony, in the wake of a power vacuum, is a worst case scenario…Small states are particularly vulnerable in this situation. [Thus,] it has been the firm belief of the then Prime Minister, now Senior Minister, Lee Kuan Yew that a small country needs powerful friends," in the context of Singapore's relationship with the United States in the new world order.[2] The historic leadership change, from Lee Kuan Yew to Goh Chok Tong, brought "no change in Singapore's foreign policy,"[3] and, unlike the rather ambivalent attitudes of Malaysia and Indonesia toward the U.S. presence in Asia Pacific, Singapore repeatedly underscored the critical importance of the United States in the region. Despite a strong emphasis on the virtue of Asian ways advocated by leading Singaporean intellectuals (recently labeled as the "Singapore School") that is oftentimes mistaken for anti-Americanism, Singapore clearly recognizes the importance of the United States for its own survival.

Professor Chan further states that "Singapore and the Unites States share the view that a viable and prosperous Pacific community is founded on a sound security arrangement in Asia Pacific," highlighting Singapore's interest in and expectation of the sound development of Asia Pacific cooperation. In fact, another leading expert on external relations in Singapore, Tommy Koh, explains that, among the seven principles of Singapore's foreign policy, is its commitment to play an active role in the evolution of the Pacific Community.

It has often been pointed out that, in a Singaporean conceptual world map, there is East Asia (including ASEAN, China, and Japan), the United States, Russia (because it used to be the U.S.S.R.), and the former colonizer, the United Kingdom, in that order. Asia Pacific, then, is truly the center of Singapore's external relations. But most of all, it is upon East Asia that Singapore attaches the utmost importance, and, because of the depth and scope of direct contact, this applies particularly to countries in Southeast Asia. It is repeatedly stressed that "Singapore must remain careful to remember that its destiny still lies with Southeast Asia, [and, thus,] Singapore needs to establish her strong commitment to ASEAN and to working for the progress of the region as a whole."[4]

Accordingly, Singapore has further strengthened its cooperation with ASEAN countries, including the much-talked-about "SIJORI growth triangle" project with Indonesia and Malaysia. The consistency between the primacy on its ASEAN relations and the support of Pacific-wide cooperation has been a constant concern of the Singapore government. In as early as 1980, Pang Eng Fong, Director of the National University of Singapore's Economic Development Center, analyzed the relative importance of ASEAN and Asia Pacific cooperation to Singapore in the following way:

> Of all ASEAN countries, Singapore is probably most likely to react positively to...forming a Pacific Community. As a globally-oriented city-state...Singapore will benefit from a consultative forum to promote cooperation among Pacific nations. But if Singapore's ASEAN partners are not enthusiastic about a Pacific

Community, it is doubtful that Singapore will emphasize the value of Pacific Basin cooperation…It would be unwise of her to take a position on the issue of a Pacific Community not endorsed by other ASEAN countries.[5]

Because of this delicate balance, Tommy Koh, in his explanation of Singapore's foreign policy principles, had to stress that "Singapore believes that its commitment to ASEAN is not inconsistent with its support for APEC and PECC. ASEAN, APEC, and PECC can co-exist as expanding and intersecting circles."[6] Endorsing these emphases on Asia Pacific cooperation, Singaporean research institutions in recent years have supported a high concentration of projects and activities that directly relate to Asia Pacific and/or the Pacific as we will see below.

II. Circumstances Surrounding Singaporean Research Institutions

Singapore has five major research institutions that are more or less policy oriented and interested in international affairs; i.e., the Information and Resource Centre (IRC), Institute of East Asian Political Economy (IEAPE), Institute of Policy Studies (IPS), Institute of Southeast Asian Studies (ISEAS), and Singapore Institute of International Affairs (SIIA). All of them claim in their annual report and brochures that they are independent, private institutions; e.g. "a nongovernmental organization" (IRC), "a nonprofit research organization" (IEAPE), "close to government but...not part of the government" (IPS), "an autonomous organization" (ISEAS), and "an independent self-governing body" (SIIA).

On the other hand, policy making and deliberation in Singapore has been dominated by the bureaucracy and, as a state under very strong, almost paternalistic government, it has not developed a tradition of open policy discussion as exists in western democracies. This is even truer in the case of foreign policy and external relations as a Singaporean political scientist, N. Ganesan writes: "foreign policy is decided, articulated and projected by a core group of elites…Issues are not often openly debated and [are] traditionally shrouded in secrecy."[7] Some even claim that "[Singaporean leaders] view that Singapore cannot afford the luxury of a more open and pluralistic system."[8] Therefore, one cannot expect Singapore's research institutions to play a significant role in the nation's policy formation and external relations.

And yet heads of these major, "nongovernmental" research institutions in Singapore often appear in various media, explaining the country's foreign policy and external relations, and they seem to enjoy the attention of the national leadership. In fact, those outside Singapore hear of them as often, if not more, as such national leaders as Lee Kwan Yew and Goh Chok Tong. For example, when Singaporeans started to argue the virtue of the Asian way, e.g., the Asian way of government, the Asian way of development, and the Asian way of "democracy," etc., at every possible occasion, often times in contrast to the problems of the western, particularly American, way, they have come to be labelled as the "Singapore school." They have been very vocal in advocating the Singaporean approach to, for example, freedom of press and human rights issues, particularly when they are criticized by the west. The most vocal, most celebrated, and most world-renowned in the "school" is Singapore's founding father, Lee Kwan Yew. With two other government leaders—Information and Arts Minister, George Yeo and Foreign Ministry permanent secretary Kishore Mahbubani—who contributed articles to *Foreign Affairs* and *Foreign Policy* in debates on East Asian patterns and civilizational clashes. *The Straits Times* identified Chan Heng Chee, Director of ISEAS as well as Tommy Koh, Director of IPS as the effective spokespersons of the "Singapore school."

To ponder on this apparent paradox, one has to pay close attention to the special relationship between the government and these research institutions. The key word here seems to be "independence." Even though major research institutions claim to be independent of the government, all of them, perhaps with the exception of IRC, have been in practice more or less closely related to the government. IEAPE was established by one of the most prominent national political leaders, Goh Keng Swee, to promote the national Confucius campaign in 1983. IPS, on the other hand, was established by Goh Chok Tong, the current Prime Minister who continues to be the Institute's patron. It received a start-up grant of S$4 million (US$2.74 million)[9] from the government of Singapore when it was founded. Sources of ISEAS's finances are, according to its 1992–93 annual report, mainly from the Singapore government's annual grant and donations from other governments, private foundations, organizations, agencies, and individuals. ISEAS's Board of Trustees also includes government officials, together with representatives of the National University of Singapore, Chambers of Commerce, and a wide spectrum of professional and civic organizations. Finally, SIIA, as an organization dedicated to promoting greater understanding and awareness of current developments in international affairs among Singaporeans, has worked very closely with the Ministry of Foreign Affairs and the Ministry of Defense, both of which are among the chief supporters of the Institute. In the western, conventional context, it would be very difficult for these institutions to maintain their independence from the government. It is obvious that the Singapore government attaches some importance to research institutions outside the government.

Closer observation of major research institutions, moreover, reveals that the leaders of these institutions are, individually, important "government" figures as well as established scholars. Tommy Koh of IPS is Singapore's Ambassador-at-Large, while Chan Heng Chee of ISEAS was Singapore's Permanent Representative to the United Nations. SIIA's chairman, Lau Teik-Soon, is Chairman of the Defense Committee of the Singaporean Parliament and one of the new generation leaders hand-picked by Lee Kwan Yew. Scholars that are close to or even a part of the government can be objects of suspicion in the western context. But in a state like Singapore where the human resource is as scarce as any other natural resource, it would be unwise of the government not to utilize the wisdom, insights, and experiences of its world-renowned intellectual experts. Both Tommy Koh and Chan Heng Chee openly admit that their respective institutes may not be able to influence the government through research reports and formal policy proposals any better than their own informal meetings and conversations with top government leaders. The dilemma, therefore, is that for these research institutions to be effective, in terms of policy impact, they must have as their representatives those intellectual leaders who are very close to the government and who can attract national leaders' attention, although these persons' presence tends to make their "independence" look rather dubious, at least from the western point of view.

Thus, the precious independence of these institutions heavily depends on the personal efforts and balancing acts of these leaders. As western-trained intellectuals themselves, they must be aware of the importance of objective research in international relations without government interference. And yet, they are fully aware of how capricious their institution's existence can be if and when they lose the government's favor. They also know how to be influential in the exclusive policy-making process. The task seems to be particularly heavy for the leaders of ISEAS since it openly claims to be a regional institution, representing the region's interests, which could be incompatible with Singapore's national interests.

Future challenges for research institutions in Singapore are two-fold. First of all, the greatest challenge for any of the major policy-oriented research institutions will be to speak openly against the few, very fundamental policies of the Republic; when this occurs the true meaning of "independence" will be tested. At the same time, it will be a major challenge for them to establish themselves, both domestically and internationally, so that they will have the government's full attention even without the help of super individuals who are closely linked with the government in addition to being outstanding scholars.

III. Profile of Major Institutions in Singapore

One feature that is distinctive to Singaporean research institutions in international relations has been their close affinity with the National University of Singapore. IEAPE is still housed physically in the Social Sciences Faculty of the university. IPS had its headquarters at the university's Department of Political Science before it moved to its present site at Hon Sui Sen Memorial Library Building on the campus. ISEAS, aside from drawing its board members from the university, frequently interacts with the university's intellectual resources. SIIA, established by a group of academics from the former University of Singapore (presently the National University of Singapore), had its headquarters at the Department of Political Science for some thirty years before it moved to its present site.

The newest addition to this list is the Centre for Advanced Studies (CAS) established in 1982 by the university's senate. Although its main feature is a post-graduate program accepting students from various countries that are broadly defined as APEC countries, it has the potential to develop into a hub of future administrative leaders in the region. It provides Asian participants with the unique experience of living and working together with, for instance, Mexican students, while it introduces the western approach to public administration to mid-career civil servants from Indo-Chinese countries.

The Information and Resource Centre (IRC) is possibly the only exception to the rule of Singaporean research institutions with close connections to the government and the National University of Singapore. It is a private limited company, having its own income-generating programs, but it claims to be "philosophically nonprofit oriented," investing its profits into its nonprofit programs. Established in 1985, it is already internationally recognized as a private, independent nongovernmental research center and, as such, it is eligible to receive grants from international foundations and corporations. As elsewhere in ASEAN countries, financial contributions from Canadian and German foundations/agencies have been remarkable, and IRC has been generously financed by the Munich-based Hanns-Seidel Foundation and the Canadian International Development Agency. IRC is also unique in its aspiration to be a regional catalyst in research, education, and human resources networking. It has a strong Asia Pacific orientation, focusing its research on sensitive issues of national and international concern which affect the evolution of the nations in the Asia Pacific region as well as the future of the region as a whole. IRC specializes in research on Indochina, the Philippines, the Southeast Asian seas and the South Pacific, as well as radical ideologies and Islam, and it is currently very active in trying to bring Vietnam into ASEAN, bringing ASEAN-ISIS delegations to Vietnam, and organizing three major conferences on the issue. Since 1992, IRC has linked up with the Singapore Institute of International Affairs, posing a grave challenge to the IRC leadership to find a balance between the nongovernmental orientation of IRC, on the one hand, and the activities and organization of SIIA which is very closely related to the Singapore government on the other.

The Institute of East Asian Political Economy (IEAPE) was established by Goh Keng-Swee, one of the right-hand aides of Lee Kwan-Yew, in 1983 as the Institute of East Asian Philosophy as part of the Singapore government's abortive drive to revive the teachings of Confucius since 1982. This drive was aimed at convincing the nation of the existence of national leaders as deities, thus, of the virtue of submitting to their guidance for economic development and prosperity. This drive, however, did not accomplish any tangible results and toward the end of the 1980s the failure of the drive became obvious. Thus, in 1989, the Institute was reorganized as an independent research institution on China's economy and politics, with John Wong, a world-renowned political scientist, as its new director, and was given its present name. Although the Institute has its own small research staff (eleven currently), its main and unique feature is some ten Chinese scholars trained in the disciplines of economics, political science, sociology, or business at the Ph.D. level, engaged in the Institute's research projects as contract researchers or short-term fellows. Another unique feature is the existence of a profit-making consulting firm within the Institute as its full subsidiary, which provides consulting services on the Chinese economy, based on a data-base constructed through the Institute's research efforts, making the Institute financially self-sustaining. Although its research is currently limited to the People's Republic of China, due to a limited number of staff, the Institute aspires to expand its programs to encompass other East Asian countries and maintains a close relationship with institutions in the region, including Chulalongkorn University's Institute of East Asian Studies in Thailand, universities and institutions in Hong Kong, and the East-West Center in Hawaii.

The Institute of Policy Studies (IPS) was established under the initiative of Prime Minister Goh Chok Tong in 1987 with the aim to be a center of policy debate and new research on underlying issues affecting Singapore and the Southeast Asian region. It is currently situated on a site on loan from the National University of Singapore, and its fourteen-member Advisory Committee includes five university faculty members. Because of its history of evolution, IPS is regarded by many as the research institution closest to the government. In fact, its current director, Tommy Koh, writes in the foreword of *Singapore: The Year in Review 1991* that it "is one of

Singapore's national think tanks" without defining it. Sasakawa Peace Foundation's 1993 study defines the IPS as "a think tank of the government," an allegation that IPS denies by stating that it is "close to the government but not part of the government." It is invited by its patron to "throw up alternative ideas and...offer constructive proposals to fine-tune existing policies;"[10] its recent research themes include a study of the impact of censorship on society. Aside from numerous research projects by its seven research staff members, including such Asia Pacific themes as subregional economic zones in Asia Pacific, economic developments in ASEAN and Asia Pacific, and trade and investment in Asia Pacific, IPS sponsors a variety of meetings, seminars, and conferences for corporate executives, journalists, and other opinion leaders, inviting senior government officials and leaders as resource persons, thus serving as "a bridge between the government, the scholars, the business community, the journalists, and other opinion-makers in Singapore."[11] It also tries to bridge the voices of Singapore's younger generation (under the age of thrity-five) to those of the older, founding father generation through a new program for the younger generation. The most recent frontier of IPS is collaboration with other institutions both within and outside of Singapore, including the Institute of Southeast Asian Studies, the Singapore International Foundation, and the Asia Society of New York.

The Institute of Southeast Asian Studies (ISEAS), by far the most well-known among the think tanks and research institutions in the region, is completely different from other research institutions located in Singapore because it is the only regional institute that is oriented toward Southeast Asian area studies. Established originally through an act of parliament as an autonomous organization in 1968, ISEAS, in the following twenty-five years, became the regional research center for scholars and other specialists studying stability and security, economic development, and political and social change in contemporary Southeast Asia. Although its infrastructure in manpower administration and other operating facilities are funded by an annual Singapore government grant, it does not receive research contracts or other project grants from the government, in order to maintain its independence. In fact, the past and present leadership of ISEAS should be given credit for developing it into a global intellectual center of Southeast Asian studies without compromising its independence in a country like Singapore where the state has consistently exercised tight control over the society. As the regional research center for Southeast Asia, ISEAS has always had a strong Asia Pacific orientation in its programs of research, fellowship, and conferences. With the Institute's ASEAN Economic Research Unit, Regional Strategic Studies Programme, Social Issues in Southeast Asia, and Southeast Asian Cultural Research Programme, many of ISEAS's projects are concentrated on ASEAN or the wider Southeast Asia and Pacific regions. Asked about the relationship between ISEAS as a regional research center and ASEAN-ISIS, Chan Heng Chee explained that individual members of the latter more or less represent their own national interests, while ISEAS does not represent any single national interest, including Singapore's. As the regional center for research and study, it grants various fellowships for Asia Pacific studies, including the Research Fellowship in Australian-Southeast Asian Relations, the Research Fellowship in ASEAN Affairs, the Research Fellowship in South-Southeast Asian Relations, and the Research Fellowship in Canadian-Southeast Asian Relations. These fellowships are funded by such organizations as the Ford and Rockefeller Foundations, USIS, and the Governments of Australia and New Zealand. Aside from these overseas institutions and Singaporean foundations, ISEAS annually receives donations and grants from such sources as the Canada-ASEAN Centre, the International Development Research Centre, Canada, and the Konrad Adenauer Foundation, again indicating substantial contributions by Canadian and German institutions in Southeast Asian intellectual endeavors. ISEAS also receives grants from Japanese foundations, i.e., the Sasakawa Peace Foundation, which is the third largest donor and the Tokyo Club Foundation for Global Studies.

The Singapore Institute of International Affairs (SIIA) is the oldest research institution in Singapore, established as early as 1961 by a group of academics from the National University of Singapore (then University of Singapore) in response to the need for a regular forum to promote greater understanding and awareness of current developments in international affairs among Singaporeans. Although it is recognized as a nongovernmental think tank, being the Singaporean founding member of ASEAN-ISIS, it is regarded to be among the closest to the government. When SIIA linked up with the above Information and Resource Centre, arguably the most independent of Singaporean institutions, some wondered if the coupling would lead to a "happy marriage." SIIA aims to promote public awareness and interests in contemporary issues of international politics and regional security through international conferences, workshops, seminars, and public lectures; to facilitate contacts among ASEAN and the wider international community of scholars, policymakers, and opinion makers; and to study international and regional issues through the preparation and publication of books and other works. As such, SIIA's program includes a number of directly Asia Pacific related projects such as international conferences on "the Japanese Role in the Asian-Pacific Region and Its Implications for the United States and ASEAN," "The Soviet Union in the Asia Pacific Region," and

"The Security of the Sea Lanes in the Asia Pacific Region." Under the new directorship of M. Rajaretnam, SIIA's operational focus will be shifted toward an inquiry of what Singapore can and should do to promote the development of other Asian countries. Aside from membership dues and various fees, SIIA receives grants and donations from Singaporean and international foundations, including the Asia Foundation, Friedrich Neumann Stiftung, and the Ford Foundation.

Notes

1. Chan Heng Chee in an interview in November 1994.
2. Chan Heng Chee, "Singapore 1991: Dealing with a Post–Cold War World," in *Singapore: The Year in Review 1991* edited by Lee Tsao Yuan (Singapore: Institute of Policy Studies, 1992).
3. Tommy T.B. Koh, "External Relations," in *Singapore: The Year in Review 1990*, edited by Tan Teng Lang (Singapore: Institute of Policy Studies, 1991).
4. Suzaina A. Kadir, " Singapore's Security Amidst Change: Problems and Prospects"at the sixth ASEAN-Japan Dialogue, Osio, Japan, 1992.
5. Pang Eng Fong, "The Concept of a Pan-Pacific Community and ASEAN: A View from Singapore" in *The Pacific Community Concept: Views from Eight Nations* (the proceedings of the Asian Dialogue at Osio, Japan, January 1980. Tokyo: JCIE, 1980, p. 82.
6. Koh, op. cit., p. 94.
7. N. Genesan, "Singapore's Foreign Policy in ASEAN" (Ph.D. dissertation, Northern Illinois University, 1989), quoted in Kadir, op. cit.
8. Economist Intelligence Unit, *The ASEAN Countries: Economic Structure and Analysis* (London: EIU, 1989), p. 160.
9. International Monetary Fund, *International Financial Statistics*, January 1995 (Washington, D.C.: IMF). Figures are based on the end of the period exchange rate for November 1994. US$1=S$1.46.
10. *The IPS Report: The First Five Years (1987–1992).*
11. Ibid.

TAIWAN

The Major Asia Pacific Research Institutions and Think Tanks in Taiwan

Hsin-Huang Michael Hsiao
Research Fellow
Institute of Sociology
Academia Sinica

I. Introduction

The main purpose of this report is to introduce and assess those major research institutions and think tanks in Taiwan for which an Asia Pacific focus can be clearly identified in recent research and exchange activities.

Generally speaking, Taiwan's research community—both public and private universities and research institutions—has not been very active in conducting studies focused on the Asia Pacific region, even though Taiwan is an integral part of this geopolitical and economic community. One reason is that Taiwan's diplomatic isolation has hindered the active and formal ties and cooperation between Taiwanese academics and their potential counterparts in many other Asia Pacific countries. Recently, however, the ascending economic status that Taiwan has enjoyed has begun to open possibilities for Taiwan to develop institutionalized scholarly exchange and cooperation with a few selected countries in the region.

The establishment of genuinely private think tanks is a rather new phenomenon in Taiwan; accordingly, the number of accredited and well-endowed nongovernment research institutions is still very small. The first private think tank—the 21st Century Foundation—was established as late as 1988. It was then joined in 1989 by the Institute for National Policy Research (INPR) and the Taiwan Research Fund in 1990. However, only the first two private think tanks have engaged in Asia Pacific related programs.

There are a few graduate institutes or centers for Asia Pacific area studies in various public and private universities, but none of those university centers have been active in developing research programs or establishing collaboration with other universities in the region. They are more or less merely faculty groups in that they provide courses for interested students or, at best, managing contract research projects on related topics.

However, there are a few governmental and semi-governmental research institutions and think tanks in Taiwan that have increased their attention to Asia Pacific regional research and exchange in recent years. Among them, the Institute of International Relations (IIR), the Chung-Hua Institution for Economic Research (CIER), and Taiwan Institute of Economic Research (TIER) are the most noticeable cases. Since 1994, Taiwan's foremost national research institution, Academia Sinica, established the Program for Southeast Asian Area Studies (PSEAAS) to facilitate and sponsor Southeast Asian research projects within humanities and social science institutes. The above six research institutes and think tanks will be the main foci of this report in evaluating Taiwan's emerging Asia Pacific research orientation.

II. Governmental Research Institutions

1. Program for Southeast Asian Area Studies (PSEAAS), Academia Sinica

Director: Dr. K. C. Chang (Vice-President, Academia Sinica)
Associate Director: Dr. H. H. Michael Hsiao, Institute of Ethnology
Address: 128 Academy Rd. Sect. 2, Nankang, Taipei, Taiwan
Tel: 886-2-789-9319, 9320 *Fax:* 886-2-785-5836, 7888911
PSEAAS, recently formed in 1994, is a multi-disciplinary and cross-institute research coordinating program in Academia Sinica. Its purpose is to encourage, support and coordinate social science research on Southeast Asia by resident research fellows in various institutes of the Academy. For its first year program, there are currently sixteen individual projects being conducted by eighteen research fellows, and the subjects include archaeology, linguistics, history, economics, sociology, and political science. PSEAAS has designated the following four general areas for its future research directions:

(1) Austronesian History
(2) Religions and Indigenous Culture in Southeast Asia
(3) Post-colonial Development in Southeast Asian Peoples
(4) Interaction between the Chinese and Southeast Asian Peoples

PSEAAS plans to publish a Southeast Asian Area working paper series, to develop contacts and exchange with research institutes in Southeast Asian countries, and to organize regional and international workshops or conferences. Though it is still in a very formative stage of development, it is Taiwan's only Southeast Asian Area Studies program. As it has the Academy's full support and is already equipped with research facilities and manpower, PSEAAS is expected to become one of the most productive scholarly Asia Pacific research centers in the region.

2. The Institute of International Relations (IIR), National Chengchi University

Direction: Dr. Yu-Ming Shaw
Address: 64 Wan Shou Road, Wenshan, Taipei, Taiwan
Tel: 886-2-939-4921 *Fax:* 886-2-938-2133

IIR was established in 1953. It began as an organ for intelligence analysis on Mainland Chinese affairs. Later, it came to resemble a special research arm of the government more than a wholly independent research institution or think tank. It is fully financed by government funds channeled through National Chengchi University. IIR regularly provides consultations to such government offices as the President's Office, the Ministry of Foreign Affairs, and the Commission of Mainland Affairs. Within IIR, there are four departments: International Affairs, Chinese Communist Affairs, International Communist Affairs, and Economic Affairs. It publishes *Issues and Studies* (in five languages), *Mainland China Studies, East Asia Quarterly*, and *America and Europe Monthly* (all in Chinese). IIR employs more than one hundred full-time researchers.

The most effective way in which IIR expands its contact and exchange with foreign academic institutions is by cosponsoring regular conferences between IIR and other concerned institutions. In addition to its well established Sino-American and Sino-European conference arrangements, IIR has also developed an institutionalized cosponsorship with the Japanese Association for Mainland China Studies since 1971, and the Asia Open Forum (Japan) since 1989. With different Korean collaborative organizations such as the Korean National Unification Board, the Institute of International Peace Studies, the Institute for East Asian Studies (Sogang University), and the Seoul Forum for Institutional Affairs, IIR has also developed regular Sino-Korean Conferences. All the above annual conferences are held alternately in Taiwan and the cosponsoring countries.

The Asia Pacific focus has increasingly become a new direction for IIR's research and consultation endeavors. Especially since the government, for both economic and diplomatic reasons, has pronounced its South-oriented external policy with

Southeast Asia a new focus of flexible diplomacy, IIR has also begun to redirect its attention to this region. It has expressed its eagerness to develop fruitful networks with research institutions, think tanks, and nongovernmental organizations in various countries in Southeast Asia.

III. Semi-Governmental Research Institutions and Think Tanks

1. Chung-Hua Institution for Economic Research (CIER)

Director: Dr. Tsong-Shian Yu
Address: 75 Chang-Hsing St., Taiwan
Tel: 886-2-735-6006 *Fax:* 886-2-733-0030

CIER was founded by the government in 1981, to act as a nonprofit and autonomous think tank. Though some of the endowment funds come from donations by private local enterprises, CIER functions more like a semi-governmental research institute with a clear designation to undertake macroeconomic studies and other theoretical work. It has more than eighty full-time researchers working in three different areas: international economic research, Mainland China economic research, and Taiwan economic research. CIER also receives government grants to study various policy issues related to Mainland Chinese and local economies. It also hosts various forums and conferences, and publishes research papers and conference proceedings.

Regarding its Asia Pacific connections, CIER has the following regular activities:

(1) Annual conference on Pacific Trade and Development with the Australian National University

(2) Annual Conference in Northeast Asia Round Table

(3) Joint Conference of CIER and the Korea Development Institute (KDI)

CIER also maintains good exchange and collaborative relations with the following government and private Asia Pacific think tanks: KDI (Korea), Nomura Research Institute (Japan), the Center for Asian Studies (Hong Kong), the Center for Policy and Implementation Studies (Malaysia), the Institute of Strategic and International Studies (Indonesia), the Center for Research and Communications (Philippines), the Institute for Southeast Asian Studies (Singapore), and the Thailand Development Research Institute. CIER has demonstrated a great interest in further developing bilateral cooperation with many other well-established research institutions in Asian countries.

IV. Nongovernmental Research Institutions and Think Tanks

1. Taiwan Institute of Economic Research (TIER)

Director: Dr. Rong-I Wu
Address: 6F, 33, Lane 11, Kuang Fu North Rd. Taipei, Taiwan
Tel: 886-2-762-7078 *Fax:* 886-2-762-6972, 886-2-768-9485

TIER was established in 1976 under the sponsorship of the Taiwan Economic Research Foundation, a corporate foundation founded by Taiwan Cement Corporation and China Trust and Investment Corporation, under the direction of the Koo family. TIER was designed to serve the needs of local businesses, academic institutions and the government for up-to-date economic information and advice. TIER consciously copied the Japanese model of combining the resources of business, government, and academia in finding answers to national economic problems. Therefore, TIER is a policy-oriented private research institute, though it receives handsome grants every year from various government agencies to carry out related research projects.

In 1985, when the Ministry of Economic Affairs proposed setting up the Industrial Development Advisory Council to help restructure Taiwan's industrial sector, TIER became a chartered research body of the government and was delegated all the research work of the new Council. TIER's research work is divided into two types, those that flow from the specific interests of individual researchers, and those that are in response to outside requests. They all deal with practical topics. The Institute's publications list is lengthy, and invariably illustrates the highly practical nature of the Institute's research. In many respects, the reports are what one could expect from a large U.S. consulting firm.

In contrast with CIER, TIER relies heavily on income from contracted research projects. Over on hundred researchers work at TIER, and are assigned to one of its seven research divisions. The seven research divisions work as independent units, and each shares half the profits of its work within the Institute. This is a rather unique responsibility and reward system.

TIER also has collaborative relations with the following Japanese research institutions:

(1) Daiwa Institute of Research, Ltd.

TIER jointly worked with Daiwa Institute to develop Taiwan's econometric model and reported the results in June 1994.

(2) The Long-term Credit Bank of Japan, Ltd.

TIER was requested to collect information on the Taiwan portion of the

"Multinational Corporations and Local Business Responses in East Asia" research project.

(3) The Export-Import Bank of Japan

TIER has planned to develop further exchange relations with this Japanese bank.

2. The Institute for National Policy Research (INPR)

Director: Dr. Hung-Mao Tien
Executive Director: Mr. Huey-Tsen Huang
Address: 5F, 111, Sung-Chiang Rd., Taipei, Taiwan
Tel: 886-2-509-9181 (-7) *Fax:* 886-2-509-2949

INPR was set up in 1989 by the Chang Yung-Fa Foundation, established by its namesake, who is chairman of the Evergreen Line and Taiwan's wealthiest shipping magnate. It was designed to be a genuine private think tank with twenty-five full-time research fellows and a number of consultants. INPR conducts in-house research on a wide range of domestic and international policy issues. The Institute is divided into two departments—administration and research. The latter has five general sections: international affairs, law and politics, finance and economy, society, and culture. According to INPR, there are five general areas with which the government has failed to deal well, and they are its main target of concern. On the domestic front, the full implementation of the ROC constitution, environment and ecology, land rezoning, social welfare, culture, and ethics reform are currently the major concerns. In the international arena, Taiwan's economic status in the world, its renewed participation in international organizations, relations between Taiwan and Mainland China, and Taiwan's integration into the political and economic community of Southeast Asia are rising to the forefront of research activities. INPR regularly hosts conferences, seminars and press conferences to publicize its research findings. The Institute also makes its research findings known through publication efforts. INPR produces *National Policy Dynamic Analysis* (a Chinese bi-weekly magazine) and the Think Tank Book Series (in both Chinese and English).

On-going research projects and publications have reflected INPR's concentration on issues in Taiwan and Asia Pacific relations. Books like: *The Breakthrough of Relations across Taiwan Straits*, *Economic and Trade Relations across Taiwan Straits*, *Taiwan's Asia Pacific Strategy*, *Information and Profile of Asia Pacific*, *Taiwan-Hong Kong Relations*, and *The Asian Regional Economy* are examples which highlight INPR's recent research efforts. In fact, INPR has even formed an Asia Pacific task force to deal with this specific research issue.

INPR's growing visibility has attracted quite a few visitors to its operations to visit its facility and has fostered the development of long-term collaborative relations with foreign scholars and think tanks.

3. The 21st Century Foundation

Chairman: Mr. Yu-Jen Kao
President: Dr. Ying-Mao Kau
Address: 9/10F, 380, Keelung Rd. Sec 1., Taipei, Taiwan
Tel: 886-2-758-6306 *Fax:* 886-2-723-5705

The 21st Century Foundation is the first private think tank in Taiwan, though it was established in the form of a foundation in 1988. The Foundation is funded by donations from Taiwan's businesses and corporations. Its overall goal, well in the mainstream of think tanks in other countries, is to act as a catalyst in the process of public policy making by integrating the scholarly community with the business and government sectors. Since its establishment, the Foundation's priorities have ranged from issues concerning parliamentary reform, Mainland policy, and the development of party politics, to financial liberalization, university law, and annual culture evaluation and assessment. It also conducts annual opinion surveys of the public's attitudes toward Taiwan's social, political, and economic conditions.

The Foundation consists of six R&D committees that focus their analytic efforts on political, legal, economic, social, cultural, and educational areas, with outside scholars as consulting members. The Foundation does not carry out in-house research because it has no in-house full-time researchers and, in most cases, it contracts out to scholars and specialists for different research projects. Therefore, the Foundation, in a strict sense, still falls short of qualifying as a genuine think tank due to its lack of high-level in-house researchers.

Nevertheless, the Foundation does have an impact on the government's policy–making process by organizing conferences on timely issues such as Taiwan-Mainland China relations, Taiwan's evolving role in the Asia Pacific region, Taiwanese investment in China, and the future prospects of Mainland policy. The Foundation is also in a position to develop more active collaborations with other research institutes and think tanks in the Asia Pacific region.

V. Concluding Remarks

As stated at the outset of this report, Taiwan's research activities on Asia Pacific were not visible until as late as the early 1990s. However, once the necessity of Taiwan's participation in the emerging Asia Pacific Regional Community was recognized, the governmental, semi-governmental, and nongovernmental research community began to pay greater attention to developing active connections with their counterparts in East and Southeast Asian countries. The interest and motivation are evident and serious, and actual steps are being taken by the research institutions and think tanks as discussed in this report. In a sense, the recent moves of Taiwan's research community into Asia Pacific regional issues have been rather late, considering the past decade or more of active involvement of Taiwanese private business in the region.

Finally, it is expected that the growing focus of interest in Mainland China and Southeast Asia will reach a new high in the near future. Therefore, research efforts on these two areas will bring about closer and more institutionalized relations between institutes in Taiwan, Mainland China, and Southeast Asian nations.

THAILAND

Independent Policy Research Institutions in Thailand

From the Viewpoint of Asia Pacific Intellectual Cooperation

Makito Noda
Senior Program Officer
Japan Center for International Exchange

I. Thailand's Asia Pacific Orientation

Recent history of Thailand's external relations has witnessed two major shifts which reflect larger changes taking place at the societal level in Thailand and its international environment. First of all, Thailand's foreign policy was released from the strong grip of a military whose utmost concern was national security, particularly vis-à-vis neighboring Indochinese countries, and became, like many other countries around the world, an instrument of economic expansion. Second, Thailand has been released from its almost obsessive preoccupation with Vietnam and Cambodia to expand its horizons to include increased multilateral relations with other ASEAN countries and the larger Asia Pacific region.

Since the end of World War II, but particularly after the Communist victory in Indochina, Thailand has found itself at the front line of an ideological contest running across Southeast Asia. The Vietnamese invasion of Cambodia in 1979, moreover, brought the threat of communism right up to its immediate eastern borders. In the cold war world, this was a threat to its very national survival, making national security, particularly vis-à-vis Indochina, the most immediate concern of Thailand's external relations. On top of these developments, historically, Thailand has always been in competition with Vietnam regarding influence over Laos and Cambodia. Thus, external relations after World War II meant, first of all, dealings with Cambodia and Vietnam, which was the domain of the military, followed by relations with major external allies, particularly the United States and China who could support Thailand against threats from Vietnam. In fact, it has been pointed out that "a rough division of labor existed in which the national security establishment took command of Thailand's immediate security and allowed the Foreign Ministry to maintain relations with the outside world,"[1] including not only the United States, China, and other major powers but also the ASEAN countries. Moreover, from the viewpoint of support in its struggle against Vietnam, the United States and China were actually given precedence in Thai diplomacy in the 1970s and 1980s, over Thailand's ASEAN partners.

The Cambodian settlement in the late 1980s was the first in a chain of important events that eventually released Thailand's foreign policy from the spellbinding concern over security, followed by the end of the cold war and the more localized effects stemming from the general liberalization taking place in Vietnam. The energy and wisdom thus wasted in its obsession with national security could now be directed to national development, making the latter half of the 1980s a period of high economic growth. Under these circumstances foreign policy was given a new role as the vehicle for economic expansion. National leaders, civilian as well as military, began to talk of the new importance of Indochina, i.e., as the field for economic advancement. They advocated the importance of developing economic relations with Indochina and bringing it into the wider community of Southeast Asian states, the beginning of a more regional, multilateral perspective. Thailand, according to them, must aspire to be an economic power in mainland Southeast Asia. Many eye-catching slogans emerged during this period, including "Thailand as the gateway to Indochina," "Thailand as a financial gateway to the region," and "Thailand's role as a bridge between mainland Southeast Asia and the outside world." A plan was proposed to develop a growth quadrangle involving southern China, Laos, Myanmar, and northern Thailand. In a conference organized for the fifth phase ASEAN-Japan Dialogue, a prominent Thai economist spoke of ATIC, meaning the Association of Thailand-Indochinese Countries, in reference to ASEAN's approach to Indochinese countries. Myanmar has also been in the scope of Thailand's Indochina policy. Regarding Myanmar as a land bridge for trade between southern China and the Indian Ocean, Thailand has attempted to integrate this self-alienating country into mainstream Southeast Asia.

Thailand's attitude toward the great powers has also undergone a significant change now that it does not have to depend so much on their support and assistance in the wake of the Cambodian issue. But, more significantly, Thailand has changed its approach to its regional partners, particularly the ASEAN countries.

Buszynski finds that "the change has been swift and has been demonstrated by the new found interest in ASEAN and Asia Pacific multilateralism,"[2] and attributes this change to two factors. First, many of the sources of tensions with other member countries were eliminated by the Cambodian settlement, most notably with Indonesia over their relations with and approaches to China. But most importantly, Thai leaders seem to have finally realized that "Thailand's regional policy required ASEAN endorsement and had to be formulated within the framework of Southeast Asian regionalism for it to succeed." Thailand's role in mainland Southeast Asia, which Thai leaders have been very concerned about, was found to be "dependent to a large degree upon Asia Pacific multilateralism and regional economic cooperation."

It was, then, very symbolic that Thailand, in October 1993, after years of close ties with the United States, quietly became a member of the Non-Aligned Movement which has been chaired by its former archrival, Indonesia. Thailand joined the Movement, according to the official announcement, because it had transformed itself from an institution for ideological advocacy under the cold war system, into an economic cooperation movement that would benefit Thailand through wider market access and a stronger collective voice in international fora. Now that Thailand's foreign policy direction has shifted from obsession with immediate security to economic expediency, on one hand, and from almost exclusive concern about its immediate northern neighbors to wider, regional cooperation on the other, Thailand's orientation toward Asia Pacific cooperation is expected to be deepened and widened. However, it may continue to have a certain degree of "Indochina bias," so to speak, for quite some time. When heads of representative research institutions in Bangkok were interviewed about their Asia Pacific–related activities in the summer of 1993, most of them first referred to, for instance, joint programs with Vietnamese institutions and exchange programs with Cambodian and Myanmar organizations.

II. Circumstances Surrounding Research Institutions in Thailand

The Non-Aligned Movement is not the only factor that Thailand shares with Indonesia. Ever since the 1932 coup that toppled the absolute monarchy and brought about the adoption of the so-called constitutional monarchy, the military has constantly played the key political role in Thailand. In fact, military leaders believe they have the responsibility to lead and guide the country through the transition to a full democracy. In place of the Indonesian concept of "dual function" of the military force, Thai politics has been based on a concept that is often referred to as "Thai-style democracy," a concept first introduced by the military leadership in the 1960s. This concept is composed of three key elements: maintenance of a political regime with the king as the sovereign; participation by the political leader that supersedes the parliament and political parties; and pursuit of the people's welfare and social justice by these leaders. This concept, thus, has provided the military with the legitimacy to intervene in politics and, when deemed necessary, take over the government. Coups d'état (eleven between 1932 and 1973) have become "an institutionalized means for political leaders to alternate in power."

In fact, over the past sixty years, politics in Thailand has evolved in a pattern that has come to be known as the "vicious cycle of politics," whereby military leaders stage a coup to abrogate the constitution in force, reintroduce participatory institutions of some kind, try but fail to keep control of such institutions, and again stage a coup to avert a "political crisis." This traditional pattern has also hampered the healthy growth of the parliament and political parties, two of the key institutions for popular political participation. Political parties were denounced by the military as "selfish special interest groups that do not genuinely represent the interests of various levels of Thai citizens" in as early as the 1960s, and they were not tolerated in Thai politics until very recently.

However, under pressure provided by economic development and growth, the Thai political system was also forced to change, and by the late 1970s, under the Prem administration, gradual political liberalization began. According to Sukhumbhand Partibatra, it was this period that witnessed "the expanding role of the private sector and nongovernmental organizations." The private sector gained the privilege of participation in policy formulation through affiliations with political parties and through government-initiated or government-related fora, such as the Joint Public and Private Consultative Committee. Nongovernmental organizations in this period also proliferated both in number and function particularly in social and economic fields that have been neglected by the government. At the same time, a "high degree of intellectual and media freedom" was attained, reducing the number of "untouchable" subjects for public discussion and liberating the production of programs and presentation of news stories. However, this period is in retrospect referred to as "liberalization without democracy" because, after all, it was not able to prevent another military intervention in 1992. This signified the fact that the guardian mentality of the military was largely preserved among its leadership, on one hand, and the delay in the development of parliamentary democratic institutions on the other. Sukhumbhand Paribatra summarizes the situation as follows:

> All this suggests that the military rejected the underlying ideals and political consequences of Western-style liberal democracy, and preferred bureaucratically guided liberalization expressed in terms of limited, controlled participation that emphasized consensus over competition, a minimally active legislature over an active and potent one, appointments over elections, and centralization over decentralization of power.[3]

But the citizens' protests which followed what many Thai watchers believe to be the last military take-over of the government, revealed to the world the emergence of a new, participatory "middle class" in Thailand. Whereas the anti-military movement of the early 1970s was led by and consisted of students and the more radical elements of Thai society, the anti-Suchinda movement in 1992 was "very broad-based both in leadership and rank-and-file participation." Most notably, it included a large number of well-dressed, professional middle-class citizens. With the emergence of this "large reservoir of well-educated, relatively well-paid people, predisposed to the principles, ideals, and practice of democracy and voluntary political participation and, when necessary, willing to make their views known," it is evident that Thai politics will undergo some fundamental changes in the years to come.

Meanwhile, the Thai economy continued to grow rapidly, despite the frequent occurrence of military coups and political instability. Many watchers attribute this phenomenon to the dominant role played by the bureaucracy in policy making and formulation. Against this backdrop, there has been little space for independent research institutions to contribute to national policy formation, particularly in the heavily security-oriented area of foreign policy. In fact, the number of independent research institutions is fairly limited, most of them being affiliated with national universities such as Chulalongkorn and Thammasat and, therefore, classified as "governmental" institutions. Directors and senior staff members of these institutions are normally professors of these universities concurrently, and they admit that they are often consulted by the government on various policy matters. But they attribute this phenomenon to their personal relationship with government and administration leaders.

It has only been in recent years that independent institutions have evolved in policy-related fields in Thailand, including the earliest Institute of Security and International Studies in 1981 and newer ones such as the Thailand Development Research Institute and the Thailand Institute of Public and International Affairs in the late 1980s.

However, with the emergence of a more participatory political culture as seen above, the need for sources of independent policy alternatives is expected to increase greatly in the coming years. The recent expansion of the role of nongovernmental organizations and initiatives in Thailand has been remarkable, transforming the civil sector from "a dirty word" into a certain social and political force. *The Asia Survey* review of Thailand in 1993 points to the "support and guidance from nongovernmental organizations" as one of the forces that have "increased the people's political awareness." The Thai government for their part has also recognized the important role nongovernmental initiatives can play, and has started supporting them financially and otherwise. In terms of the "civil society," therefore, Thailand seems to have leaped from the stone age to the very frontier. Under these circumstances, one can expect a greater role to be played by independent research institutions in the future. Particularly with the relative decline of military power in Thai politics, the field of international security will be an area open for independent, nongovernmental analysis.

III. Profile of Major Independent Research Institutions in Thailand

As mentioned above, the number of independent research institutions that conduct policy-oriented research in Thailand has been very limited. Almost all of these institutions are university-affiliated and, therefore, cannot be regarded as fully independent. Intellectuals in Thailand attribute this phenomenon to the following factors:

a. the high status attached to professorship, leading researchers to aspire toward promotion to professorship, which, ironically, has adversely affected the development of research institutions as a professional career path;
b. secure funding through the university coffer; and
c. secure supply of scarce human resources.

On top of these universally acceptable explanations, the director of a Chulalongkorn University-affiliated institute added that the independence of their study has been protected from outside interference by the prestige of the university.

However, many scholars and institute leaders believe the largest impediment to more independent institutions remains financial, particularly when "there is no tradition for private corporations to finance nongovernmental initiatives in Thailand, and, thus, those nongovernmental institutions have no other recourse than to turn to foreign funding sources."[4] The awareness of the importance of independence has already been widely shared by these intellectuals.

One institute among various university-affiliated institutions merits special attention in the current survey because of its field of specialty. The Institute of East Asian Studies (IEAS) was established in 1984 within Thammasat University by "lecturer-level young scholars who had come back from studies in Japan and felt the need to deepen Thailand's understanding of Japan's economy, politics, society, and culture."[5] It is well known that the Japanese government made a substantial contribution to the starting up of this institute. IEAS's research projects include both basic and applied research carried out by the Institute's researchers as well as by professors of various faculties in Thammasat University in the fields of Japanese studies, Chinese studies, and Korean studies, including each country's politics, economy, culture, and relations with Thailand. Recent projects include a study of the transfer of Japanese technology to Taiwan and trade relations between Thailand and Japan. It also sponsors training programs for high school teachers and teachers college students on Japan, China, and Korea. As a future plan, IEAS is considering a program for interaction between Japanese political leaders (including Diet members) and regional political leaders and scholars.

Chulalongkorn University hosts two research institutions that are relevant to the current survey: the Institute of Asian Studies and the Institute of Security and International Studies. But their status vis-à-vis the university is regarded to be somewhat more independent than the above Institute of East Asian Studies, making them quasi-independent entities. The Institute of Asian Studies (IAS) was originally established as a unit of Chulalongkorn's Faculty of Political Science in 1967, but it was promoted to a separate University Institute, a status equivalent to that of a University Faculty, in May 1985. As such, IAS functions as "an intra-university, inter-university and intercommunity organization."[6] In the *Directory of Research and Training Institutions and Organizations* compiled by the Asia Pacific Development Centre,[7] IAS is classified as "governmental but autonomous." It aims to promote interdisciplinary Asian studies and contribute to the better understanding of Asian affairs in Thailand as well as mutual understanding among Asian countries through research and other intellectual activities. Recent research themes include "Sino-Thai Entrepreneurs in Thailand: Economic and Political Involvement, 1973–Present;" "Japanese Investment in the Advertising Business: A Study of Roles and Impact on Thailand's National Development;" "The Process of Becoming NICs in South Korea, Taiwan, Singapore, and Hong Kong and the Implications for Thailand;" "Prospects for Trade between Thailand and the Indochinese States;" "Thai-Laotian Economic Relations;" "Lao Returnees of the Voluntary Repatriation from Thailand;"

"Problems of Minority Groups along the Thai-Burmese Border;" and "Trend of Investment by NICs and Japan in Vietnam and Related Problems." These themes clearly reflect the general emphasis on relations with Indochinese countries. The Institute conducts contractual research projects for various government councils as well as the National Security Council and the Foreign Ministry, but the former and current directors of the Institute believe that it is more through informal and interpersonal communications and dialogues that they feel themselves involved in policy formulation.[8] Nevertheless, the Institute frequently receives inquiries and questions from the government on their research works. As a government university unit, IAS receives allocations from national and university budgets annually, but this has proven to be short of covering the institute's total operating costs. IAS, therefore, has to rely on international as well as domestic public and private sources for some forty-five percent of their annual budget (in the case of FY1992). Among major overseas donors are American foundations (The Asia Foundation and Ford Foundation), Friedrich Ebert Stiftung, the International Development Research Centre, and Japanese individuals and institutions, including the Keizo Shibusawa Memorial Fund.

The Institute of Security and International Studies (ISIS) is the Thai counterpart of the ASEAN-ISIS network, and therefore, one of the most externally connected institutes in Thailand. ISIS was originally established in 1981 as the Southeast Asian Studies Program of the Faculty of Political Science but eventually turned into an institution officially sanctioned by Chulalongkorn University in February 1982. It aims to promote knowledge and understanding of various international and security issues, particularly those directly and indirectly affecting Thailand and Southeast Asia; help pinpoint problems, pose questions, and identify policy issues for purposes of advocacy; and enhance the general public's awareness and understanding of strategic and international issues by conducting independent, academic research on and disseminating knowledge of international and strategic issues. ISIS's major areas of research include Thailand's defense and foreign policies, various aspects of the Thai communist insurgency problem, the Cambodia conflict, and the relationship between the environment and security, areas traditionally being monopolized by the government and the military. The current director of ISIS, Dr. Kusuma Snitwongse, emphasized the importance of ISIS's independence because "the areas with which ISIS is concerned have long been monopolized by the government and, therefore, needed inquiry from the independent viewpoint."[9] Recent research projects and conferences include "Time on Whose Side in Cambodia?" "Conflict and Transition in the Vietnamese Economic Reform Program,"

"ASEAN-Pacific Cooperation and Pacific Regionalism," "Crisis in Burma," and "Future of ASEAN-Vietnam Relations." Some of these programs are conducted jointly with overseas institutions such as ISIS's ASEAN-ISIS partners, the Institute of Southeast Asian Studies in Singapore, as well as the University of California's Institute of East Asian Studies and International Institute for Strategic Studies.

ISIS is funded mainly by grants from major international philanthropic organizations, including the Ford Foundation, the Asia Foundation, and the Rockefeller Foundation. Funds provided by the university and the government are supplementary grants on a project-by-project basis.

While the above institutions are all affiliated with universities, there are two newer institutions that appear to be organizationally more independent than the above organizations. The Thailand Development Research Institute Foundation (TDRI) is regarded to be "Thailand's first policy research institute" and registered by the government as a nonprofit, nongovernmental foundation. Because TDRI was created under the initiative of the National Economic and Social Development Board (NESDB), using start-up funds provided by the Canadian International Development Agency, some claim that it is "implicitly supported by NESDB, the government," pointing to the contracted projects commissioned on TDRI (ninety percent of TDRI's annual revenue) from NESDB without competition. While policy formulation and deliberation have been monopolized by the government, it has had to commission policy-related research to universities since government agencies are "too bureaucratic for policy research," a satisfactory arrangement in terms of the quality of research but questionable in terms of continuity.[10] Against this background, TDRI was established specifically to conduct policy research. It aims to conduct and promote research into Thailand's economic and social development; to establish an information center containing updated information on relevant policy issues; to create a research network linking institutions and individuals engaged in policy research issues; and to disseminate its research findings to maximize their impact on decision-making, public opinion, and public awareness. Research projects are conducted in the program areas of energy, infrastructure, and urban development; human resources and social development; international economic relations; macroeconomic policy; natural resources and the environment; science and technology development; and sectoral economics. In the first five years, TDRI completed ninety-eight research projects, followed by forty-four projects and fifty-one projects respectively in 1990 and 1991 alone. Among recent projects which are relevant to the current survey are "Thailand/ASEAN Economic Transformation into NIC Status," "Thailand in the International Economic Community," "ASEAN-U.S.

Initiatives Study," "The Asia Pacific Project," and "Thailand's Export-led Growth." The Sasakawa study introduces Thailand's mass media's assessment that "TDRI is the real policy maker in Thailand," and attributes this prominence partly to the TDRI's Council of Trustees which is very international in composition and includes three Japanese members.

In terms of its Asia Pacific networks, TDRI closely collaborates with Harvard University's Institute of International Development, the Economic Council of Canada, as well as Japan's National Institute for Research Advancement. It is part of the Asia Forum network of think tanks set up on the initiative of the Nomura Research Institute and the Tokyo Club Foundation for Global Studies of Japan.

According to the current director, the Thailand Institute of Public and International Affairs (TIPIA) is not a research institution itself, but it tries to promote research in public and international affairs, encouraging existing research capabilities to conduct projects in these fields by providing financial and other support. It was established on the basis of the growing pluralistic nature of Thai society that demands greater cooperation among the public and private sectors in dealing with issues of national concern. It aspires to serve as a non-partisan organization which attempts to bridge the gap between the public and private sectors at both the domestic and international levels. In order to promote the generation and dissemination of information and policy options surrounding important issues and support the dissemination of perspectives on public and international issues by public, private, local, and foreign organizations, TIPIA cooperates with local and international research institutes to develop projects in the areas of public policy and international affairs, along with other programs such as a fellowship program, forum program, publication program, and outreach program. The emergence of TIPIA is a new development in Thailand, which does not have a tradition of privately funded policy-oriented research, and therefore, merits special attention from the viewpoint of the emerging civil society.

IV. Future Prospects

Although there is no guarantee that the "vicious cycle of Thai politics" will not reemerge in the future, the overwhelming trend seems to be toward more liberalization and citizen participation in politics, including the policy making process. In particular, the emergence of a middle class that is politically active will provide effective protection against the revival of a military dictatorship. Together with political liberalization, the scope of fields which have traditionally been monopolized by the government will be minimized, opening new frontiers to independent policy research. Inferring from the remarkable speed at which nongovernmental initiatives have obtained legitimacy in Thai society, there seems to be a good chance that Thailand will witness the emergence of more independent, policy-oriented research institutions in the future. One possible source of these new institutions may be those highly qualified, university-affiliated institutions which are believed to be interested in obtaining more independence as long as they can secure the funding.

Notes

1. Leszek Buszynski, "Thailand's Foreign Policy: Management of a Regional Vision" in *The Asian Survey* (August 1994), p. 722.
2. Ibid.
3. Sukhumbhand Partibatra. "State and Society in Thailand: How Fragile the Democracy?" in *The Asian Survey* (September, 1993).
4. Kusuma Snitwongse. "Thailand in 1993: Politics of Survival" in *The Asian Survey* (February, 1994).
5. IEAS Directory.
6. IAS Annual Report, 1992.
7. Malaysia country report.
8. Interview: August 10, 1993.
9. Interview: August 12, 1993.
10. Twatchiai Yongkittikul, Executive Vice President, TDRI, in an interview with the Sasakawa Peace Foundation research team.

UNITED STATES OF AMERICA

Trends in U.S. Research on Asia and the Pacific

Charles E. Morrison

Director

Program on International Economics and Politics

The East-West Center

Americans who specialize in the Asia-Pacific region frequently complain that this region receives relatively less attention from U.S. policy makers, the media, and the general public than does Europe. This is usually ascribed to European roots of the dominant culture in the United States, the long history of U.S.-European interactions of all sorts, and origins of the cold war as a struggle for European hegemony. There is little doubt that European history, culture, language, and political and economic subjects have had primary attention in U.S. international political and research attention. However, the relative attention given to Asia dramatically increased during the decades after World War II. The extension of the cold war struggle into Asia, stimulating governmental promotion of Asian studies, provided a ready market for such research, while returning veterans of World War II and the Korean War boosted the number of Americans interested in Asian research topics. Later, the region's strong economic growth attracted increased research and public attention.

Will research[1] interest in Asia and the Pacific continue to grow? Since the U.S. engagement in Asia and the Pacific during the cold war era was so dominated by security issues, it is natural that the end of the cold war has raised questions as to whether the United States will remain as deeply engaged, not only in a diplomatic and military sense but also in terms of intellectual and research interests. Many in Asia have the belief that, in comparison with U.S. relations with Europe, U.S.-Asian relationships are less deeply rooted and will be more difficult to sustain.

This essay examines trends in social science research, writing, and dialogue on contemporary topics and issues of policy relevance involving Asia and the Pacific in order to provide a sense of the sustainability of research on the region.[2] It is mainly based on a survey by the Japan Center for International Exchange (JCIE), but many of the observations are impressionistic. Our impression is that research interest in the Asia-Pacific region remains strong and, in some important areas, is growing. Asia is also being increasingly integrated into global research projects and programs, a dimension that our survey probably does not fully capture. However, despite the growing U.S. interest in Asia-Pacific topics, there are major challenges ahead in establishing research priorities, sustaining funding for certain kinds of research, and meeting national needs for research on Asia and the Pacific.

I. Regional Trends

Trends in American research interests in Asia and the Pacific track basic trends in the economic, political, and social life of the region itself and in the U.S. relationship to the region. Following are some of the more important trends in Asia Pacific and in the U.S. relationship to the region:

- The rise of the Asian economies. East and Southeast Asia continues to grow at a much more rapid rate than any other region of the world, although the center of that growth has shifted from Japan, to the Newly Industrialized Economies, to China and Southeast Asia. The region now accounts for about twenty-five percent of world gross product, putting it about on a par with Western Europe and North America as one of the major centers for world production and trade.
- The rise of Asia-Pacific regional interdependence and the phenomenon of regionalism. Economic growth in the region has been accompanied in recent years by a rapid growth in trans-Pacific and intra-Asian trade and capital flows. At the same time, a number of regional institutions designed to strengthen Asia or Asia-Pacific relations have been created or are proposed.
- Asia's growing importance in global issues. For virtually all global issues—AIDS, missile export controls, non-nuclear weapons proliferation, global warming, ozone depletion, species loss—the participation of Asian countries is now essential to the development of effective global regimes.
- The end of the cold war. With the end of the two conflicts with broad regional implications—the Sino-Soviet and U.S.-Soviet conflicts—politico-security relations are now more fragmented. Contradictory trends in the regional environment—relaxed tensions in the relations among the large powers combined with a growth in regional arms spending—create uncertainty about regional stability in the future.

- Economic and "cultural" issues have become a key dimension of U.S.-Asian relations while the public perception of the security dimension has declined except with respect to the Korean peninsula. Some Asian societies have aggressively asserted the superiority of their dominant values and attendant forms of social, economic, and political organization, usually in response to similar claims from the United States.
- A great increase in U.S.-Asian interactions of all kinds. Trade is now about forty percent above the U.S.-European level; Asians compose a significant portion of the U.S. graduate student population. Governmental, business, educational, and tourist contacts are rapidly growing. Modern telecommunications provides another important means of increasing contact.

II. Research Themes

The JCIE survey of research and dialogue activities by major institutions suggests a current research emphasis around a few principal countries or themes. These include Asian trends, U.S.-Japan relations, Korea, China, political change, economic growth and structural change, and regionalism. Some broad research activities address more than one of these topics. Most research and dialogue activities involve collaboration with Asian and other American institutions.

Asian Trends. Aside from more specific topics, there has increasingly been an effort in the United States to develop a broader understanding of the underlying dynamics of Asia's current transformation and to relate these to American interests. In recent years a number of institutions, including the Asia Foundation and the Carnegie Endowment for International Peace, have issued study group reports on U.S. Asia policy. While useful, these reports have been based more on dialogue than on substantial research effort. Other activities, including the Asia Society's Williamsburg Conference series, which began in 1971, bring together regional leaders for policy dialogue on broad regional trends and challenges.

The most ambitious project along these lines is the current two-year "Asia Project" of the Asia Program of the Council on Foreign Relations. Under this project three study groups in the areas of security, economics, and political issues were established, and a number of papers were commissioned by leading U.S. intellectuals on specific trends or challenges that impact on U.S.-Asian relations. As of this writing a number of these papers in such areas as regional security relations, environmental problems, human rights, international migration, the future of the Asian economic model, energy, foreign investment, and commercial practice have been completed in draft form. In its second year, the project will crystallize around a set of recommendations for U.S. policy makers.

This effort is significant particularly in view of the fragmentation of much of the U.S. Asia expertise, a matter that will be discussed later. With one or two possible exceptions, no individual research institution in the United States has the in-house expertise to carry out a broad-gauged Asian research program. Even the best known of these U.S. institutions, such as the Council on Foreign Relations, the Brookings Institution, or the Carnegie Endowment for International Peace, have relatively limited Asia expertise. While many larger universities have in aggregate considerably broad Asia-Pacific expertise, this expertise tends to be engaged in individual rather than coordinated research activities, nor has it been centrally recruited. The Council's effort, with generous financial support from a number of American and foreign foundations, overcomes this problem by drawing on extensive expertise around the country.

Japan and U.S.-Japan Relations. The number of U.S Japan-related research and dialogue projects is truly impressive. Most major U.S. research institutions and universities have been associated with some sort of project, study group, publication, or lecture series in recent years relating to Japan. Increasingly, U.S.-Japan projects are being carried out by broad-based institutions dealing with global issues rather than specialized Asia or Japan institutions. Increasingly also, the U.S.-Japan projects are focussed less on bilateral issues and more on cooperation on global issues (such as the environment, restructuring the United Nations, or arms control) or on the two countries' respective positions vis-à-vis a third country or region.

For example, George Washington University's Gaston Sigur Center is carrying out a major project on the U.S.-Japan Economic Agenda, which includes research on energy, the environment, and high technology as well as an associated legislative dialogue. The United Nations Association recently examined U.S.-Japanese cooperation in international crisis management through collaboration with the Asia Pacific Association of Japan. The Center for Strategic and International Studies (CSIS) has also worked with the Asia Pacific Association on a study of the U.S.-Japan Economic Relationship in East/Southeast Asia. The American Assembly and JCIE, with the collaboration of the Institute of Southeast Asian Studies in Singapore, are cosponsoring a three volume writing and dialogue activity on the United States and Japan in Asia Pacific. One edited volume has been published from this project by the American Assembly, and two other volumes as well as a special report will be published soon. The Council on Foreign Relations has sponsored research relating to security relations and labor relations. The Council and the East-West Center have done research on U.S.-Japan foreign aid collaboration. The Overseas Development Council has established a Center for U.S.-Japan Development Cooperation. This project focuses on cooperation to alleviate poverty, protect the environment, and improve the quality of governance. A Columbia University team and Japanese counterparts examined the two countries' policies in Indochina. The Mansfield Center for Pacific Affairs has sponsored a project on the impact of the media in U.S.-Japan relations and is developing a new project in collaboration with the Santa Barbara-based Pacific Basin Institute on industrial policy in Japan. The Institute for International Economics (IIE) has played an especially important role in conducting U.S.-Japan related research, usually in conjunction with broader issues.

Aside from research activities, there has been a significant growth in the number of fora devoted to special lectures or ad hoc workshops on U.S.-Japan related issues. The Japan Society, for example, organized the David MacEachron Policy Forum in 1990, bringing together leaders from Japan and the United States for a two-day meeting each year based on an important theme in the relationship. CSIS sponsors a high-level annual policy makers conference as well as three working groups on environmental cooperation, Asia-Pacific cooperation, and the future of regionalism under the framework of the U.S.-Japan Global Forum. The Program on U.S.-Japan Relations at Harvard University has a very active seminar program on U.S.-Japan related issues as do the Harvard University Center for International Affairs and Columbia University's East Asian Institute. How Japan and the United States can cooperate on human rights issues has been a particular concern of the Carnegie Council on Ethics and International Affairs. The Southern Center for International Studies in Atlanta and the Wo International Center in Honolulu are examples of regionally based institutions that sponsor annual Japan symposia.

The growing number of U.S.-Japan projects reflects at least three factors. First, Japan's economic stature makes it the most appropriate partner with which the United States should work on global and third country issues. This is particularly true on issues related to third world development where Japan has emerged as the largest donor of bilateral foreign assistance. Second, many Americans sense that Japanese research into many global issues generally lags behind that of the United States and that collaborative endeavors are a means of heightening Japanese awareness of these issues. Many of the U.S.-based projects are rooted in efforts by advocacy organizations in the United States to develop allies and strengthen sources of funding in Japan. Relatedly, and perhaps most importantly of all, with the emergence of Japanese foundations, most notably the Center for Global Partnership and the U.S.-Japan Foundation, there is probably more financial support for Japan-related research activities than for research on any other Asia-Pacific topic. The Tokyo-based Sasakawa Peace Foundation and the National Institute for Research Advancement (NIRA) also engage in Asia-Pacific research activities in which U.S. institutions or researchers play important roles. Fortunately, many of these funding organizations have defined their mission in relatively broad terms, permitting examination of the U.S.-Japan relationship in broad regional or global contexts.

The Korean Peninsula. There has also been significantly increased funding for U.S. research and dialogue efforts from Korean sources, augmented by the recent establishment of the Korea Foundation. Because of the importance of Korean security issues, the U.S. government as well as U.S. foundations also has supported Korea-related research. University-based Korean studies institutes have provided homes for much academic research on the Korean economy, government, history, and social change. Among the more important of these are those housed at the University of California at Berkeley, the University of California at San Diego, and the University of Hawaii.

There are also many dialogue-oriented activities dealing with U.S.-Korean relations. CSIS, for example, has a task force on U.S.-R.O.K. Relations; the Pacific Forum-CSIS has a U.S.-Korean Wisemen Council; and the National Bureau of Asian Research is sponsoring U.S. government supported studies on reunification issues and U.S.-Korean relations in the post-cold war world. The Carnegie Council on Ethics and International Affairs hosts a U.S.-Korea Media Forum, and IIE has launched high-level U.S.-South Korean dialogue.

A number of U.S. organizations have sought to develop relationships with North Korea with varying degrees of success. These include the Asia Society, George Washington University, the East-West Center, the University of Hawaii, CSIS, and the Nautilus Institute. The latter has been particularly effective in tracking the on-going nuclear weapons issue, maintaining an electronic data base and information service, and developing research into energy and environmental issues relating to North Korea. The Institute on Global Conflict and Cooperation, based at the University of California at San Diego, has received considerable U.S. governmental support for its efforts to engage North Korea in a broad-based "track two" Northeast Asia Cooperation Dialogue. Among the Washington-based policy-oriented institutions, the Heritage Foundation's Asian Studies Center and CSIS give priority attention to issues in U.S. relations with both North and South Korea.

China. China-related research has been bolstered by increased concern about China's future foreign policy course and the implications of China's booming economy and defense modernization. In comparison with its expertise on other Asian countries, American expertise on China has been particularly strong. In the earlier cold war period, U.S. government support for China expertise helped train and support a relatively large group of scholars, and in more recent years, this has been augmented by a growing number of mainland Chinese students with graduate training in the United States and an inclination to develop careers in U.S. academic and research institutions. Research emphases include China's economic growth and economic decision making, provincial and local governance, the military and civil-military relations, foreign policy and China's relations with other nations, and China's efforts to cope with major social issues in such diverse areas as environmental protection, population policies, the treatment of minorities, and the scope of cultural life. The course and implications of relations between the People's Republic of China, Hong Kong, and Taiwan, a triangle frequently referred to as "greater China," (although this term also sometimes includes overseas Chinese in Southeast Asia or around the world) is another area of U.S. research interest.

Virtually all the major universities maintain expertise on China, and Chinese language, politics, culture, and history are also taught at many smaller schools. Most research institutions also have at least one in-house China specialist. Among the more prominent centers of China expertise are Harvard University, the University of Michigan, and Stanford University. Among recent projects have been the Institute on Global Conflict and Cooperation's project on "The China Circle: Regional Perspectives on Evolving Relations among the PRC, Taiwan, and Hong Kong-Macau;" the Gaston Sigur Center's new project on "America, China, and Japan;" the Atlantic Council's project on "U.S. and China Relations at a Crossroads;" and the Resources for the Future's series of projects on "Risk Management in China." The National Committee for U.S.-China Relations, based in New York, maintains a very active program of dialogue and research on contemporary issues including trade, the environment, U.S.-China military relations, relations with "greater China," and the common interests of the developed countries in facilitating China's constructive engagement in global affairs. The American Enterprise Institute's Asia Studies Program, directed by a former Ambassador to China, James R. Lilley, has particular interest in China's military development, defense policies, and relations with other Asian countries.

Governance, Political Change, Democracy, and Human Rights. The growth of interest in these related areas reflects strong public and political interest in the United States in the development of democratic and legal institutions abroad. The Asia Foundation, the National Endowment for Democracy, the Luce Foundation, and the Ford Foundation are among the institutions that promote research and dialogue in these areas. Relatedly, some U.S. institutions have sought to directly facilitate the development of institutions of civil society and democratic governance such as representative parliamentary bodies, a free press, and an independent judiciary, more through training, demonstration, and dialogue than through research as such. Despite increased interest in these areas, influenced by the belief that economic development and the expansion of education and telecommunications induces political pluralism and change, research on Asian political institutions remains relatively underdeveloped in the United States.

Dynamics of Economic Growth. During the earlier cold war era, much of the economic research on Asia and the Pacific by Americans emphasized prescriptive work on how to achieve development, especially in countries in Southeast Asia regarded as vulnerable to communism. In more recent years, as a result of the dramatic economic growth in many Asian countries, the emphasis of economic research has shifted toward understanding the processes of the growth that occurred, its structural dynamics, its ramifications for development in other countries and regions, and its implications for the United States. There is continuing debate about whether the Asia-Pacific growth experience is unique or primarily represents well-understood processes of resource mobilization by increasingly efficient and modern governments.[3] A burgeoning number of political economists have given special attention to such subjects as the comparative role of the state and the market in the development process, the nature of industrial and financial policies, the role of the foreign sector, and the influence of culture and institutions. The interaction of economic and demographic factors, the implications of economic development for the environment, and resource supply issues are other important issue areas, and the East-West Center has research programs in all these areas.

Among the leading institutions in promoting an understanding of economic change and growth are IIE, the International Center for Economic Growth, the World Bank, and numerous university-based institutes and programs. It is especially in the understanding of economic dynamics that Asia is increasingly a part of the world program of programs and institutions that deal with global issues as opposed to an exclusively regional focus.

Asia-Pacific Regionalism. The development of the Asia-Pacific Economic Cooperation (APEC) forum and other cooperative regional fora has been mirrored in increased U.S. research interest in regional economic and political linkages, the institutional and organizational manifestations of regionalism, and the implications of regional institutions for economic growth and international security. IIE, whose director, C. Fred Bergsten, is serving as the chairman of the APEC Eminent Persons Group, is launching its largest project on economic and security regionalism as a follow-up to its APEC work. The East-West Center's work on regional institution-building has examined the relationship between regionalism and security, the implications of regional trading arrangements in North America for Asian countries, ASEAN regional cooperation, and the "building blocks" approach to economic regional cooperation. The Carnegie Endowment for International Peace established a study group on regionalism that produced a concise policy-oriented report in August 1994, "Defining a Pacific Community." The U.S. National Committee for Pacific Economic Cooperation, with the sponsorship of the Asia Foundation, played the leading role in developing a "Pacific Economic Outlook," a concise annual review of regional economic trends and projections based upon research and economic models. Other institutions with considerable interest in regional economic cooperation include Brandeis University, Columbia University, George Washington University, the University of California at San Diego, and the University of Washington.

The newly-established U.S. Consortium of APEC Study Centers, which links fourteen educational and research institutions, will encourage research activities on issues of regional cooperation. In general, the APEC Study Centers do not represent new structures but rather a renaming of existing programs and projects. One exception is the APEC Study Center at the University of Washington which, together with the Seattle-based National Center on APEC and the National Bureau for Research on Asia, reflects the significant interest in APEC in the Seattle area.

Aside from economic regionalism, there is also interest in regional security relations and regional cooperation, with much of the interest in this field based in think tanks as opposed to university programs. The Pacific Forum-CSIS coordinates the U.S. Council for Security Cooperation in Asia Pacific (CSCAP). The United States CSCAP committee has particular interest in research and dialogue on confidence-building measures and on Northeast Asian security issues. The United States Institute of Peace has also had a strong interest in regional security issues, including North Korea and the management of conflict in the South China Sea. The American Enterprise Institute (AEI) has also held a conference on the South China Sea.

The East-West Center has two on- going projects relating to Asia-Pacific security trends; one examines Asian conceptions of security and the other seeks to develop a security outlook modelled after PECC's Pacific Economic Outlook.

III. The Research Community

The American research community working on contemporary Asia-Pacific issues number in the thousands. According to *Access Asia,* the annual directory of Asian expertise produced by the National Bureau of Asian Research, a substantial share of the Asia-Pacific expertise in the United States is concentrated on two countries—China and Japan. There are also fairly large communities of researchers working on Korea and Southeast Asia. The number of researchers with Pacific Island interests is much smaller, and there is an absolute dearth of research activity and expertise on Australia and New Zealand.[4]

Access Asia also lists expertise by speciality. Most listings are for broad areas including politics, political economy (which overlaps heavily with politics), developmental issues, economics, trade, business, and security. There are much shorter listings for more focussed topics such as education, energy, the environment, finance, foreign investment, human rights, investment, the media, science and technology, and women's issues.

While a full survey would be necessary to establish trends in the composition and organization of the research community more definitively, impressionistic evidence suggests several important developments.

First, with the rise of Asia's importance to the United States an increased number of non-area specialists are involved in Asia-Pacific related research. This appears to be particularly true of such fields as environmental studies, health issues, and business management where experts in the discipline are finding it increasingly important to study Asia as a part of research on global trends and issues. Some established experts in these fields later become regional specialists.

Second, there does seem to be an increase in the number of individuals who are looking at the Asia-Pacific region broadly rather than at particular countries or subregions within it. While the international relations and trade fields have traditionally encouraged broad views of the region, the growth of regional interdependence and that of Asia-Pacific regionalism has encouraged country experts to give more attention to the region or their subject-country's relations with the region. Among the more prominent country specialists to address regional issues are Gerald

Curtis (Japan), Donald Emmerson (Indonesia), Harry Harding (China), Michael Mochizuki (Japan), Michel Oksenberg (China), Hugh Patrick (Japan), and Peter Petri (Japan).

Third, Asian-Americans and overseas Asian residents in the United States are of growing importance in U.S. education and scholarship on Asia and the Pacific. This is a phenomenon that probably occurs in all countries where there is a substantial inflow of foreign students at the graduate level—Australia, Canada, and several European countries—but perhaps no country provides a more attractive home for former students than does the United States. Overseas Koreans have long been prominent in Korean studies, and the growing number of Chinese residents in the United States is being reflected in increasing numbers of ethnic Chinese in U.S. research and educational positions.

Fourth, as referred to earlier, the academic community working mainly on Asia and the Pacific is geographically dispersed, but with large clusters of researchers at a few major universities, such as Harvard University, the Massachusetts Institute of Technology, Columbia University, Cornell University, Princeton University, the University of Michigan, the University of Washington, the University of California at Berkeley, Stanford University, the University of California at San Diego, and the University of Hawaii.[5] The Asia or Asia-Pacific studies centers associated with these universities help give focus to research efforts and attract funding.

Other universities and even many small colleges now employ teachers who conduct research on topics related to the Asia-Pacific region. Thus even the most rural of U.S. states have some Asia-Pacific regional expertise. Many of these combine a research specialty in Asia with broad teaching skills in a discipline or broad subject area such as the politics of developing countries. Usually, however, the small college emphasis on teaching as opposed to research, the lack of research support (such as a major research library), and isolation from daily contact with colleagues working in related fields make it more difficult for scholars working in smaller colleges to sustain their research efforts than those working in large research universities.

In contrast to universities, think tanks tend to have very limited in-house research staffs. Even such prominent institutions as Brookings have typically had no more than three Asian specialists on staff, and IIE relies heavily on visiting scholars to work with resident economists, most of whom are generalists rather than area specialists. One exception has been the East-West Center, where at the time of this writing there are about sixty resident specialists.

Fifth, the government remains a large employer of Asia and Pacific expertise. It appears that the largest single concentration of such expertise in the United States is in the Washington, D.C. area, much of it employed by government agencies. While most government Asian specialists are engaged in day-to-day work relating to government policy implementation rather than research, significant research efforts are found in such agencies as the Central Intelligence Agency, the Department of State, the Department of Commerce, the Defense Department, and the United States Trade Commission. These institutions also commission a considerable amount of research work on security and economic issues in Asia. The General Accounting Office handles special requests from Congress that now range far beyond that agency's traditional auditing function. Another Congressional agency, the Congressional Research Service (CRS), has several senior researchers on Asia and the Pacific who engage in analytic studies on issues of interest to Congress. There is also a growing demand at the CRS for short issue briefs on such subjects as U.S.-Japan trade issues and East Asian human rights problems. The Center for Naval Analysis and the National War College also have had considerable interest in Asian security issues. There is little doubt, however, that government efforts are currently more focussed on trade and economic issues rather than on traditional security issues.

Sixth, there has been a growth of research efforts on Asia Pacific issues by non-governmental organizations (NGOs). In contrast with academic research, which usually seeks to address a theoretical issue or increase the sum of human knowledge, the research carried out by NGOs usually focuses on a policy issue, summarizes existing knowledge for a less specialized audience, or is intended to provide support for an advocacy position. Some organizations with a largely public affairs function, such as the Japan Society, the Asia Society, the American Assembly, or the Foreign Policy Association, commission research or writing in association with activities that emphasize dialogue and public education.

Organizations associated with advocacy perspectives on Asian issues include Amnesty International and Asia Watch, both of which focus on human rights issues. The Heritage Foundation maintains at least one Asia specialist to provide a conservative perspective on policy issues of importance to the United States. Other organizations with a variety of political perspectives include the Cato Institute, AEI, and the Institute for Policy Studies.

Seventh, there has been a growth of Asia Pacific oriented bilateral and multinational research networks, the more permanent of these adjuncts to regional non-governmental or governmental institutions. Some of these have been previously referred to, including CSCAP with headquarters at the Pacific Forum-CSIS in Honolulu, the U.S. Pacific Economic Cooperation Council headquartered in Washington, D.C., and the newly created U.S. APEC Study Center Consortium whose secretariat is at the East-West Center in Honolulu. In other cases, U.S. institutions may be part of a regional network without a separate American component as, for example, the case of the three APEC human resource development networks on business management, industrial technology, and economic development management. Collaborative research may reflect on-going special relationships such as the University of Alabama - University of Chiba ("Chibama") work on U.S.-Japan economic and management issues.

Since much of the academic research on Asia and the Pacific is carried out by individuals or small groups there is very little coordination and certainly nothing that could be regarded as a national strategy for research on the region. However, a number of professional organizations and consortia provide fora for the discussion of research interests and needs. The Association of Asian Studies is the broadest of the professional associations of Asia-Pacific oriented researchers, but many others exist based on country or subregional focus, disciplinary focus, U.S. regional membership, or U.S. ethnic membership.

IV. Challenges

In closing, the author wishes to highlight some questions and challenges of importance to the research and research funding communities.[6] These questions cannot be answered in any definitive way, but they deserve thoughtful consideration. They are as follows:

- How should research priorities be set? In the cold war era, governmental priorities and funding heavily influenced U.S. research work on the region. In recent years, the policy agenda has become more diffused while new actors have emerged as funders, particularly Asian government or government-influenced sources. Each actor establishes general priorities although the allocation toward specific projects remains typically mediated by academic boards or foundation staff priorities.

  In many respects a greater diversity of agendas is a healthy development. At the same time, it also suggests the importance of a periodic and systematic review of research activities to identify lacunae, explore possibilities for greater synergy, or reduce duplication.
- What are the standards for relevance and quality of research? Again there can be no single standard since research serves a variety of purposes, some related to the expansion of knowledge, some to policy, and some to broader rather

than necessarily deeper understanding of issues. In the U.S. case the very openness of the policy-making system to advice or lobbying from outside the government has tended to put a premium on research directed toward issues of immediate policy significance as opposed to original research addressing issues in a broader and more conceptual frame. Correspondingly, much of the emphasis in the NGO community appears to be on dialogue and public education activities. However, since original and conceptual research is also highly relevant, its ability to attract sufficient funding should be considered.

- On a related issue, is there sufficient incentive and funding for individual research as opposed to institutional programs? There has been a strong development of collaborative projects resulting in edited volumes, but some specialists believe that solid, single-author scholarship has not similarly developed. This may reflect scholarly preferences and priorities, which are affected by the incentive structures within which researchers operate. Foundations may also have difficulty in considering individual research projects because of the greater administrative burdens in evaluating and administering them relative to their size and the small and overstretched foundation staffs.
- Finally, what is the match or mismatch between the need for American research expertise on Asia and the Pacific and the financial and human resources available to meet those needs? In the scholarly community itself, the nationality of scholars is increasingly less relevant. Americans can draw upon the best scholarship in the international community at large on Asia, and in this case, most of the best scholarship resides in Asia itself. However, it can be argued, the United States and other societies need their own expertise to tap into the international expertise, draw out the implications for their own societies and be most credible to their own publics and policy makers. While interest in Asia and the Pacific in the United States has grown enormously in the past few decades and intrinsic U.S. interests in the region have also continued to grow, it is not certain that the necessary research support for a viable U.S. research community will grow commensurately. A substantial reduction in government support for international research and exchange activities of all kinds following the 1994 mid-term elections throws this issue into strong relief.

Notes

1. Definitions of *research* differ. In this essay research is interpreted broadly to include not only efforts to expand the frontiers of understanding about the human dynamics of the Asia-Pacific region but also writing that is based upon or that summarizes such region principally for the purposes of public education or dialogue.
2. This essay does not cover substantial research of U.S. Asia and Pacific research interests including research into historical topics, the humanities, anthropology, and scientific topics related to Asia and the Pacific. The concern here is with issues of contemporary political, economic, and security policy relevance.
3. For example, see World Bank, *East Asia's Miracle Economies: Economic Growth and Public Policy* (Washington, D.C.: The World Bank, 1993), and Paul Krugman, "The Myth of Asia's Miracle," in *Foreign Affairs* (November/December 1994), pp. 62–78.
4. William B. Abnett et. al., eds., *Access Asia: A Guide to Specialists and Current Research 1994* (Seattle: The National Bureau of Asian Research, 1994), pp. 443–451. Although this data base includes non-Americans, most entries are for Americans. The listings appear to be based on how individual researchers have chosen to categorize their expertise rather than standardization by the volume compilers.
5. Ibid., pp. 443–451. Although the "location index" of this catalogue suggests the largest concentration of U.S. Asian experts are in the Washington, D.C. area, most of these work for government institutions rather than academic organizations.
6. The author addressed some of these issues in "Asia-Pacific Security Studies in the United States," in *Studying Asia Pacific Security: The Future of Research, Training and Dialogue Activities,* edited by Paul M. Evans (North York: University of Toronto - York University Joint Centre for Asia Pacific Studies, 1994), pp. 257–271.

VIETNAM

Research Institutions in the Socialist Republic of Vietnam Focusing on the Asia Pacific Region

Mark Sidel
Program Officer for Vietnam
The Ford Foundation, Bangkok

I. Introduction

Vietnam's rapidly growing engagement with the Asia Pacific region has led to significant growth in research activity on the region in Vietnam. Such activity is focused on policy research, although some scholarly research is underway as well. Most of that activity is concentrated in government ministries or the Communist Party, in research (or combined research/training) institutions directly affiliated with individual ministries or the Party, or in academic centers working at the nexus between scholarly and policy research.

In the Vietnamese system, most research institutions working on foreign issues are Party- or government-related and all receive some level of state funding. International relations and foreign affairs remain, in transitional societies such as Vietnam, very much a bastion of the state. Thus "independent" research institutions cannot be the focus of this report. Each Vietnamese policy, policy research, and academic research institution discussed in this brief survey is, to one degree or another, regime-authorized, regime-dependent and regime-enhancing.

This certainly does not mean that such institutions are the equivalent of foreign ministry information departments. As Paul Evans and others have pointed out, regime-enhancing and regime-dependent policy and academic research institutions of the types discussed here can have a key role in facilitating exploration and broadening discussion of sensitive or controversial issues, especially for internal discussion. Several examples of this facilitative function are described below.

Some definitional limitations are in order. The focus here is on policy-related research, but the limited nature of policy research in Vietnam and the close relationship of policy research to a rapidly expanding training sector led to the inclusion of certain training activities and institutions in this report.

Journalism and the media—and in particular the special role of the Vietnam News Agency and one or two publications—are closely related to the policy informing role of Vietnamese research on the region, and must be seen as a source of policy-related information and analysis. Given the relatively limited nature of policy research activities, training and journalism seem to contribute more directly to policy making in Vietnam than in countries where the research function and structures are denser.

For purposes of this report, it may be useful to emphasize those parts of the Asia Pacific region which are most important to Vietnam and reflected in sustained attention in Vietnam's foreign affairs. Thus, the focus here is on China, Hong Kong, Taiwan,[1] Northeast Asia (primarily Japan and South Korea), mainland and insular Southeast Asia, ASEAN, Australia and New Zealand, and the United States[2] and Canada.[3]

Vietnamese research on the Asia Pacific region faces numerous problems. As in many other countries, Asia Pacific research in Vietnam is generally overbalanced toward policy-related studies and leaves basic research underemphasized. Personnel are trained unevenly in specialty areas, and there appears to be little substantive contact between area and thematic researchers. Furthermore, training opportunities and funding, while increasing, are growing too slowly to meet national and institutional needs, especially at a time of decreasing national funding.

Vietnamese research on the Asia Pacific region is usually structured geographically and is carried out within the following types of institutions:

a. Political/policy institutions that conduct research on the Asia Pacific region as an integral part of their policy formulation and implementation work (such as the Vietnamese Communist Party, the Ministry of Foreign Affairs, the Office of the Government, the Ministry of Trade, and the Ministry of Defense);
b. Policy research institutions associated with political/policy institutions working on the region (such as the Institute for International Relations under the Ministry of Foreign Affairs, and the Ho Chi Minh National Political Academy, and the Institute of Marxism-Leninism and Ho Chi Minh Thought under the Vietnamese Communist Party);
c. State-funded research centers not affiliated with universities (such as units of the National Center for Social Sciences and Humanities in Hanoi and the Ho Chi Minh City Institute of Social Sciences);

d. State-funded, university-based research activity (such as at Hanoi University, Hanoi Teachers University, Ho Chi Minh City (HCMC) University, HCMC Teachers University, and HCMC Open University);
e. Privately funded research groups less formally affiliated with policy or academic institutions (such as the Vietnam Asia Pacific Economic Center); and
f. Media institutions with expanded research and analysis functions (such as the Vietnam News Agency) or an international affairs focus (such as *World Affairs Weekly*).

Because most foreign contact with the Vietnamese institutions discussed in this report is just beginning, contact information is included for most institutions described here.

II. New Developments

Those already generally familiar with Vietnamese research institutions may find the following institutional and research developments in 1993 and 1994 particularly noteworthy.

a. The Ministry of Foreign Affairs and its Institute of International Relations, discussed in detail below, have significantly expanded research and training activities and contact with the region and beyond.
b. The mixed academic and policy area research institutes in the National Center for Social Sciences have now been formally divided into five specific area institutes (including the older Institute for Southeast Asian Studies and new centers focusing on China, Japan, North America, and CIS/Eastern Europe), and are receiving some additional emphasis within the social science research network.
c. A series of small university-based research initiatives and units focusing on the region have become active in Hanoi and especially in Ho Chi Minh City.
d. The international relations department and several other faculties of the Ho Chi Minh National Political Academy, a primary Party training facility, have taken on additional research roles with strong encouragement from the Party and are seeking actively to engage with colleagues and institutions throughout the region and beyond.

III. Level and Scope of Research Activity

1. Policy Institutions which Conduct Research on the Asia Pacific Region as Part of Policy Formulation and Implementation

The Ministry of Foreign Affairs conducts extensive policy research on the Asia Pacific region. Within the Ministry, policy research is generally conducted in geographical departments. Among the geographical departments conducting extensive policy research on the region are the China Department (covering the PRC, Hong Kong, and Taiwan), the Northeast Asia Department (covering Japan, South and North Korea, Mongolia, and the rest of Northeast Asia), the Southeast Asian Department (including Australia, New Zealand, and the South Pacific), a new ASEAN Department, and other units.

Several other regional departments in the Ministry conduct related research; the Americas Department, for example, conducts research on U.S.-Asian relations, and the Russia/CIS Department covers Russian-Asian relations. The functional unit most directly involved appears to be the General Diplomatic Department, which handles some policy planning and foreign policy synthesis functions.[4]

The southern office of the Ministry of Foreign Affairs, located in Ho Chi Minh City, also conducts some limited policy research on the region. This important group, known formally as the External Relations Office of Ho Chi Minh City, reports jointly to the Foreign Ministry in Hanoi and to the Ho Chi Minh City Party and government authorities.[5]

The Vietnamese Communist Party conducts political and policy research on the region, primarily through its External Relations Commission. The Party External Relations Commission coordinates foreign affairs work and contacts for the Vietnamese Communist Party, conducts strategy and policy research, and assists a senior foreign policy strategy group headed by the Party General Secretary.

The Commission is considerably smaller than the governmental Ministry of Foreign Affairs. It includes perhaps one hundred to one hundred and fifty officials and researchers and about fifteen to twenty personnel working on the region at geographically structured Asia Pacific desks. The Commission's Asia Pacific staff is considerably smaller than that of the Foreign Ministry, and the Commission relies on the Ministry and policy and academic research institutions, including Party institutions, for policy research.

At senior levels, the External Relations Commission has sophisticated capacity to participate in foreign policy strategy development, including formulation of policy toward the Asia Pacific region.[6] At the middle and junior levels, however, the Commissions' capacity is perhaps more uneven, although that capacity is likely to be higher with respect to work on the Asia Pacific region than, for example, on the United States. Contact is more limited because the Foreign Ministry has responsibility for the prosecution of day-to-day relations and staffs the bilateral relationship. Until recently, External Relations Commission personnel and other Party staff studied only in Russia and Eastern Europe; only in the last several years have a few, very limited opportunities become available in the United States and western Europe.[7]

Other divisions of the Party, including the Secretariat, the General Office, the Party Economics Commission, and the Party Commission for Ideology and Culture, may have occasional contact with the region but do not appear to conduct policy-related research on a regular basis.

Other political and policy units conducting some research on the region include international relations staff in the Office of the Government, a special unit responsible for foreign economic policy in the Office of the Deputy Prime Minister for economic matters,[8] and the Ministry of Trade. The Ministry of Trade bases a limited number of officials in geographical departments. The Ministry of Defense carries out some research on the region as well through the Institute of Strategy Studies and other defense research and training institutions. A research institute under the Ministry of Interior is also responsible for some work on the region. The Vietnam Chamber of Commerce and Industry, a quasi-governmental foreign economic relations promotion and research body, and the State Committee for Cooperation and Investment, an extraministerial foreign economic policy formulation and investment approval group each also conduct research on Vietnam's trade and economic relations with other countries in the Asia Pacific region.

2. Policy Research Institutions Associated with Policy Institutions Working on the Asia Pacific Region

The Institute for International Relations, under the Ministry of Foreign Affairs, is Vietnam's primary international affairs research and training institution. The present Institute is the result of a merger between the former College of Foreign Affairs, in which most of Vietnam's current diplomats were trained (with supplemental training abroad or on the job), and a research-oriented institute. The Institute now enrolls several hundred undergraduates in a five-year international affairs program and trains government and Party cadre in various upgrading courses.[9]

The Institute conducts policy research for the Foreign Ministry through a series of small geographical and functional research divisions. The Northeast Asia Research Division (focusing on China and Japan, with newer work on Korea and Taiwan) and the Southeast Asia Research Division (including Australia, New Zealand, and the South Pacific) are the primary research actors. This work is almost entirely policy-oriented, and the public portion of it is published in the Institute's quarterly journal *International Studies* (*Tap chi Quan he quoc te*). Work on U.S. foreign policy toward Asia is handled through the newly merged American/European Research Division.[10]

The Institute's contacts with the region and beyond have dramatically expanded in recent years. The Institute has joined the ASEAN Institute of Strategic and International Studies (ASEAN-ISIS) network, maintains growing exchanges with several of the ASEAN-ISIS and Japanese research institutions, and is beginning to develop links with Chinese, U.S., Canadian, Australian, and other institutions.[11]

The Ho Chi Minh National Political Academy is the Party's training facility for mid-level and senior cadres, but it now has an increasing research function. The Academy trains Party cadre and sponsors research at its central campus outside Hanoi and three branch campuses in Hanoi, Danang, and Ho Chi Minh City. The Hanoi main campus includes over a dozen functional research and teaching divisions in social science fields, ranging from international relations and Marxist-Leninist theory to sociology, political studies, history, and other areas.

In recent years, the Academy has taken on a stronger and considerably more active research function at the urging of the Party. Research on the Asia Pacific region is carried out primarily in the international relations department, with research on Southeast Asia, China, and Japan, and additional work in political studies, economics, and several other departments.[12]

The Institute of Marxism-Leninism and Ho Chi Minh Thought, under the Vietnamese Communist Party, is the Party's primary research institute. It covers a wide range of functional and geographical research tasks and appears to have limited direct research capacity on the Asia Pacific region. However, its role as the Party's primary research facility provides the Institute with strong channels to policymakers. The Institute has done some translation and research work on U.S. relations with Asia,[13] and has most likely undertaken other regional work as well.[14]

The Institute of Strategic Studies and the Higher Military Academy under the Ministry of Defense each appear to conduct some policy research on the Asia Pacific region.

3. State-Funded Research Centers not Affiliated with Universities

The National Center for Social Sciences and Humanities (NCSSH) is Vietnam's primary state-funded social science research-focused institution. The Center is a ministry-level institution which conducts academic and policy research in virtually every area of the social sciences through well over a dozen functional and area institutes. Although the Center has described its mission in somewhat different ways at different times, it is perhaps most appropriate today to understand it as an institution with an academic research mission also working heavily on policy research and on the nexus between basic and applied studies. The Center also trains master's students through the research institutes, and publishes Vietnamese and English language editions of an academic social science journal.

Academic and policy research on the Asia Pacific region is conducted within the National Center primarily through the area institutes. In the late 1980s and through 1993, that work was largely carried out through two institutes. The first, a research center of long standing, is the Institute of Southeast Asian Studies. That Institute has about forty researchers with wide capacities for work on Southeast Asia, including language competence. The Institute of Southeast Asian Studies publishes an academic journal, has translated, edited, or authored numerous books, and remains one of the few Vietnamese institutions engaged in basic research on Southeast Asian countries' language, history, and culture rather than focusing more narrowly on economics, international affairs, and other applied topics.[15]

In the late 1980s and through 1993, the second NCSSH group focusing on the region was the Institute of Asian and Pacific Studies, which handled work ranging geographically "from Washington to Moscow," in the words of a senior Institute administrator. Recognizing the need for more focused and intensive area studies work, in 1993, the central government approved plans for the National Center to break up the Institute of Asian and Pacific Studies into four regional research centers, and to expand the capacity of each.

In late 1993 and early 1994, the research centers for Japanese, Chinese, North American, and CIS/East European studies were founded on the basis of research groups earlier active in the Institute of Asian and Pacific Studies and other NCSSH institutes. At this time, much of the work in NCSSH on the Asia Pacific region is carried out through the Center for Chinese Studies and the Center for Japanese Studies.

The Center for Chinese Studies has approximately fifteen to twenty researchers conducting studies of Chinese economic reform, politics, history, culture, literature, and society in four research divisions and several administrative sections. While most of the Center's work focuses on the People's Republic, some attention is given to Taiwan and Hong Kong as well, mostly in the economic and political spheres. The Center has some continuing contact with the PRC, Hong Kong, and Taiwan.

In a pattern prevalent among other China specialists in Hanoi, the older generation of researchers was trained in China in the 1950s and early to mid-1960s, speaks fluent Chinese, and has a considerably better learned and intuitive grasp of PRC issues than does the new, younger generation of Vietnamese China specialists. The younger generation has been largely trained in Hanoi and does not yet have opportunities for extensive contact with Chinese intellectual and other communities outside Vietnam.[16]

The NCSSH Center for Japanese Studies is also a result of the breakup of the Institute of Asian and Pacific Studies into four regional institutes, with some personnel added from other NCSSH centers and other units. Approximately fifteen to twenty researchers work on Japanese economics, politics, history, culture, society, and literature, including more applied topics in Vietnamese-Japanese relations. There is extensive contact with Japanese academic, research, international affairs, and government groups, and some training opportunities in Japan. Some attention is now also being paid to Korea.[17]

Numerous other NCSSH institutes have some researchers working on functional or thematic problems in an Asia Pacific context. An important group studies economies in the Asia Pacific region at the Institute of World Economy. The Institute of World Economy, like the Institute of Southeast Asian Studies, was among the first Vietnamese institutions to focus on Asia Pacific economies and economic relations with Vietnam. While in recent years the Institute of World Economy has contributed research personnel to other new institutions, such as the Centers for North American and Japanese Studies, it continues to conduct important work on the region.[18] History and ethnology work is conducted in the Institute of History and the Institute of Ethnology.

The Ho Chi Minh City Institute of Social Sciences, which has administrative ties both to local Ho Chi Minh City authorities and to the National Center for Social Sciences and Humanities, includes some researchers working on economics and perhaps other fields in the Asia Pacific region.[19] As detailed below, university-based researchers in Ho Chi Minh City are also active in work on the region.

4. State-Funded University-Based Research Centers

Research on the Asia Pacific region in university-based research centers is beginning to expand. Such units generally are not as well-staffed and remain weaker than units in the National Center for Social Sciences and Humanities and other research centers. An Asian Studies center at Hanoi University has begun some work, focusing on East and Northeast Asia. The Center for Asia Pacific Studies and the Faculty of History at Hanoi Teachers University include specialists on the region.

In Ho Chi Minh City, a Faculty of Oriental studies at Ho Chi Minh City University focuses on Southeast Asia, with some work on China and Japan.[20] The Southeast Asian studies department at Ho Chi Minh City Open University has begun to publish texts on Southeast Asia, including volumes on Thailand and Indonesia under the series title *Southeast Asia Today* (*Dong Nam A Ngay Nay*).[21] An Asian studies unit at the Ho Chi Minh City Teachers University is newly formed as well.

5. Privately Funded Research Groups Less Formally Affiliated with Policy or Academic Institutions

The Vietnam Asia Pacific Economic Center (VAPEC), a research and consulting group affiliated with the National Center for Social Sciences and Humanities, focuses on economic, trade, and investment relations with the Asia Pacific region. The Center publishes a journal, *Tap chi kinh te Chau A Tai binh duong* (Asia Pacific economic review). Several prominent academics are affiliated with the Center, including Professor Le Van Sang of the Institute of World Economy, as well as several prominent Party and economic officials. VAPEC has institute-level status at the National Center for Social Sciences and Humanities.

6. Media Activity Focusing on the Asia Pacific Region

Journalism and the media—in particular the special role of the Vietnam News Agency and one or two publications—are closely related to the policy informing role of Vietnamese research on the region. A relatively complete (though still summary) picture of Vietnamese research on the region cannot be drawn without including some information on these sources of policy research and information. Given the limited research underway, journalism (like international affairs training) contributes somewhat more directly to policy making in Vietnam than in countries where the research function and structures are more dense.

The Vietnam News Agency (VNA) is responsible for a range of open domestic reporting and publication, as well as internal reporting and analysis for all levels of the Party and government. VNA appears to maintain a small staff with experience translating, reporting on, and analyzing the Asia Pacific region. The staff has been built, at least partially, from the ranks of VNA reporters assigned to bureaus in East and Southeast Asia. This network has given VNA the direct opportunity to place personnel in the region for many years, an opportunity not available to numerous other government and research institutions.

VNA also produces a mid-level internal circulation news serial entitled *Special Reference* (*Tham Khao Dac Biet*), which contains information on international and regional affairs. The Foreign Ministry publishes a daily news headline and content service, *Tin A Hang Ngay* (*"A" News Today*), issued by the Foreign Ministry. Both publications focus extensively on the region.[22]

Vietnamese newspapers and magazines generally do not have research, writing, and analysis capacities separate from VNA on the Asia Pacific Region. Some larger newspapers (such as *Laodong* [Labor] and *Saigon Giaiphong* [Liberated Saigon]) appear to have a foreign desk or designated foreign newswriters. However, the only publications which appear to have regular research, writing, and analysis capacity on the region are *World Affairs Weekly*, a magazine affiliated with the Foreign Ministry, and *Nhan Dan* (The People), the daily newspaper published by the Central Committee of the Communist Party.

World Affairs Weekly (*Tap chi Quan he Quoc te*) was founded in the late 1980s as the monthly *World Affairs Review* by a small group of Foreign Ministry-related writers and analysts as an international affairs magazine aimed both at specialists and interested citizens. It rapidly became known for somewhat more creative foreign news analysis than other publications, and there are consistent indications that it is read by Party and government officials at relatively senior levels. Several *World Affairs Weekly* journalists have trained in Southeast and East Asia and beyond. In 1994, the *Review* signed a joint venture agreement with a Swiss publishing group and weekly publication began.

Nhan Dan is the Party's central public news and propaganda vehicle and has a foreign news department with at least some U.S. capacity. Several *Nhan Dan* journalists have traveled to or trained in Asia and the United States.

In addition, several Hanoi publishing houses are active in producing books on the Asia Pacific region. They are not research institutions, nor do they fulfill the more confidential analysis role such as that performed by the Vietnam News Agency, but they are key purveyors of book-length information about the region in the Vietnam context. One of the major publishing houses producing material on the region is the National Political Publishing House (*Nha Xuat Ban Chinh Tri Quoc Gia*), a publisher directly responsible to and supported by the Central Committee of the Vietnamese Communist Party. The National Political Publishing House publishes translations and authored volumes in politics, international affairs, law, economics, ideology, and other fields. Most output is on domestic topics, but some volumes on the Asia Pacific region have been published as well.

The World Publishing House (*Nha Xuat Ban The Gioi*) is a quasi-autonomous publisher with a long interest in foreign culture. It too has published materials on the region and will likely increase output over the next several years.

IV. Trends and Problems

Research on the Asia Pacific region in Vietnam is active but limited by uneven specialty competence. Expertise in international affairs and economics far surpasses that in other social science or policy research fields.

This uneven specialty competence both results from and further exacerbates an emphasis on policy research over basic research. Only the Institute of Southeast Asian Studies in Hanoi and several of the smaller Ho Chi Minh City units are working seriously on culture, language, history, and other aspects of basic research on the region.

There appears to be little contact between area researchers (such as in the institutes of Southeast Asian, Chinese, and Japanese studies in Hanoi) and personnel working on the region thematically in ministries and other institutes.

Training of younger personnel—especially in areas outside economics and international affairs—and funding remain perennial problems. Researchers are not sufficiently paid to work full-time on academic or policy research, and must generally seek part-time, outside employment only sometimes directly related to their research activities.

Despite these issues, research on the Asia Pacific region in Vietnam is increasing and shows no signs of slowing over the next five to ten years. With this increasing research activity will come more extensive opportunities for contact between policy and academic research personnel in Vietnam and their colleagues throughout the region and beyond.

Notes

1. For considerably more information on Vietnamese policy and academic research on China, Hong Kong, and Taiwan than is possible in this summary, see Sidel, *The Reemergence of China Studies in Vietnam, China Quarterly*, forthcoming 1995.
2. For considerably further information on Vietnamese work on the United States, see Sidel, *Vietnam's America Specialists: Policy Research, Strategy Formulation and Scholarly Activity for a New Era,* unpublished manuscript (1994) available from the author.
3. Little work on this sector is available outside Vietnam. A notable exception is Heng Hiang Khng, "Security Studies in Non-ASEAN Southeast Asia," in Evans (ed.), *Studying Asia Pacific Security: The Future of Research, Training and Dialogue Activities* (University of Toronto-York University Joint Centre for Asia Pacific Studies (Canada)/Centre for Strategic and International Studies (Indonesia), 1994). Vietnam gives sustained attention to the regions and countries listed, and relatively sporadic attention, at least at present, to North Korea, the Russian Far East, Mongolia, South Asia, Burma, the South Pacific, and Central and Latin America.
4. Ministry of Foreign Affairs, 1 Ton That Dam Street, Hanoi (fax 844-259205; telephone 844 258201). Another functional unit of the Ministry, the International Organizations Department, has led research on human rights policy.
5. Ho Chi Minh City External Relations Office, 6 Thai Van Lung Street, District 1, Ho Chi Minh City (fax 848-297785; telephone 848-225460) (Ambassador Vu Khac Bong, Director; Mr. Luong Van Ly, Deputy Director).
6. The Chairman of the Commission, Hong Ha, is a senior member of the Communist Party and of its Political Bureau and one of Hanoi's key foreign policy strategists.
7. External Relations Commission of the Vietnamese Communist Party, 1C Hoang Van Thu, Hanoi (fax 844-234514; telephone 844-258261).
8. Until recently this unit was headed by Ambassador Nguyen Trung, formerly Ambassador to Thailand and Director of the Economics Department of the Vietnamese Ministry of Foreign Affairs. Ambassador Trung is now an advisor to the Prime Minister, Vo Van Kiet, on economic matters.
9. One such series of upgrading courses for researchers, faculty, and government and Party cadre from around the country, involves foreign faculty and is supported by the Ford Foundation. The Program for International Studies in Asia of the American Council of Learned Societies cooperates abroad in selecting foreign faculty and teaching materials.
10. In early 1995 the Northeast Asia Research Division was headed by Ha Hong Hai, the Southeast Asia Research Division by Ms. Nguyen Phuong Binh, and the American/European Research Division by Bui Thanh Son who is also an Assistant Director of the Institute. It is important to note the intellectual contributions of Professor Luu Doan Huynh to the Institute's work on the Asia Pacific region and beyond over many years. A significant number of the Institute's younger leadership and more active researchers are Professor Huynh's students.

11. The Institute for International Relations is headed by Director General Ambassador Dao Huy Ngoc. It is located at Lang Thuong, Dong Da, Hanoi (fax and telephone 844-343543).
12. Professor Nguyen Xuan Son is Dean of the International Relations Department. The Academy is located at Nghia Do, Tu Liem, Hanoi (telephone 844-353331-34) (Nguyen Duc Binh, President (and member, Political Bureau, Vietnamese Communist Party); Professor Tran Ngoc Hien, Vice President).
13. The Institute's Information Division has translated the Asia Foundation's Center for Asia Pacific Affairs report on *America's role in Asia*, for example. Information Division, Institute of Marxism-Leninism and Ho Chi Minh Thought (trans. and ed.), *Vai tro cua My o Chau A* (*America's role in Asia*) (National Political Publishing House (Hanoi), 1993).
14. Institute of Marxism-Leninism and Ho Chi Minh Thought, 56B Quoc Tu Giam, Hanoi (telephone 844-258261/x3839) (Professor Dang Xuan Ky, Director (and member, Central Committee, Vietnamese Communist Party); Professor Vu Huu Ngoan, Deputy Director).
15. The Institute also does its share of research on applied topics, including Vietnam's entry into ASEAN, Vietnam's economic and trade relations with Southeast Asia, the role of Chinese investors in Vietnam, and related subjects. The Institute is located at 27 Tran Xuan Soan, Hanoi (fax 844 259071; telephone 844-267817).
16. The Center for Chinese Studies is located at Dang Tien Dong Street, Duong Thai Ha, Dong Da District, Hanoi, (fax 844-259071; telephone 844-535348/531768). The Center is headed by Professor Nguyen Huy Quy, a historian of modern China and frequent translator of Chinese political documents for distribution to Party members and others in Vietnam. Further information on the political context for Chinese studies in Vietnam, the reemergence of Chinese studies, and the role of Nguyen Huy Quy and other individuals and institutions, is available in Sidel, "The Reemergence of China Studies in Vietnam," *China Quarterly*, forthcoming 1995.
17. The Center for Japanese Studies is located at Dang Tien Dong Street, Duong Thai Ha, Dong Da District, Hanoi (fax 844-259071) (Professor Duong Phu Hiep, Director).
18. The Institute of World Economy is headed by Professor Vo Dai Luoc and located at Dang Tien Dong Street, Duong Thai Ha, Dong Da District, Hanoi (fax 844-259071).
19. Ho Chi Minh City Institute of Social Sciences, 49 Nguyen Thi Minh Khai Street, Ho Chi Minh City (fax 848-223735; telephone 848-295838/224568) (Professor Mac Duong, Director).
20. The faculty is headed by Professor Bui Khanh The. Departments within the faculty focus on Pacific, South Asian, and Australian studies; East Asian studies; and Southeast Asian studies. The faculty is located at 10-12 Dinh Tien Hoang Street, District 1, HCMC (telephone 848-291113; fax 848-222360).
21. The department is headed by Professor Nguyen Quoc Loc and located within the Open University at 97 Vo Van Tan, HCMC. Volumes published to date include histories of Indonesia, Malaysia, Singapore and Brunei, and Thailand (each by Professor Huynh Van Tong), and on the economies of Laos, Cambodia, and Myanmar (Professor Lam Quong Huyen).

22. Heng, *supra* note 3, also discusses the research and analysis role of the Vietnam News Agency and VNA internal publications. It is indicative of Vietnamese policy and research priorities that the Foreign Ministry's *Tin A Hang Ngay*, examined on numerous occasions by the author, always leads with news of the Asia Pacific region, generally culled from regional news sources as well as the British Broadcasting Corporation, Voice of America, Australian and French radio, wire services, and other sources. While these are internal publications, they are not the highest level of confidential news material and analysis since they are available to low- and mid-level researchers and officials. Several internal publications at higher classification levels are issued for more senior Personnel.

PHILANTHROPY

AUSTRALIA

Philanthropic Organizations and Corporate Philanthropy

Max Dumais
Executive Director
The Australian Association of Philanthropy

I. Overview of Philanthropy

1. The Evolution of Philanthropy

Philanthropy in Australia can best be characterized by its diversity and independence.

It is only in the last ten years or so that either private or corporate philanthropy has started to identify itself as a sector, develop a public profile, create professional roles to support its activities, work cooperatively, and develop a shared vision. The establishment of a permanent secretariat for the Australian Association of Philanthropy (AAP), in 1988, has been instrumental in further consolidating this identity and the sector as a whole.

Historically, philanthropy has operated independently and often very privately, with little or no public profile. Many individuals, private foundations and corporate-giving programmes have preferred to maintain this low profile in an effort to minimize the number of requests for support. It has not been uncommon for private funders to support the same organizations on an annual basis in order to minimize the need for research and decision making.

A number of historical factors have impacted on the growth and current practice of both private and corporate philanthropy in Australia. Australia, economically a young country, has always had a relatively small population, widely scattered geographically. The country has never experienced the great accumulation of wealth that has amassed over many generations in most other developed countries. In addition, services have traditionally been funded by government, not by individuals, religious organizations or businesses, as is more often the case in the United States, for example.

Government in Australia has never provided tax incentives or vehicles to promote the growth of private philanthropy. Current government practice indicates that it would prefer monies by way of taxation so it can determine distribution. This practice, combined with the lack of codification of taxation regulation has meant it is almost impossible to establish a tax deductible foundation in Australia. Those that are established are approved on an ad hoc and erratic basis.

The importance of tax deductibility in relation to encouraging giving in Australia is unclear. While available research indicates that tax deductibility is generally not the most important consideration in determining the willingness to give, anecdotal evidence indicates it clearly does influence its extent.

The major reasons people give have been identified as follows:

- the dynasts, those who seek to carry on the family name;
- those who feel they have greatly benefitted from society and wish to put something back into their communities;
- those who seek to give in memory of a loved one;
- those who wish to give back to an organization or to research a disease or a particular problem they may have experienced; and
- those who have inherited wealth and feel uneasy that the wealth has been unearned.

Over the past few years the government has increasingly withdrawn from funding and service provision, indicating that in a deregulating society the private sector should take greater responsibility for the disadvantaged members of the community. Unfortunately, it has not provided any tax incentives to encourage the private sector to take up this additional responsibility. The Inquiry into Charities, currently being undertaken by the Industry Commission, a federal government body, hopefully will address these issues of tax concessions and vehicles for encouraging giving.

1) Private Foundations

The number of private charitable foundations in existence in Australia is unknown as there is no central register of such bodies. It is believed, however, that the number exceeds one thousand. The majority of these are administered by trustee companies, which act either as a sole or an administrative trustee along with other external trustees.

The bulk (approximately eighty percent) of private philanthropic foundation activity in Australia takes place in the State of Victoria, for many years the economic and business centre of the country. It is believed that the activity of a number of wealthy individuals in the state's capital, Melbourne, established a critical mass of funds which acted as a catalyst for consolidation and growth. In addition, death duties in the form of probate provisions have existed longer in Victoria than many of the other states, which may have encouraged growth in the number of foundations in Victoria.

Funding from nearly all the major foundations located in Victoria are restricted to state-based activities. Very little, because of trust deed related to tax benefit, can be distributed nationally, let alone internationally.

By world standards, private foundations in Australia are relatively small. The largest private foundation, the Sylvia and Charles Viertel Foundation, has a capital base of approximately A$65 million (US$50 million).[1] This is followed by the Sydney Myer Fund (A$60 million, US$46.2 million), William Buckland Foundation (A$40 million, US$30.8 million), the Brockhoff Foundation (A$35 million, US$26.9 million) and the Helen M Schutt Trust (A$30 million, US$23.1 million), to name but a few with capital bases exceeding A$30 million.

In the financial year 1988–89, the AAP commissioned some inaugural research into levels of giving in Australia. *Giving Australia*[2] indicated that private foundation giving, at the time, was estimated at around A$122 million (US$93.9 million).

2) Corporate Philanthropy

Corporate philanthropy in Australia has not played a major role in private charitable funding.

Very few corporations have formal philanthropic foundations in place. Those seeking to establish them have been greatly frustrated by the Australian Tax Office's (ATO) reluctance to grant tax deductibility for donations to corporate foundations.

To date, corporate giving in Australia has been managed in a very ad hoc manner. A corporation's commitment to giving has largely been dependent on the personal philosophy of the chief executive, rather than on a strategic approach to corporate giving or corporate positioning in the market.

The means by which corporations have managed giving varies greatly.

Some corporations see giving as a form of sponsorship and actively seek to raise their corporate profile through such giving. Corporations falling into this category tend to fund their philanthropic activity through their marketing or corporate relations budgets. Others allocate certain monies each year specifically to charitable causes without expecting any specific corporate-related kudos in return. These givers tend to keep low profiles regarding their giving activities and often make regular grants to the same charitable organizations.

Often corporate-giving practice and directions are set by the chief executive officer—or his/her partner—with little real regard for, or research of, current community needs. Such practice therefore is an extension of personal patronage, rather than impersonal and structured philanthropy.

Recently, as with many private foundations, a trend is emerging that sees corporations professionalizing their giving activities. More strategic and clear policies are being implemented, community-need research is being undertaken to better appraise grant-seeking applications and, in certain instances, corporations are actively developing charitable projects in areas of identified need. Increasingly these corporations are committing staff and expertise to support charitable activities in the broader community.

The term *corporate citizenship* is receiving increased attention at boardroom level and many companies are beginning to integrate pro-active philanthropy into core business activity and community investment programmes.

"Smart" corporations are beginning to recognize the benefits a strategic, pro-active giving programme can bring both internally and externally, particularly as many (after the perceived excesses of the 1980s) are seeking to soften their image within the communities in which they operate as well as display greater accountability to their shareholders (increasingly more broadly based, at least in Australia).

For companies wanting to be seen as world-class performers, good corporate citizenship is starting to be viewed not as an optional extra but as a core element of successful business strategy and management.

Giving Australia estimated that businesses with over one thousand employees donated approximately A$176 million (US$135.5 million) to charitable causes during the 1988–89 financial year.

3) Individual Giving

Research undertaken by the AAP provides the most accurate and comprehensive figures available on philanthropic activity by individuals throughout the Australian community, although it should be interpreted as an indicator, rather than an exhaustive and definitive analysis, of the sector.

According to *Giving Australia*, significant amounts have been, and continue to be, donated by individual philanthropic Australians—in 1988–89 the cash amount was estimated to be over A$830 million (US$639.1 million), with 77 percent of surveyed individuals "giving something" in the surveyed period. However, the levels of giving represented a mere 0.38 percent of average household income, a percentage well below that of the United States where giving levels are running at approximately 2.0 percent of average household income. In summary, nearly half of the charitable dollars raised in Australia came from individuals.

With the diminution of government funding, greater demand is being placed on the private sector to meet the charitable funding shortfall. The pressure to meet these demands, corresponding as it does with an increase in thoughtfulness and professionalism by both corporate and private givers, means philanthropy in Australia is at a crossroads.

As a result of the above mentioned changes, the private sector is now seeking new vehicles to promote and encourage philanthropy. One such initiative meeting increasing acceptance has been the growth in community foundations, flexible tax-deductible public funds that attract large and small funding in perpetuity to be allocated for community use either through advisory boards (whose membership usually comprise prominent local citizens), or through advice from donors.

In 1994, three such community foundations were established by ANZ Trustees, a part of the ANZ Banking Group, with others certain to follow over the next few years, particularly as donors and corporations increasingly recognize the benefits of giving through such bodies.

2. The Role of Philanthropic Organizations and Corporations in Responding to Social, Political and Economic Needs in Australia

As indicated, philanthropic activity in Australia can be characterized by its diversity. At one end of the continuum both private and corporate endeavour has been very traditional and conservative. Large amounts of funding have supported the construction of major capital works programmes, typically associated with major hospitals and universities. At the other end, philanthropic activity is seen as providing venture capital for the not-for-profit sector of the community. Progressive philanthropists have initiated new projects and programmes with the aim of effecting structural change and/or new ways in which services are delivered. In addition, the ultimate goal is to prove their effectiveness and encourage government to take over their support.

Both traditional and progressive approaches play vital roles in responding to the country's community needs. With increasing pressure on the philanthropic sector to fill funding shortfalls, corporations are focusing on ensuring that what funding they offer meets clearly identified community needs, and that outcomes are carefully evaluated before additional funding is offered.

Philanthropic foundations and corporate philanthropy have played only a minimal role in responding to the political needs of the country. The activities of political organizations do not come within the legal meaning of the word charitable; funding for political parties is not tax deductible and must be publicly declared by the recipient political party.

Most philanthropic bodies in Australia would explicitly exclude funding for political parties from their charters. One of the major strengths of philanthropic activity in Australia has been the recognition that it operates outside the political process.

3. Major Players in Private and Corporate Philanthropy

There are a number of private philanthropic foundations in Australia with funding bases exceeding A$30 million (US$23.1 million). These foundations, however, do not necessarily represent the major players or those most recognized in the sector. Major participants tend to be identified as those that have developed a high public profile and which facilitate ground breaking and innovative work, work which aims to challenge and/or change government policy and/or service delivery.

In many cases this pioneering work has not required high levels of philanthropic funding, but instead has been dependent on careful planning, maximum use of existing services and, in many cases, joint funding from a number of often small foundations.

Foundations most likely to engage in this type of activity include the William Buckland Foundation, the Alfred Felton Bequest, the Myer Foundation, the Lance Reichstein Foundation, the Stegley Foundation and the Greenhills Foundation.

To date, little cooperative or joint funding of projects has occurred between private foundations and corporate-giving programmes. Corporations, until very recently, have seen little common ground between their giving and private foundation giving. This is likely to change in the future.

Many major public companies have either professionally supported strategic-giving programmes or are in the process of developing them. These companies include Coles-Myer, Mayne Nickless, Esso, Western Mining, IBM, Westpac, McDonalds, Coca Cola-Amatil, CRA, the Body Shop, Esprit, Telecom, Australian Unity, National Mutual, Rothschild, Lend Lease, Broken Hill Propriety (BHP), British Petroleum (BP) and Imperial Chemicals Industries (ICI).

Their increasing acknowledgment of the importance of developing this area of activity and incorporating it into decisions about market positioning encourages companies to look to private foundations for direction and input. The AAP can potentially play an important role in resourcing and advising professionalism in the area.

Given the difficulties individuals and families have experienced in trying to establish private foundations during their lifetime, many have chosen to give directly to those charitable activities they personally support. Much giving is done anonymously by people seeking no public acknowledgment while others either are happy to be acknowledged or who wish, through publicity for their activities, to induce others to give as well.

Australians with high public profiles for their philanthropic as well as business activities include the Fairfax, Bensen, Murdoch, Myer, Pratt, Angliss, Bushell and Gandel families, as well as Kerry Packer, Henry Roth, Ralph Sarich, Dick Smith, Phillip Wolanski, Sir Ian Potter, Henry Krongold, Isador Magid, Doug Moran and Tony and George Snow, among many others.

II. The Role of Philanthropic Organizations/Corporate Philanthropy in Promoting a Sense of Community in the Asia Pacific Region

1. Major Influencing Factors for Philanthropic Organizations/ Corporate Philanthropy to Engage in Regional Activities and Promote Regional Networks

The 1990s have been a period of substantial change in Australia's view of its place in the world. From a nation which looked to Britain, Europe and the United States for its primary social, political, cultural and even economic relationships, Australia has developed relationships with its neighbours in North and Southeast Asia at a rate unimaginable even a decade ago.

To a large extent this change has been fuelled by the economic developments in Asian countries. A seminal report produced for the Australian government by Professor Ross Garnaut in 1989, "Australia and the Northeast Asian Ascendency", noted that no economies on earth had greater complementarity than the Northeast Asian economies and the Australian in their resource endowments and the commodity composition of their trade. In 1991, the East Asian Analytical Unit was established to provide practical information based on strategic research using experts from Australia and the region. In 1992 it produced a report, "Australia's Business Challenge: Southeast Asia in the 1990s", which identified major complementarities between the economies of Australia and Southeast Asia particularly in the service sector. In 1994 a report on Australian investment in Southeast Asia identified major opportunities for the increasing number of corporations investing in the region.

Over the past decade Australian exports to Southeast Asia have grown by four hundred percent and, in the year to end June 1992, Australian investment in Southeast Asia increased by twenty-five percent. Japan and China are Australia's first and second trading partners.

This reorientation of Australia towards its Asian neighbours was engineered largely by government with a wide range of funding programmes designed to develop and support industrial, academic, cultural and humanitarian links with Asian countries. The federal government expanded its own bilateral agencies relating to Asia during this period from two to five with the establishment of the Australia Indonesia Institute (1989), the Australia Korea Foundation (1992) and the Australia India Council (1992). The strategy adopted by the bilateral agencies is to support projects and activities which can demonstrate that other funders are contributing. The experience of these agencies is that the other funders are almost never corporate or philanthropic bodies, tending rather to be other levels of government or QANGOS.

In 1991 the federal government also established an organization called the Australia Abroad Council (AAC), within the Department of Foreign Affairs and Trade, with a brief to promote Australia and its culture abroad with particular reference to Asian countries. The AAC established a series of activities designed to promote Australia in countries of the Asian region. These have been held in Korea (1992), Japan (1993) and Indonesia (1994). The promotions are managed by private organizations on behalf of the government and government funding is expected to be matched with corporate and philanthropic support. In Japan and Korea support was provided by the corporate sector but not on a scale expected by government. Corporate support tended to be provided for particular cultural, sporting and educational events, and was largely corporate promotion rather than corporate philanthropy.

The government has created an environment in which Australians in all fields of endeavour are increasingly looking to Asian countries and colleagues. It has also taken a lead in encouraging other sectors of the community to participate in joint funding arrangements for regional projects and activities. This has been an effective strategy in involving state governments and their instruments, QANGOs, and educational institutions, but as yet has not generated substantial contributions from the corporate sector.

To date philanthropic organizations and corporate philanthropy have not played an active role in supporting regional networks and regional activities. Both have been largely domestic in orientation with some notable exceptions identified in this report. As Australian business builds its investment and joint ventures in Asian countries and economic activity expands, it is likely that corporate philanthropy will also increase from the present low base.

2. Major Cooperative Efforts among Philanthropic Organizations/Corporate Philanthropy to Promote the Above Activities

In Australia to date there has been very little interaction between philanthropic grant makers to fund cooperatively in the region. This is due to the inability of the majority of private philanthropic foundations to fund outside their home states, to the small number of bodies, both private and corporate, involved in philanthropic funding generally, as well as to the belief that the first priority must be to address problems at a local and national level.

We are, however, beginning to see the beginnings of a more strategic approach to fostering our relations in the region. This move has been spearheaded by the Melbourne-based Myer Foundation which initiated Asialink and which has continued to support it.

The initial Myer funding for Asialink has been supported by the Mazda Foundation, and by the William Buckland and Truby and Florence Williams foundations, both administered by ANZ Trustees, part of the ANZ Banking Group.

This seed funding has been somewhat ad hoc, but with the emergence of organizations such as Asialink and the Asia Australia Institute, and increased professionalism in the sector, the beginnings of a strategic relationship with the region are beginning to emerge.

Other regional philanthropic initiatives that have involved Australia have been the first and second symposia on philanthropy in the region, which were held in

Thailand and Korea respectively. Likewise, the initial activities of Civicus, which has been established to develop international philanthropy, would appear to be setting the scene for more regional activity.

Individually, a number of major Australian corporations and a handful of private foundations have supported activities in the region.

In the private foundation area, a number of examples can be found. The Queensland-based Foundation for Development Cooperation, for example, is an independent, nonprofit and nonpartisan organization, whose aim is to strengthen international cooperation and development in the region. It does this by undertaking, promoting and supporting activities to improve the quality and increase the quantity of aid to developing countries, and to promote development cooperation with these countries. It claims to be the only such organization in Australia. Its counterparts overseas would include the Overseas Development Institute in the UK, the Overseas Development Council in the USA and the North-South Institute in Canada.

The core budget for the Foundation of Development Cooperation is derived entirely from private sources, although funding for specific project-related activities has also been received from government and international sources such as the Australian International Development Assistance Bureau, the World Bank, the Asian Development Bank and the United Nations Development Programme. This foundation's major activity to date has been the project "Banking with the Poor".

The Fred Hollows Foundation, based in Sydney, is another example of a private foundation with an increasing involvement in the region. It is specifically set up to eliminate avoidable blindness through skills and technology transfer in an environment of mutual respect. Currently it has services based in Nepal and Vietnam where it plans eventually to build a factory to produce interocular lenses. The factory will be owned and operated by local people, and local people will practise the surgical procedures associated with cataract blindness.

Two other foundations, ASPECT and FORESIGHT, are also involved in the treatment of cataract blindness in the region. Their concentration, however, is based more on service delivery and skills transfer, ASPECT undertakes the bulk of its work in the Pacific, whereas FORESIGHT practises throughout the region.

In line with the increasing professionalism of corporate philanthropy within Australia, several major corporations are undertaking various projects in the region. It is debatable whether all these projects are examples of corporate philanthropy in its real sense, ie whether the donor expects little or no return. Rather they appear to be attempts strategically to position these corporations in countries where they are planning to develop new markets. They all, however, do ensure substantial benefits for the host communities.

The main areas of corporate involvement that could most nearly be described as philanthropic have been environmental, health and safety, education and training, as well as enterprise development. These activities have mainly involved skills and technology transfer as well as funding support for regionally based NGOs.

An example of skills and technology transfer is the Kutubu Oilfield Project, based in the southern highlands of Papua New Guinea (PNG) and managed by Chevron Niugini and other partners including BP Development Australia, BHP Petroleum and the PNG Government.

After negotiating with the World Wildlife Fund for Nature (WWF), a partnership has been developed which will underpin a three to five year "integrated conservation and rural development project" managed by WWF. The project will be undertaken in close consultation with local landowners and communities, and with the financial and logistical support of the commercial partners.

The overall objective of the project is to facilitate the long-term protection of the region's natural environment and its considerable biological diversity by the people and communities living in the region, and to promote "sustainable economic development of these communities". The project will be funded to the level of around US$4 million (A$5.2 million) by the companies involved and it is anticipated that it will be fully operated by local people at the end of six years.

In the area of education and training, Dupont, in conjunction with the Chinese Academy of Science, has entered a partnership arrangement to produce a series of twelve documentaries, "Technology and our Daily Lives". This is the first single theme series of its type and is aimed at educating the Chinese public on the importance that science and industry play in their lives. The series is helping to build the profile of science, industry and manufacturing amongst the public at large, and at the same time is raising the public profile of Dupont and providing support for the educational facility of the Chinese Academy of Sciences.

Enterprise development is an increasing growth area which includes:

- investments in community enterprise and/or venture capital funds;
- time taken by local business leaders to serve on the advisory boards of community enterprise organizations;
- secondment and volunteer programmes for employees to work on community projects; and
- sponsorship of university and other research programmes.

Nutrimetics International, a privately held Australian skin-care product company, works with thousands of Asian entrepreneurs (mainly women) through its wholly owned subsidiaries in Thailand and Malaysia. Nutrimetics' business is based entirely on direct selling through a network of more than two hundred thousand independent consultants in Australia and six Asian countries, each of whom is able to make their own operating decisions within the broader corporate culture set by the company.

In Malaysia the company, which has as a core part of its mission statement the goal always to act ethically in business, has recently established the Nutrimetics Bumiputra Children's Fund as a tangible demonstration of its commitment to the local market and community.

3. Government Views on Philanthropic Organizations/ Corporate Philanthropy's Involvement in Promoting the Above Activities.

The federal government has established firm foundations for Australia's engagement with the countries of Asia. Economic as well as educational, scientific, medical and artistic links are encouraged and supported by government. The government has provided an environment in which Australia is orientated towards Asia and in which regional activities and networks are encouraged. Direct incentives for corporate philanthropy to become involved are not provided. However, it is likely that over time, as Australian corporations increase their offshore interests, their philanthropic activities in Asian countries will expand as will their support for networks and regional programmes.

In relation to private philanthropic activity, the federal government has done very little to stimulate the growth of local giving through foundations, let alone encouraging activity in the Asia Pacific region.

As mentioned, much of ATO's view on philanthropy stems from its basic position that deductibility for philanthropic purposes is a tax expenditure. In its terms, as stated by Assistant Treasurer George Gear, the government's position would be to assist worthy causes through the expenditure side of the budget, rather than through tax concessions.

Seen as a tax expenditure, it is understandable that the ATO views the money made available to the community by way of concessions, exemptions, or even rebates, as money which should have been collected by government and distributed through the accountability of federal parliament.

In this context, it is not surprising that the government has announced the Industry Commission into Charity. Part of the terms of reference of this inquiry is to consider the "appropriateness of present taxation treatment of charitable organizations".

The inquiry will also examine and report on

- the size, scope, efficiency and effectiveness of the services provided in Australia by charitable organizations;
- the size and scope of, and funding arrangements for, those services delivered overseas by Australian charitable organizations; and
- the administrative efficiency of charitable organizations in Australia.

Irrespective of these developments, however, Australian government agencies work closely with organizations established to deliver charitable, cultural and environmental initiatives overseas.

In addition to a failure more actively to encourage private foundation growth, the Australian government has taken a conservative view regarding distribution of income from foundations. The ATO has taken the view that the distribution of all income should occur on an annual basis unless otherwise stated in the instrument that established the foundation. Unwritten policy does, however, allow retention of between ten and fifteen percent of income to capital, but this is not encouraged.

Thus the capital growth of existing foundations has been limited, particularly as many foundations, especially those managed by trustee companies, are restricted to investment in authorized trustee investments, leading to conservative portfolios.

It has been encouraging, however, to see that over recent years trustees are playing a much more pro-active role in developing investment portfolios that encourage maximum capital growth. ANZ Trustees, for example, adopts an overall policy of achieving an annual capital growth for at least consumer price index (CPI) plus one percent. (In reality, over the last three to four years it has achieved a capital growth of at least CPI plus three percent)

III. Future Prospects

1. Role of Philanthropic Organizations/Corporate Philanthropy inFurther Enhancing a Sense of the Asia Pacific Regional Community

Given the current limitations private foundations have in funding in the region, the main opportunities for enhancing a regional community, in the shorter term, will depend on corporate willingness to take a leadership role, particularly insofar as their willingness to form partnerships with government and NGO communities.

Their ability to do this will be dependent on an increased commitment to corporate citizenship and leadership in the region.

Some of the mechanisms for increasing this activity will involve:

- establishing and/or joining Asian business partnerships;
- working with regionally focused NGOs on projects and/or policy matters;
- profiling, promoting and sharing regional "best practice" in the areas of sustainable development, corporate good citizenship and shareholder partnership; and
- developing the Australian and Asian "business leaders of tomorrow" to be socially and environmentally responsible, through company training, business partnership and/or university and business school programmes.

In order to develop a longer term vision and to begin this activity, company chief executives must initially develop a clear vision and take a leadership role, develop and implement clear policies and management systems, as well as promote greater cooperation and communication with key stakeholders.

By combining these factors companies will be well positioned to combine economic objectives with social and environmental responsibilities in ways that make sense for the company, make sense for the community and make sense for the environment.

Hopefully, the private philanthropic sector, through the Australian government's inquiry into charity, will be able to develop the mechanisms that will facilitate a broader vision.

2. Major Constraints Against Philanthropic Organizations/ Corporate Philanthropy in Engaging in the Above

In addition to the very real constraints placed on Australia's philanthropic activity in the region as a result of the relatively small amount of funding currently available, the reluctance of government to provide incentives to encourage growth in the philanthropic pool, as well as the level of need at home, there are some psychological and cultural barriers to greater involvement.

Historically, Australia has looked to the UK and Europe as a cultural reference point, rather than to Asia and the Pacific region.

Major funders, both private foundations and corporations, undoubtedly hold the view that to move into the region is too big and too hard a job, given the historic and cultural differences. At this point their vision, if indeed they have one, is narrow and limited to what they understand. This is summed up in the view that the issues confronting the broader Asia Pacific region are someone else's funding responsibility, rather than their own.

The situation is made more difficult by the particular independence, diversity and idiosyncrasies of the private foundation sector in Australia. The AAP has found it difficult productively to harness these differences and develop strong partnerships and a shared vision within Australia, let alone internationally. In addition, to date at least, Australia has little tradition of partnership building between private and corporate philanthropy.

Furthermore, both private philanthropic foundations and corporate philanthropy in Australia have had little exposure to successful funding models that have been initiated and tested in the broader region.

The lack of any infrastructure or mechanism for sharing information and transmitting knowledge about projects and programmes has acted as a major constraint to further development.

The diversity of the region has made it very difficult to identify areas of common ground. The 1990 symposia on philanthropy held in Bangkok was full of good will and the desire to develop, went a long way towards increasing Australia's understanding of philanthropy in the region, and began to identify some projects that might form the basis of funding partnerships.

Unfortunately, at the time, the identification of areas of common interest was difficult to find and the infrastructure to support any ongoing activity lacking.

3. Measures to Enhance Further the Above Efforts

To move beyond the current diffused and ad hoc approach to existing philanthropic funding activity in the region it will be particularly important for Australia to build on work already undertaken, as well as to encourage new initiatives and new involvement.

The ability to do this will depend on the identification of new and more champions for building strong regional partnerships both within Australia and within the region through existing programmes and corporate activity, as well as through links with traditional educational initiatives, such as the Colombo Plan, and exchange programmes.

Australia has built up a steady and significant alumni list within the region that should be called upon to further facilitate new activities as well as the development of a shared vision for philanthropic activity.

An immediate goal should be the formation of a formal structure to progress development. Such a structure would include member countries and could:

- systematically support activities;
- assist with the development of a shared vision;
- undertake strategic planning to support the shared vision;
- establish some regional forums around issues common to all member countries in the region, such as the environment, sustainable development, local enterprise development, health etc;
- act as a clearinghouse for both private and corporate philanthropic activity in the region; and
- provide information, education and communication about the issues, projects currently underway, and models that have been successfully tested.

Notes

1. International Monetary Fund, *International Financial Statistics.* January 1995 (Washington, D.C.: IMF, 1995). Figures given are based on end of period exchange rates for November 1994. A$1=US$0.77.
2. *Giving Australia, A quantitative exploration of the Philanthropic Sector for the 1988–89 Financial Year.* Undertaken by the Reark Research Pty Ltd for the Australian Association of Philanthropy. Printed February 1990. Out of print.

CANADA

Nongovernmental Underpinnings of the Emerging Asia Pacific Community

Donald Rickerd
President
Max Bell Foundation

I. Overview of Foundations and Corporate Philanthropy in Canada

Philanthropy in Canada is, I am glad to report, both alive and well, although somewhat subdued due to the effects of the recession—a recession that appears to have affected Canada early and whose results have lingered longer than in many other countries. That having been said, Canada and Canadians have a well-deserved reputation, both at home and abroad, for generosity and an interest in the well-being and future of others. In addition, Canada has always prided itself in its internationalism, and thus the development of NGO networks in Asian Pacific are of special interest to Canadians who have seen many examples of the benefits that such groupings can bring.

The evolution of Canadian philanthropy, both through foundations and corporations, has, to some extent, paralleled that in the United States, although with a significant lag in time and size, even when the disparity in the two countries is taken into account. There are many reasons for this difference, including Canada's much smaller population, vast distances, the much smaller number of pools of capital in the hands of corporations and extremely wealthy individuals, and a relatively mild version of the welfare state whereby most people contribute, through their taxes, to hospitals, universities, and other charitable bodies. The interventionist nature of Canadian governments at all levels has probably had a restraining effect on the overall development of philanthropy in Canada, and this is certainly true as taxation has increased so substantially over the years. One other factor of special note is that tax rates have traditionally been higher in Canada than in the United States.

To give some idea of the overall scope of charities, broadly defined, in Canada, the Canadian Centre for Philanthropy has estimated that in 1993 about C$86 billion (US$62.77 billion)[1] passed through all registered charities.[2] This is estimated to be about twelve to thirteen percent of the country's gross domestic product (GDP), or, in more vivid terms, about equal to the GDP of the Province of British Columbia. About C$40 billion (US$29.2 billion) was paid in salaries and benefits by charities to the 1.32 million people in their work force, or nine percent of the total number of Canadians employed.

To give some idea of the relative weight of charitable giving in Canada, it has been estimated by the Institute of Donations and Public Affairs Research that, in 1993, private sector donations to charity were broken down as follows:

foundations .... 5 percent
corporations .... 7 percent
individuals .... 88 percent

As far as foundations are concerned, the *Canadian Directory to Foundations*[3] lists almost a thousand active Canadian foundations. These hold assets of almost C$4 billion (US$ 2.92 billion) and make grants of about C$347 million (US$253.28 million) per annum. (These figures may be somewhat understated because of reporting variations, some foundations reporting book value of assets and others reporting current market value of assets.) There is an inordinate concentration of foundations in Ontario—about sixty percent of the national total.

One encouraging trend in Canada has been the recent establishment of a considerable number of corporate foundations, some by Canada's largest companies: the Royal Bank of Canada, Imperial Oil, and Labatt's Breweries, to name but a few. This is not to say that such companies did not give generously to charity in the past but rather to indicate that they are now recognizing their charitable commitment in a much more public way to a consistent level of donations.

Both the legal and tax structures, as they affect Canadian philanthropy, are still in an emerging phase with many gray areas yet to be adequately defined. This has made Canadians relatively cautious in the field of philanthropy, especially when it comes to involvement beyond Canada's borders, as very specific tax regulations must be adhered to where charitable funds are to flow abroad. The basic problem is, at times, complicated further by overlapping jurisdictional claims, often of a somewhat arcane nature, and by the fact that Canadian governments, at various levels, have given little visible support to the view that philanthropy is an important facet of society, something to be nurtured, encouraged and stimulated.

The development of philanthropy in Canada, both through foundations and on the part of corporations, has been marked by a number of important trends. Increasingly, over the last twenty years, both foundation and corporate boards and executives have introduced considerably more discipline into their grant making, in many instances by choosing carefully delineated program areas of activity. Concomitantly, there has been a decline in the number of organizations using a scatter gun approach, supporting whatever comes to their attention at a given moment. The ad hoc nature of this older form of grant making often prevented coping with systemic problems in favour of the random "good deeds" approach of past eras.

One further factor needs to be mentioned, and it is one that affects Canada significantly. A surprising proportion of Canadian business is owned abroad and, all too frequently, decisions on charitable donations are made in head offices, far distant from Canada. This absentee ownership phenomenon is a fact that, while not unique to Canada, is receiving increasing scrutiny at the present time, although it must be recognized that it is an exceedingly complex issue. Canada would benefit greatly from further comparative studies, which might throw light on the situation in Asia Pacific countries that are experiencing the same situation. This phenomenon has certainly contributed to a "Canada first" mentality, i.e., that Canadians have so few discretionary resources, the ones they do have should be used at home first. It is also clear that too many Canadian corporations have had only a national mandate from their foreign owners and did not operate abroad where they might have been led to "invest" philanthropic dollars out-of-country.

In recent years, Canadian foundations and large corporations have increasingly come to utilize professional staff whose specific task is to organize the philanthropic work of the entity. This is a marked change from several decades ago when very few foundations were run by anyone other than volunteers and when corporations often left their charitable giving to their corporate secretaries, their public relations departments, or the spouse of their president! Smaller sums continue to be donated by local branches and plants, usually according to strict guidelines that are nationwide in scope. This is especially true of Canada's major banks, large manufacturing companies, and resource industries. Especially for the larger foundations, there is ever-increasing reliance on professional investment managers, almost all from specialist firms operating at arm's length from the foundations, and this has resulted from much careful analysis of the investment performance of foundations in times of economic recession.

Canada's foundations and corporations have, with growing confidence, begun to attempt to be innovative in their programmatic activities, thereby breaking away from the safety of making time-honored grants to old, established institutions which came to depend on them over the years. With a resolve to be more proactive rather than merely reactive, some donors have focussed on such thrusts as program-related investments, cooperative funding by consortia of donors, donating support through the provision of gifts in kind or by way of services, and making micro credit grants. After talking for many years about taking risks, about being at the so-called "cutting edge," and being prepared to fail, some donors are now actually translating their speeches into action—and disasters have been found to be few and far between!

In addition, the activities of Canadian donor organizations have become much more open in recent years, partly as a result of voluntary action, such as the increasingly common practice of issuing public reports, and partly as a result of legal requirements, such as the filing of annual information returns which then become available for public scrutiny. The combined effect of such trends has made it possible for the Canadian Centre for Philanthropy to publish, on a regular basis, such materials as the *Canadian Directory to Foundations*—a publication of great assistance to those seeking funding support and not knowing where to look for it. It has also permitted many larger private organizations, such as hospitals and universities, to compile substantial data bases of their own, listing potential sources of philanthropic support. Through the cooperation of foreign organizations such as the Foundation Center, the Council on Foundations in Washington, D.C., and the Charities Aid Foundation in London, England, it is now relatively easy, inexpensive, and quick to obtain information on foreign sources of assistance as well as on Canadian ones.

As far as the development of new types of foundations is concerned, mention should be made of three initiatives in Canada:

a. the creation of an ever-increasing number of community foundations, all of which start small but some of which grow to substantial size, as is seen by the growth of the Vancouver Foundation and the Winnipeg Foundation, two of Canada's oldest.
b. the development of foundations within Canada's rapidly expanding ethnic communities. As immigrants to Canada have settled down and prospered, some have been able to amass sizeable fortunes and then to turn their minds to charity, utilizing the device of a foundation. This is a trend that will undoubtedly increase as immigrants make their presence felt in the business, professional, and financial worlds in Canada and often decide to pay back some of the benefits they have been able to obtain in their new homeland.
c. the establishment, in several of Canada's provinces, of so-called Crown foun-

dations which, to date, have been limited to universities. Certain universities are, by statute, able to set up a foundation that is designated as a Crown foundation and whose role is solely to assist the university that established it. Its designation, as an emanation of the Crown in the right of a province, ensures a substantially larger than normal tax benefit for donors of large sums of money to a university. While only in operation for a very few years, the results have been most impressive and, as the existence of Crown foundations becomes more widely known, their impact will become ever greater.

One additional interesting development in Canadian philanthropy has been the initiative taken by the Canadian Centre for Philanthropy in developing its "Imagine" Campaign. This is a massive effort, generously supported by corporations and foundations, to increase public awareness of the role of philanthropy and the charitable sector in Canada. Valuable advertising space has been donated to the initiative and the logo of the Imagine Campaign is now a familiar sight across Canada. The campaign is designed to increase the level of giving by both corporations and individuals, with equal stress being placed on donations of money, time, and gifts in kind. While it is extremely difficult to measure accurately the impact of such a multi-year campaign, the results appear to be most encouraging. For example, many corporations are making a public pledge to donate one percent of their pre-tax profits to charity every year.

All of the foregoing must be considered in the context of one of the monumental shifts in the history of Canada. For centuries, Canada, which was first settled by French and British people who displaced aboriginal peoples, quite naturally looked towards Europe and the Atlantic. Trade was basically with Europe, new settlers came from there, English law (and to a lesser extent French law) applied, ideas and news emanated from Europe, students went to study there, and the key languages were English and French. This relationship was intensified by the major wars in which Canada was involved, from the Napoleonic Wars through to the Second World War, as Canadian forces were almost entirely deployed to the European theater. Also, the link with the British Crown continues to be an aspect of the Canadian Constitution to this day. When trade patterns first began to alter, following the Second World War, they shifted mainly from trans-Atlantic trade with Europe to North American trade with the United States, so that the latter trading relationship has become the largest bilateral one in the world today.

Very recently, however, Canada has awakened to the reality that it is both an Atlantic and a Pacific nation. This has come about with blinding speed, a pace that has left many Canadians somewhat nostalgic for the "good old days" of centuries-old, established trading patterns and, it must be admitted, somewhat less intense competition!

Coupled with this remarkable shift in trade patterns have been a host of parallel developments: the advent of rapid and relatively inexpensive transportation routings to Asia, a new interest in the languages, cultures, and cuisines of Asian countries and, perhaps most important of all, a very rapid increase in immigration from Asian countries. Large numbers of Asian students now come to study in Canada, and these range from children in school to post-doctoral researchers. This trend is increasingly encouraged by the Canadian Government and many private organizations which have come to see the offering of Canada's excellent educational resources to overseas students as a major factor in Canada's economy. All of the foregoing changes have been cemented by major investments by Canada in Asian countries, both by corporations seeking profits and by governmental agencies involved with development projects. In addition, many Asian countries have invested heavily in Canada, often using Canada as a springboard to entry into the United States' market. Large investments in the natural resource industries and in Canada as a tourist destination have resulted in a significant flow of business executives and technical personnel to Canada, often accompanied by their families.

In many ways the symbiotic relationships between Canada and Asian countries that have developed are curious ones given their asymmetry—that is, Canada's enormous size; its extremely small, by Asian standards, population; its status as a developed country; its cold northern climate; and its European heritage. Perhaps it is remarkable that the changeover has been as smooth and harmonious as it has been!

II. Role of Canadian Philanthropic Organizations and Corporations in Promoting a Sense of Community in the Asia Pacific Region

It must be admitted at the outset that, with certain exceptions, Canadian philanthropic organizations and corporations have lagged badly when it comes to the promotion of a sense of community in the Asia Pacific region. This is particularly so when one contrasts the enormous number of initiatives that have as their goal the fostering of ties between Canada and Europe—conferences, seminars, exchanges, sports events, to name but a few. Many of the reasons for this are historical and stem from the background and history outlined earlier. With the exception of such initiatives as church-sponsored missionary efforts, some transportation links, and the sale of wheat and some natural resources, Canada's direct contact with Asia has been extremely limited over the years. While a few Japanese settled early in British Columbia, and Chinese settled in scattered lots in Canada's urban areas, the total Asian population in Canada was infinitesimal for many years, mainly as a result of Canada's unfortunate discriminatory immigration policies which favoured European, mainly British, immigrants. There was thus little trans-Pacific contact, and linguistic barriers certainly accentuated the divide.

Canadian foundations, although priding themselves as being innovative in the utilization of their discretionary funds, are actually quite slow to react to changing societal needs and social conditions. The result has been that their attention, like that of the Canadian public, to Asian matters has been, for the most part, incidental and usually a function of some other goal the foundation is seeking to achieve. With very rare exceptions, private Canadian foundations have so far ignored Asia and the Asians (I except here the rather unique Asia Pacific Foundation of Canada which was established with government funding), even though the needs, and indeed the opportunities, for innovative grant making are quite obvious.

I have had the benefit of reading a draft of the paper prepared by Professor Paul Evans of York University in Toronto for this symposium[4] and fully support his analysis of the Canadian scene. As Canada does not have a large number of foundations, applicants for financial support for projects relating to Asia have a very limited range of sources domestically. Even with the small number of foundations, it is disappointing to report that only about two percent of all foundation gifts are for international activities. As Professor Evans has pointed out, the result has been to force many Canadian applicants to seek funding abroad.

There are, however, a few Canadian foundations that do have public commitments that involve Asia Pacific. The Max Bell Foundation, for example, has since 1974, listed Asia Pacific as one of its major program areas. Since that date it has made grants in this field in the amount of C$3,247,500 (US$2,370,438). A smaller Canadian foundation, the Panicaro Foundation, has been particularly innovative in the grants it has made to promote the study of Asian matters, to facilitate a range of important meetings of participants on both sides of the Pacific, and to give encouragement to scholars. The current Lieutenant-Governor of British Columbia, the Honourable David Lam, has been most helpful in urging Canadian philanthropies to keep Asia and Asian matters in mind as far as grant making is concerned. Great support has also been derived from the Asia Pacific Foundation of Canada, although, as noted earlier, it differs in many respects from private foundations as they are known in Canada.

I would like to make one further reference to Professor Evans' thoughtful paper. It should be noted that of the ten university-based Canadian research centers he has listed, six were either started or sustained by private Canadian foundations, notably the Donner Canadian Foundation and the Max Bell Foundation, both national grantmakers based in Toronto. Both have endeavored to assist in the building of the university infrastructure and the intellectual framework that is so important if the relationship between Canada and Asia Pacific is to be a thoughtful, harmonious, and constructive one.

No one would be surprised that the financial world in Canada has a substantial interest in Asian matters. For example, the Hong Kong and Shanghai Bank of Canada has funded, amongst other projects, the new Canada and Hong Kong Resource Centre in Toronto which is an initiative of the University of Toronto-York University Joint Centre for Asia Pacific Studies, the Centre for Canada-Asia Business Relations at Queen's University, and the University of British Columbia. The Bank continues to show a very generous interest in Canada's educational initiatives as they relate to Asian matters.

The Institute of Donations and Public Affairs Research (IDPAR) has recently analyzed very carefully a number of trends in current corporate philanthropy in Canada.[5] Amongst others, it has noted that corporate donors are becoming particularly aware of the advantages of relating their donations to their overall corporate objectives. This bodes well for future funding relating to Asia Pacific matters, given the ever-increasing interest on the part of Canadian corporations to position themselves in Asia, especially in banking, insurance, telecommunications, and consulting, amongst others.

Additionally, companies are increasingly encouraging employees to contribute time as volunteers at charitable institutions, often through professional and technical skills they have learned at work. This is a trend which is growing rapidly and which has been recognized as fostering continuing and valuable relationships that go far beyond the usual direct financial contributions.

Finally, there has been a noticeable movement by corporations away from capital grants of the bricks and mortar variety towards more active projects or programs that have a defined time frame. These have led to much greater personal involvement on the part of both corporation personnel and those employed by the recipient of the assistance, a feature welcomed by both groups.

Whereas it was very rare twenty years ago for Canadian corporations and foundations to cooperate by jointly funding worthy projects, today such linkages are commonplace. Indeed, in the case of my own foundation, it is rare for it to make a major grant for a project without discovering that the applicant has made efforts, often successful, to put together a consortium of funders, typically various levels of government, major corporations, plus foundations and private donors. This is certainly the wave of the future when it comes to major initiatives in Canada, and such groupings often lead to quite unexpected, but welcome, parallel initiatives.

It is not surprising to learn from IDPAR that, while a very large number of Canadian corporations are developing a focus on Asia Pacific, this move has not yet worked its way into their donations policies. While the companies currently spend their money in Canada (where they earn it), as they move into Asia, it is almost certain they will be prepared to donate there.

It is somewhat embarrassing to have to report that the *Directory of Canadian Foundations*, under its grant categories "Asia Pacific" and "Asia" includes only two listings—the Ford Foundation and the Max Bell Foundation. Such a situation is extremely discouraging to applicants, although it must be said that sometimes grants with an Asian aspect to them may have, as their main thrust, another region of the world and deal somewhat peripherally with Asia. They would thus be listed in the *Directory of Canadian Foundations* under other headings. But however one looks at it, the world of foundations lags sadly behind the rest of Canada in coming to grips with the changing realities.

III. Future Prospects

What the situation in Canada does suggest is that there are unlimited opportunities to foster innovative steps that will lead to a more comprehensive exploration of the relationship between Canada and Asia Pacific.

a. A number of such initiatives come readily to mind, and the organizing of the Osaka meeting will, in itself, undoubtedly spark other ideas as well that can be considered, and acted upon, in Canada. It will therefore be important for the printed record of the Osaka meeting to be circulated widely to corporate and philanthropic leaders in Canada, accompanied by a concise Executive Summary.

b. There is clearly a need for an easily accessible source from which can be ascertained what current research is being undertaken in Canada so as to avoid duplication and also to permit researchers to form new linkages.

c. In addition, a more extensive compilation needs to be undertaken of funding sources, both foundation and corporate. While this step is not complex in nature, it is nonetheless extremely important for those in the field.

d. Another initiative that would have far-reaching effects would be one that would focus on media personnel so that they were more fully informed about Asia Pacific matters in general and about Asia Pacific matters as they relate to Canada specifically. A much better informed Canadian public will then slowly broaden its focus of interest to include Asia Pacific. Southam-type Fellowships in Journalism, designed specifically for those interested in Asia Pacific, would be a most valuable contribution as the media are indispensable for informing the public about the issues of the day. Such Fellowships would supplement the current short-term media program funded by the Asia Pacific Foundation.

e. Inadequate recognition is accorded at the present time to those who have made significant contributions of time, energy and ideas to the development of the Canadian-Asia Pacific relationship. The Donner medal for outstanding achievement in Canadian Studies in the United States has focussed a great deal of attention on that field and a similar initiative in the Asia Pacific field could be expected to have an equal effect. Other forms of recognition, uniquely Asian, might also be considered.

f. There is very little being done at the present time to bring together, in an informal setting, both scholars and others who are interested in Asia Pacific. An annual summer event, known as the Zavikon Asian Conference, has been held with considerable success on an island in the St. Lawrence River, but a much more extensive series of similar opportunities is greatly needed across Canada if Canadians and their Asian counterparts are to develop the personal ties that are so important in developing Canadian-Asian linkages.

g. While there are a number of Scholarship and Fellowship plans in place that permit students to study in other countries, these are for the most part limited in scope. Mobility is nowhere near as easy in the Asia Pacific area as it is for students in the European Union countries or, indeed, for those in the three North American Free Trade Agreement countries—Canada, the United States, and Mexico—if present planning is translated into reality. Initiatives in this field would go a long way to promote a sense of community where it does not currently exist.

h. While these are some excellent examples of the "twinning" of cities, a great deal more could be done to promote such linkages between much smaller centers. Again, the European example is one to be emulated.

The forgoing are but a few examples of the initiatives which might be taken in the expectation of continuing, long-term benefits leading to the fostering of a new and exciting awareness of community.

As was indicated at the outset of this review, Canadians are interested in matters international. They are innovative, experienced, and dedicated when it comes to international involvement. They can certainly be counted on to play their part in the developments that will surely follow from the Osaka meeting.

Notes

1. International Monetary Fund, *International Financial Statistics*, January 1994 (Washington, D.C.: IMF, 1995) Figures given are based on end of period exchange rates for November 1994. US$1=C$1.37.
2. *A Portrait of Canada's Charities* (Toronto: The Canadian Centre for Philanthropy 1994), p. ix.
3. *Canadian Directory of Foundations 1994-5*, 11th Edition (Toronto).
4. See Paul M. Evans's *Canadian Research Institutions and Asia Pacific* in the research institutions section of this project.
5. IDPAR, *Trends in Corporate Community Investment in Canada* (Toronto: IDPAR, 1993).

CHINA

Foundations in China
A Survey Report

Zhang Ye
Consultant

I. Background

Broadly defined, foundations are private, nonprofit organizations that obtain a certain amount of endowment funds. Their work and funding are managed by the board of trustees who may also be the major donors. The objectives of philanthropic foundations are to deliver social services in the areas of culture, education, public health, science and technology, public policy, social welfare, religion and so on.

The functions and roles of foundations are described in the *Chinese Civil Affairs Directory* as follows:

> Foundations are those mass, not-for-profit organizations that exercise management over funds donated by Chinese and foreign organizations and individuals. Their objectives are to assist the development of scientific research, education, social welfare and other public services. Foundations have several characters: (1) they are nonprofit social organizations; (2) their sources of funding come exclusively from voluntary donations; (3) a foundation should have an endowment no less than RMB 100,000 (US$12,000)[1] or foreign currencies equivalent to that amount; (4) government functionaries shall not be leaders of foundations; (5) the registration procedure for foundations has two tiers—national foundations shall apply to and be approved by the Bank of China and register at the Ministry of Civil Affairs; the provincial foundations shall apply to and be approved by the provincial governments and register at the provincial Civil Affairs Departments.

Although philanthropic foundations in the PRC did not grow up until recent years of opening and reform, many—if not all—of them qualify under most of the standards and also fall into the categories of foundation work and activities that are generally recognized in the outside world.

Like China's nongovernmental organizations (NGOs), which I have described in a separate survey report, Chinese foundations have evolved with the development of China's "reform and opening-up policy" initiated at the end of the 1970s. Rapid economic development has also given great impetus to societal pluralization. The great variety of social groups reflecting diverse social interests and expressing strong public voices have, at the same time, expanded their resource base. On the one hand, along with the process of social transformation, new social problems and the ever deteriorating social safety net originally provided by the government, require more effective and multi-channeled management. On the other hand, resources controlled by the government are diminishing due to the decentralization of power. As a result, the central government is gradually withdrawing from the area of social welfare, allowing social organizations to devise solutions to emerging problems and to secure resources to implement those remedies. It is this overall situation that creates the impulse for nongovernmental organizations, including foundations, to be established.

The China Youth Development Fund was founded in July 1981 by the Central Committee of the Chinese Youth League as the first foundation. To date, more than three hundred foundations of various types have been established throughout China, of which forty-eight are national foundations. Foundations have proved to be an effective means of soliciting and using funds available in the country and overseas to supplement the work in areas that the government is unable to manage effectively. Through the relatively independent management of the programs and the unconventional bottom-up strategies, a lot of important and cutting-edge work has been accomplished over the past few years.

One example is the Foundation for International Strategic Studies (FISS) that has succeeded in bringing together Chinese strategic planners and policy analysts and their overseas counterparts for fruitful exchange of information and ideas. In the past few years, FISS has invited scholars from the United States, Russia, Japan, Germany, Britain, India, North Korea, and Taiwan. The guests for whom they make arrangements to visit China give lectures and hold informal discussions at various research institutions and universities. For another example, the China Youth Development Foundation has succeeded over the years in providing tuition for 540,000 children and has built two hundred and four primary schools for children in underdeveloped areas. Its funds are largely raised in the society rather than provided by the government.

The development of foundations has drawn increasing attention from government agencies and various social groups. In the Ministry of Civil Affairs, the Association of Social Organizations has done tremendous comparative studies on NGOs and has drafted a "Law on Social Organizations" which is now being reviewed for approval by the State Council and the National People's Congress. The China Association of Science Foundations was established to improve the administration of foundations in the field of science and to strengthen international exchange. Several conferences on the studies of foundations have been conducted in the past two or three years. As a new form of institution, foundations, together with other NGOs, have already demonstrated, and will continue to demonstrate, their strength as an emerging social force for self-organization and self-governance. They help lay the groundwork for further structural and social change.

While giving increasing weight to NGOs, the Chinese leadership continues to emphasize political and social stability, reflected in their concern that any loosening of control over NGOs might foster dissenting political forces. *The Regulation on the Registration and Management of Social Organizations*[3] and *The Regulation on the Administration of Foundations*[4], however incomplete, both emphasize government management and control over NGOs. Like other NGOs, foundations are vulnerable to changes of the political climate in China. After the Tiananmen incident in 1989, all of the NGOs and foundations were requested to be reregistered at the Ministry of Civil Affairs or its local departments. As a result, most of the existing nongovernmental foundations have a history of no more than four years.

II. Types of Foundations

Though most of the foundations claim to be independent and nongovernmental, and many organizations call themselves "foundations," the situation is very complicated and confusing to an outside observer. As China is just moving from a planned economy to a market economy, the philanthropic culture has yet to develop. A definition suitable to one particular type of foundation may be irrelevant to other types.

For example, a Chinese foundation can be an organization that looks for funding, instead of one that dispenses an existing fund; it can be an organization that relies on government funding to implement certain programs preset by the government; it can be a company which provides some kind of public service on behalf of a government agency or an enterprise; it can also be a very flexible and loosely organized group that tries to cater to miscellaneous purposes, depending on times and circumstances.

Even so, foundations in China in general can still be roughly divided into two categories: government-funded agencies and foundations relying on social donations. The National Science Foundation and the National Social Science Fund, for example, were set up by the State Council in the late 1980s for the purpose of encouraging research achievements in the fields of natural science and social science. The National Science Foundation is managed by the Chinese Science and Technology Commission with a fund of RMB 300 million (US$35.17 million) each year, allocated by the Ministry of Finance. It is more of an independent institution, with a full-time staff, an annual work plan, and an independent review commission. The National Social Science Fund is at the moment administered by the Propaganda Department of the Communist Party's Central Committee as one division of the Department. It receives RMB 20 million (US$2.345 million) a year from the Ministry of Finance.

In principle, every research organization and individual scholar interested in natural sciences, technology, or social sciences may apply for funding from the aforementioned two foundations through a process of bidding, recommendation, competition, peer-review, and final committee decision. Both funds, however, are created to support the key projects of the national five-year plan. In addition, the government organs managing these funds design their own key projects. Therefore, applicants must adjust their research interests to suit the needs of the key projects, which are often subject to changing policy priorities and preferences of the time. Applications that reflect scholarly interests differing from the priorities set by the government are likely to be turned down.

The leaders of the two national foundations are usually well-known scientists and social scientists who are appointed to the positions. As these two are basically government agencies, their application procedures are different from nongovernmental foundations. That means that *The Regulation on the Administration of Foundations* does not apply to these government-designated foundations. They are, however, exploring ways to loosen their ties with the government in order to be able to get resources from more diverse channels. The National Social Science Fund is trying to reregister at the Ministry of Civil Affairs as a nongovernmental foundation, despite the fact that it will retain its annual funding from the Ministry of Finance. It wants to change its name into something like "China Social Science Fund" which might have less of a government ring.

Many other foundations are considered nongovernmental, or at least do not receive government funding on a regular basis. They can be roughly divided into four categories:

- Foundations that rely on membership fees and serve the interests of their members. They are usually small, local foundations such as the Tianjin Arts Foundation and the Beijing Philharmonic Orchestra Foundation.

- Foundations that rely on social contributions, but at the same time receive a large amount of government funding for their programs and administrative costs. The China Foundation for the Handicapped, for example, is one such foundation.
- Foundations relying on social donations for programs, and government subsidies for their administrative and staff salary expenses. Soong Ching-Ling Foundation is typical in this aspect.
- Foundations entirely relying on social donations, including international contributions. In this case, China Zhenhua Foundation (in the science field) is a good example.[5]

Foundations in China, though claiming to be nongovernmental, still have to maintain or establish linkages in one way or another with the government either in staffing, missions for their programs, or in their funding resources. Foundations in China therefore are very much sector oriented. They usually have little connection with one another.

Except for the purely government-funded foundations, Chinese foundations work mainly in the fields of social welfare, academic research, culture, education, public health, sports, and child and youth development.

III. Sources of Funding for Foundations

As a matter of practice, no Chinese foundation has its own self-generated endowment. Sources of funding for foundations in China come mainly from overseas. This is actually one of the major factors leading to governmental approval for incorporation. Foundations in this sense also play the role of attracting foreign funding. With China's open door policy, an increasing number of overseas Chinese are interested in supporting China's education and scientific research. Of the Ningbo-origin Chinese alone, such Hong Kong–based businessmen as Wang Kuancheng, Shao Yifu and Bao Yugang have over the years donated hundreds of millions of Hong Kong dollars. Big buildings named after them are seen everywhere in large universities and in their home province. Last November Mr. Jian Wenle, President of Hong Kong Champaign Science and Technology Groups, donated RMB 5 million (US$586,000) to the China Literature Foundation to give awards to outstanding writers. For many national foundations, donations from overseas account for sixty percent of their total financial sources.

Foreign foundations also play an important role in China. The Ford Foundation of the United States, Ebert Foundation of Germany, and the Japan Foundation all have offices in Beijing; Naumann Foundation operated its activities through the German Embassy in Beijing; and Oxfam has a representative in Kunming. Many foundations such as The Asia Foundation, Luce, MacArthur, Rockefeller and Rockefeller Brothers Fund, and Ling Nan Foundation of the United States, operate actively in China, though they have not yet opened offices in this country. They usually have very focused areas of interest and operate separately from the Chinese foundations and work mainly in the social science fields. However, they do undertake international joint funding for important projects that already receive partial funding from Chinese foundations.

Donations from the society have become increasingly common. The announcement and the solicitation of donations are usually done through the media in collaboration with the targeted groups. Newspapers, TV publicity, advertisements, and performing arts are the major propaganda means for donations.

Unlike foundations in many countries, many Chinese foundations conduct business and maintain investments. Running companies is a common practice for foundations. The China Literature Foundation, for example, runs eighteen companies ranging from big hotels to small restaurants. They generate a substantial amount of income for the Foundation. Consultancy fees have become a major source of revenue, especially for the natural science and technology foundations.

IV. Organizational Structure

Chinese foundations, like foundations elsewhere, also have a board of trustees (directors) and a full time staff. The board of trustees is supposed to be the highest authority and determines the foundation's criteria and policies. The board members are usually famous individuals in the field the foundation works in. The work of the foundation is overseen by the president and vice-president. The executive vice-president usually takes charge of the day-to-day internal administration and personnel management. In most cases, even the senior staff members of "nongovernmental" national foundations are appointed by their parent organizations in the government, and these staff members are usually on the government's pay-roll.

Normally, the board members are first elected by the steering committee, and serve on terms decided by the foundation. Either the remaining board members or the president of the foundation, or both, elect new members upon change of terms. As it turns out, the organizational structure of foundations in China is the least important. Board members have little responsibility over the foundation work, and they are mainly honorary public figures. As many foundations are quasi-governmental, most of the leaders of the foundations are current or retired government leaders despite the fact that the aforementioned *Regulation on the Administration of Foundations* prohibits government functionaries from serving as leaders of foundations. Some foundations even use the same staff as their line agencies. The China Literature Foundation's leaders, for example, are also the leaders of the China Writers Association.

V. Legacies of the Political Terminology

Such internationally popular terms as *philanthropy* and *charity* are not often used in China on formal occasions. Instead, social welfare is more commonly talked about. To some people, philanthropy has some kind of capitalist or bourgeois flavor. The term sometimes could even remind people of foreign missionaries' activities which to many people still reflect the foreign cultural and religious infiltration of the old days. And as a matter of fact, these activities are regarded by some as national humiliation of having to live on the alms of foreign forces. According to the once prevailing class analysis, the term *philanthropy* also has the nature of obliteration of class struggle. Hence, the term has never been used publicly. Much of the ideology has faded away with the pace of China's modernization drive. Chinese people have a broader and more relaxed understanding of philanthropy these days. The historical and political legacies, however, still remain.

While the term *philanthropy* may be regarded as capitalist or bourgeois, *social welfare* does have a strong socialist nature. Therefore, Chinese in most cases prefer the term *social welfare* to *philanthropy*, reflecting the current situation in which the philanthropic and charitable concept remains as yet to be developed. This is also due to the fact that in the past forty years of the planned economy the government's administrative control monopolized all the resources and did not allow other types of social activities, such as those of the foundations, to develop. The underdevelopment of a legal framework also restrains the development of charitable activities. The current tax law implemented in China does not provide tax exemption for donations from individuals or enterprises. As a result, donations from enterprises account for the smallest proportion of foundations' revenue.

Because of the cultural and historical legacies and the inadequacy of the legal framework, Chinese people are not used to the idea of giving money away to a social organization to deliver services to needy people. They are still used to looking to the government for solutions.

VI. Commonly Recognized Problems for Chinese Foundations

As mentioned earlier, foundations began to evolve as late as the end of the 1980s. In the past forty years, China had no legal or financial system to support a pluralized society or to control the disposition of decentralized financial resources because nongovernmental organizations were never allowed to play a very significant role in society. Centralized administration monopolized almost all channels of resources. Related to this phenomenon is the lack of a philanthropic concept by the leaders and the general public, and hence the lack of mechanisms to encourage the development of the philanthropic sector.

The foundations in China and their counterparts abroad therefore increasingly recognized the need for building an infrastructure to guide and facilitate the philanthropic sector. First, it is fundamentally important to establish a legal framework to regularize the foundations' autonomy and activities. Tax laws which will encourage public and corporate contributions are badly needed. The existing Regulation on the Administration of Foundations focuses more on the registration procedures and emphasizes the government's control. What is needed is a legal status for foundations and a management structure which is different from that of other sectors.

Second is the need for reform of the overall banking system. China's poor banking system has already been recognized as an impediment to further economic reform. Low efficiency and policy changes due to government intervention make the disposition and the availability of funds to foundations difficult. These problems also discourage contributions from outside China. Therefore, further development of NGOs and the philanthropic sector depends on a more complete and modern banking system.

The third major problem is the foundations' internal management. An effective organizational structure is needed to secure public accountability of foundation activities. Foundations also need to develop ways and means of identifying their objectives and methods of evaluating their achievements. Independent auditing and accounting need to be developed within the foundations. Finally, fund-raising strategies and institutional oversight of the funds are urgently needed.[6]

Notes

1. International Monetary Fund, *International Financial Statistics*, January 1995 (Washington, D.C.: IMF 1995). Figures are based on the end of period exchange rate for October 1994. US$1 = RMB 8.53.
2. *Chinese Civil Affairs Directory* (Shanghai: Shanghai Cishu Press, December 1990), p. 395.
3. See a short description in this volume; Zhang Ye, "Chinese NGOs: A Survey Report."
4. Drafted by the People's Bank and approved by the State Council.
5. Shen Xiaodan, "The Development of Fund System in Science and Technology and Private Science and Technology Foundations," in *Guide for Foundations*. December 1990 (Beijing: Chinese Workers Press, 1994).
6. These problems were also recognized by the group of American foundation executives organized by the National Committee on U.S.–China relations. See *The Rise of Nongovernmental Organizations in China: Implications for Americans*, National Committee China Policy, Series No. 8 May, 1994.

INDONESIA

Support for Indonesian NGO Programs Through Corporate Philanthropy

Andra L. Corrothers
Regional Representative for Asia
PACT, Inc. Asia Regional Office
(Private Agencies Collaborating Together, Inc.)

and

Estie W. Suryatna
Representative's Special Assistant

I. Introduction

To some observers, a mutually beneficial relationship between nongovernmental organizations (NGOs)[1] and private sector business entities[2] may appear to be a contradiction. Yet, partnerships between NGOs and corporate entities, the world over, have yielded exciting results. Private and corporate philanthropy together is estimated to amount to over $14 billion in the United States.[3] For many NGOs, corporate contributions, especially those made in a lump sum, are a large source of "unrestricted funds." For organizations that find themselves constricted by the requirements and programmatic exigencies of governmental donors, this type of assistance is highly valued. However, the benefit flow is not one way. Corporations also benefit greatly from contributions provided to the nonprofit sector. For instance:

- for multi-national or joint venture companies hosted in another country, contributions to the nonprofit sector demonstrate appreciation for host country nationals and their aspirations for improved welfare;
- NGOs generally express appreciation for private sector contributions through public announcements (media reports and press conferences, public service announcements, etc.), inclusion of the company's logo on their stationary as a

sponsor, and presentations of public service awards. Thus, private sector entities derive a large amount of publicity and community appreciation for such contributions;

- in terms of environmental or resource accountancy, companies fulfilling their responsibilities in environmental protection at industrial sites (sound chemical and solid waste disposal practices, recycling programs, etc.), and office complexes (i.e., paper recycling) also benefit in terms of accounting for excess resources utilized through contributions to environmental compensation programs;
- companies also often benefit in terms of services provided to surrounding communities or their own employees through NGO infrastructure improvement (i.e., village water supply development, skills enhancement training) or NGO-executed credit programs to candidate vendor/suppliers to these companies; and,
- many companies benefit by investing in the future of a community or a country, reaping both monetary and aesthetic benefits as a result.

Yet even though the benefit flow can be favorable for both NGOs and private sector companies, there are constraints which make such linkages difficult. Among these constraints are:

- *the business community and NGOs do not always demonstrate sufficient understanding or appreciation of each other*—i.e., NGOs do not generally know how the business community works nor do they know how to approach a company or communicate their needs and ideas, while the business community is often overwhelmed with the task of identifying deserving organizations or specific activities to support.
- *the issue of transparency (perceived lack of general public openness and accountability) constrains the relationship between NGOs and the private sector*—i.e., the business community requires assurances that funds donated actually benefit the targeted community groups and expects that NGOs will have management systems in place (i.e., fully disclosed audits) that guarantee the efficient utilization of such contributions, while NGOs often feel that companies do not often fully disclose sufficient information regarding the impact of their activities on communities or the environment;
- *often existing tax exemption and deduction regulations do not foster NGO–business linkages*—in legal systems with unclear definitions of what is or is not a nonprofit organization, unscrupulous organizations can use this vagueness to set up tax shields or buffers from public scrutiny, thereby, destroying the cred-

ibility of the nonprofit sector; additionally, without clear regulations regarding deductions for contributions to the nonprofit sector, an incentive is removed for companies to make contributions;

- *lack of resources, in terms of time and skills, in most NGOs, to adequately address the business sector partnerships*—NGOs, busy with their own activities, and lacking in both monetary and human resources, often forego linkages with the business community; and,
- *in the absence of effective and commonly recognized incentives for corporate philanthropy, the private sector needs additional, more persuasive reasons as to why giving money away is in its interest*—NGOs must concentrate on developing the language of the private sector (such as bottom line profitability, internal rates of return, opportunity costs of capital), in addition to ridding themselves of an allergy to professionalism in organizational management to erase a common business community perception that NGOs are "soft."

Additionally, through a combination of activities to educate the private sector about NGO programs, strengthen their own expertise and capacity in areas that have been identified, adapt a more entrepreneurial perspective to fund raising, and learn to speak to the private sector, effective linkages with the business community can be forged, even without a system of commonly recognized incentives.

The final constraint that needs consideration is the overall complexity of the issues affecting NGO–corporate linkages and the need to deal with them in an ordered and meaningful fashion. All elements are so interlinked that failure to address any one of them could seriously undercut the entire effort. In this sense, any cross-cutting efforts to establish corporate philanthropic mechanisms will need to deal appropriately with all the systemic constraints and limitations mentioned above, while simultaneously drawing on existing strengths and opportunities.

II. Support for the NGO Sector in Indonesia: a Historical Perspective

Indonesian NGOs have expanded significantly in number, diversity, and vitality during the past twenty-five years. As they have done so, a particular need has emerged for the expansion of the funding base to support their operations and programs. Up to now, external donors have provided an important portion of this support. Initially, it was the private foreign foundations such as *The Asia Foundation* and *The Ford Foundation*; religious entities, such as *Misereor*; or quasi-nongovernmental organizations such as the *Konrad Adenauer* and *Frederick Neumann Stiftungen* and more recently various bilateral donors such as the *United States Agency for International Development* (USAID) and the *Canadian International Development Agency* providing support to this vibrant sector.

While support from such outside entities is important during the nurturing phase of an NGO community, it should neither be expected nor required to play this role in the long run. As Indonesian NGOs continue to grow in size and importance, a more diverse, and therefore, larger base of support will be required for the sector to continue expanding its capacity to contribute meaningfully to Indonesian development efforts. A study, supported by USAID/Jakarta's Office of Voluntary and Humanitarian Programs in 1986 upheld this contention. In the final study report, Dr. Russell Betts, Development Alternatives, Inc., cited three reasons why such an expansion of the indigenous resource base was desirable.

a. First, over-reliance on foreign donors, however well-meaning, creates dependence and allows foreign entities too much input in determining Indonesian priorities. Indonesian nongovernmental organizations are sensitive to this fact.[4]
b. Second, even if the independence that undergirds concepts of self-reliance was not an important concern, current funding sources are unlikely to be able to respond adequately to the growing financial requirements of an expanding and increasingly effective Indonesian NGO community.[5]
c. Third, many activities of the Indonesian NGO community serve powerful democratizing functions by helping assure that people retain the capacity, through community-based activity, to influence not only the course of Indonesian development, but also the direction of their lives and futures.[6]

There are many options open to the Indonesian NGO community for seeking increased and diversified funding support. These options might include self-financing through related money-making programs (i.e., selling products of beneficiary programs, credit program management), or contracting their services to government and other entities for pay. The participation of the private, commercial sector, including multinational corporations in providing support is another potential sector. Much circumstantial evidence suggests that financial resources from within Indonesia will increase. Aside from multinational corporations, these resources are generally under the control of wealthy individuals and business conglomerates in the domestic commercial sector, neither of which is now being asked by the Indonesian NGO community to contribute to its full capacity. This potential resource could easily assume greater importance, much as it has in some industrialized countries, especially in the United States and the Philippines where corporate and private philanthropy has traditionally played, and continues to play, a crucially important role in sustaining the vitality of the nonprofit sector.

While inherently desirable, in practice such a resource transfer is presently not taking place to any significant degree in Indonesia. A variety of reasons can be suggested. Indonesia today lacks the tradition, experience, legal and organizational structures that could serve as a catalyst and channel for this kind of resource transfer. The resulting need for procedures and mechanisms to handle resource transfers has been recognized by various Indonesian NGO leaders who have explored means of addressing the related issues. However, these leaders have comparatively limited experience with private and private sector fund raising, and only slightly more experience outside their individual organizations in creating structures to manage the broad range of functions and responsibilities affiliated with such undertakings. Moreover, most of these leaders are preoccupied with the ongoing programs and activities of their respective organizations, and thus, cannot generally commit the time, energy, and other resources necessary to address relevant issues meaningfully. Processes, other than those that currently exist, are required to fulfill this function.

An additional need is for continued strengthening of institutional and program development among Indonesian NGOs, both in general and in relation to the resource transfer function. Indonesian NGOs, like their counterparts elsewhere, can benefit through the use of stronger administrative and management structures and more highly trained personnel. But with the focus on fund raising or resource transfer issues, these needs become especially acute. Mechanisms to assist this community of organizations to improve links to private and private sector financial support, thus, would represent a major contribution to the work of these organizations, as well as to the broader concept of overall private sector support to national development objectives.

III. Current Private Sector Supported Development Activities

Contributions for "charity," or the alleviation of current suffering, seems to be the focus of most corporate and other private sector donations currently in Indonesia. Little attention is now directed toward contributions for "development" or toward the establishment of conditions which enable people to move out of poverty. Many private sector firms appear to be ready to donate funds and, at times, equipment, supplies, staff time, and services, to relief efforts or for more highly visible problems (the physically or mentally disabled, orphans, etc.). They sometimes also contribute to programs to feed the hungry or heal the sick. The growth of corporate philanthropy usually follows such a continuum. This continuum generally starts from a response to crises and relief of immediate suffering, moves to support for institutional care for the distressed, and finally leads to efforts to prevent suffering and to empower people to improve and control their own lives. While most corporate donations in Indonesia currently focus on "charity," there is a growing perception that people require assistance to become self-reliant, and an increased emphasis on giving for developmental purposes.

Indonesian NGOs range in size and type from small village level welfare agencies to nature clubs to national level development and village mobilization organizations. They provide services to villagers and mobilize popular support for development activities. The international donor community has focused considerable attention on NGOs, and many international agencies feel that NGOs provide an effective structure for the delivery of development assistance.

However, questions have been raised about the dependence of these local development agencies on foreign assistance. There is a need to increase the independence of Indonesian NGOs from foreign sources of funding and shift the focus of local resource generation to the national level. International assistance patterns are changing and funds may not be available in the future to support Indonesian development efforts at current levels. Foreign funding sources have their own development strategies and may impose their concepts on the agencies they support. Indonesian NGOs may be subjected to questions about their nationalism, motives and objectives, if they cannot obtain support domestically.

Indonesian NGOs are beginning to recognize the need to mobilize resources locally. The multi-national and national business community is one potential source for the mobilization of such resources. However, there needs to be more communication between the business and NGO communities, and more understanding of differences in their purposes and objectives.

Within the context of the above discussion, an examination of current private sector initiatives for the support of the nonprofit sector in Indonesia is called for in order to identify gaps and appropriate additional and complementary approaches. The active involvement of the private sector is essential both in terms of policy and technical development, and in assisting with the need for local initiatives to adopt strategies to expand, diversify and localize their funding base and achieve financial self-reliance. Some of the more successful such endeavors are explored below and in the following section.

IV. Government and Private Sector Organized Philanthropy

1. *Bapak Angkat* (Foster or Adoptive Father) Program

The Directorate General, Ministry of Small Industry established the *Bapak Angkat* program six years ago to encourage large companies to provide support to small and weak enterprises. Such assistance was to be provided in the following potential areas:

- subcontracting opportunities;
- technical/managerial assistance;
- vendor development assistance;
- provision of equipment, tools, etc.;
- research and development assistance;
- provision of raw materials; and,
- marketing assistance.

Under the Decree of the Minister of Finance (issued 11 November 1989), state-owned parastatals are now required to participate in the *Bapak Angkat* program. The statutory obligation requires state-owned enterprises to provide between one percent and five percent per year from post-tax profits for these types of activities. An excellent example is that of P.T. Indosat (the satellite-based telecommunications company) which reportedly commits Rp 500 million (US$228,000)[7] per year, and has used this resource for such activities as:

- support for a wood drying facility in South Sulawesi;
- the marketing of precious stones in Central Kalimantan;
- improvement of the quality and marketing of cloth in North Sumatra;
- development of handicraft items in Irian Jaya;
- support for a picture framing business in Jakarta; and,
- contribution to the development fund established by KADIN (Indonesian Chamber of Commerce);

P.T. Krakatau Steel, another state-owned company, concluded a joint agreement in 1991 for support of a program on self-employment and micro enterprise promotion with Bank Indonesia under a program with the International Labor Organization.

2. Subcontracting/Vendor Support Initiatives

There appears to have been a considerably longer history of private sector entities establishing their own arrangement to foster small enterprise development linked to their own production and distribution needs. The following are some examples:

- *Bata Shoes*, a joint venture company, introduced a subcontract mechanism in 1963, which today links PT. Bata with more than forty small-scale shoe industries as shoe contractors in Jakarta, Bogor, Tangerang, Medan and Surabaya. This arrangement involves PT. Bata providing technical guidance and training. In addition, Bata has assisted in the establishment of over three hundred franchise retail outlets in Indonesia, through an attractive package of company support.
- *Coca Cola Indonesia* has initiated a policy of soft credit and other support for informal street vendors. In 1991, in Bali alone this involved three thousand micro-entrepreneurs.
- *Astra Group* (local manufacturer for Toyota vehicles) has established a foundation which commits resources to a wide range of community, social, and economic activities, including *Program Kait Terkait*, the *Linkage Program*, which has helped to develop a chain of suppliers for the company's production needs. Astra is also involved in assisting their own employees to set up subcontracting enterprises, and they even guarantee income for a set period.
- *Bank Expor Impor Indonesia* (The Indonesian Export Import Bank) has assisted an NGO group in Bandung with a monthly contract of Rp 3 million (US$1,368) to provide bank loan application assessment services. This involved the NGO providing five to ten assessments per month for business applicants from within the small metal industry area.
- B*ank Indonesia*, in conjunction with the German Technical Cooperation, has been involved with NGOs in helping to establish self-help groups as a mechanism for arranging credit for the most disadvantaged people in several provinces in Indonesia.
- Many large NGOs provide consultancy-for-fee services to government, multi- and bilateral development agencies and, the private sector.

V. Direct NGO and Private Sector Community Collaboration

This collaboration, while currently limited, may be the area of most potential collaboration from the NGO point of view. Several such networks are noteworthy. Among the most successful are the following.

1. Dana Mitra Lingkungan (DML)

DML, or The Friends of the Environment, was established in 1983 by prominent business leaders (bankers, industrialists, economists) and environmental activists (mostly from *Wahana Lingkungan Hidup* (WALHI, or the Indonesian Environmental Forum) with the support of the then State Minister for Population and Environment. DML's prime objective is to generate environmental awareness among the public, particularly the business sector. This objective is achieved predominately through the mobilization and management of an endowment fund. Grants and other assistance are provided for environmental conservation and sustainable development efforts. Special grant assistance and attention is given to projects submitted by NGOs.

DML has successfully collected over Rp 1.096 billion (US$500,000), which serves as the basis of its endowment fund. To date, the endowment and other fund-raising efforts have resulted in the provision of over Rp 1.754 billion (US$800,000) in assistance grants to various environmental NGOs in Indonesia. The largest portion of DML's funding is obtained from local sources. DML has a very low overhead rate, as many of its staff and board members contribute time, space and incidental expenses. DML enjoys good relations with both government and the private sector. Major corporate contributors to DML's endowment fund include: Bank Central Asia, Raja Garuda Mas Group, PT Asminco Bara Utara, PT USI/IBM, Harian *KOMPAS* (the largest daily newspaper in Indonesia), PT Bayer, and Hudbay Oil.

1) The DML-supported PEDULI (We Care) Program

In late 1989 and early 1990, the Government of Indonesia initiated two environmental impact reduction programs, namely, *Prokasih—Program Kali Bersih* (Clean River Program) and *Telasih—Teluk Jakarta Bersih* (Clean Jakarta Bay Program). These programs focused mainly on industrial polluters of Jakarta's rivers and the surrounding water shed areas, including Jakarta Bay. Thus, to complement this program, DML and other concerned environmental groups (including the Indonesian Environmental Forum, or WALHI) embarked on a program to address the problems of river and bay side inhabitants as the initial victims and as producers of environmental pollution.

While this program affected a clear impact on community awareness regarding the impact of household, chemical, and industrial pollution discharged into rivers and the bay, DML and WALHI also noted that the amount of solid waste disposed into rivers also required attention. While undertaking research toward seeking a solution to this problem, DML and WALHI encountered hundreds of scavengers which serve the municipality of Jakarta in the disposal of both household and industrial solid waste. They noted that these scavengers served an additional need in the handling of solid wastes and demonstrated the efficacy of informal sector processing of refuse.

In addition, it was discovered that scavengers handled a large proportion of the city's refuse, the remainder of which was handled by the municipal garbage disposal service organized under a group of scavenger coordinators, or *pelapak*. The scavenger coordinators usually managed a small amount of capital to buy refuse from the scavengers. The size of this capital fund varied according to the size of the operation area and the number of the scavengers coordinated. A large-scale *pelapak* might have capital amounting up to Rp 20 million (US$9,120) backed up with some two hundred scavengers. A medium-scale *pelapak* might have up to Rp 10 million (US$4,560) in capital with twenty to forty scavengers. While a small-scale *pelapak* would only have Rp 300,000 (US$137) or less and coordinate four to five scavengers, with himself also scavenging.

The scavengers generally were found operating in specific territories with traditional boundaries. Operation areas were divided thus: older, well established housing areas; real estate developments; and business districts. The waste processing cycle was as follows: the garbage was collected by the scavengers, and then sold to a *pelapak*. After classification according to the type of garbage (plastic, paper, aluminum, iron, glass or wood), the classified refuse was sold through a "wholesaler" to recycling factories.

Generally, the garbage collected by scavengers consisted of the following materials: plastic, tin, scrap metal, paper, cardboard cartons, glass, wood, and composting material. In 1992, DML's program focused on paper and plastic waste as the largest waste commodities. DML also focused its efforts on the improvement of the working capacity of the scavengers to increase their income and the utility of garbage disposed of or dumped in the Jakarta area.

NGOs involved in the program were to focus their activities on community organizing and community awareness campaigns. Campaigns were held to educate households and businesses in garbage separation and in the distribution of garbage collection receptacles. In addition, Indonesia's public television station, Televisi Republic Indonesia, provided free air time for public service messages developed by NGOs and the Matari Group (one of Indonesia's leading advertising firms).

DML has also had success in obtaining the required financing for development and acquisition of both low and high level technologies for recycling factories and first tier raw material processors (scavengers and pelapa*k*). Bank International Indonesia (BII) agreed to provide Rp 2.193 billion (US$1 million) in soft loans for these industries and entrepreneurs. Operational funds for the PEDULI Campaign were obtained in the form of grants from business/corporate sponsors (Rp 657.9 million, or US$300,000, was obtained for PEDULI).

The first stage of the Jakarta Recycling Development Program was carried out over a one year period, undertaking the following activities:

a. the development of the Scavengers' Activity Coordinating Institution; and,

b. a communication program addressing the issue of waste recycling, including the social aspects of this issue.

DML set up a "Program Task Force" to implement the program, consisting of a steering committee and an organizing committee. Members of the steering committee consisted of the sponsors' representatives (including BII), a public accountant, advertising agency executives, media executives and DML. Members of the organizing committee consisted of DML staff persons as the coordinator and representatives from various NGOs assisting scavenger groups, including Yayasan Dian Pertiwi Indonesia (a Jakarta-based NGO which assists the activities of approximately thirty thousand scavengers).

2. Business Council for Sustainable Development

Leading up to the world conference on the environment, held in Rio de Janeiro in June 1992, business leaders from all over the world joined to establish the *Business Council for Sustainable Development.* Business leaders from Norway, Chile, Argentina, Spain, Italy, Switzerland, the United States, Germany, Japan, Sweden, Great Britain, Canada, Venezuela, France, Brazil, Thailand, India, Holland, Kenya, and Indonesia attended the conference. For purposes of participating in this business council and preparing input for the Rio conference, a Business Council for Sustainable Development was initiated in Jakarta. Such prominent figures as Mohammed "Bob" Hassan (Chairman of the Indonesian Timber Association), Mr. Tanri Abeng (Executive Director of Jakarta Tourism Promotion), and Professor Dr. Emil Salim (former Minister of Population and the Environment) are members. The activities of this council involve planning for the future.

3. PT Van Melle Indonesia: Vision of Environmental Stewardship in Indonesia

The Van Melle candy company, based in Holland and with factories and markets all over the world, has pledged to pursue greater environmental stewardship and to base its values and business strategies on principles of sustainable development.[8] Building upon the assumption that global extraction, production and consumption must be made sustainable, the corporation has already taken a number of steps to reduce the environmental impacts of its operations. Thus, as part of each annual corporate report, Van Melle prepares an environmental audit of the "extractions" (primary energy, fresh water, and other primary raw materials) and "emissions" (greenhouse gases, acidifying emissions, fertilizers, solid waste, and chemical waste) of the production-consumption chain extending from the production of materials and packaging through manufacturing, distribution and consumption. These findings assist the corporation's management board to strive toward systematic, sustainable environmental management.

Van Melle's ultimate goal in this respect is to make no net contribution to environmental degradation, particularly if it is irreversible. While the company endeavors to minimize its detrimental impacts, it also acknowledges that technological limitations do not allow it to entirely eliminate negative environmental impacts of its activities.[9] Thus, Van Melle's approach is to compensate for negative environmental impact by making positive contributions to the preservation of natural resources through support for forest protection and rehabilitation efforts of NGOs.

The Van Melle Small Grants Program (VMSGP)

PT Van Melle Indonesia is eager to support forest conservation and tree planting activities in Indonesia, and has founded the Van Melle Small Grants Program (VMSGP) to support community-based forestry efforts by Indonesian NGOs. The company has chosen this focus for its environmental support efforts in Indonesia because of alarming global trends in deforestation and the associated losses of biological and cultural diversity, the ability of the world's fauna to buffer or even reverse global warming caused by greenhouse gas emissions like those from the Van Melle production-consumption chain, and the tremendous ecological, aesthetic, and socio-economic value of Indonesia's tropical forests. Furthermore, Van Melle wishes to express its appreciation to Indonesia as its host, and feels that tree planting and forest protection activities would be a meaningful contribution.

Thus, VMSGP was established. This program has a two-fold mission: to sponsor community-based forestry projects which advance both forest protection *and* people's welfare, through either tree planting or conservation activities of NGOs. The VMSGP supports field projects covering a wide variety of areas and approaches, including:

- the upgrading of agroforestry practices,
- regreening of critical upland areas,
- creation of community wood lots,
- settlement of shifting cultivators,
- marketing of non-timber forest products,
- rehabilitation of mangrove forests,
- integrated conservation and development in protected areas and their buffer zones, and
- development of ecotourism in nature reserves.

The VMSGP sponsors small-scale community-based forestry projects performed by Indonesian NGOs. The decision to sponsor NGO efforts grew from the company's belief that NGOs are well placed to implement projects in conjunction with communities, thus ensuring that projects have genuine benefits for local people and gain communities' long term support. PT Van Melle reasoned that enhanced NGO activity to complement government efforts would ultimately lead to a more dynamic and synergistic joining of forces to preserve Indonesia's tropical forests for the benefit of local, national, and international communities.

PT Van Melle envisions corporate donations approaching Rp 219.3 million (US$100,000) annually in Indonesia. Both single and multi-year proposals are accepted from NGOs; however, these applications have a Rp 21.93 million (US$10,000) per year ceiling on project costs. An Advisory Board has been set up to select and monitor the program. This Board consists of an executive officer of PT Van Melle Indonesia, two Indonesian NGO activists, and a VMSGP program coordinator.

VI. Expression of Corporate Social Responsibility: Alternative Financing of NGOs, Corporate Philanthropy and Methods of Choice

A discussion of corporate philanthropy would not be complete without reference to the means by which this generally occurs nor an analysis of how such financing can impact on the sustainability of programs or organizations. The most common method by which Indonesian NGOs currently receive financing is on a project-to-project basis. However, this type of financing does not ensure the sustainability of activities nor the organizational viability of the NGO. The figure below[10] illustrates how this method of financing affects the financial position of NGOs and influences their capacity and incentive for the development of self-reliant means of financing.

Current Financing Situation Based on Projects

Financial Resources
Largest Scale Projects
Larger Projects
Micro Projects
Small Projects
Self-Financing Income
Time
10 Years

The lessons that can be drawn from the above model are:

- The level of self-financing stagnates at a level of between five and ten percent.
- External aid fluctuates considerably, but gradually increases. However, it remains focused on short term projects.
- NGOs experience severe cash flow crises between projects.
- There is little chance that NGOs will achieve any measure of financial autonomy. On the contrary, dependence upon outside assistance increases.

1. Dependence on External Finances

If an NGO's self-financing activities do not increase, the NGO becomes increasingly dependent on external aid. The figure below illustrates this problem. As dependency on external sources increases, dependency in terms of organizational culture, technical capacity and programmatic focus also increases.

There is clearly an urgent need for new financing models for NGOs based on institutional or organizational necessities. This implies that NGOs, their corporate and their other external donors should shift the focus of financing from a *project-*

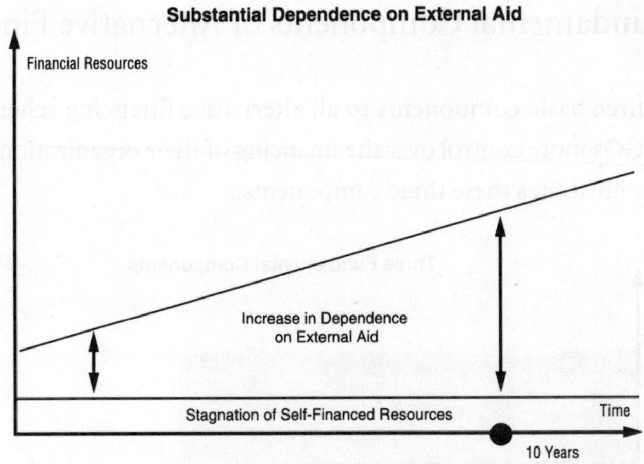

based system to the financing of the organization itself. It also implies that genuine, viable partnerships should be created between NGOs and their corporate and foreign donors that acknowledge the time and resources required to sustain these joint efforts for the benefit of communities.

For the past decade multi-lateral, bilateral and other donors to NGO programs have been concerned with the need to foster financial self-reliance among their NGO partners. But donor concern with their own internal mechanisms, which do not allow for alternatives to the project-by-project method of financing, has made finding a solution difficult. NGO financial self-reliance is not a dream; however, it is difficult to achieve. Pre-conditions for success are:

- NGOs must develop the capacity to produce long-term strategic plans, to adapt to changing circumstances, and to manage growth;
- NGOs must develop a capacity to generate reserves which can, on the one hand, produce income for their core budgets, and on the other hand, provide some degree of financial stability and security;
- NGOs must develop a capacity to choose markets for their goods and services and to sell them at a realistic level.

The private sector is in a position to assist NGOs to attain the pre-conditions for the success of their financing schemes. The private sector is a rich source of financial management, planning, and marketing expertise. Additionally, the private sector is a potential source for financial contributions, other than expertise, to NGO programs for self-reliance.

2. The Fundamental Components of Alternative Financing

There are three basic components to all alternative financing schemes, which in turn give NGOs more control over the financing of their organizations. The following diagram illustrates these three components.

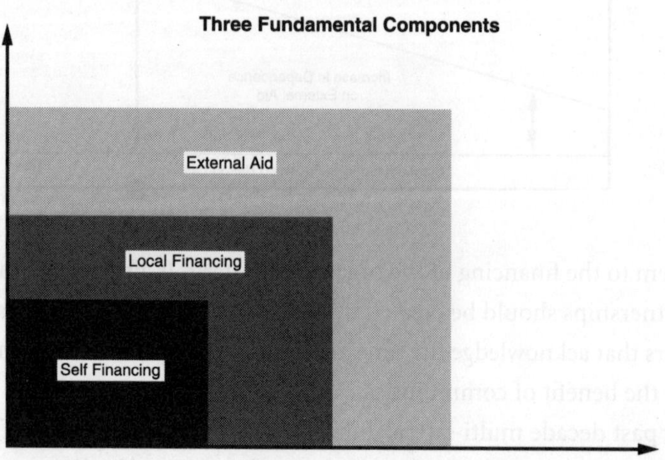

External aid: This type of assistance is generally in the form of a grant, where provisions and programs are agreed to by both parties. Multi-lateral, bilateral, or international NGO donors are the usual sources for this type of assistance. This type of assistance can be categorized as follows:

- project grants,
- program grants,
- institution building grants,
- organizational funds,
- revolving loan funds,
- credit/soft loans,
- bank guarantees.

Local financing: This type of assistance is mobilized locally, within the country, either at the national or local level. This type of assistance can generally be categorized as follows:

- contributions from the general public,
- contributions from a specific segment of the populace,
- contributions from the commercial sector,
- contributions from the local government,

- contributions from the national government,
- contributions or "hard" credit from banks or finance institutions.

Self Financing: These resources are generally mobilized internally from within an NGO. Self-generated resources are generally very flexible and controlled totally by the directors of the organization. This type of resource can generally be categorized as follows:

- membership fees,
- income generating projects (i.e., marketing products generated from beneficiary groups),
- revenue generating enterprises (i.e., specific activities designed for generating internal revenue),
- sale of services (i.e., contracting for services to be rendered for another agency, government, or company),
- investments.

Nearly all plans for self-sufficiency involve the use of one or more of these elements to some degree.

3. Alternative Financing: The Basic Approach

In order to achieve some form of financial autonomy, an organization must reduce its dependence on external sources for the majority of its support. While it is unlikely that NGOs can or should entirely eliminate external sources of assistance, it is generally agreed that some measure of self-reliance should be achieved. The basic approach to all alternative financing schemes starts from a position of heavy dependence on external financing and ends in a position in which such reliance is reduced and mobilization of alternative financing is achieved. One common element in all alternative financing schemes is the option of accumulating some funds to set up a reserve, which can be invested, or can help the organization grow.

The figure below shows growth over time of self-financed or generated fund support. Not all organizations will want to achieve the position of full financial autonomy, nor will they be able to reach such a point. However, the figure illustrates the basic approach and the underlying principles which will be discussed later.

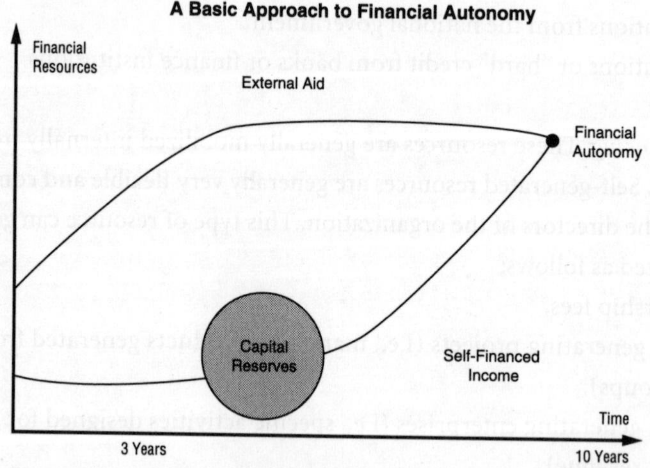

4. The Three Fundamental Components in Greater Detail

Self-financing

- membership
- income generating projects
- revenue generation enterprises
- sales of services/products
- investments

Local Financing

- general public
- specialized public
- businesses
- local government
- national government
- banks or finance institutions

External Aid

- project grants
- program grants
- institution building grants
- organizational funds
- revolving loan funds
- credit/soft loans

• bank guarantees

A book would be required to adequately describe each of these subcomponents—each is a specialized field. But an overview of the list, provides an idea of the breadth and mix of sources available in developing financing strategies within an NGO. A note of caution, before an organization decides or a potential resource organization assists an NGO to choose a strategy, an analysis should be carried out as to what type of NGO it is.

5. Types of NGOs

The first distinction of organizational difference is between an organization composed of, managed by, and representing its own members (generally referred to as a peoples' organization, or PO), and an organization which works to assist or improve the impact of the activities of POs. This latter type of organization is what is generally referred to in many countries as a development-oriented NGO. Both of these are nongovernmental and nonprofit organizations (and are sometimes both referred to as NGOs in countries which have not yet made the distinction); however, the distinction should be made when a financing strategy is chosen.

The second distinction of organizational difference is made regarding the kind of organization in relation to its activities. A few examples are shown below. These distinctions also assist potential donors, be they governmental or private sector, to decide how best to assist a recipient organization to plan for the sustainability of funds provided or the activities they support. Organizations rarely fall into well-defined, clear categories. Many organizations have elements of each characteristic; however, it is useful to understand the typology when making decisions regarding donations.

1) A Simple NGO Typology

a. Small Enterprise

These types of organizations are generally concerned with creating employment and increasing income for beneficiaries. In many cases, the organization itself derives a good portion of its resources from the production of the same goods and services that it assists target group members to produce. This type of organization can either be a PO or a development-oriented NGO.

b. Social Development Organization

These organizations assist beneficiaries or groups of beneficiaries with a variety of activities which are not linked directly to production or enterprise development. Such activities might include consciousness/awareness raising, human resources training, legal aid, literacy development, etc. These organizations are almost always development-oriented NGOs, and rarely POs.

c. Infrastructure Development Organizations

These types of organizations assist beneficiaries in building physical infrastructure such as schools, clinics, latrines, tube wells, etc. They can be either POs or NGOs.

d. Nonprofit Contractors

These organizations may engage in various development projects by providing fee-for-service assistance at the request of governments or donors to meet the needs of beneficiaries. Some examples of such services would be the provision of family planning services or supplies, food aid management, housing development, credit program management, etc. Nonprofit contractors can be either POs or NGOs.

e. Support Organizations

Support organizations assist other NGOs or POs in the development of institutional capacity or in the provision of management services. Usually through training or direct technical assistance, support organizations assist client NGOs or POs to improve the performance and impact of their development interventions. Usually support organizations are exclusively development-oriented NGOs.

6. Alternative Financing—Potential and Danger

In choosing an alternative financing option, it is necessary to anticipate the impact such a scheme would have on an organization. Equally important, donating organizations should be aware of the impact of their funding and the funding mechanism on the recipient. Impact can be both positive and negative. And while all nonprofit organizations are desirous of the type of flexible funding that alternative financing schemes provide, alternative financing takes time and effort (potentially more time and effort than is required when an organization is dependent solely on outside project-based funding). If an organization becomes so changed as a result of involvement in alternative financing schemes that it no longer expends sufficient effort on the work it was established to perform, then the alternative financing scheme itself becomes detrimental. This is a particular danger when an organization develops a fund-raising enterprise which is in a very different field in comparison to the organization's original intent. While it is entirely possible to manage such a scheme and maintain programmatic integrity, effort must then be expended on remaining true to the vision and mission of the organization. Financing strategies must be a means to an end, and not become an end in themselves. In each case, an NGO or the donor organization should review the options for the most attractive mix and fit, review the level of effort required to carry it out, consider the level of skills already existing in the organization, and examine whether the options chosen fit the vision and mission of the organization in question.

7. Towards Financial Autonomy

The following diagram shows in composite form how most alternative financing elements can be utilized. This is not a guide, but a picture to illustrate the general elements and how each element can be developed to reach autonomy.

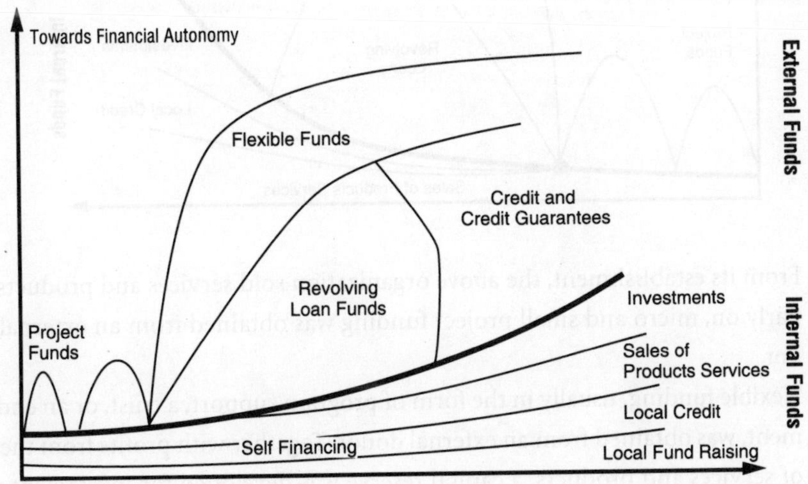

In this example:

- The above organization started out by raising some funds itself.
- It obtained some funds from external donors through support for micro and small projects early on in its life.
- Subsequently, it obtained larger, longer-term, flexible funds from external donors of which a portion was a revolving loan fund.
- From its self-generated funds, the above organization was able to build a capital reserve fund which it invested.
- Its original capital reserves increased as, over time, the organization began selling products and services and found additional funding from local resources.
- The above organization succeeded in persuading external donors to provide credit guarantees.
- Eventually, the organization gained access to local sources of credit.

The following diagrams illustrate options for specific types of organizations and may be useful in choosing a realistic mix of options.

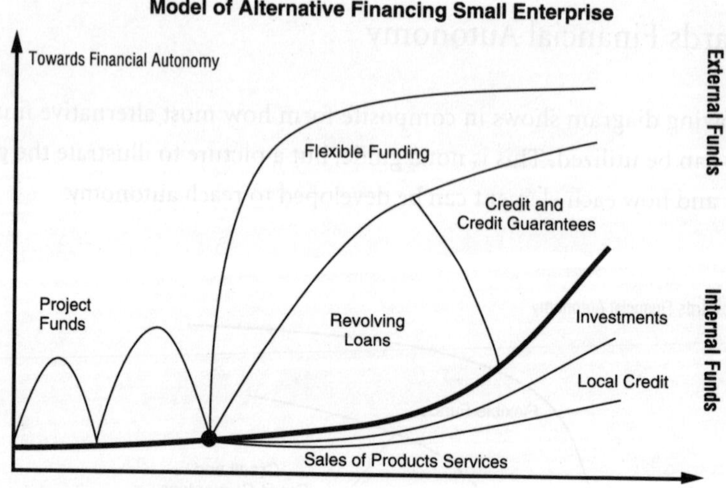

- From its establishment, the above organization sold services and products.
- Early on, micro and small project funding was obtained from an external donor.
- Flexible funding, usually in the form of program support, a trust, or an endowment, was obtained from an external donor. Together with profits from the sale of services and products, a capital reserve was developed for investment purposes.

- A revolving loan fund was obtained from an external donor.
- An external donor provided a guarantee for local credit.
- Credit was obtained directly from local credit finance institutions.

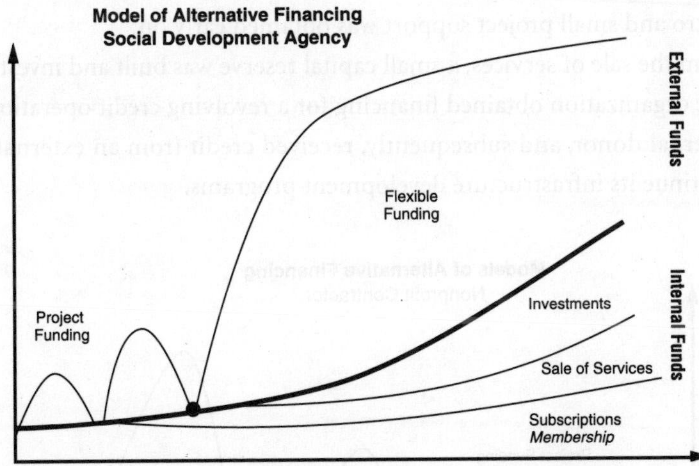

- From its establishment, the above organization obtained funds from subscriptions and membership fees.
- Micro and small project funding was obtained from an external donor.
- The sale of services was concurrent with access to project funds.
- Flexible funding, in the form of an endowment or program support, together with local fund raising and the sale of services allowed the above organization to develop a capital reserve fund which was used for investment.
- The sale of services became the largest source of finances for increasing the capital reserve.

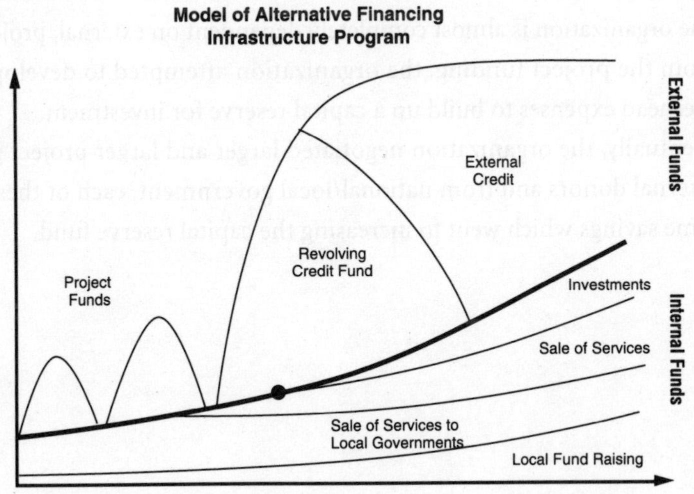

In the above example:

- From its establishment, the above organization obtained some funds from local fund-raising efforts. In addition, it also received contracts from local government.
- Micro and small project support was obtained early on.
- From the sale of services, a small capital reserve was built and invested.
- The organization obtained financing for a revolving credit operation from an external donor, and subsequently, received credit from an external donor to continue its infrastructure development programs.

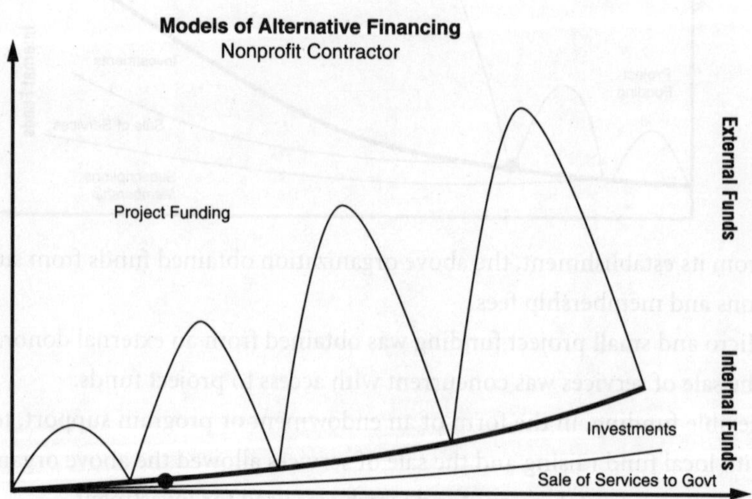

In the above figure:

- The organization is almost completely dependent on external, project funding.
- From the project funding, the organization attempted to develop savings in overhead expenses to build up a capital reserve for investment.
- Eventually, the organization negotiated larger and larger project grants from external donors and from national/local government, each of these produced some savings which went to increasing the capital reserve fund.

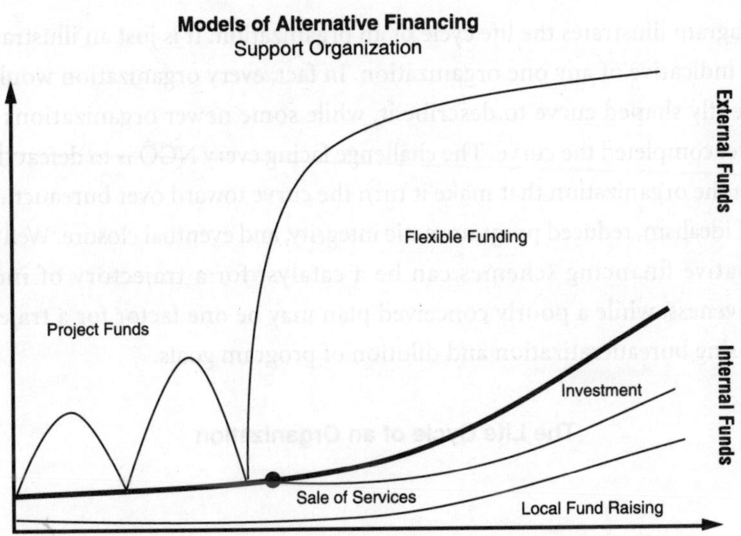

In the above figure:

- From establishment, this organization was able to obtain funds through local fund raising.
- Early on, this organization began the sale of its services.
- Furthermore, it obtained support for projects through grants from external donors.
- It obtained some type of flexible funding from an external donor, and together with its self-financing, developed a capital reserve which is invested.
- Increasingly, this organization sold its services to client organizations (who, in turn, received financing from external donors or local/national government to buy these services).

8. Strategic Planning

Good planning is a strategic element in the development of alternative financing schemes. Young and under-resourced organizations can often become overburdened to the point of closure should they undertake poorly conceived alternative financing schemes. NGOs, of every caliber and size, must expend some staff time in the development of financing for their programs. Each new effort can put some strain on the organization, thus, it is important to be realistic in analyzing "health" and competence before embarking on the development of financing of any kind. The following diagram illustrates the life cycle of an organization. It is just an illustration and is not indicative of any one organization. In fact, every organization would have a differently shaped curve to describe it, while some newer organizations will not have yet completed the curve. The challenge facing every NGO is to defeat the forces within the organization that make it turn the curve toward over bureaucratization, loss of idealism, reduced programmatic integrity, and eventual closure. Well planned alternative financing schemes can be a catalyst for a trajectory of increasing effectiveness, while a poorly conceived plan may be one factor for a trajectory of increasing bureaucratization and dilution of program goals.

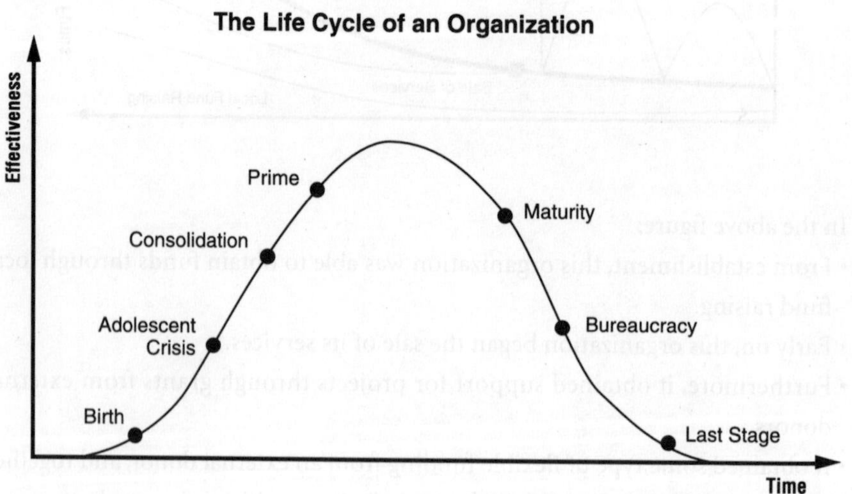

VII. Conclusions

NGOs are seen by many to be effective and innovative catalysts for development. Furthermore, some believe that NGOs offer more cost effective means by which development activities can be supported. However, if a system of funding NGOs does not sustain the continued growth and development of the NGO sector, NGOs may become more and more bureaucratic and less and less innovative in their approaches. All donors, be they public or private sector, should be aware of the impact of their funding and funding mechanisms on the NGOs they wish to support.

Partnership between NGOs and corporate entities, often catalyzed through corporate philanthropy, has yielded exciting results. Furthermore, the benefit flow is not one way. Corporations also benefit greatly from contributions provided to the nonprofit sector. At present, the corporate sector in Indonesia is not contributing to the nonprofit sector to its full capacity. And, while there have been some exciting innovations in corporate philanthropy in Indonesia in recent years, additional dialogue between corporate entities and NGOs is required to fully realize the potential in the future.

Additionally, a means should be found to sustain the impact of funds contributed to NGOs, as well as a means found to sustain the impact of NGO programs. This is not a burden that NGOs should bear alone. Public and private sector contributors should also consider how to sustain their assistance and the impact of their assistance in the long run. Alternative financing schemes that shift dependency from short-term, project-based funding to more sustainable mechanisms, and in conjunction with appropriate technical assistance in management development, can be one means by which this can be achieved.

Alternative financing scheme development is certainly one field in which NGOs can learn lessons from the private sector. Through technical assistance in financing, the private sector could contribute time to NGOs in Indonesia who wish to learn about innovations in financing and in marketing their skills and programs. Through corporate philanthropy, the private sector could contribute resources valuable to NGOs in developing more flexible and sustainable funding mechanisms. Through such a program of dialogue and support, both NGOs and corporate entities obtain a unique type of satisfaction which makes corporate and NGO partnerships both exciting and rewarding.

Notes

1. For the purpose of this paper, the term *NGO* will be used to denote Indonesian nonprofit, independent development-oriented organizations.
2. The terms *business community, private sector, commercial sector, corporations,* and *companies* have been used in this paper interchangeably to denote for-profit entities, be they multinational, international, or national.
3. "The Indonesian Business Community: The Potential for Resource Mobilization to Assist Self Employment and Micro-Enterprise Promotion Activities," SEMEP Project INS/90/002, a report to the International Labour Organization (ILO), 1991.
4. Dr. Russell Betts, "Institutional Mechanisms to Raise Funds for Indonesian Private Voluntary Organizations," Development Alternatives, Inc., 1986 report submitted to the Jakarta Mission of USAID.
5. Ibid.
6. Ibid.
7. International Monetary Fund, *International Financial Statistics,* January 1995 (Washington, D.C.: IMF, 1995). Figures given are based on the end of period exchange rate for November, 1994. US$1 = Rp 2,193.
8. Tri Nugroho, Kathy Quik, et. al, "PT. Van Melle Indonesian Small Grants Program" (1993).
9. Ibid.
10. *Towards Financial Self-reliance: An Overview for NGOs, Community Groups, and Donors,* adapted by Richard Holloway PACT Private Rural Initiatives Project Director, Dhaka, Bangladesh, from *Towards Greater Financial Autonomy—A Manual on Financing Strategies and Techniques for Development NGOs and Community Organizations,* 1991.

JAPAN

Japan's Philanthropic Development in An Asia Pacific Context

Tadashi Yamamoto
President
Japan Center for International Exchange
and
Hitomi Komatsu
Research Associate
Japan Center for International Exchange

I. Introduction—A Brief Historical Overview

Private philanthropy in Japan has relatively deep historical roots in the form of charitable giving by nobles or senior monks, dating back to the eighth century, and in the form of contributions from wealthy merchants of Osaka to private schools during the Edo period (1603–1868). A modern form of private organized philanthropy is said to have been established in 1911 on the basis of Article 34 of the Civil Code which was promulgated in 1896 as a part of Japan's modernization process dating from the beginning of the Meiji Restoration in 1868. (It is interesting to note that the basic legal framework of private foundations today still draws on the principles set down in this Code.) However, the full-fledged emergence of private philanthropy in Japan did not take place until the time of Japan's rapid economic development in the 1960s and 1970s, when a number of major corporations established foundations. Philanthropic development during this period reflected concerns of Japanese corporations, which came under attack for negative aspects of phenomenal economic development, such as environmental degradation and a steep rise in land prices and stocks due to the excessive liquidity produced by a large trade surplus. Public criticism was aroused against corporations for allegedly pursuing their own narrow self-interests. Around this time, the term "corporate social responsibility" came into the vocabulary of business leaders, and this newly acquired consciousness became a motive for the establishment of corporate foundations and increased corporate giving. In an article written in late 1974 for *Foundation News*, Tadashi Yamamoto reported as follows:

> And so, it seems that Japanese philanthropy is on the threshold of major developments. In direct response to the mounting charges against corporations, and in the hope of fulfilling their social responsibility, many large corporations have begun to allocate funds to establish "foundations." In the last several months we've seen press announcements concerning the establishment of new foundations with total assets of about $67 million, no small sum and while, by American standards, this isn't a large amount, it is for a "pioneering effort" in philanthropy in a country where there are some effective constraints on private giving.[1]

Along with the public outcry in Japan against "corporate evils," Japanese corporations in the early 1970s began to gain consciousness of the emergence of economic friction, primarily with the United States. Backlash against Japan's "economic overpresence" in Southeast Asia took the form of demonstrations and stone-throwing in Bangkok and Jakarta at the time of the Prime Minister's visit in 1974. Faced with negative reactions against Japanese economic activities abroad, Keidanren (Federation of Economic Organizations) began to coordinate fund raising for foreign institutions. Most of the corporate foundations that were established in the 1970s and early 1980s, indeed, emphasized international activities. In fact, it can be argued that Japan's philanthropic development in recent years has been influenced greatly by external factors, and foundation grant making and corporate giving have been placing a major emphasis on international outreach activities. In this connection, it is not a coincidence that the major growth in Japan's corporate philanthropy took place during the period of a surge of Japan's direct investment to the United States and Asia, which was accelerated by the sudden rise in the value of the Japanese yen in the wake of the 1986 Plaza Accord.

A study mission organized by Keidanren in cooperation with the Japan Center for International Exchange (JCIE) in October 1988 and headed by Natsuaki Fusano, Senior Managing Director of Keidanren, received intense attention within the Japanese business community. Fusano announced the creation of the One Percent Club within Keidanren at the follow-up seminar after the mission's return to Tokyo, and the Club was officially launched in 1989, headed by Mr. Shoichiro Toyoda, the present chairman of Keidanren. In September 1989, Keidanren also organized an affiliate organization called the Council for Better Corporate Citizenship (CBCC) with Mr.

Akio Morita, then chairman of Sony Corporation, to promote good corporate citizenship in the United States. In addition, Keidanren established two committees to promote philanthropic activities amongst its member companies. The Committee on Corporate Philanthropy established in 1990 was given the task to "enhance corporate understanding of grant making through seminars and public information about corporate philanthropy." This is accomplished by such activities as cooperating with the One Percent Club to increase its membership. It also advocates better tax treatment for charitable donations and less bureaucratic red tape to establish nonprofit organizations.[2] The Philanthropy Department established in April 1991 serves as "an administrative support center to assist member corporations."[3]

Given this pattern of evolution of Japan's private philanthropy, which has been predominantly propelled by corporate financial contributions, and which has been influenced by Japan's external relationship, it is natural to witness a shift in philanthropic priorities toward Asia Pacific in recent years.

Immediately after Noboru Takeshita became Prime Minister in 1987 he asked a group of private citizens to visit Southeast Asia with the aim of strengthening cultural and educational exchange with Japan. In 1989 Mr. Toshihiro Yahiro, then the vice chairman of Keidanren, supported this activity in Southeast Asia because "there was an urgent need to promote cultural exchange, as the Japanese did not sufficiently understand these countries' cultures."[4] Keidanren, in response to this sentiment, established the Committee on Promotion of Inter-Cultural Understanding. The Committee has been focusing its activities on Southeast Asian countries, particularly ASEAN countries.[5]

This brief paper, accompanying a survey project on Japan's private philanthropy will describe general trends in philanthropic development and the more recent trend of philanthropic interest in Asia Pacific.

II. A General Profile of Current Private Philanthropy in Japan

It is rather difficult to provide a definitive assessment of philanthropic developments in Japan, largely because of the lack of precise statistical materials and the ambiguous classification of nonprofit entities. There are close to twenty-five thousand nonprofit public interest corporations (*koeki hojin*) in Japan, but according to the Civil Code Article 34, all associations or foundations "relating to worship, religion, charity, science, art or otherwise relating to public interests and not having for its object the acquisition of gain may be made a juristic person subject to the permission of the competent authorities." This *koeki hojin* status is divided into *zaidan hojin* or incorporated foundation, and *shadan hojin* or incorporated association.

1. Grant-making Foundations

The total number of *koeki hojin* is close to twenty-five thousand, and about thirteen thousand five hundred are incorporated foundations (*zaidan hojin*). However, most of these incorporated foundations are considered to be operating foundations, and, according to a survey undertaken by the Foundation Library Center of Japan in 1992, there are about two hundred grant-making foundations of significant size in Japan. Aside from the number of grant-making foundations in Japan, another approach to outlining a general picture of the size of grant-making foundations in Japan is to compare the size of the twenty largest foundations in Japan as listed in Table 1. According to the Library Center of Japan, which compiled this statistical material, the combined assets of the twenty largest foundations in the United States was about twenty times the combined assets of Japan's largest foundations, according to 1990 statistics.

2. Corporate Giving

In comparison with the grant-making foundations, many of which have been established with corporate funding, direct corporate giving is considerably larger, and the number of corporations participating in philanthropic activities has also been increasing. "The results of a more recent survey (398 companies responded) on corporate social contributions reveals that the grand total of expenditure on domestic and international philanthropy by corporate members of Keidanren and the One Percent Club in fiscal 1993 was 149.4 billion yen[6] (US$ 1.51 billion).[7] Another statistical set of data that can be used to gauge the scope of corporate contributions shows that despite the fall in total expenditure of philanthropic activities during the past three years amidst the recession, the ratios of expenditure on philanthropy to recurring profits and to total sales and pre-tax profits respectively have steadily increased since 1991. For example, the ratio of expenditure on philanthropy activities to recurring profits increased from 1.72 percent in fiscal year 1990 to 3.47 percent in fiscal year 1993.[8] Moreover, observations have been made that the number

Table 1

Name of Foundation	Total Assests	Annual Grant	Year Established
1. The Sasakawa Peace Foundation	635.44	9.04	1986
2. Foundation of River and Watershed Environment Management	200.47	5.67	1975
3. Nakayama Hayao Kagaku Gijutsu Bunka Zaidan	190.80	0.34	1992
4. The Inamori Foundation	177.27	1.75	1984
5. The Vehicle Racing Commemorative Foundation	142.66	21.45	1975
6. Hoso-Bunka Foundation, Inc.	133.56	3.06	1974
7. Ishibashi Foundation	133.36	1.25	1956
8. Nagao Natural Environment Foundation	131.75	0.10	1989
9. Nippon Life Insurance Foundation	125.64	8.20	1979
10. The Toyota Foundation	123.58	5.26	1974
11. The Saison Foundation	110.68	2.07	1987
12. The Mitsubishi Foundation	105.73	4.45	1969
13. The Iijima Memorial Foundation for the Promotion of Food Science and Technology	100.68	1.27	1984
14. The Telecommunications Advancement Foundation	100.34	5.43	1984
15. Yoshida Scholarship Foundation	98.65	3.50	1967
16. International Aircraft Development Fund	94.56	70.12	1986
17. The Japan Securities Scholarship Foundation	81.31	2.38	1973
18. Shizuoka Science and Technology Foundation	80.92	3.12	1991
19. Japan Research Promotion Soceity for Cariovascular Diseases	80.39	0.21	1967
20. Rotary Yoneyama Memorial Foundation Inc.	80.08	15.82	1967
Total (of 20 foundations)	2,927.85	164.49	

Source: Foundation Library Center of Japan. *Directory of Grant-Making Foundations: Guide to Private Grant Sources, 1994.* Tokyo, Foundation Library Center of Japan, 1993.

of companies establishing a special division to promote philanthropy increased (from sixty-two companies in FY1990 to ninety in FY1993) and "the number of companies which post philanthropy expenditures as part of their annual budget increased (from twenty-eight in FY1990 to fifty-four in FY1993).[9] Similar results have been reported in the *Mecenat White Paper 1994* in which a survey on corporate cultural support reveals that both the number of companies establishing a full-time division for corporate support and that include corporate support expenses in their budget have showed an increase (rising from 36.2 percent in 1990 to 50.4 percent in 1993).[10]

Therefore, although the recession has caused the reduction of corporate earnings which in effect has resulted in the decrease in the total expenditure on philanthropic activities these companies continued to strive in their philanthropic activities.

On international giving by Japanese corporations, a list of financial contributions to overseas institutions channeled through the aforementioned CBCC provides a sense of the scale. CBCC received tax privileges as a *tokutei koeki zoshin hojin* (special public interest promoting corporation) in 1990, whereby it can receive tax-deductible contributions from corporations and individuals within limits prescribed by the law. Thus, a major portion, but certainly not all, of Japanese corporate contributions abroad can be considered to be channeled through CBCC. (There are several limitations for the use of the CBCC mechanism for tax deductibility; there have to be multiple sources of contributions for any project to be eligible to receive contributions through CBCC.) Between 1990 to 1994, corporate contributions were made to sixty-two overseas institutions for the total amount of eighteen billion yen (US$182 million).

Another indication of the size of Japanese contributions to nonprofit organizations is a list of "donation requests to Japanese corporations and industries" through Keidanren. Although Keidanren does not receive contributions from its member-corporations directly, except for a few cases, it facilitates corporate contributions to certain institutions and programs. Such a facilitating role can take the form of giving the institutions involved in fund raising a list of Keidanren members with suggestions of whom to approach for what level of funding, or it may take a more direct form, with Keidanren writing to member corporations introducing fund raisers, and tacitly encouraging their cooperation. The list containing those cases in which Keidanren has played some facilitating role is provided on request. However, since it is assumed that the predominant number of fund raisers listed have been able to receive a certain level of support from Keidanren members, the list provides a general scope of the level of support Keidanren members have provided. According to the list, in 1992 there were thirty-three requests from international programs totaling approximately 2.2 billion yen (US$22 million) and seventeen requests from domestic programs totaling approximately 3.5 billion yen. (US$35.4 million).[11]

There have also been efforts to induce corporate support of the environment as seen in the establishment of the Keidanren Nature Conservation Fund (KNCF) in 1992. The Fund provides assistance for various activities, including aid for nature conservation projects conducted in less developed countries by Japanese and foreign NGO's, training programs for Japanese business people who will work with on international nature conservation projects, and the promotion of understanding of environmental activities. Donations given by corporations and individuals through KNCF have amounted to 214.5 million yen (approximately US$ 2.17 million) distributed to eighteen projects worldwide.[12]

With regard to the support of the arts and culture, or Mecenat, the Association for Corporate Support of the Arts (Kigyo Mecenat Kyogikai) was created with 13 corporate members in 1990 and has grown to a membership of 173 in 1995.[13] "The essential function of the Kigyo Mecenat Kyogikai is to explain and popularize the Mecenat concept" and "its initial policy precluded funding artists and art troupes directly. However, from February 1994 it was granted special tax exempt status. The organization has since been able to make actual contributions. A review group within the organization has been established to review Mecenat activities of companies for consideration of tax exempt contributions. From April 1994 to March 1995, 159 corporate support activities were recognized by the Kigyo Mecenat Kyogikai, with 194.25 billion yen (US$1.96 billion) in tax deductible contributions.[14]

3. Corporate Volunteer Activities

Corporations have begun to diversify their support activities by involving themselves in areas such as supporting their employees' volunteer activities, as well as providing human and material resources. From the beginning of the 1990s corporations began to show strong interest in aiding the volunteer activities of personnel in addition to aiding societal needs with financial contributions.[15]

A large number of corporations have enacted programs such as supplying volunteer information and even supplying volunteer opportunities to employees with no experience in order to aid personnel volunteer activities. Other policies have been introduced into the corporate world to encourage volunteer activities such as volunteer commendation systems, paid holidays for volunteer activities, temporary leave of absence for volunteer activities, and volunteer matching gift systems. Another example of corporate support for volunteer activity is volunteer registration systems whereby a company is entered on a data base of volunteer activities in which employees are interested, thus establishing a referral system for various volunteer activities.[16]

According to the results of a survey conducted by Keidanren in autumn of 1991, opinions varied over whether companies should be strongly involved in volunteer activities and whether it is appropriate for a company to become involved in an employee's personal activities. Among survey respondents 45.3 percent indicated that they have some kind of employee based volunteer activity. Another 12.0 percent have employee based volunteer activities under consideration.[17] On the other hand only 2.8 percent of respondents confirmed participation in matching funds systems with 21.5 percent unaware that the system itself existed, and 65.6 percent do not support introducing such a system.

The survey reported in the *1994 Mecenat White Paper* segregated corporate support activity into five categories: funding, human resources, material resources, office space, and miscellaneous. An increase for the categories of funding, material resources, and space was reported for 1993. Total support activity categories have increased 1,866 cases in 1991, 2,462 in 1992 and 2,625 in 1993. The 1993 report was broad based covering a wide range of corporate activities.[18]

A 1994 survey sent to 2,251 companies (applicants to the Mecenat Awards, member companies of the Mecenat Council, all capitalized companies) had 376 respondents; of this number 246 companies enacted 1,786 different events. Some examples of Mecenat's Asia Pacific related corporate activities are support for a conference to preserve the Angkor Wat ruins in Cambodia, assistance to the Pacific Music Festival (PMF), the PMF orchestra's Tokyo public concert, a PMF cooperative Fukuoka public concert, and the Asia Youth Orchestra.

4. Charitable Trusts

Koeki hojin (charitable trusts) were introduced to Japan's philanthropic community rather recently, though the legal framework for this type of philanthropy had existed for some time on the basis of Article 66 of the Trust Law of 1922. Charitable trusts must be organized for the public benefit, and must have official approval for establishment. For tax purposes, charitable trusts are largely indistinguishable from organizations created under Article 34 of the Civil Code. On the other hand, unlike foundations, charitable trusts are usually created by individuals, and only seldom by corporations and local governments. In the Japanese context, this form of grant making is perhaps best suited for well-defined programs, partly because there is no need to raise an initial endowment, as is the case for foundations, nor are there cumbersome administrative procedures which are necessary for the creation of foundations.

The first charitable trust, the Imai Memorial Charitable Trust for Overseas Cooperation was established in 1977 with an endowment of two hundred million yen (US$2 million), the majority of which was donated by Mr. Yasutaro Imai, president of a small company specializing in quilts and bedding. The grant-making activities of the Imai Trust are managed by the staff of the Asian Community Trust (ACT), which was established in 1979 as the first charitable trust based on general fund raising. There are presently over four hundred charitable trusts, and it is estimated that about twenty percent of them are designated for international activities. A list of larger charitable trusts active in international giving is shown in Table 2.

III. Japan's Growing Philanthropic Interest in Asia Pacific

Japan's private foundations, corporate giving programs, and charitable trusts have been putting an increasing emphasis on Asia Pacific related programs in recent years. As indicated above, Japanese philanthropic development in general has been influenced by external factors to a considerable degree. It is quite natural, therefore, for Japanese philanthropic activities in Asia to have become more active as Japan's interest in general and its corporate interest, in particular, has significantly shifted toward Asia. Specifically, Japan's growing economic presence in Asian countries has clearly enhanced its interest in philanthropic activities related to Asia.

1. Corporate Giving

There has been a marked increase in Japanese corporate giving to Asian countries in recent years. According to Keidanren's *1992 Shakai Kouken Hakusho* publication, donation requests to Japanese corporations and industries for Asia-related programs showed a remarkable increase. During FY1988 the amount was only 3.2 percent this figure rose to 19.0 percent by fiscal 1991.

Such philanthropic activities have been facilitated by organizations such as the Japanese Chamber of Congress in Asian countries, and the aforementioned Committee on Promotion of Inter-Cultural Understanding of Keidanren's One Percent Club

Funding through CBCC also reflects this trend. Major grants donated through CBCC include:

Asian Institute of Technology .... annual contribution of US$72,000 (7.1 million yen)
UNHCR (through Private Fund for .... 1.4 billion yen (US$14.2 million) Relief of Refugees)
Japan Relief for Cambodia .... 50 million yen (US$505,000)
Chulalongkorn University............................ 470 million yen (US$4.75 million) (Automobile Engineering Dept.)
Darma Purusada University......................... 100 million yen (US$1.01 million)
IISS-Malaysia .... 96 million yen (US$970,000)

There has also been an increase in direct corporate contributions to programs of the host countries coordinating an increasing number of contribution programs. The Committee on Promotion of Inter-Cultural Understanding has encouraged corporations to provide funding for specific projects. For example thirty Japanese corporations in Thailand committed two million yen each for eleven years starting in 1990 for a total of approximately five hundred million yen (US$5 million).

Other projects sponsored by the Committee include:

- Study tours of Japan by Indonesian kindergartens, primary, and high school teachers to gain familiarity with Japanese business and daily life; twenty teachers are invited annually for the three-week visit sponsored by fifteen companies.[19]
- Assistance toward the new Center for Japanese Studies at the Institute for Strategic and International Studies in Malaysia, in a 120 million yen (US$1.2 million) funding effort supported by fourteen corporations.[20]
- Assistance to CBCC-sponsored high school programs in Singapore that teach the Japanese language, including grants to acquire equipment and for student visits to Japan.[21]
- Provision of Japanese periodicals to overseas universities and research institutes;[22] starting in 1991 Japanese periodicals have been provided to the University of Indonesia and Darma Purusada University by two corporations.[23]

Out of the eighteen projects supported by the Keidanren Nature Conservation Fund (KNCF), nine were Asia related in taking place in Thailand, Vietnam, Indonesia and the Philippines.[24]

Other projects included, collecting data on birds facing extinction, a forest conservation project and assistance to the Bird Conservation Society of Thailand; in Vietnam an environmentally friendly agricultural program and a highland forest program; in the Philippines basic research for an environmental training center; in the Philippines and Papua New Guinea nature conservation projects fostering local industries; in Indonesia the Sulawesi nature conservation project and a project to promote use of medicinal plants in Meru Betiri National Park.

There have also been efforts to encourage the dispatching of volunteers from corporations to NGOs. The Keidanren Nature Conservation Fund (KNCF) is planning to launch a program whereby it would coordinate matching volunteers with NGOs who need their support. One example of this effort is the dispatch of a volunteer from the Yasuda Fire and Marine Insurance Co. to the Wild Bird Society of Japan (Nihon Yachonokai) for a two-year term.[25] According to the *Daily Yomiuri*, the Yasuda-Yachonokai arrangement is unprecedented in that both side conducted the exchange as equal partners, taking into full consideration the benefits due to their respective organizations.

Such philanthropic activities have been facilitated by organizations like the Japanese Chamber of Commerce in Asian countries, and the aforementioned Keidanren One Percent Club.

2. Grant-making Foundations

Japanese foundations also have become increasingly interested in Asia-related programs. A major area of foundation funding has been support for Asian students either in the form of scholarships or supplementary grants for Asian students already studying in Japan but having financial difficulties. Out of forty-five foundations covered in this survey, twenty-one have been involved in such philanthropic giving to Asian students. In terms of the size of their funding, thirteen foundations provide monthly stipends of one hundred to two hundred thousand yen and eight foundations provide one hundred thousand yen or less per month. Among those that support students or offer scholarship programs, fourteen foundations specifically designate Asian countries and eight do not specify the countries of origin for the students, although the predominant number of recipients are from Asia.

The foundations that have been active in this field include the Tokyu Foundation for Inbound Students, the Rotary Yoneyama Memorial Foundation, the Hitachi Scholarship Foundation, and the Watanuki International Scholarship Foundation.

The Toyota Foundation and the Sasakawa Peace Foundation are two private foundations that send their professional staff to visit Asian countries on a regular basis, and provide substantial grants to Asia-related programs. The Toyota Foundation is particularly well known for its innovative project under the title of "Know our Neighbors" in which many academic and literary works of Southeast Asian countries have been translated into Japanese or other Asian languages. The Sasakawa Peace Foundation has been emphasizing support for NGOs both in Japan and in Asian countries. The Foundation for Asian Management Development, which was established through financial contributions of member-companies of the Electronic Industries Association of Japan, has been active in promoting entrepreneurship of small and medium industries in Asia. The Toshiba Foundation has supported a number of cultural programs in Southeast Asia. The Foundation for International Development/Relief, established in 1990, has been supporting Japanese NGOs active in Asian countries. The Saison Foundation has been supporting performing arts in Asia and exchange activities between Southeast Asian countries and Japan.

3. Charitable Trusts

As mentioned above, there is a number of charitable trusts that place primary emphasis on Asia-related programs as shown in the directory. Of particular significance in this field is the creation of ACT, which was established in 1979 as the first charitable trust depending on general fund raising from corporations and individuals. It was patterned after American community foundations, and as such, ACT's professional staff oversee the grant-making activities of a base fund given to eight trust banks that act as trustees. The ACT staff works closely with the Philippine Business for Social Progress and the Foundation for Sustainable Development in Indonesia. By the end of 1994, over 250 grants worth over 350 million yen (US$3.5 million) were provided for diverse projects carried out by NGOs in Asian countries.

There has been a pronounced interest among corporations in the Osaka and Kansai area in developing philanthropic activities in Asia countries. The Imai Memorial Charitable Trust for International Cooperation undertakes programs in developing countries in the areas of cultivation of human resources, education, health, medical care and emergency relief. Projects in Asia Pacific include preschool and kindergarten teacher training programs in Thailand and the Philippines, student scholarships in Indonesia, and health and relief activities through the Japanese Red Cross and other Red Cross Societies in Asia. The J. Kawakami Memorial Trust is primarily involved in educational programs in Asia Pacific. Other foundations active in grant making are the The Daiwa Bank Foundation for Asia and Oceania, The Osaka Community Foundation, and The Suntory Foundation. A profile of these foundations is as follows:

The Daiwa Bank Foundation for Asia and Oceania makes grants for international exchange and research study programs on political, economic, cultural, and historical relations between Japan and Asia Oceania countries. It assists joint research projects and area studies of the region by young scholars

The Osaka Community Foundation is composed of several special funds each of which was established by donations from individuals and corporations with distinct aims and businesses. A total of 15 million yen (US$152,000) in grants were disbursed in FY1993 including assistance to environmental protection (4.6 million yen or US$46,000), support for culture and sports (700,000 yen or US$7,000), and medical research and care for the handicapped and elderly (6.2 million yen or US$63,000).

The Suntory Foundation makes grants for research and study activities that are judged to be internationally significant in the fields of social sciences and humanities.

IV. Future Challenges to Japan's Philanthropic Development

Despite the significant growth of Japan's private philanthropy, its further development has been very much constrained by several factors. The biggest obstacle is a very limited availability of tax incentives for private contributions. Another major issue impeding the growth of this sector is a shortage of human resources capable of managing grant-making activities. Obviously, there is also a need to further enhance the consciousness of Japanese people, including corporate leaders, to appreciate the importance of private philanthropy for Japanese society as well as for Japan's external relationship including Japan's role in building the Asia Pacific regional community.

1. Limited Availability of Tax Incentives for Private Contributions

The fact that Japanese NGOs and research institutions have difficulty building a more solid financial base due to the limited tax incentives available for private contributions has already been mentioned. Needless to say, this relative lack of tax privileges for contributions has also put constraints on the development of private foundations in Japan. Since the 1960s, organizations operating in the fields of social welfare, education, and science have found it relatively easy to receive legal designation as *shikenkenkyu hojin* (experimental research corporations) and have also been able to receive tax-deductible contributions in order to stimulate private investment in scientific research and education. In 1988, JCIE was recognized as a nongovernmental organization eligible to receive tax deductible contributions under a new tax exemption status to promote international exchange. Later, this new tax exemption status was merged with the aforementioned "experimental research corporations," and a new category of organizations approved for tax privileges was created as *tokutei koeki zoshin hojin* (special public interest promoting organizations). Though this designation of a new category is a *de jure* broadening of tax deductibility, consideration for approval to this category is extremely rigid, and the Ministry of Finance is rather reluctant to extend this deferential tax treatment. At the time of this writing, only 833 organizations (about ten of which are in the field of international exchange and cooperation) are registered in this tax category, and it is assumed that a predominant portion of this group is made up of "independent" organizations that have been created through the initiatives of government agencies.

In recent months, some political parties have started paying attention to this lack of tax incentives which inhibits the growth of philanthropic organizations as well as the entire nonprofit and nongovernmental sector, and have been exploring possible legislative initiatives on their own. While such developments are encouraging to those in the independent sector in Japan, the process of liberalization in this field is expected to be rather slow. This situation reflects the fundamental attitude of Japan's bureaucracy, which has defined itself to be the sole arbitrator of public goods throughout Japan's modernization process. Thus, there is an underlying assumption among government officials that nongovernmental organizations are basically subsidiaries of their ministries. The development of private philanthropy, in the minds of many in the bureaucracy, will lead to the depletion of financial resources—funds which only they know best how to allocate.

2. Limited Availability of Professional Expertise in Private Philanthropy

Not unlike other types of organizations in the independent sector in Japan, Japan's philanthropic organizations and corporations engaged in philanthropic giving have very limited human resources to manage their grant-making activities. Despite a significant increase in organized philanthropy over the past few years, today there are only a handful of professional staff active in this field. There are several reasons for this situation. First, the nonprofit and nongovernmental sector is relatively new in Japan, and a professional community simply has not had enough time to develop yet. In other words, there is no nonprofit career path established for those who are interested in working professionally in this field, and there certainly is no systematic effort to develop such professional expertise. Second, there is not much recognition on the part of foundations or corporate leaders about the need for professional expertise. There are only a few funding sources that take a proactive approach in grant-making activities, and they find little reason to hire program officers for their organizations. Third, there is a belief among government ministries overseeing philanthropic organizations or among funders that it is more advisable to use as much of their available funds for making contributions, rather than spending such funds on personnel and overhead.

3. Lack of Understanding Regarding the Roles and Functions of Private Philanthropy in Japan

Although it is easy to blame the government bureaucracy for the underdeveloped nature of Japan's private philanthropy, there is also a lack of clear understanding on the part of business leaders, media, and the general public about the importance of private philanthropy, NGOs, voluntarism, and the overall nonprofit and nongovernmental sector. This again reflects the traditional pattern of public-private interaction in Japan where the private sector tends to rely on the public sector as a guardian and promoter of public interest. While this is the other side of the coin of bureaucratic dominance in Japanese society, it has gradually become clear that government agencies cannot properly deal with divergent issues facing Japanese society. There has been a rather significant private sector response to emerging new issues such as the needs of foreign workers in communities and the lack of adequate facilities and programs dealing with the rapidly aging population. There has also been an emergence of NGOs that have become active in dealing with global issues such as development assistance, the environment, and refugees. In order for these organizations to remain active or even expand their activities, it is critical that they have the support of private sources even if they have to rely on public funding to a large extent. Although there are several constraints, such as the absence of sufficient tax incentives for private contributions, many corporations have proved that they can still develop substantial philanthropy programs within the present regulatory context of Japan.

In order to promote a clearer understanding of contributions private philanthropy can make, it may, in the end, be up to private and corporate foundations as well as corporations already active in philanthropic giving to prove that they can make a substantial difference in their activities. Such endeavors will be essential in effectively responding to divergent and emerging needs within Japanese society as well as in the international context. In this connection, Japan's philanthropic activities in the Asia Pacific regional context can have a major impact on promoting understanding in Japan regarding the role of philanthropy in society, as this is the area where Japan has a long-term interest. Whether Japan will be seen as a constructive member in the region will depend on the degree of Japan's participation in the expanding network among nonprofit and nongovernmental organizations, including philanthropic entities.

Notes

1. Tadashi Yamamoto, in *Foundation News*, 1974.
2. White Paper on Corporate Philanthropy in Japan, Keidanren 1992, p. 10.
3. Ibid, p. 1.
4. *Shakai Kouken Hakusho*, Keidanren 1992, p. 227.
5. Ibid, p. 230.
6. *Results of Survey Concerning Philanthropic Activities FY1993*, Keidanren, Dec. 1994, p. 3.
7. International Monetary Fund *International Financial Statistics*, January 1995 (Washington, D.C.: IMF, 1995). Figures given are based on the end of period exchange rates for November 1994. US$1=98.92 yen.
8. *Results of Survey…*, op. cit., p. 5.
9. Ibid, p. 7.
10. International Mecenat Conference '95 booklet, p. 16.
11. *The Current State of Corporate Philanthropy in Japan*, April 1994, p. 8.
12. Keidanren Nature Conservation Fund (KNCF) pamphlet.
13. *International Mecenat…*, op. cit., p. 10.
14. Ibid, p. 9–10.
15. *The Current State…*, op. cit., p. 9.
16. Ibid, p. 9 - 10.
17. *Shakai Kouken Hakusho…*, op. cit., p. 5.
18. *International Mecenat…*, op. cit., p. 15.
19. *Shakai Kouken Hakusho…*, op. cit., p. 10.
20. Ibid
21. Ibid
22. Ibid
23. Ibid, p. 223.
24. Keidanren Nature Conservation… pamphlet.
25. *Nihon Keizai Shimbun*, 10 April, 1995; *Daily Yomiuri Shimbun*, 26 April, 1995

Table 2

Name of Trust Fund	Date Established	Total Amount	Area of Funding
Assistance Related to Foreign Students, Researchers, Research Entities, etc.			
Inohara Memorial Fund for Medicine	1988	1,671,000	foreign students enrolled in universities in Gifu Prefecture studying general medicine or dentistry
Uruma Trust Fund for Research in Science and the Humanities	1988	8,600,000	residents of Okinawa Prefecture (regardless of nationality), or native individuals of Okinawa who are conducting research or international exchange
Okayama Rotary Club International Promotion Promotion Fund	1984	1,950,000	foreign students enrolled in universities in Okayama Prefecture or researchers of Okayama universities who are conducting research abroad
Kinbara Memorial Fund for Japan-China Medical Exchange	1985	1,000,000	medical researchers/medical technology specialists from China, or for research necessary to develop the skills of a medical interpreter
Kyoto Aoi Lions Club Fund for Foreign Students	1991	—	foreign undergraduate or graduate students attending a university in Kyoto that are financing their own education and experiencing financial hardship
Koura Memorial Scholarship Fund for Foreign Students	1991	—	foreign students residing in Kanagawa Prefecture, or attending university in Kanagawa Prefecture
Kubota Fund	1984	7,680,000	foreign students from Asia, Africa, or the Middle East who are specialists in civil engineering, electrical engineering, or economic development
Shoda Memorial Scholarship Fund for Foreign Students from Asia	1989	1,140,000	foreign students from Asia residing in Tokyo or enrolled in a university located in Tokyo

Name of Trust Fund	Date Established	Total Amount	Area of Funding
Seishin Bunka Kenkyu Yanagawa Foundation	1986	2,400,00	Japanese researchers undertaking research on Asian sociocultural self-perceptions or foreign researchers undertaking research on Japanese sociocultural self-perceptions
The Public Trust Takashimaya International	1991	—	three years tuition paid plus 16,000 yen per month for a Singapore student studying distribution, design, fashion, or broadcasting (audio or visual)
Takisaki Memorial Trust	1993	10,800,000	foreign students from Asia who are enrolled in a university in Osaka and are studying science or engineering
Tsuchiura Rotary Otzuka Memorial Scholarship Fund	1988	1,050,000	foreign students from Asia enrolled at Tsukuba University or other universities in Ibaraki Prefecture and experiencing financial hardship
Koki Nagai Gakujutsu Kyoiku Kokusai Koryu Kikin	1988	18,860,000	foreign students attending a university in Chiba Prefecture, organizations
Yasuhiko Hashimoto Asia/Africa Scholarship Fund for Foreign Students	1989	1,200,000	foreign students from Asia or Africa who are enrolled in a university in Saitama Prefecture
Maeda Memorial Trust	1988	4,200,000	foreign students studying at Chiba, Keio, Tokyo, Tokyo University of Foreign Studies, or Waseda, undertaking research in the humanities or social sciences
Sataro Matsumoto Memorial Southeast Asian Students Scholarship Fund	1993	—	ten foreign students from Southeast Asia attending universities in the Tokyo metropolitan area annually receive 100,000 yen per month
Saiichi Mishima Memorial Scholarship Fund for the Study of Ophthalmology	1987	3,600,000	research students from Asia-Pacific countries studying ophthalmology, or Japanese ophthalmologists sent to Asian countries as overseas volunteers

Name of Trust Fund	Date Established	Total Amount	Area of Funding
Yasuda Wafu Memorial Asian Youth Exchange Fund	1991	—	Japanese or other Asian research students or Asian research entities undertaking research related to economic development and cooperation
Yamaha Motors International Friendship Fund	1981	13,200,000	Japanese enrolled in a university overseas, or foreign students in Japan, or for assisting indivduals reseaching transportation theory
Assistance Related to International Exchange Activities			
Kumamoto Youth Conference Center Fund for the Development of Youth Through International Exchange	1983	50,000	support of international exchange activities designed for young people in Kumamoto Prefecture
Japan-China Friendship Fund for Giving Books	1984	1,020,000	sending books and publications to Chinese schools, libraries and related educational institutions
Fund of the UNESCO Women's Center of Kobe Prefecture	1988	6,300,000	individuals or organizations promoting international exchange in Kumamoto Prefecture
Pan Pacific Fund	1979	23,288,000	organizations involved in exchange activities to promote friendship among foreign residents from Pacific Rim countries
Development Assistance and Disaster Relief			
Asian Community Trust (ACT)	1979	23,288,000	activities involving the promotion of community development, academic research, education, culture, agriculture, youth development, etc.
Imai Memorial Charitable Trust for Overseas Cooperation	1977	9,736,000	cooperation activities in sectors such as education and health care disaster relief
Kawakami Memorial Trust	1978	986,000	promotion of such efforts as educational revitalization, etc.
	Date	Total	

Name of Trust Fund	Established	Amount	Area of Funding
Kawamoto Memorial Trust of Hokkaido Xinjian-Uygur Technical Development	1986	4,125,000	technical trainees from the Xinjian-Uygur autonomous region to training in Hokkaido Prefecture, or for sending specialists to this region
Kanto Region Junior Chamber Inc. Board for International Peace	1986	4,125,000	refugees, organizations undertaking assistance activities for victims of disasters overseas as well as in Japan
Other			
Kyongju Nazare Park, Republic of Korea Fund for Assisting Japanese Wives Residing in Korea	1984	1,452,000	organizations providing assistance to Japanese wives or widows living in South Korea who are experiencing financial hardship
Moriyasu Memorial Educational Fund for Japanese Children Left Behind in China	1988	6,720,000	repatriated Japanese from China, left behind during the war, who require financial assistance to fund university or technical education
Assistance for Exchange with Countries Outside of Asia, by Foreign or Japanese Entities			
Fund for Africa	1985	3,452,000	providing social welfare or medical infrastructure in Africa, or providing support for Japanese organizations undertaking activities in African regions
Ishimori Memorial Scholarship Fund to Promote Friendship with North America	1990	1,800,000	foreign university or graduate students from North America attending a university whil living in Tokyo
Kaijima Memorial Fund for International Youth Exchange	1978	850,000	Japanese organizations in Japan or abroad promoting exchange among American and Japanese youth
Ryoichi Kojima Fund for Japanese in France	1989	4,600,000	Japanese individuals or organizations in France involved in international exchange activities, or Japan related research taking place in France
Sato Tokihiko Memorial Fund	1985	2,640,000	support for study abroad for university or graduate students of universities in Miyagi Prefecture studying civil engineering

Name of Trust Fund	Date Established	Total Amount	Area of Funding
Ryoji Saito Fund for Research in Islamic Studies	1990	2,400,000	Japanese researchers undertaking academic research in Islamic studies, or foreign students from Islamic countries studying at Japanese universities
Glaxo Holdings plc International Scholarship Fund	1990	2,400,000	Japanese university students studying medicine, pharmacy, chemistry, or biology in the United Kingdom

KOREA

Corporate Foundations in Korea

Tae-Kyu Park
Professor
Yonsei University

Presently, there are more than four thousand nonprofit foundations involved in a limited range of activities in Korea. These foundations can be classified according to two factors—the primary contributor to the establishment of the foundation and the main activities of the foundation. Classified by the first factor, foundations are divided into two groups—noncorporate foundations, established by the contributions of individuals who are not related to any corporate firm; and corporate foundations, established by the contributions of corporations or their owners. Classified by the second factor, foundations can be divided into religious, educational, scholarship-giving, medical, and social service foundations. A foundation is not limited to one specific activity and is allowed to be involved in other activities, even though it is registered with the appropriate government authority as one of the above five types. Even though Korean corporate foundations have a relatively short history compared to those in Western societies, foundations established by contributions from corporations or their owners are the most important foundations in terms of size of endowment, extent of influence on society, and variety of activities. Corporate foundations are expected to be the mainstream of nonprofit foundations in Korea in the future, considering the rapid growth in the number of corporate foundations established and the high expectation society has for their role.

I. Characteristics of Corporate Foundations

The last two decades have been a period of expansion for the Korean corporate community and of rapid growth for the national economy. Accordingly, many corporate foundations were set up during this period. Establishment of corporate foundations was primarily initiated by big business firms or groups as a result of an unbalanced economic development strategy. Therefore, it can be said that those foundations established by big corporations or big businesses are representative of Korean corporate foundations as a whole.

According to the most recent survey of corporate foundations funded by big business corporations, of the eighty-one foundations listed in the Federation of Korean Industries' *Directory of Company Sponsored Foundations*, only nine were established before 1970, and sixty-two came into existence during the 1970s and 1980s. Forty-six and seven-tenths of a percent of the total were set up in the 1980s. This trend reflects not only the short history of Korean business groups, but also the fact that, during the last decade, social expectations for corporations changed as the economy changed and political democratization proceeded. There was a tendency for the number of private foundations related to corporations to grow in response to social demands on the business sector. In the three-year period from 1990 to 1992, ten new corporate foundations were established, accounting for ten percent of the total number of foundations established in almost half a century. This fact, and the rising demand in Korean society for active participation of the business sector in social activities, indicates that the trend of establishing corporate foundations will continue in this decade.

There are three patterns of endowment contributions made to corporate foundations—contributions only by corporation owners, joint contributions by both corporation owners and corporations, and contributions only by corporations. At the time that the foundations included in this study were initially established, 51.9 percent of the total were funded by corporation owners, 33.3 percent by corporations, and 14.8 percent by joint contributions from corporation owners and corporations. However, the composition of endowment contribution types has changed and, as of the end of 1991, foundations funded by owners of corporations and those funded by corporations have been reduced to 40.4 percent and 29.6 percent respectively. On the other hand, those funded by joint contributions have increased to 29.6 percent.

Corporate foundations are registered with the Ministry of Health and Social Affairs, the Ministry of Education, and the Ministry of Science and Technology. Most of the foundations are limited to giving scholarships to students or giving research grants to university professors. Out of a total of eighty-one foundations, sixty-six are scholarship-giving or research grant-making foundations. This narrow area of corporate philanthropic activity is also reflected in the fact that sixty-one out of eighty-one foundations are registered with the Ministry of Education for the purpose of pursuing scholarship-giving and research grant-making activities. Out of the foundations established in the 1970s and 1980s, more than eighty-seven percent were funded by corporations for these activities, and even during the period of 1990–92, half of the newly established foundations specified scholarship giving and research grant provision as their main activities.

A few corporate foundations operate hospitals and health organizations, but until very recently, corporate foundations did not pay attention to supporting or operating welfare facilities or supporting welfare programs. Since the early 1980s and especially since the early 1990s, the business sector has paid special attention to providing social services, such as day care centers for low-income people and hospitals for people in remote areas. Half of the newly established foundations between 1990 and 1992 were registered with the government authority concerned with the provision of social services.

At the moment, all corporate foundations in Korea are limited to domestic activities and are not involved in any international interactions with foreign NGOs or nonprofit foundations in pursuing philanthropic activities.

The asset size of foundations varies greatly from ones with just over one hundred million won (US$125,897)* to ones with more than ten billion won (US$13 million). However, more than eighty percent of the eighty-one foundations associated with the Federation of Korean Industries had less than one million won (US$1,259) when they were set up. As of the end of 1991, foundations with assets of more than five billion won (US$6.3 million) account for almost fifty percent. When the corporate foundations were first established, there were only nine foundations with more than ten billion won (US$13 million) in assets, but this number increased to eleven in 1990 and thirteen in 1991. This shows that there has been a tendency for an increase in the assets of corporate foundations. However, most of the foundations that are registered as scholarship-giving or research grant-making are shown to have assets of less than five billion won (US$6.3 million).

It is important to understand the relationship between foundations and their founders or founding companies. In Korea, many foundations seem to be tightly managed by their parent companies, and they are controlled and operated by company managers. The foundations make regular reports to corporate headquarters and are publicized as members of the business group that established the foundation. A small portion of foundations are operating rather independent from the

* Based on the International Monetary Fund, *International Financial Statistics*, January 1995. Figures given are based on the end of the period exchange rate for November 1994. U.S.$1 = 794.3 won.

corporation that founded them. Even though the government regulates the board of directors' composition for the foundations that are in charge of decision making, this regulation has been ineffective so far.

Looking at the executive offices of the foundations, twenty-six out of eighty-one still do not have an executive body independent of the founding corporation, and are therefore pursuing their own activities, while relying on the contributing corporation for human resources in the form of management and secretarial services. Thirty-two and one-tenth of a percent of the corporate foundations are managed and operated by staff members dispatched from the contributor corporation or a corporation under the contributor's control. Only forty-two foundations out of fifty-five that have independent staff members are managed and operated by staff members who are exclusively appointed by the foundations. The remaining thirteen are supported both by staff members exclusively appointed by the foundations and staff members jointly appointed by the foundations and the contributing corporations. Currently, twenty-six foundations are dependent on jointly appointed staff members only. The average size of corporations' executive offices is relatively small; most of the foundations (sixty-three out of eighty-one) operate with no more than 5 staff members, and the average number of staff members is about 5.5 persons. Only eight of the eighty-one foundations employ more than ten persons. This is a relatively small scale of staff members of corporate foundations, considering their asset size.

On average, about ninety percent of total revenues are spent for foundation activities and the remaining ten percent for management. The revenues of foundations are mainly from fund management. In 1992, the total budget of the eighty-one foundations amounted to 105 billion won (US$132.2 million) and the average budget was 1.297 billion won (US$1.6 million), which was more than double that of the previous year. In 1991, twelve foundations spent more than one billion won (US$1.26 million) and among those, eight have more than ten billion won (US$12.6 million) in assets. Foundations that fund hospitals, day care centers, art galleries, and research institutions are spending relatively large amounts of their budget on those activities. Since 1990, the budget share for social service activities such as hospital operation and culture promotion related philanthropic activities has increased. On the other hand, the budget share for scholarship-giving or research grant-making activities has been reduced.

II. Tax and Regulation of Nonprofit Foundations

The Korean government has taken policy measures to help nonprofit foundations carry out philanthropic activities so that the private sector can contribute to social welfare improvement, along with the governmental sector. To this end, the government has tried to encourage the establishment of nonprofit foundations, especially corporate foundations, mainly by creating a tax incentive system. On the other hand, the government has found that they need to prevent nonprofit foundations from being misused as tax loopholes, justified by law, for rich families. To alleviate such concerns, the government enacted a regulation law aimed at controlling nonprofit foundations. There have been mixed evaluations of the government's policy measures toward nonprofit corporate foundations. Those who maintain a critical view of the regulation law argue that the government's policy measures have not been successful in preventing corporate foundations from taking advantage of nonprofit foundations as a legal means of tax avoidance. Even after enactment of the regulation law, nonprofit corporate foundations have been taken advantage of by parent corporations and their owners.

Owners of big business firms or groups can avoid inheritance tax by establishing nonprofit corporate foundations. The law states that inherited properties are exempt from inheritance or gift tax when they are donated for the establishment of nonprofit foundations or for the activities of established nonprofit foundations. Under the inheritance and gift tax law, a person who acquires properties through an inheritance or a gift is subject to tax rates ranging from five percent to sixty percent and from five percent to fifty-five percent, respectively. But properties that are contributed to nonprofit foundations including corporate foundations, public organizations, or religious, charitable, academic, or public welfare organizations are exempt from inheritance or gift tax, provided certain conditions are met. The properties contributed to religious, charitable, research, and public welfare activities that are operated by the Presidential Decree are exempt from inheritance or gift tax unless all or part of the earnings from the contributed properties are used for the benefit of the inheritors or their family members. But if the contributed properties are in the form of company stocks, those exceeding five percent of the total capital of the company under consideration are subject to gift tax.

Besides the inheritance and gift tax law, there are preferential tax treatments for contributions to nonprofit foundations under the income tax law, the corporation tax law, and the tax exemption and reduction control law. According to the corporation tax law and the tax exemption and reduction control law, up to ten percent of total income, two percent of one-twelfth of capital, and all contributions to nonprofit foundations or any other activities for the public good are treated as expenses and deducted in calculation of taxable income. For nonprofit foundations, up to sixty percent of income earned from profit-seeking business activities, excluding the loss carried over from the previous period, is deductible as expenses when contributed to a nonprofit foundation or any other activities for the public good. Up to five percent of income, excluding business and real estate income, can be treated as a special deduction for particular contributions. According to income tax law, up to seven percent of business income and real estate income plus two percent of one-twelfth of the total capital amount is deductible.

In Korea, both ownership and management control of large as well as small and medium size firms lie in the hands of entrepreneur families. The ownership structure in which Korean big business corporations belong to a big business group can be characterized by heavy reliance on outside financing. The low equity-to-debt ratios of the large Korean corporations makes it possible for the owner families to control corporations with relatively small amounts of capital. As a result of these characteristics of Korean big business groups, comprising dozens of legally independent companies, the owner families have exercised absolute power over personnel decisions and wielded almost complete power over the strategic and daily operations of group companies. Owners of big business groups can inherit ownership and management control of business groups by establishing nonprofit corporate foundations with tax exemption or reduction privileges. Of course, as mentioned before, the "Law on Establishment and Nonprofit Foundations" requires that no more than one-third of a board of directors which consists of two to fifteen members may be persons who have a special relationship with the founder of the nonprofit foundation. Persons who qualify as having a special relationship with the founder are (*a*) the founder himself, (*b*) relatives of the founder or a member of the board of directors, (*c*) any person employed at a corporation that is controlled by the founder or member(s) of the board of directors, and (*d*) any person who makes a living by property or money owned by the founder or member(s) of the board of directors.

But the government's policy on the control of corporate foundations has not been so effective as to prevent founders or contributors from controlling nonprofit foundations even with the stipulation on qualifications of members of the board of directors. The current regulation defines a person who has a special relationship with the founder of a foundation too narrowly and, in fact, could not rule out some persons with a special relationship from the board of directors of a corporate foundation. Therefore, the owner of a big business firm or group, and his family, have made use of nonprofit foundations through which the ownership and management control of the big business corporations or groups could be handed over to their family successors for inheritance or gift tax avoidance. Through the establishment of a nonprofit foundation by contributing a large share of a big business firm, nonprofit foundations become the largest shareholder of the firms of a business group. The owner's successor can maintain the ownership and management control of business firms or groups by controlling or occupying the board of directors of the nonprofit foundation. This argument is supported by recent survey data which shows that in many cases, nonprofit corporate foundations own large amounts of the contributing company's share ownership and are sometimes the largest stockholders of the company.

Problems associated with nonprofit corporate foundations have been raised repeatedly as a social as well as economic issue in Korean society since 1990, when many new corporate foundations were established by contributions from big business firms. The new administration, which took over power last February, in an effort to resolve this problem, has worked on designing stricter regulations related to the management and operation of corporate foundations.

There are two major measures associated with the government's policy and which are aimed at preventing nonprofit corporate foundations from being used as a loophole through which the founder can control the parent company and avoid tax burden. First, when a new foundation is established by the contribution of a company's stocks that are owned by the contributor, the maximum exemption of gift or inheritance tax has recently been reduced from twenty percent to five percent of the capital of the company under consideration. This measure, directly aimed at corporate foundations, is devised to discourage corporate foundations from being used as a device through which stocks of a company can be transferred from the founder generation to its successor. This reform is aimed at making it harder for corporate foundations to be used as a kind of holding company of the contributing company by restricting the types of assets that contribute to the establishment of corporate foundations. This new measure instituted in the regulation law of nonprofit corporations, including nonprofit corporate foundations, is expected to reduce the tax incentive of contributors who try to establish a new corporate foundation by donating some or all of their ownership share of a company. This is also expected to weaken the contributor's motivation to continuously contribute to an established foundation he has founded with his main contribution. As a result, corporate foundations are no longer to be taken advantage of by wealthy contributors who would tend to use them as ownership and management control devices of the parent companies.

Second, by nature, corporate foundations are to be established and operated fairly for the benefit of the general public, not for the benefit of a contributor or his relations. However, it cannot be totally denied that in the past corporate foundations have not been fairly managed or operated only for the cause of public good. This spirit of corporate philanthropy providing for the benefit of the public good has not been strictly abided by. This is allegedly due to the fact that the board of directors of corporate foundations can be controlled by the founder or his relations. Corporate foundations are usually tightly controlled by the founder or his relations and are operated as a subsidiary of the business firms or groups that the founder is in control of. Therefore, the new government has taken measures to alleviate the problem by reforming the regulation law stipulating qualification and structure of the board of directors. The amended law stipulates that no more than one-fifth (reduced from one-third) of the board of directors of a corporate foundation may be occupied by the founder himself and the persons with a special relationship as defined by the law. Furthermore, only one member of the immediate family of the founder, besides the founder himself, is allowed to be involved in nonprofit foundations as a member of the board of directors.

PHILIPPINES

Overview of Organized Philanthropy in the Philippines

Ma. Gisela T. Velasco
Manager
Membership and Corporate Involvement Unit
Philippine Business for Social Progress

I. Introduction

In the last twenty-five years, a dramatic change has occurred in the social landscape of Philippine development. Nongovernmental organizations (NGOs) have emerged as a credible and major force in plotting the country's socio-economic development, bringing forth the important role played by the private nonprofit sector in effecting social change. Part of this sector called NGOs are organizations whose main contribution is to provide funding to carry out development activities. This sub-sector is what is termed as philanthropic organizations.

An attempt to study this sector has posed some difficulties.[1] These impediments, however, illustrate the need for a study on grant-making organizations especially in the light of dwindling assistance from foreign donors for social development activities, and the emergence of the issue of sustainability among NGOs. This study, therefore, is an attempt to describe the organized philanthropy sector in the Philippines today and to identify the issues and challenges currently facing the sector.

The objectives of this study are to report on the major actors in the field of organized philanthropy in the Philippines, to understand the regulatory and social factors that have influenced its growth, and to explore the issues and challenges confronting the sector at this period in time.

The paper is organized into four parts: first is an overview and the historical beginnings of the practice of philanthropy in the country; second, the mechanisms currently in place to encourage or govern the practice of organized philanthropy; third, the legal and regulatory context of philanthropy in the country; and finally, the factors, constraints, and challenges facing the growth of the sector.

Defining Philanthropy

For purposes of this study, philanthropy is defined as the voluntary transfer of resources for charitable, civic and social purposes. In the Philippine context, philanthropy is of two major types: charitable and developmental grant making.[2]

Charity is what is termed as the support of other nonprofit organizations for purposes of running social, educational, charitable, or other activities serving the public good. It is characterized by a donor-grantee relationship initiated through proposals or letters of requests and forged on the basis of the donor's priorities or focus or on personal behest or preferences.

Developmental grant making, on the other hand, calls for the selective assistance to nonprofit organizations that pursue a similar or related agenda to the one defined by the grant-making organizations. It is characterized by the proactive development of partner organizations and their capability to manage programs to meet the development needs of the target area. To some extent, social investment-type activities can be considered philanthropic where resources are assigned to another organization with the end view of recovering that resource at some point in the future. Examples of this will include providing bridge financing to organizations expecting to receive long-term funding assistance from other organizations, financial advances for livelihood activities with zero or subsidized interest rates, and participation as an investor in a joint venture of a social enterprise that will yield an acceptable rate of return.

Although most of the activities of philanthropic organizations in the Philippines would still fall under the charities type, a significant percentage have started to embark on developmental grant making. This is characterized by the presence of grant-making organizations doing some form of operating function such as capacity building and project development. This take-off type of philanthropic activity has been difficult to segregate from the developmental NGOs directly undertaking programs for social development. They, nevertheless, still form part of the philanthropic sector and signal the growing shift to a proactive and long-term response.

This study is limited to philanthropic activities done either on a full-time or part-time basis by legally organized entities such as corporations, foundations, or associations. It also describes the experience of Philippine organizations that generate and manage resources drawn from their membership, original benefactors, or founders.

The role of individual philanthropists and international organizations operating in the Philippines has been excluded in this study and would hopefully be the topic of future studies on Philippine philanthropy.[3]

II. The History of Philanthropy in the Philippines

In a study on the beginnings of philanthropy in the Philippines, Callanta noted the strong influence of the Church and State in the evolution of its practice in the country.[4]

Philanthropy during the Spanish period (17th–19th century) was characterized by a strong presence of religious organizations espousing the Christian value of charity. Institutions such as orphanages, asylums, schools, and hospitals catered to the socially and physically deprived sectors of Philippine society. Although religious groups continued to operate under the American regime (1900–40), the period saw the rise of secular and voluntary organizations brought to the country by the American colonizers. Groups such as the Red Cross, the Young Women's and Men's Christian Association, and the Boy and Girl Scouts of the Philippines spearheaded activities for the sick, the young and the family.[5]

The increase in the activities of secular private volunteer organizations prompted the government to set up the Public Welfare Board in 1915 to coordinate their activities. Its establishment and that of a child care institution, the Government Orphanage, signaled the beginning of government responsibility in social welfare. The social demands during the Japanese Occupation (1941–44) further strengthened the role of government with the establishment of public agencies tasked to undertake relief operations for those who suffered from the war.

Throughout this period and until the mid-1960s, private philanthropy exercised a significant role in providing financial support to the welfare activities spearheaded by the Church, the State, and a few private voluntary institutions. Led primarily by their patriarches, notable families were at the forefront of various fund-raising activities and campaigns, contributing not only cash but also property and other material donations.

An opportunity to institutionalize these activities and to access additional resources from other donors came when the Philippine Congress enacted the Science Act of 1958. The law provided several tax incentives to private science foundations, among which was allowing the full deductibility from the donor's taxable income of contributions made to support the advancement of science and technology in the country.[6] Thus emerged the setting up of or restructuring of existing institutions to private foundations specializing in scientific research.

In the mid-1960s, a new mandate emanated from Vatican II and the social encyclicals.[7] A central idea that emerged was the enhanced participation of the laity in pursuing the mission of the Church. The responsibility to contribute in undertaking a social apostolate, especially in the rural areas, became not only that of the clergy but, equally important, that of lay individuals and communities.[8]

The late 1960s also became a period of turmoil and conflict as discontent from the student, labor, and rural sectors became more pronounced. Communism as an ideology gained ground among the disgruntled intellectuals and frustrated masses. This condition prompted the business sector to close ranks and organize themselves to prevent the social conditions from worsening. Some were motivated by lofty ideals of helping the disadvantaged or sharing their wealth or expertise. Others were worried that if they did nothing to change the situation, another ideology would take over that would not look too kindly on their way of life.[9]

The early 1970s saw the establishment of groups such as the Philippine Business for Social Progress in 1970, the Bishops-Businessmen's Conference for Human Development in 1971, and the Association of Foundations in 1972.[10] All these organizations spearheaded a new thinking among businessmen, the Church, and prominent families that operated their own foundations. This new thinking subscribed to the belief that development efforts must be coordinated rather than fragmentary, developmental rather than welfare, and should address root, rather than immediate, causes.

A major problem confronted by grant-making organizations during this period was finding "new" solutions to the worsening social problems. Economic interventions alone had been proven inadequate in solving social problems, yet, there was no proven model to fall back on in terms of a development strategy. A new philosophy for social development had to be developed.[11]

Related to this was the difficulty in attracting competent talent to development work which at that time could not provide adequate financial reward or prestige. Philanthropic organizations also had to contend with the limited absorptive capacity of requesting organizations. The limited capability of the communities to be assisted in managing projects required these organizations to invest in human resource development if they were to expect reasonably satisfying results. In some cases, the absence of credible and capable local structures prompted philanthropic organizations to transform themselves into operating foundations just so they could ensure program success.[12]

III. Major Actors in the Field of Organized Philanthropy

There are in the country today three major mechanisms in exercising organized private philanthropy. These are through corporate giving, independent foundations, and civic associations.

1. Corporate Giving

As a component of corporate citizenship,[13] the practice of philanthropy is manifested in three different modes: corporate donations program implemented by an internal unit or department of a company, activities of corporate foundations, and innovative mechanisms for practicing philanthropy.

In a study of corporate giving in the country in 1992, 249 companies reported that a total of PhP 295 million (US$12.35 million)[14] was mobilized from the business sector to support various social and charitable activities.[15] In the 1993 study, 204 companies reported an amount of PhP 306 million (US$12.81 million), a four percent increase from the previous year's total.

Education received the most assistance from the corporations for both years (PhP 53 million or US$2.22 million in 1992, PhP 68 million or US$2.85 million in 1993). From a ranking of fifth in 1992 with PhP 21.5 million (US$900,000) assistance given, health moved up to the second rank in 1993 and received PhP 58 million (US$2.43 million). Consequently, disaster response which ranked second in 1992 with PhP 52 million (US$2.18 million) slid down to third in 1993 with PhP 32 million (US$1.34 million) assistance received. Other significant changes were the drop in support for civic and community affairs (PhP 33 million or US$1.38 million in 1992, PhP 22 million or US$921,000 in 1993), the increase in assistance to livelihood programs (PhP 22.5 million or US$942,000 in 1992, PhP 30.7 million or US$1.29 million in 1993), and the rise in contributions to science and technology (PhP 5 million or US$209,000 in 1992, PhP 15.5 million or US$649,000 in 1993).

Compared to 1992 when disaster response, education, and livelihood were identified as the future areas of concern, the 1993 report indicated a shift to enterprise development, environment, and health as programs to be further pursued.

Although assistance came mostly in the form of cash (88 percent of total contributions in 1992, 74 percent in 1993), a growth in the use of in-kind donations was evident as its share in total contributions increased from 8.4 percent in 1992 to 17 percent in 1994. The donation of technical expertise was also given value as it rose from 1.6 percent (or a value of PhP 4 million or US$168,000) in 1992 to 7 percent (a value of PhP 20 million or US$838,000) in 1993.

Twenty-seven percent of the respondents projected an increase in their corporate giving budget for 1994 by 54 percent while 64 percent anticipated maintaining the same level of their corporate giving budget. This is a less optimistic response compared to 1992, where 33 percent reported an increase by 43 percent, and 60 percent indicated having the same level of giving as that of the previous year.

As a mechanism for corporate giving, a growing number of companies (thirty-six as of last count) have set up their own corporate foundations. Originally founded to promote educational and scientific research, corporate foundations today may perform one or all of three functions: to serve as the mechanism for managing the corporate giving program, to serve as the implementing arm of the company for its community relations or social development projects, and/or to generate additional resources from other agencies or organizations to expand its own program and operations. Depending on how well defined the developmental role is of the foundation vis-à-vis the mother company, a corporate foundation can do either charitable type or developmental philanthropy.

Some foundations such as the Ayala Foundation, the United Coconut Planters Bank Foundation, and Kauswagan sa Victorias Foundation are purely operating foundations, implementing programs and projects that serve specific communities or sectors. This is often true among companies with a community-at-risk, company towns, or with a specific public to serve. Among those who have remained grant-making foundations are the San Miguel (Corporation) Foundation, the SGV Foundation, and the Philippine Investments and Management Consultants, Inc. (PHINMA) Foundation. The mother companies of these foundations often have internal units undertaking the community relations function or have no specific public or sector to serve. The largest number, however, perform both functions. This enables them to work in partnership with operating NGOs, thereby limiting their overhead costs while, at the same time, maintaining projects that are clearly identified with the foundation. Among these are the Marsman Foundation, Metrobank Foundation, and the Bank of the Philippine Islands Foundation.

In 1992, the League of Corporate Foundations (LCF) was formally organized with twelve founding members. Believing in the important role of corporate foundations to bridge business expertise and social development, LCF was organized with the vision of being "...the driving force in the formation of a highly committed business sector working effectively with communities and partner institutions towards the attainment of equitable and sustainable development." The establishment of this organization was deemed important to create a climate conducive to the integration of social development ideas into the Philippine business culture.[16]

A number of companies have also initiated innovative mechanisms for promoting philanthropy while at the same time gaining a positive relationship with their employees, clientele, or customers. Citibank N.A., for example, has conducted two fund campaigns among its clients. The first, the Mt. Pinatubo Fund Campaign in 1991, was a matching scheme among its credit card members where the bank matched peso for peso every donation made by the members. The campaign generated PhP 1.5 million (US$63,000) from the bank's clients or a total of PhP 3 million (US$126,000) including the company's counterpart, enough to construct a training center in a resettlement area.

Inspired by the success of the first campaign, the bank embarked on another project to coincide with the nintieth year celebration of the company in 1992. This time, the campaign was meant to set up a Watershed Reforestation Fund and was extended to all other clients of the bank, including the general public. With the bank committing a PhP 2 million (US$84,000) seed fund, the campaign generated an additional PhP 1.3 million (US$54,000).[17]

The PHINMA group of companies has also tapped its employees in disaster response fund campaigns since 1990. Every peso raised from donations by employees was matched by another peso by the company. Moreover, the company ensured efficiency in collection by engaging systems such as "one day's pay" donations or giving up of a sack of rice from the employees regular ration.[18] Other companies have utilized cause-related marketing as an approach to promote philanthropy among its consumers while raising company or brand awareness.[19]

Another form of resource generation has been cooperative efforts to address specific issues or concerns. In 1990, the Corporate Network for Disaster Response (CNDR) was formed to rationalize business sector involvement in times of disaster. Learning from the mistakes in the 1990 earthquake relief operations, several business companies and associations set up a system for mobilizing resources that would reach actual victims of disasters efficiently and effectively. In CNDR's system, banks concentrate in receiving solicitations from individual and philanthropic donors, transportation companies provide space or actual vehicles to deliver much-needed resources to stricken areas, and manufacturing plants located nearest the disaster site provide warehousing space. Distribution is done by partner NGOs who are familiar with the area and the people most in need. This approach has enabled companies to manage their resources effectively, contributing to a collective effort rather than individual relief operations in a manner where their respective expertise can best be utilized.

2. Independent Foundations

Independent foundations are defined as grant-making organizations whose funds are generally derived from an individual, a family, or a group of individuals.[20] Among foundations, independent philanthropic foundations are the least in number. These are formed primarily to perpetuate the memory of specific individuals, usually upon the initiative of family members or friends. A number have been transformed to corporate foundations, owing to the increasing support by the companies which these individuals helped found. This is true in the case of the A. Soriano Foundation and the Ayala Foundation. In general, independent foundations directly implement projects in selected geographic areas or in response to identified issues.

3. Civic Associations[21]

Among civic organizations, the Philippine Jaycees and the Rotary Clubs are two whose thrust is service to the community. Members of the Philippine Jaycees belong to the eighteen to forty year old age bracket and have banded together with the mandate of providing leadership training through community service. As a training ground for future leaders, the chapter presidency post is a coveted position since it builds one's social and political status in society later on. The Rotary Club, on the other hand, is organized by an older but more influential membership to undertake community service projects.

Both organizations have supported projects related to *barangay*[22] development, the handicapped, or out-of-school youth. The Jaycees are better known for providing personal attention to their social projects, through voluntary services or in-kind donations. In addition, one Jaycee chapter can easily raise PhP 20,000 (US$838) a year which if accumulated among the four hundred chapters nationwide, could reach a total of PhP 8 million (US$335,000).[23]

Having a more accomplished and stable stature, Rotarians, on the other hand, easily raise more funds but are constrained from going out of their meeting halls to oversee their philanthropic activities. Donations are often coursed through organized institutions with ongoing programs. Raising PhP 500,000 (US$21,000) per chapter could easily be done realizing some PhP 125 million (US$5.23 million) per year from its approximately two hundred and fifty chapters.[24]

Despite the significant amount of funds raised, these groups often prefer short-term, high profile projects that generate media mileage for the organization and its officers. This short-term focus limits the potential of the resources in providing long-term solutions to community problems. This is largely attributed to its annual change of leaders, thereby disrupting continuity in vision and direction, and the lack of full-time staff to work on these projects. Nevertheless, the sincerity and the good intentions of members in rendering service to the community cannot be questioned and have thus contributed to their continued existence as prominent members of society.

In summary, the philanthropic organizations sector in the Philippines today is characterized by:

1) High resource generation potential

A conservative estimate of the resources readily available from local foundations and the business sector would amount to PhP 750 million (US$31.41 million).[25] This revenue can further be expanded if leveraged with international donor agencies or with individual giving.

2) Low-profile character

Philippine philanthropic organizations, unlike their Western counterparts, are less likely to engage in public disclosure except if publicity were an important concern of the sponsoring organizations, notably corporations. Even the concern for publicity, however, is tempered with the apprehension of generating unrealistic expectations from the public.

Some organizations, however, have proven that informing the public of their thrust, in effect, has made it easier for them to turn down requests not within their defined agenda. Although there are still "non-negotiable" requests, these occupy a smaller percentage of their total budget.[26]

3) Basic Social Services priorities

Scholarships are the most prevalent and preferred area of direct assistance. The majority of organizations surveyed ranked education as their primary area of concern. Health and disaster response ranked second for 1993 and 1992 respectively.

The preference can be attributed to three factors: the high demand for basic services as a public good, the inability of the government to deliver the service owing to limited resources, and the relative ease in managing these types of projects as opposed to monitoring livelihood or environmental conservation activities.

4) Limited staff

Contributing to the last two items above is the part-time or voluntary mode of management employed by most grant-making organizations. The presence of full-time and adequate staff are more often found in foundations that undertake operating functions as well. The general practice, however, is to perform the philanthropic function as a secondary concern, done during free time or with the minimum effort required.

Efforts to organize the sector through networking are already in place but still limited at the moment. Networking will have to be promoted to enable donor organizations to undertake collective projects and pursue advocacy for promoting philanthropy.

IV. Legal Incentives for Philanthropy[27]

The role of foundations in national development is duly recognized by the Philippine government as embodied in the 1987 Philippine Constitution. Section 23 of Article II of the Constitution provides:

> Section 23. The State shall encourage non-governmental, community-based, or sectoral organizations that promote the welfare of the nation.

Specific to private philanthropy, Section 11 of Article XIV states:

> Section 11. The Congress may provide for incentives, including tax deductions, to encourage private participation in programs of basic and applied scientific research. Scholarships, grants-in-aid, or other forms of incentives shall be provided to deserving science students, researchers, scientists, inventors, technologists and specially-gifted citizens.

In line with this, Philippine laws currently provide several incentives to donors providing gifts or contributions to private foundations,[28] domestic corporations, or associations organized and operated exclusively for religious, charitable, scientific, youth and sports development, cultural, and educational purposes; or for the rehabilitation of veterans; or to social welfare institutions.[29]

These incentives include deductibility for income tax purposes—up to six percent in the case of an individual,[30] and three percent in the case of a corporation—of the donor's taxable income derived from business; exemption from the estate tax; and exemption from the donor's tax.

The incentives however remain deficient and the process too cumbersome to encourage donors to increase their philanthropic activities. For example, the valuation of donations in kind such as real property is based on the schedule of values fixed by local government assessors which are oftentimes not updated to reflect real market values. A donation of already used personal property has to be valued based on its depreciated or book value, not on its fair market value (FMV) which is what the donee would otherwise pay to acquire the same product. The law is also silent on donations of properties that appreciate in value over time, e.g., paintings, heirlooms, historical memorabilia and the like, or of patents or copyrights, claims or royalties.

Of late, there are initiatives on the part of the government to revise the tax system and generate more revenues for public expenditures. The Task Force on Tax and Tariff Reforms headed by the Department of Finance has announced that among the changes being considered in the country's tax system is the decision to limit the deductions on direct business cost. Among these items are representation allowances, non-traditional advertising (including maintaining basketball and other professional club sports teams), and charity donations. The Task Force proposal is to be submitted to the President by late 1994 and if approved, will be translated into a bill for enactment by the Congress.[31]

A number of recommendations are currently being proposed to maximize tax benefits of philanthropic activities, thereby encouraging further philanthropy in the country. Among them are the use of the fair market value at the time of the donation of in-kind contributions as a basis for valuation; the provision for the valuation and deductibility of intangibles or rights; the increase in the allowable deduction to a maximum of ten percent of taxable net income; and the provision for a carryover of excess allowable deductions over a number of years, duly observing the percentage limitation in every taxable year. The concern of the Philippine government, however, for abuses of these incentives committed by unscrupulous organizations should be addressed as well.

V. The Future of Philippine Philanthropy

Philanthropy as a practice in the Philippines can be traced to two major traits or values. First is the strong kinship-based relationship prevalent in the culture. The practice of providing care and assistance to family members and relatives within an extended family structure, especially to those less privileged, can be traced back to pre–colonial society with its strong tribal organizations.[32] The expectation of being responsible to those in need becomes more pronounced as one goes up the social ladder.[33] This sense of kinship, however, can limit the scope of philanthropy to immediate relatives, the locality, or specific interest, precluding the need to extend assistance to where the need is greatest.

A second determining factor is the religious influence of doing charity and extending compassion to the "least of the brethren." For a nation marked by centuries of Christian tradition, helping the poor has evolved from being a means to gain special blessings or indulgence from heaven to that of serving as a witness to the Christian values and teachings. Whether through the Catholic teaching of charity and theology of liberation or the Protestant ethic of volunteerism, Filipino philanthropists have derived significant inspiration to share their resources from their faith.

The influence of external events such as the Mass Education Movement of Dr. Y. C. James Yen in the 1950s and the present day coalitions for the environment, women, and human rights, has prompted a rethinking of the approaches to social change and an increase in the participation of private groups. These have served as critical inputs to the development of philanthropic thinking in the country, prompting an evolution from engaging in simple charities to becoming a major actor within the development community in the country.

Among the influencing factors, the legal context for philanthropy has provided fiscal incentives to donors but is still insufficient to allow flexibility, owing to the limited scope and applicability of deductions allowed by the present provisions. Among the measures that can promote donations further are incentives such as increasing deduction to taxable income and allowing carryover of excess allowable deductions over a number of years. Better efficiency in tax collection will also generate substantial income for the government, thereby discouraging government proclivity for withdrawing exemptions from income tax.

What are some of the challenges to organized philanthropy in responding to the social, political, and economic needs of the country?

A basic issue confronting philanthropic organizations today is whether to remain a grant-making institution or be transformed into an operating foundation. Taken within the context of declining foreign assistance to the NGO sector, philanthropic organizations can contribute in sustaining the dynamic development activities in the country.[34]

It would be too presumptuous to think that the philanthropic organizations will be able to fill the void created. Their contribution, however, may lie in providing the seed funds that can be used to leverage other funds or harness indigenous knowledge and resources to support the development work in a specific locality.[35] Developmental philanthropic activities will have to be promoted to allow greater returns from the limited resources available within the country.

One avenue for doing this is by setting in motion the development and pursuance of a local development agenda. The new Local Government Code has provided the impetus for local development. This local approach works in consonance with the "immediate family" mentality present in the culture but at the same time expands the area of concern not just to basic services or livelihood but to the whole area development framework that must be addressed.

Pursuing these thrusts, however, would require from organizations a shift in the donor-grantee relationship from one of sponsorship or charities to partnership. Sponsorship is characterized by a reactive approach in giving out donations, often limited to the financial form of assistance and with the work confined within the safe walls of the offices. Partnership on the other hand puts a premium on the exchange of ideas and the joint search for solutions to problems. Financial support becomes as important, if not less important, as expertise, contacts, and linkages. As stated, although a number of foundations are already in this mode, the majority are still in the charities/sponsorship mode. Admittedly, sponsorship still has a role to play, but long-term assistance for local development would require a partnership-type of relationship where both parties can learn from one another, and gain mutual respect and understanding.[36]

Good intentions should be complemented with the capacity and skills to manage the grant-making program. On the part of the decision makers, efforts should be made to maintain contact with the actual needs of those assisted.

Corollary to this, investments will have to be made in the area of professionalizing foundation staff. The period for ad-hoc and reactive giving allowed organizations to maintain a relatively small staff with simple skills. Moving toward developmental philanthropy would require an adequate number of multi-skilled staff who can pinpoint and further develop programs that yield an impact while pursuing the organization's interest.

VI. Conclusions

In the Philippine context, the term *philanthropy* refers to a range of endeavors, from the mere act of giving away resources to any requesting party to a more directed and intentional support of activities contributing to social and economic development. This trend, which emerged alongside the development of a strong and dynamic NGO sector beginning in the 1970s, called for a shift from the traditional donor-grantee relationship to a proactive development of partners at the local level, thereby ensuring that resources are utilized for long-term and sustainable activities.

Although the resources are present and can be further expanded, the impact of this resource is constrained by the absence of a defined agenda for grant-making organizations in the country. Concentrating in specific areas (whether geographic- or issue-specific) will generate a greater impact instead of being a be-all for all. Setting institutional priorities, developing partner organizations, and further professionalizing the management can all contribute to the rationalization of the role of this sector. Networks such as the Association of Foundations, the League of Corporate Foundations, and the Corporate Network for Disaster Response should be strengthened to promote the environment for philanthropy. Only by addressing these issues can organized philanthropy in the Philippines strengthen its role in the promotion of human development in the country.

Notes

1. The author encountered difficulties in finding reference persons and materials for this study. For one, the term philanthropy connotes dole-out or welfare giving which does not relate to the proactive developmental stance undertaken by a number of grant-making organizations. Second, philanthropy implies abundant wealth. In a country where fifty percent of the population contributes only seven percent to the country's income (UNDP, *Philippine Human Development Report*, 1994), to be dubbed a "philanthropist" seems elitist and hence, inappropriate. Third, there is very limited literature on the subject available which required the author to rely on interviews and primary sources of information.
2. Interview with Sixto K. Roxas, August 1994.
3. For a study on the extent of official development assistance (ODA) channeled to NGOs in the Philippines, see G. Sidney Silliman, "Philippine Non-Governmental Organizations and Official Development Assistance," Paper prepared for presentation at the Annual Meeting of the Association for Asian Studies, 22–27 March 1994, revised 16 April 1994.
4. Ruth S. Callanta, "The Future of Corporate Philanthropy in the Philippines" in *Futuristics, The Journal of the Philippine Futuristics Society*, Volume IV (1991), p. 157–158.
5. Juan L. Arsciwals wrote in his *Taliba* (a local tabloid) column of 23 November 1928 the following: "The local elite was especially fond of supporting causes either managed by Americans or which had international appeal, such as the Red Cross, while largely ignoring local charities like the Philippine Tuberculosis Society." from Jose Ibarra Angeles, "20 Years of Corporate Citizenship," *PBSP Annual Report Volume II*, 1990, p. 10.
6. SGV & Company, "Review of Philippine Laws and Recommendations to Encourage & Promote Corporate Philanthropy," Center for Corporate Citizenship—Philippine Business for Social Progress & League of Corporate Foundations, 1994, p. 1.
7. Among these encyclicals were *Mater et Magistra* (1961) and *Gaudium et Spes* (1965). These were followed by *Populorium Progressio* (1967), *Octogesima Adveniens* (1971), the Synod of 1971 on justice in the world and the Synod of 1974 on evangelization.
8. Bishop Francisco A. Claver, S.J., "The History of the BCCs: The Philippines," in *Church of the People*, edited by Gabino Mendoza, et al. (Bishops-Businessmen's Conference for Human Development, 1988), p. 22–23.
9. Amb. Bienvenido A. Tan, Jr. in Jose Ibarra Angeles, op. cit., p. 6.
10. "The Philippine Business for Social Progress is a private, national, and nonprofit foundation established by business corporations as an expression of their corporate social responsibility. Its vision is to improve the quality of life of the Filipino poor. The Bishops-Businessmen's Conference (BBC) on Human Development was established as a forum for dialogue between the Church-related private or nonprofit sector and the corporate sector. The BBC served as the avenue for the Church and the corporate sector to address, as their common concern, social and economic problems, the ethical issues in business, and social responsibilities of corporations. The Association of Foundations is an organization of private foun-

dations which aims to foster broader public understanding of the nature of foundations as an institution in nation-building, and serves as a nerve center of information" from the AF brochure (no date).

11. Community organizing as an approach was introduced only in the 1970s. Structural Analysis, a tool for social analysis, was introduced in the country in September 1975.
12. This explains why, according to Mary Racelis, Assistant Representative of Ford Foundation, and Joy C. Duran, Executive Director of A. Soriano Foundation, a number of foundations originally doing grant making alone became operating as well.
13. For a general discussion on the practice of corporate citizenship in the Philippines, see Ma. Aurora F. Tolentino and Juan Miguel Luz, "Philippine Business in Development: From Corporate Philanthropy to Corporate Citizenship," in *Evolving Patterns of Asia Pacific Philanthropy*, edited by Ku-Hyun Jung (Seoul: Institute of East and West Studies, Yonsei University, 1993), pp. 187–216.
14. International Monetary Fund. *International Financial Statistics*, January 1995 (Washington, D.C.: IMF, 1995). Figures given are based on end of the period exchange rates for November 1994. US$1 = PhP 23.88.
15. Ma. Gisela T. Valesco, *Annual Report on Corporate Giving, 1992* (Manila: Center for Corporate Citizenship, Philippine Business for Social Progress, 1993), p. 2.
16. From the papers of the Planning workshop of the League of Corporate Foundations, 22–23 August 1992 at Marsman Estate, Davao del Norte.
17. Interview with Mr. Ramon Santos, Marketing Manager, Citibank N. A., June 1994.
18. Interview with Mr. Rene Lawenko, Director for Community Relations, PHINMA, June 1994.
19. Two of the companies that have done cause-related marketing in the past are Magnolia Corporation (ice cream, juices), which contributed a percentage of their earnings for sports development, and Philippine Cocoa Corporation (chocolates and drinks), which donated to projects for the street children a peso for every product sold.
20. Patricia E. Read, ed., *Foundation Fundamentals: A Guide to Grantseekers*, (The Foundation Center, 1986), p. 4.
21. A number of civic organizations are present in the Philippines. The following discussion, however, will concentrate on the activities of two organizations, the Rotary Club and the Philippine Jaycees, due solely to the constraints on the part of the author. There is no intention to minimize the value and extent of contributions made by other organizations. Other civic organizations operating in the Philippines include the Lions, the Kiwanis, and the Soroptimist International clubs.
22. The *barangay* is the smallest political unit in the Philippines.
23. Interview with Mr. Harry Angping, President of Rotary Club of Chinatown, Manila (1994) and Past President, Philippine Jaycees (1981).
24. Ibid.

25. The amount is based on the 1994 budget provided by foundations that participated in the survey and the *Annual Report on Corporate Giving.* Resources raised by civic organizations were not included since companies would also be one of their major donors.
26. Interview with Cecile Alcantara, President, Coca-Cola Foundation, July 1994.
27. This section is based on a study prepared by Sycip, Gorres, Velayo & Company for the Philippine Business for Social Progress - Center for Corporate Citizenship and the League of Corporate Foundations entitled "Review of Philippine Laws and Recommendations to Encourage & Promote Corporate Philanthropy," 1994.
28. "The term 'private foundation' means a non-profit domestic corporation: (i) organized and operated exclusively for scientific, research, educational, character-building and youth and sports development, health, social welfare, cultural or charitable purposes, or a combination thereof, no part of the net income of which inures to the benefit of any private individual; (ii) which, makes utilization directly for the active conduct of the activities constituting the purpose or function for which it is organized and operated, unless an extended period is granted by the Secretary of Finance; (iii) the annual administrative expense of which, does not exceed thirty percent (30) of assets of which would be distributed in the event of dissolution to another non-profit domestic corporation organized for similar purposes, or to the State for public purposes" SGV & Company "Review of Philippine Laws and Recommendations to Encourage & Promote Corporate Philanthropy," 1994, p. 4.
29. At present, for donors to avail of full deductibility of their charitable contributions, the donee institution must initially register with the Government and Tax Exempt Corporation Division (GTECD) of the Bureau of Internal Revenue (BIR). Additionally, the recipient institution must have projects listed in the National Priority Plan of the National Economic Development Authority (NEDA), which is the agency that will classify the recipient institutions as a "qualified donee institution." This is a cumbersome procedure that works against the encouragement of NGOs and other foundations, inevitably defeating the promotion of charitable giving.
30. The six percent limitation on the deductibility of donations made by individuals has been significantly restricted by Republic Act No. 7496 which adopted the Simplified Net Income Taxation Scheme (SNITS) for individuals engaged in business or the practice of a profession. Under the SNITS law, only contributions made to the government and accredited relief organizations for the rehabilitation of calamity-stricken areas declared by the President of the Republic are deductible. This does not promote philanthropic activities to other nongovernment organizations not accredited by the government or engaged in rehabilitation work.
31. *Philippine Daily Inquirer* (4 August 1944), p. 17. Prior to this, a number of bills in the House of Representatives had already been filed proposing a restructuring of the tax system by imposing a single rate of tax for corporations doing business in the country. In implementing the Gross Taxation Scheme, a company will be imposed a standard tax rate on gross income, thereby rendering void the tax benefit of deducting donations from the company's net income.

32. F. Landa Jocano, *Social Work in the Philippines: A Historical Overview* (New Day Publishers, 1980), p. 225.

33. This sociological basis for philanthropy was mentioned in the interview with Patricia Ma. Araneta, Acting Chairperson of the Association of Foundations and Joy C. Duran of A. Soriano Foundation.

34. G. Sidney Silliman, *Philippine Non-Governmental Organizations and Official Development Assistance*, pp. 21–22.

35. Interview with Mary Racelis, Country Representative, Ford Foundation, June 1994.

36. Ibid. and from the article of Chris Marsden, "Partnership: A Normal Part of Doing Business," Center for Education and Industry (CEI) Occasional Paper, 1992/1, p. 8.

Acknowledgements

The author acknowledges the assistance of Caroline Grace O. Mandac of the Center for Corporate Citizenship - Philippine Business for Social Progress, in the preparation of this report.

The author recognizes as well the following people who have provided guidance in putting together this report:

Patricia Ma. Araneta
Acting Chairperson
Association of Foundations

Armando Baltazar
Chairman
Gregorio Araneta Social Development Foundation

Amb. Howard Dee
President
Assissi Development Foundation

Juan Miguel Luz
Associate Director
Philippine Business for Social Progress

Mary Racelis
Assistant Representative
Ford Foundation

Sixto K. Roxas
Chairman
Foundation for Community Organization & Management Technology

Ma. Aurora F. Tolentino
Executive Director
Philippine Business for Social Progress

SINGAPORE

Philanthropic Organizations and Corporate Philanthropy in Singapore

Chan Tse Chueen
Research and Administration Officer
ENGENDER

The following report deals with independent philanthropic foundations and corporate philanthropic activities in Singapore. For a more in depth discussion of the nonprofit sector in general, refer to "Nongovernmental Organizaitons in Singapore" in the NGO volume of the *Survey of Nongovernmental Underpinnings of the Emerging Asia Pacific Regional Community*.

I. Narrative Report

1. Overview of Philanthropy

1) Evolution of philanthropy

The growth of philanthropy in Singapore has much in common with the evolution of NGOs in general. Its early manifestations are acts of giving that are community based and beneficiaries are selected solely on the criterion that they belong to a certain community. Altruism does not extend to all and sundry who need help, but is selective in that the recipients must possess certain qualities, be it ethnicity or language group, these qualities being mostly ascriptive. Support is given in the form of charity and welfare benefits, mostly in areas of education, health and community service, such as the building of roads and temples. It is a simple one-off donation that is not expected to have any further social impact.

Unlike the previously ad hoc nature of charitable donations, we have seen in Singapore since the 1950s, the formation of foundations that are devoted to more long-term charitable purposes, and are executed in a much more systematic way.

Yet another new development is the establishment of a foundation, such as the Tsao Foundation, that is more than a grant-making institution. Unlike other family foundations, the Tsao Foundation itself designs and runs its own community services. The foundation not only has more autonomy in deciding the ways in which the funds are to be disbursed, its provision of community service would be more flexible than others which depend on external funding.

The rise of corporate philanthropy, on the other hand, is concomitant with the rise of multinational corporations and other large businesses. The vast revenues of these corporations have become increasingly obscene and there is pressure on these giant corporations to assume responsibility for the well-being of the community they work in, and from which they have taken so much. In short, the community demands some form of return. Nowadays, the notion of a good corporate citizen has gained wide social acceptance. Corporate philanthropy is fast becoming an essential tool for the cultivation of the all-important public image of the company.[1]

2) Role of philanthropic organizations/corporate philanthropy in responding to the social, political and economic needs of the country

The Singapore government has not only successfully engineered a vibrant and voracious economy, it has also been involved in much social policy planning. An important aspect of this planning has been the concern with the redistribution of income, though in a form quite different from conventional "western" welfare systems. In fact, the government is firm in its stand against public welfare programmes modelled after those in Europe and North America and has preferred to encourage the private sector to play a larger role in contributing to the needs of the community. As Singapore's Community Development Minister Wong Kan Seng said in an article in the *Straits Times*,[2] willing individuals and community groups should be given the chance to contribute to Singapore's welfare services, while the government's role should be that of a catalyst, providing the basics and necessary funding.

In view of this persuasive encouragement by the government, philanthropic organizations and corporate philanthropic agents have been more than responsive. Various philanthropic organizations and corporations rallied to the government's call for help, in the form of donations, in kind or otherwise, sponsorships and other means of contribution. In a newspaper article, IBM pointed out that they support national causes closely paralleling government plans and policies, while Fuji Film contributed S$900,000 (US$616,000)[3] for the 1988 Courtesy Campaign. The National Ideals and Identity Campaign of 1987 was sponsored by Yeo Hiap Seng,

Singapore Petroleum Corporation, Prudential Insurance and Visa International, each contributing S$200,000 (US$137,000). These are but a handful of the many examples of such cooperation between the public and private sectors.

2. The Role of Philanthropic Organizations/Corporate Philanthropy in Promoting a Sense of Community in the Asia Pacific Region

1) Major factors influencing such activities

While philanthropic organizations and corporate philanthropic agents have been responsive to the government's directives, they have in the main been very conservative in their choice of what causes to support. The criteria set by these philanthropists concerning the selection of the kind of NGO activities to fund have tended to be mainstream. This is especially so in the case of corporations engaged in philanthropic activities as part of a strategy to build up a positive image for the company. Thus they cannot afford to focus on issues that are too thorny and controversial, and which might give them bad press; nor do they want to support causes that are unglamorous and/or not media-friendly. Developmental issues that have regional impact often do not meet their criteria.

In Singapore, the political climate is an important factor affecting the role philanthropic organizations can play in promoting a sense of community in the Asia Pacific region. Although the Singapore government has long been tireless in its support of closer economic cooperative efforts between the nation states in this region, it is nevertheless only catching up with the other aspects of society. For example, in its bid to promote Singapore as a thriving centre for the arts and entertainment, the government has taken several important first steps, including the introduction of a bi-annual Asian performing arts festival, alternating with a bi-annual festival of the arts. The government's good will towards promoting a sense of community in the region will be a great boost to efforts by the private sector. However, such good will does not come easily.

2) Government views on such cooperative efforts

As had been mentioned several times in this report, the government tends to view certain regional cooperation more fondly than it does others. With regards to philanthropic activities specifically, take for example discussion of the recently introduced Charities Bill[4] in parliament as a supplement to the existing Charities Act.[5] The bill called for a number of amendments, including to the following clauses:

- that an offence is committed when charities and other persons raise funds without a permit from the commissioner, unless they have been exempted from the requirement; and
- at present the intention is only to require a permit for fund raising for *foreign charitable purposes.* Fund raising for local charities is exempted.

In the parliamentary debate, the Minister of State for Finance (Radm Teo Chee Hean) explained why this amendment was necessary:

"To protect the interests of Singapore donors, the government intends to restrict the grant of fund-raising permits to local charities over which it has full jurisdiction as well as reputable international organizations such as UNICEF and the Red Cross which have well-established track records. Foreign charities without proven antecedents will be denied permits."

This does not bode well for the participation of Singapore philanthropic organizations in any regional cooperative network of such organizations.

3. Future Prospects

Role in further enhancement of a sense of community

A network of philanthropic organizations in Asia and the Pacific would of course facilitate cooperation and dialogue, from the exchange of information and expertise to working out strategies to ensure minimal duplication of provision of funds, such that the welfare needs of the communities are well met. Ad hoc efforts, though commendable, are not able to make any lasting impact on the development of regional ties.

A review of the philanthropic organizations and corporate philanthropy in Singapore presents the picture of an inward-looking and closeted philanthropic community. In the task of forging regional ties, Singapore would not seem a likely partner. But a saving grace is that Singapore is a city state with a well-run economy, an excellent telecommunications system, and an efficient banking centre. Regional centres of some international donor agencies have been located here, despite the fact that this is not where most of their client NGOs are based.

II. Description of Major Philanthropic Organizations/ Corporate Philanthropy

There is no comprehensive database on local foundations and trust funds, nor is it possible to have a complete list of corporate philanthropy, of which there is much. Foreign donor agencies operating in Singapore deserve a mention since it is with their resources that many regional projects see the light of day. The following compilation has been made from different sources including annual reports and brochures, the National Council of Social Services Directory of Social Services in Singapore, newspaper clippings and magazine articles.

This section is divided into three parts:

- corporate philanthropy;
- independent foundations;
- international donor agencies.

1. Corporate Philanthropy

In Singapore, the activities of philanthropic organizations and corporate philanthropy are fairly local in nature. Although corporate philanthropy is spearheaded by multinational corporations, and these MNCs usually have operations in other parts of the region, there is no concerted effort to coordinate regional programmes. For this reason, the following is by no means an exhaustive list of corporate philanthropic activities.

Some of the more popular causes that corporate philanthropy select include:

• *Environment*

This seems to attract the most money. Programmes include American Express International's Environmental Award programme, Hong Kong Bank's Care for Nature Programme and British Petroleum's several environmental projects.

• *Welfare and charities*

Corporations such as United Overseas Bank, Hewlett Packard, Coopers and Lybrand, Citibank and Hard Rock Cafe have made donations to the Community Chest and/ or the various charities under it.

• *The arts*

Contributions have been made towards the sponsorship of concerts, plays, fashion events and creative writing programmes, from Singapore Press Holdings, Esso, C K Tang and Chase Visa.

2. Independent Foundations

Even before the Charities Bill was introduced, the causes supported by these philanthropic organizations would invariably be for mostly local programmes. Although many of the foundations mentioned here are not regional/international, they are still included on account of the abysmal lack of a substantial regional foundation.

1) Lee Foundation

Address: 65 Chulia Street, #44-01 OCBC Centre, Singapore 0104
Tel: 535-4055 *Fax:* 535-3552
Contact person: Secretary

The Lee Foundation was established in 1952 by rubber and pineapple tycoon Lee Kong Chian, with S$3.5 million (US$2.4 million). At the end of 1990 the foundation had an accumulated fund of nearly S$10 million (US$6.8 million). Its gross income from investments totalled S$9.5 million (US$6.5 million) and it disbursed S$9.1 million (US$6.2 million) to charitable causes. Its constitution prohibits the donation of any grant or assistance to any political organization.

It was set up to:

- give financial support to charitable, educational and medical institutions. It played a large role in setting up schools in Singapore;
- support many of the country's charitable organizations as well as research projects;
- donate money to schools and hospitals. In the 1980s the focus was on medical institutions while in the 1990s its focus is on helping Singapore's growing elderly;
- give donations to various institutions affiliated to the Singapore Council of Social services;
- give donations to schools, universities, colleges, libraries, sports and cultural groups;
- help in welfare and relief work, such as aid to victims of fire, flood and other calamities in Singapore and elsewhere;

- provide for needy individuals who for technical reasons are not eligible for government public assistance; and
- provide financial aid to students in accredited institutions of higher learning that recommend and sponsor their applications. Grants are given under certain conditions and remitted directly to the educational institutions and not to the students.

2) Shaw Foundation

Address: 1 Scotts Road #10-00 Shaw Centre Singapore 0922
Tel: 235-2677

The Shaw Foundation was established in 1957 with the idea of "giv[ing] back money to the public" according to its founder, Tan Sri Runme Shaw, the late entertainment magnate. The Shaw Foundation does not have a start up fund but has key real estate assets—the Shaw Centre and the Shaw House—whose revenue go to the foundation.

- For 1990 the Shaw Foundation donated S$10 million (US$6.8 million) to three hundred funds and organizations in Singapore.
- In 1992 it donated S$16.5 million (US$11.3 million) to 350 recipients including S$1 million (US$0.68 million) to the Institute of Policy Studies.
- Donation recipients included schools and institutes of higher learning, children's homes, homes for the aged, welfare homes, hospitals and medical institutions, and Community Chest charities.
- S$30,000 (US$20,500) is awarded annually for scholarships.

3) Hong Leong Foundation

Address: Hong Leong Building, 16 Raffles Quay, #18-04, Singapore 0104
Tel: 220-7377 *Fax:* 224-1703
Contact person: Company Secretary

Established in 1980 by the Kwek family, the foundation is limited by guarantee and was incorporated under the Companies Act, Cap. 50 on 12th December 1980. Its objectives and activities include:

- conducting charitable activities regardless of race, language and religion;
- making grant donations to approved charitable organizations and to deserving projects;

- paying visits to charity homes and the organization of outings for the aged, disabled and children; and
- the distribution of Hong Baos to social welfare recipients before every lunar new year.

4) Lien Foundation

Address: c/o Mandarin Hotel, 333 Orchard Road Singapore 0523
Tel: 7374411
Chairman: Mr Lien Ying Chow
Founded in 1980 by millionaire banker Lien Ying Chow, who gave forty-eight percent of the shares in his family holding company to the foundation to "support education and charities". The foundation made donations amounting to S$334,500 (US$229,110) in 1990.

5) Tsao Foundation Ltd

Address: 100 Beach Road, #20-01/03 Shaw Towers, Singapore 0718
Tel: 294-7770 *Fax:* 299-7809
President: Dr Mary Ann Tsao
Billionaire Frank Tsao leads a consortium of Hong Kong tycoons developing the S$1.7 billion (US$1.2 billion) Suntec City in Singapore, and the foundation was set up by his family to provide a wide range of health care to Singaporeans, particularly workers and the elderly.

Headed by his daughter and funded by the Tsao Trust, the Tsao Foundation is a family as well as an operational foundation whose objective is care for the elderly. Its programmes and activities include:

- the awarding of scholarships;
- the running of workshops, community based social services, training for family members on care for the elderly, the organization of conferences and conventions, and the education of the public through publications;
- the sharing of experience and expertise with other groups with similar concerns.

6) Chen Su Lan Trust

Address: 257 Selegie Road, #15-279 & #15-182, Selegie Complex, Singapore 0718
Tel: 336-4033/4/5 *Fax:* 338-1392

Contact person: Secretary

This philanthropic trust fund was set up by Dr Chen Su Lan to carry out programmes of Christian charity. It was founded in 1952 in fulfilment of a vow and as an expression of gratitude to God for the founder's deliverance from the dangers of World War II. The trust serves to

- propagate the teachings of Jesus Christ, to help the poor and the needy, those in need of moral and social rehabilitation, and those who are victims of calamities;
- contribute to any charitable institutions whose objectives are similar to those of the trust; and
- make financial contributions to health, education, welfare and church-related institutions.

7) Rajabali Jumabhoy Foundation

The Rajabali Jumabhoy Foundation was incorporated in May 1992 in the name of the patriarch of the four-generation Jumabhoy family of listed Scotts Holdings. The foundation provides support for the poor and needy, medical research and services, as well as promoting educational advancement through donations and scholarships. It made its first donation of S$96,000 (US$66,000) to ten charities and two schools in January 1994.

Other independent foundations in Singapore include the Khoo Foundation, the Tan Joo Kee Trust Fund, the Singapore Chinese Chamber of Commerce and Industry Foundation, the Ngee Ann Kongsi Foundation and the Tan Kah Kee Foundation.

The bulk of the money from independent foundations in Singapore goes to NGOs that run local programmes, although some, such as the Lee Foundation and Shaw Foundation which have funded the Institute of Southeast Asian Studies, also give grants to regional organizations. Foreign funding for NGOs, on the other hand, remains lean. UNDP's Development Cooperation 1987 Report (released in 1988) revealed that 78.1 percent of externally financed technical assistance was from bilateral programmes (government to government). Financing from UNDP accounted for 12.9 percent, while that from UN systems other than UNDP accounted for 7.8 percent. Funds from other foreign NGOs accounted for only 1.2 percent of total technical assistance.

3. Foreign Donor Agencies

Foreign donor agencies play an important role in consolidating the Asia and the Pacific as a region, because they give priority to (or at least some part of their budget is reserved for) projects that are regional. The relevance of the inclusion of these foreign donor agencies in a country report of philanthropic organizations in Singapore should be obvious. Since there is no comprehensive list of foreign aid received by all NGOs in Singapore, do note that the following list is not an exhaustive one. The information is compiled from the following organizations' annual reports, brochures, and information sheets.

1) Asia Development Bank (ADB)

The ADB is an international partnership of forty-seven member countries engaged in promoting the economic and social progress of its developing member countries in the Asia Pacific region. It was established in December 1966 with its headquarters in Manila, Philippines. It is owned by the governments of thirty-two countries from the Asia Pacific region and fifteen countries from Europe and North America. In its twenty-three years of operation, the bank has become a major catalyst in promoting the development of the most populous and fastest growing region in the world today.

The bank's principal functions are:

- to make loans and equity investments for the economic and social advancement of developing member countries;
- to promote investments of public and private capital for development purposes;
- to respond to requests for assistance in coordinating development policies and plans of member countries; and
- to provide technical assistance for the preparation and execution of development projects and programmes and advisory services.

In its operations, the ADB is required to pay special attention to the needs of smaller or less developed countries and give priority to regional, sub-regional and national projects and programmes which will contribute to the harmonious economic growth of the region as a whole.

The bank's financial assets consist of ordinary capital resources, comprising subscribed capital, reserves and funds raised through borrowings; special funds, comprising contributions made by member countries, accumulated net income, and amounts previously set aside from the paid-in capital. Loans from the ordinary capital resources, which account for sixty-six percent of the bank's lending, are generally made to member countries which have attained a somewhat higher level of economic development. Loans from the Asian Development Fund are made on highly concessional terms and are almost exclusively made to the poorest borrowing countries.

ADB's operations cover the entire spectrum of economic development, with particular emphasis on agriculture, energy, development, financial institutions, transport and communications and social infrastructure. Most of the bank's financing is designed to support specific projects. The bank also provides programme, sector and multiproject loans.

2) The Asia Foundation

The Asia Foundation is a private, non-profit grantmaking organization with its headquarters in San Francisco and twelve field offices in Asia, with programmes in twenty-eight Asian and Pacific island nations. The foundation supports Asian initiatives to strengthen institutions concerned with representative government, effective legal systems, human rights, market economies and independent and responsible media. The foundation also supports nongovernmental organizations that encourage broad participation in public life and it promotes leadership development through internships, graduate training and study tours. The foundation's Centre for Asian Pacific Affairs promotes U.S.-Asian dialogue on political, economic and security issues affecting the region.

Governed by a board of leading American citizens, the foundation is funded by contributions from the private and public sectors in the United States and Asia.

3) International Development Research Centre (IDRC)

Address: Regional Office for Southeast and East Asia, 7th Storey RELC Building
30 Orange Grove Road, Singapore 1025

Tel: 235-1344 *Fax:* 235-1849

Canada's IDRC, through its support for research, assists scientists in developing countries to identify long-term practical solutions to pressing development problems. Support is given directly to scientists working in universities, private enterprises, government and nonprofit organizations.

IDRC is directed by an international board of governors and is funded by the government of Canada. IDRC provides funding for projects which are managed by

Third World researchers affiliated with universities, governments and NGOs. Its proposed activities aim to:

- be relevant to local or national development priorities;
- strengthen national capacities;
- involve applied rather than basic research; and
- promote collaboration with other donor groups and/or Canadian partners.

4) Canadian International Development Agency (CIDA)

Address: Canada-ASEAN Centre, 80 Anson Road # 15-02 IBM Towers, Singapore 0207

Tel: 225-7346 *Fax:* 222-7439

CIDA is the federal government agency responsible for implementing Canada's official development assistance (ODA) policies and administering most of the ODA budget. The agency reports directly to the Minister for External Relations and International Development and to the Secretary of State for External Affairs. It was established in 1968.

The ASEAN-Canada Fund

- provides financial assistance to nongovernment organizations in ASEAN in support of innovative small-scale development programmes which have a regional focus;
- supports development-oriented as opposed to welfare-oriented proposals with the view of promoting and fostering regional cooperation;
- finances small projects that require limited financial inputs and yet have significant impact on the beneficiaries in both the short term and the long term.

Because of the regional nature of the fund, many requests are in support of training workshops and activities dealing with the environment, natural resources management, adaptation of technology, human resource development or the cultivation of leadership potential.

The ASEAN-Canada Women's Initiative Fund

- supports national and regional women's organizations (GO/NGO or academic) from the ASEAN region to better address issues of importance to them;
- supports regional workshops, conferences, networking and regional project activities;
- assists in the development of collaborative research, data collection or information sharing;

- provides training assistance in specific skills in new technology/enterprise;
- aims to enhance women's participation in decision-making.

5) Friedrich-Naumann-Stiftung

Address: East and Southeast Asia Regional Office, #08-803 RELC Building
30 Orange Grove Road, Singapore 1025
Tel: 732-6927 *Fax:* 235-2142

This is a German foundation devoted to the principles of freedom and liberty, and the promotion of these principles to the various regions of the world. In carrying out this work, it has more than five hundred partner organizations in over eighty countries. Its activities include publications on human rights, democracy and women's issues, as well as the conducting of workshops to enhance dialogue on these issues.

6) Canadian High Commission, Singapore

Address: 14th Floor, IBM Towers, 80 Anson Road, Singapore 0207
Tel: 225-6364 *Fax:* 225-2450

7) Australian High Commission, Singapore

Address: 25 Napier Road, Singapore 1025
Tel: 737-9311 *Fax:* 733-7134

Apart from these, other foreign donors that have funded NGOs in Singapore include the Global Fund for Women, the International Planned Parenthood Federation, International Centre for Economic Growth, Tokyo Club for Global Studies, Hans-Seidel-Foundation, Ford Foundation, Japan International Cooperation Agency, MacArthur Foundation, the Rockefellar Foundation, the Swedish International Development Authority and the various UN system agencies (ESCAP, FAO, ILO, UNEP, UNESCO, UNHCR, UNICEF, UNV, WHO, UNIFEM, UNDP, UNFPA).

III. Conclusion

The emerging sense of community in the Asia Pacific region is only good in so far as it helps point to a way of better relations, over and above economic ties, that will help to solve the quite alarming problems associated with current development processes. Problems such as population displacement, rapid resource depletion and ecological disasters, prostitution and AIDS, to name but a few. Therefore NGOs and philanthropic organizations that actively promote this sense of community inherit an enormous task in the face of such heavy responsibilities.

Notes

1. Maureen Woon, "Corporate sponsorship: good deed or good 'deal" in *Mirror* (15 July 1991).
2. Wong Kan Seng, "Government's role in welfare services should be that of 'catalyst' " in *Straits Times* (23 March 1990).
3. International Monetary Fund *International Financial Statistics,* January 1995 (Washington, D.C.: IMF, 1995). Figures given are based on end of period exchange rates for November 1994. US$1=S$1.46.
4. Singapore National Printers. *Republic of Singapore Government Gazette Bills Supplement—Charities Bill* (Singapore: SNP Ltd, 1994).
5. Singapore National Printers. *The Statutes of the Republic of Singapore—Societies Act (Chapter 311): Revised edition 1985* (Singapore: SNP Ltd, 1986).
6. National Council of Social Services. *Directory of Social Services 1992* (Singapore: NCSS, 1992).

TAIWAN

The Emerging Asia Pacific Regional Activities of Taiwan's Foundations

Hsin-Huang Michael Hsiao
Research Fellow
Institute of Sociology
Academia Sinica

I. Introduction

The purpose of this report is to present a profile of how Taiwan's foundations carry out their Asia Pacific regional networks and activities by illustrating some noticeable examples.

Of the 309 foundations that participated in the survey, about one-third have experience in exchange activities with related foundations or organizations in foreign countries. Frequent exchange activities include cosponsoring programs and exchanging information, publications, and visits. Popular counterparts for foreign contacts are research institutions, NGOs, and foundations with similar objectives to Taiwanese foundations. Taiwan's foundations have the greatest number of contacts with related organizations in the United States, followed by Northeast Asia and Southeast Asia respectively. The Asia Pacific regional activities of Taiwan's foundations, by and large, have not been very active. In most cases, such activities as exchanging information and cosponsoring joint programs are not well institutionalized. Nevertheless, like research institutions, think tanks, and NGOs, Taiwan's foundations in recent years, have gradually developed greater interest in promoting regional networks in Asia Pacific.

Taiwanese foundations are divided into three classifications: independent foundations, corporate foundations, and semigovernmental foundations. Illustrations of each type of foundation are given below.

II. Independent Foundations

1. Buddhist Compassion Relief Tzu-Chi Fund

Chair: Master Hsi Cheng Yen
Address: 21, Kang-Lo Village, Hsin-Chen Hsiang, Hua-Lien County, Taiwan
Tel: 886-38-561-825 *Fax:* 886-38-267-776

The Tzu-Chi Fund is an independent Buddhist charitable foundation, established in 1980 from a small local Buddhist charitable organization set up in 1966. As of 1993, it has over three million sponsoring members throughout Taiwan. The history of this Buddhist foundation's development is full of amazing stories. It is now the wealthiest private foundation, and enjoys both national and international recognition. The Buddhist nun, the Master Cheng Yen, is apparently a charismatic spiritual leader.

The Fund is designated to promote charitable activities, medical care, education, and culture. It provides financial and medical relief to the poor both in Taiwan and overseas. It has built a hospital and medical college, a nursing school, and a children's development center. In addition it has also established a culture center for organizing Buddhist and public interest activities.

Since the mid-1980s, the Fund has been visited by Buddhist and philanthropic organizations from Japan, Korea, Malaysia, Thailand, Hong Kong, Singapore, Nepal, and even Mongolia. The Fund has a strong Asia Pacific regional community sense in its provision of important overseas assistance. As of 1994, the Fund has branches in Singapore, Japan, and Hong Kong. It has even established a Buddhist monastery and nursing home in Korea. Since 1990, the Fund has provided overseas relief assistance to Nepal, Thailand, Mainland China, and Mongolia.

2. S. Y. Tao Memorial Foundation

Chair: Mr. Kuan-Hsiung Wu
Address: 4F, 227, Roosevelt Rd. Sect. 3, Taipei, Taiwan
Tel: 886-2-363-1536 *Fax:* 886-2-363-0230

The S. Y. Tao Foundation was established in 1970, as the first cancer foundation promoting public knowledge of and research on cancer prevention. Mr. Tao, former ROC Minister of Economic Affairs died of cancer, and this foundation was formed in memory of his courageous struggle against the disease. This private foundation has been actively engaged in public education about cancer, and in providing free checkups for the general public. It also provides grants for cancer researchers and medical doctors to attend regional and international conferences related to cancer.

The Foundation also invites directors of cancer research or cancer societies in Japan, Korea, Australia, the United States, Canada, England, and France, to visit Taiwan. It plans to hold an international conference on cancer prevention in Taiwan.

By and large, this foundation has a steady and institutionalized exchange network with similar organizations in the Asia Pacific region as a whole.

3. Lung Cancer Foundation in Memory of Dr. K. S. Lu

President: Mr. Kuang-Rei Luo
Address: 201, Hsi-Pai Rd., Sec. 2, Taipei, Taiwan
Tel: 886-2-875-7533 *Fax:* 886-2-875-7100

The Dr. K. S. Lu Lung Cancer Foundation, another cancer prevention organization, was formed in 1980. It provides opportunities for Taiwan's lung cancer experts to attend regional and international meetings, invites overseas scholars and experts to Taiwan, and finances conferences organized by local medical associations. Professor Huyata from Tokyo Medical University is one of the invitees who has been asked to give lectures in Taiwan. However, the Asia Pacific regional network has not yet become a focus for the activities of this foundation.

4. Peng's Foundation for Culture and Education

Chair: Dr. Ming-Min Peng
Address: 15F, 99, Jen-Ai Rd., Sec. 2, Taipei, Taiwan
Tel: 886-2-357-6511 *Fax:* 886-2-341-1344

Peng's Foundation for Culture and Education is a very new foundation established in 1994, aiming to promote the establishment of a new order and world vision for Taiwan's future. Peng had been in exile in the United States for nearly thirty years, because of his political dissent from the ruling Kuomintang. The Foundation's inaugural conference on "Taiwan and Japan: Past, Present and Future," which invited many Japanese scholars to present papers, was a success.

It is expected that this foundation will serve as an effective forum for envisioning Taiwan's future and its role in the Asia Pacific regional community.

5. Sun Yat-senism Foundation for Scholarly Exchange

Chair: Dr. Ling-Ling Tsao
Address: 9F, 160, Min-Chuan East Rd., Taipei, Taiwan
Tel: 886-2-792-3399 *Fax:* 886-2-792-3366

The Sun Yat-senism Foundation for Scholarly Exchange, established in 1992, is designated to promote the thoughts of Sun Yat-sen around the world. Since its inception, it has organized conferences on Sun Yat-senism and the 21st Century in Hong Kong, Peking, Nanking, and Tokyo. The foundation's goal to hold conferences in as many cities as possible in Mainland China seems to be very ambitious. The Asia Pacific region is likely to be the focus of attention for its future activities, but due to its specific objectives, the Foundation's reach will be quite concentrated on the Chinese communities in the region.

6. Shih Ho Cheng Folk Culture Foundation

Chair: Mr. Shih Ho Cheng
Address: 3F, 62-3, Hsi-Ning North Rd., Taipei, Taiwan
Tel: 886-2-552-3973 *Fax:* 886-2-552-5528

With the clear objectives of research on as well as preservation and promotion of folk culture, the Shih Ho Cheng Folk Culture Foundation, established in 1980, has actively engaged in investigating various forms of Taiwanese and Chinese folk culture and art. The main targeted area for its collaborative efforts so far has been Mainland China and the scholarly communities focused on Chinese folk culture in the Asia Pacific region.

It has published a series of books on folklore and theater, and has organized an Asia Pacific regional conference on Chinese Festival Rituals and Performance, with overseas participants from Singapore, Japan, and China.

Due to its financial constraints, it is unlikely that the Foundation's existing research networks with China can be developed further.

7. Chinese Floral Arts Foundation

Chair: Ms. Chien Tsao Chen
Address: 1F, 285, Chien-Kuo South Rd., Taipei, Taiwan
Tel: 886-2-705-6312 *Fax:* 886-2-704-4873

The Chinese Floral Arts Foundation, established in 1986, is unique in its own right.

It is set up to promote Chinese floral arts and flower arrangement. Most of its promotional activities, such as floral arts exhibits, lectures, and auctions for charity, are in Taiwan. However, it has developed an exchange network with many art museums and galleries in San Francisco, Honolulu, and Chicago, and it also has close relations with the Ryukyu Floral Arts Association where it has held an exhibit.

Given its sound financial condition, the Foundation is expected to further promote Asia Pacific regional networks and collaborative efforts.

III. Corporate Foundations

1. The Cultural Foundation of the United Daily News Group

Chair: Mr. Tih-Wu Wang
Address: 9F, 563, Chung-Hsiao East Rd., Sec. 4, Taipei, Taiwan
Tel: 886-2-756-9063 *Fax:* 886-2-756-9070

The United Daily News Group consists of eight newspapers: *The United Daily News, The Economic Daily News, The Min Sheng Daily,* and *The United Daily Evening News,* which are all published in Taipei, Taiwan; and four other newspapers published around the world, *The World Journal* in North America, *The Europe Journal* in Paris, *The Universal Daily News* in Bangkok, and *The United Daily News* in Hong Kong. Altogether, the United Daily News Group publishes close to three million copies of Chinese newspapers every day to reach the Chinese reading public wherever they are. Therefore, this news group has become the largest Chinese newspaper chain in the world.

The Cultural Foundation of the United Daily News Group was established in 1982 to requite the support from and encouragement of its readership and society in general, this has enabled the role of these newspapers to grow.

The Foundation remains dedicated to working with Chinese at home and abroad to build upon a cultural foundation via cross-Straits and East-West cultural exchange, creating a greater epoch for Chinese culture.

Foundation activities include support projects to upgrade the development of domestic journalism, a cross-Straits cultural exchange program, a cultural forum series, an academic conference series, a cultural lecture series, an international figures invitation program, and dialogues between domestic and foreign scholars.

In 1993, the Foundation organized the following large-scale conferences: Traditional Chinese Culture and the Future Cultural Development, Evaluation and Prospect of Taiwan's Cultural Development, and Chinese Literature, 1949–1993. The last conference included Chinese scholars invited from Mainland China, Hong Kong, and the United States.

A review of the Foundation's overseas grant making activity reveals an evident focus on scholars from Mainland China. Two such grants are available: one is a publication grant, and the other is a visiting research grant.

2. United Overseas Chinese Commercial Bank Foundation for Culture and Philanthropy

Chair: Mr. Yi-Wu Ho
Address: 65, Kuain-Chien Rd., Taipei, Taiwan
Tel: 886-2-312-555 *Fax:* 886-2-331-1093

Another typical corporate foundation was established in 1980 by the Overseas Chinese Commercial Bank. Its activities include scholarships for overseas Chinese students in Taiwan's universities; publication grants for topics on financial, business, and legal issues; lectures and conferences on enhancing overseas Chinese investment in Taiwan; research grants for areas such as national development, financial structures, overseas Chinese economy, and overseas Chinese policy; and program grants on culture and the arts. The Foundation also invites prominent overseas Chinese to visit Taiwan, and it has provided assistance to Chinese schools in northern Thailand.

It is clear that the Chinese communities in Southeast Asia are the main target groups for this foundation's external networking activities.

3. Himalaya Foundation (HF)

Chair: Mr. Hsiao-Chung Han
Executive Director: Mr. Hsien-Hsin Chiang
Address: 6F, 167, Fu-Hsin North Rd., Taipei, Taiwan
Tel: 886-2-718-7061 *Fax:* 886-2-718-5777

The Himalaya Foundation (HF) was formed by the Himalaya Corporation in 1990. In the last two years, HF has devoted its efforts to compiling and publishing valuable yearbooks of Taiwan's Foundations (1993, 1994), and it also provided financial assistance to the US-Asia Research Institute's (New York) publication of *Asian Affairs: An American Review* (a quarterly), and the Japan Center for International Exchange's "Survey on Nongovernmental Underpinnings of the Emerging Asia Pacific Regional Community."

By reviewing HF's recent activities and self-defined role, one can expect that HF will be an accredited and active foundation to promote collaborative efforts in the Asia Pacific region in the near future.

4. Dimension Endowment of Art (DEOA)

Chair: Mr. Geoffrey T. C. Huang
Address: 7, Hsin-Yi Rd., Sec. 3, Taipei, Taiwan
Tel: 886-2-325-6283 *Fax:* 886-2-325-6405
The Dimension Endowment of Art (DEOA) was founded in 1989, by Mr. Geoffrey T. C. Huang, the president of Taiwan Pineapple Group. It began as an endowment dedicated to art education and dissemination in Taiwan. Several activities, such as the "Seminar on Regulations and Practices of the Arts," "Lectures on Contemporary Arts of Pan-Pacific," "Parents-Children Arts Potential Campus," and the "Seminar of Administrative and Professional Practices of Arts," were undertaken during the past few years. In 1993, in cooperation with Musée Marmattan, Paris, DEOA sponsored an exhibition of the "Works of Claude Monet and the Masters of Impressionism" that attracted over 310,000 visitors to the National Palace Museum.

It also collaborated with the Memorial Hall of Xu Pei Hong to sponsor an exhibition of this famous Chinese painter in Taipei in 1994. In 1990, DEOA cosponsored a symposium on contemporary arts in the Pan-Pacific with the National Central Library. A Japanese arts scholar was on the list of speakers. DEOA plans to establish an Art Library for the purpose of collecting domestic and overseas art information. In addition, a study project on the "Trend of Development of Arts in Pacific and Southeast Asia and the Active Exchange Model" is under way.

DEOA is a well-established institution expected to engage in more regional collaborative efforts in the field of arts and art education.

5. Lin Nai-Ong Foundation

Chair: Mr. Ching-Fu Lin
Address: 346, Min-Chuan East Rd., Sec. 3, Taipei, Taiwan
Tel: 886-2-503-7111 *Fax:* 886-2-503-4917
The Lin Nai-Ong Foundation was established in 1985 with a handsome endowment from Mr. Ching-Fu Lin, a successful business man who has a joint venture with the Mitsubishi Company of Japan. The Foundation has devoted all its efforts to preserve, collect, and exhibit Taiwan's aboriginal culture. It is the sole financial

supporter to establish for the public the Hsuen-Yi Museum for Aborigines Culture in Taipei. In its overseas grant-making activities, the Foundation provided a program grant to the Institute of Oriental Culture, University of Tokyo, to initiate the Research Group of Taiwan's Aborigines. It is a four-year program grant, from 1993 to 1997.

6. King Car Educational Foundation (KCEF)

Chair: Mr. Tien-Chai Lee
Address: 230, Roosevelt Rd. Sec. 3, Taipei, Taiwan
Tel: 886-2-368-0273 *Fax:* 886-2-365-9053

The King Car Educational Foundation (KCEF) was set up in 1980, by the King Car Company, a soft drinks manufacturer. Its main tasks are to organize activity camps for young people and provide program grants to local environmental, consumer and charity groups for their respective public interest activities. It also made a donation to help establish the Tzu-Chi Medical Research Center.

KCEF's Asia Pacific activities are limited to Mainland China, and it sponsors a concert tour in Shanghai and Peking.

7. Foundation of Chinese Dietary Culture (FCDC)

Chair: Mr. Tsao-Shi Ong
Address: 145, Chien-Kuo North Rd., Sec. 2, Taipei, Taiwan
Tel: 886-2-503-1111 (ext. 5616) *Fax:* 886-2-505-7095

The Foundation of Chinese Dietary Culture (FCDC) was founded in 1989 by Mercuries and Associates, Ltd., for the promotion of study on Chinese dietary culture. It has sponsored two annual international conferences on Chinese Dietary Culture, to which it invited scholars from Japan, Korea, Hong Kong, the United States, and Mainland China. A library of Chinese Dietary Culture has been established for public use under FCDC.

In the area of international exchange, Japan seems to be the main country for possible networking in the Asia Pacific region. FCDC intends to develop further collaborative relations with Korea, but so far regional collaborative efforts are still very informal and have no institutionalized networking arrangement.

IV. Semigovernmental Foundations

1. Straits Exchange Foundation (SEF)

Chair: Mr. Chen-Fu Koo
President: Dr. Jen-Her Chiao
Address: 16F, 156, Min-Shen East Rd., Sec. 3, Taipei, Taiwan
Tel: 886-2-718-7373 *Fax:* 886-2-514-9962

The Straits Exchange Foundation (SEF) was established in 1991 by government funds and corporate donations, to act as a semigovernmental foundation "dedicated to promoting the contacts and exchange between the Chinese on both sides of the Taiwan Straits." Therefore, it is devoted solely to the activities of "people to people" exchange between Taiwan and Mainland China. SEF also serves as a front line for the Taiwanese government to deal with Mainland China's counterpart organizations. It promotes understanding of the current socio-cultural conditions in China through its bimonthly magazine *Exchange*, provides research grants on various issues in China, organizes conferences and seminars in Taiwan and China, and mostly, extends invitations to Chinese scholars and cultural figures to visit Taiwan. It also organizes study tours to China for Taiwanese youth, artists, and scholars.

Evidently, Mainland China is the primary concern for SEF's overall programming and activities.

2. Chiang Chin-Kuo Foundation for International Scholarly Exchange (CCK Foundation)

Chair: Mr. K. H. Yu
President: Prof. Yih-Yuan Li
Address: 14F, 106, Hong-Ping East Rd., Sec. 2, Taipei, Taiwan
Tel: 886-2-737-7292 *Fax:* 886-2-737-7294

The Chiang Chin-Kuo Foundation for International Scholarly Exchange (CCK Foundation), established in 1989 by government funds and corporate donations, is the wealthiest national foundation in Taiwan. Its main goal is to provide grants for collaborative efforts in research, programming, conferences, and publication. It is open to applications from around the world, including Asia Pacific. From 1992 to 1994, the CCK Foundation provided grants for twenty-four projects of all sorts to Asia Pacific research institutions and universities. The grant recipients in this region include: the University of Santo Tomas, the University of the Philippines (Philippines), National University of Singapore (Singapore), Ho Chi Minh University, the Association of Literature Teachers and Researchers in Ho Chi Minh City (Vietnam), Griffith University, the University of Melbourne, Macquarie University, Edith Cowan University, the University of New South Wales (Australia), the Chinese University of Hong Kong, the Technology University of Hong Kong, Hong Kong University, and Hong Kong Polytechnic (Hong Kong).

Within the field of international scholarly exchange, the CCK Foundation is undoubtedly the most effective and active foundation in Taiwan. CCK Foundation's status as a national foundation has won for Taiwan a prominent international reputation through its ambitious and well-endowed overseas grant-making activities.

3. Pacific Cultural Foundation (PCF)

Chair: Mr. Huan Lee
President: Mr. Yu-Sheng Chang
Address: Suite 807, 346 Nanking-East Rd., Sec. 3, Taipei, Taiwan
Tel: 886-2-752-7424 *Fax:* 886-2-752-7429

The Pacific Cultural Foundation (PCF) was established in 1974 by government, private, and corporate donations, to serve as a grant-making foundation specifically for scholarly and cultural exchange in the Asia Pacific region. It provides grants for research, publication, writing, and seminars. PCF also sponsors programs in performing arts, art exhibitions, and cultural excursions held in Taiwan. During the past twenty years, PCF has been one of the more prominent cultural foundations active in promoting international research and cultural and arts exchange between Taiwan and the rest of the world, especially the Asia Pacific region.

PCF should be considered a good potential contact foundation for other research institutions, NGOs, and foundations in the Asia Pacific region, to develop further collaborative networks.

V. Concluding Remarks

Several observations on the emerging concept of the Asia Pacific Regional Community can be drawn from the above descriptions of seventeen independent, corporate, and semigovernmental foundations:

1. It is quite clear that a sense of Asia Pacific community is not yet reflected in the activities among the three types of foundations in Taiwan. So far, no foundation

has been designated to promote such a concept in its stated objectives or programming.

2. There are some exchange, networking, and collaborative efforts that have been undertaken by various foundations, but they remain either bilateral or randomly organized, and are not vigorously institutionalized.

3. It is ironic that, being an integral part of the Asia Pacific region, Taiwan has not really paid enough attention to this regional community. However, in recent years, progress has been made by a few research institutions and NGOs to develop more collaborative efforts with their counterparts in the region. Some of the foundations described in this report have also expressed interest in enhancing regional networks and exchange activities. All these new efforts demonstrate that a sense of community with the Asia Pacific region is steadily emerging among the research institutions, NGOs, and foundations in Taiwan.

THAILAND

Philanthropy in Thailand

Amara Pongsapich
Head of the Department of Socio-Cultural Affairs
Chulalongkorn University

I. Overview of Philanthropy

1. History of Philanthropy in Thailand

The development of philanthropy and nonprofit development organizations in Thailand can best be understood through historical perspectives. Traditional Buddhist temples performed philanthropic functions by providing for the needy and serving as community centers. However, different forms of organizations appeared after the immigration of western missionaries and of the Chinese. The impact of the West, the presence of the Chinese, and the spread of communist ideology brought about changes in philanthropic activities in the country. Threats to Thailand's national security were the main fears of the government regarding the role of philanthropy.

1) Early Buddhist influence

Throughout the seven hundred years of the Sukhothai, Ayutthaya, and early Bangkok periods, Buddhism played a vital role in helping to maintain cultural and political stability in the country. Religion established the foundations of philanthropy and propelled a socialization process conducive to merit making. From the earliest times, the monks and their monasteries functioned as centers for intellectual, cultural, recreational, and community life. Boys learned to read and write, and men and women exhibited their artistic talents, performed their religious rituals, and relaxed and enjoyed themselves when getting together at the temple. Seen through the eyes of the children, temple grounds were their playgrounds, and to performers they were theaters during festivities. Travelers took refuge at the "temple hostels," receiving both food and lodging. While temples often functioned as health centers when someone fell ill and needed traditional medicine and treatment, they also operated orphanages for poor and helpless children. The philanthropic nature of temple activities was obviously part of the community life, but formal philanthropic organizations were not seen until much later.

Since the thirteenth century, during the Sukhothai period, Buddhism in Thailand existed as a syncretized religion with Buddhism, Brahminism, and animism as its three main components. The first kings of the Sukhothai era invited Buddhist monks from neighboring kingdoms to propagate Buddhism in Sukhothai. From that time on, Buddhism was an integral part of the monarchy. Not only did Buddhism spread throughout the Sukhothai kingdom, within the Sukhothai center, Buddhist and Brahmin rituals were practiced with intensity. The concept that Great Tradition existed at the core of the kingdom and was propagated and propitiated by the palace while little tradition exhibited itself with large followers outside the palace and in peripheral areas, was clearly supported. In terms of administration and control, the kings established a monastic hierarchy parallel to the structure of the monarchic ruling. Two main classifications were followed, i.e., the city monastery and the forest monastery. The monks themselves were also given titles parallel to the positions held at the different ministries. The parallel structure of religious hierarchy and the monarchy helped strengthen and support each other. Buddhism was integrated and merged to become the ruling ideology and at the same time penetrated into the everyday lives of the Thai people.

During the Ayutthaya period which followed, Buddhism and Brahminism became stronger. The *Devaraja* or the "divine king" concept from Brahminism was adopted and strengthened. The king was seen as a divine person with special god-like characteristics, to be revered and treated in a highly respected manner. At the same time, monks and priests were representatives of religious and divine beings and had to be treated in a respected manner as well. Thus, the ruling class and the religious class were two distinct groups of people belonging to a category of human beings separate from the ordinary people. As society evolved, one can see the integration of the ruling class and monastery classes in the Ayuthaya era. The monasteries and the hierarchy of the religious leaders and monks became more differentiated following the more complex structure of the lay ruling class. The close relationship between the monarchy and the monasteries was maintained until the emergence of the open door policy toward the West in the late ninteenth century.

The monastic class exhibited their benevolent characteristics through the teachings and practice of Buddhism. The monastery functioned as a community's center for social welfare. People also made merit at the monasteries, and the sacred and profane aspects were inseparable. Philanthropy was also part of everyday life because one is supposed to make merit through giving. It can therefore be said that giving to fellow human beings in need was one of the first forms of philanthropy seen in early Thailand.

When King Rama V of the Bangkok era (1868–1910) introduced administrative structural reforms, many modern structures such as the Ministry of Education and the Ministry of Health were introduced. The role of the monasteries was subsequently reduced. At the same time, the monastery structure needed to be revised to follow the administrative structure. The Monkhood Law, promulgated during this period, stated that the committee of high ranking monks called the *Maha Thera Samakhom* or the Great Thera Association (*Thera* means monk) be established as an advisory committee to the king regarding religious affairs. When the Monkhood law was changed in 1941 and again in 1962, the role of the Thera Association was changed. Presently, all Buddhist monk affairs are under the supervision of the Thera Association.

2)Impact of the West

Although Thailand was never colonized, it is undeniable that a westernization process took place and had certain impacts on Thai society as a whole. King Rama IV (1851–1868) and King Rama V (1868–1910) both intentionally sent their sons to the West to learn about different ways of life and to bring change to their country. At the same time, missionaries from the West also came to Thailand, intending to bring changes which would lead to religious conversion. Catholics and Protestants both came, but the impacts they made were very different.

a. The Catholics

The first Catholic missionary came to Thailand in 1567–68 from Portugal, followed by missionaries from Spain and France. In 1662, records indicated that there were approximately two hundred Catholics in the country, most of whom were non-Thais. The first mission in Thailand, called the Siam Mission, was officially declared in 1669, and the first cardinal came in 1674. During that period, a hospital and youth group were also established. The exploratory period was considered unsuccessful, with no Thais being converted and none of the philanthropic activities introduced by Catholic missionaries integrated into Thai society. In fact, during the first two centuries after their arrival, Catholic missionaries had no impact upon Thai society.

After World War II, the Catholic Church faced difficulties gaining recognition and acceptance by the public; they realized the need to reform. Between 1959–65 intensive consultations in the form of seminars and workshops were carried out. One important outcome was the shift in emphasis of the conceptual frame. Instead of putting emphasis on faith, religion should be viewed as a vehicle to bring solutions to social problems. In other words, the message for salvation was being reinterpreted. Religion would have to reach people and society. Western Catholic ideology would have to recognize other existing cultural ideologies. Local culture and indigenous knowledge became important prerequisites for development workers to learn and find ways to integrate with the Catholic concept of salvation. Subsequently, the organizational structure of the Catholic Mission in Thailand, as is the case in other countries, was revised. Divine institutions and human institutions are two obvious institutional types within the Catholic mission in each country. In addition, cooperation at the regional level is being maintained, and the Federation of Asian Bishops Conference was established. In Thailand, one important reform activity included the establishment of the Major Seminary in 1975 to educate and prepare Thais to become Catholic priests. The whole preparation process taking place within Thailand helped bring about a better understanding of Thai culture and society and a better integration of Catholic teaching into Thai society.

b. The Protestants

Protestant missionaries came into Thailand for the first time in 1828, and the first exploratory phase is classified to have been between 1828–78 when King Rama V announced Freedom of Religious Belief in the country. The London Missionary Society was established in Bangkok, and the Chinese in Bangkok were identified as the first target group to be approached. Leaflets printed in Chinese were distributed, medicine for cholera, pneumonia, and small pox were made available. Bibles and other documents were also translated.

The American Presbyterian Mission arrived and began their activities during 1835–1940. Outstanding activities included the establishment of clinics to treat deadly diseases of the time. The first operation in Thailand took place in 1836. The missionaries of the American Presbyterian Church also helped bring about many innovations including the first newspapers for high class Bangkok readers, called the *Bangkok Recorder*. The first American Consulate was a Presbyterian missionary who helped established two churches and a school. The Bangkok Christian Boys School was established in 1901 and was the outcome of the efforts of two missionaries and the first Chinese to be baptized.

The Modern Phase of the Protestant Mission covered between 1878–1934 from the year of the Declaration of Freedom of Religion to the year when the Church of Christ in Thailand was established. At that time, it was necessary to have Thai nationals involved in the organization because of the nationalistic movement after World War I and after the Russian Revolution. Similar to the Catholic Mission, the Protestant Mission expanded the propagation work in the form of preaching; building hospitals, schools, churches, and leprosy centers; and working with other minority groups in addition to the Chinese with whom they had already established a close relationship.

The Contemporary phase of the Protestant Mission started the year the Church of Christ of Thailand was established. Thai nationals became members of the working committees with the assistance of the American Presbyterian Mission and the Disciple Mission which were finally dissolved in 1957 and 1962 respectively.

The role of Catholic and Protestant missionaries in the organization of ethnic organizations became very clear. Even though the Catholics came earlier, they were working with Thai people and were not as successful. The Protestants, on the other hand, came later and started their mission by working with the Chinese first and hill people later. It became very clear that ethnic minorities, being marginal to Thai society and culture, willingly turned to the missionaries if the missionaries could provide them with social and moral support. The Protestants were very successful in converting the Chinese and the Karen to Christianity.

3) The Chinese and philanthropy

Governments up until World War II viewed Thailand as an ethnically homogeneous country consisting of Thai people only. Those who were non-Thai ethnically were outside the Thai social structure. They lived as separate groups but intermixed with Thais, having free cultural and economic exchanges. Among lowland groups, cultural borrowing, adoption, and assimilation had been observed, accepted, or even welcomed. The questions of ethnic differences became important only after the formation of a nation-state.

The nationalist movements which took place after World War I and World War II brought about many conflicts and mistrust among the people of different ethnic origins. The first group to be identified was the Chinese "secret societies" organized both in China and overseas. In Southeast Asia, secret societies became powerful during the early ninteenth century. From the government perception, they operated as a gang robbing people and demanding ransom from villagers as protection money. They were considered "outlaws" and needed to be taken care of by the government. On the other hand, from the perception of poor Chinese immigrants, activities of the "secret societies" may have been viewed as philanthropic in the sense that they provided assistance and protection to a certain group of people. The activities of the secret societies reached their peak during the first half of the ninteenth century and became less active with the colonization activities.

The speech-group associations played an important role in the expansion of Chinese education in Thailand. As mentioned earlier, Western-type education was introduced into Thailand by the American Protestant and French Catholic missions. Their first schools were attended largely by Chinese. The impact of mission schools on the Chinese community became important toward the end of the nineteenth century. In particular, the French-operated Assumption College and the American-operated Bangkok Christian Boys School (later College) became popular with Chinese boys hoping to enter Western business houses and banks.

Later, because of the threat of communist ideology among overseas Chinese, the Thai government introduced laws and regulations in an anti-foreigner manner for reasons of national security.

The Chinese reaction to the economic depression and the government's "Thaiification" policies involved two developments of importance to the social structure. First, hard times led shopkeepers and merchants in almost every trade to organize in a manner similar to what had been observed earlier. According to Skinner, the Tung-yeh-hui (same business association) became the most widespread type of Chinese formal organization. Through them, members of trade associations could exchange information, formulate concerted action in the face of government regulation, operate to avoid excessive competition, and restrict entry of new entrepreneurs into the trade. The other Chinese response took the form of secret societies. These were organized along speech-group lines with the primary aim being the preservation of each group's share in the rapidly diminishing economic plums. The legitimate trade associations were established almost exclusively in Bangkok, while secret-society activity was, up to 1937, largely restricted to the provinces.[1]

One of the most notable developments in Chinese formal organizations during the early 1900s was the rapid increase in the number and scope of mutual help and welfare associations. Since the Thai government was slow in extending public social welfare facilities, local Chinese society fostered intracommunity self-help activities. Poor Chinese still counted on raising their occupational status and became upwardly mobile. The social values of the average laborer were not radically inclined toward the struggle to get ahead. Nevertheless, Skinner felt that the poor were still poor and inadequately provided for. The elite, who could achieve full prestige according to Chinese values, therefore, provided assistance through generous philanthropy, morally motivated. This paternalism and highly sanctioned philanthropy formed the foundation of most of the Chinese associations founded or expanded during the twenties and thirties.

Another type of philanthropic organization which became prominent in Bangkok at that time was the benevolent society. Several small benevolent societies were founded in the nineteenth century on strict speech-group lines, but by the early 1920s, one of them, the Pao-te Shan-t'ang, became recognized as the benevolent society in Bangkok. Based on highly eclectic (Confucian, Buddhist, and Taoist) religious sanctions, its major activities were the collection and burial of corpses found on the streets and of unclaimed dead from the T'ien-hua Hospital, the provision of free coffins and burial to destitute families, and the organization of relief to victims of fires and floods. It maintained a free cemetery on the outskirts of town.

Since the Thai government adopted a capitalist development ideology, the Chinese or Thais of Chinese ancestry have been able to respond to governmental policy and become a prominent and influential mechanism in Thailand's development process, instead of organizing clan and speech group associations; commercial associations and trade associations established earlier became more active. The Chinese readily adjusted.

2. Recent History

During the twentieth century, Thailand was compressed between the expansion of British power in the west and of French power in the east. It was during this period that modern philanthropy, which functioned differently from traditional religious groups, was seen. A group of women led by royalty petitioned King Rama V in 1885 to set up the Sapa Unalom Daeng, which has become the Thai Red Cross, to care for wounded soldiers and provide medical and other supplies. Thus, the first formally recognized philanthropic organization was established. Furthermore, King Rama V was aware of the need to modernize the country, and in his extensive travels to Europe, he realized that some of the European institutions could contribute to the modernization process.[2]

1) The 1932 coup d'état

Other than the establishment of the Boy Scouts during the reign of King Rama VI, and Sapha Unalom Daeng, which was established in 1890 and later became the Red Cross, in general, activities of the associations established in the early twentieth century were mainly social services, and there was no formal registration system until after the 1932 coup d'état which changed Thailand from a monarchic government to a "democratic" government. The Women City Club (Samakhom Satri Thai Haeng Sayam) was formally established in 1932 by the woman editor of *Ying Thai*, a daily women's newspaper. The office was set up at the office of the Tram Labor Association.[3]

After World War II, with the threat of communism, Buddhist ideology was brought into confrontation with communist ideology. Buddhist institutions, being philanthropic in nature, were promoted, while most other organizations were closely controlled. Political stability was the main concern of the government.

The Women's Cultural Club was set up by the Prime Minister's First Lady in 1943. The objectives were to promote cultural and social activities among members and provide welfare for those in need. During this period many more organizations came into existence. In addition to the philanthropic and housewives' groups, there were also school alumni groups and organizations based on vocation. In 1956, the Women's Cultural Club, which had branches in almost all provinces in the country and was headed by the provincial governors' wives, was reorganized resulting in the establishment of the National Women's Council of Thailand. This group represents organizations of high class people who provide social services to the poor and destitute.

Thera association was re-established in 1962 to monitor religious (Buddhist) activities and institutions within the country. During the nationalist period (WWII–1960) and during the military dictatorship (1960–73), only philanthropic activities were promoted.

"Development" activities which have taken place since the first national development plan in 1961 affected people in the various socio-economic classes differently. Among the high class, business associations were formed with very few local groups found in rural areas. Associations and organizations established between the end of World War II and 1973 usually had the objective of working for the improvement of members of the societies. Most of them were considered organizations of the high society group, however.

There were also clubs and associations that were organized around social and business gathering activity but at the same time were supporting social development activities by providing contributions and/or giving continuous support with or without members of the clubs or associations participating in the activity in person. International clubs such as Rotary, Lions, and Sontas are included in this group. The Rotary and Lions Clubs had separate chapters in other provinces but were considered as belonging to the same association. Similarly, religious groups—missionary or otherwise—also have organizations with branches in other provinces in the country. They formed their networks working for the same cause and many times sharing the financial support from the same sources.

During the 1960s, when the country was under military rule, students were not active and did not engage in political activism. However, some of them found working for rural summer camps an outlet for their politico-social propensities. The camps enabled many youth from the upper and middle classes to familiarize themselves with rural poverty and disparity.

2) The 1973 student coup d'état and the 1976 counter coup

After the student coup d'état took place on 14 October 1973, the Thai people became politically active. Many nongovernmental organizations established during this period were run by committed people from various professions who viewed development from the social development point of view. Most of them are not registered, however. This group of organizations differs from the philanthropic groups organized earlier, and will be discussed in a separate paper under the heading "Nongovernmental Organizations." However, it needs to be mentioned here that the counter coup taking place in 1979, repressed the activities of these liberal nongovernmental organizations, and many of them died while a few others were revived after the amnesty law was announced in 1980.

II. The Role of Philanthropic Organizations

1. Changing Government Policies and Strategies 1825–1980

Discussion in Section I of this report indicates quite clearly the role which philanthropy played in Thai society. Traditionally, nonprofit organizations were religious and philanthropic in nature, and the government saw no reason to intervene. Later, when the Christians and the Chinese came, nonprofit organizations serving the needs of marginal non-Thai people were viewed by the government as a threat to national security. However, during the monarchic rule and before administrative reforms were introduced by King Rama V (1868–1910), no legal action was introduced. As part of the modernization process, King Rama VI (1910–25), a nationalist leader who viewed the Chinese as a threat to the economic security of the country, introduced the Civil and Commercial Code in 1925. The Civil and Commercial Code included sections on foundations and associations. This was the first attempt to control the activities of nonprofit organizations. Sections 81–97 of the Code are concerned with foundations and Sections 1274–1297 are concerned with associations. Details concerning registration, operation, and termination of foundations and associations are described in the law.

During World War II, with the threat of communism from China, the government appointed the National Cultural Commission of the Ministry of Education to oversee activities of nonprofit organizations in an attempt to control philanthropic organizations even further. The National Cultural Act of 1942 was promulgated to take care of nonprofit organizations whose objectives were to propagate cultural heritage and to provide welfare and social services in the form of clan associations, as well as religious organizations.

However, associations formed by the Chinese to help people in the same business or the same trade, functioned somewhat differently from other associations. It was then felt necessary to create a separate law. The Trade Association and Chamber of Commerce Act was promulgated in 1966 during the military regime.

When grassroots groups formed cremation associations at the village level, during the 1960s and early 1970s, the National Cultural Commission had no way to register and/or control them. After the student led coup d'état in 1973, with strong communist penetration in the countryside, the need to control grassroots cremation associations was felt. The Cremation Act of 1974 was promulgated, giving authority to the Department of Public Welfare to oversee the activities.

In addition, labor movements activated after 1973 created labor unrest and the government then promulgated the Labor Relations Act in 1975.

To summarize, nonprofit organizations were under the government's close control until 1980. The responsible government agencies include:

Type	Registration	Law
1. Foundation	Ministry of Interior and the National Cultural Commission	1. Civil and Commercial Code, 1925, Sections 81-97 2. National Cultural Act, 1942
2. Association	Director General of Department of Police and the National Cultural Commission	1. Civil and Commercial Code, 1925, Sections 1274-1297 2. National Cultural Act, 1942
3. Trade association	Director General of Department of Internal Trade	Commercial Association Act, 1966
4. Cremation association	Director General of Department of Public Welfare	Cremation Welfare Act, 1974
5. Labor union	Ministry of Interior Department of Labor	Labor Relations Act, 1975

According to the laws identified above, legally, only three types of organizations are recognized and registered by the Thai government: associations, labor unions and federations, and foundations. Other terms exist such as councils and leagues, but to acquire legal status they must register under one of the three legally acceptable terms.

Tax exemption for registered nonprofit associations and foundations is granted by the Ministry of Finance. To qualify for tax exempt status, an organization must submit an application, it must have been in existence for more than three years, and its books must have been endorsed by a certified accountant during that period. Salaries paid to employees are not exempt. Donations to registered nonprofit organizations are tax deductible, upon the consent of the Ministry, but only up to one percent of earnings or profits. Donations are tax deductible only when made to qualified organizations granted tax exempt status by the Ministry of Finance.

Maintenance of registered status, and therefore of tax exemption and deductibility status, is dependent on submission of annual reports, meeting minutes, and budgets. In 1991, under an announced policy of promoting philanthropic activities, the interim government established a committee to review much of the legislation governing nonprofit organizations including tax incentives and related matters.

2. Formation of Networks and Cooperative Efforts among Philanthropies in Response to Government Policies

The need to organize and work together in the form of loose networks was felt each time the government promulgated new laws or regulations. The Chinese cooperate among themselves in the form of trade groups, linguistic groups, and clan associations. The Christians also form pacts to strengthen themselves. Sometimes these groups function beyond national borders because their ethnic and religious affiliations go beyond national boundaries. Earlier cooperative efforts were based on ethnic and religious membership while later affiliations have been in the form of worldwide membership associations such as the Rotary, Lyons, and Sontas Clubs, and similar high-class membership associations.

Umbrella organizations, both registered and unregistered, also form part of the Thai nonprofit sector. Calling themselves councils and leagues, some register as associations with the National Cultural Commission in Bangkok or with provincial government offices. Registration of these organizations helps legitimize some of the activities carried out. Many of the non-Thai groups felt the need to acquire legal status to enable them to work safely and with reasonable comfort. Religious, ethnic, and vocational identities tend to be criteria for establishing networks and affiliations. These organizations focus on common issues and objectives aimed at improving the well-being of specific target groups or of the people in general.

The establishment of umbrella organizations is deemed necessary when there are many organizations working on similar issues or carrying out similar activities. At present, there are many types of nongovernmental and nonprofit organizations. As mentioned above, legally, only three types are recognized and registered by the Thai government: associations, labor unions and federations, and foundations. In 1989, there were 8,408 general nonprofit associations registered with the National Cultural Commission, 373 commercial associations and a small number of employers' associations registered with the Department of Internal Trade, and 2,773 cremation associations registered with the Department of Public Welfare. The labor groups include labor unions, federations, and councils; all are registered with the Department of Labor. In 1989, there were 2,966 foundations registered with the National Cultural Commission. Almost half of them focused on funding cultural and educational activities.

In addition, there are also unregistered nonprofit groups organized for specific purposes but without legal status. They may be called projects, working groups, or forums. They tend to be small and dedicated to public welfare, community development, and campaign advocacy issues such as human rights, the environment, and cultural promotion. Grassroots organizations and advocacy groups usually do not register because of the burdensome endowment or membership requirements. Furthermore, many development groups prefer not to register because then they need not report to anyone. They may, on occasion, combine under umbrella councils or coordinating committees.

Umbrella organizations, both registered and unregistered, also form part of the Thai nonprofit sector. Registered umbrella organizations are presented in Table 1. However, many of those on the list are very specific in nature and do not have much impact on Thai society in general. Seven out of nineteen are religious organizations; five are trade or vocational in orientation; three focus on specific target groups, e.g., women, children, and the aged; and the other three are leagues of foundations, associations, and councils of social welfare. It is clear that except for those focusing on specific target groups and the National Council of Social Welfare, development-oriented and advocacy groups do not register.

Table 1: Registered Umbrella Organizations in Thailand

Council	Year Registered
Hindu Dharma Sabha Bangkok	1943
Council of Church of Christ Association	1943
The Netherlands Chamber of Commerce	1955
Board of Trade	1955
Council of Buddhist Propagation Foundation	1955
National Council of Women	1956
National Council of Social Welfare	1959
National Council of Young Buddhist Association	1960
Spiritual Assembly of the Bahais of Bangkok	1963
The Foundation of the Church of Christ	1965
Research Officer Association of the Territorial Defense Department	1966
League of Foundations	1967
The Congress of Parents and Teachers Association	1972
National Council for Child and Youth Development	1985
League of Associations	1986
Council of International Popular Culture Association	1989
Senior Citizens Council	1989
Council of Catholic Education	1989
Council of Science and Technology Association	1989

III. Umbrella Philanthropic Organizations with Specific Target Groups

The discussion in this section will be divided according to issues. However, for each issue the historical development of philanthropic activities also reflects the evolution of issues considered to be important over time. The establishment of umbrella philanthropic groups also indicates the need to coordinate the efforts of volunteers and development workers on the same or related issues and activities. The umbrella philanthropic organizations discussed in this paper include only the relief or welfare-oriented types. Religious organizations are not included.

1. Philanthropy and Women's Activities

The National Council of Women of Thailand (NCWT)

The Women's Cultural Club was set up by the Prime Minister's First Lady in 1943. The objectives were to promote cultural and social activities among members and provide welfare for those in need. After World War II, many more organizations came into existence. In addition to the social welfare and housewives groups, there were also school alumni groups and organizations based on vocations. In 1956, the Women's Cultural Club which had branches in almost all provinces in the country headed by the provincial governors' wives, was reorganized, resulting in the establishment of the National Council of Women of Thailand (NCWT). The Council came under the Royal Patronage of Her Majesty the Queen in 1961. Later on, NCWT became an affiliated council of the International Council of Women, which has consultative status category I with the Economic and Social Council of the United Nations.

The objectives of NCWT are:

a. To exchange and coordinate among women's organizations, nationally and internationally, in order to promote safety, general well-being, and understanding among all humankind with an emphasis on women.

b. To help raise the standard of living and capabilities of Thai women as well as seek to obliterate problems and obstacles hindering the development of the associations and women's organizations.

In order to achieve the objectives identified above, NCWT will not intervene in the activities and objectives of member associations.

There are approximately one hundred and twenty member associations in the Council. In addition to the board of the council, there are fifteen sections: education and morals, social welfare, health, housing, children and family, migration, home economics, music, arts, economics and vocations, law, mass media, peace and international relations, women and labor, and economics and energy. Each year a number of projects are identified and differ from year to year depending on the policy of the Board. The Chairperson is responsible for recruitment of volunteers and actual implementation of each project. In addition, there are regional chairpersons representing member associations in the respective regions as well as chairpersons of the districts in the Bangkok Metropolitan Area.

After the announcement of Women's Year in 1975, NCWT was recognized as a women's nongovernmental organization, and at certain times, it represents the government in some UN activities. NCWT was fully involved in the struggle for the establishment of a national mechanism for women's activities in Thailand. When the government designated the National Economic and Social Development Board and later on the Department of Community Development to be the secretariat of the National Commission on Women's Affairs, NCWT was recognized as one of the two representatives of women's NGOs. The announcement by the United Nations of Women's Decade (1985–95), and of other international promotion schemes, forced the Thai government to set up a permanent office to function as the secretariat for the National Commission for Women's Affairs in 1989. It is now located at the newly established Division for the Promotion and Coordination of Women's Affairs in the Office of the Permanent Secretary of the Office of the Prime Minister.

During the late 1980s, NCWT recognized the need to evaluate past performance and review policies and strategies for the effective future development of women's activities in general, and NCWT in particular. A long-term plan was drawn up and activities become more development oriented. In general, the activities of member associations of NCWT are still considered along the line of cultural conservation and oriented toward welfare. The more liberal women's organizations do not join NCWT.

Other organizations deserving mention here include the Thai Girl Guides Association, the Association for the Promotion of the Status of Women, the Women Lawyers' Association of Thailand, the Institute for Gender and Development Studies, the Friends of Women Group, and the Women Foundation. The first three are also members of the NCWT while the other three are not. The Thai Girl Guides Association has long been active, especially in rural areas, in the sphere of nonformal, vocational programs for women. Its latest venture has been the promotion of women as health care providers for the family and community. The Association for the Promotion of the Status of Women has been instrumental in setting up an emergency home for distressed women and children which has offered shelter to many prostitutes escaping from brothels and provided support to battered wives. It operates an occupational training center which is aimed at the rehabilitation of women who have taken up dubious professions. The Friends of Women Group created greater interest in women's development through its publications and organization of various seminars. They work with women factory workers and provide legal assistance to those in need. The Women Lawyers' Association also provides legal advice to women. The Women Foundation, established and operated jointly with the Women Information Center, also works with battered women and has set up a rescue center for women in distress. It is also trying to cope with the problem of forced prostitution, especially child prostitution. The group also networks with organizations in other countries on the issue of trafficking of women. Collaboration has been established between receiving countries such as Japan and countries in Europe, and supplying countries such as Thailand, the Philippines, and Sri Lanka.

The Gender Research and Development Institute functions to carry out action research and collaboration with both government organizations (GOs) and NGOs, with the objective of more equity and justice in the workplace and the social environment. In addition, many universities have Women's Studies Programs on campus. Most of them are informal groups trying to set up curricula on women's studies and carrying out research projects. Most of these university groups are classified as borderline cases of GOs and NGOs. All of them may be said to be working for the betterment of women, to do away with discrimination, and some try to influence government policies on issues related to women. These issues are, for example, the period allowed for maternity leave, leave with and without pay, equal wages, and sexual behavior in relation to AIDS.

When important issues concerning women are recognized, these groups join hands and establish quite a strong network working for causes of concern to all women.

2. Philanthropic Organizations Working on Children and Youth Issues

As in the case of philanthropy related to women, organizations working for the welfare of children and youth have been developed since the early stages of philanthropy in Thailand. Part of the reason is the sympathy most people have toward helpless children. Activities related to children and youth range from the provision of food and lodging for orphans and disabled children to scholarships for children in schools, and more recently, to activities helping street children and child prostitutes. The number of organizations working with children and youth is large and some kind of organizational body is certainly needed to facilitate coordination of similar and related activities.

The Council of Children and Youth Development Organizations

The Council of Children and Youth Development Organizations was initiated in 1984 after the need for a coordinating body of children and youth activities was voiced in many seminar sessions. The National Children and Youth Bureau, a government organization responsible for the coordination of activities related to children and youth, together with administrators of some of the nongovernmental organizations, and twelve professionals in the field, formed a working group to draw up bylaws and regulations for the administration of a coordinating body. The draft proposal was examined by participants of the national meeting of children and youth organizations in June 1984. After approving the proposal, the Council was formed with twenty-one temporary board members responsible for the establishment of the formal organization. The Council was formally established in 1985.

The objectives of the Council are:

a. To function as a coordinating center for policies, programs, and projects of nongovernmental organizations working on children and youth activities;
b. To function as the data and information center for activities related to children and youth;
c. To function as the center for the promotion, support, and implementation of children and youth-related activities;
d. To represent nongovernmental organizations in promoting and in coordinating with government organizations, as well as foreign and international organizations; and
e. To disseminate information in newspapers and other media on activities based on the objectives of the council.

To achieve the above objectives, the Council set up policies and guidelines to focus its activities in three areas: coordination, research and monitoring, and promotion and support. Nongovernmental organizations are invited to join the activities by becoming members. At the annual meeting, members are invited to become involved in the policy-making process by serving as board members for three years. The board establishes policy guidelines and implementation plans while the secretariat carries out the actual implementation by pooling financial and human resources from member organizations and/or funding agencies.

There are 63 members (31 regular and 32 associated). The board consists of 14 persons with 12 advisors. There are also 11 subcommittee members with 2 advisors. The secretariat has 6 staff members.

3. Community Development and Social Development Organizations

Some of the organizations classified under this category focus on the general topic of development but at the same time are concerned with specific issues such as women, children and youth, and human rights. These organizations focus on development activities which may be either integrated or sectorial. They might have started the activities sectorially and expanded to more integrated activities. An example is the Population and Community Development Association, one of the largest, if not the largest, nonprofit development agencies in the country. It was one of the first of the private nongovernment agencies started in family planning and has had an important role to play in the area of community services in the rural areas. The activities include family planning, health, agriculture, primary processing industries, and marketing, with education as an integrated part of each activity. In this section, only the National Council of Social Welfare will be discussed. This umbrella organization encompasses most of the philanthropic organizations in the country. Even a smaller umbrella organization such as the Council of Organizations for the Disabled also belongs to the Council of Social Welfare. Therefore, the smaller umbrella organizations will not be discussed separately.

The National Council of Social Welfare of Thailand

The National Council of Social Welfare of Thailand was officially registered in 1960 by the Department of Public Welfare, with a number of philanthropic organizations. The main objective was to form a coordinating center for the promotion of social welfare organizations in Thailand. The Council came under the patronage of His Majesty the King in 1961, and Her Majesty the Queen became the Honorary President of the Council the following year.

His Majesty the King donated one million baht (US$40,000)[4] as an endowment fund for the construction and bestowed "Mahidol" as the name of the building to house the office of the Council. The name was bestowed in honor of his father, Prince Songkhla Mahidol, for his contribution in the area of social welfare. His Majesty the King also donated four hundred baht (US$16) a month for the rent of the land where the building is constructed. The donation started in September 1963 and continues to the present. The building was officially opened by His Majesty the King and Her Majesty the Queen on 5 March 1965.

The Council has the following nine objectives:

a. To promote coordination and cooperation of activities related to social welfare, social problems, and social development;
b. To support the role and participation of nongovernment member organizations in activities related to social welfare, social problems, and social development;
c. To support education, research, and planning activities in areas related to social welfare, social problems, and social development;
d. To promote joint efforts in community welfare activities, to help the needy, to assist in social development, and to raise consciousness among the people and different groups to have mutual concern for each other;
e. To assist the disadvantaged and those with problems to become able to help themselves by providing assistance as necessary and appropriate, both material and non-material, both short-term and long-term;
f. To cooperate with the government and other agencies in solving social problems affecting the living conditions of the people, the peaceful Thai society, and national security;
g. To improve the efficiency and administrative and management capability of the Social Welfare Council and to promote efficient work ethics of committee members, staff, and volunteers of the Council;
h. To provide information on objectives, policies, projects, and management plans of the Social Welfare Council and member organizations and to disseminate proper knowledge and understanding on social welfare, strategies to solve social problems, and social development; and
i. To support social development strategies according to the ideologies known as "Dharma Land, Golden Land, and Sustainable Development" and to achieve balanced and integrated development spiritually, socially, and economically. Spiritual development will be the basis to bring about quality of life, peace, and national stability. The ultimate goals are to maintain the nation, religion, monarchy, and democracy.

There are nine policies:

a. cooperation and coordination
b. promotion and support

c. education, research, and planning
d. community welfare funding
e. welfare for the disadvantaged and those with social problems
f. social problem solving
g. management
h. public relations
i. social development strategies on
—the Dharma Land, Golden Land ideology
—human resource development
—family
—health
—education
—religion and culture
—national security
—the environment
—sustainable development

There are two types of membership, i.e., regular and affiliated. Regular member organizations have to be formally registered and to have been in operation for at least one year. Affiliated members need not be formally registered but have to have been in operation for at least one year. There are 512 regular members—192 in Bangkok and 320 in the provinces—and 125 affiliated members—16 in Bangkok and 109 in the provinces.

The National Council of Social Welfare receives government support every year. The Council also raises funds for its activities and for the Community Welfare Fund, as well as for contributions to support the activities of Her Majesty the Queen.

Activities of the Council take place both in Bangkok and in the provinces depending on member organizations. The *Council of Social Welfare News* comes out regularly to provide information to member organizations and the public. Linkages with international social welfare networks are also carried out through exchange of visits and attendance of meetings on social welfare and related activities.

4. Health and Health-Related Philanthropic Groups

The Primary Health NGOs Coordinating Committee (PHC)

The 1992 data indicate that there are approximately 170 organizations working on health-related issues. Of these, 130 are foundations, 30 are associations, and 10 are not registered. The large number of foundations clearly reflects the dominance of the philanthropic and charity nature of health activities. This group sees no need to formally organize because charity work can be carried out individually. However, the more liberal groups, composed mostly of young and newly graduated doctors and pharmacists, were not content with dealing with health issues along charity lines. They saw the need to advocate for certain health issues to inform the public of the harm caused by misuse of drugs and other consumer products.

In an attempt to provide health care to the people in the rural areas more adequately, the Ministry of Public Health launched many programs. Two related programs are the provision of rural hospitals at the district level (both thirty-bed and ten-bed) and internship programs where new graduates in the fields of medicine, dentistry, and pharmacology are required to work in rural areas as health personnel for two years. In the late 1970s and early 1980s, after the programs were implemented, these highly motivated young graduates were very ambitious and wanted to help bring about development to the country. Some of them set up a health-related nongovernmental organization in the district where they worked and recruited volunteers from local clinics and health centers to work on health-related development issues.

In 1981–82, a group of health-related nongovernmental advocacy organizations met and formed a coordinating body under the name Primary Health NGOs Coordinating Committee (PHC). Since the founding members, a few of whom received the Best Rural Doctor of the Year Award, were mostly personnel of the Ministry of Public Health fulfilling their internship requirement, there was a strong link between this coordinating committee and the Primary Health Care Office of the Ministry of Public Health. PHC later became a very active health advocacy group. There are about twenty member organizations at the moment.

The objectives of the Coordinating Committee are:

a. To function as the center to coordinate information to support primary health development;

b. To coordinate the dissemination of information to the public and make the people realize the nature of health problems and be willing to help solve related problems;

c. To coordinate the dissemination of concepts, activities, and views of primary health NGOs to the public; and

d. To coordinate to promote and improve efficiency in the management of member primary health NGOs with academic and resource support.

Activities of the Coordinating Committee include training programs, seminar and forum sessions, a health development database center, publication of the *PHC Newsletter* (bi-monthly) and *Health Journal* (tri-monthly), and campaigning for advocacy issues in an attempt to influence certain government policies. The issues advocated include anti-smoking policy, appropriate medical consumption practices, nutritious food, etc.

IV. Conclusion: Future Prospects

Philanthropy in Thailand has existed since early history with religion as the basis for many of the activities. Non-religious groups were ethnically organized in the form of Chinese secret societies and clan organizations. During the 1930s, when liberals demanded more freedom, resulting in the 1932 coup when Thailand changed from an absolute to a democratic monarchy, liberal philanthropic groups were also established.

At the formation stage, the government tried to maintain the form and function of philanthropic activities by putting them under state control. The National Cultural Act was promulgated in 1942 to register and legalize nonprofit and nongovernmental organizations. Their activities were also supposed to be non-political. The Trade Association and Chamber of Commerce Act of 1966 was promulgated to control the activities of the Chinese. Many of the Chinese groups found trade associations to be an alternative for their group activities. During the 1960s when Communist ideology penetrated the rural and remote areas of Thailand, villagers also formed themselves into groups. With the introduction of cremation associations as membership groups (in which a villager joins to pay dues when someone dies to insure that when he or she dies, a cremation will be paid for by other members), the government felt the need to control these village groupings as well. The Cremation Act of 1974 was promulgated, requiring cremation associations to register. Similarly, the Labor Relations Act of 1975 was promulgated to control the labor unions.

The establishment of umbrella nonprofit and nongovernmental organizations reflected the need of the organizations to empower and strengthen themselves in dealing with government rules and regulations. On the other hand, the government also encouraged the formation of umbrella organizations to enable it to have a contact point for coordination and/or control.

During the Fifth National Development Plan (1981–85), when the government adopted poverty eradication programs, the role which nongovernmental organizations played in rural development activities became very clear. In its Sixth and Seventh National Development Plans (1986–90 and 1991–95) the government formally acknowledged the role of nongovernmental organizations in rural development. Among other things, the plans promote the establishment of local groups to carry out development activities. Previously, the only areas allowed for nongovernmental organizations were for-profit business and investment.

Of the umbrella organizations described in this report, the National Council of Women of Thailand and the National Council of Social Welfare of Thailand were both encouraged by the Department of Public Welfare. They both receive annual government budgetary support. In addition, the Council of Children and Youth Development Organizations was established with the assistance of the Children and Youth Bureau. The other groups, to be discussed in the paper on "Nongovernmental Organizations," were encouraged by other counterpart agencies. For example, the National Coordinating Committee of Nongovernmental Organizations for Rural Development was established jointly by the National Economic and Social Development Board and other liberal nongovernmental organizations. The Local Development Institute is under the auspices of the National Education Board. The Urban Community Development Office is partly nongovernmental and partly supported by the National Housing Authority with its budget coming from the government.

It is undeniable that, at present, cooperation between governmental and nongovernmental sectors is being recognized by all concerned to be very important. Each needs the support of the other. Attempts are being made to convince the government of the need to provide financial support for activities to be carried out by the nongovernmental sector. At the same time, support from the for-profit sector is also being sought. However, both the Government Budget Bureau and the business sector still need a certain degree of convincing.

In terms of international linkages, these umbrella organizations have contacts with similar organizations in other countries. When issues warrant international cooperation, they join together and organize international symposia and/or joint activities. Symposia on street children and child prostitutes have been organized both in Manila and Bangkok. International funding agencies are willing to support activities which will help bring about public awareness and action programs. Preliminary assessments indicate that international efforts to promote cooperation among local philanthropic groups to join together to promote the social well-being of the disadvantaged groups have been appreciated both by the volunteers and philanthropic organizations as well as by the general public.

Notes

1. William G. Skinner, *Chinese Society in Thailand: An Analytical History* (Ithaca: Cornell University Press, 1962).
2. Vitit Muntarbhorn, "Occidental Philosophy, Oriental Philology: Law and Organized Private Philanthropy in Thailand" in *Philanthropy and the Dynamics of Change in East and Southeast Asia,* edited by Barnett F. Baron (New York: Occasional Papers of the East Asian Institute, Colombia University, 1991).
3. Siriporn Skroebanek, "Feminist Movement in Thailand (1855-1932)" in *Satrithat,* Vol. 1, No. 3 (August-October, 1983).
4. International Monetary Fund, *International Financial Statistics,* January 1995 (Washington, D.C.: IMF). Figures given are based on the end of period exchange rate for November 1994. US$1 = 25.05 Baht.

Selected Bibliography

Chintakanond, Nareewan

"Approaches to Cooperation between Government Agencies and Nongovernmental Organizations in Thailand" in Government–NGO Cooperation in Social Development Proceedings of the Seminar on Cooperation between Government Agencies and Non-governmental Organizations in the Planning and Delivery of Social Services, 4–11 December 1990, Hong Kong. New York: United Nations, 1991.

Chula Unisearch, Chulalongkorn University

Public-Interest Non-Government Organizations in Thailand: A National Survey. Bangkok: Chulalongkorn University, 1988.

Khumthaweeporn, Chatchai

"Christianity in Thailand" in *Belief and Religion in Thai Society.* Bangkok: Sukhothai Thammathirat University, 1990.

Muntarbhorn, Vitit

"Occidental Philosophy, Oriental Philology: Law and Organized Private Philanthropy in Thailand" in *Philanthropy and the Dynamics of Change in East and Southeast Asia* edited by Barnett F. Baron. Occasional Papers of the East Asian Institute, Columbia University, 1991.

National Council on Social Welfare of Thailand

Social Welfare Council News Bangkok: National Council on Social Welfare of Thailand (various issues).

National Council of Women's Organization

The National Council of Women's Organization under Her Royal Patronage. Bangkok: NCWA Newsletters (various issues).

National Economic and Social Development Board

Status and Operation of Nongovernment Organizations. Bangkok: NESDB, Rural Development Coordination Division, 1992.

Pongsapich, Amara

Defining the Nonprofit Sector: Thailand. The Johns Hopkins Comparative Nonprofit Sector Project. Working Paper Number 11, 1993.

Pongsapich, Amara and Nitaya Kathaleeradaphan

Nonprofit Sector and Corporate Funding in Thailand. Bangkok: Chulalongkorn University Social Research Institute, 1994.

Skroebanek, Siriporn

"Feminist Movement in Thailand (1855–1932)" *Satrithat,* Vol. 1, No. 3 (August–October, 1983).

Suwana-adth, Malee

The NGO Sector in Thailand and the Potential Role of NGOs in National Development. A Study Report for the Project on the Role of NGOs in Development sponsored and supported by the Asian and Pacific Development Center and the Asian NGO Coalition for Agrarian Reform and Development, 1991.

Tongsawate, Maniemai and Walter E.J. Tips

Coordination between Governmental and Non-governmental Organizations in Thailand's Rural Development A study of planning and implementation of integrated rural development at the local level. Bangkok: Asian Institute of Technology, Division of Human Settlements Development. Monograph No. 5, 1985.

Update Interdenomination, Ltd.

Update Christian Directory 1988–1989. Bangkok: Update Interdenomination, Ltd, 1989.

UNITED STATES OF AMERICA

U.S. Philanthropy and the Asia Pacific Region

Gordon Jay Frost
Editor, International Philanthropy
Senior Consultant, CDA/Investnet

Foreword

"The best philanthropy is a search for cause, an attempt to cure evils at their source"

—*John D. Rockefeller*

"Apart from the ballot box, philanthropy presents the one opportunity the individual has to express his meaningful choice over the direction in which any society will progress."

—*Unknown*

"I have tried to keep things in my hands and have lost them all, but what I have given into my Lord's hands I still possess."

—*Martin Luther King, Jr.*

American motivations for philanthropy have always ranged from the civic, to the political, to the religious. Calls for the people to address basic needs, both at home and abroad, date from the earliest days of settlement in the 1600s. In our interdependent world, where the burgeoning independent sector has been increasing its demand for voluntary contributions to support its efforts, every citizen has an opportunity to be involved in a cause.

This paper attempts to provide a window on the trend to internationalize American institutional philanthropy in Asia, beginning with a review of the origins and motivations of domestic and international giving, then examining contemporary avenues for philanthropy, and finally observing the professional associations and political and economic forces that are trying to direct and promote the growth of the sector. In addition, recent developments in U.S. philanthropy's relationship to the Asia Pacific region will be examined. In order to conform to the other papers provided for this conference, the three sections focusing on foundations, corporations, and philanthropic associations will address their unique role in promoting a sense of community in the Asia Pacific Region.[1]

Information for this paper has been gathered from the most applicable sources and analyzed, with special attention given to the major factors influencing nonprofits as they engage in regional activities and promote regional networks. This paper will also look at significant cooperative eVorts (such as overseas grant-making activities, workshops, symposia, etc.). In addition, the role of government's views or actions to promote or discourage activity in the Asia Pacific region will also be investigated.

I. Introduction

Philanthropy—literally *love to mankind* in its original Greek—has taken on many meanings in contemporary America. These range from giving cash donations to national charities or volunteering for homeless shelters to corporate support for ballet and large independent foundation support for development projects around the globe. The origins of philanthropy in the United States are variously ascribed both to religious traditions carried from European ancestors, such as "tithing,"2 and to democratic traditions. While "tales of altruism, charity, and philanthropy can be found in every culture and every community," organized giving and voluntarism are more pronounced in America than anywhere in the world.[3] In the following pages, we will examine the history that led the United States to its current state of institutional giving and voluntarism, along with the primary donation mechanisms. We will also consider the associations that are promoting the growth of philanthropy today. In addition, each section will focus on one of the most important charitable relationships: U.S. philanthropic activity in or related to the Asia Pacific regional community.

II. A Brief History of American Giving Abroad

American giving first emerged in the mid-1600s, distinguishing itself by its independence from the government and coordination by civic groups and concerned citizens. Before the twentieth century, American campaigns for contributions had aided Santo Dominican refugees, earthquake victims in Venezuela, Greeks battling for independence, and Irish suffering in the great potato famine.

The first major Asian event to inspire American charity was a disastrous food shortage in India in 1897, which took three million lives. This event was concurrent with the growth of American relief organizations.[4] What generated such a significant response to this crisis was the fund-raising technique, which both popularized the cause and made it seem relevant to American individual donors regardless of their own ethnic background. The appeal was directed at the emotions and charity of ordinary citizens employing techniques such as displaying photographs of starving children, and featuring headlines such as "India's Dying People," thus encouraging maximum participation even at small amounts ("Every dollar saves a life").

In quick succession, famines occurring in both China and Japan followed the crisis in India. China's famine and floods in the early 1900s left more than two million dead and more than a million without food. A newly reorganized national Red Cross raised $327,897 in aid. *The Christian Herald*, a U.S. newspaper, provided $427,323. The Japanese famine inspired the creation of a Japanese-American committee fund-raising effort, which was able to mobilize $241,822 from T*he Christian Herald*'s efforts and $245,865 through the Red Cross.

In the 1920s, with the advent of organized philanthropy, through both the individual and foundation giving activities of Carnegie, Ford, Luce, and others, nonrelief philanthropy assistance began in Asia. Colleges established by Americans in China, India, and Japan received $3 million from the Laura Spellman Rockefeller Foundation and other donors. Henry Luce brought together approximately $2 million for Yenching University, and several other schools benefited from a $2.5 million bequest from the estate of Mrs. Stephen Harkness in 1926.

In 1923, Tokyo experienced a massive earthquake and fire which killed two hundred thousand people, seriously injured half that number, and left two million homeless and in danger of starvation and rampant disease. While twenty-eight nations responded with nearly $10.5 million, voluntary contributions from the United States alone totaled over $11.6 million. Two trends important to future international giving were already becoming visible: corporate giving and ethnic philanthropy. Many of the gifts came from large corporations who saw that in rebuilding Japan they could build relationships within the country as well. Meanwhile, $1.4 million was contributed by the small but close-knit Japanese-American community. In later years, ethnic contributions continued to be of increasing significance, such as the

$30 million raised in five years by the Chinese-American community during the war years for famine relief in Asia. these trends in both corporate and ethnic activity have continued in the United States.

Recent large-scale pop and rock music fund-raising events have acted as catalysts for foreign emergency donation activities by groups and individuals. U.S. Aid for Africa, whose anthem "Feed the World" was broadcasted globally, is the best remembered public event of this type and represents a new feature of philanthropy in the United States. The Concert for Bangladesh, organized by musician and former Beatles member George Harrison set the stage both for the involvement of pop stars in promoting global causes and for using music to interest a new generation of donors in international needs and issues.[5]

At present, especially with the growth of global networks among major relief and development organizations—such as Save the Children, Childreach, World Vision, Christian Children's Fund, CARE, and many others—such donor opportunities as child sponsorship, annual membership, planned gifts, major gifts, and programs targeted to constituencies with a special interest in the region where the charity is being conducted, have continued to inspire not only new philanthropists but also a greater feeling of international belonging among Americans.

III. An Overview of U.S. Philanthropy Today

Despite some notable charity scandals, a recent recession, and increased congressional oversight on nonprofit organizations, America's strong commitment to philanthropy has not wavered. According to the 1994 edition of *Giving USA*, an annual compendium on American philanthropy produced by the American Association of Fund Raising Counsel (AAFRC), estimated philanthropic contributions in 1993 reached $126.22 billion.[6] Of this amount, an overall increase of 3.55 percent over 1992, 81.2 percent or $102.55 billion was given by individuals. Another 6.8 percent of gifts were made in the form of bequests, making the total amount of gifts from individuals, nearly 90 percent of all charitable donations in the United States. This pattern reflects early historical trends in American philanthropy. Corporate giving, which was the source of $5.92 billion (4.7 percent), was flat, and foundations accounted for $9.21 billion (7.3 percent), representing a slight increase from $8.64 billion in 1992.

IV. Foundations

An analysis of the data in the latest edition of *Grants for Foreign & International Programs*, which is drawn from The Foundation Center's grants database on the thousand largest foundation in the U.S., provides some insight into the pattern of international giving in general and to Asia in particular.[7] Among its findings in the 1992–93 period:

- There were 6,532 grants of $10,000 or more totaling $664,643,616 by 488 foundations to foreign and international programs.
- Total giving to international projects in the United States was $410,773,038 for 4,288 grants. The majority went to organizations in New York ($131.4 million in 1,234 grants), the District of Columbia ($94.8 million in 950 grants), and California ($40.5 million in 457 grants).
- Total giving outside of the United States totaled $253,870,578 for 2,244 grants. Top recipient countries include England ($15.8 million for 198 grants), Mexico ($21.6 million for 150 grants), and South Africa ($15.8 million for 139 grants). The largest amount of money, $23 million, went to Brazil.
- The top five foundations in foreign and international giving collectively distributed 32 percent of the total number of grants and 48 percent of the dollars of all foundations in the top 1,000. Those foundations are as follows: Ford Foundation ($135,553,133 for 986 grants), MacArthur Foundation ($60,899,799 for 354 grants), Kellogg Foundation ($52,648,840 for 160 grants), Rockefeller Foundation ($43,054,616 for 499 grants), and the Mellon Foundation ($28,376,020 for 112 grants).
- Major areas of interest, by percentage of giving in dollars, were international affairs ($203.7 million), health ($96 million), social sciences ($69 million), education ($66.3 million), environmental protection ($59 million), and animals and wildlife ($45.4 million).

  Of the types of organizations that received this funding, two stand out as clear leaders—colleges and universities ($189.5 million in 1,360 grants) and international organizations ($187.3 million in 2,285 grants.

Obtaining information on U.S. nonprofit interest in and support for projects in and related to Asia has been challenging. However, data analysis reveals that the world's most populous region received only nineteen percent in grant dollars disbursed abroad by U.S. foundations and only twenty percent of the grants (see Table 1).

Table 1: Grants to Asia

Country	Grant Dollars	Number of Grants	Country	Grant Dollars	Number of Grants
Australia	3,170,722	32	New Zealand	173,288	3
China	13,519,000	106	Papua New Guinea	740,353	4
Hong Kong	53,462	2	Philippines	5,622,509	60
India	10,111,132	118	Singapore	150,000	2
Indonesia	4,680,875	35	South Korea	202,550	3
Japan	1,595,621	18	Sri Lanka	2,267,625	12
Korea	60,000	1	Taiwan	110,000	4
Laos	90,000	1	Thailand	4,283,040	41
Malaysia	210,000	5	Vietnam	445,000	5
Nepal	800,500	10			
			Totals: 18	$48,285,677	462

(Source: *Grants for Foreign & International Programs*)

Many foundations take a programmatic view rather than a regional one to international giving. At the John D. and Catherine T. MacArthur Foundation, one of the county's largest international givers, for example, a staff member said, "we do very little funding in Asia. What we do has to do with arms control and regional security." When asked about cooperative activities, she added, "We don't work with any other foundations."[8] A representative of the Compton Foundation said "Asia is not one of our focuses of interest…for our Peace and World Order program, [the focus] is international conflict resolution and the prevention of proliferation of weapons of destruction. In population work, our geographic focus is on Mexico, Central America and sub-Sahara, as well as environmental giving."[9] The S.H. Cowell Foundation, formerly made grants to the Philippines, but it is now focusing on northern California because, according to foundation representatives, their work in the Philippines was completed so the program was discontinued.[10] The Ford Foundation, founded in 1936, maintains an interest in preserving peace and advancing human welfare and has developed strong regional programs to address these concerns. The Ford Foundation has an endowment of more than $6 billion and has given more than $7 billion worldwide to more than nine thousand institutions and individuals from offices in seventeen countries.

For some foundations, regional efforts are a reflection of programmatic focus or reflect one of several principal personal interests. One example is The Burma Project, one of many programs supported by the New York offices of the Soros Foundations—arguably the largest philanthropic endeavor aimed outside the United States in the history of American giving. One of several projects in Central Asia, The Burma Project both generates its own programs and supports endeavors by "individuals and organizations already working on Burma issues." Specific efforts include encouragement for grassroots groups working for the restoration of freedoms in the country, education programs for students, and professional training for young Burmese seeking to build a future democratic Burma. Other programs that have been supported include a Burmese-language newspaper in Asia, a Burmese-language radio station beaming from Norway, a bi-monthly magazine focusing attention and dialogue on the country, educational grants and internships for Burmese refugee students, education for Burmese women by indigenous NGOs, and grants for translation as well as electronic communication links between groups working on Burma around the world.[11]

Another foundation active in Asia is The Henry Luce Foundation. Founded in 1936 by the late Henry R. Luce, the co-founder and editorial driving force behind Time Inc., the Foundation was established in tribute to his parents, who were educational missionaries in China between 1897 and 1925. The foundation maintains links to Asia through the Luce Scholars Program, the United States-China Cooperative Research Program, and Asia Project Grants. Giving for these China programs totaled $6,408,971 for 1993, or about one-third of total foundation grants. In its efforts to promote "understanding between the people of East Asia and the United States," the foundation attempts to "propagate international, intercontinental cross-fertilization, particularly with East Asia."[12] One of the ways this is accomplished is through cooperative arrangements, such as contract with The Asia Foundation in San Francisco to conduct elements of the Luce Scholars Program through its staff representatives in Asia. Grants to Henry Luce Scholars provide opportunities for young American scholars at U.S. institutions to work as interns throughout Asia in their chosen field. Examples of giving to institutes in the 1992–93 period were a grant of $120,000 to Huazhong Normal University in Whan, Hubei Province, People's Republic of China, in support of a research center dedicated to the history of Christian universities and Christianity in China and $20,000 to Pacific Theological College in Suva, Fiji Islands, to support the publication of a book on the history of Christianity in the Pacific. In the first half of 1994, the following grants were announced: $650,000 to the Institute of International Education (as a result of this grant women from public service organizations in China, Hong Kong, and Taiwan will be able to participate in an exchange and training program); $180,000 for Bridge to Asia which provides for an electronic information transfer station to serve research and teaching needs of Chinese legal scholars; and $360,000 to the United Board for Christian Higher Education in Asia, for a faculty exchange program with the United States. All three are multi-year grants.

The Rockefeller Brothers Fund has also shown a keen interest in Asia, and more specifically, in promoting cooperation in the Asia Pacific region, especially in the independent sector. In 1993 alone, the Fund made several notable grants: $120,000 to the Japanese NGO Center for International Cooperation for general support; $80,000 to the International House of Japan in support of the Dartmouth-International House Conference on "The United States and Japan on the Eve of the 21st Century: Prospects of Joint Leadership;" and, $47,150 to Yonsei University in Seoul in support of a symposium on the development of philanthropy in East Asia. According to Russell Phillips, the executive vice president, the Fund has a "declared interest…in the promotion of philanthropy and has a budget for it…in the Asia Pacific and Eastern and Central Europe." Five pages of the Fund's current report include listings of grants to encourage philanthropy, several of which are focused on Asia. Along with the Ford Foundation, the Rockefeller Brothers Fund was a supporter of the conferences that led to the Osaka Symposium and have "for a long time been interested in Asia Pacific but have not clustered grants there" because the opportunity did not exist.[13]

Smaller family foundations are often a highly effective way for individuals to establish giving in particular areas of interest, thus establishing a tradition of institutional giving for succeeding generations of family members and philanthropists with similar interests. Many such organizations have emerged in recent years with an interest in Asia, although only a handful have established a network of contacts that enable them to target the impact of their giving by cooperating with other philanthropic entities in the region. The Albert Kunstadter Family Foundation is an example of one foundation that has done precisely that.

Founded in 1952, this private family foundation supports international organizations, particularly those with projects related to Asia. Most grants are seldom over $5,000 and support general operations or broad program areas. In FY1991, a total amount of $346,593 was disbursed. Mr. John W. Kunstadter, President and Treasurer, said "I would say that the only [recent] tendency we have experienced is to increase grant making in Vietnam...[At present Ms. Kunstadter] is visiting a number of grantees, mostly in Hanoi: English language training programs, architects seeking to do urban rehabilitation, etc."[14] Often information about small scale funding requests comes from the Ford Foundation office in Bangkok which does not work with small grants. According to staff at the U.S.-Indochina Reconciliation

Project, the only other significant funders in Vietnam, Laos, and Cambodia are the Christopher Reynolds Foundation, Luce Foundation, The Asia Foundation, Ford Foundation, and the United Nations Development Program. The Gere Foundation, founded by actor Richard Gere, is another example of an organization whose predominant focus is on Asia. All of the foundation's grant making—$94,600 in 28 grants in 1992—is devoted to Tibet.

Many of the foundations expressing a singular interest in donation activity in Asia or in the Asian American community are those established by Asian Americans themselves. Although no accurate accounting of such institutions exists, Dr. Robert Lee estimated that in 1990 there were at least 124 with combined assets of approximately $66 million and $5 million in grants.[15] Although there is a natural connection between many Asian Americans and the nations from which their ancestors originated, an emerging generation of philanthropists have demonstrated an interest in the needs of their own communities in the United States.

Some Asian American foundations that are working in Asian Pacific American communities include:

- The Edna & Yu Shan Han Charitable Foundation, which made $81,500 in grants, primarily for scholarships to assist needy students in studies of Chinese culture, art, or history, with a preference for students of Chinese ancestry;
- The Kawaguchi-Kihara Memorial Foundation, a family foundation established in 1979 in Los Angeles. It awarded $98,000 in grants in FY1992.
- The Ishiyama Foundation gives money to educational organizations and to schools that promote exchange between the United States and Japan. In addition, it gives money to organizations where there is a personal family connection.
- The Goel Foundation, an Indian-American family foundation established in 1990, made $200,000 in grants last year, close to fifty percent of which was related to Asia—and most of that related directly to India. The foundation's programs provides funds for school, clothing, and education, and provides monetary loans to parents.

According to Asian Americans and Pacific-Islanders in Philanthropy, "only 0.2 percent of America's philanthropic dollars between 1983 and 1990 went to organizations working in Asian Pacific American communities, and most of this funding came from five foundations." The amount in dollars totaled only $34,660,040 out of $19,433,342,253 in foundation support over that period. Possible explanations offered by the group stress that while the number of recent Asian-American immigrants in poverty is quite substantial, most Americans, including some Asian Americans, perceive Asian immigrants as a monolithic, model minority whose economic performance is strong. Thus, support for philanthropic activities in the United States is generally weak.

With regard to cooperative efforts with foreign grant makers, one Asian American foundation representative expressed dismay over the lack of giving by Asian companies and foundations, especially members of the Affinity Group on Japanese Philanthropy of the Council on Foundations, for Asian-American related needs. The representative further added that support by Asian philanthropy groups for entities like the Japan Society and similar organizations is not seen as addressing the needs and concerns of Asian Americans. It is possible that foundations affiliated with a parent Asian company have been careful not to be seen targeting their philanthropy to any one particular ethnic group in recognition of frequent American misperceptions about giving. However, properly executed, such support could go a long way toward addressing basic needs in America and toward cultivating relationships with the fastest growing American population with the greatest personal affinity to Asia.

V. Corporate Giving

While there is no accounting for the precise amount of dollars going into the Asia Pacific region, the following is a brief, annotated listing of a number of different overseas corporate giving programs and the specific work they are doing in Asia.

*Aetna Foundation: Acc*ording to Diana Kinosh, who works with international and direct corporate contributions, "Aetna has international initiatives in countries where the company has operations…we carry out education and immunization programs in these areas which merit support. In Asia, our focus is on Hong Kong, Taiwan, Korea, Indonesia, and Malaysia. However, our charitable focus is limited. Grants of note in 1993 include $25,000 to Peking University in China and $15,000 to the Social Welfare Council Sara Wak in Malaysia.

American Express Foundation: Examples of interest in the Asia Pacific region include joint support with the World Monuments Fund, UNESCO, and a Sophia University team for the reconstruction and preservation of Angkor Wat, an ancient Hindu-Buddhist site; and restoration of the Vigan Heritage Village in the Philippines. Total contributions in 1993 totaled $21.1 million. Many of American Express' programs have a tourism industry orientation. The fund for China is budgeted for $600,000 between 1994 and 1997, supports tourism education, and promotes small business development in travel and tourism.

AT&T: According to official company materials, as "AT&T's global business grows, so does our philanthropic support to institutions in those countries where we have a significant business presence."[16] Grants to the Asia Pacific region in 1994 to date include: $100,000 to the Asian Youth Orchestra in Hong Kong, $50,000 to the Bell Shakespeare Company in Australia, $100,000 to the Hara Museum of Contemporary Art in Japan, $50,000 to the Art Tower Mito Contemporary Art Center in Japan, $50,000 to the Information Science and Technology Exhibition Center in Taiwan, and $100,000 to the Institute for International Economics in Washington, D.C. to support studies exploring the prospects for an Asia Pacific Economic Community. In addition, AT&T supports numerous international institutions in the United States, including The Asia Foundation. With employees outside the United States constituting approximately seventeen percent of AT&T's total workforce—and international revenues accounting for about twenty-five percent of total revenues—AT&T expects regional contributions in the near future to better reflect this growing overseas interests, particularly the countries in the Asia Pacific Region, namely China, Japan, India, Australia and Taiwan.

Bank of America: While Bank of America does not fund outside the United States, it does support Asia-related activities in locations where it has a presence, particularly in California, Texas, Oregon, Illinois, New York, and Arizona. In 1994, grant recipients included the Japanese American Community & Culture Center, Japanese American National Museum ($20,000 over five years), The Asia Foundation (two grants totaling $130,000 over two years), the Korean Youth Center ($10,000), Lao Kmhu Association ($5,000), Wahmei School ($1,500), and the Chinese Newcomer Service Center ($10,000). The primary interests of the foundation include economic development, arts and culture, community services, and education.[17]

Bankers Trust Foundation: In June, Bankers Trust Foundation announced a $575,000, five-year grant to the China Youth Development Foundation in Beijing. This contribution is part of an overall corporate strategy to diversify its giving from a previous focus on Latin America. The foundation has expressed an interest in Japan, Hong Kong, China, Korea, Singapore, and other parts of Asia Pacific. Recently, the foundation's president met with the Japan Center for International Exchange to explore options for activities in the Asia Pacific region.

Chevron: With gifts of $3.1 million, Chevron is the fifteenth largest international corporate giver in 1991, according to the Conference Board. Chevron's giving in Asia dates back to grants to Indonesia in the 1950s. Caltex, Chevron's operating company, carries out grant making in the Asia Pacific region, with representatives in each country making independent proposals for prospective projects. According to a staff member, Caltex enjoys a high degree of autonomy because it is not a wholly owned subsidiary, and thus not a part of the Chevron budget.

DuPont: DuPont has one of the oldest and largest corporate grant-making programs, having begun its grant making in 1918. Current giving abroad totals $4 million, and an increase of two and a half times that amount by the year 2000 is projected for programs that include the Pacific Rim. Programs in Asia have included a joint project with the Carter Center to eradicate Guinea worm disease through water purification. Corporate giving in Asia, for various reasons, also represents sound business strategy for DuPont.

Exxon Corporation: Exxon, with $17 million in grants, was rated the second largest international corporate giver in 1991 by the Conference Board. All contributions outside the United States are made by subsidiaries and affiliates in other countries. In Asia, $2.7 million was given in the areas of education and health, welfare, and community services. Among its programs, major participation in a $500,000 research program on Little penguins, the only such bird native to Australia. "Contributions are one way [we direct] resources to assist host countries with their significant social and economic problems,"[18] explained Edward Ahnert of the contributions office.

IBM: IBM is ranked number one in corporate contributions at home and abroad according to the Conference Board report—with a giving level of $37.6 million (down from $46.6 million a year earlier). IBM targets Asia Pacific as its second most important regional recipient with $11 million going to seventeen countries. Programs include fellowships for graduate study in the region,;support for persons with disabilities in Japan; donated computers in Taiwan, Indonesia, and the Philippines; and an educational focus through equipment donations in Australia and New Zealand. As James G. Parkel, director of corporate support programs, told the Conference Board, "Consistent with our business objectives, IBM's goal is to be a national asset and a recognized worldwide leader in helping address societal issues...We foresee more and more corporate giving overseas."[19]

Hewlett-Packard Company: According to Brad Whitworth, HP public affairs manager, "philanthropy, like most everything else at HP, is highly decentralized. We feel that decisions should be made at the lowest possible level in the organization, by the people who are closest to the situation. The same applies to grants activities... We establish a tone and a direction for the entire company, and try to see that everyone follows the same general pattern. Programs vary a little from country to country, region to region. But, if you look at them on aggregate, the efforts in Singapore look a lot like what we do in France or here in the U.S." Giving is also based on a local construct. According to Mr. Whitworth, "We have local committees (elaborate in some countries, small in others), representative of the make-up of the local organization, who research requests, qualify recipients, determine funding, install equipment, and follow up with funding recipients."[20]

Levi Strauss: Levi Strauss demonstrates "a strong commitment to the well-being of communities in which its employees live and work."[21] That commitment now extends to more than forty-five countries, including eight in Asia Pacific: Australia, Hong Kong, Japan, New Zealand, Pakistan, the Philippines, Singapore, and South Korea. According to company sources, "The scope of our international philanthropy is expanding to match the growth of our international operations." Resources are allocated through various programs. One which is relevant to Asia is the Community Involvement Team; led by employee volunteers at almost every company location, CITs raise funds for community projects which they identify where they work. In one example in the Philippines, a school for 2,500 children without fresh water received a $14,300 grant which provided for a water line which now provides for new washrooms and a vegetable garden. Giving in the last reported cycle included approximately $770,000 in support to programs in Australia, Hong Kong, Japan, Malaysia, New Zealand, Pakistan, Philippines, Singapore, South Korea. All grants were directed to groups in the target areas identified by people working in the community and therefore able to determine need and ability to carry out the project.

Newman's Own: Since launching his salad dressing to the market at the urging of friends ten years ago—and deciding that all profits would go toward charity—Newman's Own has given away over $60 million in the United States and around the world. A primary interest of the company's giving is children. Giving outside the United States is based on corporate relationships with the community, and Australia is the largest recipient of grants. According to program representatives "...we have given to Australian charities about $3 million...we also give in Hong Kong and Japan..."[22] When ask about program activity in Asia Pacific or utilization of a regional approach to funding, Ms. Hotchner, a program officer, was not aware of dialogue on an Asia Pacific regional community concept for philanthropy at all.

Merck & Co.: Merck & Co. is responsible for $5.1 million in contributions outside the United States concentrated at the local level—mostly in the form of product donations. A number of Asian countries are listed as recipients of gifts by the company. In Australia, Merck established a foundation to support science and medical research, which involves bringing Australian health officials to the United States for six months of work at the National Institutes of Health. In China, Merck is making available manufacturing technology for a hepatitis B vaccine. Japan is also being evaluated for future funding opportunities.

In summary, the diversity of corporate giving mechanisms is nearly as great as the variety of companies themselves. What most have in common appears to be an interest in decentralization, namely a shift towards community level decision-making involvement by local employees while retaining an overall corporate focus from headquarters, and an increased involvement in giving abroad that is a reflection of operations and profits made around the world. This demonstrates an effort to bring corporate giving into line with corporate objectives by expanding the variety of styles of giving to address issues more creatively and cost effectively. In short, contributions are moving from what is generally regarded as philanthropy among private foundations and individuals to various forms of commercial, voluntary and in-kind support which can achieve the same objectives in different ways. Due to this increasing corporate interest in seeking out opportunities for social investment, this new approach may have more immediate success than many other philanthropic entities in establishing effective partnerships with organizations around the world.

VI. Professional Organizations

A number of professional organizations have been formed over the last few decades to promote collaboration between and among grant seekers and grant makers.

In the fund-raising progression, which has become an integral part of the U.S.

nonprofit sector, several associations have played a leadership role in coordinating increased international dialogue. Among these are the Council for the Advancement and Support of Education (CASE), which provides educational and fund-raising network opportunities for colleges and universities; the National Society of Fund Raising Executives (NSFRE), whose thirteen thousand members represent a wide variety of nonprofit organizations, from museums to social service agencies; and the Association for Healthcare Philanthropy (AHP), whose rapidly growing membership comprises hospital and health care professionals.

Each of these organizations has a growing international component that can facilitate greater cooperation among nonprofits and enhance their ability to increase revenues from philanthropic entities. CASE in conjunction with HEERA, its British counterpart, holds an annual conference in England, which brings together groups from throughout Europe. NSFRE also holds an annual international conference drawing a large constituency from Mexico, where it has a chapter, and Central and South America, as well as Australia, England, and other countries. AHP's annual gathering and membership is being augmented by increasing amounts of fund raising from Canadian hospitals. Together with the World Fundraising Council, an organization comprised of fund-raising association leaders and fund-raising counsel from around the world, these organizations provide information to others in the field around the world, collaborate on training, and provide professional exchange opportunities.

Perhaps the most promising global effort based in the United States that brings together all three components of the sector—citizen groups, donor organizations, and individuals—is CIVICUS. Founded officially in 1993, CIVICUS is an international alliance of organizations and individuals whose mission is to strengthen philanthropy and community service through local voluntary initiatives throughout the world. Led by a twenty-member board of directors representing six regions of the world and directed by Miklos Marschall, the organization involves both grant makers and recipient organizations. Its First World Assembly will be held in Mexico City in January. The emergence of CIVICUS is a sign of both the desire for interchange between practitioners and scholars and the respect for philanthropic efforts by funders from all over the world.

While none of these efforts has focused specifically on Asia, the major reason for that omission is the absence of a professional network of fund raisers or grant makers in Asia with whom these associations might be able to interact. Both the Osaka Symposium on Nongovernmental Underpinnings of the Emerging Asia Pacific Community and the CIVICUS conference offer the best chance to address this tremendous disparity in information sharing between philanthropy groups in the West and those in the East.

VII. The Future of American Philanthropy Toward the Asia Pacific Region

While the concept of an Asia Pacific regional community has evolved in trade and regional security issues since the 1980s, the phrase is never cited in literature on U.S. philanthropy. In all the books, trade publications, interviews, and on-line searches consulted in preparing this paper, the Asia Pacific regional concept never surfaced. This is not to suggest a lack of interest in Asia by participants in the U.S. independent sector. Rather it reflects the fact that philanthropic giving has historically defined its program priorities independently, and this has delayed the development of a comprehensive approach to its programs as a sector.

In order to understand why American philanthropy has not yet developed a collaborative approach to Asia, it might be useful to review how foundations, corporations, and individuals participate in charitable giving to the Asia Pacific regional community. In addition, it is useful to review the government relationship with the independent sector. Other factors that impact on the development of the independent sector, such as hosting international conferences, conducting reciprocal study missions, promoting greater involvement from individual local actors, and encouraging the involvement of professional associations, will also be investigated.

Foundations: With few exceptions, foundations give support to an individual vision or mission. They are primarily concerned with measurable success on particular issues and do not conduct their activities for the benefit of nations or regions. In those cases where foundations have a similar outlook and interest in a particular country, joint activity can develop, however this has been coincidental and not part of a conscious pan-Asian scheme. For example, John Kunstadter states that his foundation's only tendency "is to increase grant making in Vietnam," and he notes that " the majority of grants are coming through our friends who are working there very actively. Not too many others are working in this politically sensitive area."[23] Other foundations, such as the John D. and Catherine T. MacArthur Foundation, say that they "do very little funding in Asia. What we do has to do with arms control and regional security. We support the scientific arms control community in China and also some work on research in Vietnam...We don't work with any [other] foundations."[24] As one foundation president said succinctly: "We look at what's happening; where it's happening is not particularly relevant."[25] Notable exceptions to the "issue vs. vision" pattern among foundation programs are the several groups that promote philanthropy in certain geographic areas, such as the foundation members of South African Grantmakers in Philanthropy, which collectively awarded $42 million in grants in 1992, or AAPIP, which is striving to increase giving to the Asian-American community. However, the persistent perception that Asia is a successful veteran of development—and thus a monolithic economic power, that does not need philanthropic assistance—may have a negative impact on collaboration in the United States and among countries within the Asia Pacific region itself.

Corporations: Corporations are involved where they have an economic interest. As noted earlier in the paper, U.S. companies are increasing their giving where they have operating locations. Due to the fact that there are many corporations with operations in Asia, philanthropic dollars in the region will inevitably grow. However, since this giving is highly decentralized—with many corporate headquarters not even in possession of documentation on grant recipients on a country by country or even a regional basis—the opportunities for an Asia Pacific plan for giving as a part of an overall global corporate strategy may be limited. Some companies are notable for a different approach that combines global corporate strategies, including working as a good corporate citizen with the Asia Pacific region, with involvement by local office personnel. Examples include Levi Strauss, which has regional plans for philanthropy and people who help to carry them out; AT&T, which is increasing its international role; and Hewlett-Packard, where headquarters sets the "tone and direction for the entire company, and [then] tries to see that everyone follows the same general pattern. It is in this area, and also the future of defining corporate philanthropy and the budgets from which it will emanate, that the biggest questions remain. But one thing is clear: corporations give in order to be perceived as good citizens and, being in competition with one another, do not tend to work collectively as foundations can and sometimes do. For this reason, it is unlikely that corporate giving, no matter how firmly aligned with the Asian community, will be an organizing force in building an Asia Pacific regional community.

Individuals: Individuals give to causes and institutions reactively. Rather than trying to build communities, they tend to respond to urgent appeals—starving children on telethons, earthquakes in Armenia, etc.—and focus to a lesser degree on trying to build bridges with individuals in other countries as they seek to share what they have. This bias on emotionally elicited individual donations explains the success of child sponsorship programs, and a growing interest in foreign affairs. What might harness this inherent interest and help shape it into a force for advancing the Asia Pacific regional community concept is for nonprofit organizations, both in the U.S. and from Asia, to set a new tone in the dialogue with individual donors. Currently, most people perceive the world in terms of the evening news. Asia is seen as a trading block, with occasional elements of political or cultural interest. NGOs—not government—will have to change this perception.

Government: The U.S. government lets the independent sector remain independent. The government's only effort to encourage the sector has been through the Common Agenda scheme, which is supportive of collaborative efforts between U.S. and Japanese NGOs, and which will potentially have a great impact upon developing countries in Asia. Organizations that receive money from USAID must also receive a certain percentage of their support from other sources as well, encouraging these groups to solicit public as well as corporate/foundation contributions. This helps to some extent to maintain their independence from the government. In addition, the United States Information Agency has invited and arranged national tours for individuals associated with nonprofit organizations and philanthropic entities from Asia and other nations to help those people better understand the United States and also to form relationships with American counterparts. The only other effort where the government is directly influencing the role of U.S. philanthropy toward the Asia Pacific region, as well as the rest of the world, is in continued consideration of eliminating tax deductions for foreign charitable contributions. This would have an extremely detrimental effect upon the trend toward more corporate contributions abroad. Aside from these issues, the government takes a very hands-off approach to U.S. philanthropic interests.

Professional Associations: Professional associations are contributing to dialogue. Associations in the field of American philanthropy are increasingly internationalizing their activities. Many organizations focus on particular issues, as manifested in the Canadian interest in fund raising for health-related activities and membership in the Association for Healthcare Philanthropy and Latin American participation in NSFRE conferences. There is much more that can be done, however, in expanding chapters of these associations abroad by, for example, sending study missions to Asia, and exploring joint research projects led by practitioners as well as scholars. Both the CIVICUS and Osaka Symposium on Philanthropic Development meetings are efforts in this direction.

Barnett Baron, in his introduction to *Philanthropy and the Dynamics of Change in East and Southeast Asia*, identified areas of collaboration between Asian, American, and other international foundations to promote the "growth and increased professionalization of private philanthropy"[26] in the region. Suggested methods included establishing or strengthening networks of philanthropic organizations within individual nations; scheduling occasional meetings among these independent national networks to exchange ideas and compare experiences, as well as more regular contact between East Asian and U.S. foundations and corporate givers to discuss specific issues of substance; providing internships or short-term practical training opportunities by U.S. grant makers and major NGOs for staff members of Asian foundations; and establishing training centers to provide training in nonprofit management. Perhaps most significant to our inquiry was the recommendation that, "American foundations should experiment with the use of matching formulas to stimulate local counterpart funding from private Asian sources."[27]

In that spirit, the following are some additional considerations for expanding cooperation among U.S. philanthropy organizations for activities within the Asia Pacific Community.

Nonprofits: If people need support, they must ask for it. If Asian organizations wish to receive support from U.S. philanthropic institutions, they should do as their American counterparts do: cultivate relationships with potential funders…and ask. Donor priorities are defined in part according to demand, and there is little evidence to suggest that Asian nonprofit organizations are engaged in any concerted effort to tap into U.S. philanthropy. According to the Ishiyama Foundation, a Japanese American family foundation, requests for funding are almost exclusively from U.S. charities for Japan-related projects, and they "have not received any requests from Japanese institutions" for support. A corporate giver said simply that they are always looking for potential recipients. While Asian nonprofits must decide for themselves how they should appeal for money in the contexts of their own cultural and financial concerns, American fund raisers and grant makers can best assist them by offering training, organizing conferences, facilitating exchanges of practitioners to provide leadership and guidance in establishing relationships with prospective donors, preparing case settlements and proposals that best reflect their organizations, and developing standards for measuring the success of their programs and conveying that to their supporters.

Reciprocal Study Missions: Reciprocal study missions should be conducted, through the support of host governments or prominent foundations. For years, U.S. foundations and corporate giving programs have welcomed the Japanese staff of emerging philanthropic entities in Japan. These study missions helped Japanese philanthropic personnel gain a sense of the professionalization of philanthropy and then adapt what was applicable upon their return. Americans should also seek opportunities to meet with other counterparts overseas, if only to learn of which areas would benefit from collaboration. Host countries overseas should make overtures to welcome U.S. philanthropic representatives, thereby establishing links to the U.S. independent sector.

Conferences: International Conferences dealing with independent sector issues should be held and made open to all interested parties. Dialogue between practitioners and scholars is essential in providing for increased cooperation among nonprofit and philanthropic entities. As useful as closed colloquia may often be, more conferences need to be open to debate. Just as published guidelines for a giving program help fund raisers to know which programs to approach and which discard, increased meetings between those who study the independent sector, including those who work in the sector and support it, would help to enhance the relationships among all the related actors and support the emergence of a more efficient and enlightened community of philanthropy. This is especially true with regard to international meetings, as there is already far too little information on international giving and receiving.

Summary and Conclusions

Philanthropy and voluntary association are not uniquely American ideas. As Lester Salamon pointed out in his article, "The Rise of the Nonprofit Sector,"[28] citizen associations in China date back to the eighth century, and the first foundation in Japan was established nearly a century before the first American foundation. What makes America's independent sector unique is its relationship with the government and accessibility to the public, both of which have set the stage for America's explosion in philanthropic activity over the last century.

First, nonprofit organizations act as partners with the government. The government is a leading source of financial support for nonprofits, viewing the nonprofit sector as a cost eYcient provider of services to society. In addition, the government provides tax incentives for others entities to support the sector through private donations and enables the organizations themselves to operate with a tax-exempt status. Although the organizations may receive government support, and philanthropic institutions may receive tax breaks for giving, neither are beholden to the government or obligated to support any of its policies. They are responsible only to their own boards of directors which are almost entirely independent of government involvement or representation.

Second, these organizations are generally open and accessible; whether through membership, donations, public events, publications, or volunteer activities, individuals have access to charitable organizations one way or another. Membership provides individuals with a sense of empowerment that emboldens them to express themselves, have a voice in political, scholarly and cultural debate, and to press for change when necessary. As Salamon writes, "virtually all of America's major social movements, for example, civil rights, environmental and consumer issues, and women's rights have had their roots in the nonprofit sector."[29] Thus philanthropic organizations in the United States have been agents of social change in society.

We are now witnessing a rapid growth of the independent sector around the world which, according to Salamon's article "may prove to be (as momentous) to the latter twentieth century as the rise of the nation-state was to the latter nineteenth."[30] The intellectual community's interest in this development is reflected in various publications, for example articles by Craig Smith in *Harvard Business Review* on corporate giving and Yuko Iida Frost in *The Brookings Review* on Japan's nonprofit sector. This interest in the independent sector by academia is accompanied by government interest, especially in countries where individuals, foundations, and corporations will have to play a role in providing talent, time, and money to address basic social and cultural needs.

Ironically, in America, where the sector has blossomed over the past century, signs of concern have emerged due to scandals in the independent sector. In addition, state governments seeking additional tax revenue are exploring the idea of taxing nonprofits. Even the federal government is eliminating the tax advantages for giving to family foundations at the end of this year. These developments can be seen as indications that America is retreating from its historical support for philanthropy, despite the trend towards internationalization explored above in the evolution of its independent sector.

At the NSFRE International Conference this March, Stanley Katz of the Council of Learned Societies went so far as to ask fundamental questions about international giving such as "Why should we in the United States be so interested in philanthropy abroad, and, in particular, why should we be so committed to the promotion of philanthropy abroad? Until recently the primary reason seems to have been a cold war influenced, poorly articulated assumption that if philanthropy contributes to democracy at home, it will also help to support and possibly even to create democracy abroad."[31] The end of the cold war has fundamentally changed these basic assumptions and initiated a process of redefinition of purpose within the independent sector in the United States. In the case of the government, many people are beginning to question the efficacy of tax money being applied to development abroad when poverty, infant mortality, child inoculation, and literacy rates in the United States are alarmingly similar to those of many nations we are supporting. Articles in the *New York Times* on the subject and an exposé by "Sixty Minutes," a leading television news program, featuring a report on alleged USAID financial support for the relocation of U.S. manufacturing jobs to low wage developing nations, have fueled public resentment and negatively impacted on support for foreign assistance.

UNICEF, in response to this growing mood in the United States is acting proactively to use its international relief experience in America's inner-cities and direct U.S. contributions to that effort. As Marilyn F. Solomon, executive director of the Los Angeles chapter of the U.S. Committee for UNICEF told the *Los Angeles Times*, "We can't just talk about children 'over there' because those children live here now. We have the same problems."[32] Ms. Solomon characterized the effort as an attempt to "forge the gap between local and international efforts for youth."

Despite these trends, however, the generosity that underlies American giving—and which pressures the U.S. government to act cooperatively in accordance with this basic sentiment—has not changed. If the American people are made aware of the needs that exist in Asia they would respond positively just as they historically have since the turn of the century. However, it is incumbent upon those in Asia and the United States who recognize these needs to articulate them in order to inform the public, as well as develop cooperative structures for addressing these needs which promote efficiency and eliminate duplication of effort, and involve everyone in the sector in this effort. Only in these ways can an increasingly inward-looking American public be reoriented to the historically global trend of its corporate and foundation givers—to see ourselves as part of the fabric of the world.

Notes

1. Individual giving is the core of philanthropy in America, making up more than eighty-five percent of all charitable contributions. As individual contributions to activities in Asia are difficult to quantify, and the intention of this project is to focus on institutional giving, these contributions are not covered in the final draft of this paper.
2. "One tenth given to the church," according to the *Oxford English Dictionary*, a *tithe* referring to a tenth of one's production, usually salary.
3. James A. Joseph, *The Charitable Impulse* (New York: The Foundation Center, 1989), p. 3.
4. For more information on the three stages of U.S. NGO growth and its impact on U.S. voluntary assistance abroad, see Yuko Iida Frost's "American Nongovernmental Organizations (NGOs) and Their Relationship with the Asia Pacific Regional Community," also provided for the O*saka Symposium on Nongovernmental Underpinnings of the Emerging Asia Pacific Community*, 1994.
5. The Concert for Bangladesh also foreshadowed the danger of special events fund raising for international causes. While it raised nearly $175,000, most of the money never reached the needy and has been tied up in litigation. The event's major success was in drawing the entertainment community into efforts to raise the awareness of the American public to the needs of impoverished people abroad.
6. Ann E. Kaplan (ed.),*Giving USA* (New York: American Association of Fund Raising Counsel, 1994) pp. 59–73.
7. "Facts and Figures," in *Grants for Foreign & International Programs* (New York: The Foundation Center, 1994–1995).
8. From a telephone interview with a staff member of the John D. and Catherine T. MacArthur Foundation, 14 October 1994.
9. From a telephone interview with a staff member of the Compton Foundation, 14 October 1994.
10. From a telephone interview with a staff member of the S.H. Cowell Foundation, 14 October 1994.
11. "The Burma Project," a brochure of the Open Society Institute, George Soros, Chairman, 1994.
12. The Henry Luce Foundation, Inc.: *1992–1993 Biennial Report*, 1994.
13. From a telephone interview with Russell Phillips, Executive Vice President, Rockefeller Brothers Fund, on 2 November 1994.
14. From a telephone interview with John Kunstadter, 17 October 1994.
15. Robert Lee, *Guide to Chinese American Philanthropy and Charitable Giving Patterns* (San Rafael: Pathway Press, 1990).
16. AT&T International Program Guidelines, 1994.

17. From a telephone interview with a staff member of the Bank of America Foundation, 14 October 1994.
18. Anne Klepper, Report Number 1019: *Global Contributions of U.S. Corporations.*
19. Ibid.
20. From a fax interview with Brad Whitworth, 6 October 1994.
21. *Levi Strauss & Co. Social Investment Report,* 1994.
22. From a telephone interview with Ursula Hotchner, Senior Vice President, Newman's Own, on 2 November 1994.
23. From a telephone interview with John Kunstadter, President, Kunstadter Foundation, 12 October 1994.
24. From a telephone interview with a staff assistant at the John D. and Catherine T. MacArthur Foundation, 12 October 1994.
25. From a telephone interview with Quincey Tompkins of the Foundation for Deep Ecology, 17 October 1994.
26. Barnett F. Baron (ed.), *Philanthropy and the Dynamics of Change in East and Southeast Asia* (New York: East Asian Institute, 1991), pp. 16–17.
27. Ibid.
28. Lester M. Salamon, "The Rise of the Nonprofit Sector," in *Foreign Affairs,* July/August 1994, pp. 109–122.
29. Ibid.
30. Ibid.
31. Stanley N. Katz, "Philanthropy and Democracy: Which Comes First," in *Advancing Philanthropy,* Summer 1994, p. 34.
32. Jocelyn Y. Stewart, "UNICEF Knocks on New Doors For Support: What Began as a Halloween Tradition to Help Children In Foreign Countries Tackles Same Problems at Home," *Los Angles Times,* 1994.

UNITED STATES of AMERICA

The Role of U.S. Foundations in Asia Pacific
A Historical Perspective

Hiroshi Peter Kamura[1]
Executive Director
Japan Center for International Exchange (U.S.A.)

I. Introduction

This paper is intended to complement Jay Frost's overview piece which broadly surveys international activities of organized American private and corporate philanthropy. This paper will focus on the role major U.S. foundations have played in Asia Pacific in both prewar and postwar years in the fields of:

(1) the development of American interest and expertise
(2) economic, social, and human resource development
(3) regional linkages and networking
(4) the development of the nonprofit sector including private philanthropy

This survey is not intended to be exhaustive. Rather, it seeks to shed some light on the kinds of roles U.S. organized philanthropy has played in the aforementioned areas through a historical perspective.

International largesse has been one of the most salient features of U.S. philanthropic activities since the early years of the twentieth century. However, it is important to remember that only a small number of foundations (and corporations in recent years) have been active in international affairs and only a handful of these grant makers are currently involved in Asia Pacific related programs in specific.

Today, there are more than thirty-five thousand grant-making foundations in the United States. The *1992 Directory for International Grantmakers*, compiled by the Council on Foundations, identified 145 grantmakers (private foundations and corporate foundations/giving programs) who are involved in international activities in the United States and abroad.

The Japan Center for International Exchange, as part of its survey project entitled, "Nongovernmental Underpinnings of the Emerging Asia Pacific Regional Community," compiled the *Directory of U.S. Private and Corporate Foundations Active in Asia Pacific* in 1995. The directory identified fifty-nine grant makers either active or interested in Asia Pacific related programs. Of the fifty-nine, about half are private foundations and the rest comprise corporate foundations or their giving programs. We have also noted, as of late a significant growth in the number of corporate grant makers becoming active in Asia Pacific related programs both in the United States and in the region itself.

Given the large number of foundations that exist in the United States, the community of foundations oriented internationally in general and towards Asia Pacific related programs in particular remains quite small in the U.S. philanthropic world.

Nevertheless, some foundations, especially, the Rockefeller Foundation and the Ford Foundation, and some other large ones, including the Rockefeller Brothers Fund and the Henry Luce Foundation, have played a significant role in cultivating American interest and expertise, and developing institutions and human resources in education, science, and culture in the region. Although a small philanthropy, the Albert Kunstadter Family Foundation became active in the late 1980s in supporting, initially China-related projects in the United States and China, and, most recently, educational programs in Vietnam.

II. The Prewar Roots of U.S. Foundation Work in Asia

The postwar years were marked by a considerable expansion of the international programs of the Rockefeller Foundation (established in 1913) and the Carnegie Corporation of New York (established in 1911), as well as the entry into the international affairs field of the Ford Foundation (established in 1936 but a regional foundation in Michigan until 1950). Of these "big three," the Rockefeller Foundation was the only one that had done major work in Asia prior to World War II. Carnegie's involvement was mainly in Africa where it concentrated on education. The Henry Luce Foundation started grant-making activities in 1937, focusing on China.

a. The Rockefeller Foundation

The Rockefeller Foundation was created "to promote the well-being of mankind throughout the world." While most efforts by Rockefeller philanthropies were devoted to causes within the United States, their overseas work in Asia also began before the war.

John D. Rockefeller, Jr. and the Rockefeller Foundation provided substantial financial support to three new international affairs organizations in their formative stage of institution-building: the Council on Foreign Relations (1921), the Foreign Policy Association (1918), and the Institute for Pacific Relations (1925), the first organization oriented to East Asia.

1) China

In 1914, the China Medical Board was founded by the Rockefeller Foundation to train a whole generation of Chinese doctors. The Peking Union Medical College, the "Johns Hopkins of China," funded by the Foundation, was opened in 1921 for the training of medical students. Rockefeller Junior himself visited Peking for its dedication. During the same trip he and Mrs. Rockefeller visited Japan and Korea.

The Foundation supported Christian missions and educational institutions in China. Rockefeller also made gifts for the restoration of the Forbidden City and to Lingnan University in southern China. In the field of agriculture, in 1935 the Foundation, in collaboration with several other universities and organizations, initiated a rural reconstruction program in China based at Nanjing University. Through this program several hundred young Chinese received training fellowships, a few to the United States. More than one million dollars was invested by the Foundation in agriculture. By the termination of these programs in 1949 with the Communist takeover, the Foundation had spent $45 million in China, most of which was for the medical school and training.

2) Southeast Asia

In the 1920s and 1930s, the Rockefeller Foundation helped finance medical education and training at the Royal Medical School in Siam, the Hong Kong Medical School, and the King Edward VII Medical School in Singapore. In the prewar period, the Foundation supported extensive public health efforts in Asian countries including the Philippines and Malaya. Such efforts included programs to control deadly diseases such as yellow fever, malaria, and typhus. (Dr. Hideyo Noguchi's research on yellow fever was conducted at the Rockefeller Institute for Medical Research [today's Rockefeller University] in New York, funded by the Rockefeller Foundation.)

3) Japan

Rockefeller made an important contribution to Japan, too. In light of the complete destruction of the library of the Tokyo Imperial University by the 1923 Kanto earthquake, Rockefeller provided $1.5 million for its restoration.

4) Fellowship Program

Rockefeller fellowship programs in the field of social sciences also started worldwide in 1914—sending carefully selected students to some of the best institutions in the United States and Europe. The program was the single most important device for the training of competent personnel for intellectual leadership. The Foundation spent $28 million for some ten thousand fellowships in seventy-five countries prior to 1950. Many of these fellowships were administered by the National Research Council and the Social Science Research Council (SSRC). The Asian fellowship program became an integral part of the human resource development efforts of the Rockefeller Foundation. The Asian fellowships, especially those of economics, became critical in the postwar years to produce a cadre of leading economic scholars and policy makers in Asian countries.

5) Area Studies

By the 1930s, the United States, unlike several European countries, had not yet developed a school for the study of modern Asian languages and cultures. In 1933, a grant was made to the American Council of Learned Societies (ACLS) to strengthen the Library of Congress as a center for students of Japanese and Chinese languages. Beginning in 1934, with Foundation aid, a series of summer institutes was initiated at Harvard, Columbia, California and Cornell universities for intensive training of young scholars in Japanese and Chinese languages and cultures. This movement spread and by 1941, twelve universities had developed special courses in one or both of these languages. Such efforts proved to be a critical basis on which to build to meet the acute demand for knowledge of East Asia and its languages. One might say that this marked the beginning of area studies of Asia in the United States.

b. The Henry Luce Foundation

The Henry Luce Foundation was founded in 1936 by Henry R. Luce, founder of Time, Inc. With current assets of some $500 million, the Foundation consistently devotes thirty percent of its annual budget to Asia-related programs. It is particularly active in China-related programs, reflecting the Luce family interest in the country. Henry R. Luce's father was born to missionary parents in China and was a Presbyterian missionary who taught for thirty years at a missionary college there. In 1935, one year prior to the establishment of the Foundation, Luce gave $50,000 to Yenching University in Peking as part of an endowment to honor his father, a leader in the establishment of this missionary-founded academic institution. There was no specific giving plan during the first phase of the Foundation's history other than that some form of help to China was a major concern. Between 1936 and 1945, the Luce Foundation gave $83,000 toward Asian affairs, of which $73,000 went to the China Institute of America; $60,000 went to U.S. religious institutions; and support for Christian colleges in East Asia included $12,000 to the Associated Board of Christian Colleges in China.

The Luce Foundation's work in China was terminated in 1949 with the Communist takeover, though it reentered the country in the 1970s. For more than twenty years thereafter, the Foundation moved throughout other parts of East Asia, supporting and building educational and religious institutions. As a part of a studied plan, it also embarked upon a program of grants to U.S. educational institutions that were mainly concerned with East Asia.

Thus, in addition to the enormous ongoing voluntary giving of American citizens to Asia, especially China, through disaster relief or missionary activities, some U.S. foundations had already initiated formative programs in Asia before the outbreak of World War II. Given the value of the U. S. dollar at the time, their contributions were indeed impressive.

III. U.S. Foundation Activities in Asia in the Postwar Period

1. Development Assistance–Related Institution-Building and Human Resources Development

The U.S. foundations earned the most enduring place in Asia by their work in development assistance programs closely linked to institution-building and human resources development. Notably, the Ford Foundation and the Rockefeller Foundation played the most active and important roles in the postwar years. Later joining in this effort was the Rockefeller Brothers Fund (RBF); the Asia Foundation, established in 1954 and federally funded but managed privately; and the Public Welfare Foundation. The China Medical Board, after the 1949 Communist takeover of China, moved into eight countries in East and Southeast Asia, providing support for medical research and training. Its fellowship program enormously assisted in the training and education of Asian doctors in public health. The board has reinstated its work in China and other Asia Pacific countries and is presently providing major support to HIV and AIDS related programs.

a. The Ford Foundation

In 1950, when the Ford Foundation grew into an independent national foundation with both national and international concerns, the trustees adopted five broad areas of Foundation action. The first area was "the establishment of world peace." The grant programs would be "overseas development, international training and research, and international affairs." In the same year funds were appropriated for its Overseas Development Programs in South and Southeast Asia and the Middle East. The program was extended to Africa in 1958 and to Latin America in 1959 with the belief that the Foundation would make more effective use of the experience it gained in Asia.

It is widely recognized that the development program is by far the most significant contribution the Ford Foundation has made in international affairs. This is particularly relevant for Asia Pacific. Of the $2.1 billion the Foundation allocated to international programs from 1950–81, three quarters was spent on its Overseas Development Program and most of that went directly overseas. Over $400 million of the $2.1 billion was used for Asia Pacific related development programs. It is estimated that this figure would reach some $500 million by 1995.

In the field of Ford's program for human resources development with an emphasis on building individual capacity, the Foundation provided social science fellowships for young scholars in Asian countries to study in U.S. graduate schools for training. In the 1960s and 70s, some one hundred young Japanese social scientists were awarded fellowships. The program not only helped build up their research and teaching capabilities, but also greatly assisted them in broadening their contacts with the worldwide intellectual community in the postwar years, which was also a concern of the Foundation.

Over many years, Ford has maintained field offices in Asia to implement its programs—Bangladesh, China, India (also covering Nepal and Sri Lanka), Indonesia, Thailand, and the Philippines. A new field office is planned to open in Vietnam in the fall of 1995 where Ford has already been substantially involved in recent years.

During the past four and a half decades, the Foundation's largest commitments in Asia have been in rural poverty and resources; its second focal point has been reproductive health and population. In Asia, as in elsewhere in the world, Ford has worked to advance social justice by removing legal and cultural barriers to the rights of women and the poor. It has provided major support for the preparations of the 1995 UN Conference on Women to be held in Beijing.

The Foundation's past development assistance was especially important in Southeast Asia to help build local competence to deal with problems of food production, rural poverty, population growth, education, natural resource management, and social and economic policy. It helped Indonesia's efforts in food production research in several fields at national and provincial universities. Many Indonesian economists and other social scientists have been trained with Ford support. In both Thailand and Indonesia, Ford also supported efforts to improve the educational system. More than 125 young social scientists from several Southeast Asian countries received awards in the 1960s and 1970 through the foundation's Southeast Asia Fellowship Program for advanced training and studies of national and regional problems.

To help Southeast Asian countries cope with environmental and natural resources problems, it supported training and research at the Bogor Institute of Agriculture in Indonesia, the University of the Philippines, and other institutions. Ford's funds assisted work on such problems as river-basin management, rehabilitation of upland areas, forest and grasslands management, and pest control. In Malaysia, the foundation supported language studies and public administration training. Further, grants were made to strengthen the participation of Asians in international economic affairs.

During the period of 1952–79, the Ford Foundation invested more than $40 million to enhance the understanding of China through various programs, which are discussed in other sections of this paper. In 1979, after the normalization of diplomatic relations between China and the United States, the Foundation began a program of direct support for academic and professional exchanges. The main purpose of Ford-supported activities during the period of 1979–88 was to strengthen academic and professional competence in China in the fields of economics, law, and international relations. About $18 million was spent. Since the opening of the Foundation's Beijing field office in 1988, the program has been enlarged to include the economic development of poor areas and the improvement of reproductive health and child survival. Another $10 million was committed for the 1988–90 period.

The Chinese Academy of Social Sciences (CASS) and the Chinese Academy of Agricultural Sciences (CAAS), were the two original principal grantees. Later the

Foundation broadened its scope of funding to include leading universities, State Councils, and Ministry research institutes. The major grantees in the United States were the National Academy of Sciences for the activities of the Committee on Scholarly Communication with the People's Republic of China (CSCPRC), Columbia University for the U.S.-China Arts Exchange, and the Agricultural Development Council (now Winrock International Institute for Agricultural Development).

b. The Rockefeller Foundation

In the 1950s, the Rockefeller Foundation and the other Rockefeller family philanthropies guided by John D. Rockefeller, 3rd ("JDR") shifted from aiding European institutions in the early postwar years to focusing on the "poor" countries of the world and their needs for development. The Foundation concentrated its grant-making programs on conquering hunger and famine by focusing on food production and agricultural research reproductive biology and population and higher education development. One of the most successful and best remembered development programs of the Foundation is the educational assistance program in Asia, which ran from 1963 to 1980. Several universities in Indonesia, the Philippines, and Thailand were targeted. The Foundation made long-term commitments of over ten years to build institutions of higher education in these countries, especially in the areas of agriculture, public health, biomedicine, and social sciences.

The Foundation was substantially involved in the implementation of such programs resembling an operating foundation—sending Foundation staff and hiring leading American professors to teach at these universities. This was skillfully combined with Rockefeller's fellowship program. Thousands of students and faculty members received fellowships to study in their own countries, and hundreds were able to study in U.S. or European universities. Of specific importance were the economics fellowships since they produced a number of leading economists and policy planners who later became leaders of nation building in their respective countries. Rockefeller's university development program is to date regarded as a model development effort in institution-building and human resources programs.

The Rockefeller Foundation program at Thammasat University is particularly well known. It began in 1964, at first spread broadly across different departments and disciplines, but after the first few years it began focusing on the Economics Department. Developing the capacity for economic policy planning to achieve economic development was chosen as one of the highest needs of the country at the time. They practically started from scratch, as the university had only a handful of full-time faculty members and a large number of students. Curricula were rigid and outdated. Dr. Puey Ungphakorn, former governor of the Bank of Thailand and a dynamic intellectual leader who became the new dean, worked closely with Foundation representatives to formulate a "five-objective, four-stage program" for the economics faculty.

The objectives were: to improve the quality of undergraduate programs; establish a master of economics program in the English language; promote policy-oriented research; develop the faculty as a leading sector to strengthen the university as a whole; and make the graduate program a regional training center.

By 1981 when the Rockefeller program was terminated, the university was well staffed and had respectable undergraduate and graduate programs and improved research capability. After the Rockefeller's departure, domestic support grew and other foreign donors joined in supporting it. The Ford Foundation and the Japan Foundation have become regular sponsors for visiting professors. Particularly notable is the importance of Ford's research grants under its New International Economic Order program.

c. The Population Council and the Agricultural Development Council

The 1950s and 1960 marked a period of institution-building that goes hand in hand with human resource development. In this period, JDR, in collaboration with the Rockefeller Foundation, and often on his own, engaged in institution-building efforts related to Asian development. Two institutions created by his vision are the Population Council and the Agricultural Development Council (ADC).

1) The Population Council

In the 1950s, the danger of population explosion was little understood in the world, yet, JDR recognized the importance of population control and reproductive biology. It was too sensitive an issue at the time for the Rockefeller Foundation to enter this field in a major way. So, in 1952 JDR decided to create an organization, the Population Council ("Pop Council"), to undertake social and health sciences programs and research relevant to population and reproductive problems. JDR made a personal contribution of $1.4 million as seed money with a pledge to provide $250,000 per annum. The Ford Foundation joined JDR's efforts by making a first grant to the Council in the amount of $600,000 in 1954, then in 1957 $1 million to support research and training activities. RBF also made a first grant of $54,000 in 1956. Thanks to the Ford grant, the fellowship program expanded significantly.

The Council has become the world's preeminent institution in the population field. While it operates worldwide, Asia Pacific has been, by far, the largest beneficiary of the Council's work.

2) The Agricultural Development Council (ADC)

Next, JDR established the Agricultural Development Council (ADC) in 1953. This research and training organization involved in agricultural economics and planning and rural development grew out of his concern with an overpopulated, poverty-stricken postwar Asia with a serious food shortage. This concept stemmed from his earlier vision of a "Far Eastern Food Research Institute." JDR, again, made an initial personal commitment of $1.25 million with a pledge of $250,000 per annum over a five-year period. Further, RBF approved a grant of $500,000 annually for seven years and later, gave $250,000 annually for general support until 1973. ADC, was merged into Winrock International Institute for Agricultural Development in 1985.

ADC, in collaboration with JCIE, sponsored a series of five seminars in the late 1970s and early 1980s as a joint endeavor of American, Japanese and Asian social scientists and agricultural economists. The National Institute for Research Advancement (NIRA) in Tokyo, RBF, and Ford provided the financial support.

ADC's most important and long-lasting contribution to Asia was its Asian Fellowship program. Along with the Asian fellowship programs of the Ford and Rockefeller Foundations, ADC's Asian Fellowship is widely recognized as a "success story" of foundation work in Asia. ADC, from its inception to 1985, provided nearly 400 fellowships to Asians from thirteen countries, including Japan in the social sciences, especially, agricultural economics. According to Abe Weisblat, program administer for decades, many former Asian fellows are currently serving as leaders in government, universities, and research and training organizations, playing critical roles in socioeconomic policy in their respective countries of origin.

As seen in the preceding section, the roles played by the Ford Foundation and the Rockefeller Foundation in Asian development is impressive. As occasionally noted, these two foundations and RBF have funded the same organizations regardless of origin. One of the most important of such philanthropic cooperation can be seen in the 1958 agreement concluded between the Ford Foundation and the Rockefeller Foundation with the Republic of the Philippines to build and run the International Rice Research Institute (IRRI) in Los Banos. In 1960, the year of IRRI's founding, Ford provided the capital funds of $6.9 million and Rockefeller the operating budget. IRRI opened in 1962 and Ford and Rockefeller have continued to provide substantial support over the years. What should be noted about this joint foundation work is its multiplier effect. Other donors who have joined IRRI's funding include the U.S. and Japanese governments, the International Development Research Center (IDRC) of Canada, and other governments and multilateral financial institutions.

2. Promoting Cultural and Educational Exchanges

JDR's lifelong fascination and preoccupation with Japan and Asia, which had taken root before the war was the driving force in creating cultural and educational institutions to promote exchanges between the United States and Asian nations. JDR became the very embodiment of an "institution builder" of Asia-U.S. affairs.

a) JDR Japan Projects—The Japan Society and the International House of Japan

In 1950, JDR agreed to join a U.S. mission to conclude the peace treaty with Japan, which was led by John Foster Dulles, then the new chairman of the Rockefeller Foundation. JDR was charged with the responsibility for the cultural, educational, and informational aspects of U.S.-Japan relations. He was to propose projects in the cultural field that would help build mutual friendship and respect between the two nations over the long term. In January-February 1951, he joined the Dulles delegation to Japan. While there he met many Japanese public and private leaders and renewed his acquaintance with Shigeharu Matsumoto who he first met at the IPR conference in Tokyo in 1929.

JDR's report on cultural recommendations for Japan was submitted to the State Department. It analyzed cultural relations and interests, stressing mutuality and the "free and voluntary interchange of ideas and information" with an emphasis on the "two-way street" and the need for Americans to learn about Japan. His ideas for the private sector included a "cultural center" in each country, International House(s) in Japan, an exchange-of-intellectuals program, and an English-language teaching program in Japan.

1) Japan Society

With advice from his aide, Ed Young, the Japan Society in New York, which was closed down during the war, came to JDR's attention as the most promising organization concerned with Japanese society and culture in the country. So, instead of creating a new "cultural center," he decided to revive the Society. In March 1952, the Japan Society was reinstituted with the new board including Dulles (chairman), JDR (president), and Edwin Reischauer.

Under the leadership and generous financial aegis of JDR, the Society grew into the largest and most important organization of Japanese-American affairs in the nation. A joint program with the International House of Japan, which began shortly after the Society's revival and was endowed by JDR, the Intellectual Interchange Program between Japan and the United States, took a number of prominent intellectual and cultural leaders to each other's country. Also, for many of the earlier years, he provided an annual grant of $60,000 to the Japan Society to support English-language teaching in Japan. Furthermore, JDR donated the land for the Japan Society's present location on East 47th Street, where it has been housed since 1971.

The U.S.-Japan Leadership Program, initially funded by the U.S.-Japan Foundation, brings potential American national leaders to Japan for an intensive program to acquaint them with Japan. Over the years, other U.S. foundations, including the Starr Foundation, RBF, and the Pew Charitable Trusts, have funded the program. The Society's extensive U.S.-Japan exchanges and public affairs programs are supported by individuals, companies, and foundations in the United States and Japan.

2) The International House of Japan

JDR concurrently worked with Shigeharu Matsumoto to create the International House of Japan in Tokyo, "I-House", modeled after the International Houses in New York, Berkeley, Chicago, and Paris, as an international center for intellectual and cultural exchanges with housing and library facilities. The Rockefeller Foundation approved a grant of $676,121 (250 million yen) to be matched by 100 million yen to be raised in Japan through the Japan Committee.

The I-House was chartered in 1952 and construction began on a two-and-a-half acre plot in central Tokyo. I-House worked closely with its sister organization, the Japan Society, to cosponsor the Intellectual Interchange Program. Also, it administered the Grew Scholarship program for Japanese students to attend U.S. colleges; and later, starting in the late 1970s, the Nitobe Inazo Fellowships for Japanese social scientists to pursue post-graduate work in the United States. This program was jointly established by the Toyota Foundation and the Ford Foundation. It has also run numerous exchange programs and seminars including the Dartmouth Conference, the Williamsburg Conference with the Asia Society, and the Japan Seminars of the Aspen Institute.

b. Asia Society

JDR's interest in and commitment to Japan quickly extended to other Asian countries. Under his leadership, the Asia Society was incorporated in 1956, with JDR himself as president, to foster cultural interchange between the United States and Asia, promote greater knowledge of Asia in the United States, and generally serve as a center of information on Asia. By 1960, JDR had contributed nearly $2 million, averaging $400,000 a year, and gave another $1 million almost entirely to the fund for renovating the building acquired by him to house the Asia Society and the Japan Society. In the early years, the Society restricted its activities to social and cultural affairs—exhibits, publications, lectures, and seminars. It defined "Asia" as the Far East and South and Southeast Asia, but not the Middle East, and formed "Country Councils" around which special programs for specific Asian countries were carried out. With the passing of time, the Society gradually developed programs dealing with contemporary politics and economics of Asia. By the 1970s, in addition to Rockefeller sources, other donors, including the Andrew W. Mellon Foundation and the Ford Foundation, joined in supporting the Society.

The Society also has sponsored an Asian Fellows program to bring mid-career Asian professionals to New York to provide an Asian perspective to the Society's programs. Many current projects of the Society are addressing issues facing the post–cold war Asia Pacific and its relations with the United States. These projects are funded by not only major U.S. foundations such as Ford, Rockefeller, Luce, and Starr, but by Japanese and other Asian foundations as well.

c. Asian Cultural Council

In 1963, JDR founded a small foundation, the JDR 3rd Fund, specifically to promote cultural and artistic exchange between the United States and Asian countries. Entirely funded by JDR ($1.2 million annually for the first ten years), the Asian Cultural Program provided $500,000 in grants—fellowships for Asians, projects for the preservation of Asian cultural traditions, exhibitions and performances of Asian works in Asia and the United States, and exhibitions and performances of American works in Asia. After JDR's death in 1978, the Program was reconstituted in 1980 as a separate organization, the Asian Cultural Council, which has been affiliated with RBF since 1991. Now supported by individuals, corporations, and foundations, the Council remains the only American foundation devoted specifically to Asian American cultural exchange. It provides close to $2 million annually for grants in support of fellowships and institutional and collaborative projects. The Council has recently established several new program initiatives to expand opportunities for Asian American cultural dialogue and strengthen institutional linkages throughout the Asia Pacific region.

d. Magsaysay Award

Inspired by JDR, RBF established the Ramon Magsaysay Award in 1957 in memory of the late president Magsaysay of the Philippines and founded the Ramon Magsaysay Award Foundation, headquartered in Manila, to administer the program. Since its formation, up to five awards of $50,000 annually have been presented to individual Asians who distinguished themselves in five areas: government service; public service; community leadership; international understanding; and journalism, literature and creative communication arts. They are today regarded in the region as the "Nobel Prizes" of Asia. In 1987, the program for Asian Projects was created to fund projects in Asia that exemplify the spirit of the Foundation and RBF's program interests. In 1993, RBF provided $150,000 for five Awards and $130,000 for thirteen projects.

e. Luce Scholars Program

Established by the Henry Luce Foundation in 1974, the Luce Scholars Program is a commitment by the Foundation to create Asia-aware professionals who will assume leading roles in U.S. society. This program is unique in that annually it carefully selects fifteen talented young Americans under the age of thirty to work in professional internships, or in what the Foundation characterizes as "apprenticeships," in an East or Southeast Asian country for one year on a grant made by the Luce Foundation and administered by the Asia Foundation. Several of the scholars go to Japan annually. The program was instituted by the Luce Foundation with the belief that in the course of their careers, Americans in leadership roles are likely to have some interaction with Asia, yet most of them have had no prior experience with it.

The heart of the program lies in the internships and job placements (not academic programs for degrees) that are arranged for each Scholar on the basis of his or her individual career interest, experience, training, and general background. As of 1994, approximately 250 young men and women had received this fellowship. Since the program's inception in 1974, the Foundation has invested close to $5 million.

f. National Committee on U.S.-China Relations

Founded in 1966, the National Committee on United States-China Relations is a public, nonprofit organization that encourages the understanding of China and the United States among citizens of both countries. The Committee focuses its exchange, educational, and policy activities on economic development, international relations, education administration, global issues, and communications. Since its formation, the Ford Foundation has been the largest and longest sustained funder of the Committee's work. Other major donors include the John D. and Catherine T. MacArthur, Kunstadter, Luce, and Starr Foundations, RBF, and U.S. government agencies.

The National Committee has carried out numerous binational exchange programs and studies. Beginning in 1980, it has conducted the Scholar Orientation Program, in which some seven hundred Chinese scholars and students have participated. The Committee also administers the annual Fulbright Summer Seminars Abroad Program by sending elementary and secondary school teachers to China for five weeks.

The Committee has sponsored the U.S.-China dialogue program annually since 1984 as a joint project with the Chinese People's Institute of Foreign Affairs (CPIFA), the Committee's oldest counterpart. The project, funded by the Ford Foundation, has aimed to increase mutual understanding among senior leaders in the United States and China, and build a network for interpersonal relations.

Another recent significant program was the Foundation Executives Delegation to China in July 1993 to examine the development of philanthropy and the emergence of NGOs in China. This project was partially funded by the Starr and Henry Jackson Foundations. The National Committee and the Atlantic Council jointly undertook a year-long policy project in 1992 and released a policy paper entitled United States and China Relations at a Crossroads, in 1993, which made specific recommendations for U.S. policies. The project was supported by the Ford Foundation, the Luce Foundation, and RBF.

g. Other Bilateral Organizations

The China Institute of America, founded in 1926, is known as "the granddaddy of all China exchanges and educational institutions." The Luce foundation has given long, sustained support to the Institute, including its major gift to the construction of its China House in New York as the "cultural center" of Sino-American relations.

Modeled after the Japan Society, the Korea Society was established in 1957 to promote greater awareness, understanding, and cooperation between the Untied States and South Korea. Its programs include education, public policy, business, the arts, and media. The Society is supported by U.S. and Korean corporations and foundations. Another more recent creation is the America-China Society, a high-level group, which was charted in 1987 by Henry Kissinger and Cyrus Vance.

3. Promoting Intellectual and Policy Dialogue

In the postwar years, as Russell Phillips of RBF noted, American philanthropic leaders became acutely aware that there was a virtual vacuum of intellectual and policy dialogue between the United States and Asia; American leaders did not know their Asian counterparts and Asians themselves did not know each other within the region. Hence, various efforts were initiated to address these problems. Private philanthropy in the promotion of international, interregional, and region-U.S. dialogue has played a very important role.

a. Intellectual Interchange Program

The earliest postwar Intellectual Interchange Program began in 1952 under the leadership of Matsumoto of the I-House and JDR, who provided the endowment. The Japan Society with the selection committee at the East Asian Institute of Columbia University became the U.S. counterparts of the I-House in running the programs. A number of prominent intellectual leaders have visited each other's country through this program.

b. Dartmouth Conference

Matsumoto also worked with John Dickey, then-president of Dartmouth College, to organize the 1962 Dartmouth Conference, perhaps the first of the intellectual exchange conferences between Japan and the United States. Some of the subjects discussed there included the problems of Communist China, disarmament, economic and trade relations, and the status of democracy in Japan and the United States. Around that time, a few other intellectual exchange or policy dialogue programs started, often with funding from U.S. donors such as the Ford Foundation and the Rockefeller Foundation. In 1993, RBF made a grant of $80,000 to I-House toward two conferences with Dartmouth's Nelson Rockefeller Center for the Social Sciences.

c. Williamsburg Conference

One example of very early Asia Pacific regional dialogue activity is the Williamsburg Conference series. Initiated in 1971 by JDR, the conference provides a high-level forum for candid, off-the-record discussions on key issues affecting the Asia Pacific region. Its model was the Bilderberg Conferences for U.S. and European leaders. The original co-conveners were JDR, Saburo Okita, and Soedjatmoko. The 1994 annual conference, its twenty-second round, was held in March 1994 in Hanoi. Some fifty participants from fourteen Asia Pacific nations attended the meeting, currently co-convened by Tommy Koh, Yoshio Okawara and Cyrus Vance. The I House, Tokyo and the Asia Society administered the conference. Initially funded by JDR, the conferences have also been supported by U.S. and Asian foundations and corporations.

d. Shimoda Conference

In the 1960s with Japan's rapid economic growth, accompanied by increasing friction with the United States over trade, security, and other policy issues, Japan and its relations with the United States started attracting the attention of private and public American leaders. The first national conference on Japan and the United States was organized by the American Assembly of Columbia University, largely funded by the Ford Foundation. Its follow-up conference, the first American-Japanese Assembly, which later came to be known as the Shimoda Conference, was sponsored by the Assembly and the precursor group of JCIE. The U.S. cosponsor later became the Japan Society. It was probably the first high-level, large-scale U.S.-Japan policy dialogue.

The latest round, Shimoda IX, was held in the fall of 1994 in Awashima, Japan, as a part of a three-part conference series on the theme of "Japan and the United States in Asia Pacific," through cooperation with the American Assembly again and the Institute of Southeast Asian Studies in Singapore. Shimoda IX thus expanded the hitherto U.S.-Japan bilateral conference to a broader Asia Pacific policy forum focusing on the United States, Japan, and Asia Pacific. The Ford Foundation, an original funder along with contributions from several Japanese businesses, has continued to support Shimoda, while other U.S. and Japanese donors, including RBF, the

Luce Foundation, the MacArthur Foundation, the Japan Foundation, and the Center for Global Partnership have joined in supporting it.

Following up on a recommendation made at Shimoda I by Senator Mike Mansfield, JCIE and Columbia University, with a ten year funding commitment from the Ford Foundation, established the U.S.-Japan Parliamentary Exchange Program in 1978. It is now in its twenty-seventh year and is cosponsored by the Japan Society with broad support from U.S. and Japanese foundations and corporations.

Above are just several examples of earlier and better known intellectual exchange and policy dialogue programs involving American, Japanese and other Asian leaders. Today, there are numerous such programs. For example, since 1990 the Japan Society has sponsored the annual seminar of the David MacEachron Policy Forum bringing together leaders from Japan, the United States, and other Asia Pacific countries to discuss key policy issues in U.S.-Japan relations in a broader context. The U.S.-Japan Global Forum of the Center for Strategic and International Studies (CSIS), begun in 1991 as an evolutionary transformation of "The Quadrangular Forum," is funded by CGP and other U.S. foundations. The forum has sponsored high-level policy-makers' conferences on the global environment, regionalism, and Asia Pacific cooperation. The Stanford University Asia/Pacific Research Center (A/PARC) in 1994 initiated an annual Asian-U.S. Leaders Conference, a small but top-level leaders' policy-oriented intellectual dialogue. It is funded by the JL Foundation in Los Angeles.

IV. Developing Research Institutions and Policy Dialogue in Asia Pacific

Independent research institutions are a very important leg of a civil society. They ensure pluralistic, alternative sources of the public policy-making process as well as nongovernmental, intellectual, and policy dialogue. Particularly in the field of international relations, independent research institutions can be very effective facilitators of unofficial diplomacy, as eloquently demonstrated by the role the Royal Institute of International Affairs and the Council on Foreign Relations played in postwar Atlantic relations. However, in the countries whose philanthropic sector is underdeveloped, as is the case in most developing countries, it is very difficult to manage independent research. Often times, institutions have to rely on income sources that may hamper their independence. Thus, in the absence or shortage of domestic funding sources, assistance from international philanthropy can have a profound effect on the development of this part of a civil society.

1. Institution-Building

It is a well-known fact that U.S. foundations have played a critical role in developing these institutions in East and Southeast Asian countries. In fact, it is believed that some of the institutions in Asian countries that have since become major players in this field, may not have even survived their embryonic state without U.S. foundations' generous and timely support. The genesis of the IRRI and the role of the Ford and Rockefeller Foundations was discussed earlier. Somewhat less known than the case of IRRI is the role of the Ford Foundation in the establishment of the Indonesian Institute of the Sciences (LIPI) which hosts more than twenty research centers, including the Centre for Political and Regional Studies and the Centre for Economic and Development Studies. The Ford Foundation helped to establish the LIPI, which is now a governmental institution and expected to provide the basis of the establishment of the country's National Academy of Sciences.

2. Support for Regional Intellectual and Policy Dialogue

Practically all of the major research institutions in East and Southeast Asian countries, particularly those policy-oriented, international-minded institutions that are the major subjects of the current project, have benefited greatly from the generous assistance of U.S. foundations. For instance, participants of the conference on "The Future of Asia Pacific Security Studies and Exchange Activities" (12–15 December 1993, Bali, Indonesia) noted that in Asia Pacific, "the United States' thirteen foundations provide almost all of the private funding available for security studies, and of these, six provide over ninety percent."[2]

In 1991, major U.S. foundations donated a total of $5.2 million to security studies in the region, while the figure went up to $6.4 million in 1992. This situation is not at all confined to the field of security studies, and more or less a similar observation can be made of various fields such as economic development and other social sciences. In the year 1992–93, a total of $34.6 million was granted from U.S. foundations for the Asia Pacific countries as defined in the current project. This grant total occupies 7.5 percent of the total grants for foreign and international programs by U.S. foundations, while 13.2 percent ($25.8 million) was provided for projects in Asia Pacific in 1993–94. These figures represent a substantial increase from ten years ago (i.e., $7.7 million in 1983 and $9.1 million in 1984).

The list of grants of the Asia Foundation, the Ford Foundation, and the Rockefeller Brothers Fund in the past few years include a large number of Asia Pacific research institution grantees. Most notably, a large number of Chinese research institutions are listed as recipients including the gigantic Chinese Academy of Social Sciences (CASS), the Beijing Institute of International Strategic Studies, the Institute of International Relations, Peking University's Institute of International Relations, the Shanghai Academy of Social Sciences, the Shanghai Institute for International Studies, the China Center for International Studies, the China Institute of Contemporary International Relations, and the China Institute of International Studies. An expert on China can testify that this is by itself a list of major research institutions in China. In recent reform movements, CASS institutes, which used to be financed one hundred percent by the government, are now forced to finance two-thirds of their budgets by nongovernmental sources.[3] Under these circumstances, the presence of the Ford Foundation, whose annual budget for China alone exceeds $7 million, has been critical.

Next to China, institutions in ASEAN countries have relied heavily on grants from U.S. foundations. The Institute of Southeast Asian Studies (ISEAS), indisputably the most well known research institution in Southeast Asia and perhaps the world's leading regional research center on Southeast Asian studies (founded in 1968 with Ford seed money), for instance, appears often in the grants lists of major U.S. foundations, particularly of those aforementioned three and the Rockefeller and MacArthur Foundations. In 1989, ISEAS received from U.S. foundations grants of $780,369 or 38.6 percent of total donations and grants received in the year, $564,556 (27.2 percent) in 1990, and $849,810 (30.3 percent) in 1991. In 1992, the Ford Foundation alone donated $960,886 which was 41 percent of the total grants and donations received.

Similar things can be said about most other major research institutions in Southeast Asia, including the Centre for Strategic and International Studies, Jakarta; the Institute of Strategic and International Studies (ISIS), Kuala Lumpur; the Institute of Strategic and Development Studies, Philippines; the Singapore Institute of International Affairs; and Chulalongkorn University's Institute of Security and International Studies, Thailand. Together, in 1988, these five institutions formed a nongovernmental forum, the ASEAN Institutes of Strategic and International Studies (ASEAN-ISIS).

Today, ASEAN-ISIS has developed into one of the world's most effective regional nongovernmental organizations whose achievements include the launching of the ASEAN Regional Forum (ARF), the first regional governmental-level security forum in Asia Pacific that encompasses diverse economic and political systems. The ARF is a product of ASEAN-ISIS's proposal to the ASEAN Post-Ministerial Conference (ASEAN-PMC) regarding the initiation of discussions on critical but sensitive issues including regional politico-security dialogue. It has been pointed out that this formidable ASEAN-ISIS is, essentially, a product of friendship among heads of major research institutions who frequently meet and get acquainted in international conferences and other programs sponsored by either one of the respective institutes or by American institutions. One of the characteristics of U.S. foundations' grants on these ASEAN institutions has been the outstanding number of international conferences and other forms of intellectual dialogue for which these grants are used. Therefore, it is by no means an exaggeration to state that ASEAN-ISIS would not have emerged without the contributions from U.S. foundations.

V. Promoting Asia-Related Regional Studies in the United States

1. Asian Studies

In the early postwar period, in the field of Asian Studies, some major universities harbored a nuclei of scholars who had studied Chinese literature or history. There was also a handful of language and area experts trained to carry on activities by the war efforts. Many of the "second generation" of Japan specialists belonged to this group. The study of Southeast Asia had barely begun and, among social scientists, only historians and anthropologists had been involved in foreign area studies.

The emergence of the United States as a global power after World War II underscored the national need for competence and expertise in "non-Western" societies. Some foundations, notably Ford, decided that knowledge about foreign areas could be best developed by supporting training and research within universities.

Between the 1950s and 1970s, Asian studies grew and thrived in U.S. colleges and universities. Much of this growth was financed and encouraged by the largesse, first of major foundations, some of which had helped to pioneer U.S. academic interests in Asia, and on the massive scale of the deferral government (especially through Title VI of the National Defense Education Act of 1958, and later through the Higher Education Act of 1965 and Fulbright support. Title VI has been the major federal initiative for strengthening American education in foreign languages, and in area and international studies.) In the 1960s and 1970s, this growth was further impelled by expanded support, both foundation and federal, for international educational exchange involving both students and faculty from the United States and Asia. There are at least ninety centers for Asian Studies that currently exist.

However, since the 1980s, there has been a long-term erosion of federal financial support, along with more recent budgetary pressures affecting universities and their priorities. For Title VI, the budget declined from $64 million in 1967 to $28 million in 1991. The Foreign Language and Area Studies Fellowships (FLAS) component of Title VI, which supports academic year and summer fellowships for graduate training, was reduced from more than 2,500 FLAS fellowships in the mid-1960s to 600–800 per year in the mid-1980s. Major foundations, including the Ford and Mellon Foundations, have terminated their programs and moved into other fields of new concerns including Eastern European, Middle Eastern, and Latin American studies.

Against this generally gloomy trend, however, U.S. involvement in Asia has increased significantly over the last two decades and is expected to grow in the years to come, given the growing trade and investment relations between the United States and Asia Pacific. For example, in spite of the shrinking budget, the number and quality of applications for the Fulbright program for doctoral research in the Asia Pacific has been rising as has the number of students registering for courses on Asia in many universities and colleges.

A notable recent trend shows that foundation support for research, exchange, and dialogue has grown and continues to focus more on broader regional and global issues of Asia Pacific rather than country-specific programs. The Luce Foundation remains firmly committed to the support of Asian Studies through its Fund for Asian Studies, U.S.-China Cooperative Research Program, and the new Fund for Southeast Asian Studies. Corporate leaders have recognized the value of international education, and hence, corporate support is likely to increase. Finally, considerable growth has developed in philanthropy in Asia and some foundations have begun to assist U.S. institutions in area studies. It seems that this new trend will continue in the future.

The Role of Foundations in Developing Asian Studies

During the period of growth and prosperity for Asian studies between the 1950s and 1970s, foundation support for the training of individuals and the improvement or creation of institutions was substantial. The most active funding sources included the Ford, Rockefeller, Mellon, Starr, and Luce Foundations. Like Ford, the Mellon Foundation followed a long-term approach with endowment grants in 1977 and 1986 providing ongoing support for East Asian studies (China, Japan, and Korea), totaling $9.25 million on a matching basis to nine universities.

1) The Ford Foundation's Foreign Area Studies Program

The Foreign Area Studies program is one of the two most important contributions made by the Ford Foundation in its international programs and is especially relevant for Asia Pacific, according to Frank Sutton (who is presently writing a book on the history of the Ford Foundation). It had an enormous impact on U.S. graduate education in the field of international studies, as many Asian studies centers or country studies centers at major universities were either created or substantially supported by Ford. The Association of Asian Studies and other country-specific associations and consortia were also started with Ford funding.

In the 1980s, by which time the area studies program had been phased out, Ford spent over $400 million on foreign area studies. Of this sum, $62 million was spent on Asian area studies programs. Almost all of this money was used in the United States. Its strategy was to first move toward supporting the training of individuals, and then to try to improve or, if necessary, create institutions. It aimed to support both the development of experts through training and the development of knowledge through research. Ideally, these goals coincide with the fellowship program when advanced degree students prepare their dissertations. The Foundation's Foreign Area Fellowship Program, which awards American and Canadian students' graduate training involving overseas research, began in 1952. The amount given totaled $45 million, which included not only Asia, though Asia fellows were by far the largest group. The fellowships carried considerable prestige, and a high proportion of today's foreign-area scholars are alumni of the program. The program was administered by ACLS and SSRC.

Another major component of the Foreign Area Studies program was the support to universities, specifically to area studies and notably to Asian studies. Beginning in 1960, multimillion-dollar grants went to Asian studies centers at such universities as Harvard, Chicago, Columbia, California (Berkeley), UCLA, Stanford, Cornell, Michigan, MIT, Indiana, and Yale. Smaller grants went to Princeton and the University of Pennsylvania. Other recipients included Duke, Denver, Washington, Michigan State, and Pittsburgh. These grants totaled some $190 million. (Its more specific role in support of Chinese studies and Southeast Asian studies is discussed below.)

2) Henry Luce Foundation—Fund for Asian Studies
Much smaller than Ford, the Luce Foundation currently devotes over 30 percent of its annual budget to Asia-related programs. In the 1970s, U.S. universities were beginning to weaken their Asian programs. This was due to cut-backs of federal funding and declining foundation support. The Foundation then established the Luce Fund for Asian Studies in 1975, committing $3 million over a seven-year period to increase "the understanding of U.S.-Asian relationships at every level: historical, economic, cultural, and political." Eleven academic institutions concentrating on East Asian studies were specifically chosen to be recipients of the Foundation's support. The breakdown of the $3 million expended was: China ($828,000), Japanese studies ($529,500), East Asia general ($459,500), Southeast Asia ($346,000), all-Asia ($334,000), Korea ($320,000), Philippines ($140,000), and Taiwan ($64,000). The eleven designated institutions included (in the order of the size of receipts): Columbia, Harvard, Michigan, Chicago, Cornell, Stanford, and Princeton.

Although the Fund was closed in 1982, the Luce Foundation has continued to fund various Asia projects ($6 million in 1992–93)—research, cultural and scholarly exchange, and public education and public policy programs. The Foundation also established the Luce Fund for Chinese Scholars, the U.S.-China Cooperative Research Program, and the newest Luce Fund for Southeast Asian Studies. (These programs are also discussed below).

2. Japanese Studies

a. Overviews

A comprehensive study has been done on the status of Japanese studies in the United States by the Japan Foundation with the Association of Asian Studies. The most recent study has been summarized by Professor Patricia Steinhoff in the Japan Foundation's *Japanese Studies in the United States: Directory of Japan Specialists and Japanese Studies Institutions in the United States and Canada* (1995). According to Dr. Steinhoff, there were some 1,858 Japan experts (thirty percent more than in 1989) and 841 Ph.D. candidates (nearly twice as many as in 1989) in Japanese studies in the United States and Canada as of 1994. Most of these Japanese studies specialists belonged to universities and/or other advanced institutions. The number of Japan specialists in the United States in 1975 was 846. That number increased to 1,025 in the 1982–83 academic year, and to 1,224 in 1988. Though it is not possible to compare these numbers with other area specialists, this is a rather impressive rate of expansion. Today, the field of Japanese studies in the United States is widely dispersed or laterally spread; educational programs on Japan are available in nearly every state of the Union. Steinhoff reported in 1988 that thirty-five large Japanese studies programs were available in the United States, and that there has been a pronounced westward shift over the past thirty years.

While it is reported that in 1974 the number of the institutions with eight or more Japan specialists in the entire United States was 26, the number of institutions with more than ten specialists had increased to 35 by 1989. The institutions with a large number of Japan specialists include: the University of Hawaii (67 Japan specialists), the University of Michigan (46), the University of Southern California (35), Ohio State University (32), Columbia University (31), Stanford University (29), the University of Wisconsin (24), the University of Chicago (24), Brigham Young University (24), and UC Berkeley (23). They all have major Japanese studies centers or Japan programs within Asian studies centers. The number of American institutions with at least one Japan specialist was as high as 304 as of 1989. The number of specialists in the social sciences concentrating on contemporary Japan has substantially increased, opening the way for policy-oriented dialogue and intellectual exchange between Americans and Japanese.

b. Funding Sources

As for the financial sources of these Japanese studies in the United States, the 1988 report indicates that two-thirds of the funding comes from American governmental and private sources with private foundations contributing as much as one-third. Contributions from Japanese sources were a little over twenty percent in the same year. In the 1982–83 academic year, financial contributions from Japan comprised approximately three-fourths of the entire funding for Japanese studies, due to the large number of grants and donations from the Japan Foundation and several Japanese corporations. However, the same report speculates that if all the miscellaneous costs of Japanese studies (such as salaries and indirect costs) were included, it would be clear that most of the burden has been borne by American funding sources. Furthermore, trips to Japan, for instance, were mostly financed by American sources.

The Japan Foundation has been an important source of support. The addition of The Center for Global Partnership (CGP), an affiliate fund, has extended substantial funding in the field of policy studies, as well as advanced research through the SSRC-administered Abe Fellows program.

Another important source of funding for Japanese studies on the U.S. side is the Japan-United States Friendship Commission, a government foundation. Congress created the Commission in 1975 to strengthen the cultural and intellectual foundations of the U.S.-Japan relationship. Of the four program categories established in 1977, Japanese studies in American Education received the highest ratio of annual budget allocation—about forty percent. The Commission has annually provided $1.5 to 2 million for this purpose. The single largest beneficiary over many years is the Inter-University Center for Japanese Language Studies in Yokohama, Japan, the leading and most effective institution for advanced training of American graduate students in the Japanese language, with annual support averaging around ¥50 million.

The 1989 report claims that, quite aside from its own findings, "there are indications that both public and private U.S. support is declining, while Japanese support in increasing." Japan is by far the best funded area studies field in the United States and this is primarily due to the initiatives of Japanese government and corporate foundations. CGP has added substantial funding in the field of policy studies, as well as fellowships through the SSRC-administered Abe Fellowship Program. Investment in Japanese studies by Japanese has been much based on the theory that better American understanding of Japan will help to sustain this critical bilateral relationship.

While the increase of the contributions from Japan is undoubtedly welcome, this tendency should be carefully observed to determine whether it is a sign of declining interest in Japanese studies on the part of U.S. foundations. In fact, several American participants at a conference on U.S.-Japan intellectual exchange, organized by RBF in September 1990, expressed concern over what seems to be a shift of emphasis away from Japanese studies in recent grant making by American foundations.

Shortage of funds indeed seems to be a serious concern among traditional American Japanologists, and Professor Marius Jansen, chair of the Asian Studies Department at Princeton University, decries the relative decline and absolute shortage of funding for Japanese language instructors and improving specialized libraries.[4] He claims that "additional support for libraries, for language study, and for research possibilities, are neither 'innovative' nor attractive for funding agencies, but they are urgent for the continued health of the field," and urges the American foundations and other funding agencies to continue supporting these activities.

3. Chinese Studies

a. Overview

Even prior to President Nixon's trip to China in 1972, which reopened the door, both private and federal funding sources in the United States invested heavily in contemporary China studies during the late 1950s and 1960s, and had already built up a substantial scholarly and institutional base for understanding China. According to Terrill Lautz of the Luce Foundation, this is an excellent example of the foresight of U.S. philanthropy. In 1991, forty percent (2,285) of the 5,713 members of the Association for Asian Studies (AAS) were listed as China specialists. During the period 1952–79, for example, the Ford Foundation invested more than $40 million to promote the understanding of China. Support was given for major university centers of Chinese studies, including the Fairbank Center at Harvard, the Center for Chinese Studies at Michigan, the East Asian Institute at Columbia, and the Institute of East Asian Studies at UC Berkeley. Funding was also provided for SSRC's China Committee, ACLS, and AAS. Since the late 1960s, Ford has also made grants to the Committee on Scholarly Communication with the People's Republic of China (CSCPRC) and to the National Committee on U.S.-China Relations, two organizations that have played a prominent role in Sino-American relations.

As U.S.-China relations have matured over the past decade, the funding patterns of U.S. foundations have shifted from support for China studies at U.S. universities toward China itself. Also, foundations appear more interested in new areas—exchanges, training, and development and research programs in China—rather than Chinese studies per se. The 1989 Tiananmen incident did not change U.S. foundation programs as grant makers believed that engagement offered the best chances for ongoing reform.

The Rockefeller Foundation supports research programs in China in the fields of agriculture, health, population, and the environment. Ford has addressed the development of sociology, economics, and international relations in China; it is now turning to issues such as rural poverty and women's health. These programs have certainly enhanced American understanding of contemporary China, but the problem is that support for American students and scholars in the academic study of China has become a by-product, rather than the chief objective, of development assistance in China. Given the shrinkage of external funding for area studies in general, in addition to the above complexities, the picture of Chinese studies has become more complex and difficult. In fact, many U.S. universities with extensive involvement with their counterparts in China find it increasingly difficult to maintain the costly infrastructure for China studies on their own campuses.

b. Funding Sources

Today, over twenty major China or East Asian study centers exist, but they have faced cut-backs of both federal and foundation support. ACLS and SSRC have curtailed the number and size of their grants for area studies programs.

Major donors for China studies have been on the private side, the Ford, Luce, MacArthur, Mellon, Rockefeller, Starr, Lingnan, and Kunstadter Foundations, RBF, and the United Board for Christian Higher Education in Asia; and on the federal side, CSCPRC, U.S.I.A., the National Science Foundation, and the National Endowment for Humanities. Only two new "players" have joined. One is the Freeman Foundation, and the other is the Taiwan-based Chiang Ching-kuo (CCK) Foundation for International Cultural Exchange, which has become a major new source of funding for China studies in the United States. It provides, for example, approximately $300,000 per year to ACLS in support of fellowships in Chinese studies.

There is no formal group or consortium of U.S. foundations in support of China studies or related programs, although there have been some informal groups that meet primarily for information exchange. Russell Phillips of RBF has sponsored occasional breakfast meetings with several key foundations interested in Asia in general, not just China. The "Lingnan Luncheon Club" chaired by Douglas Murray, Lingnan Foundation president, regularly meets to exchange information and share experiences of participating China-related institutions. Over seventy members from foundations and exchange, academic, and educational groups belong to the group.

Still another is the occasional "China Grantmakers Meeting", jointly organized by Douglas Murray and William Sawyer, president of the China Medical Board. Senior executives of fifteen foundations interested in China are members and meet for information exchange and the discussion of major issues facing U.S. grant makers in China.

During the "development decade," as characterized by Terrill Lautz, from 1959 to 1970, Ford invested $23.8 million; the U.S. government, $15 million; and U.S. universities, $15 million in China studies. Ford's strategy was to concentrate on a limited number of key university centers, as discussed above. Funds were mainly channeled to nine institutions and national research and fellowship programs administered by SSRC and ACLS. Ford's grants were also given to the U.S. National Academy of Sciences for scientific and scholarly exchanges with PRC. It moved away from funding China studies in the United States during the mid-1970s due to budget cuts and changing priorities. Ford has since developed sizable training and development programs in China, and established the first U.S. foundation office in Beijing in 1988.

The MacArthur Foundation has provided substantial support for international relations and policy studies programs concerned with China. RBF supports environmental and international relations projects dealing with China and other parts of Asia. The Starr Foundation had funded many excellent China-related projects, including some based at universities (major funding to renovate Columbia's East Asian Library, now The Starr Library, is one example). The Dodge Foundation has funded an innovative program to introduce Chinese language instruction at the high school level for the past several years. The Kunstadter Foundation provided modest but well-chosen assistance to various China projects. In the late 1980s, the Wang Corporation sponsored a postdoctoral fellowship program for American scholars.

The United Board for Christian Higher Education in Asia has supported many Chinese students and visiting scholars at U.S. institutions of higher education. The Lingnan Foundation supports programs at Zhongshan University in Guangzhou, the Chinese University of Hong Kong, and Lingnan College in Hong Kong. The Asia Foundation has sponsored training programs for Chinese specialists in the fields of law, foreign affairs, and business management. Over the years, both Ford and Mellon have invested several million dollars in grants for ACLS/SSRC-sponsored China programs.

The Luce Foundation has had a long-standing interest in China and U.S.-China relations. It has worked, primarily through support for research and academic exchange programs at the post-doctoral level, to improve Americans' understanding of China. During the 1980s, Luce funded a program for senior PRC scholars to visit U.S. campuses, called The Luce Fund for Chinese Scholars. A cluster of projects on the history of Christianity in China has been another area of special interest. Under the U.S.-China Cooperative Research Program, Luce has more recently supported many three-year cooperative research projects between Chinese and American scholars in the humanities and social sciences (thirty projects totaling more than $5 million since 1988).

4. Korean and Southeast Asian Studies

a. Korean Studies

Korean studies is far less developed than Japanese and Chinese studies in the United States and has remained quite small even in recent years. As South Korea has emerged as a major economic power in Asia Pacific, more attention has been gradually given to the development of the field of Korean studies, which is badly understaffed. There are not many teaching and research centers actively involved to date. However, many observers think that Korean studies is likely to grow, especially given the fact that the Korea Foundation, a new large foundation, and the Korea Research Foundation have been aggressively investing in developing the field at U.S. universities as the Japan Foundation has done in Japanese studies. The former gave $9 million to Harvard two years ago for the endowment of a chair in Korean studies.

b. Southeast Asian Studies

Southeast Asian studies remains largely underdeveloped in the United States. One expert interviewed for this report said that Southeast Asia is an "orphan" of Asian studies. The reasons behind this are (*a*) diversity of the region in terms of culture and language, (*b*) the history of colonialism, which is often still a politically divisive issue, and (*c*) the Vietnam war experience. Given the virtual absence of any academic programs on Southeast Asia in prewar American universities, the development of area and international studies in the 1950s and 1960s significantly increased the number of scholars and students, as well as university programs, focusing on the region.

By the late 1960s, there were Southeast Asia centers at seven or eight institutions and over five hundred Southeast Asia specialists. In 1988, the AAS membership included 630 Southeast Asia specialists. Compared with overall membership growth in the AAS membership, including Japan and China specialists (over 1,800 and 2,200 respectively), the number of Southeast Asianists has been declining. There was even a withdrawal of some Southeast Asian studies programs and fellowships after 1975. Only in the late 1980s, ten years later, was there a revival of interest in Southeast Asian studies. This is mainly because of (*a*) dynamic economic growth of the region, (*b*) the huge number of immigrants from the region resettled in the United States, and (*c*) a gradual opening up of and access to countries like Vietnam, Cambodia, Laos, and Myanmar. The first generation of immigrants' children are now attending U.S. universities and demanding such study centers or study programs.

To respond to such a new need and challenge, the Luce Foundation in the late 1980s earmarked $8 million to the Luce Fund for Southeast Asian studies. It then provided an additional three to four million dollars for eleven universities singled out because they already had existing centers for Southeast Asian studies that needed to be revitalized and improved. They indeed needed a boost. Yale and Cornell universities were strong in the 1950s but badly needed new sources of funding by the 1980s. Luce's beneficiaries have been Arizona State, Cornell, Northern Illinois, the Northwest Regional Consortium for Southeast Asian Studies (Oregon and Washington), Ohio, UC Berkeley, Hawaii, Michigan, Wisconsin-Madison, and Yale. Terrill Lautz believes that perhaps Luce had a greater impact in Southeast Asian studies than in Chinese studies because the former is a smaller field with much greater fundamental needs on the part of universities. The Foundation has given seed money for faculty positions, library development, and student fellowships.

VI. Broadening Regional Intellectual Interaction

In the late 1970s the concept of pan-Pacific cooperation, advocated by the late Japanese prime minister, Masayoshi Ohira, and by influential groups in the United States and Australia, received little interest or attention in the ASEAN region and the Pacific Rim area. However, by the late 1980s and especially in the early 1990s, there has been a growing interest in the Asia Pacific regional community. This has been enhanced by fundamental changes in the international and regional environments and subsequently has raised new and real challenges to public policy making within the region. It has also encouraged many private research and academic institutions to undertake an increasing number of joint research projects and policy-oriented dialogue in recent years on political-security issues, economic issues, global and common issues.[5] It should be noted that many of these important endeavors were initially supported by U.S. foundations, with subsequent participation by private and public sources of funding in Asia.

One significant development in joint-research and dialogue in recent years is the active participation of or even initiatives taken by emerging economic powers in Asia, such as ASEAN countries. It was noted at the time of the Asian Dialogue (currently the ASEAN-Japan Dialogue Program) meeting, in Oiso in 1980 organized by JCIE and supported by the Ford Foundation, that, "serious attention to the possibilities of expanded Pacific economic cooperation was confined to relatively small circles in Japan, Australia, and the United States," and "in particular, the ASEAN perspective was conspicuously lacking."[6] This new assertiveness of Asian intellectual leaders reflects substantial changes in intellectual interactions within the region in this new era. Indeed, the prospects of the emergence of some form of regional community presents a new and challenging set of research agenda which have to be addressed jointly by intellectual leaders of the countries in the Asia Pacific region.

There have been a considerable number of joint research projects and conferences on the theme of the Pacific economic community over the years. In the early years, the Pacific Basin Economic Council (PBEC) was formed in 1967 by business leaders from the five advanced Pacific nations to discuss issues raised in regional trade and investment, and greater cooperation between public and private interests; the Pacific Trade and Development Conference series (PAFTAD) followed in 1968 involving policy-oriented economists which provided a forum for policy-relevant discussions on trade, investment and development issues in the Asia Pacific region; and in 1980 the Pacific Economic Cooperation Committee (PECC) was formed with the tripartite participation of academics, businessmen, and government officials at the initiative of Japanese Prime Minister Ohira and Australian Prime Minister Fraser. PAFTAD and PECC, both aided by Ford, The Asia Foundation and RBF, among others, have paved the way for the founding of the Asia Pacific Economic Cooperation (APEC) forum.

These conferences and research projects have considerably enhanced collaboration among economic research institutions as well as economists, researchers, and practitioners of the region's nations. With a new set of critical policy issues in trade, investment, development assistance and other economic spheres, there is a greater amount of interaction among research institutions and economic departments of universities within the region. According to JCIE's survey, it is clear that the absence of a sufficient number of institutions that can undertake these activities is a major constraint in the further promotion of such critical activities. Similarly, it is clear that these joint studies and dialogue programs require a new cadre of intellectual leaders in most of the countries in the region. The situation is further exacerbated by a serious shortage of scholars and experts who can effectively participate in these programs, thus creating a situation of same old faces coming together in different parts of Asia Pacific.

A study of data collection in connection with JCIE's survey project also indicates a marked increase of joint research and policy-oriented dialogue in the security field in recent years. One recent effort, an enormous contribution in providing a comprehensive picture of the growth of regional intellectual interaction in Asian Pacific security issues, is a joint project undertaken by the University of Toronto-York University's Joint Centre for Asian Pacific Studies, and the Centre for Strategic and International Studies in Jakarta. This study project resulted in a major publication entitled *Studying Asia Pacific Security: The Future of Research Training and Dialogue Activities*[7] based on the Bali Conference in December 1993, "The Future of Asia Pacific Security Studies and Exchange Activities."

The conference involved some sixty participants from universities, research institutes, foundations, and government agencies in seventeen countries. The conference and publication were jointly financed by the Ford, Asia, MacArthur, Sasakawa Peace, and Chaiyong (Bangkok) Foundations, RBF and CGP. Subsequently, the Ford Foundation made a grant to Dr. Evans and his Joint Centre for the "Dialogue Monitor"—An Inventory of Multilateral Meetings on Asia Pacific Security Issues. Its first issue, which was released in July 1995, has identified more than two hundred ongoing dialogues. There is also an increasing number of regional joint studies and dialogue on regional security matters.

These efforts include, in 1988, the establishment of ASEAN-ISIS, an organization of security research institutes, and its Asia Pacific Roundtable held annually in Kuala Lumpur, and most recently CSCAP (Council for Security Cooperation in Asia Pacific) in 1993, a broader group of ten research institutes. Most member institutes of ASEAN-ISIS have been heavily supported by the Ford Foundation and other U.S. foundations. Ford also provides partial funding for ASEAN-ISIS conferences.

Not unlike the problems related to research and dialogue on economic issues, a dearth of research institutions, a shortage of experts, and inadequate financial support constrain these security-related activities, which have increased in demand. It is noticeable that U.S. foundations continue to play a major role in this field, as they have done in the past, although there are some signs of increasing support from Japanese funding sources such as the Sasakawa Peace Foundation and CGP.

As of late, there has been an exploration for a new regional security arrangement to broaden participation of existing regional organizations, thus expanding consultations on security cooperation, and establishing new structures and processes to address issues related to regional security cooperation. Formation of the ASEAN Regional Forum (ARF) and its first meeting in Bangkok in 1994, is a first step in this direction. There is clear recognition at the government level, as well as in the private sector, that there should be concerted efforts to promote dialogue on regional security issues.

In addition to economic and security issues, there is the growing importance of a new set of issues that may come under the rubric of "global issues," which are gaining more salience in regional community building. Environmental issues are perhaps the most critical for the Asia Pacific region. Another "global issue" in the region is related to demographic changes in the region creating the serious challenge of migration movements. Still other region-wide concerns are the questions associated with changes or potential changes in political values and rights. Divergent approaches to such issues, as exist between the United States and Japan, can have deep political, as well as economic, implications. Addressing such issues in a dispassionate and analytical manner will be a necessary requirement in the process of building a regional community. Other issues with regional implications that are gaining importance in Asia include AIDS, improved cooperation in combating terrorism and the exportation of drugs, facilitating Asia Pacific cooperation in science and technology for development, and developing regional labor standards.

As documented in the details of the Morrison paper and the JCIE directory, the writer simply wants to note that U.S. foundations, research institutions and NGOs have already started addressing many of the political-security and economic issues, as well as regional and global issues. It is valuable to emphasize that these projects are financed not only by U.S. foundations but also by Asian sources and involve research institutions and researchers in Asia. It is hoped that they will also contribute to the promotion of regional intellectual interaction. Some of the most notable and current "giant" projects include the Asia Program of the Council on Foreign Relations, the Asia Pacific regional economic integration project by the Institute for International Economics, Brookings Institution's world economic integration project focusing on Asia Pacific, and the Rockefeller Foundation initiatives on nuclear monitoring in Asia Pacific—including in North Korea—as part of its global environment program.

As the Asia Pacific region moves to a new era with potential for the emergence of a regional community, there will be a growing number of region wide issues that will need to be addressed. There will clearly be a need for much greater intellectual interactions in the form of joint studies and dialogues. Building the capacity to carry on such tasks is obviously the fundamental challenge facing the region. Philanthropic cooperation will serve a special purpose to enhance such regional efforts

VII. Promoting Private Philanthropy in Asia

Several U.S. foundations, notably, the Ford and Asia Foundations and RBF, have put high program priority on supporting efforts to develop and expand the community of private philanthropy and nongovernmental institutions in Asia Pacific.

a. JCIE's International Philanthropy Project

JCIE launched the International Philanthropy Project in 1974 to help develop private philanthropy and good corporate citizenship in Japan and promote U.S.-Japan philanthropic cooperation. In recent years, such efforts have been broadened to promote good corporate citizenship by Japanese corporations in the United States and Asia. Most currently, through its 1993–94 survey project, "Nongovernmental Underpinnings of the Emerging Asia Pacific Regional Community," JCIE's efforts are being directed to promote Asia Pacific philanthropic cooperation.[8]

A point of special note is that JCIE's philanthropy project has been generously supported by U.S. foundations, especially Ford and RBF. Also, the Council on Foundations has effectively assisted JCIE in its program efforts whenever needed. The Council, in the initial stage of JCIE's project, not only sponsored the 1994 study mission by Japanese foundation and corporate officials to the United States, but also helped to select participants for the first international conference on private philanthropy, organized by JCIE in 1995. It has cosponsored several other JCIE conferences, as well.

JCIE's past activities to promote philanthropic cooperation in Asia Pacific include a survey report on "Activities of Japanese Nonprofit Organizations in Southeast Asia" (1977); a survey report on "Research Institutes and Development Organizations in Asia (1978); a survey on "Cooperative Activities of American and European Foundations in Asia" (1979); a study mission by foundation and corporate representatives to Southeast Asia (1978); an international symposium on "Priorities for Philanthropy in Southeast Asia" (1979); the establishment of the Asian Community Trust (ACT) (1979); a study mission by Japanese foundation representatives on "Needs of Universities and Research Institutes in Southeast Asia" (1981); a survey on voluntary organizations in Asia (1984); cosponsoring the Keidanren mission on corporate philanthropy in the Asia Pacific region (1992); and a survey project on the "Nongovernmental Underpinnings of the Emerging Asia Pacific Regional Community (1993–94) and the culminating International Symposium in Osaka (1994).

b. Asian Community Trust (ACT)

The Asian Community Trust (ACT) was established in 1979 under JCIE's initiative as Japan's first charitable trust based on general fund raising, and aims to encourage sustainable social and economic development in the Asian community. It is a private, international grant-making organization exclusively devoted to Asia and modeled after the American community foundation concept. ACT provides support to indigenous, locally based NGOs in Asia, and is designed to promote grassroots efforts to develop self-reliant communities. It also seeks, through its grant-making activities to enhance mutual understanding and promote a sense of community among the peoples of Japan and other Asian countries.

By 1994, ACT had made 270 grants worth 340 million yen to NGOs in developing countries in Asia. It has recently received a tax-exempt status comparable to the U.S. 501(c)(3) and is expected to renew its efforts to consolidate the organization. An initial grant made by the Ford Foundation to ACT was for personnel and staff development.

c. Council on Foundations (COF)

In addition to its invaluable assistance to JCIE's philanthropy project, COF has, over the years, provided advice, guidance and technical assistance to many Japanese foundations, scholars, and study missions. From the mid-1980s to the early 1990s, in collaboration with the Sasakawa Peace Foundation, the Council's Institute for New Staff sponsored training workshops specifically tailored for nonprofit staff from Japan and other Asian countries.

Though overall COF programs are designed for member foundations in the United States and COF is not active internationally, in 1982, it formed the Committee for International Grantmakers as one of the standing committees within the Council. Before 1982, it was an ad hoc group of foundations concerned about expanding the number and effectiveness of grants for international purposes. Now renamed as the International Committee, it serves as a planning and advisory group for international programs at the Council. The Committee also sponsors international programs at the annual conference of the Council with some past sessions related to Japanese philanthropy. It has published a guide for international grant making and the Directory for Int*ernational Grantmakers.*

The Council and the International Committee together with the Johnson Foundation cosponsored a conference in 1991, "Western Grantmakers in China" at the

Wingspread Center in Wisconsin to assess U.S. foundations' evolving relationship with China, and to examine the prospects for future grant-making initiatives. As a whole, the Council's and the Committee's interest in Asia Pacific remained marginal. However, in 1994 the Council decided to undertake a major project on Asia for 1995, which is described below.[9]

d. Affinity Group on Japanese Philanthropy (AGJP)

A national affinity group of the Council on Foundations, AGJP, was formed in 1991 as an association of grant-making organizations to provide professional development opportunities to those involved or interested in Japanese philanthropy. It sponsored the seminar "Philanthropy in Japan and Japan in Philanthropy" in 1993 at the Council's annual conference among several other seminars on subjects related to Japanese philanthropy, corporate citizenship, and volunteerism. The Group organized a study tour to Japan for one week in the fall of 1994 which was hosted by the Japan Federation of Economic Organizations (Keidanren). JCIE cooperated in organizing the main programs. The current membership of AGJP, comprising corporations and foundations, is about thirty.

e. Hong Kong Conference: "Corporate Citizenship in Asia Pacific"

Initiated by Delwin Roy of the Hitachi Foundation, an active member of COF's International Committee, the Council decided in early 1994 to implement a special program related to corporate grant making in East Asia—a conference to be held in the fall of 1995. The Joint Working Group on International Corporate Philanthropy was organized under the chairmanship of Dr. Roy. Thus far, three planning meetings have been held, beginning in March 1994. The Council will sponsor a conference on "Corporate Citizenship in Asia Pacific" in Hong Kong—a meeting for a hundred and fifty senior level officers and managers making decisions about corporate giving and corporate community involvement in Asia Pacific. The conference will examine existing and emerging practices of corporate philanthropy and citizenship in Asia Pacific. It will provide an opportunity to exchange perspectives with participants from a variety of U.S. and Asia Pacific corporate foundations, giving programs, and community affairs departments in many different industries. This is the first major undertaking on Asia Pacific by COF.

f. Asia Pacific Philanthropy Consortium (APPC)

The Asia Pacific Philanthropy Consortium (APPC) was launched in December 1994 in conjunction with JCIE's Osaka Symposium, the culmination of the survey project entitled the "Nongovernmental Underpinnings of the Emerging Asia Pacific Regional Community."

Preceding the Osaka Symposium were two international symposia on organized private philanthropy in East and Southeast Asia in Bangkok in 1989 and Seoul in 1993. They were funded by the Ford, Toyota, and Asia Foundations and RBF. Building on these two symposia and extensive discussions with representative foundation executives in the United States, Japan, Korea, Hong Kong, the Philippines, and Thailand, four institutions long involved in supporting the development of private philanthropy in Asia, formed APPC. The founding institutions are, namely, The Asia Foundation, the Institute of East and West Studies at Yonsei University, Korea, JCIE, and the Philippine Business for Social Progress. Barnett Baron of The Asia Foundation provided effective leadership in the process of APPC's formation.

The Consortium is governed by a multinational Executive Committee. Designed to promote and strengthen the role of philanthropy, as well as philanthropic cooperation in the Asia Pacific region, APPC will engage in networking and exchanges, research activities, clearinghouse and data base services, and technical support. Partial funding for APPC has thus far been obtained from a dozen foundations in the United States, Japan, Korea, and Australia. It is hoped that the Consortium will grow into a premier regional institution in these endeavors.

VIII. Conclusion

The purpose of this paper has been to review U.S. foundation activities vis-à-vis Asia Pacific related research and dialogue in a historical perspective, and not to evaluate such programs. However, the track record of foundations, as documented above, speaks for itself.

As we observed, U.S. foundations' operating philosophies and leadership, have taken different approaches, dependent on size. The Ford Foundation, RBF, and the Luce Foundation have emphasized the importance of regional programs. Asia Pacific as a region has been an integral part of their international affairs programs. The Rockefeller Foundation invested an enormous amount of its funding in development and cultural exchanges in the postwar years, but in the 1980s left Asia as a regional program. This does not mean that it has withdrawn from Asia from a programmatic perspective. The approach of the Rockefeller and MacArthur Foundations, and the Pew Charitable Trusts is a functional one. They do not support regional or country programs in Asia, but support of specific fields is a part of their program interests. For example, the Rockefeller Foundation supports agriculture and biomedical programs in China, not because it is China, but because agriculture and medicine are their fields of interest worldwide. Similarly, the Foundation is involved in North Korea's nuclear monitoring project because it sees it as part of their global environment effort. MacArthur and Pew provide grants for Asia Pacific in the fields of security and the environment.

Ford and RBF are interested in the concept of the Asia Pacific regional community, while Luce takes the more traditional approach of providing support for academic and cultural programs on Asia. A small family foundation, the Kunstadter Foundation, given its limited resources, focuses on some highly selected areas of family interest and provides support to organizations over the period of several years.

In the field of development assistance, Ford and Rockefeller, as their rich resources have allowed, concurrently engaged in massive institution building and human resources development in Asia in the 1960s and 1970s. RBF, much smaller than the former two, has taken the approach of first concentrating on building individual capacities, then on step-by-step institution building, and finally on projects using those human resources and institutions built up over the years.

Still, some foundations are very specialized. The China Medical Board centers its attention on Asia's medical training and education. It has embarked on programs to deal with AIDS in the Asia Pacific region. Luce is very Asia oriented, especially towards China, reflecting its founder's legacy. The foundation supports academic and cultural programs rather than policy studies. The United Board for Christian Higher Education in Asia is involved with a significant number of giving programs, albeit solely in the field of higher education.

These foundations and others mentioned in the preceding sections comprise the community of foundations playing a substantial role in the Asia Pacific region. According to several executives of these foundations, they are the "major players" and the field has not been expanded. The only significant new player is the Freeman Foundation. With assets of $400 million, this foundation appears to take a major interest in Asia. It has recently given several widely publicized major gifts related to Asia, including $2 million to the Asia Society to support Asian studies in U.S. elementary and secondary schools; $750,000 to the East-West Center for its New

Generation Seminar involving future leaders in the Asia Pacific region; and $175,000 to the Institute of International Education for the U.S.-Japan women community leaders exchange program cosponsored by JCIE.

Private philanthropy has been an essential element in building post–World War II Atlantic relations. U.S. private foundations have played a crucial role in Asia; independence, pluralism, and pragmatism are important features used to undertake their grant-making programs. As most foundation officials who were interviewed emphasized, the virtues of foundations are "flexibility, the ability to provide a quick response, and a willingness to take risks." This study has demonstrated an impressive record of U.S. foundations in support of new initiatives, the strongest of which have become self-sustaining over time.

Foundations first supported population and reproductive biology programs. These were politically and religiously sensitive issues that governments and public agencies could not tackle. Foundations still support newer, non-traditional programs in Asia, for example, the environment and human rights. Again, only foundations can support programs of human rights, say, in China, because of the sensitivity issue. Luce and Ford are funding some such programs. Luce's earlier effort to facilitate U.S.-North Korean private dialogue; Rockefeller's North Korea initiatives; the Soros Foundation program in Burma in support of an "open and free society"; and the Ford Foundation program in Vietnam since the 1980s are other examples of issues that can only be pursued unofficially in a low-key way. Support for research institutions by foundations is especially important to ensure their independence. When the RAND Corporation, previously a one hundred percent government military contract think tank, went through its transition to become an independent public policy organization like Brookings, back in 1948, Ford provided a loan guarantee to assure its survival.

On the other hand, some serious inherent problems lie in the fact that foundations usually cannot provide ongoing support for many years. Grants typically decline or are terminated as the newness of topics wears off, or when a field or an institution is no longer at a critical stage of development. Occasionally, foundations themselves face budget cuts. We have witnessed such examples in the sections above.

Today, U.S. foundations face challenges to redefine their international programs in the post–cold war world. Given the ongoing, drastic cuts for international development, education, and exchange in the U.S. federal budget, it is possible that foundations may come under pressure to provide funds for NGOs who may lose traditional government funds. Likewise, budget cuts for domestic spending will also increase the demands of educational and cultural organizations whose programs are not international.

Finally, will U.S. foundations continue to engage in the Asia Pacific region? The overwhelming consensus is "yes." The questions then become: how much; in what form; and for how long? U.S. interest in Asia Pacific, economically, politically, and culturally, will only increase in the years to come. Hence, more exchange and dialogue will be needed. Although U.S. foundation officials do not foresee any major increase in their giving for the Asia Pacific, they believe that U.S. corporations, with their burgeoning business and trade interests in the region, are becoming more active in supporting Asia Pacific related programs and this trend is likely to continue to grow. Concurrently, we have been observing the emergence of private and corporate philanthropy in the dynamically expanding Asia Pacific economies, beginning in Japan, and now in Korea, Taiwan, and Southeast Asian countries. It is hopeful that overall philanthropic money will grow and Asia Pacific philanthropic cooperation will increase the common pie for the promotion of regional dialogue and cooperation.

The review of foundation programs and Asia Pacific related activities by nongovernmental organizations shows that most of these efforts are not specifically intended to aid in the creation or integration of the Asia Pacific regional community comparable to the European Community, at least not at the present moment. However, many of the foundation people this writer interviewed believe that these kinds of sustained and expanded Asia Pacific programs and activities, along with networking and cooperative projects, will cumulatively contribute to fostering a sense of community over the long run. This is the very basis of the movement toward community building in the future. "Making Haste Slowly" seems a most viable approach in this process.

Especially important is the well-accepted fact that one of the principal pillars in the process of promoting an Atlantic community in the postwar era was philanthropy. Any sort of effort toward building an Asia Pacific community will also require that there be full-fledged philanthropic development and cooperation in Asia and across the Pacific.

Notes

1. The writer wishes to acknowledge with many thanks the invaluable contributions and guidance of Tadashi Yamamoto and Makito Noda, JCIE/JAPAN. Research was ably assisted by Karin Wilcox, JCIE/USA.
2. Paul Evans, *Studying Asia Pacific Security* (North York: University of Toronto - York University Joint Centre for Asia Pacific Studies, 1994).
3. See the report on research institutions in China in this volume.
4. The Japan Foundation, "Japanese Studies in the Late 1980s—Problems and Prospects" in *Japanese Studies in the United States* (Tokyo: The Japan Foundation, 1988).
5. See Charles Morrison's paper on research institutes in the United States and JCIE's *Directory of U.S. Research Institutions Active in Asia Pacific Studies.*
6. Charles E. Morrison and Anne F. Miyashiro, "Issues in pan Pacific Cooperation" in *The JCIE Papers: The Pacific Community Concept: Views from Eight Nations,* chapter 1.
7. Evans, op. cit.
8. See JCIE's *Twenty-Fifth Anniversary: 1992–1994 Program Report* and *International Philanthropy Project—A Case Study, 1991.*
9. Many Japanese and Asian donors and donees have benefited from the work of the Foundation Center, COF's close collaborating group. As a part of the Cooperating Collections Network, the Foundation Center Library of Japan and ANZ in Australia maintain collections of Foundation Center publications for free public use.

APPENDICES

APPENDIX A

List of Researchers and Cooperating Organizations

(in alphabetical order of the country)

Australia

Max Dumais
Executive Director
The Australian Association of Philanthropy
(organized philanthropy)

Jenny McGregor
Director
Asialink Center
(NGOs/research institutions)

Canada

Allan Arlett
Ingrid van Rotterdam
Partners
The Arlett van Rotterdam Partnership
(NGOs)

Paul Evans
Director
University of Toronto - York University Joint Centre for Asia-Pacific Studies
(research institutions)

Donald Rickerd
President
Max Bell Foundation
(organized philanthropy)

China

Shohei Muta
Program Officer
Japan Center for International Exchange (JCIE)
(research institutions)

Makito Noda
Senior Program Officer

Zhang Ye
Consultant
(organized philanthropy/NGOs)

Hong Kong

Yue-man Yeung
Director
Hong Kong Institute of Asia Pacific Studies
(research institutions)

Makito Noda
Senior Program Officer
JCIE
(NGOs/organized philanthropy)

Indonesia

Andra Corrothers
Regional Director for Asia
PACT, Inc. Asia Regional Office
(NGO/organized philanthropy)

Estie W. Suryatna
Representative's Special Assistant

Makito Noda
Senior Program Officer
JCIE
(research institutions)

Japan

Toshihiro Menju
Program Officer
JCIE
(NGOs)

Takako Aoki
Research Associate

Tadashi Yamamoto
President
JCIE
(organized philanthropy)

Hitomi Komatsu
Research Associate

Makito Noda
Senior Program Officer
JCIE
(research institutions)

Korea

Hye-Kyung Lee
Professor of Social Welfare
Institute of East and West Studies
Yonsei University
(NGOs)

Ku-Hyun Jung
Director
Institute of East and West Studies
Yonsei University
(research institutions)

Tae-Kyu Park
Professor of Economics
Institute of East and West Studies
Yonsei University
(organized philanthropy)

Malaysia

Lim Tech Ghee
Professor
Institute of Advanced Studies
University of Malaya
(NGOs)

Makito Noda
Senior Program Officer
JCIE
(research institutions)

New Zealand

Peter Harris
Executive Director
Asia 2000 Foundation of New Zealand
(NGOs/organized philanthropy)

Nicky Thomson
Programme Manager, Business
Asia 2000 Foundation of New Zealand
(research institutions)

Philippines

Segundo E. Romero
Vice President
Institute of Strategic and Development Studies
(NGOs)

Rostum J. Bautista
Research Assistant

Ma. Gisela T. Velasco
Manager, Membership and Corporate Involvement Unit
Philippine Business for Social Progress
(organized philanthropy)

Makito Noda
Senior Program Officer
JCIE
(research institutions)

Singapore

Chan Tse Chueen
Research and Administration Officer
ENGENDER
(NGOs/organized philanthropy)

Makito Noda
Senior Program Officer
JCIE
(research institutions)

Taiwan

Hsin-Huang Michael Hsiao
Research Fellow
Institute of Sociology
Academia Sinica
(NGOs/organized philanthropy/research institutions)

Thailand

Amara Pongsapich
Director
Social Research Institute
Chulalongkorn University
(NGOs/organized philanthropy)

Makito Noda
Senior Program Officer
JCIE
(research institutions)

U.S.A.

Gordon Jay Frost
Editor, International Philanthropy
Senior Consultant, CDA/Invest
(organized philanthropy)

Yuko Iida Frost
Publisher, International Philanthropy
Consultant, Save the Children
(NGOs)

Hiroshi Peter Kamura
Executive Director
Japan Center for International Exchange, Inc.
(organized philanthropy)

Charles Morrison
Director
Program on International Economics and Politics
The East-West Center
(research institutions)

Vietnam

Mark Sidel
Program Officer for Vietnam
The Ford Foundation
(NGOs/organized philanthropy)

APPENDIX B

Osaka Symposium

Regency Ball Room E, 3F.
Hyatt Regency Osaka

Sunday, December 11

18:30 Opening Buffet Reception [Regency Ball Room B, *3F.*]

Welcoming Remarks: Yoshimasa Umemoto, *Advisory Councillor to Takeda Chemical Industries, Ltd.; former Chairman of the Corporate Philanthropy Committee, Keidanren (Japan Federation of Economic Organizations)*

Monday, December 12

9:30–10:30 Session 1: Asia Pacific Community Building and the Role of the Independent Sector

[Regency Ball Room E, *3F.*]

Panelists

Stephen W. Bosworth, *President, United States-Japan Foundation*

Yuji Suzuki, *Professor of International Politics, Hosei University*

M. S. Kismadi, *Executive Director, Foundation for Sustainable Development*

Moderator

Tadashi Yamamoto, *President, Japan Center for International Exchange*

10:45–12:15 Session 2: Regional Cooperation among Research Institutions

Panelists

Paul Evans, *Director, University of Toronto–York University Joint Centre for Asia Pacific Studies*

Somsakdi Xuto, *Former Director, National Institute of Development Administration*

Moderator

Ku-Hyun Jung, *Director, Institute of East and West Studies, Yonsei University*

12:30 Buffet Lunch [Sapphire, *2F.*]

14:30–17:00 **Session 3**: Emergence of NGOs and Their Regional Cooperation

Panelists

Paiboon Wattanasiritham, *President, Foundation for Thailand Rural Reconstruction Movement; Former Chairman, NGO Coordinating Committee on Rural Development (NGO-CORD)*

Victoria P. Garchitorena, *Executive Director, Ayala Foundation*

Michio Ito, *Managing Director, Japanese NGO Center for International Cooperation*

Vivienne Wee, Programme Director, ENGENDER—Centre for Environment, Gender and Development

Moderator

Russell A. Phillips, Jr., Executive Vice President, Rockefeller Brothers Fund

18:30 Dinner [Regency Ball Room D, *3F.*]

Speech: Asia Pacific Community Building—a Cultural Perspective

Masakazu Yamazaki, *Playwright and Professor of Literature, Osaka University; Member of the Board, Suntory Foundation*

Tuesday, December 13

9:30–12:00 **Session 4**: Issues of Philanthropic Development in Asia Pacific [Regency Ball Room E, *3F.*]

Panelists

Feng You, *Vice President and Secretary General, China International Medical Foundation*

Carrillo Gantner, *Vice President, Myer Foundation*

Krisda Piampongsant, *Director, External Cooperation Division I, Department of Technical and Economic Cooperation*

Sixto K. Roxas, *Vice Chairman, Foundation for Philippine Environment; Chairman, Foundation for Community Organization and Management Technology*

Barnett Baron, *Executive Vice President, The Asia Foundation*

Moderator
Peter F. Geithner, *Director of Asia Programs, The Ford Foundation*

12:30–14:30 Lunch [Regency Ball Room E, *3F.*]

Session 5: Patterns of Japanese Philanthropic Development

Panelists
Natsuaki Fusano, *Senior Managing Director, Keidanren (Japan Federation of Economic Organizations)*
Masaaki Honma, *Professor of Economics, Osaka University*
Chimaki Kurokawa, *Managing Director, Toyota Foundation*

Moderator
Tadashi Yamamoto

15:00–16:00 Session 6: Strengthening the Management of Asia Pacific Philanthropy

Panelists:
Delwin Roy, *President, Hitachi Foundation*
Pedro Roxas, *President, Central Azucarera Don Pedro Corporation; Chairman, Membership Board Committee, Philippine Business for Social Progress*

Moderator
Nelson Young, *Chairman, Hsu Chung Ching Educational Foundation of Hong Kong*

16:15–17:45 Session 7: Future Strategies of Philanthropic Development and Cooperation in Asia Pacific—Asia Pacific Philanthropy Consortium

Panelists
Barnett Baron
Ma. Aurora F. Tolentino, *Executive Director, Philippine Business for Social Progress*
Ku-Hyun Jung

Moderator
Tadashi Yamamoto

18:00–19:00 Closing Cocktail Reception [Sapphire, *2F.*]

Participants from Foreign Organizations

Amara Pongsapich	Vice President for Research Affairs Chulalongkorn University (Thailand)
Barnett F. Baron	Executive Vice President The Asia Foundation (U.S.)
Margaret Bell	Member of the Board of Directors CIVICUS President International Association for Volunteer Effort (Australia)
Stephen W. Bosworth	President United States-Japan Foundation (U.S.)
Page Chapman III	President Bankers Trust Foundation (U.S.)
John J. Deeney	Director The Hong Kong-America Center (Hong Kong)
Max Dumais	Executive Officer Australian Association of Philanthropy (Australia)
Paul M. Evans	Director, University of Toronto–York University Joint Centre for Asia Pacific Studies (Canada)
Feng You	Vice President and Secretary General China International Medical Foundation (China)
Carrillo Gantner	Vice President The Myer Foundation (Australia)
Victoria P. Garchitorena	Executive Director Ayala Foundation (Philippines)
Peter F. Geithner	Director of Asia Programs The Ford Foundation (U.S.)
Harold H. C. Han	President Himalaya Foundation President Himalaya Investment Corporation (Taiwan)
Peter Harris	Executive Director Asia 2000 Foundation of New Zealand (New Zealand)

Pamela G. Hollie	Philippine Representative The Asia Foundation (U.S.)
Chang-Soon Hwang	Senior Researcher Korea Institute for Youth Development (Korea)
Jerry L. Inman	Japan Representative The Asia Foundation (U.S.)
Ku-Hyun Jung	Director Institute of East and West Studies Yonsei University (Korea)
Kamjorn Chaowarat	Businessman and Philanthropist (Thailand)
M. S. Kismadi	Executive Director Foundation for Sustainable Development (Indonesia)
Krisda Piampongsant	Director External Cooperation Division I Department of Technical and Economic Cooperation (Thailand)
P.B. Krishnaswamy	Executive Director National Foundation for India (India)
Hye-Kyung Lee	Director of Philanthropy Program Institute of East and West Studies Yonsei University (Korea)
Chi Ho Lew	Auditor-General Korea Foundation (Korea)
Michael Liffman	Executive Officer The Myer Foundation (Australia)
Jenny McGregor	Director Asialink Centre (Australia)
Horacio R. Morales, Jr.	Member of the Board of Directors CIVICUS President Philippines Rural Reconstruction Movement (Philippines)
Ernest J. Notar	Director of Philanthropic Services International Youth Foundation (U.S.)
Paiboon Wattanasiritham	President Foundation for Thailand Rural Reconstruction Movement (Thailand)

Tae-Kyu Park	Professor of Economics Yonsei University (Korea)
Russell A. Phillips, Jr.	Executive Vice President Rockefeller Brothers Fund (U.S.)
Donald S. Rickerd	President Max Bell Foundation (Canada)
Helen Riha	Assistant Director Himalaya Foundation (Taiwan)
Pedro E. Roxas	President The Central Azucarera Don Pedro Corporation Chairman Membership Board Committee Philippine Business for Social Progress (Philippines)
Sixto K. Roxas	Chairman Foundation for Community Organization and Management Technology, Inc. President SKR Managers & Advisors, Inc. (Philippines)
Delwin A. Roy	President Hitachi Foundation (U.S.)
Mark Sidel	Program Officer for Vietnam The Ford Foundation, Bangkok (Vietnam)
Somsakdi Xuto	Former Director National Institute of Development Administration (Thailand)
Jae-Ik Suh	Program Officer Samsung Welfare Foundation (Korea)
Pei-Yu Teng	Executive Director Lotus Foundation (Taiwan)
Nguyen Van Thanh	Executive Vice President Vietnam Union of Friendship Organizations (Vietnam)
Ma. Aurora F. "Rory" Tolentino	Executive Director Philippine Business for Social Progress (Philippines)
Anthony Tsui	Director The Croucher Foundation (Hong Kong)

Stephen Tyler	Senior Program Officer Southeast Asia Regional Office International Development Research Centre (Canada)
Mark Vermilion	Director for Corporate Affairs Sun Microsystems (U.S.)
Vicharn Panich	Director Thailand Research Fund (Thailand)
Keiko Watanabe	Tokyo Representative International Youth Foundation (U.S.)
Vivienne Wee	Programme Director ENGENDER—Centre for Environment, Gender and Development (Singapore)
Elizabeth A. Wong	Program Coordinator of International Programs Council on Foundations (U.S.)
Nelson Young	Chairman Hsu Chung Ching Educational Foundation of Hong Kong (Hong Kong)
Zhang Ye	Consultant on NGOs Researcher, Chinese Academy of Social Sciences (China)

Participants from Japanese Organizations

Ronni Alexander	Professor Graduate School of International Cooperation Studies Kobe University
Takayoshi Amenomori	Director Toyonaka Association for International Activities and Communication
Jun'ichi Aoyagi	Senior Staff Writer Cultural News Department *Nihon Keizai Shimbun* (Nikkei)
Masayuki Deguchi	Secretary General Suntory Foundation
Norihiko Fujii	Managing Director Sumitomo Life Wellness Foundation
Takashiro Furihata	Manager Planning Department Osaka International House Foundation
Masafumi Furuichi	Executive Director Mitsubishi Bank Foundation
Natsuaki Fusano	Senior Managing Director Keidanren (Japan Federation of Economic Organizations)
Naohiro Higuchi	Assistant Manager, Public Relations Takeda Chemical Industries
Masaaki Homma	Professor of Economics Osaka School of International Public Policy Osaka University
Hitoshi Iikawa	Assistant Manager Council of Local Authorities for International Relations (CLAIR)
Shuichi Ikeda	Manager Research Institute of Culture, Energy & Life, Osaka Gas Co., Ltd.
Kotaro Inoue	Special Staff Manager Public Relations Section Sumitomo Life Insurance Company
Akira Iriyama	President The Sasakawa Peace Foundation

Michio Ito	Managing Director Japanese NGO Center for International Cooperation
Takashi Ito	Director Assistant Planning Division The Japan Foundation Center for Global Partnership
Tomoyuki Kafuku	Executive Director and Secretary Kansai Research Foundation for Technology Promotion
Shisei Kaku	Executive Director of International Relations Planning and Coordination Department Osaka Prefectural Government
Yoshio Kasamatsu	Adviser Sumitomo Life Social Welfare Services Foundation
Katsuakira Kihara	President Nara Machizukuri Center, Inc.
Jun'etsu Komatsu	Deputy Executive Director The Japan Foundation Center for Global Partnership
Chimaki Kurokawa	Managing Director The Toyota Foundation
Minoru Kusuda	Director Kusuda Office Former Executive Director The Japan Foundation Center for Global Partnership
Masaki Nagasawa	Executive Director The Daiwa Bank Foundation for Asia and Oceania
Yoshihiro Mishima	Executive Director The Osaka Community Foundation
Hidekazu Ohnishi	Assistant Manager General Office of Community Relations and Development, Kansai Electric Power Co., Inc.
Kiyoshi Segami	Standing Director Yamada Science Foundation
Masahide Shibusawa	Director East-West Seminar

Osamu Shiragami	Senior Executive Director The Asahi Glass Foundation
Hideyuki Suwa	Executive Director Osaka Gas Foundation of International Exchange
Yuji Suzuki	Professor of Sociology Hosei University
Chuichi Takanashi	Secretary General CIBA-GEIGY Foundation (Japan)
Haruhiko Tanaka	Associate Professor, Faculty of Education Okayama Univesiry
Masami Tashiro	Deputy Director Corporate Philanthropy Department Keidanren (Japan Federation of Economic Organizations)
Yoshimasa Umemoto	Advisory Councillor Takeda Chemical Industries, Ltd. Former Chairman Committee on Corporate Philanthropy Keidanren (Japan Federation of Economic Organizations)
Yoshiko Wakayama	Program Officer The Sasakawa Peace Foundation
Hideo Yamaguchi	Executive Director Foundation Library Center of Japan
Tadashi Yamamoto	President Japan Center for International Exchange
Naoto Yamauchi	Associate Professor of Economics Osaka School of International Public Policy Osaka University
Masakazu Yamazaki	Playwright and Professor of Theatre Studies Osaka University Member of the Board Suntory Foundation

APPENDIX C

Philanthropy in a Multiethnic Society: The Case of Malaysia

Edmund Terence Gomez
University of Malaya

I. Introduction

The measure, mode, and major features of philanthropic activity in Malaysia have primarily been determined by the ethnic division of society into the *Bumiputeras* (literally translated, this means "sons of the soil" and refers primarily to the Malays though the term includes all other indigenous people of the country) and the non-*Bumiputeras*, such as the Chinese and Indian communities. While the Chinese have a history of philanthropy in the time of their migration into the country from the nineteenth century, such practices among the *Bumiputeras*, apart from the Muslim *zakat*, are only a relatively recent feature. This disparity is largely due to historical factors, such as the different conditions of migration into Malaysia of the various non-*Bumiputera* communities and the impact of colonial rule on the communities as well as on the *Bumiputera* community. Other factors consist of the impact of state policies, especially in the economic, cultural, and educational spheres of life of the different ethnic communities. Philanthropic patterns have also been determined by intra-ethnic class and sub-communal divisions as well as the varying levels of political and economic power of the various ethnic communities.

In view of the ethnic nature of most of the major political parties in Malaysia, philanthropic activities have also been an important recourse through which these parties have tried to forge a communitarian spirit, which transcends class and sub-communal divisions, as a means to mobilize support. However, while this has been particularly evident among the non-*Bumiputera* parties who are members of the ruling *Barisan Nasional* (National Front) coalition, i.e., the Malaysian Chinese Association (MCA) and the Malaysian Indian Congress (MIC), such activities have not been necessary for the leading Malay party, the United Malays' National Organization (UMNO). This is attributable to UMNO's hegemonic role in the coalition which has enabled it to use the state apparatus to protect and promote the welfare of the *Bumiputeras*. Thus, to understand the nature of philanthropic activity in Malaysia is then to understand the evolving nature of (Malay-dominated) state-society relations. [1]

II. Philanthropic Practices in Malaysia: A Historical Review

The reasons for the late development of philanthropy among the *Bumiputeras*, especially the Malays, stem in part from the limited impact of British colonialism on the essentially feudal structure and subsistence-oriented agricultural economy of the community. In addition, the fact that the colonizers encouraged the Malays as a race to continue with their work in the rural sectors of the Malaysian economy, primarily those in the production of rice and fish, while restricting the efforts of Malay farmers enterprising enough to venture into rubber production, profoundly circumscribed the development of indigenous capital and continued to restrict Malays to traditional economic activities.

The British colonizers also encouraged mass migration of Chinese into the country from the second half of the nineteenth century to feed labor for the tin mines.[2] In response to the generally unsympathetic or indifferent colonial administration, many Chinese businesses found that they had to adopt frontier community institutions and relations to meet the needs of economic organization. These businesses, most of them small- or medium-sized, over time came to be associated with particular families. In spite of the impediment posed by British capital to the development of Chinese business, several Chinese acquired prominence in the tin and rubber industries.

Growing British interest in the plantations in the early twentieth century was responsible for the large scale transportation of primarily Tamil Indians from what was then British India. Although these Indians predominantly consisted of indentured laborers to work in the rubber estates, a small number of them were also occupied in urban mercantile trade, money lending, and the lower civil service.[3] By the time of Malaysian Independence in 1957, almost three-fifths of the Indian population in the country was entrenched in positions within plantation agriculture, while only one-fifth was involved in either government service or commerce.[4]

While the British colonialists, by allowing for the large-scale migration of Chinese and Indian workers into the country, contributed inevitably to the ethnically heterogeneous composition of Malayan society, they nevertheless did little to encourage mutual interaction among the communities. In fact, limited ethnic integration was the necessary consequence of the British-driven separation or segregation of the races through economic specialization. The Chinese were mainly sent to work in the tin mines, the Indians channeled to self-contained semi-rural plantations, while most of the Malays remained as peasants in rural areas. Further, the need for integration was also absent since many of the Chinese and Indians felt that their sojourn in Malaysia was at best a temporary one. Since they were to return "home" to China or India after accumulating enough savings, they naturally did not conceive of Malaya as their new homeland.

Given such an ethnically polarized environment, the non-Malay communities, particularly the Chinese, set up various associations with the purpose of safeguarding their educational, cultural, and economic interests. Heng[5] identifies seven principle types of Chinese-based voluntary organizations in Malaya by the early twentieth century: the dialect/territorial associations formed at the state, provincial, and village level; the clan/surname associations; the trade guilds and Chambers of Commerce; the cultural, dramatic, and musical societies; the social and recreational societies; the religious and/or moral uplifting societies; and the mutual aid and funerary societies. Heng[6] goes on to note that of these various associations, the Chinese Chambers of Commerce (CCC) were the largest and most important organizations.

This was in view of the fact that the Chinese businessmen who led the various Chambers of Commerce were also at the forefront of other organizations and were thus primarily responsible for the advancement of Chinese welfare through philanthropic activities. Probably the most well known of these Chinese philanthropists was Tan Kah Kee, who helped initiate the China Relief Fund through which most Chinese Chambers of Commerce and individual businessmen were mobilized to fund relief efforts in China, especially during the Sino-Japan War. Such philanthropic work also involved the setting up of hospitals, though most of it was centered around the advancement of Chinese education.

Tan Kah Kee's son-in-law, Lee Kong Chian of the Lee Rubber Group, was known to have donated "not less than $5 million per year," in the form of bursaries to charitable organizations, and to the promotion of Chinese education.[7] Another prominent philanthropist was Aw Boon Haw, who donated large sums of money towards social causes. His philanthropy was also largely influenced by the state of affairs in his homeland of China. He donated generously towards helping Nationalist China in its war effort against the Japanese. In times of natural crisis, when China was stricken by the calamities of drought or floods, Aw galvanized fund-raising campaigns through his newspaper, *Sin Chew Jit Poh*, and the Hakka Association, an association of Chinese who spoke his dialect. He also played a prominent role in the setting up of several schools in Singapore (Chung Cheng High School, the Catholic schools, and the Methodist and Anglican schools). Nanyang University in Singapore was also established through the financial assistance of Aw, together with other businessmen, who strongly felt that the time had come when "the Chinese needed their own university."[8]

The keen need felt by businessmen to promote the cause of education was in large measure founded on the belief that their own role as businessmen would suffer in an environment where it would be difficult for them to look for suitable educated personnel to help them run their own businesses or implement the new infrastructure needed to meet the challenges posed by modern enterprise.

Further, in a situation where the British colonial administration contributed very little to the financing of Chinese education (the British, however, wholly financed Malay primary education and partially financed English education), the Chinese community was thrust with the responsibility of sponsoring Chinese education.[9] By 1949, government aid per student was as follows: Chinese schools—$8.72, Indian schools—$55.84, Malay schools—$67.88, English schools–$187.88.[10]

The financial implications were obvious since many more Chinese children and youths attended Chinese-medium schools than English-medium ones. Enrollment figures for 1938, for instance, list 91,534 Chinese students in Chinese schools in contrast to only 26,974 students in English-medium ones. Almost ten years later, in 1947, it was estimated that fifty-five percent of all Chinese primary school students were enrolled at Chinese schools, in comparison to the ten percent who attended English schools.[11]

The situation of the ethnic Indians was altogether different. Unlike the Chinese community whose members were sufficiently funded and united to form self-help or communitarian-based organizations, the Indians were divided along subcommunal and caste lines. Further, their negligible impact on the Malaysian economy, in terms of wealth accumulation and the creation of a capitalist class, contributed to only middling philanthropic activity within the community.

The Indian-based organizations that were eventually formed in the early twentieth century had a strong urban middle-class orientation. For example, the Selangor Ceylon Tamil Association was formed in Kuala Lumpur in 1900 while the Taiping Indian Association was established in 1906 and the Selangor Association in 1909; subsequently, numerous such associations were established in other major urban areas in the country.[12] Set up and headed by professionals, these bodies were mainly interested in organizing cultural and recreational facilities for mostly urban-based Indians, consciously alienating themselves from the plight and concerns of Indian laborers in the plantations; however, some of these associations, with the help of a few Indian philanthropists, were also responsible for establishing Tamil primary schools in urban areas.[13]

The convergence of several of these urban-based Indian organizations and four Indian Chambers of Commerce and Merchants' Associations gave rise to the creation of the first major Indian organization in the country. In spite of its predominantly middle-class leadership, the Central Indian Association of Malaya (CIAM), established in 1936, took up the cause of exploited Indian plantation labor and also attempted to address the social ills afflicting the other poor sections of the Indian community. Although it met with little success in this area, CIAM's agenda was also motivated by the need to initiate social reform either through legislation or private effort. To this end, it highlighted the problems associated with excessive toddy-drinking, Hindu marriage legislation, and the lack of educational provisions for the community.[14]

In the area of education, Tamil schools (the problems were especially severe for those in the plantations) were generally poorly organized and rarely received financial support from the community. The British colonial government's insistence that the management of plantations set up Tamil vernacular schools in the estate, however, was viewed as being part of a strategy to encourage Indian plantation laborers into taking up long-term residence in the country. Moved by the obvious benefits to them from this, rubber and coffee planters were, from 1900 onwards, voluntarily setting up schools in their plantations. To those not so easily persuaded, the Labor Code of 1923 made it obligatory for them to provide educational facilities if there were ten or more resident children of school-going age—between six and twelve years old.[15]

The majority of the classes in the Tamil schools run by the management were, however, not conducted under proper "school" conditions, while most of the staff were neither qualified nor trained well enough to teach. Urban Tamil schools fared much better in that the drive to promote Tamil education was spearheaded by Christian missions, Hindu associations, and individual philanthropists.[16]

Philanthropic activity within the Malay community in the pre- and post-Independence periods was very limited, due in large measure to the distinct manner of development of the Malayan economy. Although the colonial economy flourished to such a degree that it became the single most profitable colony of the British Empire, the creation of colonial monopolies had thwarted the growth of a local capitalist class which could produce for the local market. Local businesses were instead actively urged to engage in production for the purposes of export, commerce, and usury. Most of these newly emerging business opportunities were, however, seized by the more urbanized and commercially better connected Chinese. The Malays, together with the Indians, were largely sidelined by the burgeoning capitalist sector. It was only the elite of both communities who were mobilized into the colonial state apparatus, while the masses were left to languish in their peasant occupations. Thus, the scant commercial involvement of the Malays as well as the small number of prominently successful businessmen in the community gave rise to a situation where much of the philanthropic activity of the community had to be made heavily reliant on government support and assistance.

One of the most distinctive as well as pivotal features of Malay philanthropic activity derives from the Muslim religion itself; Islam in effect mandates that Muslims contribute a portion of their wealth towards charity. The *zakat* is among the more significant forms of such a contribution.

Zakat is the state-organized capital levy on idle capital and constitutes an integral aspect of Islamic advocacy of collective provision for the welfare of the poor. It constitutes the minimum financial obligation of a prosperous person towards the society in which he lives. *Zakat*'s dual purpose is the creation of self-discipline and the provision against destitution. It aims to eliminate poverty, promote public well-being, financially bolster those on the brink of insolvency, and feed the hungry. The proceeds from *zakat* are to be used primarily for redistributive purposes since Islam abhors selfishness and material acquisitiveness; *zakat* thus promotes the ideal of sacrifice to cleanse those of selfishness and plutocracy. The obligatory feature of *zakat* is responsible for it frequently being referred to as *regular charity* or the *poor-due*. Although it is the duty of the state to make this collection of *zakat*, penalties for non-payment are weak and its enforcement is not actively instituted.[17]

The law and rulings pertaining to *zakat* in Malaysia generally cover the collection of four different types of *zakat*—the *zakat* on income, the *zakat* on crops (paddy), the *zakat* on assets, and the *zakat* on businesses. A number of states have provisions for other types of *zakat*, for instance, the *zakat* on gold and livestock.[18] Since every state has its own *zakat* organization, estimates of the amount paid in the form of *zakat* are difficult to establish. One recent estimate, however, is that about RM70 million was collected for the whole country in 1991.[19] The *zakat* collected is distributed to various social causes, including assistance for the poor and needy, new converts, and missionary activities. In the past, all funds distributed were channeled solely to Muslim beneficiaries. It is, however, not yet certain if this inclination towards religious exclusiveness has been influenced by the country's multiethnic and multi-religious society.[20]

III. Political Philanthropy

Since the late 1940s, philanthropic activity in Malaysia in the main has been associated with the country's principal political parties, especially the non-*Bumiputera* parties, namely the MCA and the MIC. There are two distinct periods during which philanthropic activities have proven particularly useful as a means to galvanize support: in the pre-Independence period when these political parties were first established and during the period 1970 to 1990, characterized by the vigorous implementation of state policies which increased state participation in the economy, the heightening of Malay political hegemony, and the rapid growth of a Malay capitalist class with a correspondingly growing dominance over the economy.

The MCA was established in 1949 as a consequence of the British-driven need to form an alternative organization to the predominantly Chinese-supported Malayan Communist Party (MCP). The British turned to the Chinese elites and members of the Chinese Chambers of Commerce to establish such an organization since it was also in their economic interest to ensure that MCP did not come to power and since Chinese capitalists already had an established reputation as leaders of most Chinese-based organizations. Inevitably, the MCA included among its membership some of the most successful Chinese businessmen and leading professionals in the country who were also at the helm of the Chinese Chambers of Commerce of most Malayan states as well as important Chinese associations (the Selangor Chinese Assembly Hall, the Perak Chinese Association, the Penang Chinese Town Hall, and the Johor Bahru Chinese Association). These MCA leaders were also playing key roles in trade guilds, cultural, social, and recreational associations, and the numerous dialect and territorial associations.[21]

The MCA, however, at the time of its inception, served primarily as a welfare body. Its principal objective between the years 1950 and 1953 was to assist the British administration in the relocation of almost half a million rural Chinese to the almost 500 newly formed, semi-urban "New Villages" in the hope that such a move would sever any possible ties established between these rural Chinese and the communist insurgents. For the purposes of funding such a massive relocation exercise, the MCA was granted permission in 1950 to operate a "million dollar Social Welfare lottery. Since the hugely popular lottery was open only to members of the MCA, it helped to augment both the party's membership and its influence among the Chinese.[22] In fact, when the inaugural lottery was drawn in February 1950, the party's membership had swelled by fifty percent. By mid-1953, the MCA had already raised several million ringgit, four million of which was used to construct and maintain schools, build houses, and provide amenities such as piped water, dispensaries, and recreational facilities within the New Villages.[23] However, the same year, in the wake of protests from other political parties, at the forefront of which was the multiracial Independence of Malaya Party (IMP) led by the influential Onn Jaafar, that the proceeds from the sweepstake supplied the MCA with an unfair pecuniary edge over other parties during electoral campaigns, it was subsequently banned.

The Alliance—predecessor of the Barisan Nasional—first formed between the MCA and UMNO (and later including the MIC), also stemmed from an act of philanthropy by the former. In July 1952, arising out of discussions between the Chinese elites and British on the need for non-Malay assistance in improving the economic welfare of the Malays, the MCA channeled RM500,000 from the proceeds of its Social Welfare lottery into a Malay Welfare Fund.[24] Although the fund was initially created for the purposes of welfare work, which included the setting up of vocational training centers for the Malays, it was eventually utilized to further secure the MCA's ties with UMNO through the newly-formed Alliance by making it finance a major portion of the Alliance's administrative and election expenses.[25]

The MIC, like its Chinese counterpart, also has a long history of involvement in business activities, professedly for welfare purposes. The business involvement of the MIC was, however, precipitated by the decision of foreign plantation owners to hastily dispose of their interests in the country, given its imminent Independence. This led to the swift fragmentation of rubber plantations and the mass unemployment of Indian laborers. The MIC's response to this crisis was the setting up of a cooperative, with funds generated by the estate workers themselves, to buy into the plantation sector, thus enabling them to become landowners and acquire an interest in the rubber industry. The National Land Finance Cooperative Society (NLFCS), though far from being a major business institution, is still in operation currently.

The MIC's essentially middle-class orientation was responsible in large measure for its meager support from the Indian working class, especially those in the plantations whose workers made up the majority of the Indian community. The fragmentation of the plantations, therefore, provided the party with excellent grounds for mobilizing support for the party from this vital segment of the community. The NLFCS's early success considerably bolstered the MIC's appeal among working-class Indians, who remain today the party's main base of support.

Even UMNO, following its inception in 1946, launched into an economic development program which, among others, proposed the setting up of a Malay Savings Bank, a lorry, a bus and motorboat transport company, and a trading company. Aimed at improving Malay welfare and increasing their involvement in business. the program, however, failed to make much headway due to poor governmental support and the lack of Malay business acumen.[26] By the end of the decade, UMNO had also initiated a party lottery, but the project met with very little success owing to the lottery's heavily circumscribed appeal among the party's predominantly peasant and working-class membership.[27]

In spite of the steadily expanding post-Independence Malayan economy, Malays still stood to benefit little, both in terms of the ownership as well as the management of business operations in the country. By December 1961, official statistics indicate that of the 84,930 sole proprietorships, only 12 percent, or 11,648 of these, were owned and managed by Malays, and that less than 5 percent of the total partnerships of 16,103 fell under Malay control. It was also estimated that the ratio of Malay to non-Malay firms was a glaring one to seven.[28] All this clearly demonstrated that the Malays were still excluded from the mainstream Malaysian economy even a decade after Independence. Many of them were still peasants in rural areas.

The economic condition of the Malays failed to improve appreciably even by the mid-1960s. They wielded only negligible control of the economy, hardly participated in the professional sector, and constituted the largest numbers in the poverty category. In view of these circumstances, there were anxious calls within UMNO for more direct state involvement in business. These demands were premised on the professed belief that unregulated market forces would impair social cohesiveness by perpetuating imbalances in the ethnic ownership of the country's economy. UMNO members also blamed the state for not providing adequate support to bolster the existing scant Malay participation in business activity and their meager ownership of the economy. Although a number of new public enterprises were set up with the aim of placating the discontented in UMNO, there was very little change to the Malay position in the post-independence economy.

The 1969 race riots eventually led to the awaited expansion of state involvement in the economy. In the field of politics, UMNO attained greater hegemony at the expense of MCA's diminished influence with the expansion of the tripartite Alliance into the Barisan Nasional, comprising around a dozen parties some of which also had much Chinese support. The state now had to assume the critical role of ensuring economic redistribution. To this end, the New Economic Policy (NEP), promulgated in 1970, was the course of action proferred by the state to help it achieve economic parity between the races. The NEP's ultimate objective was to achieve national unity through poverty eradication, irrespective of race, and inter-ethnic economic equity through a "restructuring" enterprise. The NEP emphasized wealth restructuring through social engineering. It was the government's hope of creating a "viable" Malay entrepreneurial community and thirty percent *Bumiputera* corporate ownership of the economy by 1990 that provided the undeniable momentum to the NEP.

Only a few years into the NEP, there was already mounting non-*Bumiputera* apprehension over their economic future when public enterprises began mushrooming into most sectors of the economy—the number of public enterprises had eventually swelled from 10 in 1957 to 841 in 1986—and government-controlled trust agencies, created to acquire equity on behalf of the *Bumiputeras*, began to dominate pivotal areas of the economy. Chinese and Indian grievances over governmental policies were heightened in the mid-1970s when legislation such as the Industrial Coordination Act (ICA) and monitoring agencies like the Capital Issues Committee (CIC) were introduced to secure vigorous implementation of the NEP. While the ICA provided the government with the power to ensure that companies adhered to stipulated ethnic ownership and labor quotas, the CIC was responsible for advancing the "indigenization" of corporate stock .[29]

The corresponding relationship between UMNO's rising political hegemony and the state's growing involvement in the economy simultaneously contributed to the creation of an influential Malay capitalist class and to increasing non-*Bumiputera* disfavor with the NEP. Despite these fears, the Barisan Nasional was returned to power in subsequent national elections and UMNO's growing hegemony over the state allowed for a political environment which was slowly being reorganized to cater to the vested interests of particular individuals. What this in effect entailed was to transfer the rein on resources as well as the national economy to the hands of those who were politically dominant and to that sector of the *Bumiputera* community which enjoyed the benefit of close ties with the political elite and many of whose members in fact functioned as proxies for these politicians.

In the cultural and educational spheres, with growing Malay hegemony, the non-Malays began to fear that government policies would impede the promotion of Chinese and Tamil education and practices. For instance, it is evident that the sovereignty of the Malay language has been seen by both Malays and non-Malays as a symbol of the Malay nature of the state and of Malay predominance in it. Thus, the Malays rejected the continued use of Tamil and Chinese in the education system on the grounds that it perpetuated non-Malay exclusiveness and obstructed the formation of a truly national community. At the same time, some Chinese and Tamil groups feared the loss of their cultural identity with the decline of Chinese and Tamil education. Thus, although since 1971 all primary schools were required to progressively adopt Malay as a medium of instruction—Chinese and Tamil primary schools have also been allowed to function with the vernacular as the main medium of instruction, though Malay also became a compulsory language—and all government bodies were required to use the Malay language as the official correspondence language, Malay has progressed more as an official language rather than as a national language.

A similar situation arose when the government proposed a National Culture Policy in the early 1970s. The policy was based on three principles: first, that it was to be based on the cultures of the people indigenous to the region; second, that elements from other cultures which were suitable and reasonable were to be incorporated into the national culture; and third, that Islam was to be an important element in the national culture. This, however, resulted in a heated debate over the predominantly Malay-Muslim nature of the proposal, and the policy was strongly criticized by most non-Malay organizations. By the late 1980s, a study undertaken by a local university indicated that while most Malays supported the policy, only a minority were in favor of an amalgam of cultures.[30]

The heightening of Malay dominance over the state, particularly accelerated state involvement in business and the ensuing concentration of wealth in the hands of a politically well-connected *Bumiputera* elite inevitably led to the involvement in business of the MCA and MIC, purportedly to acquire wealth on behalf of the communities they professed to represent. By the late 1960s and early 1970s, the MCA, in response to increasing state control of the economy, had begun to mobilize Chinese capital so effectively under a "corporatization movement" that its efforts at doing so were construed by Malay leaders as constituting a grave threat to the development of *Bumiputera* capital.[31]

The corporatization movement was so successful that when the MCA incorporated Multi-Purpose Holdings Berhad (MPHB), then its major holding company, to pool Chinese resources with the objective of entering business to safeguard and advance Chinese capital, it managed, for the first time in its history, to capture the imagination of the working class who were made to be convinced that the MCA had, through MPHB, found a means to check the gravitation of economic power towards the UMNO-dominated state.[32] The MCA began to propound the ethic of self-help among working- and middle-class Chinese. This ethnic line, especially when MPHB rapidly prospered during the economic boom of the early 1980s, considerably enhanced the MCA's appeal among the Chinese. By the mid-1980s, however, leading Chinese politicians—including the MCA president himself—who had been at the vanguard of MPHB (as well as that of other institutions developed under the auspices of the corporatization movement) were convicted on charges of criminal breach of trust, which pushed the company to the edge of bankruptcy.

The MCA, however, still plays a prominent role today in helping to raise funds from the Chinese for the cause of promoting Chinese education and sustaining Chinese schools. The party managed to raise RM50 million for its two principal educational projects—the expansion of the already existing Tunku Abdul Rahman (TAR) College and the Langkawi Project—which were initiated to assist the poor in financing their education. The party had in early 1995 instituted another educational fund to aid the development of the numerous independent Chinese secondary schools.[33]

Like the MCA, the MIC too has established several cooperatives with the professed objective of helping to increase Indian ownership of and participation in the national economy. Cooperatives in fact appear to be the community's most favored form of capitalization. Among those established and controlled by the various party leaders are Syarikat Kerjasama Nesa Pelbagai (Nesa), set up in 1974; Koperasi Belia Majujaya (M) Berhad, a multipurpose cooperative launched in 1977; and Koperasi Pekerja Jaya (KPJ), founded in 1979. Among the activities that these cooperatives are involved in are the construction of affordable houses for its members, the promotion of small Indian businesses, and investment in major corporate ventures. In addition to this, the party has also launched the MIC Unit Trusts Berhad, which operates a few unit trust funds that invest in the local bourse; the Malaysian Institute for Educational Development (MIED) to improve the educational prospects of Indians; and an investment holding company, Maika Holdings Berhad, to increase Indian equity ownership of corporate wealth and involvement in business.

All these organizations, with the exception of the NLFCS, were established after 1970, the year of the NEP's inception. Since the NEP sanctioned the UMNO-led government to intervene directly in the economy to promote *Bumiputera* capitalism, the MIC launched these business ventures on the ostensible basis that these too could play a similar role for the Indian community. Further, given the limited impact of government policies like the NEP in redressing the pressing economic woes of the Indian community, the MIC found that it was faced with the urgent need to promote such organizations.

However, although the inability of the Indians to raise their corporate ownership to a satisfactory level has been the professed reason for the party to foray into business, the party's commercial involvement has until today done very little to revive the community's economic status. By the end of 1990, Indians had in fact ownership of less than one percent of their country's corporate wealth, an actual relative decline when compared to their one percent corporate ownership way back in 1970. Most of these business enterprises have, unfortunately, functioned as vehicles for patronage and for the promotion of the vested political interests of MIC leaders. Despite the dismal performance of these organizations, the MIC continues to promote several fund-raising projects and business ventures to help alleviate the problems and hardships faced by Tamil schools as well as to promote the general welfare of the Indians.

IV. Current Philanthropic Practices

Most current philanthropic exercises in Malaysia appear to follow their antecedents in the manner of their operation, mode of involvement, and type of leadership. For instance, among the most prominent non-politically associated Indian organizations are the Education, Welfare and Research Fund (EWRF); the Sri Murugan Centre (SMC); and CHILD, the last two of which are believed to have been set up by leaders who had broken away from the EWRF. All three organizations possess a middle-class leadership, a trend which is discernible in most post-colonial Indian based institutions, like CIAM and the MIC.

The EWRF was founded in 1981 by several Indian professionals and academics on the encouragement of MIC President S. Samy Vellu. The fund is primarily involved in the cause of education for the Indians although its other concerns revolve around correcting the social ills experienced by the community such as the problem of alcoholism, the poor educational standards of the Indians, the subservient status of Indian women within the home and in society, and the dissolution of families.[34] Funded chiefly by donations from the public, the EWRF provides educational loans and hostel facilities for students, administers pre-school programs, and undertakes research on the social problems affecting the Indians.

The SMC was established in 1982 by a group of Indian university academics and students who continue to dominate its leadership. The center's main activity lies in the providing of tuition facilities to financially impoverished students so as to enhance their performance capacity in school and prepare them for government examinations. More than 110,000 students have benefited from the tutelage provided by the SMC. The center currently has more than 300 branches, most of which are situated in the plantations, with a volunteer staff of around 2,500, the majority of whom are graduates from the local universities, who help prepare at least 25,000 students per year for government examinations.[35]

CHILD, established in 1984, is also led by prominent professionals and academics in the community. Funded primarily through donations, the organization is involved in providing pre-school education to financially beleaguered Indians. Apart from helping to ensure adequate training for the teachers in these pre-schools, CHILD also helps to equip these schools with the necessary teaching facilities and material, including books. CHILD also produces reference books for primary-level education and conducts youth programs to enhance writing and leadership skills.

The MIC, notwithstanding the limited success of most of its projects to promote Indian social and economic interests, continues to voice its interest in establishing and operating various funds and companies;[36] of late, most of these funds are set up primarily to help establish and run institutions which provide technical training. The party's more recent efforts to try to get the government to focus attention on the predicament of the Indians and to institute policies that would specifically deal with their problems have not proven very successful.

With the advent of highly successful Malay capitalists and the growth of numerous Malay-owned or controlled business corporations following the NEP's implementation, philanthropic activity within the community is on the rise. Most of these philanthropists, however, are businessmen whose close ties with the ruling party have transformed them, almost overnight, into major corporate players. At the 1993 UMNO General Assembly, for instance, party treasurer Daim Zainuddin announced that nineteen businessmen had donated a sum of RM24 million to help the government set up the *Bumiputera* Entrepreneurs Foundation which would help train and develop self-reliant and informed Malay businessmen.[37] Renong Berhad, a publicly listed company controlled by Halim Saad, a protégé of Daim Zainuddin, emerged in the late 1980s as one of the country's leading construction concerns and went on to help establish the Renong Group Scholarship Trust Fund in 1992. The Fund has awarded scholarships to students of all races.[38] There are other minor Malay-controlled foundations. Examples of these are the Tunku Abdul Rahman Foundation, which was founded in 1936 to help fund secondary and tertiary level education, and the Tun Razak Foundation.

Philanthropic activity is still prevalent and remains most active within the Chinese community. By the early 1990s, there were more than 4,000 Chinese organizations in Malaysia that were concerned with the promotion of Chinese culture and, more importantly, with the advancement of Chinese education. Although most of them are funded by the Chinese, some of the more non-traditional organizations among them have increasingly pursued less Chinese-based activities.[39]

Several of the major Chinese companies also operate funds that contribute to charitable and welfare activities. For instance, the Kuok Foundation, instituted by the prominent Chinese tycoon Robert Kuok, and the Kuala Lumpur Kepong (KLK) Group, controlled by the family of the late rubber baron, Lee Loy Seng, are noted for their philanthropic work.[40] More recently, the MUI Group, controlled by Khoo Kay Peng, set up the Hope Foundation in 1990 while the Loy Hean Heong's MBf Group launched the MBf Caring Trust in 1993. The initiation of both funds was seen to be in line with the government's campaign to promote a "caring society". According to Deputy Prime Minister and Finance Minister Anwar Ibrahim, the institution of such funds by the corporate sector would reflect its new attitude of combining "profits with social responsibility." In such a way, added the Deputy Prime Minister, the private sector could also play a key role in helping to redress social problems, particularly the eradication of poverty.[41]

The MCA also continues to raise funds for the purpose of sponsoring educational activities and institutions. Among these are the expansion and upgrading of the Tunku Abdul Rahman (TAR) College, an institution established in 1967 when the MCA failed to get government approval to set up a Chinese university, Merdeka University; the official medium of instruction in the TAR College is, however, English. Through the TAR College, the MCA hopes that Malaysians will have greater opportunities to pursue tertiary and professional courses. The Langkawi Project has also been set up for the purpose of providing scholarships to the children of the poor, though the fund, like the TAR College, is open to students of all races.

At the national level, the government established the National Welfare Foundation in 1982 under the auspices of the Welfare Ministry.[42] However, the Foundation's attempt in 1987 to promote the Malaysian Philanthropic Campaign as a means to create a "common chest" proved unsuccessful, mainly because organizations were concerned that the distribution of funds would not be in accordance with the percentage of funds raised by them for the proposed "common chest."[43] Despite this, it appears that philanthropic activities in the country are perceived to be increasingly less ethnic-centered, in spite of the fact that most Malaysian organizations still remain ethnically based. For instance, the most prominent of the non-ethnic-based organizations in the country are the urban-based Rotary and Rotaract Clubs which have a multi-racial membership and participate in welfare activities that transcend racial lines.

Although it is probably presumptuous to attempt to draw strong conclusions on the actual nature and mode of philanthropic activities in Malaysia in view of the dearth of information on such activities, it is evident that there is still a strong link between non-Malay political parties and philanthropic activities, especially on the issue of promotion of education in the vernacular. However, other non-politically linked Indian and—in particular—Chinese associations that have long been concerned largely with issues pertaining to culture and education continue to play a significant role in their respective ethnic communities in preserving and promoting their language and cultural practices. Despite this, in the area of welfare work, the largely ethnically-based nature of such activities seems to be diminishing; even organizations that are still ethnically based appear to be adopting a multiethnic perspective in their activities.

Notes

1. Hsin-Huang Michael Hsiao, "Chinese Corporate Philanthropy in East and Southeast Asia," in *Evolving Patterns of Asia-Pacific Philanthropy*, edited by Ky-Hyun Jung (Seoul: The Institute for East and West Studies, 1994), p. 80–81.
2. John Gullick and Bruce Gale, *Malaysia: Its Political and Economic Development* (Petaling Jaya: Pelanduk Publications, 1986), p. 52–56.
3. Sinnappah Arasaratnam, "Malaysian Indians: The Formation of Incipient Society," in *Indian Communities in Southeast Asia* by K.S. Sandhu and A. Mani (Singapore: Institute of Southeast Asian Studies, 1993).
4. Frank H. Golay et al., *Underdevelopment and Economic Nationalism in Southeast Asia* (Ithaca: Cornell University Press, 1969) p. 348.
5. Heng Pek Koon, *Chinese Politics in Malaysia: A History of the Malaysian Chinese Association* (Singapore: Oxford University Press, 1988) p. 18–19.
6. Ibid.
7. Chan Kwok Bun and Claire Chiang, *Stepping Out: The Making of Chinese Entrepreneurs* (Singapore: Simon & Schuster Asia Pte Ltd, 1994), p. 314–15.
8. Ibid. p. 123.
9. Heng, op. cit., p. 22–23.
10. Kua Kia Soong, *A Protean Saga: The Chinese Schools of Malaysia* (Kuala Lumpur: The Resources & Research Center, Selangor Chinese Assembly Hall, 1990), 54–55.
11. Heng, op. cit., p. 22–23.
12. Sinnappah Arasaratnam, *Indians in Malaysia and Singapore* (Kuala Lumpur: Oxford University Press, 1980), p. 83-84. Rajakrishnan Ramasamy, *Sojourners to Citizens: Sri Lankan Tamils in Malaysia, 1885-1965* (Kuala Lumpur: Rajakrishnan Ramasamy, 1988), p. 146-48.
13. Arasaratnam, *Indians in Malaysia*, p. 182–83.
14. Rajeswary Amapalavanar, *The Indian Minority and Political Change in Malaya, 1945-1957* (Kuala Lumpur, Oxford University Press, 1981), p. 152–53. Arasaratnam, *Indian Communities*, p. 199.
15. T. Marimuthu, "The Plantation School as an Agent of Social Reproduction," in *Indian Communities in Southeast Asia* by K.S. Sandhu and A. Mani (Singapore: Institute of Southeast Asian Studies, 1993), p. 468.
16. Arasaratnam, *Indian Communities*, p. 202.
17. Donald L. Horowitz, "The Qur'an and the Common Law: Islamic Law Reform and the Theory of Legal Change," *The American Journal of Comparative Law* (spring 1994): 291–92. S.J. Gilani, "Redistribution and Consumer Welfare in an Asian Islamic Framework," *Kajian Ekonomi Malaysia* XXII, 1 (1985): 38. Amin Omar, "Perfection Only in Giving," *Malaysian Business* (October, 1983): p. 45.
18. Lim Teck Ghee and Tan Poo Chang, "Private Philanthropy in Malaysia," in *Evolving Patterns*

of Asia-Pacific Philanthropy (Seoul: Institute of Southeast Asian Studies, 1994), p. 166.

19. Ibid.

20. Ibid., p. 168.

21. Heng, op. cit., p. 64–65.

22. Gayl D. Ness, *Bureaucracy and Rural Development in Malaysia* (Berkeley: University of California Press, 1967), 53, 59.

23. Richard Stubbs, "The United Malays National Organization, the Malayan Chinese Association, and the Early Years of the Malayan Emergency, 1948–1955," *Journal of Contemporary Asia* Vol. 10 (1979): 77-88. Heng, op.cit., p. 108–09.

24. Heng, op.cit., p. 164–65.

25. Ibid., p. 165.

26. N.J. Funston, *Malay Politics in Malaysia: A Study of the United Malays National Organisation and Party Islam* (Kuala Lumpur: Heinemann Educational Books, 1980), p. 80–87.

27. Heng, op. cit., p. 164.

28. Mohd. Fauzi Haji Yaacob, "The Development of Malay Entrepreneurship Since 1957: A Sociological Overview," in *Economic Performance in Malaysia: The Insiders View*, edited by manning Nash (New York: Professors World Peace Academy, 1988), p. 132.

29. James V. Jesudason, *Ethnicity and the Economy: The State, Chinese Business and Multinationals in Malaysia* (Singapore: Oxford University Press), p. 136–147.

30. *The Star*, 12/6/95.

31. Bruce Gale, *Politics and business: A Study of Multi-Purpose Holdings Berhad* (Petaling Jaya: Eastern Universities Press, 1985). Yeoh Kok Kheng, "A Study of the Malaysian Chinese Economic Self-Strengthening (Corporatisation) Movement—With Special Reference to MPHB, Other Communal Investment Companies and Cooperatives," Malaysian economy discussion at the University of Malaya in Kuala Lumpur, 1987.

32. Ibid. Edmund Terence Gomez, *Political Business: Corporate Involvement of Malaysian Political Parties* (Queensland: Centre for Southeast Asian Studies, James Cook University, 1994).

33. *New Straits Times*, 9/4/95.

34. Lim and Tan, op. cit., p. 169-70.

35. *The Star*, 10/9/95.

36. Ibid., 9/3/92.

37. *New Straits Times*, 6/11/93.

38. Ibid., 8/11/94.

39. Lim and Tan, op. cit., p. 163.

40. *New Straits Times Press*, 24/4/76.

41. Ibid., 15/3/93, 18/5/95.

42. Ibid., 25/4/87.

43. Ibid., 8/5/87.

References

Amin Omar (1983)
"Perfection Only in Giving", *Malaysian Business,* October.

Arasaratnam, Sinnappah (1980)
Indians in Malaysia and Singapore, Kuala Lumpur: Oxford University Press.

Arasaratnam, Sinnappah (1993)
"Malaysian Indians: The Formation of Incipient Society", in K.S. Sandhu and A. Mani *Indian Communities in Southeast Asia,* Singapore: Institute of Southeast Asian Studies.

Chan Kwok Bun and Claire Chiang (1994)
Stepping Out: The Making of Chinese Entrepreneurs, Singapore: Simon & Schuster (Asia) Pte Ltd.

Funston, N.J. (1980)
Malay Politics in Malaysia: A Study of the United Malays National Organisation and Party Islam, Kuala Lumpur: Heinemann Educational Books.

Gale, Bruce (1985)
Politics and Business: A Study of Multi-Purpose Holdings Berhad, Petaling Jaya: Eastern Universities Press.

Gilani, S.J. (1985)
"Redistribution and Consumer Welfare in an Asian Islamic Framework". Kajian Ekonomi Malaysia, XXII (1), 37–42.

Golay, Frank H., Ralph Anspach, M. Ruth Pfanner and Elizabeth B. Ayal (1969)
Underdevelopment and Economic Nationalism in Southeast Asia, Ithaca: Cornell University Press.

Gomez, Edmund Terence (1994)
Political Business: Corporate Involvement of Malaysian Political Parties, Queensland: Centre for Southeast Asian Studies, James Cook University.

Gullick, John and Bruce Gale (1986)
Malaysia: Its Political and Economic Development. Petaling Jaya: Pelanduk Publications.

Heng Pek Koon (1988)
Chinese Politics in Malaysia: A History of the Malaysian Chinese Association, Singapore: Oxford University Press.

Horowitz, Donald L. (1994)
"The Qur'an and the Common Law: Islamic Law Reform and the Theory of Legal Change", *The American Journal of Comparative Law,* Spring issue.

Hsiao Hsin-Huang, Michael (1994)
"Chinese Corporate Philanthropy in East and Southeast Asia", in Ku-Hyun Jung (ed) *Evolving Patterns of Asia-Pacific Philanthropy,* Seoul: Institute for East and West Studies.

Jesudason, James V. (1989)
Ethnicity and the Economy: The State, Chinese Business and Multi-nationals in Malaysia, Singapore: Oxford University Press.

Kua Kia Soong (1990)
A Protean Saga: The Chinese Schools of Malaysia, Kuala Lumpur: The Resources & Research Center, Selangor Chinese Assembly Hall.

Lim Teck Ghee and Tan Poo Chang (1994)
"Private Philanthropy in Malaysia", in Ku-Hyun Jung (ed) *Evolving Patterns of Asia-Pacific Philanthropy*, Seoul: Institute for East and West Studies.

Marimuthu, T. (1993)
"The Plantation School as an Agent of Social Reproduction" in K.S. Sandhu and A. Mani *Indian Communities in Southeast Asia*, Singapore: Institute of Southeast Asian Studies.

Mohd Fauzi Haji Yaacob (1988)
"The Development of Malay Entrepreneurship Since 1957: A Sociological Overview", in Manning Nash (ed) *Economic Performance in Malaysia: The Insiders View*, New York: Professors World Peace Academy.

Ness, Gayl D. (1967)
Bureaucracy and Rural Development in Malaysia, Berkeley: University of California Press.

Rajakrishnan Ramasamy (1988)
Sojourners to Citizens: Sri Lankan Tamils in Malaysia. 1885–1965, Kuala Lumpur: Rajakrishnan Ramasamy.

Rajeswary Amapalavanar (1981)
The Indian Minority and Political Change in Malaya: 1945–1957, Kuala Lumpur: Oxford University Press.

Stubbs, Richard (1979)
"The United Malays National Organization, the Malayan Chinese Association, and the Early Years of the Malayan Emergency, 1948 1955", *Journal of Contemporary Asia*, Vol. 10, 77–88.

Yeoh Kok Kheng (1987)
"A Study of the Malaysian Chinese Economic Self-Strengthening (Corporatisation) Movement—With Special Reference to MPHB, Other Communal Investment Companies and Cooperatives." M.Ec. diss. University of Malaya.

Newspapers and Magazines

The New Straits Times

The Star

Malaysian Business

APPENDIX D

Financial Contributors

The Asia Foundation (San Francisco)
East-West Seminar (Tokyo)
Ford Foundation (New York)
Himalaya Foundation (Taipei)
The Hitachi Foundation (Washington, D.C.)
Japan-U.S. Friendship Commission (Washington, D.C.)
John D. and Catherine T. MacArthur Foundation (Chicago)
Rockefeller Brothers Fund (New York)
Sasakawa Peace Foundation (Tokyo)
Suntory Foundation (Osaka)
Ushiba Memorial Foundation (Tokyo)
Weyerhaeuser Foundation (Tacoma)

APPENDIX E

ASIA PACIFIC PHILANTHROPY CONSORTIUM

Building upon two earlier conferences on organized private philanthropy in East and Southeast Asia, which took place in Bangkok in 1989 and Seoul in 1993, the Asia Pacific Philanthropy Consortium was launched in March 1995 as an informal association of like-minded institutions, each independent , but jointly pursuing a set of common objectives. Initially consisting of The Asia Foundation (United States), the Japan Center for International Exchange (JCIE), the Philippine Business for Social Progress (PBSP), and the Institute for East and West Studies of Yonsei University (Korea), the Consortium now includes institutions throughout the Asia Pacific region. It is governed by a six-person executive committee consisting of members from Australia, Korea, Japan, the Philippines, Thailand, and the United States. "Lead agencies" within the region are responsible for specific programs organized under Consortium auspices.

The Consortium seeks to promote the role of philanthropy in addressing critical issues in the Asia Pacific region; to increase the flow and effectiveness of philanthropic giving within and to the region; to respond to the institutional strengthening needs of existing and emerging Asia Pacific philanthropies through networking, human resource development, and research; and to facilitate efforts by philanthropic organizations in the region to identify and collaborate in addressing issues of mutual concern.

To accomplish these objectives, the Consortium will support four types of activities; (1) human resource development through technical support, training, or internships in the management of philanthropic organizations; (2) research to address critical issues affecting the nonprofit sector and to encourage wider discus-